T0390701

A HISTORY OF POLITICAL CONFLICT

A

HISTORY

OF

POLITICAL
CONFLICT

ELECTIONS &

SOCIAL INEQUALITIES

IN FRANCE, 1789–2022

JULIA CAGÉ
THOMAS PIKETTY

TRANSLATED BY STEVEN RENDALL

The Belknap Press of Harvard University Press
CAMBRIDGE, MASSACHUSETTS | LONDON, ENGLAND   2025

EU GPSR Authorised Representative
LOGOS EUROPE, 9 rue Nicolas Poussin, 17000, LA ROCHELLE, France
E-mail: Contact@logoseurope.eu

First printing

Library of Congress Cataloging-in-Publication Data

Names: Cagé, Julia, author. | Piketty, Thomas, 1971– author. | Rendall, Steven, translator.
Title: A history of political conflict : elections and social inequalities in France, 1789–2022 /
Julia Cagé and Thomas Piketty.
Other titles: Histoire du conflit politique. English
Description: Cambridge, Massachusetts : The Belknap Press of Harvard University Press, 2025. |
Translation of: Une histoire du conflit politique: élections et inégalités sociales en France, 1789–2022. |
Includes bibliographical references and index.
Identifiers: LCCN 2024051490 (print) | LCCN 2024051491 (ebook) | ISBN 9780674248434 (cloth) |
ISBN 9780674300590 (pdf) | ISBN 9780674300606 (epub)
Subjects: LCSH: Voting—Social aspects—France—History. |
Right and left (Political science)—France—History. |
Government, Resistance to—France—History. | Equality—France—History. |
France—Politics and government—1789– | France—Social conditions.
Classification: LCC JN2959 .C2313 2025 (print) | LCC JN2959 (ebook) |
DDC 324.944/09—dc23/eng/20250303
LC record available at https://lccn.loc.gov/2024051490
LC ebook record available at https://lccn.loc.gov/2024051491

CONTENTS

ACKNOWLEDGMENTS

A great many people have given us their support for this research project, in particular with regard to the compilation of the body of electoral and socioeconomic data on which this study is based (the data are available online and can be accessed at unehistoireduconflitpolitique.fr). We are especially grateful to Alena Lapatniova, Tatyana Shukan, and Maria Emanovskaya for their valuable work collecting the electoral registers in the French National Archives, and to all the marvelous teams at the National Archives who welcomed us in recent years and without which this study could not have been carried out. We also thank Éloïse Alluyn, Thomas Carrié, Lorenzo Catalano, Inès Cliquot de Mentque, Guillaume Guinard, Marwa Kheddouci, Sacha Martinelle, Antoine Richard, and Claire de Rosamel, as well as Jean-Laurent Cadorel, Jeanne Dorlencourt, Romain Morgavi, Eva Salavera, Alexandre Verlet, and, of course, Hardish Bindra.

By providing us with sources they had already digitized, or their expertise on this or that particular point, many of our colleagues were of enormous help. We are especially indebted to Serge Aberdam, who gave us access to valuable data on the referenda of 1793 and 1795, which he had digitized on the basis of electoral registers in the revolutionary period, and who so kindly shared his enthusiasm and knowledge about this founding moment. We also want to thank Guillaume Blanc, Carles Boix, Florian Bonnet, Pierre-Henri Bono, Paul Brandily-Snyers, Charlotte Cavaille, Thomas Corpet, Hyppolite d'Albis, Abel François, Pauline Grosjean, Saumitra Jha, Jean Lacroix, Miren Lafourcade, Eric Monnet, Etienne Pasteau, Gilles Postel-Vinay, Frédéric Salmon, Nicolas Sauger, Aurélie Sotura, Mara Squicciarini, and Timothy Tackett for their help. Thanks also to Caroline Piketty for having guided us through the twists and turns of the various electoral registers concerning elections in the national and departmental archives.

It is not always easy to map the data; thanks to Agathe Denis for her indispensable help with Python (and her unfailing patience), and more generally to all the PhD candidates and young researchers (including Edgard Dewitte, Moritz Hengel, Felipe Lauritzen, Élisa Mougin, and Olivia Tsoutsoplidi) who energetically aided us in our work on a daily basis. Thanks to Lucas Chancel, Amory Gethin, Clara Martinez-Toledano, Rowaida Moshrif, and all the members of the World Inequality Lab for supplying the irreplaceable intellectual environment. Without the splendid teams at WeDoData, the site unehistoireduconflitpolitique.fr would not exist; thanks to Karen Bastien for agreeing to work with us and for once again mapping the data; and thanks to Brice Terdjman and Mattia Longhin for their fantastic work.

A project of digitizing historical archives on such a large scale would not have been possible without major public financial support. We thank in particular the European Research Council (in the context of ERC Grants 856455 and 948516), as well as the François-Simiand Center for Economic and Social History and the World Inequality Lab. We are, of course, extremely indebted to the university institutions to which we have been so lucky to belong, the École des hautes études en sciences sociales, the École d'économie de Paris, and Sciences Po Paris, and especially everyone who has allowed us to carry out our work and who made possible its material organization (notably, Cathy Bernard, Pilar Calvo, Loïc Da Costa, and Diane Gabeloteau).

And, of course, we are grateful to all the teams at our publisher, Le Seuil, for their steady trust and solid support in this large-scale undertaking, and in particular to Séverine Nikel and Vassili Sztil for their invaluable guidance.

This book has also been a personal and familial adventure. Without her big sisters and her grandparents, our little Piana might sometimes have found her parents a little too absorbed in their research. Thanks to her for making a big splash! She'll find out soon enough what her parents were doing at that time, and in the interim she'll continue to make us the happiest of lovers.

A HISTORY OF POLITICAL CONFLICT

Introduction

Who votes for whom, and why? How has the social structure of the electorates of the various political tendencies in France evolved between 1789 and 2022? To what extent have the diverse coalitions in power and in opposition been able to bring together the lower, middle, and wealthy classes and federate divergent interests, and how has that contributed to the process of the social, economic, and political development of the country? How have the multiple characteristics of social class and sociospatial inequalities (size of the urban area and the municipality, sector of activity and occupation, level of property and income, age and gender, education and degree, religion and origin, and so on) determined the ways individuals vote—as well as whether or not they participated in elections?

Such are the fundamental questions that this book seeks to answer. It has both a retrospective and a prospective interest. With its five Republics and the multiple changes in its governmental system since 1789, France is an incomparable laboratory for the study of the vicissitudes of modern political life in general, and of electoral democracy in particular. Election by majority vote or by proportional representation, direct or indirect democracy, a parliamentary or a presidential system, representative democracy or referenda, multiple coalitions between the Left, Right, and Center—France has tried them all in the course of the last two centuries. It was the first country to experiment on a large scale with quasi-universal suffrage for men, in the 1790s, and then in a quasi-permanent way starting in 1848; it was also one of the last to extend the right to vote to women, in 1944. France has had legislative assemblies constituted by a large majority of monarchist deputies (in 1871) and others in which the Communist and Socialist deputies were by far the most numerous (in 1945). If democracy is a promise never completely fulfilled, always an ongoing project, an imperfect attempt to regulate social conflicts by deliberation and voting and always to move further down the road toward social and political equality, then the French laboratory offers an ideal framework for better understanding the complex paths and unfinished bifurcations that this hope can take.

Thanks to its precocious unification as a territorial and administrative state, a process largely begun under the Old Regime and then accelerated and consolidated by the French Revolution, the country also has well-preserved electoral archives going back to 1789 that make it possible to study at the level of the municipalities almost all the results of the votes that took place over the past two centuries. The very rich collection of data produced by censuses and diverse administrative, educational, religious, social, financial, and fiscal sources also enables us to analyze in detail the structure of sociospatial inequalities and their relation to political behaviors since the revolutionary period.

An Unprecedented Database: unehistoireduconflitpolitique.fr

On the basis of an unprecedented project of digitalizing electoral and socioeconomic records covering more than two centuries, an enterprise that had never before been carried out in such a systematic way and encompassing such a long period, this work offers a history of electoral behaviors and sociospatial. inequalities in France from 1789 to 2022. All the data collected from the approximately 36,000 municipalities in France, from raw documents (electoral registers preserved in the National Archives in manuscript form) to homogenized, finalized files, are available online at unehistoireduconflitpolitique.fr, and anyone can consult the site to obtain the digitized versions of all the graphs and illustrations presented and analyzed in this book. This site also contains hundreds of other maps, graphs, and tables that we have chosen not to include in this book in order to limit its size, but interested readers can refer to them to deepen and refine their own analyses and hypotheses. Readers can also generate maps and graphs of their own choosing—for instance, to determine the political movements characterized by the most working-class or the most bourgeois votes, election by election and political tendency by political tendency, over the last two centuries.

The municipal and cantonal data we put online relate to the quasi-totality of the legislative elections carried out from 1848 to 2022 (a total of forty-one legislative elections),[1] all the presidential elections from 1848 to 2022 (a total of twelve

---

1. This includes the legislative elections of 1848, 1849, 1871 (two elections), 1876, 1877, 1881, 1885, 1889, 1893, 1898, 1902, 1906, 1910, 1914, 1919, 1924, 1928, 1932, 1936, 1945, 1946 (two elections), 1951, 1956, 1958, 1962, 1967, 1968, 1973, 1978, 1981, 1986, 1988, 1993, 1997, 2002, 2007, 2012, 2017, and 2022. The data were collected at the level of 3,000 cantons for 1848, 1849, and February 1871 (because not all the municipal data were preserved for these three elections, which were held in the cantons' main towns) and then, starting in July 1871 (with a few exceptions connected with problems of preservation for certain years or departments), at the level of 36,000 municipalities. For the legislative elections held from 1789 to 1799, we have utilized the departmental data collected by Marvin Edelstein and have not undertaken new collections. Furthermore, we have not attempted to digitize the data for the legislative elections under the monarchies from 1815 to 1848 (in which only 1 to 2 percent of adult males had the right to vote) or those held under the Second Empire from 1852 to 1869 (conducted under the system of universal male suffrage, but in an authoritarian framework that left only limited space for candidacies that were not official).

presidential elections),[2] .and five significant referenda that took place from 1793 to 2005.[3] For the period from 1993 to 2002 we have reproduced the official municipal data digitized and published by the Ministry of the Interior, with a few minor corrections concerning the political subtleties used. But for the period before 1993, before now, none of the election data at the municipal level had been digitized and put completely online, so the database presented here with free access online is totally unprecedented.[4]

Rethinking Bipolarization and Tripartition on a Historical Scale

In addition to its historical interest and the new database that it provides, this work offers a new way of seeing the crises of the present and possible ways of resolving them. In recent years, and moreover almost constantly over the course of the last two centuries, certain political actors have thought it clever to explain that the ideological and sociological cleavages of the past have been definitively transcended. That Left and Right were now meaningless notions, et cetera. In reality, political conflicts are always multidimensional and can never be reduced to a unidirectional Left-Right axis, in part because social class is itself a multidimensional concept (taking in the size of the agglomeration and the municipality, occupation, income, wealth, age, gender, origin, religion, and other factors) and in part because electoral conflict bears on extremely diverse questions (about the political system, border system, property system, fiscal system, and educational system, for example) and is

---

2. We refer to the presidential election of 1848, and then those of 1965, 1969, 1974, 1981, 1988, 1995, 2002, 2007, 2012, 2017, and 2022. The data collected for 1848 are at the level of the cantons (for the same reasons as for the legislative elections), and starting with 1965, at the level of the municipalities.

3. We refer here to the referenda conducted in 1793, 1795, 1946, 1992, and 2005. The data were collected at the level of the districts (groups of cantons) for 1793 and 1795, cantons for 1946, and municipalities for 1992 and 2005. The data for 1793 and 1795 issue from collections made by Serge Aberdam.

4. All the details on the sources used and the procedures of digitalization and homogenization are available online. In the body of the text we will return to the most important sociopolitical aspects connected with the constitution of this database (and in particular, to the attribution of political labels to the candidates, especially on the basis of the press of the time; see chapter 8). We would like to thank all the students, young researchers, and colleagues of all ages who have assisted us in this project, and of course the National Archives' splendid teams, without whom no research of this kind would be possible. Their names appear in this book's acknowledgments and on the site. Let us add that in this book we limited ourselves to elections conducted in Metropolitan France; the elections carried out in the overseas territories and the former colonies during the last two centuries raise specific questions and deserve to be the subject of a full-scale study in their own right.

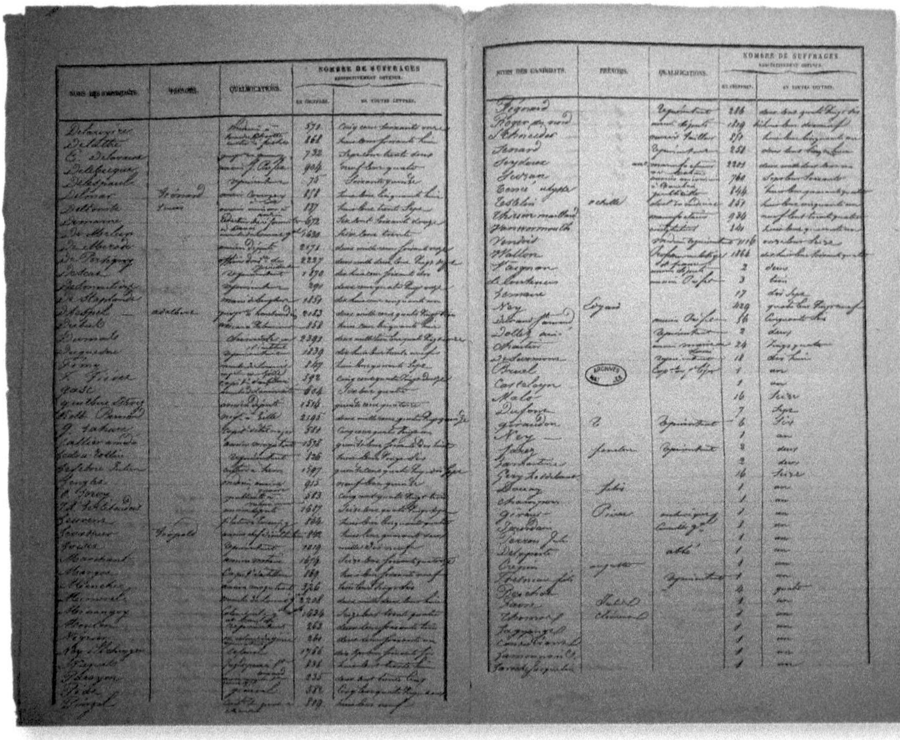
NOMBRE DE SUFFRAGES
NOMBRE DE SUFFRAGES

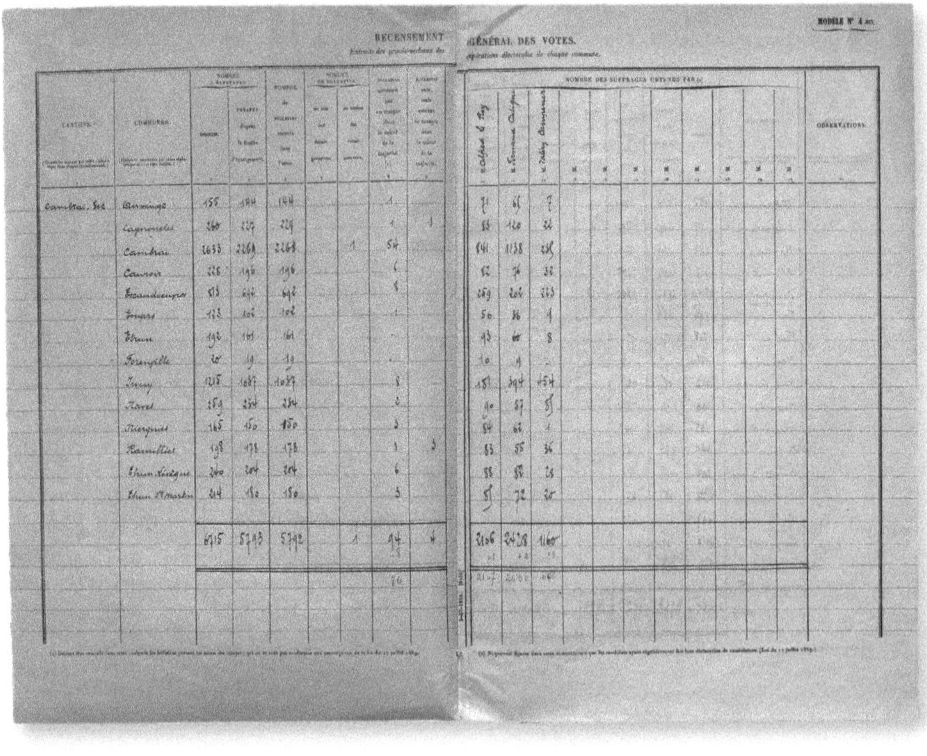
MODÈLE N° 4 bis.
RECENSEMENT GÉNÉRAL DES VOTES
OBSERVATIONS

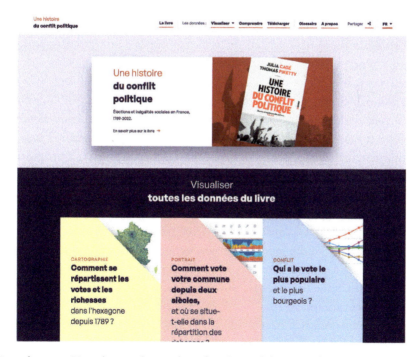

Reproduction 1: The raw materials used: Electoral records

1a (*left top*) Legislative elections of 1849 (Canton of Cambrai-Est. Nord)
1b (*left bottom*) Legislative elections of 1910 (Canton of Cambrai-Est. Nord)
1c (*above*) Presidential election of 1981 (Canton of Cambrai-Est. Nord)

The figure reproduces the electoral records for the legislative elections of 1849 (1a) and 1910 (1b), as well as for the election of 1981 (1c) for the Canton of Cambrai-Est in the department of Nord.

Reproduction 2: The website unehistoireduconflitpolitique.fr (screenshot)

constantly developing. Even so, the cleavages of the past are never completely absent. On the contrary, it is always on the basis of this heritage that the structure of political conflict and the plural and changing conceptions of Rights, Centers, and Lefts continue to be redefined and rearticulated around worldviews and divergent socioeconomic interests whose importance does not seem about to decline.

Apart from this structural multidimensionality of political conflict, there are historical periods in which one main axis may take precedence over the others. In particular, this may involve a socioeconomic conflict between the working classes and the property-owning classes as a whole, in which case, the electoral confrontation takes the form of a Left-Right bipolar conflict that may to a certain extent merge with a conflict between rich and poor. We shall see that this "classist" type of bipolarization is generally structured around inequalities of property (even more than around inequalities of income) and always leaves an autonomous role for the rural-urban conflict and the religious and educational conflicts, and obviously for the complexity of individual experiences and subjectivities. This "complexified classist" configuration has occupied an essential place in France beginning around 1900–1910 (with the rise in the power of the Socialist Party and then the Communist Party) and continuing until 1990–2000. It played a maximal role from 1958 to 1992, a period during which almost no political tendency could exist outside the Left-Right bipolarity, particularly in the emblematic elections of 1974, 1978, and 1981, when the Left-Right structure of the voting in relation to wealth was indeed very marked. If we take a long-term view, we have to admit that this bipolarization, which was especially strong between 1910 and 1992, had a deciding and largely positive impact on the country's democratic, social, and economic development over the course of the century. It fed a prolific competition to set up multiple essential public policies while at the same time permitting more peaceful democratic transfers of power at the head of the state. One of this book's essential goals is to better understand the socioeconomic and political-ideological contexts and the strategic choices made by actors capable of explaining why and how this type of bipolar conflict is constructed or deconstructed.

The question is all the more important because there are also historical periods—at the end of the nineteenth century and the beginning of the twentieth, and once again in this beginning of the twenty-first century—for which a ternary (or sometimes quaternary) structure is more suitable for describing the multiple political currents and subtleties involved. In particular, the presidential and legislative elections held in France in 2022 brought out a relatively clear tripartition of political life, with a green-social bloc on the left, a liberal-progressive bloc in the center, and a nationalist-patriotic bloc on the right, each of them representing about a third of the votes.[5] The choice of terms is of course open to question, and indeed, the debate about words represents one of the central stakes of political conflict: some people accuse others of being part of the "false Left" (*fausse gauche*), while others claim to be the "true Right." Almost everyone describes their adversaries as being in the hands of extremists or the powerful. We try to avoid these strategies that seek to disqualify, define, or essentialize any group; in our view, there is no true Left or true Right, but rather a moving plurality of political tendencies. We shall use the terms "Lefts," "Centers," and "Rights" (in the plural) in a flexible and evolving way, starting with the ways in which actors—voters, parties, media, and others—have tended to use them to designate themselves in different periods. We shall insist on the particularity of each political tendency or nuance (generally speaking, we can distinguish about ten significant political nuances in most of the legislative elections that took place from 1848 to 2022), which we will assign, as much as possible, by using the names they use for themselves or which are, in any case, acceptable to their supporters (when supplementary groupings appear to be pertinent). For that reason, we will avoid using the terms "extreme Left" and "extreme Right," because there are no political actors who choose to designate themselves as extreme.

In the case of the tripartition resulting from the 2022 elections, it is natural to connect it with older ideological bases. We shall see that in large measure, it refers to three of the principal ideological families that have structured political life since the nineteenth century: socialism, liberalism, and nationalism. For two centuries, liberalism has emphasized the role played by private property and the domestic and international markets in promoting individual emancipation and industrial development, with occasional successes on the economic level but sometimes also with considerable social damage. Nationalism responds to the resulting social crisis by emphasizing the importance of the nation and local and ethnonational

---

5. If we add up the votes for the candidates from left-wing and green parties (LFI, PS, PCF, EELV, LO, NPA), we get 32 percent of the votes cast in the first round of the presidential election. Adding up the votes for the outgoing president (who came from the LREM party) and the candidate of the LR party (Les républicains), we also obtain 32 percent of the votes. We arrive at exactly the same result of 32 percent if we add up the three candidates of the nationalist-patriotic candidates (RN, Reconquête, and DLF). If we divide up the three blocs the 3 percent of the vote that went to the unclassifiable ruralist candidate (Jean Lasalle), we end up with three almost perfectly equal thirds. To a large extent, LR is halfway between the liberal-progressive bloc and the nationalist-patriotic bloc, and could be classified with the latter. Obviously, a fourth bloc is constituted by those who abstained, and we will also study in detail the factors that determined participation in voting.

solidarity, whereas socialism attempts, not without difficulties, to promote an alternative socioeconomic system founded on sharing power and property and on universal emancipation through education. Each of these three main tendencies seeks in its own way to provide plausible answers to the social question as it has been formulated since the Industrial Revolution and constantly redefined over the last two centuries in light of both the different blocs' experiences in power and socioeconomic transformations. The tripartition of 2002 also bears the mark of new issues that became fully important only in the last few decades (ecology and climate, as well as migration and cultural identity), which have helped redefine the old political tendencies, as new issues do in every historical period.

But the central point is that the current tripartition can be correctly analyzed only by looking back two centuries. Over the long term, we find different forms of tripartition between 1848 and 1910 (around a triptych composed of Socialists and Radical-Socialists on the left, Moderate and Opportunistic Republicans in the center, and conservatives, Catholics, and monarchists on the right), then a bipolarization (with the disintegration of the Socialist-Communist Left, the rising power of the European and ecological question, and the emergence of new migratory and identitarian cleavages).

We shall also see that the existence of a ternary electoral confrontation, rather than a binary one, in no way implies the weakening of the class cleavage. On the contrary, the vote for the central liberal-progressive bloc registered in the election of 2022 appears in the available data to be one of the most "bourgeois" observed for two centuries (probably even the most "bourgeois" in all of French electoral history) in the sense that it brought together in unprecedented proportions a group of voters much more privileged than the average. The propensity to vote for this bloc, for example, is a strongly increasing function of the municipality's wealth (as measured by either average income or average property value), with an unusually steep slope in comparison to the preceding historical periods. Thus, in 2022 the Ensemble vote was more than 1.7 times higher than its national average in the richest 1 percent of the municipalities, or more than what we find for the Right in 1924, 1962, or 1993; above all, it is systematically and greatly lower than its national average in the least affluent 60 percent of municipalities, whereas the Rights of the past generally succeeded in gathering more significant support from their own ranks (see figure I.1).

The other particularity of this new tripartition is that the working classes are deeply divided between the two other blocs. Simply put, we can say that the urban working classes voted for the Left bloc and the rural and peri-urban working classes

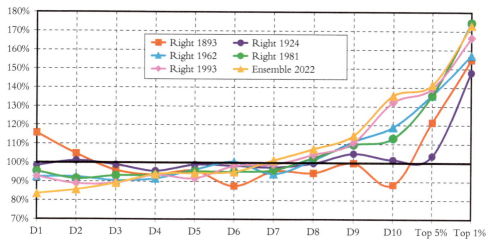

Distribution of the population by deciles as a function of municipal income per inhabitant

FIGURE I.1. Was the 2022 Ensemble vote the most bourgeois in French electoral history?

The vote for the Ensemble-UDI bloc in 2022 increases strongly with income. The slope is on the whole comparable with the vote profiles for the right wing observed in the past, with the difference that the latter generally got better results in the poorest municipalities (particularly in the poorest rural municipalities, but not only there).

Note: The results indicated here are after controls for the size of the conurbation and municipality.

Sources and series: unehistoireduconflitpolitique.fr

voted for the Right bloc.[6] We find certain aspects of similar electoral structures in earlier episodes of tripartition in the nineteenth century and at the beginning of the twentieth century, before bipartition became dominant during much of the twentieth century. In this work, we shall try to show in particular that it is by meticulously comparing these different configurations and their transformations that we can better understand the tensions at work today and envisage several trajectories of development for the coming decades. We shall emphasize especially the fact that in the past, the union of the rural and urban working classeswas achieved on the basis of ambitious programmatic platforms that aimed to reduce social inequalities in all their dimensions, taking into account the particularities of the different territories—and the same will probably hold true in the future.

6. See chapters 11, 13, and 14 for a detailed analysis of the recent elections and of these historical comparisons. The conclusion obtained concerning the Ensemble vote is even more striking in the absence of any monitoring of the size of the agglomeration and the municipality. See chapter 11, figures 11.30–11.31.

Surveys, Electoral Data, and Sociospatial Inequalities

Before going further in this direction, let us begin by clarifying the procedure and methods that we will use, as well as the way our work is situated within the vast literature in social sciences (especially history and political science) that is devoted to elections and to political ideologies. Generally speaking, how can we know who votes for whom? We can distinguish two principal and complementary methods: one starts from the surveys conducted at the individual level, the other from electoral and socioeconomic data observed at the most granular level possible.

The most direct method consists in conducting surveys at the individual level, ideally with a representative sample of the population—generally, a few thousand people who are asked questions relating to their socioeconomic characteristics (occupation, income, age, sex, religion, and so on) and their recent electoral choices. Since 1950, surveys of this type have been conducted regularly after most of the elections in the main Western countries, particularly in the United States, France, and the United Kingdom, and were then generalized in almost all the countries where there have been pluralistic elections since 1980–1990. These so-called postelectoral surveys (usually conducted in the days or weeks following the election studied)[7] have given rise to exciting, innovative kinds of research, particularly in French political science since the 1950s, notably by Jacques Capdevielle, Nonna Mayer, Guy Michelat, and many other authors.[8] In the context of a collective project in which we participated that involved about twenty researchers, and fol-

---

7. This generally makes it possible to conduct longer interviews and ask more questions than in the exit polls conducted by news organizations when voters are leaving the polling place.
8. An initial, relatively detailed survey of voting and occupations was organized in France by the Institut français d'opinion publique (IFOP) after the legislative elections in 1951. Then more and more sophisticated postelectoral surveys were organized following the legislative elections in 1958, generally in partnership with the Fondation nationale des sciences politiques (FNSP) and its various research centers, particularly the Centre de recherches politiques de Sciences Po (CEVIPOF). The 1978 survey introduced detailed questionnaires on inheritances—crucial information that was unfortunately absent from most of the surveys carried out in other countries. On this long tradition of research, on which we base our own work to a large extent, see, in particular, M. Duverger, *Partis politiques et classes sociales en France* (A. Colin, 1955); G. Michelat and M. Simon, *Classe, religion et comportement politique* (Presses de la FNSP, 1977); J. Capdevielle and E. Dupoirier, "L'effet patrimoine," in *France de gauche, vote à droite?* (Presses de la FNSP, 1981); D. Gaxie, *Explication du vote. Un bilan des études électorales en France* (Presses de la FNSP, 1985); D. Boy and N. Mayer, *L'électeur a ses raisons* (Presses de Sciences Po, 1997); S. Crépon, A. Dézé, and N. Mayer, *Les faux-semblants du Front National* (Presses de Sciences Po, 2015); and M. Foucault and P. Perrineau, *La politique au microscope. 60 ans d'histoire du Cevipof* (Presses de Sciences Po, 2021).

lowing on from earlier studies, the postelectoral surveys conducted from 1948 to 2020 in fifty countries on every continent were recently assembled and systematically used to compare the transformations of the structure of the electorates, specifically concerning the link between electoral behavior and the level of education, income, and inheritance.[9]

Unfortunately, this first method, based on surveys carried out at the individual level, suffers from two drawbacks that are serious and even crippling, considering the historical and spatial perspective adopted in this study. No representative survey of this type exists before World War II, so this method prevents us from going back to the interwar period or the beginning of the twentieth century (and a fortiori to the nineteenth century or the end of the eighteenth century) and taking a long-term approach, which is the primary objective of this book. In addition, the limited size of the samples used in these surveys allows us to bring out certain general tendencies, but it weakens the subtle comparisons between one election and another, and in particular, it keeps us from correlating in a statistically reliable way the territorial criteria (such as the size of the municipality and the agglomeration) with socioeconomic criteria (such as the sector of activity, occupation, income, or wealth), even though the correlation of spatial and socioeconomic criteria plays a central role in the transformations that we are going to highlight, especially those concerning the political division of the rural and urban working classes and its transformations over time. This lack of historical depth and sociospatial representation also applies to individual surveys of the ethnographic type, which are based on detailed interviews with small samples and provide uniquely rich material for a subtle understanding of individual trajectories and processes of politicization, but which are unfortunately not available consistently over a long period.[10]

The second method consists in using electoral data at the most detailed spatial level possible (such as cantons, municipalities, and polling stations) and putting

9. See A. Gethin, C. Martinez-Toledano, and T. Piketty, eds., *Clivages politiques et inégalités sociales. Une étude de 50 démocraties, 1948–2020* (EHESS / Gallimard / Seuil, 2021). All the results are available in the World Political Cleavages and Inequality Database (wpid.world). The chapters of this work also provide points of entry into the very rich international bibliography founded on postelectoral surveys.

10. For fascinating examples of ethnographic surveys concerning recent elections, see E. Agrikoliansky, P. Aldrin, and S. Lévêque, *Voter par temps de crise. Portraits d'électrices et d'électeurs ordinaires* (Presses Universitaires de France / Irisso, 2021). See also Collectif SPEL, *Le sens du vote. Une enquête sociologique (2011–2014)* (Presses Universitaires de Rennes, 2016). There also exist multiple studies combining surveys of a representative sample and detailed ethnographic interviews. See, in particular, C. Braconnier and N. Mayer, *Les inaudibles. Sociologie politique des précaires* (Presses de Sciences Po, 2015).

them in correspondence with the socioeconomic data observed at the same level. In this way, it is possible to compare the votes of the poorest and richest municipalities (defined by the level of their average income or average property values, for example), or the most agricultural and the least agricultural municipalities, or the most and the least industrial, and so on. The results thus obtained must always be carefully interpreted because this method, by construction, does not enable us to observe electoral behaviors at the level of the individual, but only to compare averages at the level of municipalities or the other geographical units used. In comparison with the method based on surveys, this second approach, based on localized electoral and socioeconomic data, nonetheless has immense advantages. In particular, electoral results at the local level have generally been well preserved in most countries since elections have existed, so it is possible to go back to the beginning of the twentieth century, to the nineteenth century, and even to the end of the eighteenth century in certain cases (especially in France) where the right to vote was generalized early on and where the archives have been especially well preserved. Then it becomes possible to write a history of electoral behaviors and social inequalities covering more than two centuries and not just a history centered on the post-1950 period, which changes the perspective in an extraordinary way and makes it possible to renew the thinking and problematics of the present period, which is in certain respects closer to the situation that prevailed at the end of the nineteenth century and the beginning of the twentieth than it is to that of the Trente Glorieuses. Considering the magnitude of the work of collecting data for this project, it seemed to us materially impossible to carry it out on a comparative basis, and that is why the present work concerns only France (and specifically, Metropolitan France). However, we hope that it will encourage similar research projects on other countries and enlighten our understanding of the political conflicts at work today in many Western democracies.

Ideally, this method based on localized electoral and socioeconomic data should be conducted at the level of the polling station. Unfortunately, this kind of data that cover a long period are not available.[11] On the historical scale, most of the

---

11. In France, electoral data at the level of the polling station have been systematically digitized by the Ministry of the Interior only since 2002. For earlier periods, electoral records preserved in the National Archives pertain to only the municipalities, and not the polling stations, with a very small number of exceptions (such as the residential neighborhoods within Parisian arrondissements). In any case, the local cartography of polling stations has changed a great deal and does not seem to have left a homogeneous mark over a long period, not to mention that the socioeconomic data that can be used for analyzing the voting is generally not available at that level (with the exception of data from very recent years).

sources are available solely at the level of the municipality, which in the French context already constitutes an extremely detailed and pertinent level of analysis.[12] For example, with about 36,000 municipalities it is possible to compare, for all sizes of agglomeration, hundreds of very poor and very wealthy municipalities, others that are highly agricultural or highly industrial, those that rely largely on private education and those that do not, and so on. We will also use, secondarily, the cantonal level (generally about 3,000 cantons), which allows for analyses that are less detailed than at the municipal level but nonetheless pertinent in the rare cases where the municipal data are not available. On the other hand, it is impossible to use such a method rigorously if one only has data at the level of the department (around 90 to 95 departments, depending on the period) or electoral districts (generally, about 500 districts). As soon as we try to correlate several variables (the size of the municipality and the agglomeration, income and real estate, the sector of activity and occupation, religiosity and education, for example)—and this is indispensable if we are to have any hope of sorting out the different factors—only the municipal level or possibly the cantonal level allows us to envisage a satisfying analysis.

From the History of Ideologies to the History of Electorates

Why wasn't the work of collecting electoral data and analyzing the socioeconomic structure of electorates over a long period, as we propose in this book, done earlier on this scale? Certainly there are intellectual factors that are connected with an unwarranted separation of the disciplines and methods within the social sciences (particularly between economic and social history, and between political and cultural history), but another possible explanation is that such a project of digitization and data collection is much more conceivable today than it was just a few decades ago, considering the new human and material means (in particular, digital means) at the disposal of researchers in the social sciences.

---

12. All the electoral and sociodemographic data are also available at the level of the twenty Parisian arrondissements, which we have treated as separate municipalities in the context of this study. On the other hand, the data concerning the arrondissements of Lyon and Marseille are not available consistently over a long period, and we have therefore had to treat these two cities as whole municipalities, as we also did for all the other large cities, which constitutes an important limit of the analysis. More detailed data at the level of neighborhoods or cantons would benefit from being further utilized for certain cities and subperiods, and they are available at unehistoireduconflitpolitique.fr.

Without overestimating its significance, the issue of resources is no doubt important, and it can help explain why there are a great many works on the history of political-ideological tendencies in France since the Revolution and relatively few on the social history of the electorates that given their votes to these different tendencies. However that may be, this imbalance seems to us regrettable, insofar as the two approaches are obviously complementary. In particular, the social history of electorates may make it possible to better understand the most significant political-ideological and programmatic characteristics of the parties and coalitions as they have been perceived by voters, which can in turn illuminate the history of ideologies and lead us to propose new interpretations of the history of the Lefts, the Rights, and the Centers. With regard to the history of the different political families, there are in all countries a great many works—in France, for example, in the lineage of René Rémond's research on the history of the Rights or Gilles Richard's more recent works, which put more emphasis on the renewal of tendencies from a sociohistorical point of view than on their supposed fixity. This domain of research includes a very rich literature composed of multiple monographs and synthetic works on the histories of both the Rights[13] and the Lefts,[14] on which our characterization of the different political tendencies will be largely based. We will also make use of the classic sources on these questions: parliamentary debates, the press, manifestos, and electoral programs.

Let us recall in particular that the first use of the notions of Left and Right to characterize different political tendencies goes back to the French Revolution. The decisive moment is traditionally situated in the session of 28 August 1789, which was devoted to the question of the royal veto, shortly after the taking of the Bastille on 14 July 1789 and the abolition of aristocratic privileges adopted during the night of 4 August. While the deputies tried to agree on a new constitution for the kingdom, the representatives favoring the king's absolute right to veto in future legislative processes sat on the right side of the assembly hall, while those who were

---

13. See G. Richard, *Histoire des droites en France de 1815 à nos jours* (Perrin, 2017). See also R. Rémond, *Les droites en France* (Aubier, 1982), a revised version of the classic study first published in 1954 under the title *La droite en France de 1815 à nos jours. Continuité et diversité d'une tradition politique*. See also the collective work coordinated by J. F. Sirinelli, *Histoire des droites en France*, 3 vols. (Gallimard, 1992).

14. See the collective work coordinated by J. J. Becker and G. Candar, *Histoire des gauches en France*, 2 vols. (La Découverte, 2004). See also M. Winock, *La gauche en France* (Tempus, 2006); J. Julliard, *Les gauches françaises 1762–2012* (Flammarion, 2012); J. Mischi, *Le parti des communistes. Histoire du PCF de 1920 à nos jours* (Hors d'atteinte, 2020). On the structuring role of the triptych socialism-liberalism-nationalism, see B. Karsenti and C. Lemieux, *Socialisme et sociologie* (EHESS, 2017).

opposed to it and demanded that the Assembly have full and complete sovereignty sat on the left side.[15] Some authors point out that this Left-Right topographical division had already been adopted in 1787–1788, during the meetings of the Assembly of Notables, an Areopagus constituted by representatives of the nobility, the clergy, *parlements,* and the cities of the kingdom. It was convened by Louis XVI for the purpose of adopting fiscal measures that sought to save the Old Regime (without success), and it ended with the convocation of the Estates General in 1789.[16] What is certain is that the Left-Right conflict over the political and constitutional system was from the outset inseparable from a Left-Right of the socioeconomic type about the question of taxes, the privileges of the nobility and the clergy, the Church's ownership of properties and the educational system, and more generally, the distribution of property, wealth, and power in the society. What the supporters of the royal veto feared was obviously that an excessively sovereign Assembly might set about redistributing wealth and power limitlessly, or more generally radically challenging the social order, on the basis of a simple decision made by a majority vote. We shall see that the effects of the political-constitutional and socioeconomic dimensions have continued in combination (but without ever completely coinciding) in the ideological and programmatic history of the Lefts, the Centers, and the Rights since 1789.

Siegfried, the Question of the Republican Vote, and Influence

Unfortunately, studies concerning the social history of electorates are much less numerous. The work closest to the project developed here is no doubt the *Tableau politique de la France de l'Ouest sous la Troisième République,* published in 1913 by the political analyst and geographer André Siegfried. In this classic book, which is foundational for modern political science, the author sets forth a meticulous study of the votes observed in the legislative elections from 1871 to 1910, canton by canton in the fourteen departments of western France, from the Vendée in Brittany and extending though Anjou and Normandy. On the basis of data collected by hand and carefully mapped, Siegfried attempts to answer a central question: Why do certain rural cantons vote massively for monarchic or conservative candidates,

---

15. In the end, a compromise was found in the framework of the monarchical constitution that officially went into effect in September 1791, which included a right to issue a suspensive veto (for a maximum of two legislative sessions, or four years) that did not apply to financial and budgetary questions.

16. M. Denis, "1815–1848. Que faire de la Révolution française?," in Sirinelli, *Histoire des droites,* vol. 1.

whereas others continue to vote heavily for republican candidates, even within a single department and within cantons that are geographically close and apparently similar? To account for these observations, Siegfried uses two sets of socioeconomic indicators that he also took care to collect at the cantonal level: on the one hand, the data issuing from the real estate tax relating to the distribution of agricultural land in 1883 (making it possible to measure the influence of large properties, defined as the farms larger than forty hectares in the total area of the canton) and on the other hand, the data issuing from a ministerial survey of primary schools for girls in 1911 (making it possible to measure the share of girls enrolled in private schools in the canton).

The thesis Siegfried defends by using his maps is the following: In cantons where land has remained concentrated in the hands of the great landowners, who are often of noble origin, and where the Church has retained its influence, especially through its control over educational institutions, voters support monarchical and conservative candidates. Inversely, in cantons where the redistributions carried out since the Revolution have made it possible to establish small farms and to loosen the grip of the large landowners and the clergy, the peasants vote for republicans.[17] This thesis is debatable, and it can be challenged especially insofar as it presents a purely passive view of the conservative vote, which, as Siegfried sees it, can be analyzed only as the result of the ascendancy of the elites over the rural working classes (which raises several difficulties, as we shall see later). No doubt this can be attributed in part to the fact that Siegfried himself was an unsuccessful republican candidate for a seat in the deputation from Basses-Alpes, facing an aristocrat known for his clientelism (the Count of Castellane), and then again in 1910 in Normandy, where he was also unsuccessful.[18]

Still, Siegfried's work, carried out with limited means, is extremely innovative and impressive, and it has long deserved to be continued and systematized with the aid of supplementary resources. Unfortunately, although this work has often been celebrated, it was not followed by similar research.[19] In 1921, Gaston Génique

17. See A. Siegfried, *Tableau politique de la France de l'Ouest sous la IIIe République* (A. Colin, 1913).

18. See A. L. Sanguin, "Entre contexte personnel et contexte professionnel: André Siegfried et le *Tableau,* une perspective biographique," in *"Le Tableau politique de la France de l'Ouest" d'André Siegfried. Cent ans après, héritages et postérités,* ed. M. Bussi, C. Le Digol, and C. Voillot (Presses Universitaires de Rennes, 2016).

19. For a long time, Siegfried himself planned to extend his 1913 study to other parts of France, in particular in the context of a project devoted to all the departments of the Mediterranean South—a goal he never realized. However, see the partial results published in A. Siegfried, *Géographie électorale de l'Ardèche sous la IIIe République* (A. Colin / Presses de la FNSP, 1949).

published an interesting study on the distribution of votes in the legislative elections of 1849, using, as we do, the electoral reports preserved in the press archives of the time in order to determine the political tendency of the candidates (democrats-socialists, republicans-constitutionals, conservatives).[20] However, the work produced relates to only the departmental level (and not the cantonal level), and contrary to Siegfried, the author does not seek to bring together socioeconomic indicators that might be able to explain the votes observed. In 1937 and 1946, François Goguel, one of Siegfried's main followers at Sciences Po, published his classic works on the French Senate and party politics under the Third Republic. Then in 1951 and 1970 he published very interesting sets of maps indicating the distribution of votes by political tendencies, from the legislative elections of 1871 to those of 1958.[21] Unfortunately, there again, data were gathered only at the department level, with no attempt to relate them systematically to socioeconomic indicators. Starting in 1980 and 1990, Hervé Le Bras and Emmanuel Todd published several stimulating works that analyzed the impact of familial structures (not just social class) on the geography of voting. However, the historical data collected mainly relates to the departmental level, which makes it difficult to rigorously separate the effects of the different variables.[22] Several authors have also published electoral atlases describing the results of elections at the departmental (and sometimes the cantonal) level, but without seeking to connect them systematically with voters' socioeconomic characteristics.[23]

In addition to the factors already mentioned, the fact that Siegfried's approach has not gained widespread acceptance can probably be explained in part by the meteoric rise in postelectoral surveys after the 1950s and 1960s (along with the revival of interest in the history of political tendencies and ideologies). As we have already noted, these surveys permit an analysis at the individual level of the links between socioeconomic characteristics and political behavior, and have led to very rich works. The price to be paid for this methodological innovation is that it may have helped diminish interest in the method based on spatialized electoral data,

20. See G. Génique, *L'élection de l'Assemblée législative en 1849. Essai d'une répartition géographique des partis en France* (Rieder, 1921).

21. See F. Goguel, *Le rôle financier du Sénat français. Essai d'histoire parlementaire* (Sirey, 1937); *La politique des partis sous la IIIe République* (Seuil, 1946).

22. See F. Goguel, *Géographie des élections françaises de 1870 à 1951* (A. Colin, 1951); *Géographie des élections françaises sous la IIIe et la IVe République* (A. Colin, 1970).

23. F. Salmon, *Atlas électoral de la France (1848–2001)* (Seuil, 2002), which includes interesting maps at the departmental level (and even at the cantonal level for some elections). Unfortunately, the corresponding data have not been made public and are not available online.

and in that way, focused attention on the post-1950 period (when it does not focus on more recent periods) and reduced the import of research on the transformations of electorates over long periods.[24] Moreover, even for the recent period, the approach using surveys does not permit us to correlate the variables in a satisfactory way (by taking into account simultaneously income and land, or education and property, for example), or to study the characteristics of the electorates of small parties, because of the size of the samples; by comparison, the use of variations at the municipal level makes such an approach possible.

Understanding the Divisions of the Working Classes, 1789 to 2022

Although the method developed by Siegfried has not really been followed and systematized since his foundational work was published in 1915, several important studies carried out on the level of smaller areas (but with more diversified sources and greater historical depth) have made it possible to go into more detail and, on some points, to revise his conclusions on the origins of the republican electorate and the monarchist or conservative electorate. We refer in particular to the book that Paul Bois devoted to the department of the Sarthe.[25] Like Siegfried, Bois seeks to understand why, under the Third Republic (and, for that matter, under the Fourth Republic as well), the vote for right-wing candidates was much greater in municipalities in the western part of the department than in the eastern part. However, Bois introduces an additional explanatory factor—namely, the profound disillusionment of a large part of the rural working class with regard to the French Revolution. In particular, he shows that peasants in the western part of the department, far from being dominated for all eternity by the traditional elites, were on the contrary the ones who expressed themselves the most virulently in the *Cahiers de doléance* of 1789 and formulated the most pressing demands concerning the clergy and the nobility, especially regarding fiscal injustices and the redistribution of land.

On these two decisive points, the peasants would be deeply disappointed. The general philosophy of the new powers that issued from the French Revolution con-

---

24. A comparable phenomenon for works devoted to the distribution of incomes and inheritances. The development of surveys conducted on households, starting in the 1950s and 1960s, probably delayed the use of fiscal and administrative data, which—despite all their defects—have the immense advantage of going back as far as the nineteenth century and allow more long-term historical perspectives. T. Piketty, *Les hauts revenus en France au 20e siècle* (Grasset, 2001), 23–27; *Le capital au 21e siècle* (Seuil, 2013), 39–40.

25. See P. Bois, *Paysans de l'Ouest. Des structures économiques et sociales aux options politiques depuis l'époque révolutionnaire dans la Sarthe* (Mouton, 1960).

cerning fiscal matters was to reduce indirect taxes (the *gabelle*, which was deeply unpopular, as well as the various duties and indirect taxes weighing on urban areas in particular) and to shift the fiscal burden to the new direct tax system, which was to be based mainly on a property tax proportional to the value of the agricultural land and real estate held. Nothing in this program guaranteed that poor peasants would emerge winners, considering that the new authorities rejected the principle of progressive taxation (that is, levying higher taxes on rural and urban elites than on the rest of the population). In practice, starting in 1791, many peasants encountered higher taxes and fees, not the decreases they had hoped for, especially since the landowners often shifted the new fiscal burden to agricultural rents. The disappointment was even greater regarding the redistribution of land. When the Church's properties were nationalized in 1790, the most important issue for the government in Paris was to refill the state's coffers, not to redistribute land free of charge to the poorest citizens. Church properties were to be auctioned off, and it was largely the urban bourgeois classes that benefited from this and increased their power, much to the displeasure of impoverished country people.

Using especially the records of electoral assemblies in the revolutionary period, Paul Bois convincingly showed that this disappointment was particularly great in the western cantons of Sarthe, where ecclesiastical lands (notably, those owned by the monastic orders, which were particularly unpopular, and on which many hopes were based in the *Cahiers de doléance*) had historically been the largest. Resentment directed toward the urban bourgeois was, of course, encouraged by the clergy and the noblesse, who found it easy to condemn the hypocrisies of the new government, accusing it of ruining the Church and its social works in order to enrich itself, all in the name of justice and equality—as was right and proper. When the authorities in the capital decreed in February 1793 the conscription en masse of 300,000 new draftees, the cantons in the West swung over into royalist insurrection. They retained a long-lasting distrust of republican elites from the cities. Inversely, Bois shows that the ecclesiastical lands were few in number in eastern Sarthe (where noble properties were predominant and were largely spared), such that the resentment directed toward bourgeois who had bought national properties was much less pronounced and was expressed more against the traditional nobility.[26]

---

26. By collecting more data concerning the distribution of land in the cantons of the Sarthe, Bois also shows that in certain cases, a greater concentration of land in the hands of nobles can increase the number of votes for left-wing candidates (not for right-wing candidates, as Siegfried thought). We will return to this question on the national level and confirm to a large extent both Bois's results and the nonsystematic nature of the connection found by Siegfried. See chapter 8.

In addition, even before the Revolution, the eastern cantons were more closely connected with the city through the rapidly developing, multiple activities of weavers in the countryside, which encouraged a greater proximity to the urban world and voting behaviors more favorable to republic tendencies.

The classic work on the Vendée uprising published in 1964 by Charles Tilly confirms Bois's conclusions concerning the deep postrevolutionary disappointment of a large part of the rural working classes.[27] In this case, Tilly is interested in a set of cantons located south of Angers, in Maine-et-Loire, and in particular in the striking contrast between Mauges, west of Layon, the region in revolt par excellence, and the area around Saumur to the east, which remained loyal to the republic and to which we can attach Val (the right bank of the Loire). Tilly also takes as his basis real estate sources and the records of electoral assemblies, and he confirms that the selling off of national properties played a foundational role in the formation of political representations. The urban bourgeoisie succeeded in getting their hands on ecclesiastical lands in a particularly crushing way in Mauges, where the peasants were too poor to be able to buy anything at all, whereas a few of them were able to purchase land in Val-Saumurois, a region that was historically wealthier. Mauges continued to be overtaxed under the Revolution, contrary to the hopes expressed in the *Cahiers de doléance*.[28] Tilly also shows that the poverty in Mauges led to the exclusion of a large proportion of the peasants from the electoral process, which strengthened the grip of the urban bourgeoisie and rich individuals in the countryside on assemblies and elective offices. The military conscription initiated in February 1793 infuriated the peasants of Mauges, who demanded that those who had bought ecclesiastical properties be the first to be sent off to the far reaches of the country and that they cease to benefit from various exemptions. In the first days of March, columns of thousands of peasants took up arms against the government in Paris. This brutal conflict between the countryside and the cities continued to feed resentment and the right-wing vote in Mauges

---

27. See C. Tilly, *The Vendée: A Sociological Analysis of the Counter-Revolution of 1793* (Harvard University Press, 1964) [*La Vendée. Revolution et contre-révolution* (Fayard, 1970)].

28. This is explained in part by the rejection of progressive taxation, which could have benefited poor regions like Mauges, as well as by the fact that the new authorities feared that the new fiscal system (based notably on proportional taxes on land) might lead to excessively large redistributions among territories, so they adopted a system of departmental quotas intermediary between the taxes paid under the Old Regime and the taxes implied by the new bases in force, with a very gradual convergence of the two systems.

during the Third Republic, whereas Val-Saumurois kept its distance from the insurrection and subsequently voted for republican candidates and for the Left.[29]

Without denying the electoral influence of the elites and the importance of the phenomena of manipulation and capture analyzed by Siegfried, phenomena that play a central role in political processes at the end of the eighteenth century and during the nineteenth, as they still do in the twenty-first century,[30] it seems to us that this thesis of a postrevolutionary disappointment and more generally of the "hypocrisies of the Left" (and in particular, of certain "left-wing elites" or groups perceived as such—in this case, the urban bourgeoisie benefiting from the Revolution) deserves to be taken seriously. In particular, the Left has been regularly accused by the Right of taking pleasure in making abstract remarks about social justice that ultimately enable it to present itself in a favorable light while at the same time pursuing its own interests. This kind of discourse always contains a grain of truth, and we begin by analyzing the social and political conditions of its diffusion and efficacy, just as we do for other discourses (in particular, those on the hypocrisies of the different right-wing groups and their elites). In addition to the case of Siegfried, who, as a good republican of the triumphal Third Republic, tends to demonize the monarchist or conservative vote (which cannot be solely the effect of the elite's influence) and to conclude that the republican vote is the only one in conformity with the interests of the working classes (while at the same time remaining wary of the socialist vote), since 1789 there has been a repeated tendency to consider the rural world as structurally conservative, eternally in thrall to the powerful and perpetually resistant to progress and democracy, whereas the urban world is supposed to be the bearer of the values of modernity and change, of solidarity and respect for difference. These prejudices are all the more widespread because they have been diffused both by the urban, liberal bourgeoisie (which is often sure of its right and of the legitimacy of its civilizing mission with regard to the rural masses, who are considered backward) and by many socialist and working-class tendencies (which are often persuaded that only the urban proletariat was

---

29. In an interesting way, the economic and political balance was inverted at the end of the twentieth century and the beginning of the twenty-first: Val-Saumurois, which was formerly more prosperous than Mauges, lost its industrial jobs and swung over to a strong vote for FN and then RN, whereas Mauges handled its conversion more successfully, continuing to support the traditional Right or the Center-Right. See J. Prugneau and E. Bioteau, "Une 'frontière de l'Ouest intérieur.' Cent ans après Siegfried, retour sur le Layon," in Bussi, Le Digol, and Voillot, *"Le Tableau" . . . d'André Siegfried.*

30. See J. Cagé, *Le prix de la démocratie* (Fayard, 2018).

the bearer of revolutionary changes, whereas the peasantry is doomed to be conservative and submissive with regard to the elites old and new).

Such prejudices do not survive analysis. Generally speaking, in the eighteenth
century, peasant revolts played a central role in the process leading to the French
Revolution and then as the Revolution unfolded. The National Assembly's abolition of privileges on 4 August owed a great deal to the peasant revolts in the
summer of 1789, which attacked lords and chateaus and began to burn the titles
to property that they found there, which ultimately convinced the deputies meeting
in Paris that they had to act as quickly as possible and put an end to the discredited institutions of feudalism. These revolts themselves followed decades of peasant
rebellions that the divided government was less and less able to control, particularly during the summer of 1788, when the question of the modalities of the election for the Estates General was finally clearly raised, in a quasi-insurrectional
atmosphere (amid the occupations of parcels of land and communal properties
and anti-landowner violence).[31]

If so many peasants later turned their backs on the Revolution, it is not because
they suddenly became conservatives. It is because their hopes of gaining access to
property and being able to stop working for other people had been dashed, and
because the peasants were marked by what they perceived as an unbearable hypocrisy on the part of the so-called revolutionary urban elites who had taken the
lead. This foundational disappointment, well studied by Bois and Tilly, is essential for understanding the initial formation of partisan and electoral structures and
their later developments. We should also note that in several regions we see a
strong Socialist and Communist vote in the nineteenth and twentieth centuries,
particularly in the legislative elections of 1849 (which saw a rural left-wing vote
that frightened many property owners) and then in the interwar and postwar
periods with the vote for the French Communist Party.[32] This reminds us that
nothing is set in stone; everything depends on the way in which political
organizations succeed or fail in mobilizing electorates around collective projects.

---

31. See J. Nicolas, *La rébellion française. Mouvements populaires et conscience sociale, 1661–1789*
(Gallimard, 2002), which lists eighty-seven antiseigneurial rebellions in 1730–1759 and 246 in
1760–1789. See also G. Lemarchand, *Paysans et seigneurs en Europe. Une histoire comparée,
16e–19e siècles* (Presses Universitaires de Rennes, 2011), which emphasizes the role of peasant
revolts on the European scale, in particular during the years preceding the wave of revolutions
in 1848.

32. See, for example, L. Boswell, *Le communisme rural en France. Le Limousin et la Dordogne de
1920 à 1939* (Pulim, 2006). See also J. Mischi, "Ouvriers ruraux, pouvoir local et conflit de
classe," in *Campagnes populaires, campagnes bourgeoises,* Agone 51 (2013), 8–33.

We will also see that over the past two centuries, participation in elections has been structurally greater in the rural world, a phenomenon that has moreover been seen as early as the revolutionary period, which shows that the demand for democracy has never been limited to the world of the cities—on the contrary. The diverse working classes, average or well-off, rural or urban, have always had reasons to adopt this or that political behavior, and it is above all important to begin by understanding these reasons, in 1789 as in 2022, rather than seeking from the outset to stigmatize or essentialize them.

Multidimensionality and the Metamorphoses of Sociopolitical Cleavages: Rethinking Political Conflict on the Basis of Geosocial Classes

That is why in this book we will emphasize the multidimensionality of sociopolitical cleavages from the French Revolution to the present and the necessity of understanding the different points of view on the current conflicts. To sum up, social class exists, and it has never stopped playing a crucial role in political confrontation. However, to be productive, it must be seen in a multidimensional and spatial perspective. For analyzing the developments of socioeconomic inequalities as well as for examining the structure of political conflict and its transformations, the pertinent concept of social class corresponds in reality to a geosocial (or sociospatial) class whose contours are constantly being redefined by economic processes, and especially by the ongoing political experiences and lessons that each individual draws from events. The concept of a geosocial class that we will use includes, of course, the question of the relation to the territory and to natural resources, means of transportation, and sources of energy (in connection with the analyses developed by Bruno Latour, for example).[33] But it is a notion that must be understood in the broader sense, in its socioeconomic dimensions. It includes in particular the question of inequalities of access to social transfers and public services (schools, hospitals, athletic and cultural facilities, public infrastructures, and so on), the questions of possession of the means of production, of the hierarchy of salaries and incomes, of access to property and housing, of fiscal and social justice—subjects that all have a strong territorial dimension.

Within the rural world, as in the urban world, disparities between social classes thus appear as multiple and changing, especially in relation to the sector of activity involved, to what the different groups have and the ways in which they fit into the

---

33. See B. Latour and N. Schultz, *Mémo sur la nouvelle classe écologique. Comment faire émerger une nouvelle classe écologique consciente et fière d'elle-même* (La Découverte, 2022).

social and spatial fabric, to their hopes and expectations. Beyond broad statements of intentions (the end of privileges, the establishment of a fairer fiscal system and a better distribution of wealth and opportunities), successive governments find themselves obligated to negotiate complex arbitrages and to create countless frustrations as soon as they actually exercise power, as were the new authorities issuing from the Revolution of 1789. From the outset, the fundamental political conflict is not unidimensional (the poor versus the rich). It is at least bidimensional (the poor versus the rich; country people versus city dwellers), with very different ways of seeing the world and different expectations among the rural working classes and urban working classes, the former often tending to fear that they will be neglected in comparison with the latter (sometimes with good reason), as well as among the rural and urban wealthy classes. This bidimensional conflict immediately defines a structure with at least four large geosocial classes and not two (poor country people, wealthy country people; poor city dwellers, wealthy city dwellers), not to mention intermediary classes, which multiply accordingly the possible coalitions and the different forms of bipartition or tripartition. We can even say that the initial conflict that resulted from the Revolution was tridimensional (at least), because the experience of the rural working classes was not the same depending on whether, historically speaking, they had had to confront ecclesiastical property owners (whose goods were often acquired by the urban bourgeoisie after 1789, whence particular resentments against the urban world) or noble landowners (which, depending on the attitude of the local nobility and the development of the successive mobilizations, might have helped feed various political positions).

For two centuries, this initial complexity had undergone multiple transformations on the same scale as the profound social, economic, and political changes that the country had experienced since 1789. However, the overall structure retained some of its original aspects. The feelings of abandonment—regarding the absence of public services in rural areas, the difficulty of gaining access to property and wealth, and the accusations of hypocrisy made against various camps, for example—all continued to play a structuring role. At times, and in particular during periods of bipolarization in the course of the twentieth century, certain political movements succeeded in convincing the rural and urban working classes that what bound them together was more important than what divided them, thus imposing a conflict based on class. But generally speaking, the rural world's distrust of the urban world remained very strong. In 1793, the peasantry feared being despoiled by the cities, and specifically by the urban bourgeoisie. In 1848 and 1871, rural voters attributed the worst goals to the zealots and the new proletarians in the cities: the destruction of the private property to which they aspired, and a fresh challenge to the family and religion. In 2022, voters in villages and towns attributed to voters in the working-class suburbs and the metropoles intentions that were hardly more reassuring: ethnic quotas, urban privileges, abolition of the police, welfare, Islamo-leftism, and "wokism." This immense incomprehension often has something excessive about it, but it always has its reasons, rooted in socioeconomic disparities and contradictory worldviews that must be analyzed publicly. Usually, it plays the game of the elites, who can benefit from these confrontations to keep themselves in power and perpetuate a high degree of inequality, in the nineteenth century as in this beginning of the twenty-first century. In theory, we can always imagine after the fact programmatic platforms that might have made it possible to unite rural and urban working-class voters in the various periods. But the task is clearly more complex in contemporary reality than in a retrospective analysis. Our primary objective will be, first, to understand the reasons for these divisions and the logics presiding over their transformations, hoping, naturally, that that might help renew our perspectives on the crises of the present.

Our analysis is also inspired by the works of the political analysts Seymour Lipset and Stein Rokkan, who set out in the 1960s to analyze party systems and their evolution by adopting a multidimensional view of electoral cleavages. Their classification is based on the idea that modern societies have been marked by two major revolutions: the national revolution—through the construction of a centralized state power and of the nation-state—and the Industrial Revolution. According to Lipset and Rokkan, these two revolutions gave rise to four great political cleavages, whose importance varied depending on the countries involved: the cleavage between the center and the periphery (the central regions, or those close to the capital, and the regions that saw themselves as peripheral); the cleavage between the centralized state and the churches; the cleavage between the agricultural and the industrial sectors; and finally the cleavage concerning the ownership of the means of production, which opposed the workers to employers and to property owners.[34] Today, we must add the migratory and identitarian cleavage, the cleavage over globalization and international economic integration, and of course the cleavage over the environment and climate change. There, too, we will seek in each case to understand how the different socioeconomic characteristics help structure worldviews and contradictory expectations on all these questions.

---

34. See S. Lipset and S. Rokkan, "Cleavage Structures, Party Systems and Voter Alignments: An introduction," in *Party Systems and Voter Alignments: Cross-national Perspectives* (Free Press 1967.

A Central Hypothesis: The Classist Conflict Makes the March toward Equality Possible

Even so, in this book we do not intend to simply reject all beliefs and all discourses. Understanding different points of view does not exclude trying to analyze the measure in which the different electoral configurations have contributed to good democratic functioning and more generally to socioeconomic development. In particular, we will see that the tendency to bipolarization observed during the twentieth century, from 1900–1910 to 1990–2000, and particularly between 1958 and 1992, was accompanied by broad participation in voting and by a powerful movement toward greater socioeconomic equality, a movement that has historically been inseparable from movement toward greater collective prosperity. It corresponds to phases in which the spatial divisions tend to disappear behind social divisions, and in which both the former and the latter tend to diminish. Inversely, the phases of tripartition observed in the nineteenth century and the beginning of the twenty-first century have been accompanied by unequal participation (like the decline in turnout seen in the course of recent decades, which is unparalleled for two centuries), increased inequalities, and relative social and economic stagnation.

In summary, bipartition and classist conflict allow democracy to function and continue the march toward equality and social and economic progress.[35] Inversely, tripartition often feeds on a division of the working classes on the basis of spatial and identitarian conflicts, which tends to prevent the peaceful, democratic devolution of power and to hobble the movement toward equality and the resolution of tangible problems that arise.

Let us say at the outset that all electoral configurations (bipartition, tripartition, quadripartition, and so on) have their advantages and disadvantages, and especially that they have their own reasons and logics, such that it would make no sense to rank them in a strict hierarchy. The central hypothesis presented in this work seems to us the most coherent with the historical materials at our disposal, and we will try to weigh patiently all the elements pushing us in this direction or another. But it must be considered a historical hypothesis, reasonable and supported

---

35. Let us emphasize in passing that, contrary to what theorists of populism like Ernesto Laclau and Chantal Mouffe claim, the classist and multidimensional approach of the opposition between the humbler and the more privileged is a more pertinent way of reading social inequalities than the one that would consist in simply opposing "adversaries" separated by purely political borderlines and not socioeconomic borderlines. In particular, the classist approach enables us to consider the possibility, by establishing economic and social policies that are appropriate and clearly explained, the transcendence of antagonisms.

by arguments, and not an absolute and intangible law. The social sciences are above all historical sciences; they are not experimental sciences, and therefore we are not going to replay the electoral and political history of the past two centuries, replacing bipartition with tripartition or inversely. In theory, we could very easily imagine a democratic world where bipartition and tripartition would both have disappeared in their current forms, and where differences of opinion and beliefs would depend entirely on the deliberative process itself and no longer on socioeconomic characteristics. But none of that seems able to be materialized within a visible horizon. Political opinions are certainly never reducible to socioeconomic determinants. They always depend in large measure on the subjective, private experience of each individual, on meetings and exchanges, on the hopes and the worldview that flow from it. The fact remains that the individual socioeconomic variables (including the size of the agglomeration and the municipality, the sector of activity and occupation, the level of property and income, age and gender, education and diploma, and religion and origin), understood in the broad sense, have lost none of their importance in the past two centuries—quite the contrary. We will see that their explanatory power has even had a tendency to increase in recent decades. There is nothing astonishing about that, and it must not be interpreted as a sign of selfishness or self-absorption; it is legitimate that the multiple social experiences help feed the different worldviews that people subsequently bring to the table of democratic deliberation and the electoral confrontation, especially in periods of intense transformation.

From this point of view, the immense advantage of a bipolar, Left-Right conflict of the classist type—primarily between the working classes and the wealthy classes, or else between the most disadvantaged classes and the less disadvantaged classes, defined by, for example, their levels of real estate and financial capital, income, or diploma, independent of their geographic or cultural origins—is that it provides "grist for the mill." In other words, conflicts intermediated by social class are potentially solvable in redistribution and economic and social transformation, whether it is a matter of incomes, salaries, or property, the circulation and sharing of power, the amelioration of working conditions and participation, or egalitarian access to education and healthcare. It is certainly never simple to set the cursor at the right level on these different questions. But an assumed democratic confrontation between several classist parties contributing points of view and complementary experiences can contribute to it. If there is something healthy about classist conflict, that is clearly not because the working-class bloc wants to go too far in redistribution, or that the bourgeois bloc is too timid. There are also and especially an infinite number of variations in the methods of structuring redistribution and of organizing the property system and the fiscal system, the educational system and the real estate system, the healthcare system and the retirement system, and so on. Historical experience suggests that in the face of such complexity, a democratic confrontation between two coalitions defined on a principally classist basis may allow us to work out solutions and advance toward the construction of a new social and economic system, in the context of a driving dialectic.

By comparison, the tripartition of political life is often accompanied by a division of the rural and urban working classes around identitarian conflicts based on geographical origins or ethnic or religious identities. The problem is that such conflicts often do not admit of any solution other than the exacerbation of the conflict itself or the destruction of one camp by the other. This can lead to political dead ends, such as situations in which the privileged classes remain in power by playing on the divisions between the two camps, or, more generally, blockages preventing the adversaries from finding solutions to the great socioeconomic problems of the moment (inequalities, education, the environment, security, and so on). However, it would be a mistake to attribute all "identitarian" conflicts to a form of tribalism from which there is no escape. Taking into account in a rational way the multiple forms of sociocultural and ethnoreligious differences sometimes requires the invention of new politics based on respect for diversity and common rules, the battle against discriminations, and the shared need for individual and collective security. In the same way, it would be absurd to reduce every form of rural-urban cleavage to an identitarian conflict. As we have already noted, the origin of rural-urban conflict often lies in misunderstandings, frustrations, and sociospatial hypocrisies that must be examined closely and generally admit of socioeconomic solutions—the reorganization of public services and a better redistribution of medical and educational infrastructures in the field, for example. In addition to examining the question of bipartition and tripartition, we will seek above all to improve our understanding of the multiple dimensions of political conflict and the reasons why the different social classes have adopted this or that electoral behavior in France over the past two centuries.

Finally, let us emphasize that all the hypotheses and interpretations presented here require, of course, ample discussion. Our objective in this work is to open a debate on a new empirical and historical basis, and not in any way to end it. We hope that the interpretations defended in this book, along with the data put online, will make it possible for everyone to clarify their own hypotheses and will help provide material for the essential future democratic confrontation over these complex questions.

The Outline of This Book

The rest of this work is composed of fourteen chapters in four parts. The first part, titled "Classes and Territories: Sociospatial Inequalities in France since the Revolution," consists of four chapters. The objective of this first part is to set up the general framework in terms of sociospatial inequalities, which will be used in the following parts to study the transformations of electoral behaviors. Chapter 1 analyzes what is no doubt the most striking structural development on the level of the right to vote and political equality as well as the redistribution of wealth and socioeconomic equality—namely, the existence of a limited but real advance toward greater social equality in France since the Revolution. Chapter 2 introduces the spatial dimensions and shows that this limited progress toward equality over the long term is located in the context of a growing polarization of the population and the rise of territorial inequalities in the course of recent decades. Chapter 3 introduces the metamorphoses and persistence of educational inequalities, as well as the structuring role of the public-private cleavage and the religious question of religion. Finally, Chapter 4 introduces the new identitarian cleavages connected with national or ethnic origins and their interaction with the other dimensions.

The second part, "The Rise and Fall of Democratic Mobilization: Electoral Turnout in France, 1789–2022," consists of three chapters. Chapter 5 begins by studying the general evolution of electoral participation since the Revolution by examining one after the other the three main categories of national elections analyzed in this work—namely, legislative elections, presidential elections, and referenda. Chapter 6 examines the socioeconomic factors determining participation in the framework of the legislative elections conducted from 1848 to 2022, emphasizing the existence of a rural participation that has been structurally greater for the past two centuries (with interesting exceptions) and the unprecedented disconnect between the participation of the poorest municipalities and that of the richest ones since 1980–1990 (a phenomenon largely unknown earlier). Chapter 7 extends this analysis to the participation in presidential elections and referenda.

The third part, titled "Between Bipolarization and Tripartition: Two Centuries of Legislative Elections in France," offers a general analysis of the socioeconomic determinants of the vote for the various political tendencies from the legislative elections from 1842 to 2022. Chapter 8 begins by providing an overview of the general structure of coalitions and political families as expressed in legislative elections since 1848. Chapter 9 takes a more detailed look at the socioeconomic structures of the vote during what might be called the first major period of tripartition

(1848–1910). Chapter 10 analyzes the difficult process of building a system based on Left-Right bipolarization during the period 1910–1992. Finally, chapter 11 examines trends toward a new form of tripartition between 1992 and 2022 and analyzes different scenarios for future developments.

The fourth part, "Between Representative Democracy and Direct Democracy: Political Cleavages in Presidential Elections and Referenda," examines the role of presidential elections and referenda in the transformations of the socioeconomic determinants of voting. Chapter 12 begins by analyzing the case of the presidential election of 1848 and its reinvention between 1965 and 1995. Then chapter 13 examines the metamorphosis of the presidential elections from 2002 to 2022. Finally, chapter 14 analyzes the role of referenda in electoral and socioeconomic cleavages, with particular emphasis on the role of the European referenda of 1992 and 2005, which were a powerful catalyst for the tripartition of recent decades, and this leads us back to the question of possible future developments.

In order to facilitate reading, only the main sources and references are cited in the text and the footnotes. Readers who want to obtain detailed information on all the sources and methods used in this book are asked to consult the site unehistoireduconflitpolitique.fr, where they will also find the complete database of electoral and socioeconomic information constituted in the framework of this research project, along with numerous supplementary materials. In particular, each individual will be able to download all the graphs, tables, and maps presented in the book, as well as all the corresponding series and all the information and computer codes that make it possible to reproduce them, from the raw data to the final series. Hundreds of supplementary graphs and maps will also be available, along with an interface enabling everyone to explore the data in their own way—for example, by producing maps and graphs showing the evolution of the structure of voting and the level of wealth for a chosen municipality over the last two centuries. The database and the tools made available will be regularly updated, and we thank in advance users who are so kind as to inform us, via the interface provided for that purpose, of any observations, reactions, and suggestions they might have with a view to possible improvements.

PART I

Classes and Territories

SOCIOSPATIAL INEQUALITIES IN FRANCE
SINCE THE REVOLUTION

CHAPTER 1

A Limited and Tumultuous Advance toward Equality

Before studying the transformations of voting behaviors, in the first part of this book we will analyze the main lines of the evolution of sociospatial inequalities in France since 1789. Political attitudes are in fact part of a social structure undergoing a profound reconfiguration, and it is essential to begin by assessing its importance, especially since political choices will themselves influence these transformations. In this chapter we will first analyze what is probably the most striking structural development: a limited but real advance toward greater equality in France on the political, social, and economic levels since the Revolution, albeit with an interruption and the beginning of a new rise in inequalities in recent decades that today arouses profound concerns. In the following chapters we will examine the other most striking transformations, emphasizing the growing polarization of the population nationally and the return of territorial inequalities; then the persistence of educational inequalities and the historical roles of the public-private cleavage and the religious question; and finally the new identitarian cleavages connected with origins and how they interact with other dimensions.

An Uncompleted Advance toward Political Equality

Let us begin with what is probably the best-known transformation, and also the most fundamental one: a real but incomplete advance toward greater political equality since 1789. This advance may first be seen in the quantitative evolution of the right to vote. The population of Metropolitan France (in its current territory) has risen from about 28 million inhabitants in 1789 to 66 million in 2022, and the adult population (by today's standard—that is, eighteen years old and older) has risen from about 18 million in 1789 to 52 million in 2022, following a relatively slow and regular increase that has been accelerating since 1945, ultimately almost tripling the population in a little more than two centuries.[1] The population

---

1. Between 1789 and 2022, the average growth rate of the total population was 0.4 percent per annum, as opposed to 0.6 percent per annum in Europe and 0.9 percent per annum on the global level over the same period.

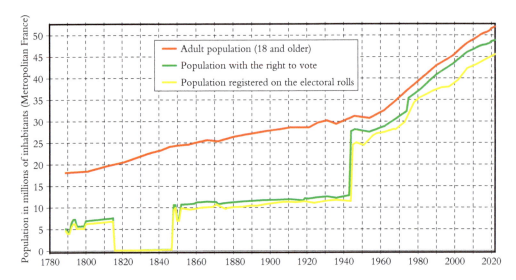

FIGURE 1.1. The right to vote in France, 1789–2022

The population with the right to vote was about 5–6 million in France under the Revolution, fell to 0.1–0.2 million under the Restoration (censitary suffrage), and then grew to more than 10 million in 1848 (universal male suffrage), almost 28 million in 1944 (universal female suffrage), and 48 million in 2022 (for an adult population of 52 million).

Sources and series: unehistoireduconflitpolitique.fr

that has the right to vote evolved in a clearly less linear way. During the French Revolution and the Empire, from 1789 to 1815, the country had around 5–6 million potential voters—that is, adult men with the right to vote. This number fell to 0.1–0.2 million under the Restoration and the monarchies based on censitary suffrage (1815–1848), before bouncing back to 10 million with the establishment of universal male suffrage following the Revolution of 1848, and then to nearly 28 million in 1944 with universal female suffrage. Since then, the number of potential voters has followed the evolution of the population, except for the little leap connected with the lowering of the voting age from twenty-one to eighteen in 1974 (see figure 1.1).

On the whole, if we examine the proportion of the adult population that has the right to vote, we note a substantial but chaotic advance in the last two centuries. About 30–40 percent of adults had the right to vote under the Revolution and the Empire, then that proportion fell to less than 1 percent under the Restoration and the censitary monarchies before rising again to 45 percent in 1848 and more than 90 percent in 1944. Since then, only individuals of foreign nationality have not had the right to vote, so the proportion of potential voters in the adult

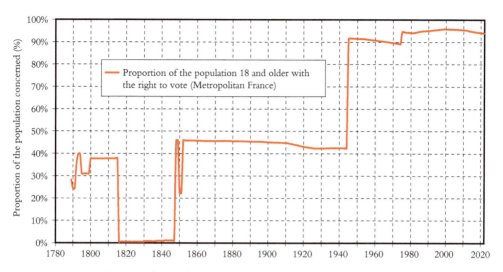

FIGURE 1.2. The long march toward universal suffrage

The proportion of the adult population aged eighteen and over) with the right to vote was about 30–40% in France during the Revolution, fell to 0.5–1% between 1815 and 1848 (censitary suffrage), then grew to about 45% in 1848 with the implementation of universal male suffrage and more than 90% in 1944 with universal female suffrage.

Sources and series: unehistoireduconflitpolitique.fr

population is around 90–95 percent, depending on the evolution of the proportion of foreigners (see figure 1.2).[2] If we limit ourselves to the adult male population, we see that between 1789 and 1815 the proportion of adult males with the right to vote was around 60–80 percent, before falling to 1–2 percent between 1815 and 1848 and then stabilizing around 90–95 percent, where it has remained since 1848 (see figure 1.3).

The Hopes and Limits of the Revolutionary Assemblies

Several points regarding these developments must be stressed at the outset. First, we have to emphasize that the French Revolution truly constitutes the birth of electoral democracy on the global scale. It was the first time in history that such a

---

2. In 2022, foreigners represented about 8 percent of the adult population—that is, 92 percent of the adult population had the right to vote. Here, we are not taking into account persons of French nationality who were deprived of their civil and electoral rights (a rare and temporary measure).

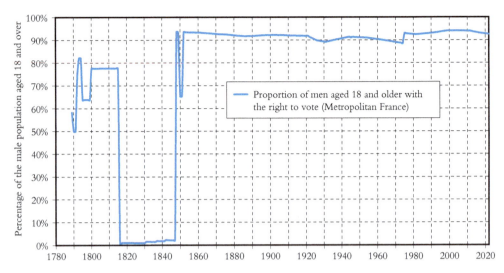

FIGURE 1.3. Male suffrage in France, 1789–2022

The proportion of the adult male population (aged eighteen and over) with the right to vote was about 60–80% in France during the Revolution, fell to 1–2% between 1815 and 1848 (censitary suffrage), then rose to 90% in 1848 with the implementation of universal male suffrage.
Sources and series: unehistoireduconflitpolitique.fr

large number of persons (between 5 and 6 million between 1789 and 1815, and even a little more than 7 million in 1792–1794) was called to the polls, in a regular and recurring way, in order to decide the destiny of a large country populated by nearly 30 million people. In comparison, Athens and the other cities of antiquity had at most a few tens of thousands of citizen-electors. When the French Revolution began, the United Kingdom had scarcely 300,000 electors (out of a total population of 14 million) and the United States had about the same number (out of a population of 3 million, including slaves).

To be sure, having the right to vote did not mean that one actually had political power. First, one had to be registered on the voters' lists—which for the last two centuries in France has generally been the case for about 90 percent of those who have had the right to vote—and above all, one had to go vote and make one's voice heard. In the second part of this book, we will analyze in detail the development of the rate of voter registration and the rate of turnout. During the Revolution, turnout reached 30–40 percent, then climbed and stabilized at around 70–80 percent from 1848 to the 1980s and 1990s, and then underwent a marked decline starting in 1990–2000, with less than 50 percent turnout among registered voters in the last legislative elections.[3] At this point, let us simply note that the rate of turnout on the order of 30–40 percent seen under the Revolution is far from negligible, considering the defective organization of the voting system. Moreover, this turnout was greater in the countryside, which shows a particularly strong form of rootedness and democratic appropriation.

We must also emphasize that the Revolution of 1789 set up a very extensive election system in which people were voting constantly and on everything—municipal, cantonal, and departmental elections, legislative elections, elections for justices of the peace, officers of the National Guard, and so on—passing by way of the administrators of districts and departments, directors of polling stations, priests, and bishops. The US historian Marvin Edelstein, the author of the standard work on elections under the French Revolution, calculates that in all, there were about 1.2 million elective offices that had to be filled during the first years of the Revolution in 1790–1791. This veritable elective frenzy that seized the country between 1789 and 1799 was accompanied by a new division of the territory, within which there were organized incessant electoral assemblies that met at the level of the municipality or the main city of the canton, the district, or the department.[4]

This ambitious elective system was not without contradictions and hypocrisies. In addition to excluding women, the electoral system eliminated a non-negligible fraction of the poorest men (between one-quarter and half the adult men, depending on the period). Initially, the regulation of January 1789, established in view of the elections to the Estates General, granted the right to vote to all men over twenty-five who resided in the municipality and were registered on the *rôles de contributions*—that is, those who paid a direct tax in the municipality (no matter how small this tax was). In practice, the regulation excluded young adults, persons who were itinerant or had no stable residence, and all servants. Among the male

---

3.   See chapter 5, figure 5.2.

4.   See M. Edelstein, *La Révolution française et la naissance de la démocratie électorale* (Presses Universitaires de Rennes, 2013). See also M. Crook, *Elections in the French Revolution: An Apprenticeship in Democracy, 1789–1799* (Cambridge University Press, 1996); S. Aberdam, *L'élargissement du droit de vote entre 1792 et 1795 au travers du dénombrement du comité de division et des votes populaires sur les constitutions de 1793 et 1795* (Paris I, 2001); S. Aberdam, *Démographes et démocrates. L'oeuvre du comité de division de la Convention nationale* (SER, 2004); S. Aberdam et al., *Voter, élire pendant la Révolution française 1789–1799. Guide pour la recherche* (CTHS, 2006); P. Gueniffey, *Le nombre et la raison. La Révolution française et les élections* (EHESS, 1993; repr., Cerf, 2020). The districts were the groups of cantons in force from 1789 to 1799; they were replaced in 1800 by arrondissements, units intermediary between the canton and the department, corresponding today to the subprefectures.

population over eighteen years old, it is estimated that nearly 15 percent of the men were excluded by the age requirement and about 25 percent by other requirements, such that the proportion of potential electors was on the order of 60 percent. The foundational elections took place all over the country in March and April 1789, at the same time that the *Cahiers de doléance* were being composed. Shortly after the meeting of the Estates General in Versailles, and then in Paris, in May and June 1789, the elected representatives of the Third Estate constituted themselves as the National Assembly, where after many debates they were joined by the elected representatives of the nobility and the clergy (who, with 2 percent of the population, had as many representatives in the Estates General as the Third Estate did with 98 percent of the population).[5] The Assembly then set about writing a constitution. The electoral law adopted in October 1789 outlined the main rules applicable to the legislative elections conducted over the following decade.

In summary, for all the legislative elections held from 1789 to 1799, notably in 1791, 1792, 1795, and 1798, the general principle was that the election of deputies took place in two stages. All men who had the right to vote (around 60 to 70 percent of men older than eighteen) were first called on to meet in a primary assembly in the canton's main town in order to designate the departmental electors. Then those electors met in the department's main town, usually one week later, and it was that departmental assembly that designated the deputies who would have seats in Paris. The problem was that access to the office of departmental elector was reserved for a relatively restricted group, generally the richest 10 percent of male adults. In other words, participation in the primary assemblies seems to have been relatively open, and in fact it was, for the period, with 60 to 70 percent of the men eligible to vote, but at the crucial moment, only the richest 10 percent of men remained on stage. Thus, the sole function of the poorest voters was to choose who among the richest men would represent them (or more precisely, who among the richest would meet in the departmental assembly to choose the deputies) and to create a false and hypocritical first impression that it was a democratic representative system when actually it was centered on the richest few.

---

5. When the meeting of the Assembly of Notables was closed by Louis XVI in 1787–1788, the question of voting by orders or voting by heads during future Estates General still had not been resolved (confronted by the opposition of the notables and the jurists of the Parisian *parlement,* they simply continued the rules of voting by orders that had been applied to the preceding Estates General in 1614), but it was nonetheless decided to double the number of representatives of the Third Estate, a fateful decision considering that the representatives of the Third Estate were going to impose de facto voting by heads.

Initially, the electoral law adopted in October 1789 foresaw a third threshold. Access to the primary assemblies was reserved for men who were twenty-five or older, resided in the municipality, and paid a direct tax equal to three days' work (three livres),[6] a threshold that did not exist for the elections to the Estates General. This brought the proportion of potential electors among adult men to below 60 percent.[7] To be designated as a departmental elector, one had to pay at least ten livres in direct taxes (about 25 percent of adult men met this requirement),[8] and to be elected as a deputy, one had to pay at least one *marc d'argent,* or fifty livres (less than 5 percent of adult men met this requirement). The rule of the *marc d'argent* provoked vigorous reactions, particularly among the urban lower and middle bourgeoisie, who approved of the exclusion of landless peasants and the poorest city dwellers (who were confined to the primary assemblies or completely excluded from the process), but considered themselves to be perfectly qualified to participate fully in the elections. This rule was finally abolished in 1791, but after bitter negotiations, the threshold for serving as a departmental elector was raised so high that only 10 percent of adult males could meet it.[9]

Then events accelerated. In June 1791, just as the new monarchical constitution was going into effect, the king was caught trying to escape abroad. Not without reason, Louis XVI was accused of attempting to join the exiled nobles and of plotting with European monarchies to snuff out the Revolution by military means. After that, he was never able to completely restore confidence. While the threat of war was approaching, the insurrection of 10 August 1792 led to Louis XVI's arrest, and he was guillotined five months later, in January 1793. Under pressure from the insurgents, who invaded both the Tuileries Palace and the National Assembly (which still included supporters of the constitutional monarchy), the Assembly decided on 11 August to dissolve itself and to hold an election for a

---

6. The price of a day's work was set at a maximum of one livre in large cities and a maximum of a *demi-livre* in the countryside. At the time, the average national income per inhabitant (men, women, and children lumped together) was close to 200 livres per year (or 200 gold francs, considering that the *franc germinal* instituted in 1803 and used until 1914 had the same metal content and approximately the same purchasing power as the *livre tournois,* which had been in circulation since 1726.

7. More precisely, by comparison with the elections to the Estates General, the proportion of potential electors fell by approximately 75 to 65 percent among men over twenty-five and from 60 to 50 percent among those over eighteen. But the new rule was nonetheless more open than the one set for the municipal elections of 1787 (ten livres to be an elector, thirty livres to be eligible.

8. This same threshold was applied for access to other elective offices that were not legislative.

9. This threshold was set at twenty-five livres for rural property owners and fifty livres for urban property owners, in a context where direct contributions, too, were increasing.

National Convention to be entrusted with writing a new, republican constitution. The right to vote was immediately extended to all men twenty-one or over who resided in the municipality, without a minimal tax payment. However, servants were still excluded, and the two-level election system still applied. The primary assemblies were convoked on 26 August, followed by departmental assemblies on 2 September. Any of the electors in the primary assemblies, who now represented more than 70 percent of adult males, could in principle be elected as a departmental elector and then as a deputy, but this revolutionary development, announced two weeks before the elections, was rarely applied. The Republic was officially proclaimed by the Convention on 20 September 1792, the very day of France's victory in the Battle of Valmy. The republican constitution adopted in June 1793 and ratified by referendum in July 1793 instituted quasi-universal male suffrage (more than 80 percent of adult men, including servants) and direct election of deputies by the totality of the electors, without passing through the departmental assembly and without any tax threshold.[10] However, this new system did not last long enough to be applied; it was replaced in 1795 by the Directory's constitution, which reintroduced censitary rules similar to those of 1791, with a double tax threshold for participation in primary assemblies (about 60 percent of adult men) and in the departmental assemblies entrusted with designating the deputies (between 5 and 10 percent of adult men).

The Battle for Universal Suffrage and Power Sharing

Generally speaking, the battle for universal suffrage has always been inseparable from a broader debate about the organization of public authorities and the rules of the devolution of political power. The electoral system set up in 1789, with more than a million offices to be filled by elections held throughout the country, represented a relatively ambitious form of participative democracy. The primary assemblies not only aimed to provide for the most diverse offices but also were sites where wishes and petitions could be discussed and approved. The constitution adopted in June 1793 also provided that the primary assemblies might under certain conditions take up a law directly within forty days of its adoption by the par-

---

10. The new constitution extended the right to vote to all men twenty-one and over who had resided in the municipality for more than six months, without the requirement that they be on the tax rolls. In order to protect against the risks of future manipulation, it provided that the legislative districts would be established on the basis of 40,000 inhabitants per deputy (between 39,000 and 41,000 inhabitants, to be precise) over the whole territory, with direct election of representatives by the citizens.

liament and proceed to reexamine it, thus introducing possibilities of direct and participative democracy.[11] During the referendum of July 1793 (concerning the adoption of the constitution)—the only election in which it was possible to apply quasi-universal male suffrage, and the national election with the greatest turnout of the whole revolutionary period—the primary assemblies designated some 7,000 envoys assigned to transmit to the Convention the results of the deliberations as well as the most diverse wishes, all with compensation planned for transportation and lodging in Paris so that even the humblest citizens could make the trip (a system that had already been introduced in 1792 for the deputies, and extended to all in 1795). An analysis of the minutes of the primary assemblies shows the strength of the demand for political participation, in particular among the sharecroppers and the poorest peasants, who were often excluded from the assemblies of 1790–1791 and who tried in 1792–1793 to make their voices heard demanding a fairer fiscal system and a better division of land and the national assets.[12]

Despite these promising innovations, the institutional system that was tried out during the Revolution had important limits. For a large part of the elites, whether urban or rural, it was inconceivable to let the working classes, who were poor and little educated, elect the deputies directly, or, worse yet, to let them come to Paris to occupy seats in the assembly themselves. The goal of the twofold system consisting of a primary and then a departmental assembly was precisely to prevent them from doing that. It followed also from the idea, widespread at the time, that in order to avoid manipulations, the vote had to take place in small assemblies (of a few hundred people), in full view of everyone. For the same reasons, this system functioned without candidates being announced beforehand. In other words, to avoid the application of pressure, candidates for seats as departmental electors and then as deputies could be made known only on the day of the primary assembly and the day of the departmental assembly.[13] This system had its logic, but it precluded

---

11. The Girondins' draft constitution, proposed in February 1793 and advocated by Condorcet, proposed a mechanism of legislative intervention by the primary assemblies that was still more extensive than the one that was ultimately adopted in the Montagnards' constitution of June 1793 and that could lead to a referendum on a proposed law if a sufficient number of citizens asked for it (rather than to a reexamination by the primary assemblies, a complex and ill-defined procedure). Neither of the two proposals had enough time to be applied.

12. For a detailed analysis of these wishes and petitions, and of the meeting of the 7,000 envoys of the primary assemblies in Paris on 10 August 1793, see S. Aberdam, *L'élargissement du droit de vote*, 647–730.

13. The possibility of announcing candidacies in advance was introduced during the legislative sessions of 1797, while at the same time the possibility of declaring one's candidacy on the day of the election, and of voting for someone who had not declared his candidacy, was preserved.

any debate before the elections and was ultimately a failure.[14] The Revolution's other great institutional debacle was even more serious. The omnipotence accorded to the Assembly and the absence of a clear separation between the legislative, executive, and judiciary powers, in a context where the whole of the jurisdictional system (largely consisting of offices that had been venal and inheritable under the Old Regime) was in the process of being completely reworked, and moreover, in the context of a war at home and abroad, were to make a major contribution to the traumatic experience of the Terror in 1793–1794, with decisions regarding arrests and executions being made in the middle of a session of the Convention or by its committees or provincial envoys. Later on, the establishment of strict procedures defining the separation of powers and the rule of law made it possible to avoid a return to such practices.

Nonetheless, the debate initiated under the Revolution concerning the best way to connect universal suffrage, the organization of public authorities, and the sharing of political power never left people's minds. In 1795, the experience of the Terror was instrumentalized by supporters of the Directory to restrict universal suffrage (which was blamed for everything that went wrong) and to return, to a varying extent, to censitary voting for the designation of the deputies. However, universal suffrage played no role in the events, because there was never enough time to apply it. After his coup d'état in November 1799, Bonaparte decided to do away with elections almost completely and to put an end to the ambitious election system of 1789–1799. In the name of the verticality of power and the rejection of electoral and parliamentary chaos, the members of legislative assemblies were henceforth named directly by him, so the chambers lost all autonomy with regard to the execu-

---

Not until 1799 did all candidates have to declare themselves in advance and in a single district, all other votes being considered null and void. Previously, the main candidates for seats in the legislature (for example, Bonaparte in 1848, and Gambetta, Thiers, and Boulanger in 1879 and 1880) could be elected in multiple districts and departments, a mechanism that was used to increase their notoriety on the national scale.

14. Some authors, such as Patrice Gueniffey, defend the idea that the interdiction of candidacies declared in advance expresses a structural rejection of political pluralism. In reality, as Melvin Edelstein has shown, the model of electoral assemblies without candidacies declared in advance, which is found at that time in the young republic of the United States in the form of the "town meeting," reflects in both cases a rejection of the corruption associated with political parties on the British model. See Edelstein, *La Révolution française,* 275–311. Although imbued with negative preconceptions about revolutionary assemblies and the French Revolution in general (see the astonishing foreword added in 2020), the work Gueniffey published in 1993 remains a valuable reference. See Gueniffey, *Le nombre et la raison.*

tive authority.[15] The same went for mayors and other offices to be filled, which were now appointed by the central government and the prefects. Electoral frenzy was followed by a frenzy of verticality. Interestingly, Napoleon nonetheless decided in 1799 to reestablish a male suffrage broader than it had been under the Directory, with about 80 percent of adult males having the right to vote.[16] This suffrage was very theoretical because the electors were essentially convoked to ratify, in referenda-plebiscites, the emperor's constitutional choices. But in broadening male suffrage, Napoleon inaugurated an ideological tradition that was to play a long-lasting role: Bonapartism presented itself as a continuation of 1789 (with no return to the old nobility's privileges, and priority given to merit and to new talents), and for all that, it relied on a direct rapport between the leader and the people, who alone were capable of according him their confidence directly by voting for his essential choices, as opposed to a representative model in which a small parliamentary elite confiscates power and highjacks the people's sovereignty.

Political Equality, between Parliamentary Democracy and Direct Democracy

In 1848–1852 Napoleon's nephew, Louis-Napoléon, was to play the same score with just as much ability, succeeding in this way in embodying a president-emperor who was close to the people and who defended universal suffrage when it faced new forms of feudalism. In the meantime, the monarchical Restoration had transformed the political landscape in 1815 with Louis XVIII (Louis XVI's brother, who had been living in exile in the various courts of Europe for a quarter of a century), and then, when he died in 1824, with his successor, his brother Charles X, who was deposed in 1830 in favor of their cousin Louis-Philippe (son of the regicide Philippe d'Orléans, who had voted to execute the king in 1793, whence a long-lasting quarrel between the two dynastic branches). Above all, the period 1815–1848 marks the triumph of the censitary principle. Along with the Chamber of Lords (Chambre des Pairs), which gathered together the very high nobility (like

---

15. More precisely, the members of the Senate were appointed directly by Napoleon, and the members of the legislative body were chosen by the Senate from the lists of candidates emerging from a process of censitary voting involving several degrees.

16. In 1795, the Directory had retained lower voting age of twenty-one that had been decided in 1792, but it had also reestablished a minimum tax threshold, which was repealed in 1799, with the return to an election system close to that of 1793 and a somewhat stricter residency requirement (one year instead of six months).

the British House of Lords), the Chamber of Deputies was elected between 1815 and 1830 solely by men thirty or older who paid at least 300 francs in direct taxes (that is, scarcely 1 percent of adult males). To be a deputy, one had to be forty or older and pay at least 1,000 francs in direct taxes (less than 0.2 percent of adult males met this condition).[17] Since the main direct tax was the real estate tax, this system privileged rural landowners (in particular, the nobility) over the urban and industrial bourgeoisie. Between 1830 and 1848, the Orléanist dynasty claimed to be closer than the Legitimists to the urban elites and business circles and decided to extend suffrage very slightly: the fiscal thresholds were set at 200 and 500 francs, so the number of electors rose to 2 percent of adult males and the number of those eligible rose to 0.4 percent. In comparison to the very extensive right to vote in the period 1789–1815, this was a considerable regression that was to fuel future revolts.

The Revolution of February 1848 marks the definitive advent of the universal male suffrage. The Constitutive Assembly elected in April 1848 established a republican constitution founded, first, on a president of the Republic elected by direct universal (male) suffrage—an election that took place in December 1848 and saw the triumph of Louis-Napoléon Bonaparte—and second, on a legislative National Assembly also elected by direct universal (male) suffrage, a single chamber endowed with the legislative power without which the president could not govern.[18] The legislative election took place in May 1849 and resulted in the victory of the Party of Order, a conservative coalition basing itself on the rural vote and bringing together former Legitimists and Orléanists as well as Bonapartists. But the Democratic Socialist electoral lists (again, following the terminology used at the time) achieved excellent results, not only within the urban proletariat, which was on a roll, but also in several rural areas. The fear of the Red vote and an impending Socialist victory was amplified by their excellent results in the by-elections

---

17. The law of the "double vote" promulgated in 1820—and then repealed in 1830—also introduced the possibility for a quarter of the wealthiest censitary electors (that is, approximately all those eligible) to vote a second time to designate part of the deputies. The double vote is far from being peculiar to France. It remained in force until 1948 in the United Kingdom, where it took the form of "university seats," whereby the men who held diplomas from the most prestigious universities were authorized to vote for their representatives in Parliament in addition to their geographical vote. See J. Cagé, *Le prix de la démocratie* (Fayard, 2018).

18. As Alain Garrigou reminds us in his *Histoire sociale du suffrage universel,* the establishment of universal suffrage in 1848 took place in the Hôtel de Ville under the threat of armed insurgents. Announced by Lamartine on 25 February 1848, the decree creating universal suffrage was published on 5 March. See A. Garrigou, *Histoire sociale du suffrage universel en France. 1848–2000* (Seuil, 2002).

of 1849–1850. This was notably the case in the elections of 10 March 1850, which resulted in the victories of twenty-one Democratic Socialists for thirty vacant seats, including all the seats of Saône-et-Loire and several key seats in Paris, and which ended up convincing the Party of Order that the tidal wave was on its way and that it was urgent to act.[19] The conservative majority then resorted to the ultimate weapon by adopting the law of 31 May 1850 (aka the Burgraves' Law),[20] reserving the right to vote for electors who could prove at least three years of residence in the canton, as it was understood that this had to be proved by producing a certificate of taxation, which in practice excluded a large number of poor electors. Out of the approximately 10 million electors registered in 1848, about 3 million were excluded from the lists. The proportion of adult men who had the right to vote thus fell from almost 95 percent to less than 65 percent, which represents an enormous retrogression (see figure 1.3). In large cities such as Paris and Lyon, where many newcomers had no homes in their own names and did not pay personal taxes (the equivalent of the *taxe d'habitation* today), the effects were still greater: the number of electors was divided by three.

Like his uncle in 1799, Louis-Napoléon presented himself to the country as the defender of universal suffrage against the parliamentary elites, whom he said were guilty of having confiscated power in the name of a representative system that was falsely democratic. Furious that the Assembly had rejected the constitutional amendment that would have permitted his candidacy in the presidential election of 1852 (the constitution of 1848 provided for a single term, nonrenewable), in the early morning on 2 December 1851, the day of his coup d'état, he had the text of his famous decree plastered on the walls of Paris: "The National Assembly is dissolved. Universal suffrage has been reestablished. The law of 31 May is abrogated." Playing cleverly on the people's hostility to the parliamentary elites who had just revealed to the country their true nature and their class egotism with the Burgraves' law (and other social and fiscal measures to which we will return), he then had ratified, by a referendum with universal suffrage, a new constitution and then a return to the Empire. Parliamentary power was thereby reduced to next to nothing, and it was by means of repeated referenda-plebiscites that the prince-president (who became Emperor Napoleon III in 1852) would succeed in establishing his

---

19. See B. Ménager, "1848–1871. Autorité ou liberté?," in *Histoire des droites en France,* ed. J. F. Sirinelli (Gallimard, 1992). By-elections were very frequent until 1899 because deputies were elected in several districts.
20. In 1848, the right to vote was based on a requirement of only six months' residence (as in 1793), and all the ways of proving it were accepted for registration on the lists.

power until 1870, relying on the model of a direct relationship to the people already used between 1799 and 1815.[21]

From the Senatorial Republic to the Presidential Republic

In September 1870, the military defeat at the hands of Germany led to the fall of the Second Empire. The Assembly elected in February 1871 by male universal suffrage was clearly conservative, but the tendencies favorable to a monarchical or imperial regime were divided into three groups (Legitimists, Orléanists, Bonapartists). Unable to agree on a dynasty, in 1875 the majority finally rallied to the idea of a republican regime, which was to become the Third Republic. After the disastrous experience of 1848, the prospect of a presidential election by universal suffrage was out of the question. The president was thus to be elected by the National Assembly (the Chamber of Deputies and the Senate meeting together). In order to limit the power of universal suffrage, the most important decision made by the conservative majority consisted, in fact, of creating two chambers, one elected by direct universal suffrage (the Chamber of Deputies) and the other elected by indirect suffrage by a college of great electors constituted by municipal and cantonal advisers and structurally overrepresenting the countryside (the Senate).[22] The decisive point was that the Senate had a right of veto over the totality of the legislation: to go into force, all laws had to be adopted in the same terms by the two chambers.

In practice, from 1875 to 1940, the Senate blocked numerous social and fiscal reforms of the greatest importance, sometimes for several decades. An example often cited is that of the income tax, which was finally accepted by the Senate in July 1914 as World War II approached, but there were many bills that were long debated and then adopted by the Chamber of Deputies but rejected by the senators, notably the Doumer bill in 1895–1896 and the Caillaux bill in 1907–1909. A still more striking example was women's right to vote, adopted by the Chamber in 1919, then repeatedly put on the parliamentary agenda during the interwar period

---

21. A notable difference from his uncle is that Napoleon III maintained legislative elections with direct universal suffrage in 1852, 1857, 1863, and 1869, though a system of official candidacies and monitoring of the press left little room for opposition.

22. When it was created in 1875, the Senate included a large group of irremovable senators appointed by the Assembly, the last of whom died in 1918. During the discussions of 1873–1875, it had also been envisaged to have the senators elected by a college composed of the taxpayers who paid the most taxes at the level of each municipality, before a system based on the municipal and cantonal councilors was imposed.

and rejected every time by the Senate. Let us note in passing the importance of interactions between socioeconomic questions and institutional questions; in both cases, regarding the income tax and the vote for women, France was almost the last Western country to adopt these reforms, which are today considered essential, and in both cases, they would have been adopted several decades earlier had the Chamber of Deputies had the last word. From the point of view of the partisans in the Senate, the main objection was that a chamber elected by universal suffrage and left to itself might end up adopting hasty and demagogic legislation—an argument which, though it is understandable, obviously has its limits.

The fact remains that in 1945–1946 it took a strong Communist and Socialist parliamentary majority produced by universal suffrage and two referenda to finally get a new constitution adopted, that of the Fourth Republic, whose main difference from that of the Third Republic is precisely that the Senate completely and definitively lost its right to veto legislation. This crucial choice was repeated in 1958 in the constitution of the Fifth Republic. Since 1946, the Senate's only power has been to propose amendments to various bills, but ultimately it is for the National Assembly (the new name adopted by the Chamber of Deputies in 1946 to mark its recovered preeminence) to decide and impose its text in the event of disagreement.[23]

Along with women's right to vote and the end of the senatorial veto, the third great politico-constitutional upheaval since World War II is obviously the presidential election's grand return to universal suffrage. In the interwar period more and more political actors, in particular those on the right side of the assembly halls, emphasized, in the name of democratic efficiency, the need to endow France with a more stable executive power. But this theme of the "reform of the state" struggled to find outlets, so strong was the specter of 1848, the fear of Caesarism, and the attachment to the parliamentary model, especially in the center and on the left. In 1946, de Gaulle alleged that the constitution of the Fourth Republic favored the return of the party system and parliamentary instability. Under cover of the Algerian crisis, in 1958, he succeeded in establishing the election of the president of the Republic by an electoral college that was far larger than just the members of the parliament, with more than 80,000 great electors who came from

---

23. With the important exception, however, of constitutional amendments, which in the constitution of 1958 must in principle be approved in identical terms by each of the two chambers, by simple majority, before being subjected to either a two-thirds vote in the two chambers meeting in a joint session or a ratification by referendum. In the 1946 constitution, the National Assembly could also override the opposition of the Conseil de la République (equivalent to the Senate) and subject an amendment to a referendum.

the general and municipal councils (the same electoral body as the Senate), thus giving him a political legitimacy distinct from that of the parliament. In 1962, de Gaulle transformed the experiment by having the president elected by direct universal suffrage ratified by a referendum.[24] Vigorously contested at the time, this popular decision ended up becoming customary, especially after the transfer of political power in 1981 and the election of François Mitterand. Somewhat as Bonapartism had done, but in a very different sociohistorical context and with a much greater recognition of the role of the parliament, Gaullism succeeded in winning acceptance for the idea that the representative and parliamentary model is not the only form in which universal suffrage is expressed; it can also be manifested in a direct relationship between voters and the leaders they choose. Since 2002, presidential and parliamentary elections have taken place every five years and in that order (first the presidential election, then the parliamentary election), and they now set the French electoral rhythm.

An Ongoing Conflict regarding Democracy and Political Institutions

One conclusion emerges from this brief historical reminder: the movement toward greater political equality has not been a long, peaceful river since 1789, and this conflictual and uncertain process is far from coming to an end. It is sometimes said that today, the conflict over institutions has calmed, insofar as no political tendency really considers depriving voters of the power to elect the president and entrusting this role once again to the parliament.[25] More generally, no matter what defects the institutional system in place might have, no major political movement is seriously proposing to challenge the electoral principle itself and to return to an authoritarian or dynastic regime. For that matter there are

---

24. Let us recall, however, that this constitutional amendment, no doubt the most important of the Fifth Republic so far, was made on the basis of de Gaulle's blatant violation of the constitution (which the Constitutional Council he had appointed had no difficulty pardoning), because nothing said (or says today) that such an amendment can be decided by referendum without the prior approbation of the two chambers (an approbation the latter would never have given). Nonetheless, this observation must not be overdramatized, insofar as the same can be said about virtually all the important constitutional amendments made since 1789; for example, nothing in the rules of the Old Regime said that the Third Estate could constitute itself as a National Assembly and put an end to the privileges of the other two orders.

25. In theory, many other options could be considered, including a collective executive, like the Federal Council of the Swiss Confederation, but no alternative of that kind has so far been the object of a significant political movement. Furthermore, the maintenance of the current system obviously does not exclude a rebalancing of the executive and legislative powers.

many other points within the present electoral system about which there is absolutely no consensus.

Generally, the chronic dissatisfaction with the representative and parliamentary model has in reality never ceased, and since the Revolution it has fed the hope for a democratic model that is more participative and permits more citizens to have a voice in choices that concern them, a hope that the presidential election—and more broadly, electoral democracy[26]—does not in any way exhaust—on the contrary. The feeling of a growing distance between electors and elected officials has increased over recent decades and now poses a grave threat to the country's democratic balance, as the collapse of turnout in elections shows. This dissatisfaction goes back a long way, and it is doubtless partly explained by the fact that the social position of members of parliament relative to the society of their time has always been very elevated. This has never been fully accepted, and these days it is accepted less and less.

Fifty-four percent of the members of the first National Assembly (formed in June 1789 by the meeting of the elected representatives of the Third Estate and those of the other two orders) were members of the nobility or the clergy. This proportion declined to 12 percent after the legislative elections of June 1791, which constituted a substantial democratic progress.[27] However, we must add that the officials of the Third Estate came mainly from relatively wealthy bourgeois classes. Analysis of documents for some of the departments shows that about 70 percent of the members of the assemblies of the revolutionary period paid direct taxes at least equal to the *marc d'argent* (that is, 5 percent of adult men at the time).[28] The available sources on the occupations of the members of parliament (including lawyers, industrialists, senior managers, and members of liberal professions) suggest that these orders of grandeur—about 70 percent of the members of parliament were descended from the richest 5 to 10 percent of individuals at that time—apply rather well to the deputies of the Third Republic as well as to those of the Fourth

---

26. As we have already noted, in this book we have chosen to study political conflict from the angle of electoral democracy. To be sure, this approach is far from the only one possible, and participation may take various forms besides the ballot box, ranging from demonstrations to associative activity, the organization of boycotts, and other forms of protest. See, for example, R. Sénac, *Radicales et fluides. Les mobilisations contemporaines* (Presses de Sciences Po, 2021).

27. Edelstein, *La Révolution française*, 373–410. The proportion of nobles among the deputies later increased to more than 50 percent at the Restoration. See P. B. Higonnet, "La composition de la Chambre des Députés de 1827 à 1831," *Revue Historique*, 1968.

28. Gueniffey, *Le nombre et la raison*, 424–428. This analysis covers the members of the departmental assemblies and is the number is no doubt higher for those who were elected deputies.

and Fifth Republics.[29] The other deputies usually came from the middle classes (for example, teachers) and not from the working classes. The only period in which we see a significant proportion of workers and employees[30] is between 1945 and 1980 (about 10 percent of the elected officials, which remains very low for a group that at the time represented 60 percent of the electors), when the French Communist Party had a large group in the parliament. The proportion of employees and workers among the deputies has declined steeply since 1970–1980, returning to nearly nil over recent decades.

However, the experience of parity between men and women shows that voluntarist measures can make it possible to improve the representation of groups that have been historically underrepresented.[31] In theory, one could imagine a system of social parity that would force parties to present at least 50 percent of their candidates from among the workers and employees (or approximately their share in the current working population), on pain of dissuasive sanctions.[32] The measure

---

29. On the social origins of the members of parliament, see M. Dogan, "L'origine sociale du personnel parlementaire Français," in *Partis politiques et classes sociales en France,* ed. M. Duverger (A. Colin, 1955); M. Dogan, "Political Ascent in a Class Society: French Deputies 1870–1958," in *Political Decision-Makers,* ed. D. Marvick (Glencoe, 1961); E. Anceau, *Les députés du Second Empire. Prosopographie d'une élite du 19e siècle* (Champion, 2000); J. M. Mayeur, J.-P. Chaline, and A. Corbin, *Les parlementaires de la IIIe République* (Publications de la Sorbonne, 2003); J. Garrigues, *Histoire du Parlement de 1789 à nos jours* (A. Colin, 2007), 133–190.

30. *Ouvriers et employés.* These terms designate blue-collar industrial workers and low-skilled workers in the service sector. These categories play an important role throughout the book.

31. An initial, relatively modest law (providing that no sex can occupy more than 75 percent of the seats in the list system) was adopted in 1982, but it was censured by the Constitutional Council because it violated the principle of equality. Escape from this dead end did not occur until the constitutional amendment of 1999. The law of 2000 established complete "chabadabada" parity for list-system elections, as well as financial sanctions for parties that presented too few women candidates in district elections—sanctions that turned out to be insufficient to be fully effective, but which nonetheless made it possible to move the situation along; see, for example, Q. Lippmann, *Les femmes au pouvoir. Que change vraiment la parité en politique?* (CEPREMAP, 2023). Then the government tried to require parity in other contexts (such as boards of examiners), but it was censured again. A second constitutional amendment adopted in 2008 permitted the application of quotas for access to social and professional responsibilities rather than political offices alone. In general, the Constitutional Council has played, on several occasions since the 1980s, a conservative role similar to that of the Senate under the Third Republic on many socioeconomic questions of the first importance, in particular concerning the wealth tax (see chapter 13).

32. Cagé, *Le prix de la démocratie,* 418–431; J. Cagé, *Libres et égaux en voix* (Fayard, 2020), 146–154. The absence of employees and workers from the Assembly in no way reflects what might be characterized as the citizens' preference for elected officials who come from the wealthiest classes; instead, it reflects the fact that the parties did not present any (or presented very few) candidates who were employees or workers.

may seem to be radical and problematic, but in a certain way it is on the same scale as the present radical exclusion of the working classes in parliamentary assemblies. In any event, the case of gender parity shows that the advance toward political equality is a process that is still ongoing, and whose rules remain largely to be invented.

We must note that in addition to this lack of social representativity among members of parliament, the question of the invention of new forms of direct, participative democracy has advanced little since the French Revolution. Regarding the referendum by citizen initiative (RIC), largely associated with the *gilets jaunes* (yellow vests) movement in 2018–2019, we are not much more advanced today than we were at the time of the republican constitution of 1793 (which was never applied). The constitutional amendment of 2008 certainly introduced the possibility of a referendum by shared initiative (RIP), which can in principle be launched at the request of one-fifth of the members of parliament and one-tenth of the registered voters. But in practice, this threshold is so high that it has proven inaccessible. Despite repeated requests by several political movements on the left as well as the right, the successive majorities have refused to lower the threshold, no doubt in part because deep down, many deputies refuse to share their power, but also because such a provision raises complex questions and should be carefully framed. At the time of the *gilets jaunes* movement, among the examples of RIC frequently mentioned were possible referenda on the cancellation of public debt and on immigration. No matter how legitimate they might be, it is very clear that such questions can become the subject of a referendum only after a great deal of discussion, formulation, and collective deliberation. For example, one could imagine a new form of "deliberative referendum" in which a vote would take place after a citizen assembly chosen by lots had publicly organized a debate of arguments and expert opinions, all with a system of access to the media and financing of campaigns making it possible for the different points of view to be expressed in an equitable way.[33] As with all institutional and democratic innovations of this kind, some people will be wary of the risks of the adventure and prefer to stick to the current status quo, while others will argue for the necessity of change without being quite

---

33. Cagé, *Libres et égaux en voix,* 79–92. The absence of such rules in California or Switzerland (where the threshold for launching a referendum by popular initiative is about 2 percent of the registered voters) shows the manipulations to which these systems can sometimes lead. On the different forms that deliberative democracy could take, see also H. Landemore, *Open Democracy: Reinventing Popular Rule for the Twenty-First Century* (Princeton University Press, 2020).

sure what form it will take, and only historical experimentation on a grand scale will make it possible to resolve the uncertainties.

The Question of Influence and Money in Politics

We must emphasize that the question of the influence of the powerful and of money in electoral processes has never really been dealt with in a completely satisfying way. Yet, it has been asked since the first steps toward electoral democracy were taken. The minutes of the primary assemblies of the revolutionary period show how property owners, going beyond the existing rules, often succeeded in excluding from these assemblies the poorest of their fellow citizens, notably share-croppers, whom they tried to assimilate to domestic servants and who were officially excluded from assemblies.[34] Alexis de Tocqueville, a deputy from La Manche (where his family owned the chateau and the domain of Tocqueville, in the municipality of the same name) under the censitary monarchies, tells candidly in his memoirs how he succeeded in keeping his term of office as a deputy when universal suffrage was instituted in 1848. On the day of the election, he led the peasants himself to the polling station, where he was elected without difficulty.[35] When in 1913 Siegfried referred to the influence of the traditional elites, he was undoubtably wrong in making it the sole determinant of the conservative vote (or even the main determinant), but he nonetheless based his view on a certain number of concrete elements. Thus, research has shown that despite the secrecy of the ballot, which had been officially in place since 1848, hundreds of cases of vote invalidation

---

34. See S. Aberdam, *L'élargissement du droit de vote*. See also P. Bois, *Paysans de l'Ouest. Des structures économiques et sociales aux options politiques depuis l'époque révolutionnaire dans la Sarthe* (Mouton, 1960); C. Tilly, *La Vendée. Revolution et contre-révolution* (Fayard, 1970).

35. "The people had always been well intentioned toward me, but this time I found them affectionate, and I was never surrounded by more respect than I was since brutal equality was plastered on all the walls. To vote, we had to go together to the town of Saint-Pierre, a league away from our village. The morning of the election, all the electors, that is, the whole of the male population over twenty years old, met in front of the church. All the men lined up in pairs, following alphabetical order; we left behind us only the children and the women; there were a hundred and seventy of us in all. When we arrived on the top of the hill where one looks down on Tocqueville, we stopped for a moment; I realized that they wanted me to speak. So I climbed up on the edge of a ditch, they stood in a circle around me, and I said a few words that the circumstances inspired in me. I reminded these good people of the gravity and importance of the act they were going to perform. . . . All the votes were given at the same time, and I have reason to think that almost all of them were for the same candidate. Immediately after casting my own ballot, I bade them farewell, and, getting into the carriage, left for Paris." A. de Tocqueville, *Souvenirs,* 23 April 1848.

were recorded during the period from 1871 to 1914, notably in western France, generally involving property owners and sometimes members of the clergy. The number of cases seems to decrease steeply during the interwar period, no doubt in part thanks to the efforts made by political organizations, the press, and civics textbooks to disqualify these practices.[36] The law of 1913 instituting the obligatory passage through the voting booth also helped limit the potential for pressuring voters.

Although the direct coercion of voters seems to have largely disappeared, the question of the power of influence through the financing of campaigns or in the media has never been truly dealt with. To be sure, several laws regarding political financing have been adopted, starting in 1988, but the ceilings remain extremely high: each member of a household can contribute up to 7,500 euros per annum to finance political parties, and more than 4,600 euros for each electoral campaign. Amounts like these are beyond the reach of most voters, and in fact, the 10 percent of the French with the highest incomes represent more than half of all political donations—that is, far more than their share of the total of incomes, and more than five times more than their supposed share in the community of citizens. If the objective were really to put voters on an equal footing, it would be necessary to limit donations to a few hundred euros at most, or even to institute "bonds for democratic equality" of the same amount for everyone, which citizens could freely allocate every year to the parties or movements of their choice. Let us add that in France, political donations are accompanied by major fiscal advantages: a political donation of 7,500 euros is accompanied by the right to a tax deduction of 5,000 euros, which amounts to having two-thirds of the political preferences of the richest people subsidized by the rest of the taxpayers. This astonishing system never ceases to amaze, given that the vote of ordinary citizens entitles them to only one or two euros per vote in the public funding for political parties.[37]

One could also think that the legislation put in place in 1988 that legalizes—and in reality, even subsidizes—private political donations without really trying to reduce them has succeeded in giving a new legitimacy and increased influence to

---

36. N. Dompnier, "Les paradoxes de la liberté de vote," in *"Le Tableau politique de la France de l'Ouest" d'André Siegfried. Cent ans après, héritages et postérités,* ed. M. Bussi, C. Le Digol, and C. Voillot (Presses Universitaires de Rennes, 2016).

37. See Cagé, *Le prix de la démocratie;* Cagé, *Libres et égaux en voix,* 2020. Moreover, these tax deductions concern only the richest half of the population, the half that has to pay income tax, and not the taxpayers who are limited to paying indirect taxes, VAT, the CSG (generalized social contribution), supplemental social security contributions, even though these levies are much heavier<<AU: much more lucrative?>> in terms of total receipts.

the role of money in politics. Even if it is difficult to quantify this effect precisely, this development made it possible to tilt political programs in a direction unfavorable to the working classes more than in the preceding decades, and in that way to contribute to the observed decline in their turnout in elections. It would certainly be absurd to make the power of money the only determinant of the vote. But it would be just as unjustified to claim that it has no importance and that the rules cannot be improved. For example, Emmanuel Macron, who won the 2017 presidential election, received more donations from French expatriates living in London than the cumulative total from all the large provincial cities.[38] It is difficult to imagine that this has no relation to the order of priorities he set forth—for example, the suppression of the "exit tax" weighing on the expatriates in question.[39] Obviously, the question of political equality and a more democratic way of sharing power will continue to fuel complex political conflicts in the coming decades, as it always has ever since 1789.

The Unfinished March toward Socioeconomic Equality

The movement toward political equality, as incomplete as it may be, has made immense progress since the French Revolution. It has also helped nourish a move-

---

38. The data of the National Commission on Campaign Accounts and Political Financing (CNCCFP) indicate that in 2016–2017 the candidate elected in 2017 and his party received more donations from French expatriates in London alone (990,000 euros) than the total of donations from residents in the cities of Lyon (238,000 euros), Toulouse (96,000), Marseille (93,000), Nantes (58,000), Bordeaux (57,000), Strasbourg (52,000), Lille (49,000), Montpellier (48,000), Nice (48,000), Tassin-La-Demi-Lune (47,000), Sappey-en-Chartreuse (40,000), Aix-en-Provence (36,000), Rouen (29,000), Rennes (29,000), Grenoble (28,000), and Fourmies (24,500) taken together (with cities—all outside the Île de France region— listed in decreasing order of donation amounts). French citizens expatriated in New York contributed more (more than 200,000 euros) than the inhabitants of Toulouse and Marseille taken together. On the geography of political donations in France, see J. Cagé and M. Guillot, "Is Charitable Giving Political? Evidence from Wealth and Income Tax Returns" (CEPR Discussion Paper no. 17597, 2022).

39. On the influence of campaign expenses on electoral results in France, see Y. Bekkouche, J. Cagé, and E. Dewitte, "The Heterogeneous Price of a Vote: Evidence from Multiparty Systems, 1993– 2017," *Journal of Public Economics,* 2022; on the effects of campaign donations on the candidates' speeches, see J. Cagé, C. Le Pennec-Caldichoury, and E. Mougin, "Corporate Donations and Political Rhetoric: Evidence from a National Ban," *American Economic Journal: Economic Policy,* 2023. Let us also note that the question of political financing is not foreign to that of (the absence of) social representivity among the elected officials; if, in order to run for office, citizens are no longer expected to pay a minimal contribution, the lack of resources for financing a campaign often acts as a barrier to entry for the least privileged, including in local elections.

ment toward greater socioeconomic equality, which is also very incomplete and at the same time very real. Over the course of the last two centuries there has been, notably, a general rise in the standard of living, as well as the general level of health and education. The studies and diplomas that used to be reserved for a tiny elite have been opened to broader and broader strata of the population (we will come back to this in subsequent chapters). Generally speaking, the most striking phenomenon, in France as elsewhere in the whole of European and Western societies, and to a certain extent on the global scale, is that the advance toward greater collective prosperity has developed inseparably from a power movement toward greater equality, simultaneously on the political, social, and economic levels, carried forward by popular mobilizations.[40]

However, as with the march toward political equality, the breadth of this movement toward socioeconomic equality must not be exaggerated—and in some of its dimensions, it has even tended to retreat in recent decades. Let us begin by examining the evolution of the division of property in France since the end of the eighteenth century, which can be studied, notably by taking successoral archives as a starting point (see figure 1.4).[41] The evolution observed shows that there is a movement toward more equality over the long term, and at the same time, that this evolution is anything but linear and that the concentration of inheritances has always been extremely high.

Let us examine things more closely. We note first of all that the share of the richest 10 percent in the totality of private properties (that is, in the totality of properties of all kinds: land, real estate, business, industrial, and financial, clear of debts) decreased only slightly after the Revolution. It remained at an astronomical level all through the nineteenth century and up to the beginning of the twentieth, with a tendency to rise during the decades preceding World War I. The wealthiest 10 percent alone held around 85 percent of the totality of properties in France in the 1780s, shortly before the Estates General, then around 85 percent between 1800 and 1810, and almost 90 percent during the first years

40. See T. Piketty, *Une brève histoire de l'égalité* [A brief history of equality] (Seuil, 2021).
41. These results are based on an important collection of data in the successoral archives of the Parisian and departmental archives. See T. Piketty, G. Postel-Vinay, and J. L. Rosenthal, "Wealth Concentration in a Developing Economy: Paris and France, 1807–1994," *American Economic Review,* 2006; T. Piketty, G. Postel-Vinay, and J. L. Rosenthal, "Inherited vs. Self-Made Wealth: Theory and Evidence from a Rentier Society (Paris 1872–1927)," *Explorations in Economic History,* 2014. These works are part of an ongoing research program since the interwar period, at the intersection of the *Annales* and the British American school of economics. See Piketty, *Une brève histoire de l'égalité,* 13–18.

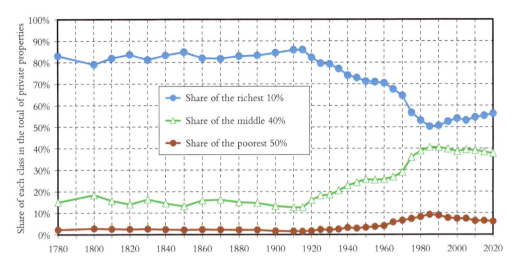

FIGURE 1.4. The distribution of property in France, 1780–2020: The difficult emergence of a "patrimonial middle class"

The share of the richest 10% in the total of net private wealth (real estate, occupational, and financial assets, net of debt) was 80–90% in France between 1789 and 1914. The deconcentration of wealth began after World War II and was interrupted in the early 1980s. It was carried out chiefly to the benefit of the "patrimonial middle classes" (the middle 40%), defined here as the intermediary groups between the "lower classes" (the poorest 50%) and the "upper classes" (the richest 10%). Sources and series: unehistoireduconflitpolitique.fr

after 1910, on the eve of the Great War (see figure 1.4). In Paris, where considerable financial and industrial fortunes were accumulated at the end of the nineteenth century and during the Belle Époque, the concentration of fortunes was still greater than in the rest of France, reaching astronomical levels (particularly at the level of the richest 1 percent).[42]

Then the wealth share of the wealthiest 10 percent began a steep decline, starting from World War 1 and during a large part of the twentieth century, falling from nearly 90 percent in 1914 to scarcely more than 50 percent in the 1980s, before beginning to rise again over the last decades of the century and finally reaching about 55 percent in 2020. In addition, we note that the deconcentration seen over a long period benefited mainly the next wealthiest 40 percent, not the poorest 50 percent, who, to sum up, have almost never possessed anything substantial. The share of the poorest 50 percent was barely 1–2 percent of the total of properties in

42. The portion held by the richest 1 percent then exceeded 65 percent in Paris, as opposed to about 55 percent in France as a whole. See Piketty, *Une brève histoire de l'égalité,* figure 4.

the nineteenth century. Today it is just 5 percent, which constitutes progress, to be sure, but very small progress. Most of the redistribution benefited the 40 percent of the population located between the poorest 50 percent and the richest 10 percent, whose share of the total patrimony rose from scarcely 10 percent in the nineteenth century to about 40 percent today, despite an erosion since 1990.

Over a long period, the progress toward greater equality is incontestable, and it is reflected materially in the emergence of a "patrimonial middle class," as we can call the 40 percent of the population located between the lowest 50 percent (the "popular classes" or "working classes") and the top 10 percent (the "wealthy classes"). This was a considerable transformation, and its social, economic, and political import must not be underestimated. Specifically, the fact that such a group, comprising 40 percent of the population, now holds on the order of 40 percent of the private wealth means, by definition, that its members possess on average the equivalent of the average wealth at the national level, or about 200,000 euros of net wealth per adult today. In practice, the members of this patrimonial middle class are at the head of patrimonies ranging from approximately 100,000 euros to 300,000 euros per adult, consisting overwhelmingly of real estate or sometimes a small company (see figure 1.5). Though they are not very rich, these people are far from having no property at all, and they are naturally very attached to this new status, which they fear losing all the more because the position of this patrimonial middle class has been eroded over the course of recent decades. The existence of such a group that is simultaneously remote from both the poorest and the richest is a considerable historical novelty with major political implications, particularly concerning the difficulties of making groups with such disparate hopes and experiences stick together in a single political coalition. We shall see that this reality can explain in part the new electoral divisions between the world of towns and villages (where property is broadly diffused) and the world of the suburbs and great cities, and to a certain extent, the rise of tripartition.[43] In a certain way, the situation was simpler and less fragmented in the nineteenth century and at the beginning of the twentieth, insofar as the differentiations within the poorest 90 percent were less marked and the working and middle classes were relatively close to one another in comparison with everything that opposed them to the property-holding classes.

Yet, even if it is undeniable over the long term, the progress toward greater socioeconomic equality must not be exaggerated. The truth is that despite some advances, the concentration of property has always been extremely high. The

43. See especially chapters 11 and 13.

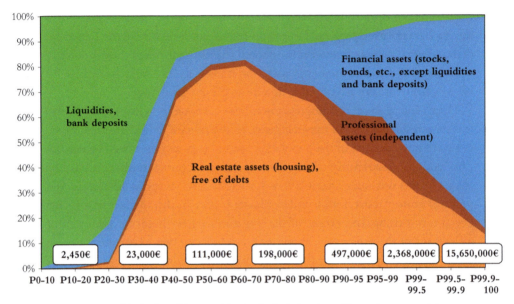

Distribution of the population by deciles in function of the patrimony per adult

FIGURE 1.5. The composition of property in France in 2020

In 2020 the smallest patrimonies (e.g., those between the 10th and 20th percentiles, with an average amount of 2,450 euros) consisted chiefly of liquidities and bank deposits, middle-level patrimonies consisted of real estate assets, and the large patrimonies consisted of financial assets.

Note: The distribution indicated here is that of the patrimony per adult (the patrimony of couples divided in half).

Sources and series: unehistoireduconflitpolitique.fr

richest 10 percent currently own around 55 percent of total wealth, or more than ten times the share owned by the poorest 50 percent (scarcely 5 percent) even though they are, by definition, five times more numerous. This signifies a difference in the average wealth between these two groups that ranges from about one to fifty.[44] Let us add that these considerable patrimonial inequalities are only very partially connected with age; the gaps are almost as great within each age group

_____

44. Or about 20,000 euros on average for the poorest 50 percent, and 1.1 million euros for the richest 10 percent. The share held by the richest 1 percent alone was about 25 percent of France's total patrimony in 2020, or five times more than that of the poorest 50 percent, who are fifty times more numerous, producing a gap in average patrimony between the two groups ranging from 1 to 250 (20,000 euros versus 5 million euros). See Piketty, *Une brève histoire de l'égalité*, figure 4. See also the World Inequality Database (WID.world) for detailed series by percentile.

(twenty-five to thirty-four, thirty-five to fifty-nine, and sixty and older).[45] Let us also add that the issues here greatly exceed a simple question of monetary inequality. The question of how property is distributed has implications that also and especially concern the distribution of power within society. People who own almost nothing, or worse yet, have nothing but debts, are in a very weak bargaining position with regard to others and to their own lives. For example, they are forced to accept jobs that correspond neither to their training nor to their need for work-family balance, in order to pay their rent and provide for those close to them. Inversely, a society where the poorest 50 percent holds a substantial part of the total wealth would also be a society where a larger number of people would have access to more diversified opportunities and options in life, such as buying an apartment, launching a personal project, or beginning a new occupational activity. But what we see today (we shall return to this at length) is a simultaneous return of economic inequalities—albeit at levels far lower than those seen just a century ago—and political inequalities. They fuel each other.

The French Revolution and Inequalities: An Ambiguous Balance Sheet

We return now to the past to try to better understand the reasons for the differing evolutions observed in the distribution of property since 1780 (see figure 1.4). In particular, the fact that the French Revolution had such a limited effect in terms of the reduction of socioeconomic inequalities may surprise readers today. However, it is a reality that is important to assert, because it had a crucial impact on the structuration of political conflict and electoral behaviors in the nineteenth century and, to a large extent, up to our own times. Let us explain first that, of course, the Revolution made possible a considerable leap forward in matters of equality in numerous dimensions, beginning with the right to vote and political equality. The end of the nobility's fiscal privileges and the establishment of a unified tax system also constituted a major change, even if its real financial import must not be exaggerated, insofar as the nobility was already subject to several levies under the Old Regime such as the poll tax and the *taille tarifée,* which was a kind of graduated income tax based on the standard of living of the different classes.[46] To truly change the distribution of the fiscal burden and make it

---

45. Piketty, *Une brève histoire de l'égalité,* 68; Piketty, *Capital et idéologie* (Seuil, 2019), 647–648, figure S11.18.

46. See M. Touzery, *L'invention de l'impôt sur le revenu. La taille tarifée (1715–1789)* (CHEFF, 1994).

easier for the lower classes to bear, it would have been necessary to go much further in transforming taxes by setting up a highly progressive fiscal system that weighed more heavily on the richest (nobles and bourgeois), a development defended by certain deputies but which the majority of the members of the assemblies of the revolutionary period were not yet ready to accept, and which they saw as a dangerous and potentially uncontrollable adventure.[47] The end of the nobility's jurisdictional privileges and of the venality of offices and the establishment of a public justice system were also transformations of great import, all going in the direction of equality, but there again, they were insufficient to allow a rapid reduction of socioeconomic disparities.

Concerning the structure of property, the principal measure adopted under the Revolution was the nationalization of the Church's property in the form of national goods and their sale by auction. This was a transformation of considerable breadth, no doubt the deepest and most structural of all. Under the Old Regime, the Church was by far the leading property owner in the kingdom. It held about one-quarter of the lands and properties of the country, if we include the value of the ecclesiastical *dîme,* which was also abolished.[48] To its detractors, it was a quasi-state, more powerful than the state itself, and it was high time to put an end to it. This point of view won out, and in the autumn of 1789 the National Assembly decided to nationalize the clergy's goods. For the state, this solution had the immense advantage of settling a large part of its financial problems and allowing it to confront the enormous public debt that had led to the convocation of the Estates General.[49] The political cost of this decision was immense, but it was considered lesser than the alternative, which consisted in massively raising taxes in a context where fiscal rebellions and peasant revolts were multiplying and people were already having great trouble agreeing on a tax system acceptable to everyone. With the civil constitution of the clergy, which was adopted in July 1790 by the National Assembly and which Louis XVI tried in vain to veto, the deputies decided that the state would henceforth pay members of the clergy. This new system, applied until 1905, was supposed to compensate the Church in part for the loss of

---

47. On the fiscal measures proposed by Condorcet, Paine, and other less known actors, as well as on the beginnings of their application in 1792–1794, see Piketty, *Capital et idéologie,* 138–142.

48. Under the Old Regime, the *dîme* was a levy of about 8–10 percent on the product of lands (including those of the nobility) paid directly to the ecclesiastical institutions.

49. The amounts were comparable: about one year of national income for public debt and about the same amount for the Church's property. See Piketty, *Capital et idéologie,* 119, figure 2.3.

the *dîme* and the income from its properties, even if in practice the resources received were far smaller (we will return to this).

For the defenders of the Church and its social role—such as the Abbé Sieyès, a member of the clergy but elected from the Third Estate, and the author of the famous pamphlet *Qu'est-ce que le Tiers État?* published in January 1789—the abolition of the *dîme* and the sale of ecclesiastical goods (often at low prices) amounted in reality to the transfer of hundreds of millions of *livres tournois* to the benefit of rich private landowners (bourgeois or nobles). All this was to the detriment of the poorest classes, who had often been the primary beneficiaries of dispensaries, schools, collective grain storage, and other forms of social assistance that were run by the Church. The question is complex, insofar as the ecclesiastical incomes were in fact used to finance not only the sometimes excessive lifestyle of the bishops and monasteries (which Sieyès was prepared to trim), but also the social and educational services that were among the only ones available at the time. For actors like Sieyès, it would have been preferable to attack the nobility's property and leave to the Church the means necessary to perform its task. In theory, it would also have been possible to imagine that the state might use these resources to organize education and healthcare services. But in fact, that is not what happened; the government did not fully assume this role until the late nineteenth and early twentieth centuries. In the short run, the main outcome of the sale of the Church's properties was to enrich those who had the means to buy them, partially confirming Sieyès's criticism.

These different factors explain why the French Revolution ultimately led to only a very limited reduction in socioeconomic inequalities. In certain parts of the territory, the poor peasants benefited from a few meager redistributions of lands, mainly in 1792 under the Convention, which developed a more extensive interpretation of the seigneurial privileges that were to be abolished, without compensation, only during other periods of the Revolution.[50] But basically, property transfers took

---

50. The emblematic case is that of the corvées—that is, the days of unremunerated work that peasants owed their lords in exchange for the right to use their lands. In 1792–1794 the Convention tried to establish the idea that these feudal vestiges had to be abolished without compensation for the lords, in which case the peasants would become full-fledged owners of the lands they worked. However, in the majority of the cases, under the influence of doctrines promoted in 1790–1791 and again starting in 1795, the corvées were transformed into rents (a corvée of one day per week becoming, for example, a rent equal to one-sixth of the produce of the land cultivated by the peasant) and did not lead to any transfer of ownership. See R. Blaufarb, *The Great Demarcation: The French Revolution and the Invention of Modern Property* (Oxford University Press, 2016).

place in the context of the auctioning off of the national goods (that is, mainly ec-clesiastical goods, supplemented by the Crown's goods and certain goods belonging to exiled nobles) and merely reproduced or aggravated the existing patrimonial in-equalities. Moreover, the legal and fiscal system bequeathed by the Revolution con-tinued to be applied during the whole of the nineteenth century and until the be-ginning of the twentieth century without any major discontinuity, notably in regard to the rejection of fiscal progressivity (despite a few efforts made in 1848 and 1871). This helps explain the maintenance until 1914 of a very strong concentration of property close to or superior to the levels observed at the end of the eighteenth century, taking into account the new possibilities of accumulation opened up by industrialization, international financial investments, and the colonial empire.

Furthermore, this strong concentration of fortunes and its perpetuation by the Revolution was well known at the time. In a way, recent research in successoral ar-chives confirms and illuminates the feelings of disappointment expressed by poor peasants in the minutes of the revolutionary assemblies studied by Bois, Tilly, and Aberdam. The theme of the concentration of property and the social hierarchies it outlines are also omnipresent in nineteenth-century literature, whether in Balzac's novels (which are most often set in the 1820s or 1830s) or in Proust's (whose action takes place in the Belle Époque and on the eve of 1914), and which represent in both cases a society founded on immense patrimonial inequalities. We can also note that strong presence of the theme of the "profiteers of national goods" in the collective imagination of the nineteenth century. In Balzac's novels, characters who have made their fortunes by buying up these goods at bargain prices are everywhere (for example, in *Eugénie Grandet, Le cousin Pons, Le curé de village,* and *Les pay-sans*). In addition, this theme nourished the pessimism and political conservatism of the novelist, who explains in 1842, in the preface to the *Comédie humaine,* that Christianity seems to him the best way to fight "man's depraved instincts"—a Chris-tianity that he thinks should be allied with the Crown, with a moderate use of elec-tions. More generally, this theme refers to the "Black Band," a term derived from a semi–conspiracy theory for the supposed association of speculators who agreed under the Revolution to purchase abbeys, chateaus, and the most valuable artworks at low prices in order to resell them for a profit or demolish them and sell off the materials. This theme was especially popular among the Romantics, and in 1823, while he was in his monarchist period, Victor Hugo wrote an ode about it.[51]

---

51. "Quand de ses souvenirs la France dépouillée, / Hélas! aura perdu sa vieille majesté, / Lui dispu-tant encore quelque pourpre souillée, / Ils riront de sa nudité!" Hugo, *Odes et ballades,* a collec-tion of poems he wrote in his youth.

The "Great Redistribution" (1910–1990) and the
Construction of the Welfare State

We now come to the phase of a sharp reduction of socioeconomic inequalities that unfolded during most of the twentieth century, from the 1910s to the 1980s–1990s—and which, as we shall see, is characterized by a political system based on the rise in power of the Left-Right bipolarization. We have noted that the wealth share of the wealthiest 10 percent dropped from almost 90 percent in 1914 to just 50 percent in the 1980s (figure 1.4). We find the same compression of inequalities if we examine the distribution of income (see figure 1.6). Generally, we observe that the concentration of incomes is always less extreme than that of wealth, and that the movement toward greater equality has been more conspicuous for income than for wealth. The share of the total income of people with the lowest incomes was scarcely 10 percent in the nineteenth century and at the beginning of the twentieth, and since the 1980s–1990s it has been around 20–25 percent. During the same period, the share of the 10 percent of the highest

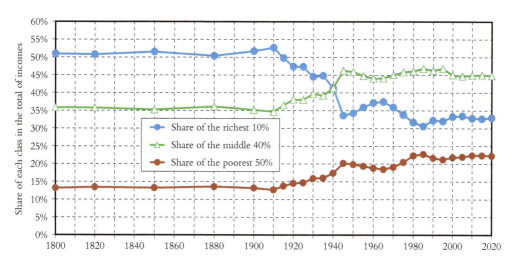

FIGURE 1.6. The distribution of incomes in France, 1800–2020: The beginning of a long-term movement toward equality?

The share of the highest 10% of incomes in the total of incomes, including income from work (salaries, income from unsalaried work, retirement pensions, unemployment benefits) and from capital (profits, dividends, interest, rents, capital gains), was about 50% in France between 1800 and 1914. The deconcentration of incomes began after the two world wars and was carried out to both the benefit of the "working classes" (the lowest 50% of incomes) and the detriment of the "upper classes" (the highest 10%).

Sources and series: unehistoireduconflitpolitique.fr

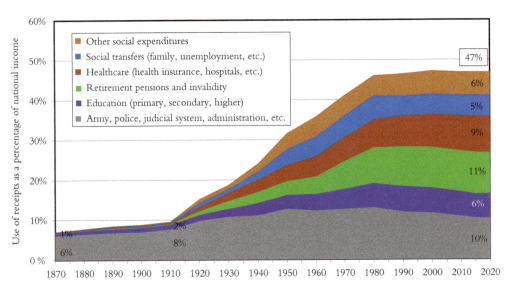

FIGURE 1.7. The rise of the welfare state in Europe, 1870–2020

In 2020, fiscal receipts represented 47% of the average national income in Western Europe and were spent this way: 10% of the national income for regalian expenses (army, police, judicial system, general administration, basic infrastructure such as roads, etc.), 6% for education, 11% for retirement pensions, 9% for healthcare, 5% for social transfers (excepting retirement), 6% for other social expenditures (housing, etc.).

Note: The development indicated here is five-year average for Germany, France, the United Kingdom, and Sweden.

Sources and series: unehistoireduconflitpolitique.fr

incomes has declined from more than 50 percent to about 35 percent. To be sure, that remains considerable for a group that is by definition five times less numerous than the poorest 50 percent; our current society remains very hierarchical, in a particularly massive way so far as property is concerned, but just as clearly for incomes. Nonetheless, it remains that the movement toward greater equality is incontestable.

How can we explain this steep reduction of socioeconomic inequalities observed during the period 1910–1990? Many research projects have tried to answer that question. The main explanatory factor is the development of the welfare state, a major phenomenon that we can see in all the countries of Western Europe during this period (see figure 1.7).[52] Multiple other factors have also played an essential role and helped make this transformation possible, such as the development of the

52. The evolutions indicated in figure 1.7 pertain to the five-year averages observed for four European countries, which makes it possible to abstract from short-term shocks and to concentrate on the

progressive tax on income and wealth (which has allowed the reduction of inequality, notably at the summit of the distribution, while at the same time making much more acceptable the general increase in tax levies indispensable for building the welfare state) and the establishment of a social system granting rights far more extensive than before to salaried workers and their representatives (including, in certain countries, in the managerial authorities of enterprises, and more generally in the framework of collective negotiations making it possible to organize social protection and to participate in determining salary scales and working conditions).

Several elements deserve to be emphasized. First of all, the amount of the fiscal receipts (all tax incomes taken together: such as income taxes, other taxes, and social contributions) increased strongly in Europe over the long term, rising from less than 10 percent of national income before World War I to about 45–50 percent of national income since the 1980s–1990s. At the end of the nineteenth century and until 1914, regalian expenditures (on army, police, justice, administration, for example) absorbed almost the totality of tax incomes. In France, as in other countries, the progression of social expenditures was extremely slow and followed only very gradually the progress of universal suffrage. On the eve of the war, education expenditures were still at very low levels, around 0.5–1 percent of the national income in France, as in Germany, the United Kingdom, and Sweden. By design, such low expenditures could finance only extremely elitist and hierarchized educational systems, in which the great mass of students had access only to a relatively rudimentary and poorly financed primary education, and only a minuscule elite could benefit from secondary or higher education. Starting in the 1920s and until the 1980s, this progress accelerated, to the point that expenditures for education reached about 5–6 percent of the national income in all the countries of Western Europe in the 1980s–1990s. The key to this was quasi-universal access to secondary education and the much greater openness of higher education. We observe evolutions just as spectacular for healthcare expenditures, retirement, and other social expenditures (see figure 1.7). All these developments made powerful contributions to the reduction of socioeconomic inequalities, both in terms of income and in terms of wealth. They also made possible an unprecedented growth of collective prosperity and productivity, notably thanks to investment in education, which over the long term appears to be the primary determinant of social

---

long-term trends. For the same reasons, the exceptional expenditures connected with COVID in 2020 have not been taken into account.

and economic development on the global level.[53] In all, the construction of the welfare state has been an immense success in Europe in the twentieth century, which is also demonstrated by the fact that no major political movement proposes to return to the situation of a hundred years ago, when levies represented less than 10 percent of the national income. The debate is now about whether it is advisable to continue the historical development of the welfare state or to stabilize its size at the current level (which is difficult enough), not to massively reduce it.

Will the Growth of the Welfare State Continue in the Twenty-First Century?

Will the growth of the welfare state continue in the twenty-first century, or should we try to maintain the present situation and limit ourselves to stabilizing and rationalizing what was constructed over the past century? This is one of the most defining political debates for the future, perhaps even the most crucial of all. In support of the thesis that we should seek to continue the development of the welfare state, we can note that the relative stagnation of educational expenditures since the 1980s and 1990s despite the rapid increase in the number of students is the most convincing explanation for the structural decrease in economic growth observed the course of the last two decades. More generally, it is striking to see the extent to which the development of the welfare state was paused in European countries as a whole, despite the growing demands in sectors like education, healthcare, and retirement, and also despite the fact that recourse to the private sector raises serious problems in these domains, both in terms of equality of access and in terms of collective efficiency. For example, we can note the exorbitant cost of private healthcare in the United States (and its poor performance in terms of healthcare indicators), and also the repeated failures of for-profit structures in education (such as Trump University), which seem to be explained by the need to find support in the actors' intrinsic motivations in numerous sectors (in education, but also in healthcare, culture, the media, social action, transportation, environment, and energy), and not in commercial motivations alone. To a large extent, the historical success of the welfare state is also that of a gradual and incomplete process of decommodification.

---

53. The advance in education allows us to explain, on the one hand, the enormous gap in productivity and national income per inhabitant between the United States and Europe over the twentieth century, and on the other hand, the convergence between 1950 and 1990. See Piketty, *Une brève histoire de l'égalité.*

Nonetheless, that does not mean that the historical growth of the welfare state can easily continue, without limit or obstacle. In theory, we can certainly imagine that the movement toward equality and the quantitative growth of the welfare state might continue, the keys being decisive new stages in matters of real and verifiable educational justice, the redistribution of inheritances and wealth, and power sharing in enterprises and the city, as well as on the international level—all this in a context in which each country would set social, fiscal, and environmental conditions in pursuing economic exchanges with other countries. Taking into account the changes observed in the twentieth century, nothing prevents us from imagining that the welfare state might amass resources ultimately reaching 60 or 70 percent of the national income (or more), while at the same time developing new forms of decentralization and collective participation in decisions on matters of common interest.[54] The questions of the organization and democratic governance of these public services, at least as much as the questions connected with the social acceptability of their financing and with the temporary losses in purchasing power that might result from putting international economic integration in question, nonetheless raise issues that are important and very complex. It seems to us that these challenges are surmountable, but on the condition that we take their measure and equip ourselves with the means to move beyond them, without seeking to underestimate the difficulties or make rapid progress.

Regarding such a complex question, it is natural and even indispensable that contradictory points of view be expressed. According to a view that can be qualified as liberal or conservative, the constraints of globalization and international competition forbid us to envisage any increase in levies, especially on the most mobile and most enterprising actors, because otherwise the country would lose its competitivity, and the whole of the population would suffer from that (starting with the most vulnerable). To be sure, this point of view on the necessity of stabilizing public spending sometimes reflects shortsighted social self-interest hiding behind the appearance of the common interest (and the trickle-down dogma). But it does not lack good arguments, and it must also be heard—as must criticisms of the efficiency of public action. To many citizens, probably to a majority of them, the idea that it would be strictly impossible to go farther in social redistribution and to ask the richest to contribute more no doubt seems excessively conservative and ultimately unconvincing, especially if one takes into account, on the one hand, the visible prosperity of the multimillionaires and the managerial classes, and on the other hand, the considerable objective needs in the sectors of education, health-

54. Piketty, *Une brève histoire de l'égalité.*

care, and housing, as well as in the areas of the environment and the fight against climate change. What is certain is that in the future, these debates will continue to fuel very intense political and electoral conflicts, as they have always done in the course of the construction of the welfare state, from the nineteenth century up to our own times.

The Role of Political and Electoral Conflict in the Reduction of Inequalities

To what extent are the development of the welfare state and the reduction of socioeconomic inequalities over the course of the twentieth century in France, and more generally in European societies, due to the transformations of the political and electoral landscape, and in particular to the emergence of new political parties, notably the Socialist Party and the Communist Party in the case of France? It is obviously impossible to answer such a question in all rigor, considering the complexity of the sociohistorical processes at work and the multiplicity of the events that have combined their effects. Still, the political factors, and in particular the coming to power of new social actors, have clearly played an essential role in the rise of the welfare state and the reduction of socioeconomic inequalities. Even before World War I, the growth of public spending on education was one of the prime objectives of the governments in power during the first decades of the Third Republic, even if the pace of growth remained very slow. The Socialist Party's rise to power and the pressure thus exerted on the Radical Party made it possible to accelerate the social agenda, with, for example, the adoption in 1910 of the law on "workers' and peasants' retirements." In 1908, in the conclusion to *Histoire socialiste de la France depuis 1789, which he had just edited, Jean Jaurès emphasized that after the successes registered on the level of political equality—with a definitive weakening of monarchical, censitary, and Caesarist ideas—the movement toward socioeconomic equality was able to get underway, as was shown, according to Jaurès, by the establishment in 1901 of a progressive inheritance tax, which he saw as the first stage of a structural transformation of the property system.*[55] *In 1936, the coming to power of the Popular Front, a coalition led for the first time by the Socialists, allied with the Radicals and the Communists, led to the adoption of emblematic measures*

---

55. J. Jaurès, "Le bilan social du 19e siècle," in *Histoire socialiste de la France contemporaine de 1789 à 1900,* vol. 12 (Rouff, 1908). The creation of a progressive tax on inheritances (law of 25 February 1901) preceded that of the progressive income tax (law of 15 July 1914), finally accepted by the Senate to finance the war. Initially set at 2.5 percent, the rate applied to the largest inheritances was raised to 6.5 percent in 1910 to contribute to the financing of pensions for workers and peasants.

on paid vacations and collective bargaining, salaries, and the length of the work day. Ten years later, the very strong position of the Communist Party and the Socialist Party in the parliamentary assemblies that issued from the legislative elections of 1945–1946 was to play a crucial role in the establishment of French-style social security.

In other European countries, we find at the same time the crucial role of the electoral victories of the Social Democrats in Sweden in 1932, which led them to institute a welfare state system that was one of the most complete tested up to that time, as well as the victory of the Labour Party in the United Kingdom in 1945, which resulted, notably, in the creation of the National Health Service. In both cases, these electoral triumphs led to new social groups, and authentic workers' parties came to power in countries where the political systems were shaped by strong elitist and aristocratic traditions.[56]

It must also be emphasized that the development of the welfare state sometimes occurred under the direction of political movements other than the Socialist, Social Democratic, or Labour Parties, and that in this case, the parties often played a major role by exerting strong pressure. For example, we might mention the case of Germany, where the Social Democrats are rarely in control of the federal government, and where it was rather the Christian Democrats who presided over the establishment of the founding social laws adopted during the postwar period. This is true, for instance, for the laws of 1951 and 1952 on co-management (introducing up to half the seats for representatives of salaried workers in the managerial authorities of the largest companies), adopted by Christian Democratic majorities to the dismay of the stockholders, and also under pressure from the syndical movement and the Social Democrats, who strengthened the legislation after they took power in 1976. In France, the great social laws of 1936 on paid vacations and collective bargaining were adopted almost unanimously by the Chamber of Deputies, even if the initial impulse came, obviously, from the Popular Front's electoral victory and especially from the strikes and occupations of factories that followed it. Another interesting case to which we shall return is that of the "blue horizon" chamber that resulted from the elections of 1919, which was one of the most right-wing in French electoral history, but in which the National Bloc majority voted, in June 1920, for one of the most progressive tax reforms ever adopted in France. Clearly, the competition with the left-wing parties played a decisive role

---

56. Immediately after World War II, the British Labour Party had among its elected officials a large share of workers and employees, who represented more than one-third of the Labour MPs in 1950. See Cagé, *Le prix de la démocratie,* 411, figure 66. See also J. Cagé and E. Dewitte, "The Rising Demand for Representation: Lessons from 100 Years of Political Selection in the UK" (working paper, Sciences Po Paris, 2023).

in this, just as much as did the new social and financial context that issued from the war, at a time when workers' salaries till had not regained their prewar purchasing power, and when new strikes threatened to block the country's way forward. The existence of the Communist countermodel since the Bolshevik Revolution of 1917 also made the danger of generalized expropriation more concrete and tended to transform the progressive income tax and the social welfare measures into a lesser evil in the political landscape of the 1920s, as it did during the whole Soviet period.

We also note the major role played by the social movement in catching up in the areas of salaries and French-style social protection, which began after the historic mobilizations in May 1968 and continued until the elections in May 1981, in an overheated social and electoral context where the existing government constantly feared being replaced by a Socialist-Communist coalition. When that coalition finally took over in 1981, a considerable part of its salary program had already been applied, which added to the feeling of disillusionment.[57] New social rights were put in place for salaried workers, and a new educational ambition was emphasized (with the objective, formulated in 1985, of reaching 30 percent of the age class at the level of the high school diploma over the course of the following decades), but the disappointment with this program was obvious when compared with the expectations raised by the promises of a complete transformation of the socioeconomic system. The Socialist governments that emerged from the elections of 1988, 1997, and 2012 subsequently tried to implement new social advances such as a wealth tax, a minimum guaranteed income, and universal healthcare, even if the scope of their redistributive ambition was increasingly called into question. We will return at length to this when we study how the structure of the votes and the political options available evolve over a long period.

To sum up, the reduction of socioeconomic inequalities in the twentieth century cannot be attributed to a single political camp, or in this case, to the increase in the power of the Socialist, Communist, Social Democratic, or Labour Parties, depending on the variable configurations in the different European countries. The reduction of inequalities must instead be examined in the broader perspective of a political ecosystem characterized by a bipolarization between a Social Democratic or Socialist bloc and a Christian Democratic or liberal-conservative bloc,

---

57. Between 1968 and 1983, the purchasing power of the minimum salary increased by 130 percent, as compared with about 50 percent for the average salary (which itself rose faster than the production per worker, if we add the increases in social contributions). See T. Piketty, *Les hauts revenus en France au 2oe siècle* (Grasset, 2001), 201–202.

with the two blocs alternating in power in a system of virtuous competition that has historically allowed collective experimentation and the successful development of the welfare state, all under the determining pressure of the social and syndical movement, and in a context marked by geopolitical competition on the world-wide scale. Inversely, the movement of a generalized economic liberalization adopted on the European and global scale over recent decades has greatly contributed to the limitation of the range of socioeconomic options. One of the central objectives of this book is to improve our understanding, in the case of France, of how the electoral coalitions and programmatic platforms at the origin of this ecosystem were established in the course of the twentieth century, notably by opposition to the different forms of tripartition observed in the nineteenth century or at the beginning of the twenty-first, which have in a way hobbled and still hinder the historical march toward equality, and how this system was subsequently weakened and could be reborn in the future. Before doing that, however, we must pursue our analysis of socioeconomic inequalities and their transformations over a long period, emphasizing more than we have up to now the spatial and territorial dimensions that have always played a central role in this long history, on the social and economic levels as well as on the political and electoral levels.

CHAPTER 2

The Return of Territorial Inequalities

In this chapter we will study the main lines of the evolution of socioeconomic inequalities on the territorial and spatial level in France over a long period. First, we will take the measure of the growing polarization of the population in the national territory over the past two centuries, a structural evolution within which each individual will need situate himself or herself. Then we will analyze the evolution of territorial inequalities, such as those that can be measured by the distribution of production, property values, income, and occupations and sectors of activity. We will see that territorial inequalities had reduced significantly since the nineteenth century, though it is true that they were extremely high to start with. They have begun to rise again since the 1980s–1990s, in a more pronounced way than the inequalities of income and wealth at the national level. This general context offers us an indispensable key for understanding the transformations of electoral behaviors that will be studied in the rest of this book, and we will see that they depend crucially on the interaction between the level of wealth and the place in the territory concerned (villages, towns, suburbs, and cities).

The Increasing Polarization of the Population in the Territory

The first structural evolution that we should emphasize is the increasing polarization of the population in the national territory. In other words, over the last two centuries, an ever-growing proportion of the population has accumulated in certain parts of the territory, whereas on the contrary, other segments of the country have had a tendency to empty out. This evolution is well known, but it nonetheless constitutes the fundamental framework within which perceptions of space and distance, notions of belonging and identity, and sometimes feelings of abandonment and disappearance have developed since the Revolution. It is therefore important to start by taking its measure.

We can begin by assessing the polarization between departments and between regions. For that purpose, and on the basis of information emerging from censuses regularly carried out since 1801 and the first counts made in connection with the French Revolution, we have collected data series bearing on the population of some

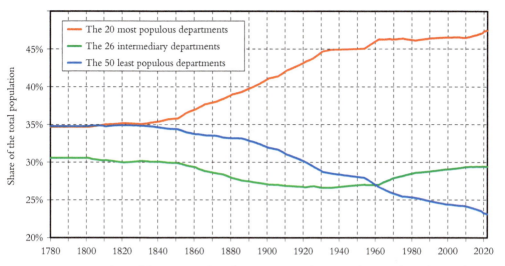

FIGURE 2.1. The share of the most populous departments rose from 35% of the total population of Metropolitan France in 1800 to 47% in 2022. That of the 26 following departments was 30% in those years, and that of the least populous 50% fell from 35% to 23%.

Note: The distribution of the population was calculated for the whole period on the basis of the 95 departments in 2022 and current territory of Metropolitan France.

Sources and series: see unehistoireduconflitpolitique.fr

36,000 municipalities in France from 1780 to 2022.[1] Then we distributed these municipal populations among the ninety-six departments of the current metropolitan territory in order to study the structure of the population on a stable basis.[2] We note that in 1800, the twenty most heavily populated departments had 35 percent of the population, and that today their share is 47 percent. Over the same period, the share of the fifty least populated departments fell from 35 percent to 23 percent, whereas that of the twenty-six intermediary departments remained stable at around 30 percent (see figure 2.1).

---

1. Taking into account creations, disappearances, and fusions of municipalities, the exact number of municipalities has changed only slightly since the Revolution: it was about 37,000 in the nineteenth century and the beginning of the twentieth, before decreasing very slowly and settling at around 36,000 at the end of the twentieth century and about 35,000 at present. To simplify our exposition, we will usually refer to the "36,000 municipalities in France." The series on municipal populations are less precise for the end of the eighteenth century and the beginning of the nineteenth, but that is of no importance for the general developments presented here.

2. Since the creation in 1968 of new departments in the area around Paris (Hauts-de-Seine, Seine-Saint-Denis, Val-de-Marne, Essonne, Yvelines, Val-d'Oise, Seine-et-Marne, and Paris), the departments of Metropolitan France have been numbered 1 to 95, with ninety-six departments in all, taking into account that in 1975 the former department of Corsica (20) was divided into two departments

The increase in the share of the twenty most densely populated departments is explained mainly by the strong demographic growth of Île-de-France, which represented around 5 percent of the total population in 1800, then gradually rose from 5 percent to 19 percent between 1830 and 1970, and has stabilized at that level ever since (currently, it has about 12 million inhabitants).[3] The decrease of the share of the fifty least populated departments corresponds to a more diffuse phenomenon that can be found in most regions, with the emergence of departments that are very sparsely populated in comparison to the others. In 1800, most departments were home to around 1 percent of the national population (between 0.7 percent and 1.3 percent, approximately). In 1900 and still more in 2022, we find all over the territory departments with extremely small populations—less than 0.3 percent of the total national population, for example.[4] Taking into account the fact that the total population itself has grown greatly since the Revolution (from 28 million to 66 million), most of the departments whose share of the total has declined have nonetheless seen increases in their numbers of inhabitants over the long term. In other words, it is often a question of a relative decrease in a world in full development, and not an absolute decrease. Nevertheless, there are sixteen departments that have suffered an absolute decline in their population between 1800 and 2022, including six departments that have seen losses of more than 30 percent (Cantal, Creuse, Lozère, Lot, Meuse, and Orne), which is considerable.[5]

Municipalities and Conurbations in France over a Long Period

The movement polarizing the population also took place within each department, between urban centers and rural territories. An initial way of seeing it is to examine the evolution of the distribution of the population among the 36,000 municipalities. We note that the 10 percent of municipalities with the largest populations constituted 42 percent of the total population in 1800, and that this share rose to

---

(2A and 2B, corresponding to Corse-du-Sud and Haute-Corse, respectively). In order not to distort the trends, all the series shown here refer to the current territory of Metropolitan France for the whole of the period concerned. Let us recall that Savoie, Haute-Savoie, and Alpes Maritimes were not part of the national territory between 1815 and 1860 (2 percent of the population), nor were Haut-Rhin, Bas-Rhin, and Moselle between 1871 and 1918 (4 percent of the population).

3. The share of the total population of the other twenty-one current regions has been relatively stable or slightly declining for the past two centuries, except for the Provence-Alpes-Côte d'Azur, which rose from 4 percent to 8 percent between 1890 and 2000. See unehistoireduconflitpolitique.fr, figures B1.1a–B1.1b.

4. For example, this is the case of Meuse and Haute-Marne, or, again, Creuse. See unehistoireduconflitpolitique.fr, map C2.1.

5. The ten departments that have suffered an absolute decrease of less than 30 percent are Ariège, Aveyron, Corrèze, Gers, Haute-Loire, Haute-Marne, Haute-Saône, Jura, Manche, and Nièvre.

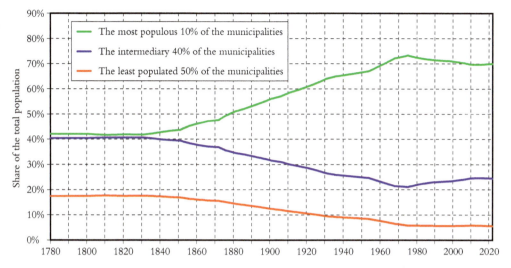

FIGURE 2.2. The share of the 10% of the municipalities with the greatest population in the total population of Metropolitan France rose from 42% in 1800 to 73% in 1975, and then decreased to 70% in 2022. The share of the 50% of the municipalities with the lowest population fell from 17% of the total population in 1800 to 6% in 2022.

Note: The distribution was calculated for the whole of the period on the basis of the current territory of metropolitan France.

Sources and series: unehistoireduconflitpolitique.fr

70 percent in 2022. During this time, the share of the next-largest 40 percent of municipalities declined from 41 percent to 24 percent, and that of the smallest 50 percent of municipalities declined from 17 percent to 6 percent (see figure 2.2).

Another way of seeing this is to look at the evolution of the share of the national population represented by each of these municipalities. If the population was distributed in a completely equal way among the 36,000 municipalities, then each of them would represent a little less than 0.003 percent of the total population. In 1800, most of the municipalities had between 0.001 and 0.002 percent of the total population, which corresponds to a relatively balanced distribution. In 2022, on the contrary, more than three-quarters of the municipalities had less than 0.001 percent of the population. In other words, a large part of the territory no longer counts for much in terms of its demographic contribution to the country (see map 2.1).

In all, more than half the municipalities have seen absolute decreases in their populations between 1800 and 2022, and about one-quarter saw decreases of more than 50 percent. If these declines are particularly striking in a number of departments—like Côtes d'Armor, Mayenne, and Sarthe—we also see a very great heterogeneity within departments, as in Alpes-Maritimes (see map 2.2). This polarization took place gradually; thus, a number of territories underwent diminutions of their populations between 1950 and 2022 (some of them only since the beginning

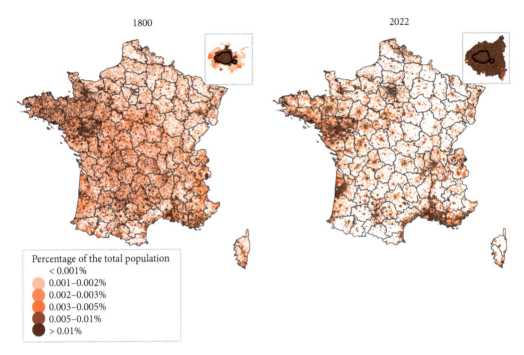

1800

2022

Percentage of the total population
  < 0.001%
  0.001–0.002%
  0.002–0.003%
  0.003–0.005%
  0.005–0.01%
  > 0.01%

MAP 2.1. The increasing polarization of the population in the territory, 1800–2022

From 1800 to 2022, an increasing share of the territory has been constituted by municipalities bringing together a very small fraction of the population (less than 0.001% of the total population).

Sources and series: unehistoireduconflitpolitique.fr

of the twenty-first century), but compared with the beginning of the nineteenth century, their populations are larger today.[6] Later on, we will examine in detail the impact of this territorial polarization on electoral behaviors, but let us stress here what the absolute decline of the population of a municipality means concretely: the closure of classes in schools and then the closure of the schools themselves, the gradual disappearance of local public services, small shops going out of business, town centers where drawn shutters little by little replace public and private activity, and a sense of emptiness that gradually overtakes a disappearing history.

It will nonetheless be noted that in terms of the total population, the share of the 10 percent most populous municipalities peaked around 73 percent in 1975 and since then has slightly declined, to the benefit of the next most populous 40 percent of municipalities (see figure 2.2). This is explained especially by the fragmentation of the populations of some city centers to the benefit of suburban municipalities. In fact, since the municipality is going to constitute our elementary

6. See unehistoireduconflitpolitique.fr, maps C2.2 and C2.3.

1800–2022

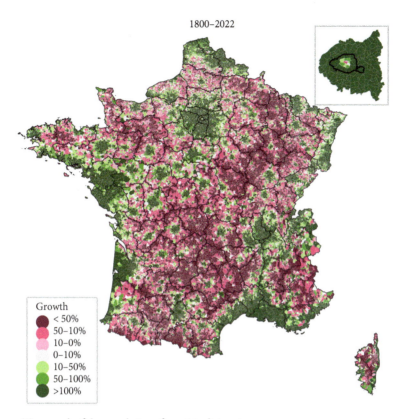

MAP 2.2. The growth of the population of municipalities, 1800–2022

The map represents the change in the size of the population of municipalities from 1800 to 2022. The municipalities in violet lost population during this period (and the darker the violet, the more they lost), while those in green gained in population (and the darker the green, the more they gained).

Sources and series: unehistoireduconflitpolitique.fr

unit for studying both electoral behaviors and socioeconomic inequalities, it is naturally very important to take into account the way in which these municipalities come together to form conurbations. For municipalities with the same number of inhabitants, say, 500 or 5,000, some are in fact part of a large conurbation, whereas others are isolated—which leads to very different perceptions of their places in the territory, as well as specific inequalities in access to public services such as education and welfare. This is often accompanied by considerable differences in terms of socioeconomic characteristics and political behaviors. To study these questions, we will use the definition of the conurbation established by the National Institute of Statistics and Economic Studies (INSEE), which is based on the existence of a conurbation in terms of the continuity of buildings. To simplify, a conurbation (also called an urban unit) is defined as the set of adjacent

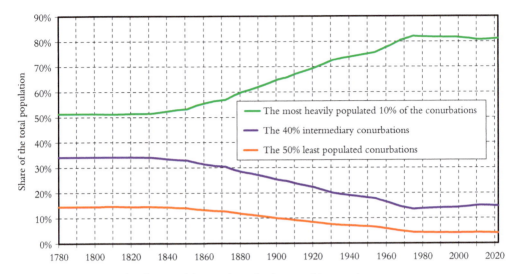

FIGURE 2.3. The distribution of the population by the size of the conurbation

The share of the total population in the 10% most populated conurbations grew from 51% in 1800 to 82% in 1975, then dropped slightly to 81% in 2022. The share in the least populated 50% fell from 14% in 1800 to 4% in 2022. Note that the share is calculated for the whole period on the basis of the current territory of Metropolitan France. The conurbations are defined as adjacent municipalities not separated by a built-up area of more than 200 meters (INSEE, 2020).

Sources and series: unehistoireduconflitpolitique.fr

municipalities that covers without interruption a built-up area of more than 200 meters.[7] In order to obtain results that are as comparable as possible over the whole period being studied, we rely on the list of conurbations (and the municipalities constituting them) drawn up by INSEE in 2020.[8] Specifically, the 10 percent of conurbations with the greatest populations saw their share of the total population rise from 51 percent in 1800 to 82 percent in 2022, while the share of the 40 percent with the smallest conurbations fell from 14 percent to 4 percent (see figure 2.3).

---

7. With exceptions for bridges, parks, business activity zones, collective facilities, and so on. All the methodological details are available online at the INSEE site, www.insee.fr/en/accueil.

8. The geographical proximity of the municipalities is by design unchanged since 1789. As for the continuity of the built-up area, it is impossible to define rigorously a notion that can be consistently measured over time. because we lack adequate maps, whence the choice here to apply the same list of conurbations to the whole of the period. This implies that certain conurbations studied here were probably not entirely conurbations in 1800 or 1900 (in the sense of the continuity of the built-up area), and thus that the growth of conurbations was in reality even more rapid than indicated here.

The distribution of the population among conurbations has been broadly stable since the mid-1970s; since then, conurbations of all sizes have advanced at roughly the same pace, which can be explained by the limits encountered by urban hyper-concentration and by a transformation of public policies on the subject.[9] A representative case is Paris, which, with its 431 municipalities, included nearly 11 million inhabitants (out of 12 million in the Île-de-France region) in 2022, and whose share in the national population has stabilized at around 17 percent since the 1970s. The same goes for the next ten most populous conurbations (Lyon, Marseille-Aix, Lille, Toulouse, Bordeaux, Nice, Nantes, Toulon, Douai-Lens, and Strasbourg), which included nearly 600 municipalities between them, and whose share in the total population has been steady since 1970 at around 14–15 percent (though with a slight increase), after having tripled between 1830 and 1970.[10] The increasing polarization of the population at the level of the conurbations, which had advanced rapidly over the course of the preceding century and a half, thus has slowed over the last fifty years. However, we should note that the polarization at the level of the department, for its part, continued, with the share of the fifty least populated departments in the total population having continued to fall since 1970 (see figure 2.1). Over the long term, we also observe that for the past two centuries, the quasi-totality of the rise in population has taken place in conurbations of more than 10,000 inhabitants, and for the most part, among those with more than 200,000 inhabitants. Since the 1970s, the distribution of the rise has been much more balanced among conurbations of different sizes (see figure 2.4).[11]

---

9. Let us mention particularly the invention of the "urban policy" in the early 1970s, with a complete overhaul of town and country planning policy, the development of the territory, the condemnation of large-scale urban development projects, and the implementation of suburban housing programs (such as the *Chalandonettes,* named after Georges Pompidou's minister of public works, Albin Chalandon). The desire to put an end to "mass" construction projects is also reflected in the 1972 Common Program (*Programme pour un gouvernement démocratique d'union populaire* [Éditions sociales, 1972]), which emphasizes that development must have as its mission to correct imbalances: "to develop and reanimate mining and border regions, to rebalance the Paris region, and to bring the West and Center out of their regional underdevelopment." Quoted in R. Hésnin, "Années 1970: Une décennie charnière?," in *Aménagement du territoire. Changement de temps, changement d'espace* (Presses Universitaires de Caen, 2008).

10. See unehistoireduconflitpolitique.fr, appended figures B1.4e–B1.4g. Alongside these giant conurbations including dozens or sometimes even several hundred municipalities, most of the conurbations consist of only a few towns. On the basis of the built-up area, INSEE has divided the 35,000 municipalities active in 2020 into about 30,000 conurbations consisting of 27,500 isolated municipalities and 2,500 multimunicipality conurbations including 7,500 municipalities (or three municipalities, on average, for each of these multimunicipality conurbations).

11. If we define the urban population as those living in conurbations of over 10,000 inhabitants, then the urbanization rate has risen from 23 percent in 1800 (4 percent in the twenty least

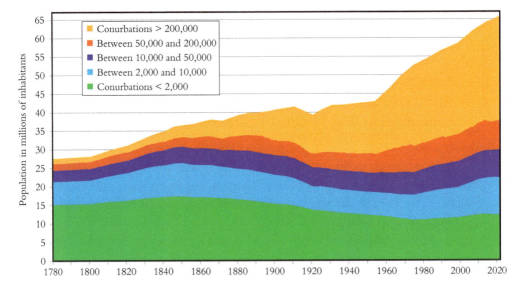

FIGURE 2.4. The population by the size of the conurbation

Between 1800 and 2022, the total population of Metropolitan France (current territory) rose from about 28 million to 66 million. The population of conurbations of less than 10,000 inhabitants remained more or less stable at about 22 million. All the demographic growth took place within the largest conurbations, and for the most part, within conurbations of more than 200,000 inhabitants.

Sources and series: unehistoireduconflitpolitique.fr

Villages, Towns, Suburbs, and Metropoles: First Points of Reference

When we study the determinants of electoral behaviors and the connections with other socioeconomic characteristics of municipalities, we will take care to correlate with as much precision as possible the effects of the size of the municipality

urbanized departments, 57 percent in the twenty most urbanized) to 66 percent in 2022 (27 percent in the former, 87 percent in the latter) between 1830 and 1970, and has remained virtually stable since 1970. See unehistoireduconflitpolitique.fr, figure B1.2c. We could also use groupings of municipalities combining criteria of built-up continuity and employment structure, such as the notion of urban area, which includes, according to INSEE definitions, not only the municipalities of a given conurbation (defined by the continuity of the built-up area) but also municipalities that do not belong to the same conurbation in the sense of the built-up area, if at least 40 percent of their employed resident population work in the conurbation in question (the so-called *couronne périurbaine* constituted by these additional municipalities). The notion is pertinent, but it is usable only for the recent period; the available data do not allow us to resort to the long term. Taking into account the historical perspective we have adopted here, we have therefore chosen to concentrate on the notions of municipality and conurbation.

and the size of the conurbation, taking into account the exact position of the different municipalities within the distribution of the sizes of the municipality and the conurbation, centile by centile, or ventile by ventile (that is, by arranging the municipalities and conurbations in twenty groups of the same size). We will also occasionally resort to presentations of our results founded on a small number of categories, making possible a simpler, more intuitive way of visualizing the principal conclusions. To that end, we will use in particular a distribution of the population into four large categories of habitats: villages, towns, suburbs, and metropoles (or metropolitan centers). These notions are all the more useful because of the opposition of the vote in the suburbs in favor of the Left bloc and the vote in the towns and villages for the Right bloc, which is currently found in the contemporary political debate in France, especially since the emergence of an electoral tripartition after the elections of 2002. Therefore, it is particularly interesting to study the way the realities have evolved over a long period.

The reference categorization we will use is the following: villages group together the inhabitants of conurbations of fewer than 2,000 inhabitants; towns group together the inhabitants of conurbations comprising between 2,000 and 100,000 inhabitants; suburbs group together the inhabitants of secondary municipalities of conurbations of more than 100,000 inhabitants outside the principal municipality (all the municipalities except the principal municipality); and metropoles group together the inhabitants of the principal municipality of conurbations of more than 100,000 inhabitants (the most heavily populated municipality, generally corresponding to the metropolitan center in the geographical sense of the term). If these definitions are adopted, we can see that France's 66 million inhabitants in 2022 are distributed in a relatively balanced way: 12 million in villages, 22 million in towns, 21 million in suburbs, and 11 million in metropoles. In 1800, the 28 million inhabitants of France lived chiefly in villages (15 million) or in towns (11 million), and many fewer in metropoles (1 million) or suburbs (1 million). See figure 2.5, and also map 2.3 for the geographical distribution of villages, towns, suburbs, and metropoles.

In all, between 1800 and 2022, the share of the population living in villages fell from 54 percent to 19 percent, and the share living in towns from 38 to 34 percent. Over the same period, the population living in suburbs rose from 4 percent to 31 percent, and that living in metropoles rose from 4 to 16 percent (see figure 21.6). Here, too, we note a relative stabilization of the distribution of the population since the middle of the 1970s in comparison to the massive changes that occurred in the preceding century and a half. To sum up, since the middle of the 1970s, villages and towns have included about half the French population (we will sometimes refer to the "rural world," meaning this most rural half of the country during

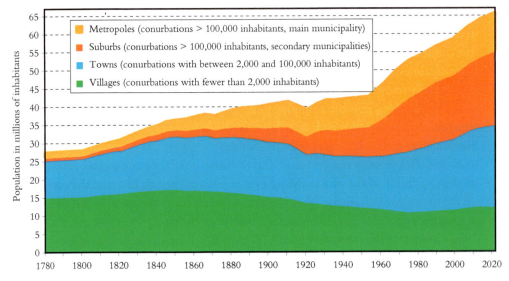

FIGURE 2.5. Villages, towns, suburbs, and metropoles (population in millions)

In 2022, out of a total population of 66 million inhabitants, about 12 million lived in villages (defined here as conurbations of less than 2,000 inhabitants), 22 million in towns (conurbations with between 2,000 and 100,000 inhabitants), 21 million in suburbs (secondary municipalities of conurbations with more than 100,000 inhabitants), and 11 million in metropoles (main municipalities of conurbations with more than 100,000 inhabitants). In 1800, using the same definitions, a total population of 28 million was divided among 15 million inhabitants in villages, 11 million in towns, 1 million in suburbs, and 1 million in metropoles.

Sources and series: unehistoireduconflitpolitique.fr

the recent period, even if towns are not, strictly speaking, rural municipalities, and indeed constituted the most important part of the urban world at the time of the Revolution), whereas the suburbs and the metropoles made up the other half of the population (the "urban world").

However, within this generally stabilized landscape, we note a significant and unprecedented recovery in recent decades of the towns' share (to the detriment of the villages' share, which continues to decline) and a continuing increase in the suburbs' share at the expense of the metropoles, whose share in the population is undergoing an erosion that is also unprecedented, declining from 20 percent in 1970 to 16 percent in 2022. The case of the Paris conurbation is emblematic. Its share of the national population has been stable at around 17 percent since 1970, but during same time, the city of Paris's share has fallen from 5 percent to scarcely more than 3 percent (following a historical decline that began during the interwar period), a decrease that has been entirely offset

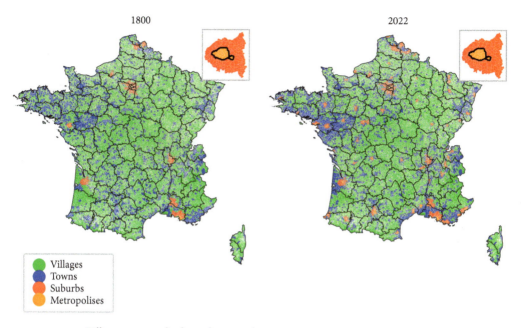

MAP 2.3. Villages, towns, suburbs, and metropoles

The map represents the municipalities classified as villages (conurbations with fewer than 2,000 inhabitants), towns (conurbations with between 2,000 and 100,000 inhabitants), suburbs (secondary municipalities of conurbations with more than 100,000 inhabitants), and metropoles (main municipalities of conurbations with more than 100,000 inhabitants). In 1800, 54% of the population lived in villages, 38% in towns, 4% in suburbs, and 4% in metropoles; in 2022, 19% lived in villages, 34% in towns, 31% in suburbs, and 16% in metropoles.

Sources and series: unehistoireduconflitpolitique.fr

by the continual growth of the share of the Parisian suburbs.[12] Let us add that the stabilization of the overall distribution in no way implies the end of mobility; within each generation, some people born in villages or towns move to metropoles or suburbs, and vice versa.[13]

12. The population of the city of Paris reached its zenith between 1910 and 1960 with about 2.8 to 2.9 million inhabitants, before falling abruptly from 2.8 million to 2.2 million between 1960 and 1980, and then stabilizing at around 2.2 million from 1980 to 2020. Taking into account the sharp rise in the national population, the share of the city of Paris has fallen by more than half in one century, passing from 7 percent of the total population in 1920 to hardly more than 3 percent in 2022. Over the same period, the Paris conurbation's share of the total population grew from 13 to 17 percent. See unehistoireduconflitpolitique.fr, figures B1.3e and B1.4g.

13. Unfortunately, the sources available do not allow us to measure this mobility in a perfectly comparable way over the long term. Nonetheless, examining the structures of populations by age and sex enables us to sketch its contours and lines of evolution. See chapter 3.

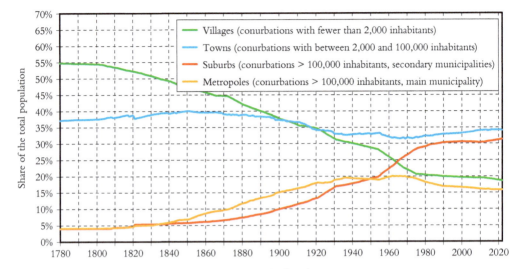

FIGURE 2.6. Villages, towns, suburbs, and metropoles (in %)

The share of the population living in villages (defined here as conurbations with less than 2,000 inhabitants) fell from 54% in 1800 to 19% in 2022; the share living in towns (conurbations with between 2,000 and 100,000 inhabitants) fell from 38% to 34%; the share living in suburbs (secondary municipalities of conurbations with more than 100,000 inhabitants) grew from 4% to 31%; and the share living in metropoles (main municipalities of conurbations with more than 100,000 inhabitants) rose from 4% to 16%.

Sources and series: unehistoireduconflitpolitique.fr

This distribution of the population in four categories has the advantages of being relatively simple, intuitive, and suitable for being used transparently for a long-term analysis. We will see that this mode of analysis provides an efficient framework for studying political behaviors if it is correlated with other criteria, notably in terms of wealth. In other words, it is essential to emphasize that in every period there are poor villages and rich villages, poor towns and rich towns, poor suburbs and rich suburbs, poor metropoles and rich metropoles. Of course, the precise thresholds used for these definitions are debatable, like all categorizations of this type. In particular, the threshold of 100,000 inhabitants may seem relatively small for defining conurbations of suburbs and metropoles. One might prefer a threshold of 200,000 or 300,000 inhabitants, but that would raise other problems. It is difficult to use the term "town" when referring to conurbations as large as these, and moreover, when we go back two centuries, there are very few conurbations that big. We might also use a single variable, for instance by defining the inhabitants of suburbs and metropoles as the inhabitants of the twenty-five largest metropoles in each period, which would correspond to a threshold of about

50,000 in 1800, 100,000 around 1900, and 260,000 in 2022.[14] All these definitions have their advantages and disadvantages, and we have been careful to verify
that all the results presented in the rest of this work remain valid, whatever the
chosen definition might be. In practice, the choice of the threshold does not make
much difference; in the long run, the rise in power of the suburbs and metropoles
is everywhere the same in all cases. Specifically, whatever threshold is chosen among
those mentioned above, the share of the national population living in metropoles
and suburbs has risen from about 5–10 percent around 1800 to 35–55 percent currently, with an increase occurring for the most part between 1830 and 1970 and a
relative stabilization since 1970 (see figure 2.7).[15]

Measuring Territorial Inequalities: Production, Property Values, Income

Let us now turn to the question of the measurement of territorial inequalities. In
the following chapters we will look closely at educational inequalities and those
related to religion and origins. At this stage, we are going to concentrate on the
strictly socioeconomic dimensions, using several indicators that allow us to shed
a complementary light on a complex reality that involves production, property
values, income, occupation, and the sector of activity. We will begin by examining
what can be said about the territorial distribution of production (in the sense of
the GDP). Using in particular the great industrial and agricultural surveys
organized all over the territory from the middle of the nineteenth century on, researchers have tried to assess the distribution of the GDP at the departmental
level, starting in 1860. Although these assessments must, of course, be used with

---

14. By comparison, the number of conurbations concerned passes with a fixed threshold of
    100,000 inhabitants grew from about ten in 1800 to about fifty in 2022 (and from three to
    thirty with a threshold of 200,000, and from one to twenty with a threshold of 300,000). To
    analyze the contemporary period, the geographer Christophe Guilluy has proposed the inclu-
    sion of the "France of the metropoles," comprising the twenty-five largest conurbations (or
    more precisely, the twenty-five largest urban areas), with the rest of the territory constituting
    "peripheral France." See C. Guilluy, *La France périphérique. Comment on a sacrifié les classes
    populaires* (Flammarion, 2014). The division into four categories proposed here (villages,
    towns, suburbs, metropoles) seems to us richer and more operative in a historical perspective,
    especially if we take care to clearly distinguish rich and poor municipalities within each cate-
    gory, which Guilluy tends to forget to do, the better to emphasize the frontal opposition
    between his two sets.
15. We are going to concentrate on the definition obtained with the intermediate threshold of
    100,000 inhabitants, but we have taken care to ensure that all the results presented below
    remain qualitatively unchanged if the other thresholds are adopted. See unehistoireduconflit-
    politique.fr.

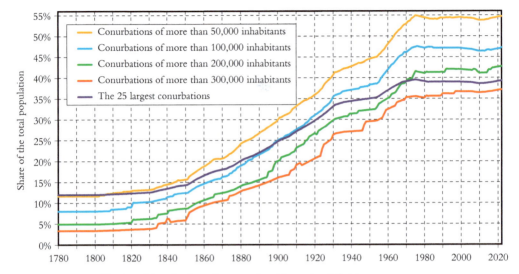

FIGURE 2.7. The rise of the suburbs and metropoles: Alternative definitions

No matter what definition is adopted for metropoles and their suburbs (conurbations of more than 50,000, 100,000, 200,000, or 300,000 inhabitants, or the twenty-five largest conurbations every year), their share of the total population has generally increased steadily over a long period, from around 5–10% of the total population in 1800 to around 35–55% of the total population in 2022. Sources and series: unehistoireduconflitpolitique.fr

caution, they nonetheless provide interesting orders of magnitude.[16] We note, for example, that the average GDP per inhabitant of the ten richest departments (in the sense of the GDP per inhabitant) was 3.1 times higher than that of the ten poorest departments in 1860. This ratio then gradually diminished from 3.1 in 1860 to 2.2 in 1990, before increasing again to 2.7 in 2022. Here we find the same overall curve and the same rise of territorial inequalities since 1900 if we examine the ratio between the twenty richest departments and the twenty poorest, or between the five richest and the five poorest (see figure 2.8).

The increase in the gaps in GDP has been particularly great since 1990 when we compare the five richest and the five poorest departments. This is explained mainly by the recent, unprecedented concentration of the production of wealth

16. Here we rely mainly on the estimates of the departmental GDP for 1860, 1896, and 1930 by P. P. Combes, L. Lafourcade, J. F. Thisse, and J. C. Toutain ("The Rise and Fall of Spatial Inequalities in France: A Long-Run Perspective," *Explorations in Economic History,* 2011), which we complete using the estimates of the regional and departmental GDP carried out by INSEE and Eurostat since 1960.

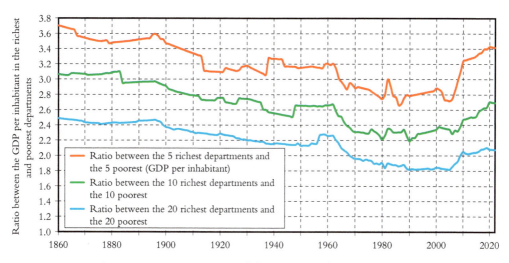

FIGURE 2.8. The increasing gaps in GDP per inhabitant between departments since 1990

In 1860, the average GDP per inhabitant in the five richest departments (in terms of GDP per inhabitant) was 3.7 times higher than in the five poorest departments; this ratio fell to 2.7 in 1985 and then rose to 3.4 in 2022. The ratio between the average GDP per inhabitant in the ten richest departments and the ten poorest departments fell from 3.1 in 1860 to 2.2 in 1990, and then to 2.7 in 2022.

Sources and series: unehistoireduconflitpolitique.fr

in the most prosperous departments in Île-de-France (especially Paris and Hauts-de-Seine). To be sure, these territories have always been appreciably richer than the national average, but since 1990 there has been an unprecedented decline in comparison with earlier periods. The available data allow us, for instance, to estimate that the GDP per inhabitant of Paris was on the order of 2.5 times greater than the national average from 1860 to 1980–1990, and then that this ratio continued to increase and reached about 3.2 at the beginning of the 2020s. The case of Hauts-de-Seine is still more spectacular: the GDP per inhabitant was 1.6 to 1.8 times higher than the national average in the years 1970 and 1980, then it began a particularly rapid rise, to the point that the department slightly overtook Paris in the 2010s. It was 3.3 times the national average at the beginning of the 2020s. Considering that the poorest departments have a GDP per inhabitant that is on the order of half the national average, that means that Paris and Hauts-de-Seine now have a GDP per inhabitant that is six or seven times higher than the poorer territories. Interdepartmental gaps have not reached such levels since 1860.

It is particularly striking to note that at the end of the nineteenth century and for most of the twentieth, the country's most prosperous departments were distributed in a relatively balanced way over the whole of the national territory, whereas today they are almost all located in the Paris region.[17] That reflects structural transformations of the organization of the economic system and of the productive fabric, with the decline of the major industrial centers located in the provinces (for example, in Seine-Maritime, Bouches-du-Rhône, and Nord) and the rise in the power of the financial sector and of the headquarters of the great multinational groups located in Île de France. We find similar results in the works of the sociologist Olivier Godechot, who has shown, based on salary records drawn from businesses' declarations of social welfare payments, that the highest remunerations are now concentrated in an unprecedented way in Paris and Hauts-de-Seine (especially in finance and in the top management of the big groups), whereas in the 1970s a large share of the highest salaries was found in provincial departments (for example, in management positions at industrial sites).[18]

In general, there have been many territorial recompositions in France since the nineteenth century. The first cartographies of socioeconomic inequalities between departments, made in the 1820s by the geographers Adrien Balbi, Conrad Malte-Brun, and Charles Dupin, emphasized the famous Saint-Malo–Geneva line, with higher levels of both education (measured by, for example, the number of students in royal colleges per inhabitant) and industrial development northeast of this line.[19] If we examine the map of the GDP per inhabitant in 1860, we also find that levels of development are generally higher northeast of this line (for example, in Normandy, in the Paris basin, and in the north or northeast of the country) than they are in the southwest (for example, in Brittany, the Massif Central, and the Southeast), even if there were already exceptions. The renewal of

---

17. See unehistoireduconflitpolitique.fr, figure B6.2g. As for periods predating the creation of new departments in the area around Paris in 1968, the GNP of the department of Seine was divided between Paris and the departments of the *petite couronne* (the set of departments immediately surrounding Paris) based on the differences in the share of the GNP per inhabitant observed in 1968 and on the development of other indicators available for the period between 1860 and 1968 (in particular, the share of property values per inhabitant). We have proceeded in the same way for Seine-et-Oise, which was divided again in 1968, between Yvelines, Essonne, Val-d'Oise, and *la petite couronne*.

18. In 1860, the five richest departments were Paris, Seine-Maritime, Marne, Hérault, and Bouches-du-Rhône. In 2022, they were Hauts-de-Seine, Paris, Rhône, Val-de-Marne, and Yvelines. The poorest departments in 1860 were Corrèze, Ariège, Haute-Corse, Savoie, and Hautes-Alpes. In 2022, they were Haute-Saône, Creuse, Meuse, Tarn-et-Garonne, and Aisne. See unehistoireduconflitpolitique.fr, map C2.4.

19. See O. Godechot, "Is Finance Responsible for the Rise of Wage Inequality in France?," *Socio-Economic Review,* 2012; O. Godechot, "Financiarisation et fractures socio-spatiales," *L'Année sociologique,* 2013.

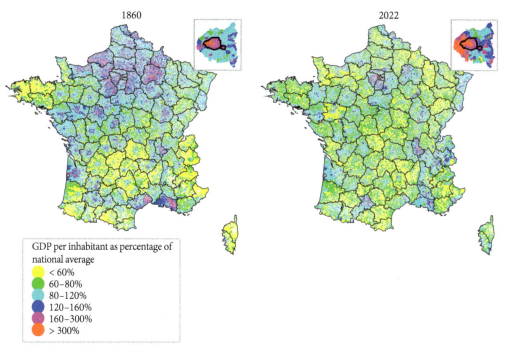

MAP 2.4. GDP per inhabitant as percentage of national average, 1860–2022

This map represents the GDP per inhabitant of each municipality as a percentage of the national average. The departmental GDPs have been distributed within departments as functions of the relative income of each municipality.

Sources and series: unehistoireduconflitpolitique.fr

the productive fabric and in particular the decline of the old industrial sectors of the north and northeast of the country was to lead to very marked recompositions in 1930 and especially in 2022, when the Saint-Malo–Geneva line seemed to be virtually inverted, with levels of GDP par inhabitant now higher in large parts of the west, the southwest, and the southeast of the country than in the north and the northeast. Maps also illustrate that the territories where the GDP per inhabitant is higher than the national average are now much more highly concentrated in the Paris region than they used to be (see map 2.4).[20]

Generally, it is important to emphasize that the territorial inequalities of the GDP per inhabitant reflect not only the effects of economic specialization, but also political choices and relationships of power and domination between territories

20. See also unehistoireduconflitpolitique.fr, map C2.5, for the distribution of the GDP per inhabitant in 1930.

and social groups. For example, the policies of financial deregulation adopted in the 1980s and 1990s have contributed to the growth of the financial sector and particularly of market activities, which are strongly concentrated in the Paris region, and which have begun to attract a growing segment of the most highly educated workers from all over the country and to inflate the GDP of the area around Paris in relation to other regions. Far from being purely technical, the question of the size of the GDP and the valorization of the various economic activities (including within a single enterprise) also reflects power relationships and collective choices. For example, if a large group succeeds in increasing the remuneration of its managers in its headquarters in the Paris region while at the same time reducing the salaries of its employees in its establishments and branches in the provinces, then the GDP in the Paris region will rise at the expense of the provincial GDP, without Île-de-France having necessarily become more "productive" than the provinces. The same goes for the valorization of public services in the GDP, which results above all from a collective choice in connection with objectives of social and territorial development.[21]

In all, over the long term, the diminution of territorial inequalities of the GDP per inhabitant is explained in part by the same factors that account for the movement toward greater equality at the national level, starting with the development of public services unified over the whole of the territory (especially in education, healthcare, and transportation infrastructure) that began at the end of the nineteenth century and continued throughout the twentieth century. In comparison with the compression of vertical inequalities measured between centiles of income or patrimony at the national level (see chapter 1, figures 1.4 and 1.6), the reduction of the disparities in the GDP per inhabitant between departments has nonetheless been less important historically, and especially the increase in inequalities since 1980–1990 was considerably larger for territorial inequalities than for vertical inequalities. We must also emphasize that the rather limited decrease in disparities in the GDP per inhabitant between departments over a long period has taken place in a context marked by a growing polarization of the population. If we examine the distribution of the total GDP (not the GDP per inhabitant), we

---

21. In national accounting, the value of public services (for instance, education, healthcare, and policing) is measured by their production cost, and then in particular by the salaries of the agents concerned. A country that chooses to reduce the salaries of its teachers will thus reduce the value of the GDP issuing from teaching (as measured in the official national accounts), even if nothing has changed in the social and collective value of the corresponding educational services.

see that all through the period from 1860 to 2022 there was a tendency toward an increasing concentration of the wealth produced in one small part of the territory.[22]

The Rise in Territorial Inequalities in Property Values since 1980–1990

Using the departmental GDP yields some interesting lessons but also raises multiple difficulties. In particular, it requires a relatively complex statistical formulation, and moreover, it can be calculated only at the level of relatively large territories like the department. It is very hard to estimate the GDP at the municipal level without taking into account that the considerable differences between the place of production and the place of habitation make interpretations difficult. If we want to distribute the departmental GDP at the municipal level, the most convincing way to proceed is probably to do so on the basis of the average income of each municipality (see map 2.4). Generally speaking, to measure socioeconomic inequalities at the municipal level, we will rely on two main indicators: income and property values. The latter is particularly interesting because it is the indicator for which we have the most complete sources over the long term. The reason for this is simple: the new fiscal system set up by the French Revolution was based chiefly on the property tax, a direct tax on the value of housing and land possessed by each individual. Introduced in 1790–1791, the property tax continues to be applied today, with rules virtually unchanged for more than two centuries. A proportional tax at low rates that make it possible to assert one's right to own property, the property tax represented the ideal tax for major property owners in the nineteenth century, as opposed to progressive taxes on wealth that potentially seek a redistribution.

In 1791, the fiscal administration started collecting the information required to set up a property tax and to publish numerous departmental tables regarding the distribution of tax bases. All through the nineteenth century—approximately every ten years—it organized large inventories of properties, thus enabling us to determine the value of all the goods concerned including houses, apartments and other buildings, and agricultural land.[23] We digitized the whole set of departmental and

---

22. Between 1860 and 2022, the share of the next twenty richest departments fell from 27 to 24 percent, and that of the fifty poorest departments fell from 27 to 16 percent. This growing concentration of the GDP was briefly interrupted between 1960 and 1990, when it resumed its historical course. See unehistoireduconflitpolitique.fr, figure B6.2a.
23. Of course, the property tax (like today's equivalent) was applied to housing property as well as to business assets (such as agricultural land, shops, and factories), except that machines and equipment were not taken into account (only the value of land and buildings was taxed), so

municipal data taken from these property inventories that start at the beginning of the nineteenth century.[24] These are extremely reliable data, especially for the oldest periods, when inflation was low and the value of goods was relatively stable over time. However, the data concerning the tax bases become less interesting for the last decades of the twentieth century and the current period, because the cadastral values used for the property tax have not undergone a general review since 1970. For recent decades, we have thus resorted to the fiscal and notarial databases, which now permit us to follow the totality of property transactions and the market values of dwellings exchanged at the municipal level.[25] In all, the data collected provide an unprecedented observation post that allows us to analyze the evolution of the distribution of property capital (in the sense of the value of housing) between departments and between municipalities over the last two centuries.[26]

But this indicator is ambiguous from the point of view of economic prosperity and the level (and the quality) of the inhabitants' lives. To be sure, the fact that property values per inhabitant is very high in this or that territory testifies to a

---

when this system was introduced in 1790–1791, the industrial sector was taxed less than the agricultural sector. In theory, this was supposed to be compensated by the *patentes* tax on trading licenses and certain occupations (which would later be renamed *taxe professionnelle*, or business tax); in practice, the taxation of the different sectors would not be balanced until a system of taxes of incomes and profits was created in 1914–1917.

24. We should clearly distinguish the tax bases (that is, the values of the properties, which is what interests us here) from the departmental quotas represented by the receipts paid by each department as its property tax. The receipts were in theory supposed to be proportional to the tax bases, in accord with the fiscal reform of 1790–1791, but it soon became apparent that that would have led to territorial redistributions enormous in comparison with those of the disparate fiscal system of the Old Regime, which—as we have already noted—led to the adoption of departmental quotas intermediate between the two systems. In the late nineteenth century, these systems gradually converged toward tax bases, at the price of incessant political battles. All the details on the data and the methods used are available at unehistoireduconflitpolitique.fr. On the question of tax equalization between departments under the Revolution, see the classic studies by R. Schnerb, *La péréquation fiscale de l'Assemblée constituante 1790–1791* (Bussac, 1936); and "De la Constituante à Napoléon: Les vicissitudes de l'impôt indirect," *Annales ESC*, 1947.

25. For recent years, we have drawn in particular on the DVF (Demande de valeurs foncières) database issuing from the registration fees and published by the fiscal administration at the level of individual transactions (with address, price, and the characteristics of the good concerned).

26. Because the available data on occupational property is not homogeneous over time (for example, agricultural land was relatively highly taxed at the beginning of the nineteenth century, but from the end of the nineteenth and during the twentieth century this tax gradually decreased) and raises many problems of interpretation, we have chosen to concentrate on property values in the sense of housing.

kind of prosperity, especially regarding what concerns property owners, and to a certain extent, wealthy renters who can afford to live in these territories and who also help drive up prices. On the other hand, for renters with modest incomes, living in a territory where the average value of housing is very high is not necessarily good news—far from it. Let us recall that it is the more modest members of society who suffer the most from the unavoidable expenses—particularly rent—that make up the largest part of their budget. We will therefore have to correlate this indicator with other information, in particular the average income of the municipality in question, which no doubt constitutes a better gauge of the wealth and poverty of territories. We will also correlate this information with the proportion of property owners, which is a particularly pertinent indicator on the socioeconomic level as well as on the political level.

Let us begin by examining the results obtained at the departmental level. We note that the inequalities of property values between departments were extremely great in the nineteenth century, but between 1910 and 1920 they began a sharp decrease that continued until the early 1980s, and then started to rise strongly again in 1980s and 1990s. For example, the ratio between the property values per inhabitant in the five richest departments (in terms of property values per inhabitant) and that of the five poorest departments rose from 8.0 in 1800 to 9.5 in 1900, fell to 2.8 in 1985, and rose again to 5.1 in 2022 (see figure 2.9).

In general, during the interwar and immediate postwar periods, the data issuing from the general income tax instituted by France in 1914 (and first used for the income tax of 1915) applied only to taxable households—that is, to about 10 to 20 percent of the households during the interwar period, a proportion that gradually rose starting in 1945 and reached about 50 percent in the 1950s. It was only after the early 1980s that the incomes of all households (whether taxable or nontaxable) were declared and registered systematically. For the period 1860–1980, we have estimated the development of average incomes in each department, using information about the income of taxable households (which provides useful indications regarding the evolution of the departments' prosperity, starting in 1915) and other available information (such as the departmental GDP starting in 1860). Although small variations must be interpreted prudently, the large lines of evolution are not very dependent on the details of the hypotheses made.[27] Concerning the post-1990 period, the most significant fact is that the rise in disparities of income between departments is much more limited than the increase in disparities

---

27. The results obtained are close to those presented by F. Bonnet H. d'Albis and A. Sotura, "Les inégalités de revenus entre départements français depuis cent ans," *Économie & statistique,* 2021.

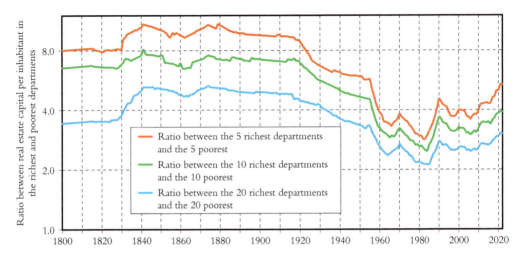

FIGURE 2.9. The increasing disparities in real estate capital between departments, 1800–2020

The ratio between real estate capital (total value of housing) per inhabitant in the five richest departments and the five poorest departments rose from 8.0 in 1800 to 9.5 in 1900, fell to 2.8 in 1985, and then rose to 5.4 in 2022. The ratio between the ten richest and the ten poorest departments rose from 6.5 in 1800 to 7.2 in 1900, fell to 2.5 in 1985, and rose to 3.9 in 2022. The ratio between the twenty richest and the twenty poorest passed from 3.4 in 1800 to 4.9 in 1900, to 2.1 in 1985, then to 3.0 in 2022. Note: The distribution has been calculated for the whole period on the basis of the territories of the ninety-six departments in 2022.

Sources and series: unehistoireduconflitpolitique.fr

in property values or GDP per inhabitant. It is equally striking to note the extent to which the disparities in income decreased significantly between 1950 and 1990, and were much larger than the disparities in GDP per inhabitant during the same period (see figure 2.10). This can be explained by a combination of several factors, including the development of different forms of the distribution of income (which tend to reduce the disparities in income of households as compared with disparities in GNP)[28] and, especially, a growing disconnection between the place of production and the place of residence. For example, the rapid growth of the GDP per inhabitant in Paris and in Hauts-de-Seine over the course of recent decades is only partly reflected in the growth of the income received by the inhabitants of these departments, because part of the wealth thus produced feeds the salaries paid to the residents of neighboring departments (or of other countries, in the case of the payment of dividends). A particularly striking case is that of Seine-Saint-Denis, whose

28. However, this effect must not be exaggerated, because here we are examining disparities of average municipal income after taking into account retirement pensions and unemployment benefits, but before income tax is taken into account.

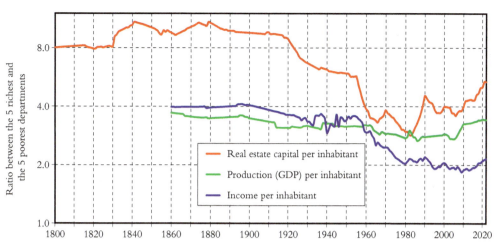

FIGURE 2.10. Measuring disparities in wealth among departments: Real estate capital, production, income

The ratio between real estate capital (the total value of housing) per inhabitant in the five richest departments and the five poorest passed from 9.5 in 1900 to 2.8 in 1985, then to 5.4 in 2022. The same ratio defined with production (GDP) per inhabitant passed from 3.5 in 1900 to 2.8 in 1985, then to 3.4 in 2022. The ratio defined with income per inhabitant moved from 4.1 in 1900 to 1.8 in 2010 and then to 2.2 in 2022.

Sources and series: unehistoireduconflitpolitique.fr

rank in the hierarchy of GDP per inhabitant is relatively high and has even tended to improve in recent years, whereas its rank in the hierarchy of income per inhabitant has collapsed to the extent that the department is now among the poorest in the country.[29] Furthermore, the growing role played by retirees must be noted. If elderly people retire to departments other than those in which they participated in production, as they usually do, then that can help equalize incomes among departments in comparison to the disparities in GDP per inhabitant.[30]

29. Seine-Saint-Denis was ranked twenty-first for GDP per inhabitant in 1980, twentieth in 2000, and seventh in 2022. In terms of income per inhabitant, the department was ranked ninth in 1980 and fiftieth in 2022 (out of ninety-six departments). This reflects the considerable difficulties encountered by the department's residents in finding well-remunerated work, and it puts into question statements made by people like Christophe Guilluy, who sees in "the emergence of a petite bourgeoisie issuing from Maghrebin and African immigration" (an "emergence" he makes no attempt to quantify) the consequence of the economic activity of the suburbs that are supposed to benefit from their centrality and from the "dynamics of the globalization of the metropoles." See C. Guilluy, *Fractures françaises* (Bourin, 2010).

30. See F. Bonnet and A. Sotura, "Spatial Disparities in France: From Diverging Production to Converging Income" (working paper, Paris School of Economics, 2019). See also L. Davezies,

Nevertheless, it would be a big mistake to overestimate this movement of the equalization of incomes among departments. For one thing, this movement has clearly ended: the extensive compression of disparities of income observed between 1950 and 1990 was clearly interrupted in the 1990s and 2000s. We can even note that since 2010 there has been a significant increase in these disparities, which marks a major historical rupture in comparison to the earlier trends (see figure 2.10). In addition, although it is true that social welfare transfers have partially offset the effects of the ongoing recompositions of the productive fabric, we must not neglect the fact that the psychological impacts can be very different. In other words, retirement pensions or unemployment benefits can help attenuate the extent of income decreases connected with deindustrialization or the loss of economic activities, but this kind of compensation can only be partial and temporary, and they cannot replace the feelings of pride and identity that come with participation in the country's productive structure.[31]

Rich Municipalities, Poor Municipalities: Property Values and Income

Let us now turn to inequalities among municipalities. In the framework of this book, they are the essential issue, because it is by working at the level of the 36,000 municipalities (and not the ninety-six departments) that we can hope to make progress in our understanding of the socioeconomic determinants of political behaviors. The most complete and most comparable data over the long term are those that pertain to property values per inhabitant—that is, the average value of housing in the municipality in question (no matter whether this housing is occupied by its owner or by renters); therefore, we will begin there. We note first that with respect to property values, the municipal inequalities have followed approximately the same profile as the departmental inequalities over a long period. The disparities between the richest and the poorest municipalities were extremely high (and slightly rising) in the nineteenth century and at the beginning of the twentieth,

---

"Les inégalités de développement territorial: Énigmes et menaces," in *Les inégalités territoriales,* ed. M. Talandier and J. Tallec (, 2022).

31. Moreover, monetary compensations cannot mask the loss of status. Between 1980 and 2022, Meuse fell from fifty-fifth to ninety-third in terms of GDP per inhabitant, and from sixtieth to eightieth in terms of average income; Ardennes fell from fifty-second to eighty-sixth in terms of GDP per inhabitant, and from sixty-sixth to eighty-eighth in terms of average income. In addition, some authors question the sustainability of the mechanisms that reduce territorial inequalities, especially because of the increase of the public debt. See, for example, L. Davezies, *La crise qui vient. La nouvelle fracture territoriale* (Seuil, 2012).

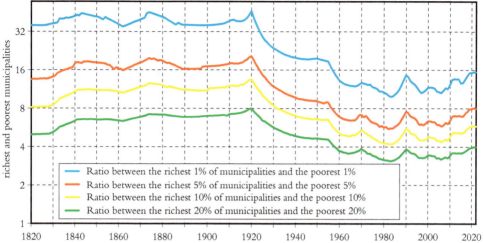

FIGURE 2.11. The increase in disparities in real estate capital between municipalities, 1820–2022

From 1820 to 1920, real estate capital (the total value of housing) per inhabitant of richest 1% of municipalities (in terms of real estate capital per inhabitant) was more than thirty times higher than that of the poorest 1% of municipalities; this ratio fell below 10 in the early 1980s, and then rose to about 16 in 2022. Similar developments are observed for other ratios.

Sources and series: unehistoireduconflitpolitique.fr

before beginning a significant decline between 1920 and 1980 and then rising again, starting in 1980–1990. For example, property values per inhabitant of the richest 1 percent of municipalities (in terms of property values per inhabitant) was more than thirty times higher than in the poorest 1 percent of municipalities between 1820 and 1920. This ratio then fell to less than 10 at the beginning of the 1980s before rising to about 16 in 2022 (see figure 2.11).

We should also note that the municipal inequalities remained at very high levels. They testify to the considerable scope of the spatial and residential segregation of the country. In 2022, the disparities from 1 to 16 between the poorest and the richest municipalities correspond to an average value of housing on the order of 50,000 to 60,000 euros for the former, and around 800,000 to 1 million euros for the latter (even more than 1 million for some municipalities). In the first group, we find, for instance, Aubusson (Creuse), Château-Chinon (Nièvre), and Vierzon (Cher), where average housing unit costs just 60,000 euros. The second group includes municipalities like Marnela-Coquette (Hauts-de-Seine), Saint-Jean-Cap-Ferrat (Alpes-Maritimes), and Saint-Marc-Jaumegarde (Bouches-du-Rhône), where the average value of a housing unit is more than 1.2 million euros. We also find considerable disparities within the great conurbations, in particular in the Paris

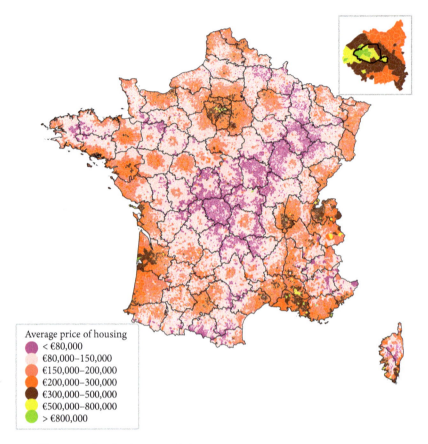

MAP 2.5. The geography of real estate capital

The map represents the average price of housing observed in real estate transactions in the various municipalities (national average: 219,500 euros).

Sources and series: unehistoireduconflitpolitique.fr

region, where the average housing unit is worth 150,000 euros in Clichy-sous-Bois (Seine-Saint-Denis) and in Évry (Essonne) and reaches 1.3 million euros in Paris's 7th arrondissement, for a disparity of 1 to 9 within a distance of just twenty kilometers.[32] At the level of the country as a whole, the average value of housing units is close to 220,000 euros, but in most of the territories we find very large disparities around this average (see map 2.5).

---

32. The disparities in the price per square meter are almost as high (1 to 8). Let us note again here that—especially for renters, but also for first-time buyers—the value of property is an ambiguous indicator of the standard of living of the inhabitants of a given territory.

The immense advantage of working with 36,000 municipalities is that the groups consisting of the poorest 1 percent of the municipalities and the richest 1 percent each includes hundreds of municipalities, just like all the centiles of the hierarchy of municipalities in terms of property values per inhabitant (or the centiles corresponding to other indicators), which will allow us to study in an extremely detailed way the relations with other socioeconomic and political variables, and in particular, voting.[33] It will also be noted that the disparities in property values remain very large, even when we move away from the extreme centiles, with a disparity of more than 4 in 2022 between the poorest 20 percent and the richest 20 percent of municipalities, for example (see figure 2.11).

If we now compare the municipal inequalities in property values and income, we see first of all that the former have always been larger than the latter, just as in the case of departmental inequalities. We also see similar evolutions over the long term. The disparities in incomes among municipalities decreased significantly over the course of the twentieth century, particularly between 1950 and 1990, before stabilizing in the 1990s and 2000s and then beginning to rise again in the 2010s.[34] In 2022, the average income of the richest 1 percent of the municipalities is thus more than eight times higher than that of the poorest 1 percent of the municipalities, whereas this disparity was barely higher than 5 in the early 1990s (see figure 2.12).

Specifically, this disparity of 1 to 8 corresponds to the fact that the average income is scarcely 7,000 to 8,000 euros per year and per inhabitant in the poorest 1 percent of the municipalities, whereas it reaches 60,000 to 70,000 euros per year in the richest 1 percent.[35] The average income exceeds even 100,000 euros per year

33. So that the developments are not distorted by small municipalities, all the centiles indicated in figure 2.11 and all the graphs of the same type have been defined taking into account the size of the municipality. In other words, the richest 1 percent means the 1 percent living in the richest municipalities, and so on.

34. We have complete data on the incomes of all households (taxable and nontaxable) at the municipal level only since the early 1980s. For the period 1860–1980, we have used the estimates of the average departmental income described above and we have assumed that the position of the municipalities within the departments had evolved from 1860 to 1980 in the same way for the intradepartmental distribution of income as for the distribution of property values. The positions of the municipalities within the intradepartmental distributions being relatively stable over time, alternative hypotheses would have very little impact on developments as a whole. All the detailed results connected with these estimates are available online on the site unehistoireduconflitpolitique.fr.

35. The fiscal income considered here includes all the incomes appearing in the declarations of income (such as salaries, incomes from unsalaried activity, retirement pensions, unemployment benefits, interest, rents, and dividends), before any allowances or deductions (in particular,

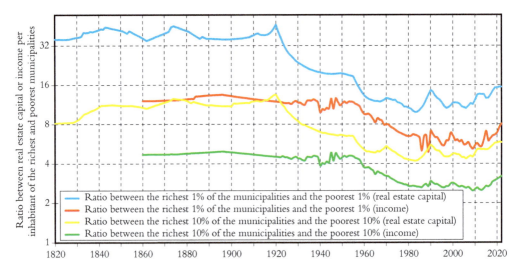

FIGURE 2.12. Municipal inequalities: Real estate capital vs. income, 1820–2022

From 1820 to 1920, the real estate capital (the total value of housing) per inhabitant of the richest 1% of municipalities was more than thirty times higher than that of the poorest 1% of municipalities; this ratio fell below 10 in the early 1980s, and then rose to about 16 in 2022. Similar developments are observed for other ratios.

Sources and series: unehistoireduconflitpolitique.fr

and per inhabitant (including children) in the 7th and 8th arrondissements of Paris and 80,000 euros in Neuilly-sur-Seine (Hauts de Seine), the richest metropoles and suburbs. We also find all over the territory dozens of municipalities where the average income is around 60,000 to 70,000 euros, like Saint-Cyr-au-Mont-d'Or (Rhône), Pechbusque (Haute-Garonne), le Touquet (Pas-de-Calais), Tourgéville (Calvados), le Vésinet (Yvelines), Bois-Guillaume (Seine-Maritime), Uffheim (Haut-Rhin), and Barbizon (Seine-et-Marne). They are often suburbs or well-off towns, and sometimes villages. At the other end of the scale, there exist hundreds

---

before the 10 percent deduction for occupational fees), divided by the number of members of the household (adults and children taken together). Nontaxable transfers of money (basic welfare benefits, family benefits, housing benefits) represent 3–4 percent of the national income and have only a limited impact on disparities in the average fiscal income between municipalities. See A. Bozio, B. Garbinti, J. Goupille-Lebret, M. Guillot, and T. Piketty, "Predistribution vs. Redistribution. Evidence from France and the US" (CEPR discussion paper no. 15415, 2020), figure 12b. We will return in chapter 4 to the spatial distribution of government subsidies.

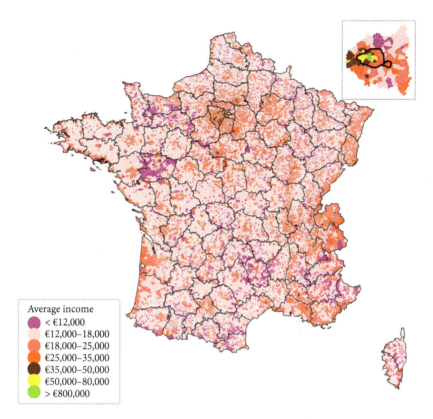

MAP 2.6. The geography of income per inhabitant, 2022

The map represents the average income per inhabitant of each of the municipalities (total taxable income before any deductions, divided by the number of inhabitants, including children; national average: 19,200 euros).

Sources and series: unehistoireduconflitpolitique.fr

of municipalities all over France where the average income is around 7,000 to 8,000 euros per year per inhabitant (that is, close to the poverty threshold), like Beaumesnil (Eure), Creil (Oise), Grande-Synthe (Nord), Bény-Bocage (Calvados), Noyant (Maine-et-Loire), Grigny (Essonne), and the 3rd arrondissement of Marseille. Scarcely any better off, with less than 9,000 euros per year and per inhabitant, are municipalities like Roubaix (Nord), Stains (Seine-Saint-Denis), and Chesne (Eure). There, too, both towns and villages count among the poorest in the country. For the country considered as a whole, the average income is almost 19,000 euros per year per inhabitant, a level that is found in many parts of the territory (see map 2.6).

The Convergence toward the Bottom of the Poor Suburbs and Poor Towns

Let us now correlate more systematically the information about wealth (property values and income) and about the sizes of municipalities and conurbations. The first result is that on average, metropoles and suburbs have always been richer than towns and villages, both in terms of average property values per inhabitant (see figure 2.13) and in terms of average income per inhabitant (see figure 2.14).

This result is striking: it shows that the economic hierarchy of the territory has always coincided with the spatial hierarchy that opposes the urban world to the rural world. This conclusion must, however, be qualified, because these average disparities between the urban and rural worlds have had a tendency to decrease over the long term (while remaining at a high level),[36] and also, and especially, because inequalities have always been very large within these categories—between rich and poor suburbs, rich and poor towns, and so on—and these are inequalities that the averages do not allow us to see.

Concerning the disparities in average property values, at the beginning of the nineteenth century the metropoles were situated very far beyond the rest of the country (between three and four times the national average), at a time when they constituted a very small part of the total population. The disparities decreased at the end of the nineteenth century and over the course of the twentieth, with regard to both the suburbs and the towns and villages. Despite an increase over recent decades, today they remain much smaller than they were in the nineteenth century (see figure 2.13). Concerning the disparities in average incomes, which have always been less extreme than the inequalities of property values, they also diminished over time, despite, there too, a recent rise in the incomes in metropoles in relation to the average. In the end, today, the disparities might seem relatively modest. In 2022, the average income in the metropoles is 115 percent of the national average (which is currently 19,000 euros per year per inhabitant); that equals 108 percent of the national average in the suburbs, 94 percent in towns, and 91 percent in villages (see figure 2.14). But the fact is precisely that it doesn't make much sense to stick

---

36. The share of metropoles and suburbs in the totality of the country's property values rose from 23 to 52 percent between 1860 and 2022 (whereas their share in the population rose from 15 to 47 percent). If we define the "urban world" as including the 50 percent of the population living in the largest conurbations in the country at each point in time, then the share of the urban world remained relatively stable at around 60–65 percent of total property values over a long period of time (with a small decrease), while its share in the total income decreased a little more clearly (from 55–60 percent to less than 55 percent). This reflects in part the fact that the correlation between the size of the conurbation and property values per inhabitant diminished slightly. See unehistoireduconflitpolitique.fr, figures B1.5n–B1.5w, B6.5f, and B7.4g.

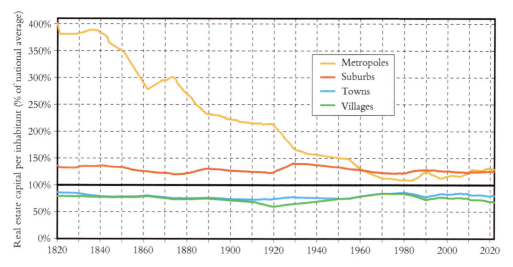

FIGURE 2.13. Villages, towns, suburbs and metropoles: The development of real estate capital per inhabitant, 1820–2022

From 1820 to 1920, the real estate capital (total value of housing) per inhabitant of the richest 1% of municipalities was generally highest in the metropoles (main municipalities of conurbations of more than 100,000 inhabitants), followed by the suburbs (secondary municipalities of more than 100,000 inhabitants), towns (conurbations with 2,000–100,000 inhabitants), and villages (conurbations of fewer than 2,000 inhabitants), but with a net reduction in disparities over the long term. Sources and series: unehistoireduconflitpolitique.fr

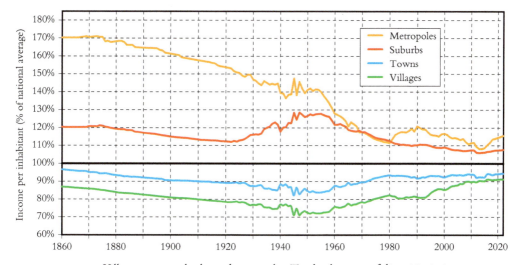

FIGURE 2.14. Villages, towns, suburbs, and metropoles: The development of disparities in income per inhabitant, 1860–2022

From 1860 to 2022, income per inhabitant has generally been highest in the metropoles, followed by the suburbs, towns, and villages, but with a reduction in disparities over the long term. In 2022, the average income was equal to 115% of the national average in the metropoles, 108% in the suburbs, 94% in towns, and 91% in villages. Sources and series: unehistoireduconflitpolitique.fr

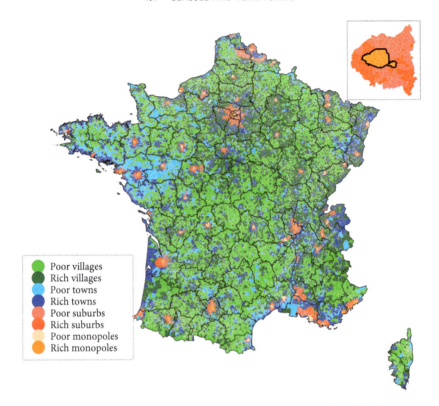

MAP 2.7. Villages, towns, suburbs, and metropoles, poor and rich: Geographical distribution, 2022
The map represents municipalities classified as villages, towns, suburbs, and metropoles (see map 2.3). Poor villages correspond to the half of the villages with the lowest incomes per inhabitant, and rich villages correspond to villages with the highest incomes per inhabitant, and so on for poor towns and rich towns, poor suburbs and rich suburbs, and poor metropoles and rich metropoles. Sources and series: unehistoireduconflitpolitique.fr

with these averages. Within each of these categories and in the whole of the territory, we can find municipalities where the average income is as much as 60,000 to 70,000 euros and others where it is scarcely 7,000 to 8,000 euros. If we adhere to a general opposition between the metropoles, suburbs, towns, and villages, we are in danger of missing the most important social inequalities. To stick to relatively simple categories, we can, for instance, consider rich metropoles and rich suburbs (defined as the richest halves of the metropoles and suburbs) in contrast with poor metropoles and poor suburbs, and proceed in the same way with towns and villages (see map 2.7).[37] The social geography that flows from this becomes immedi-

37. Here again, to avoid the biases connected with small municipalities, these definitions take into account the size of the municipalities. In other words, the poorest 50 percent of the villages means the 50 percent of the population living in the poorest villages, and so on.

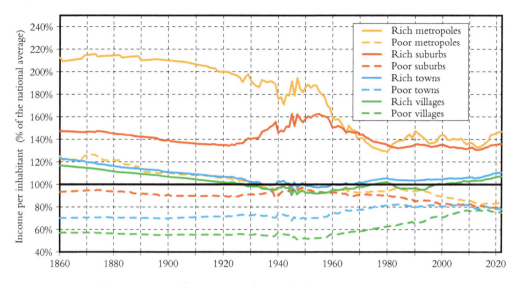

FIGURE 2.15. The convergence of poor towns and poor suburbs

The rich metropoles and rich suburbs (defined as the half of the metropoles and suburbs with the highest incomes per inhabitant) have always been clearly richer that the national average. Since 1980, rich towns and villages have become considerably richer than poor suburbs and metropoles, which have inversely become as poor as the poor towns and villages.

Sources and series: unehistoireduconflitpolitique.fr

ately more subtle and intelligible. We see first that rich metropoles and rich suburbs are clearly above the rest of the country (around 140 to 150 percent of the national average income in 2022), and the disparities separating them from the national average increased significantly in recent decades. Rich towns and villages are close to the national average (about 110 percent of the national average income in 2022), but we also see that they enriched themselves more quickly than the rest of the country did in the recent period. Inversely, since 1980–1990, we find a clear deterioration of the position of the poor suburbs and the poor metropoles, as well as a stagnation of poor towns, so that all these categories end up at approximately the same level as the poor villages in the 2010s and the beginning of the 2020s, with an average income around 80 percent of the national average (see figure 2.15).

Poor Towns and Poor Suburbs: Common Economic Interests

This fundamental economic proximity of poor suburbs and poor towns (as well as poor villages and poor metropoles) is a particularly striking result, especially if we consider the fact that the political behaviors of these different territories have diverged greatly over the course of recent decades, as we will show in detail in the following pages. One of our main objectives is precisely to improve our understanding of the reasons for this paradox, and also the possible ways of resolving it. We note here that these different poor territories have many features in common that have become more important in recent decades, beginning with their disadvantaged socioeconomic situation. Such shared interests could in theory fuel common political mobilizations, and it is essential to better understand the other motives for diverging that have prevented this regrouping and the ways in which these realities might develop in the future. The general increase in territorial inequalities between the urban world and the rural world over recent decades can, of course, be one explanation for this paradox, because this phenomenon can feed the (false) perception that the urban world as a whole has enriched itself at the expense of the rural world.

If we continue the analysis and examine the poorest 20 percent of the poorest suburbs, we see that these very poor suburbs have moved slightly below the very poor towns since the beginning of the 2000s (and below very poor villages since the early 2010s). In 2022, the former's income was about 65 percent of the national average income, and the latter's was about 70 percent. Inversely, the very rich suburbs (the richest 20 percent) have moved far beyond the rest of the country (around 170 percent of the national average), followed by very rich towns and villages (about 130 percent).[38] The most striking phenomenon of recent decades is the increase in inequalities within each category.

We must also emphasize that these comparisons of average income do take into account differences in the cost of living, and especially the cost of housing. For example, when we note that the average income in the poor suburbs and poor towns (in the sense of the poorest 50 percent of the suburbs and towns) is approximately the same, we must add that the average value of housing is almost twice as high in the former as it is in the latter (see figure 2.16). For all the households that rent their homes and have no choice but to devote a fourth or a third of their incomes to housing (if not more), and moreover, for households that are in the process of buying homes and will have to devote the same sums to repaying their loans, this means considerable differences in living conditions for the same average income. In other words, after correction for differentials in the cost of living, the average income in the poorest suburbs is in reality significantly lower than that in the equivalent poor towns.

---

38. See unehistoireduconflitpolitique.fr, figure B1.5k.

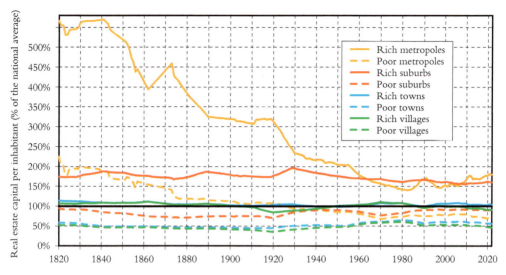

FIGURE 2.16. Major inequalities with regard to the price of housing

The value of housing has always been much higher in rich metropoles and rich suburbs (defined as the half of the metropoles and suburbs with the highest real estate capital [the total value of housing] per inhabitant) than in the rest of the country. Note that the value of housing in the poor suburbs is close to the national average, and almost twice as high as in poor towns and villages.

Sources and series: unehistoireduconflitpolitique.fr

Villages and Towns with Large Proportions of Property Owners, Rich Metropoles and Suburbs with High Incomes

Generally, when studying territorial inequalities, it is essential to take into account inequalities with regard to both incomes and property values, because they are imperfectly correlated and both of them have a major impact on living conditions, and also because they feed imaginations, worldviews, and political behaviors that are not exactly the same. From this point of view, the major fact is that the spatial hierarchy with respect to real estate property has always been rigorously the opposite of the hierarchy with respect to income. More precisely, the proportion of households that own their housing has always been greater in villages, followed by towns, then suburbs, and finally metropoles (see figure 2.17). In general, the geography of the proportion of homeowners coincides only very imperfectly with that of income or property values per inhabitant (see map 2.8).

Let us add that the data issuing from census returns enable us to follow the evolution of the proportion of homeowners at the level of the 36,000 municipalities only since the beginning of the 1960s, and that we do not have analogous information for

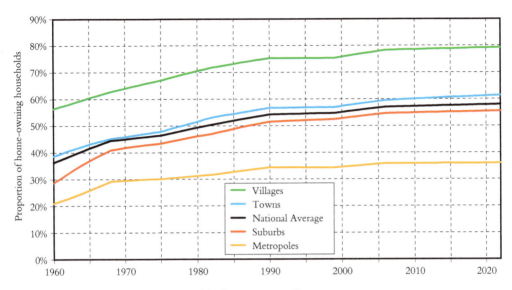

FIGURE 2.17. Villages and towns with high proportions of homeowners

Between 1960 and 2022, the proportion of home-owning households rose from 37% to 58% in France. This proportion has always been highest in villages, followed by towns, suburbs, and metropoles.

Sources and series: unehistoireduconflitpolitique.fr

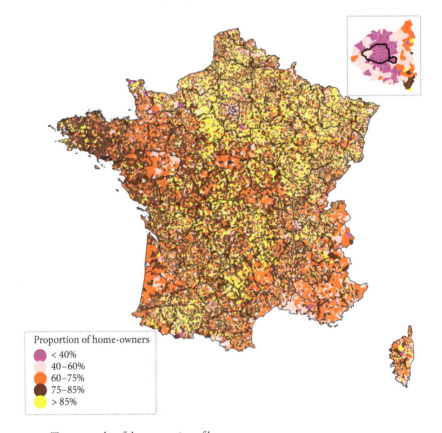

Proportion of home-owners
- < 40%
- 40–60%
- 60–75%
- 75–85%
- > 85%

MAP 2.8. The geography of the proportion of homeowners, 2022

The map represents that proportion of households owning their own home, by municipality, in 2022 (national average: 58%).

Sources and series: unehistoireduconflitpolitique.fr

earlier periods.[39] However, the data from successoral archives in the context of the TRA project show that the situation was much the same before. All through the nineteenth century, in the same way as in the twentieth century, the proportion of successions including real estate (houses or agricultural lands) was much higher in the rural world than in the urban world, where the immense majority of the deaths in the nineteenth and early twentieth centuries did not lead to any bequest (or where it did, to minuscule bequests limited to a few personal effects).[40] We can also see that in France, the proportion of households owning their own homes rose from 37 percent to 58 percent between 1960 and 2022, a sign of general enrichment and the emergence of a "patrimonial middle class." Nevertheless, this proportion has remained virtually unchanged since the middle of the 2000s. Generally speaking, the increases observed have been comparable in size in the different parts of the territory, though the diffusion of property ownership has been more limited in the metropoles. In 2022, the proportion of households owning their own homes reached 79 percent in villages, but only 37 percent in the metropoles (see figure 2.17). It is equally striking to note that the proportion of homeowners is approximately the same in poor villages and rich villages (within the 50 percent of villages that have the lowest average income or the highest), and that it is also just as low in rich metropoles as it is in poor metropoles. The world of towns, like that of suburbs, is much more diversified with regard to property ownership. While it is true that the proportion of property owners is on average a little higher in towns than in the suburbs, the criterion of income still plays a determining role. For example, the proportion of homeowners in wealthy suburbs is significantly higher than it is in poor towns.[41]

We must add that the inverted hierarchy with regard to property in the territories concerns only the proportion of property owners, not the value of the properties. Property values per inhabitant is twice as high in the metropoles as it is in

---

39. Here we use the digitization of the census data at the municipal level carried out by INSEE starting with the census of 1962. Theoretically, it is possible to envisage similar digitizations for the censuses of the early twentieth century and the nineteenth century, but that could probably apply to only certain parts of the territory, considering their different states of preservation and the lack of centralization of the corresponding documents. In general, on the prospects for the future enrichment of the database collected in the context of this book, see the technical appendices available online (unehistoireduconflitpolitique.fr).

40. See J. Bourdieu, L. Kesztenbaum, and G. Postel-Vinay, *L'enquête TRA, histoire d'un outil, outil pour l'histoire* (INED, 2013). The TRA project is based on the digitization of successoral documents and vital statistics since the beginning of the nineteenth century of individuals whose patronyms begin with the letters *T-R-A*.

41. See unehistoireduconflitpolitique.fr, figure B1.6b.

villages, and these disparities have grown much larger over recent decades (see figure 2.13). That is, property owners in the metropoles (and especially in the richest ones, where prices have shot up compared to other territories) possess real estate, and more generally, patrimonies, whose market value is much greater than that of the goods owned by property owners in villages.[42] Moreover, the fact that the proportion of property owners is so much higher in the villages and towns than in the metropoles is partly explained by the low level of real estate prices, which allowed people to buy property much more easily, especially in the suburbs. Nonetheless, an extremely significant difference continued to exist on the economic and the sociopolitical levels, especially since it could be one of the decisive elements motivating the choice to take up residence in the metropole or to remain in the villages and towns. Taking on long-term debt to buy one's house, along with the effort required to save and to establish one's occupational and personal stability that that implies, also helps forge the values and identities that are defined in part by contrast to other groups that have not set out on such a trajectory. The fact that these perceived differences are partly artificial (the rents paid in the suburbs or the metropole often demand "efforts" that are at least equivalent to those required to meet the loan payments made by people living in towns and villages) does not in any way reduce their burden in a world where the knowledge of other sociospatial classes and their concrete life experiences are by nature relatively limited because of the lack of fully adapted intermediations (political and syndical organizations, media, and schools, for example).

Different Productive Specializations

Inequalities with respect to property reflect not just choices, imaginations, and distinct sociocultural traditions; they are also part of different productive specializations that refer to a long heritage from the past. If the proportion of property owners is historically just as high in villages, that is partially because the supply of real estate is abundant and the prices of land and houses are more affordable, but also because agricultural activity is closely associated with owning an individual farm. Under the Revolution, access to land was the peasants' first demand, and the immense disappointment that followed the urban bourgeoisie's appropriation of national goods was one of the main factors explaining the hostility of a large part of the peasant classes with respect to the political forces associated with these events. Subsequently, the peasants' wariness of Socialists and Communists, who

---

42. See unehistoireduconflitpolitique.fr, figures B1.5f–B1.5g.

were suspected—not without reason—of wanting to challenge the peasants' desire to own the land they worked (or at least of not supporting it enthusiastically enough), also played a crucial role in the structuring of political behaviors all through the nineteenth and twentieth centuries (we will return to this at length). Over the long term, a large proportion of the inhabitants of the rural world finally succeeded in gaining access to property ownership, even if this happened much more slowly and on a smaller scale than they would have wished, and without the political support they were counting on.

At the beginning of the twenty-first century, this long history has continued to play a structuring role, especially since the transformations of productive specializations and the historical decline of agricultural activity took place only very gradually, as is shown by the data issuing from the censuses. In 1800, about 65 percent of the working population was active principally in agriculture. The share of agriculture in total employment was still 32 percent in 1950; in 2022, it was barely 5 percent (including the food processing industry).[43] Construction and industry (excluding food processing) have followed a familiar bell-shaped curve, rising from about 20 percent in 1800 to a high around 37 percent in the early 1970s before falling back to 17 percent in 2022 (see figure 2.18).[44] In the middle of the twentieth century, employment was distributed in three almost perfectly equal thirds: 32 percent for the primary sector in 1950, 33 percent for the secondary sector, and 35 percent for the tertiary sector (services).

It was, moreover, at just that time that this representation of employment in three sectors was popularized, grouping together the activities called "services" in a single bloc, a regrouping that today seems dated and artificial, but continues to feed perceptions. Within this enormous bloc, we can distinguish two main components that are characterized by considerable development over a long period: first, education, healthcare, and social welfare activity (medico-social housing, elder care, the personal care industry), whose proportion of total employment has risen from scarcely 2 percent in 1800 to 9 percent in 1950 and 25 percent in 2022; and second, shops, hotels-cafés-restaurants, leisure activities, culture, and transportation, whose proportion has risen from 5 percent in 1800 to 15 percent in 1950, and 29 percent

---

43. Of which about half (a little more than 2 percent of total employment) is for agriculture properly so called, including forestry and fishing, and the other half is for food processing.

44. Work in the textile industry, which had played a dominant role within the industrial sector in the nineteenth century and at the beginning of the twentieth century, began its decline in 1950, and then was joined by other industries (including the steel industry, the chemical industry, and the auto industry) starting in 1970. By comparison, construction has remained relatively stable at about 5–10 percent of total employment over the long term (7 percent in 2022).

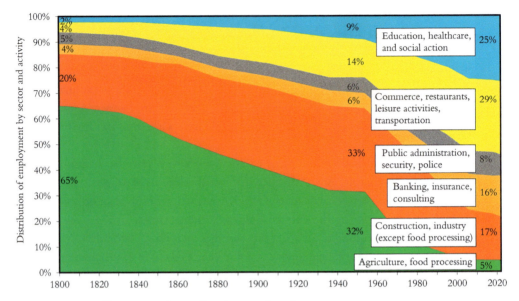

FIGURE 2.18. The metamorphoses of employment since 1800

Between 1800 and 2022, the share of agriculture and food processing fell from 65% to 5% of total employment and construction and industry (except food processing) fell from 20% to 17%, while the share of banking, insurance, real estate, and consulting rose from 4% to 16%, public administration rose from 5% to 8%, commerce, restaurants, culture, leisure activities, and transportation from 4% to 29%, and education, healthcare, and social action from 2% to 25%.

Sources and series: unehistoireduconflitpolitique.fr

in 2022 (see figure 2.18). In all, these two fundamental blocs have thus risen from hardly 7 percent of employment in 1800 to 24 percent in 1950 and 54 percent in 2022. By comparison, the share of public administration, which groups together the sovereign functions of the state and collectivities (such as general administration, security, and justice has not moved over the long term: 4 percent in 1800, 6 percent in 1950, 8 percent in 2022. Finally, the bloc constituted by banking, finance, real estate, consulting, and services to businesses has recently grown considerably, from 4 percent in 1800 to 6 percent in 1950, and 16 percent in 2022. This is explained in part by the externalization of certain functions by other sectors, in particular by industry and construction, which would otherwise continue to include about 20–25 percent of total employment.[45]

---

45. The services said to be "directed chiefly toward enterprises" (such as accounting and law) have been included in the banking-finance-real estate-consulting sector, even though some of them concern households and could have been attached to the education-healthcare-social welfare or commerce-restaurants-culture-transportation sectors.

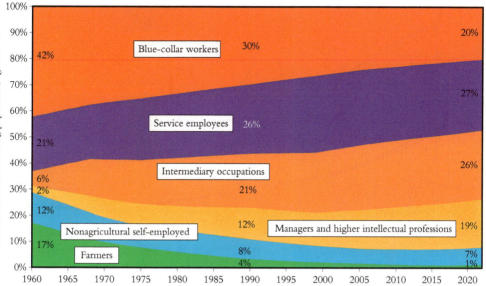

FIGURE 2.19. Socio-occupational categories since 1960

Between 1960 and 2022, the share of blue-collar workers in the active population aged twenty-five to fifty-four decreased from 42% to 20%; conversely, the share of service employees rose from 21% to 27%, intermediary occupations rose from 6% to 26%, and managers and higher intellectual professions from 2% to 19%. The share of nonagricultural self-employees fell from 12% to 7%, and farmers fell from 17% to 1%.

Sources and series: unehistoireduconflitpolitique.fr

In addition to distributing employment by sector, it is also helpful to make use of classifications by socio-occupational category, which have undergone rapid development in France starting with the censuses of 1946 and 1954.[46] For this category, the data are also available at the level of the 36,000 municipalities from the beginning of the 1960s, making it possible to analyze the transformations of the spatial distribution of occupations. At the national level, we see a sharp decline in the number of self-employed workers, both agricultural and nonagricultural (such as craftsmen and merchants), whose share in the active population has fallen from 29 percent in 1960 to 8 percent in 2022 (see figure 2.19).[47] Unsurprisingly, the self-employed have

---

46. The censuses conducted before 1946 were not made in accord with a grid of occupations and socio-occupational categories that was preestablished and homogeneous over time, so the results are difficult to use over a long period, except for the sectors of activity.

47. Let us add, however, that the liberal professions (physicians, lawyers, and others, who make up 2–3 percent of the working population, depending on the periods) are counted among the "managers and superior intellectual professions," and not among the self-employed, whose share would slightly exceed 10 percent if they had been included.

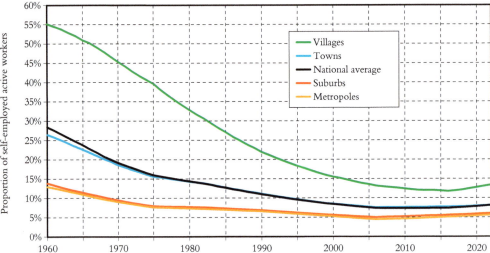

FIGURE 2.20. Self-employed agricultural and nonagricultural workers structurally more present in the rural world

The proportion of independent, self-employed workers (agricultural and nonagricultural) in the working population as a whole fell from 29% in 1960 to 8% in 2022. In 1960, this proportion was maximal in the suburbs, followed by metropoles, towns, and villages; in 2022, it was maximal in towns, followed by villages, suburbs, and metropoles.

Sources and series: unehistoireduconflitpolitique.fr

always been overrepresented in the rural world; their proportion of the active population has always been minimal in the metropoles and suburbs, followed by towns and villages (see figure 2.20).[48]

From this point of view, the case of manufacturing blue-collar workers (*ouvriers*) and low-skilled service employees (*employés*) illustrates a more complex situation. Whereas farmers and self-employed workers are a structurally larger contingent in the rural world and managers and intermediary professions are more present in the urban world, blue-collar workers and employees are in an intermediary geospatial situation whose contours have been largely redefined over time. At the national level, the sharp decline in the number of blue-collar workers since 1960 has been partly offset by the rise in the number of employees, so that on the whole, the proportion of blue-collar workers and employees in the active population has declined less steeply than is sometimes imagined (63 percent in 1960 and still

48. This has to do, notably, with the strong presence of farmers in poor villages (that is, in the 50 percent of villages with the smallest incomes) at the beginning of the period, and to a lesser degree in poor towns. See unehistoireduconflitpolitique.fr, figures B1.6d and B1.6g.

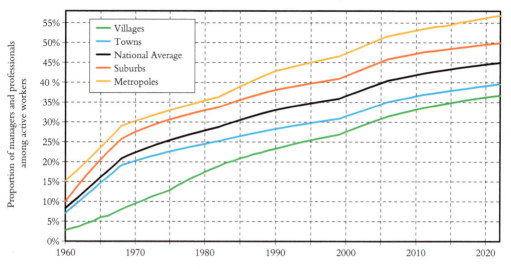

FIGURE 2.21. Managers and intermediate occupations most structurally present in the urban world
The proportion of managers, higher intellectual professions and intermediate occupations among employees rose from 8 percent to 45 percent between 1960 and 2022. This proportion has always been maximal in metropoles, followed by the suburbs, towns, and villages.
Sources and series: unehistoireduconflitpolitique.fr

47 percent in 2022). However, their spatial distribution has been totally trans-formed. In 1960, the proportion of blue-collar workers and employees was greatest in the suburbs, followed by the metropoles, and then towns and villages. In 2022, it was greatest in towns, followed by villages, then suburbs and metropoles (see figure 2.22). It will nonetheless be noted that the disparities have been greatly re-duced over time: above all, we see a kind of averaging of blue-collar workers and employees, who are now strongly present more or less everywhere in the territory, including in villages, where they were historically absent because of the preponder-ance of the self-employed. The world of villages and towns, which used to be agricul-tural and self-employed, has thus become largely the domain of blue-collar workers and employees. It will also be noted that the proportion of blue-collar workers and employees varies greatly over the whole of the territory, not only between depart-ments but also within each department (see map 2.9).

In fact, it is crucial for our investigation to emphasize that social inequalities take on a considerable magnitude within each spatial category. In wealthy metropoles and wealthy suburbs (the 50 percent with the highest incomes), man-agers and intermediary occupations now represent almost 60 percent of those working, as opposed to just 35 percent for blue-collar workers and salaried em-ployees (mainly the latter). Conversely, in the poor suburbs (the 50 percent with

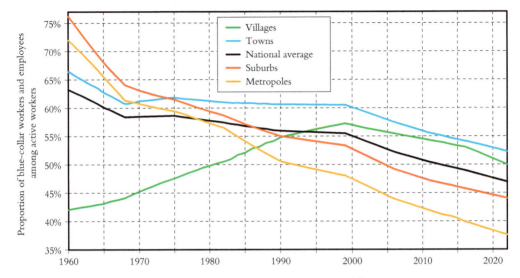

FIGURE 2.22. Blue collar workers and service employees in sociospatial change.

The proportion of blue-collar workers and service employees rose from 63 percent to 47 percent between 1960 and 2022. In 1960, this proportion was maximal in the suburbs, followed by the metropoles, towns and villages. In 2022, it was maximal in towns, followed by villages, suburbs, and metropoles.

Sources and series: unehistoireduconflitpolitique.fr

the lowest incomes), the proportion of blue-collar workers and employees is about 55–60 percent of the active population, roughly the same level as in poor towns and poor villages.[49] Employees are nonetheless somewhat more numerous in the poor suburbs than in the poor towns and villages, and the inverse is true for blue-collar workers. The magnitude of these disparities must not be exaggerated, but this still reflects different productive specializations in the metropoles and suburbs—that is, services rendered by some of the residents of the suburbs for the benefit of residents of the rich metropoles and suburbs, and inversely, a more prominent role for industry and food processing in the towns and villages (in part because industrial development arrived later to these areas).[50] These differences

---

49. See unehistoireduconflitpolitique.fr, figures B1.6f and B1.6h.

50. The proportion of blue-collar workers in the suburbs falls between 1960 and 1990, whereas it rises in villages and is maintained in towns, such that during this period the villages and towns exceed the suburbs in terms of the proportion of blue collar workers. This disparity has remained at the same level since 1990, in a general context of the decline of the proportion of blue-collar workers. See unehistoireduconflitpolitique.fr, figures B1.6q–B1.6r.

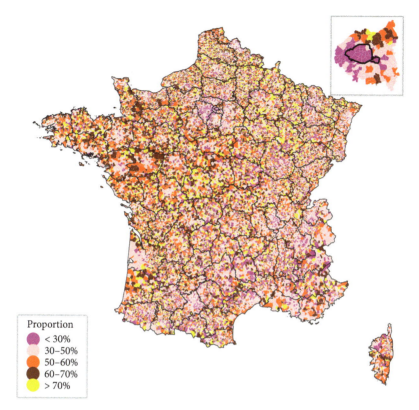

MAP 2.9. Geography of blue-collar workers and service employees, 2022
This map represents the proportion of blue-collar workers and service employees in the working population by municipality (national average: 47%).
Sources and series: unehistoireduconflitpolitique.fr

in productive specialization potentially have major consequences for the different worldviews and political perceptions, including, for example, a greater sensitivity to questions of international competition and industrial delocalization in towns and villages, and inversely, a greater proximity to trajectories of promotion through public employment and higher education in the suburbs and metropoles. Along with the question of the relationship to property ownership, this is one of the objective factors that can contribute to the opposition of these different territories and explain, for example, why employees in the suburbs and blue-collar workers in towns and villages now vote for different political blocs, in spite of everything that might draw them closer together.

The Return of Territorial Inequalities:
The Cause or the Consequence of Tripartition?

Let's sum up. After a significant reduction in disparities over the course of the twentieth century, territorial inequalities have grown larger since the 1980s–1990s from the point of view of the distribution of production, property values (the value of housing), and income. The increase in inequalities among territories is greater and more striking than the increase in vertical inequalities at the national level analyzed chapter 1. In particular, in the 1980s and 1990s the concentration of the production of wealth in a few departments around Paris reached levels never seen before. To this day, the disparities in property values and incomes remain smaller than those observed in the nineteenth century or the beginning of the twentieth century, but they are growing rapidly. Generally speaking, territorial inequalities have always been at very high levels. In the early 2020s, we find all over the territory hundreds of municipalities in which the average income barely reaches 7,000 to 8,000 euros per year and per inhabitant, and others where the average income exceeds 60,000 to 70,000 euros (or even, occasionally, 100,000 euros). In recent decades we have seen inequalities increasing between rich suburbs and poor suburbs and between rich towns and poor towns, as well as at the levels of villages and metropoles.

This general way of framing the issue will play an essential role in studying electoral behaviors and their transformations since the Revolution. Let us say it at the outset: the relation between socioeconomic inequalities and electoral attitudes always moves in both directions. The former helps forge the latter, which in return helps shape political choices influencing the former. Over the last two centuries, the feeling of abandonment experienced by the inhabitants of rural and peripheral territories or disadvantaged urban zones has constantly fueled the political attitudes of both groups (and sometimes a lack of participation). The unprecedented concentration of the production of wealth in Île de France and a few large metropoles over recent decades has naturally contributed to the development of new spatial fractures and the voters' rejection of parties of the Right and the Left that have exercised power. In fact, the evolution of inequalities always reflects political choices. Far from being the consequence of natural or exogenous forces (like "globalization" and "technological progress"), it flows largely from the policies pursued, whether they are structural decisions regarding commercial openness, the deregulation of the financial sector, or policies of public investment (for example, giving priority to high-speed trains for the inhabitants of the metropoles instead of regional trains, or viewing the location of hospitals, schools, and public services in towns and villages as structurally unfavorable), which can help explain the development of inequalities between territories in recent years. The increasing power of questions about energy and climate has also led to a sharpening of the tensions between territories, as shown by the *bonnets rouges* crisis in 2013 (following a tax on heavy trucks and multiple social welfare plans in the food-processing industry), and especially by the *gilets jaunes* movement in 2018–2019, following the introduction of a carbon tax and an increase in the price of fuels that de facto weighed much more heavily on the inhabitants of towns and villages than it did on metropoles and suburbs.

In return, the new political divisions between the rural world and the urban world, and especially between the popular classes in towns and villages on the one hand and those in suburbs and metropoles on the other, along with the system of electoral tripartition that they entail, have also contributed to the political blockages and the lack of choices that would allow us to cope with these inequalities, which are both social and territorial. Let us add that the question of whether it is possible or even desirable to further reduce territorial inequalities is also one of the central questions of political conflict. Ultimately, it is a debate rather close to the one discussed in chapter 1 concerning the continuation of the welfare state's expansion in the twenty-first century. For these political movements and the voters most convinced by liberal theses, the obligatory levies have already reached a level too high to maintain the country's competitiveness ranking, and any attempt to increase taxes on the most prosperous actors and territories, and to strengthen policies of redistribution, would be doomed to fail and would end up being turned against the most vulnerable. Conversely, for many citizens, particularly in the poorest suburbs, towns, and villages, it is not only possible but essential to mobilize supplementary resources to invest more in the most disadvantaged territories. For these voters and the political tendencies supporting these discourses, both on the left and, more and more often, also on the right of the political chessboard, it is perfectly possible to find supplementary resources, either by raising taxes on the wealthiest, who often escape taxes that are supposed to be paid by everyone, or by reducing unjustified public expenditures, which they say benefit chiefly the most privileged classes and territories.

It is interesting to note that this conflict is found among geographers and specialists in territorial development. For some of them, territorial redistribution has already reached its limits. The most dynamic and prosperous metropoles in the country (starting with the Paris metropole) are already overtaxed to come to the aid of territories that are not very productive, and any attempt to go further in this direction would risk killing the golden goose and lead to unhitching these driving regions from international competition. If we add to that the growing public debt, everything would seem to encourage us to conclude that putting regions that lag behind on perfusion must stop and not be increased.[51] For other geographers, such an analysis is biased and reflects a quasi-naturalist view of the GDP and market forces. If the GDP of Île-de-France seems so elevated, that may not be because its inhabitants (or rather the inhabitants of certain wealthy areas within it) are by nature tremendously productive; it is also and perhaps especially because they have benefited from public policies, from infrastructures and investments much more favorable than those in other parts of the country, without taking into account the fact that financial and commercial deregulation has also helped concentrate production in certain territories and valorizes certain activities more than others.[52] The second analysis seems to us a priori more convincing, but the fact is that the complexity of the subject authorizes, once again, contradictory and nevertheless plausible interpretations. Only political and electoral conflict will make it possible to settle the debate collectively and to model the future trajectory. One of the central questions is whether the different categories of territories that consider themselves to have been abandoned, in particular the suburbs and towns, will be capable of uniting and putting aside their disagreements in order to establish a new voluntarist policy of reducing territorial inequalities. But before going any further in this analysis of the intersecting relationships between economic and political developments, we must pursue our study of socioeconomic inequalities and their transformations in France over the long term, taking a special interest in inequalities of education, and then in the emergence of new cleavages connected with origins.

---

51. See, for example, Davezies, *La crise qui vient.*
52. For an overview of these conflicts among geographers, see, for example, T. Courcelle, Y. Fijalkow, and F. Taulelle, *Services publics et territoires. Adaptations, innovations et réactions* (Presses Universitaires de Rennes, 2017), 29–45.

CHAPTER 3

The Metamorphoses of Educational Inequalities

We turn now to educational inequalities and their metamorphoses. The major phenomenon over the long term is the persistence of very strong sociospatial inequalities in education in a context of an unprecedented expansion of the general level of access to knowledge and written culture over the past three centuries. These socioterritorial disparities partly intersect with those connected with production, real estate capital (total value of housing), income, sector of activity, and occupation, which we studied in chapter 2, without, however, merging entirely with them. Today, they help fuel powerful tensions between social classes and territories, as well as an unsatisfied demand for a real democratization of the educational system and access to the best programs of study and to the best-equipped schools. We will also examine the principal stages of the cleavage between public and private education that has played a structuring role in shaping political attitudes and educational inequalities in France from the nineteenth century up to our own time.

The Educational Cycles and the Persistence of Stratification

First, we must assess the very long-term movement constituted by progress toward a broader and more open education. Teaching has a great collective history, involving families and their desire for recognition and social advancement, the churches and their projects for the moral and spiritual training of society, and finally, more and more clearly from the nineteenth century, the state. Over the course of the twentieth century, the public resources devoted to education, expressed as a proportion of the national income, were multiplied by more ten in France, from just 0.5 percent in 1900–1910 to almost 6 percent since 1980–1990.[1] This unprecedented expansion has made it possible to transform an elitist educational system that was restricted to a minority into a system that is capable of providing universal access to primary and secondary education. Today most members of the new generations can enter higher education (but not without difficulty, considering the stagnation of resources invested in training over recent decades). The important point is that at each of these stages (learning to read, a long primary education, a

---

1. See chapter 1, figure 1.7.

short and then a long secondary education, then a short higher education, and tomorrow a long higher education), new forms of stratifications and hierarchies appeared, with considerable challenges and tensions along the way.

To gauge educational inequalities over the long term, and especially the evolution of the literacy rate, the oldest sources we have are spouses' signatures on marriage certificates. These signatures were found in the parish and vital statistics registers in almost all the current departments at several dates since 1686, in particular in the context of the Maggiolo inquiry conducted in 1877–1879.[2] The results must be interpreted with caution, but the orders of magnitude and the general evolutions are relatively clear. In France, the proportion of spouses signing their act of marriage rose on average from 23 percent in 1686 to 37 percent in 1786, 72 percent in 1870, and 97 percent in 1905. We will see that a large part of the historical progress toward literacy was already accomplished before the Third Republic enacted the great laws on cost-free, obligatory schooling (which does not mean that these laws did not have a decisive impact in completing this evolution, and especially in paving the way for later stages). We must also emphasize that the inequalities among departments remained enormous for a long time. At the time of the French Revolution, the proportion of spouses who signed their marriage certificates was scarcely more than 10 percent in the twenty least literate departments (as shown by marriage certificates), whereas it already exceeded 70 percent in the twenty most literate departments (see figure 3.1).[3]

---

2. The rector of the Académie de Nancy from 1868 to 1871, Louis Maggiolo, received the official support of the Ministry of Public Instruction (now called the Ministry of National Education) for his inquiry, which allowed him to make use of the help of almost 16,000 teachers, to whom he entrusted the task of compiling a list of marriage certificates covering seventy-eight departments and 32,000 municipalities in 1686–1690, 1786–1790, and 1816–1820—data that can be completed by a count of the registers of vital statistics established by the Ministry of the Interior, starting in 1854. See M. Fleury and P. Valmary, "Les progrès de l'instruction élémentaire de Louis XIV à Napoléon III, d'après l'enquête de Louis Maggiolo (1877–1879)," *Population*, 1957. See also F. Furet and J. Ozouf, *Lire et écrire. L'alphabétisation des Français de Calvin à Jules Ferry*, 2 vols. (Minuit, 1977).

3. For the geographical distribution of these departments in 1686 and at the time of the French Revolution, see unehistoireduconflitpolitique.fr, map C3.1. Many historians have studied the reasons for these great geographical inequalities—between departments, but also within departments—in the development of literacy in France. Although issues of schooling naturally play a major role, particularly the acceptance or rejection of the "public" financing of school under the Old Regime—and more generally, the reticence of certain bourgeois and aristocratic milieus in regard to the education of peasants—they are not the only factors. Multiple chapters in a study of the history of literacy in France edited by François Furet and Jacques Ozouf call into question the very nature of schooling and stress the mediocrity of the educational institution in the eighteenth century—an institution that was unstable, precarious, and often very unequally attended. Furet and Ozouf, *Lire et écrire*.

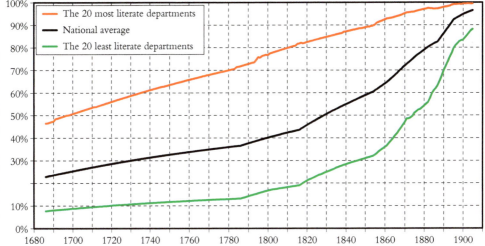

FIGURE 3.1. The long march toward literacy: The proportion of spouses signing their marriage certificates, 1686–1905

The proportion of spouses signing their marriage certificates rose on average from 23% in 1686 to 72% in 1870, and then to 97% in 1905. In the twenty most literate departments it rose from 46% in 1686 to 71% in 1786, then to 99% in 1905. In the twenty least literate departments it rose from 8% in 1686 to 13% in 1786, and to 88% in 1905.

Sources and series: unehistoireduconflitpolitique.fr

The counts carried out also allow us to see major disparities between men and women in their rates of signing marriage certificates, even if in the end these disparities appear to be clearly lower than the territorial disparities between departments.[4] The considerable territorial inequalities reflect a multitude of factors, such as the distance or proximity of the principal axes of commercial and cultural circulation, the strategies of ecclesiastical and state actors facing the educational stakes and the challenge posed by Protestantism, and, of course, the no less considerable resources of families, parishes, and collectivities for financing schools. In addition to marriage certificates, the other classic source that makes it possible to measure literacy over the long term is the aptitude tests organized by the military for young conscripts, which resulted in regular statistics from 1827 on. These documents enable us to determine the proportion of conscripts who knew how to read

---

4. See unehistoireduconflitpolitique.fr, figures B3.1a–B3.1b. The disparities in the rates of signature between women and men are on the order of ten to twenty percentage points in the eighteenth and nineteenth centuries, compared with disparities of sixty to seventy points between the least literate departments and the most literate departments.

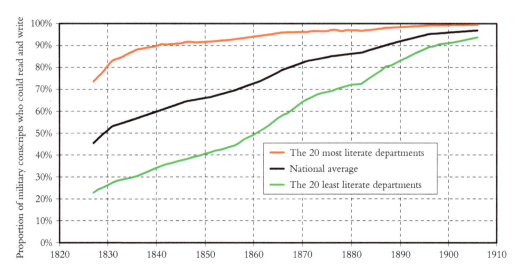

FIGURE 3.2. The long march toward literacy: The proportion of military conscripts who could read and write, 1827–1906

The proportion of military conscripts who could read and write rose on average in France from 45% in 1827 to 97% in 1906. In the twenty most literate departments it rose from 23% 1827 to 94% in 1906.

Sources and series: unehistoireduconflitpolitique.fr

and write (as judged by the military institution), and by definition, they apply only to males. These results must be interpreted prudently. However, we see trends that cohere very well with those demonstrated by the marriage certificates, concerning both the general level of literacy in the various subperiods and its evolution over time (see figure 3.2). The departmental classifications and the magnitude of the disparities are also virtually the same, no matter which of these two sources is used, even though they issue from very different origins and conceptions, which suggests that the territorial inequalities thus highlighted are relatively robust.

Starting in 1866, we also observe in population censuses detailed information regarding the levels of education of the whole of the population (no evidence of that kind was available in earlier censuses).[5] In the censuses from 1866 to 1946, the main available measure concerns the proportion of the population who knew how to read and write (as gauged by the census employees and the persons concerned). The questions regarding the level of education were refined in the census of 1954. Then, starting with the 1962 census, we have, for the 36,000 municipali-

5.   The first general census of France's population was carried out in 1801 by the Bureau des statistics, created the preceding year by Lucien Bonaparte, who was the minister of the interior.

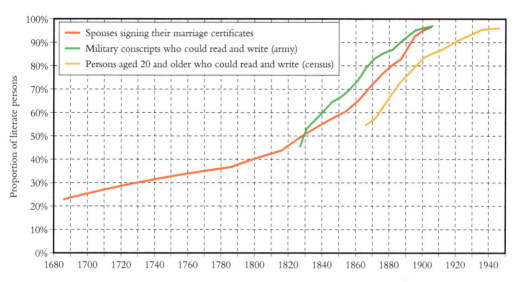

FIGURE 3.3. The long march toward literacy, 1686–1946

The three available ways of measuring literacy over the long term (using evidence of spouses who signed their marriage certificate, military conscripts who could read and write, persons aged twenty and older who could read and write according to the censuses) yield coherent results. To sum up, literacy exceeded 90% for the generations born starting in 1890–1900, and for the whole adult population starting in 1920–1930.

Sources and series: unehistoireduconflitpolitique.fr

ties in France, detailed information about the distribution of diplomas, particularly regarding people who held a secondary school degree (*baccalauréat*) or a higher education degree. Concerning the censuses of 1866–1946, it is striking to note how late in coming was the quasi-universal literacy of the population, if we take the whole of the population into account. In the census of 1866, scarcely 55 percent of the population twenty years old or older was registered as knowing how to read and write. Not until 1920–1930 did literacy exceed 90 percent in the adult population (see figure 3.3).[6]

It will also be noted that the territorial inequalities of achieving literacy remained considerable until the middle of the twentieth century. In the twenty least literate departments, only 30 percent of the adult population knew how to read and write in

6. The disparities in the literacy rates observed using the data of the conscripts or the signatures of marriage certificates are explained by the fact that in this case, we are concerned almost uniquely with younger generations, whereas the data of the census take into account the whole of the adult population.

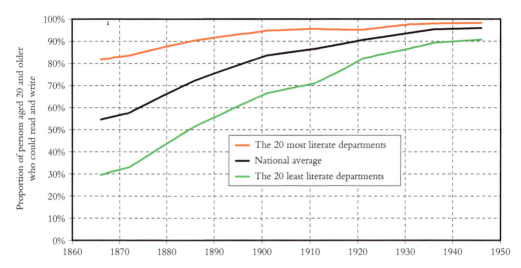

FIGURE 3.4. Large territorial inequalities and literacy

The proportion of people aged twenty and older who could read and write (as measured by censuses) rose on average in France from 55% in 1866 to 96% in 1946. In the twenty least literate departments, it rose from 30% in 1866 to 91% in 1946.

Sources and series: unehistoireduconflitpolitique.fr

1870 (as opposed to 80 percent in the twenty most literate departments). This shows that it took several generations for the laws on free and obligatory schooling passed at the beginning of the Third Republic to produce all their effects, including within the oldest segments of the population. It will also be noted that the territorial inequalities once again appear to be greater and more persistent than those connected with gender.[7] If we examine the geographical distribution of the levels of education, we see that the famous Saint-Malo–Geneva line observed for the distribution of production, real estate capital, and incomes remained relevant for a long time. In 1786 as in 1906, the territories situated northeast of this line were on average more literate than those in the southwest, though there were already several exceptions.[8] If we examine the geography of higher education degrees in 2022, we find, as for economic wealth, a very different distribution, and to a certain extent, a complete turnaround with respect to the initial line, with large parts of the west and southwest of the country overtaking the traditionally literate and industrial regions of the northeast (see map 3.1).

---

7. See unehistoireduconflitpolitique.fr, figures B3.1d–B3. Between 1866 and 1946, the disparities in literacy between women and men are on the order of five to ten percentage points, at most.
8. See unehistoireduconflitpolitique.fr, maps C3.2–C3.3.

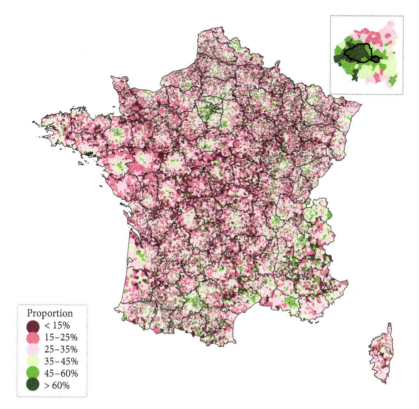

MAP 3.1. Spatial inequalities in education: The proportion of higher education degrees, 2022

The map represents for each municipality the proportion of persons holding higher education diplomas among the population aged twenty-five and over (national average: 34%). Note the substantial variations between departments and within them.

Sources and series: unehistoireduconflitpolitique.fr

Access to Secondary School and Higher Education Degrees, from Villages to Metropoles

In studying spatial inequalities in education, it is particularly instructive to examine the distribution of diplomas at the level of the 36,000 municipalities, and this information is available thanks to the censuses carried out since the early 1960s. First, we must emphasize the impressive diffusion of the secondary school diploma at the level of the 36,000 municipalities over the past sixty years, which was even more rapid and spectacular than the rise in literacy, which was spread over more than two centuries. In 1960, barely 4 percent of the adult population held a secondary school diploma, a degree that was then less widespread in the country than literacy was in the time of Louis XIV. In 2022, the proportion of those with this degree reached 50 percent among people older than twenty-five. old. It now exceeds 80 percent among the younger generations, in conformity with the objective set in 1985 by the Socialist government (an objective that seemed at the time very optimistic, even utopian, and dangerous for many people), and it will automatically reach this level for the whole of the adult population a few decades from now. The proportion of those over twenty-five years old holding a higher education degree has risen from less than 2 percent in 1960 to more than 34 percent in the early 2020s. Everything seems to indicate that it will reach this level for the whole of the population in the decades to come (all age groups taken together). Today, no one knows whether or if access to higher education will cross the threshold of 90 percent reached at the beginning of the twentieth century for literacy, but it is a real possibility, perhaps before the end of the twenty-first century.

This very substantial progress on the whole must not, however, mask the fact that new inequalities and social stratifications have been reconstituted at each stage of educational expansion. A first way of taking the measure of the sociospatial disparities consists in examining the evolution of the proportions of secondary school and higher education diplomas, using the same categories as the ones introduced in chapter 2: villages, towns, suburbs, and metropoles.[9] We note that the proportions of secondary school graduates have always been greatest in the metropoles, followed by the suburbs, then the towns and villages. In other words, between 1960 and 2022, the diffusion of secondary school and higher education diplomas has been very substantial more or less everywhere, but the hierarchy between territories has not changed, and the absolute disparities have even tended to grow over time (see figures 3.5–3.6).

However, this way of representing educational inequalities is incomplete, because, as in the case of economic disparities, it is essential to take into account the existence of deep divisions within each of these categories. Rich metropoles and rich suburbs (defined as the half of all metropoles and suburbs with the highest average incomes) are characterized by a considerable advantage over the rest of the country in terms of diplomas, an advantage that has grown over time. In 2022, the proportion of higher education diplomas is approaching 60 percent in the rich metropoles, whereas it is hardly more than 20 percent in the poor towns and

9. A reminder: villages are defined as agglomerations of fewer than 2,000 inhabitants, towns as agglomerations of between 2,000 and 100,000 inhabitants, suburbs and secondary metropoles as agglomerations of more than 100,000 inhabitants, and metropoles as the principal municipalities of these agglomerations of more than 100,000 inhabitants. See chapter 2.

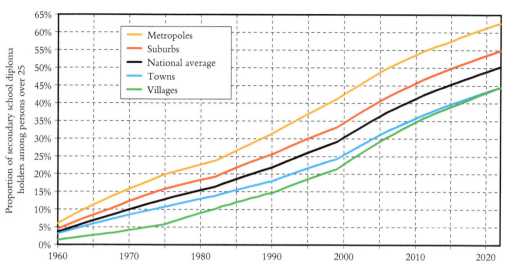

FIGURE 3.5. Villages, towns, suburbs, and metropoles: the development of the proportion of secondary education graduates, from 1960 to 2022.

The proportion of secondary school graduates rose at the national level from 4 percent to 50 percent between 1960 and 2022. It has always been maximal in metropoles, followed by suburbs, towns, and villages. Note. The definition of villages, towns, suburbs and metropoles is the one introduced in chapter 2 (conurbations of more than 2,000 inhabitants, conurbations of between 2,000 and 100,000, secondary and principal communes of conurbations of more than 2,000 inhabitants).

Sources and series: see unehistoireduconflitpolitique.fr

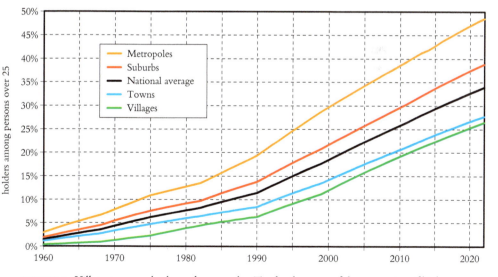

FIGURE 3.6. Village, towns, suburbs, and metropoles: The development of the proportion of higher education graduates

The proportion of higher education graduates among persons over twenty-five (as measured by censuses) rose from a national average of 2 percent to 34 percent between 1960 and 2022. It has always been maximal in metropoles, followed by suburbs, towns, and villages.

Sources and series: unehistoireduconflitpolitique.fr

poor villages.[10] Here we are dealing with disparities almost as extreme as those observed between the least literate departments and the most literate departments at the time of the French Revolution. The situation is very different if we examine the poor metropoles and especially the poor suburbs, and if we compare the poor suburbs to the rich towns and rich villages. All through the period 1960–2022 we observe, for example, that the proportion of those holding secondary education or higher education degrees has always been higher on average in rich towns (the richest half of all towns) than in the poor suburbs (the poorest half of suburbs). Since the beginning of the 2000s, the rich villages have also outstripped the poor suburbs in terms of the proportion of holders of both secondary school and higher education degrees.[11] For education, as for income and real estate capital, it is above all the disparities within each spatial category (villages, towns, suburbs, metropoles) that have tended to grow larger over the course of recent decades, which shows how essential it is to correlate these categories with social criteria.

Poor Territories Disadvantaged with Regard to Education

Generally, for educational inequalities, as for inequalities of income and wealth, we must stress everything that unites all the disadvantaged social classes, whether they live in the poor suburbs, poor towns, or poor villages. Regarding incomes, we have already noted that the average income in the poor suburbs (the 50 percent of the suburbs with the lowest incomes) continued to decrease relative to the national average over recent decades, and since the beginning of the 2010s it has been at the same level as the average income of poor towns and villages (defined in the same way).[12] Today, the very poor suburbs (the poorest 20 percent) have an average income even inferior to those in their equivalent towns and villages.

The poor suburbs nevertheless remain significantly ahead of the poor towns and poor villages with respect to diplomas held.[13] How can this lead in education be explained, and why isn't it reflected in the disparities in income? Several factors seem to be involved. Regarding the advance in education, we have to take into account the fact that the inhabitants of the suburbs benefit from greater proximity

10. See unehistoireduconflitpolitique.fr, figures B1.7a–B1.7d.

11. See unehistoireduconflitpolitique.fr, figures B1.7a–B1.7d.

12. See chapter 2, figure 2.15.

13. In 2002, among the inhabitants of the poor suburbs who were more than twenty-five years old, about 45 percent held secondary school diplomas and 30 percent had higher education degrees (as opposed to scarcely 40 percent and 2 percent in the poor towns and poor villages). See unehistoireduconflitpolitique.fr, figures B1.7a–B1.7d.

to facilities at the metropolitan universities, which can help explain why access to diplomas is easier for them than for the inhabitants of towns and villages.[14] The educational lead of poor suburbs is, of course, already achieved at the level of the proportion of secondary school degree holders, but it could also reflect in part the existence of easier access to higher education. Moreover, although the inhabitants of towns and villages have in principle access to the same public system of primary schools, middle schools, and lycées as do the inhabitants of the metropoles and suburbs, the conditions for access are not always similar in practice, starting with the time students spend getting to and from school, which can have negative effects on academic success.[15] Let us also emphasize that young people from villages and towns who undertake advanced studies are often move to metropoles during their studies, and subsequently may never return, considering the development of their sociability and their careers, which automatically contributes to finding a smaller proportion of diplomas in the rural world. It will also be noted that the population of the metropoles is more female than that of towns and villages.[16] Furthermore, the population of the metropoles—and to a lesser degree, that of the suburbs (and particularly the poor suburbs)—is more female than that of towns and

14. Thus, in his *Fractures françaises,* Christophe Guilluy claims that the inhabitants of sensitive urban zones (ZUS) would benefit—according to him, because of the new centrality of the suburbs in the heart of the wealthiest and most active urban areas—from the richest range of studies (as well as the most dynamic job markets), emphasizing, though without quantifying it in any way, "the explosion of the number of young diploma holders from these neighborhoods." C. Guilluy, *Fractures françaises* (Bourin, 2010).

15. Several studies show that young people from rural environments more frequently attend schools outside their municipalities of residence than do young people who live in cities, and that they travel distances that grow larger as they progress from primary school to lycée—from nine to twenty-three kilometers, on average, to reach a school situated in a different municipality. Ninety-four percent of young people from rural areas—as compared with half of young city dwellers—have to change to a different municipality when they enter lycée, and therefore travel on average twenty-three kilometers a day. See "Entre ville et campagne, les parcours des enfants qui grandissent en zone rurale" (INSEE Première no. 1888, 2022). On the negative effects of the distance to school on academic results, see, for example, T. Flach, P. Lujala, and B. Strom, "Geographical Constraints and Educational Attainment," *Regional Science and Urban Economics,* 2013.

16. See unehistoireduconflitpolitique.fr, figures B2.1a–B2.1i. The proportions of women are strictly the same in all sizes of conurbations, among children (biological proportion 49 percent), but diverge among adults, with shares ranging from 47–48 percent in villages to 52–53 percent in metropoles, all through the period 1960–2022 (with the suburbs and towns located in an intermediary position, and the former exceeding the latter since 1990). On student migration among women, see É. Guéraut, F. Jedlicki, and C. Noûs, "L'émigration étudiante des 'filles du coin': Entre émancipation sociale et réassignation spatiale," *Travail, genre et sociétés,* 2021.

villages.[17] These specific demographic characteristics are associated with the most advanced degrees and explain a non-negligible part of the disparity between poor suburbs and poor towns and villages (between one-third and half).[18] They can also help explain the absence of higher incomes. More generally, migratory trajectories allow us to explain partly the greater academic investment in suburbs and the urban world. This holds true for migrations from other countries and in particular for extra-European migrations. The *Trajectoires et origines* (Trajectories and origins) studies have shown how these careers are associated with very large investments in education (in comparison with autochthonous people of equivalent social origin), without the diplomas obtained necessarily leading to jobs and supplementary salaries.[19] This can also be applied to internal migrations: young men and women with diplomas who move from towns and villages, more than those who have remained in their rural territories, bring with them a project of mobility and social promotion through education that can be transmitted to following generations.

Let us add that the greatest proximity to public jobs in the education, hospitals, and administrative sector, which is particularly demanding in terms of diplomas, can also help explain why the suburbs have an educational advantage over towns and villages, but again, without this advantage leading to higher incomes. Regarding the relation to property and to the type of productive specialization, the relation to training and diplomas is one of the objective factors involved in the opposition between the towns and villages on the one hand and the suburbs

---

17. See unehistoireduconflitpolitique.fr, figures B2.2a–B2.2j.

18. Women in fact hold more degrees than men at the national level, and the youngest more than their elders, because of the democratization of access to higher education in recent years. Technically, if we estimate the impact of the size of an agglomeration on the level of education, the coefficient of the rank-rank regression between the proportion of degree holders and the size of the agglomeration (controlling for the average municipal income by ventile) is reduced by 30–50 percent, depending on the years and the specifications when one controls for the structure by age and gender of the municipality. See unehistoireduconflitpolitique.fr, figure B3.3i.

19. See, for example, C. Beauchemin and P. Simon, "Histoires migratoires et profils socioéconomiques," in *Trajectoires et origines. Enquête sur la diversité de la population française* (INED, 2015). Why aren't these educational investments always subsequently reflected in professional careers? If the existence of discrimination in hiring could not be the sole explanatory factor, it is clear that it plays an important role here. Various studies conducted in France have shown that—for a given diploma—job candidates whose surnames sound Maghrebin have a much smaller chance of obtaining a hiring interview than candidates whose patronymics are of French origin. See, in particular, M.-A. Valfort, *Discriminations religieuses à l'embauche: Une réalité* (Institut Montaigne, 2015); M.-A. Valfort, "Discrimination à l'embauche des personnes d'origine supposée maghrébine: Quels enseignements d'une grande étude par testing?" (Note IPP no. 76, 2021). See also T. Piketty, *Mesurer le racisme, vaincre les discriminations* (Seuil, 2022).

and metropoles on the other. In the following chapters we will see the importance of these divergences, with respect to both participation in voting and the formation of political preferences.

Nonetheless, we must stress that in the end, the disparity in training between poor suburbs and poor towns and villages is relatively small in comparison to everything that opposes these disadvantaged territories to the richest suburbs and metropoles.[20] This observation holds not only for the inequalities in diplomas and in wealth, but also for the educational resources actually allocated to the different territories, especially in matters of primary and secondary education. Contrary to what is sometimes said, the most socially disadvantaged territories are often found to receive smaller allocations of public funds than the most privileged territories at the level of primary and secondary education. For example, if we examine public middle schools in the Paris region, we see that the percentage of teachers on temporary contracts (who have less training and are paid less than the permanent staff and new teachers) is barely 10 percent in the most privileged departments (Paris, Hauts-de-Seine) and reaches 50 percent in the least privileged departments (Seine-Saint-Denis, Val-de-Marne). Studies based on National Education pay stubs have recently made it possible to demonstrate the extent to which the system is moving backward on the national scale. If we calculate the average salary of teachers in different schools and lycées, taking into account the small bonuses applied in priority zones, but also all the other elements of remuneration connected with seniority, the diploma held, status (temporary or permanent contract), and so on, we see that the higher the percentage of students from the privileged social classes, the higher the teachers' salaries.[21] The smallest average salary of teachers in disadvantaged zones is sometimes counterbalanced by a smaller number of students, but the available studies suggest that a smaller class does not always suffice to compensate for a teacher with less experience or more limited training. We must also emphasize that the fundamental inegalitarian mechanism—namely, the

---

20. The disparity is five and ten percentage points in the first case, whereas it is more than thirty percentage points in the second. See unehistoireduconflitpolitique.fr, figures B1.7a–B1.7d.

21. In middle school, the average remuneration of teachers (including all bonuses) is less than 2,400 euros per month in the 10 percent of middle schools with the smallest percentage of socially privileged students, then it rises gradually to reach 2,800 euros in the 10 percent of middle schools with the highest percentage of socially privileged students. In lycées, this same average remuneration rises from less than 2,700 euros per month in the most disadvantaged 10 percent to almost 3,200 euros a month euros per month in the most privileged 10 percent. See A. Benhenda, "Teaching Staff Characteristics and Spending per Student in French Disadvantaged Schools" (working paper, Paris School of Economics, 2019); A. Benhenda, *Tous des bons profs: Un choix de société* (Fayard, 2020).

flight of the most experienced teachers, the ones with the most degrees and the best paid, to the most privileged schools, and in particular to the city centers and the wealthy suburbs—disadvantages in comparable proportions all the disadvantaged schools, whether they are in poor suburbs or poor towns and villages (and perhaps even more the former).[22] For the same reasons, a recasting of the policy on the allocation of resources in order to change this situation might potentially benefit all the poor territories. To sum up, there are objective factors that can contribute to the opposition of poor towns and poor suburbs, and there are also and especially common interests and policies of social and educational justice that could in theory bring them together.

Is the Battle for the Democratization of Education before Us?

More generally, it is important to emphasize that the battle for the democratization of education is in large measure before us and not behind us. Too often, educational expansion serves as a screen to hide the sometimes abyssal hypocrisies that characterize the educational system. When Pierre Bourdieu and Jean-Claude Passeron published *Les héritiers* in 1964, inequalities in higher education were simple and brutal: less than 1 percent of the children of farmworkers became university students, as opposed to 70 percent of the children of industrialists and large business owners and 80 percent of the children of the liberal professions. Sixty years later, the massive expansion of access to the university system has complicated the debate. Attempts are now made to present educational inequalities as legitimate, under cover of the notions of merit and equal opportunity. In reality, the higher education system in France is nonetheless particularly hypocritical, because although it adorns itself in the garb of "republican" equality, it succeeds in investing three to four times more public resources per student for students admitted to selective programs of study (preparatory classes, *grandes écoles*) than for those embarking on the ordinary university programs—between 12,000 and 15,000 euros per year for students in the best-funded programs, and less than 4,000 euros for those in less-funded programs. But it turns out that on average, the former group has much more privileged social origins than the latter, especially the students in the most sought-after programs and the most selective schools, access to

22. The results established by Asma Benhenda do not include the explicit decomposition by the size of the agglomeration, but the available elements (in particular those regarding the proportions of temporary teachers by department) suggest that teachers' average remunerations are particularly low in the poor suburbs in comparison to the poor towns and poor villages (for the same percentage of socially disadvantaged students).

which has absolutely not been democratized over recent decades, despite repeated assertions that it has.[23] Public funds thus contribute to the exacerbation of the initial inequalities rather than reducing them—with a clear conscience, and contrary to the official discourses.[24] If children from socially disadvantaged classes are not admitted to preparatory classes today—as used to be the case with higher education in general—that is not because they naturally prefer playing soccer to studying, but rather because it is precisely when they are still young children that the public service of education should compensate for the inequalities of inherited social and educational capital. But in fact, for disadvantaged students from both the rural world and the urban world, the opposite occurs.

If we take into account all public expenditures for education, from nursery school to higher education, we find considerable inequalities within an age group: the 50 percent of students who currently benefit from the smallest expenditures receive between 60,00 and 100,000 euros each, whereas the 10 percent that benefit from the largest expenditures receive between 200,000 and 300,000 euros each. However, we must emphasize that this concentration of funds for education to the benefit of a minority is less extreme than it was at the beginning of the twentieth century, when only the children of the bourgeoisie had a chance to be admitted to secondary and higher education, and when the mass of the population had to be content with an education that was basic and inadequately financed. Around 1900–1910, the 10 percent of the best endowed students thus benefited from 40 percent of the total expenditures on education, as opposed to about 25 percent for the 50 percent of the least endowed. The latter were, however, five

---

23. According to the latest information available, children from disadvantaged social categories (36 percent of n age group) represent 20 percent of all university students, but only 8 percent of the students at Sciences Po Paris, 7 percent at ENS Ulm, 3 percent at HEC, and o percent at Polytechnique. Inversely, those who come from very privileged social categories (23 percent of an age group) constitute 47 percent of all university students, but 73 percent at Sciences Po Paris, 75 percent at ENS Ulm, 89 percent at HEC, and 92 percent at Polytechnique. See C. Bonneau, P. Charousset, J. Grenet, and G. Thebault, *Quelle démocratisation des grandes écoles depuis le milieu des années 2000?* (IPP, 2021). In addition, the study notes that there has been no measurable progress in matters of social mixture since 2000, except for a few modest effects connected with the agreements established by Sciences Po with disadvantaged lycées. On the costs of the different programs, see G. Fack and E. Huilery, *Enseignement supérieur: Pour un investissement plus juste et plus efficace* (CAE, 2021). See also P. Pasquali, *Héritocratie. Les élites, les grandes écoles et les mésaventures du mérite (1870–2020)* (La Découverte, 2021).

24. "Quantitative" inequalities of access to higher education have thus been replaced by "qualitative" inequalities connected with the nature of the course of study pursued (which go hand in hand with inequalities in hard cash for financing). See C. Peugny, *Pour une politique de la jeunesse* (Seuil, 2022), 69.

times more numerous (by definition), which consequently corresponded to disparities in investment per student between these two groups ranging from 1 to 8. At the beginning of the 1920s, the 10 percent of the best endowed students received about 20 percent of the total expenditure, as compared to almost 35 percent for the least endowed 50 percent, which corresponds to a disparity in investment per student ranging "only" from 1 to 3. This inequality nonetheless remains considerable, and hardly in conformity with contemporary discourses on the equality of opportunity.[25]

Of course, we can in theory imagine a fairer system that would also allow greater social mobility and a stronger economic dynamic. There again, such an alternative system could be in the common interest of all the disadvantaged social classes, whether they reside in the poor suburbs, towns, or villages, or even, ultimately, in the interest of society as a whole. That would probably require a substantial increase in the total resources devoted to higher education,[26] as well as fairer and more transparent procedures of allocating resources and students to the various programs, taking into account in a balanced way students' preferences and abilities as well as their social backgrounds and the obstacles they confront in finding housing and transportation. However, in declaring these objectives, we immediately see the magnitude of the task and the sociopolitical tensions that might flow from it. The search for the ideal compromise between these different objectives will demand time and much trial and error. To a large extent, this is a never-ending process that must be repeated over and over. It is perfectly legitimate and healthy that within this process, skeptical points of view regarding the advisability of an unlimited expansion of education, and the considerable difficulties involved in financing and organizing it, are expressed.[27] In particular, the mobilization of supplementary resources raises the same difficulties and the same criticisms as those already mentioned in the preceding chapters on the subject of continuing the growth of the welfare state and the struggle against territorial inequalities. In the eyes of those who are the most convinced by the liberal theses,

25. See T. Piketty, *Une brève histoire de l'égalité* (Seuil, 2021), 137, figure 14, and 259, figure 32.
26. Let us recall that reduced to the number of students—and there, too, contrary to the announcement effects—public investment in the university system has been declining in France since 2010. This is a political choice that not only prevents us from envisaging a reduction in educational inequalities but also prepares us for the future very poorly.
27. In addition to the question of cost, there is the question of the frustrating gap between the degree received—in particular in comparison with the one obtained by one's parents—and the reality of the job obtained (and the qualifications actually required). On the feeling of frustration that arises from the devalorization of academic degrees, see, in particular, C. Peugny, *Le déclassement* (Grasset, 2009).

the obligatory levies have already reached the maximal point conceivable, and the educational system must henceforth continue its development by resorting to registration fees and financing from the students themselves and their families, along with businesses and rich donors. Conversely, the proponents of redistribution see it as preferable to ask more from those who can afford to give by introducing more progressive income taxes, so that the resources in question benefit all and not a minority. As often happens in such cases, the principal issue is not so much how to describe theoretically what an ideal system based on fiscal and educational justice would look like (although that exercise has its utility), but imagining political trajectories that allow coalitions to have the legitimacy necessary to demonstrate practically what it is possible to do. What is certain is that the considerable transformations of education seen over the past three centuries have been possible only at the price of political upheavals of enormous scope, and that this will very certainly continue to be the case in the future.

The Religious Cleavage and the Public-Private Conflict

Let us now go back and examine a little more closely some of the political conflicts that have studded this long history. If we examine the controversies surrounding the organization of the educational system in France since the Revolution, the most central conflict, and the most structuring one, is incontestably the one opposing public, secular education to private, religious education. Ultimately, the key question has long been whether the church or the state should be in charge of organizing the education of young people. The answer may seem obvious today, because since the end of the nineteenth century a mainly public system has overseen an unprecedented expansion of education, financed by considerable fiscal resources. But it is important to realize that for a long time, the answer to this question was very uncertain, because the state took little interest in educational affairs, and because extensive political experimentation was necessary to allow the state to demonstrate its ability to organize a large-scale educational system.

To improve our understanding of these uncertainties and this trajectory, which is ongoing, we must once again return to the foundational period of the French Revolution. Under the Old Regime, the Catholic Church had considerable resources (about a quarter of the kingdom's land and buildings, in addition to the ecclesiastical tithe), which allowed it to play the role of society's spiritual and moral monitor, not only by financing the churches, priests, bishops, and monasteries, but also with a vast network of schools, hospitals, and charitable works. Without seeking to exaggerate the extent of the charitable work it performed (which we can legitimately deem modest in comparison to the state's educational and health-care record during the twentieth century), we are obliged to note that in the eighteenth century and at the beginning of the nineteenth, the Church was still the principal collective organization that was truly concerned with questions of education. In particular, in the sixteenth and seventeenth centuries the Catholic Church had set about developing a large network of elementary parish schools, partly to achieve its general objective of the population's spiritual and moral elevation, and partly to respond to the competition and the challenges represented by Protestantism, which, by emphasizing universal access to written culture and by radically attacking the hierarchical chain leading from the papacy to the bishops and parishes, was then threatening to challenge one of the principal pillars of the country's religious, territorial, and institutional organization.

The decision made in autumn 1789 to nationalize the Church's property holdings and transform them into national assets would totally upset this balance. At the same time, the constitutive assembly chose to confer on the new administrative authorities (municipalities and departments) the Church's control over the schools, while failing to transfer the resources that would have enabled them to fulfill this role. The national assets were sold to the highest bidder, chiefly to the benefit of members of the bourgeois or noble classes who had the means to purchase them. Essentially, these sales served neither to redistribute land to poor peasants nor to finance new public services. In 1794, the Convention adopted legislation providing for the state to pay teachers, but this law was abandoned in 1795 for lack of funds, so the financial burden fell on families, the municipalities, and the Church. The latter had succeeded in keeping a few assets, which it reconstituted in part with the gifts and legacies of the faithful, and thereafter it received from the state a budget that sought to compensate it (very partially) for the loss of its assets and tithes. All through the nineteenth century, and especially during the period of the censitary monarchies (1815–1848) and the Second Empire (1852–1870), the Church did all it could to recover its past moral and political preeminence by getting fully involved in questions of education, and especially in the education of girls, which had been particularly neglected by state and secular authorities, as well as the persistent lack of schools to train female teachers. In 1808, the Napoleonic decree organizing the system of public education stipulated that all schools "shall take as the basis of their teaching the precepts of the Catholic religion."[28] In 1816, the monarchical state decided, in its ordinance on teaching, that the certifi-

---

28. See J. N. Luc, J. F. Condette, and Y. Verneuil, *Histoire de l'enseignement en France, 19e–21e siècles* (A. Colin, 2020), 48.

cates of morality issued by the ecclesiastical authorities were sufficient to confer the right to teach, which made it possible to accelerate the development of Catholic schools, especially for girls. In 1833, the Guizot law introduced the obligation for municipalities to pay a minimal remuneration for the teachers in municipal schools, but the amount was set at such a low level that the supplements paid by families and the human and material resources provided by the Church continued to play a central role.[29]

In 1850, in a context in which the leaders of the conservative Republic were wary of the socialist contagion and asked prefects to dismiss thousands of "Red" teachers, the Falloux law provided new support for the development of Catholic schools. In particular, it extended the ordinance of 1816 by giving the certificates of morality issued by mother superiors the same legal value accorded teachers' certificates of competence. For the Catholic camp, incarnated around 1850 by Charles de Montalembert, one of the authors of the Falloux law, the ultimate objective was to obtain "freedom to teach"—that is, in the end, to kick the state out of education, in the same way that it was to be kicked out of the spheres of production and property, in order to protect "freedom to work" in a context where conservatives fought hard to impose the forced closure of the national workshops (*ateliers nationaux*) in 1848.[30] The field of education was thus supposed to become once again the business of the churches, which had always been the protectors of written culture and of morality, and they were to receive a budget suited to that mission if they could not recover the properties they owned under the Old Regime.[31] Conversely,

---

29. The law of 1833 set a minimum salary of 200 francs per year to be paid by the municipalities, which was not very different from the minimum salary of 150 livres set by the royal declaration of 1698 (which was never really applied uniformly over the whole territory). In comparison, the legislation of 1794 had set a remuneration to be paid by the state:1,000 livres for female teachers and 1,200 livres for male teachers (also never applied, because it was cancelled in 1795). To get an idea of the orders of magnitude, the national average income per inhabitant (including all men, women, and children) rose from about 200 livres per year (or 200 gold francs) in 1780–1800 to 400–500 francs in 1850, and 1,000–1200 francs in 1900–1910. The minimum salary of 200 francs set in 1833 thus seems particularly insufficient; the amounts set in 1794 are much more ambitious—so ambitious, in fact, that paying them would have required a vast fiscal reform and redistribution of wealth.

30. We will return to this in chapter 9. This forced closure played an important role in the broad victory of Louis-Napoléon Bonaparte in the presidential election of December 1848, as the workers sought to ensure the elimination of General Eugène Cavaignac, the "butcher" of the ateliers.

31. The idea of restoring the national assets to the Church was abandoned in the First Restoration in 1814, officially because of the fear of setting the country ablaze, and no doubt also because the new elites in power were satisfied with a regime based on private property and not on ecclesiastical property.

the secular camp defended the role of public schools, but without really gauging how much it would cost.

In the middle of the nineteenth century, at a time when a little more than half of French children aged six to eleven were really attending school,[32] the system of primary education was composed in practice of a great diversity of more or less well-financed schools. Along with entirely private schools run by religious congregations (the private congregationalist schools) and a few secular private schools, we find among the so-called public schools (that is, those receiving public subsidies from the municipalities under the framework of the Guizot law of 1833) some secular public schools and many congregationalist public schools—that is, schools operated by religious congregations that nonetheless received public funding that enabled them to provide schooling for girls at a lower cost. Taking into account the low level of the subsidies provided, almost all the schools asked the parents to make large financial contributions (with a few rare exceptions for the poorest families). In practice, many so-called public schools could be more expensive for parents than the supposedly private schools, which had access to large sums given by religious institutions that made education their priority, which sometimes amounted to more than the impoverished municipalities provided (or more than certain municipalities that were richer but cared little about educating the masses). Between 1852 and 1870, the schools run by religious congregations, benefiting from rapidly rising public subsidies, enrolled a growing proportion of the students, thus realizing in part the Catholic camp's program.

The Battle for Public Education, 1875–1914

At the beginning of the 1870s and the Third Republic, the proportion of children attending secular public primary schools (of all children attending school) was about 50 percent. This average conceals great disparities: the proportion is 70 percent for boys and only 30 percent for girls. In other words, the private Catholic schools, many of which benefited from public subsidies provided by the municipalities, had gained a clearly dominant position in the schooling of girls. That was notably the case for the *salles d'asile* (nursery schools), where the religious congregations had ultramajorities, but also for elementary schools if we

---

32. From the surveys carried out at the time by the Ministry of Public Education, it can be estimated that the attendance rate of children aged six to eleven years old was about 40 percent in 1830–1840 (with large variations between summer and winter because of work in the fields), 50–60 percent between 1850 and 1860, 70 percent in 1870, and 80–90 percent starting from 1880–1890.

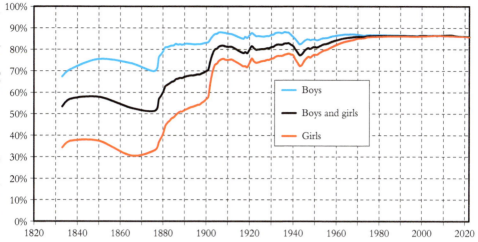

FIGURE 3.7. The development of the proportion of children attending public primary schools

The proportion of children attending secular public primary schools (among all children attending primary school) declined under the Second Empire and was about 50% at the beginning of the Third Republic (30% for girls, 70% for boys), and then rose to more than 80% in 1910 (75% for girls, 85% for boys). After a decrease in public school enrollments under the Vichy regime, the establishment of private education under contract in 1959 led to a stabilization of the public / private balance since the 1960s, with a slight decrease in public school enrollment in the recent period. Sources and series: unehistoireduconflitpolitique.fr

include all the private Catholic schools. This reflects in large measure the secular state authorities' lack of sufficient motivation to develop education, especially the education of girls. The great construction project of the Third Republic was to change this situation radically. The proportion of children attending public schools rose from about 50 percent in 1870 (30 percent girls, 70 percent boys) to 80 percent in 1910 (75 percent girls, 85 percent boys). This was a considerable transformation that took place in two stages: first at the end of the 1870s and during the 1880s, then between 1900 and 1910 (see figure 3.7).

In the first stage, governments took measures allowing public schools to be made more affordable and attractive to families. The Jules Ferry laws of 1881 and 1882 introduced completely cost-free secular primary schools and obligatory attendance until the age of thirteen, and on top of that, the state was to pay the teachers. The Paul Bert law of 1879 had paved the way by increasing funding for the normal schools entrusted with training teachers and by requiring that there be at least one normal school for girls in every department. The law led to the creation of six new normal schools for boys and sixty-seven for girls. The new laws

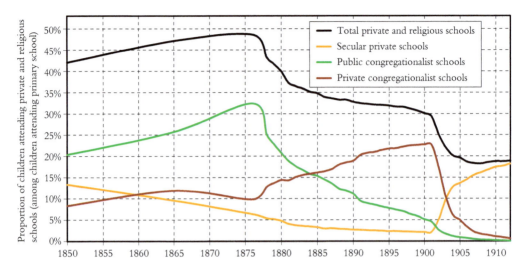

FIGURE 3.8. The battle for public education, 1850–1914

Several categories of private and religious schools coexisted before 1914: private secular schools, public congregationalist schools (i.e., operated by religious congregations but receiving public subsidies), and private congregationalist schools. In the late 1870s and 1880s these subsidies stopped, and the public congregationalist schools became private. Then between 1900 and 1910, congregationalist schools were closed and became private in the current sense of the term.

Sources and series: unehistoireduconflitpolitique.fr

also sought to secularize public schools entirely and to gradually do away with the congregational schools that had benefited from public funding for decades. The 1882 law determined that religious education would henceforth take place outside the public schools, with one day a week devoted to the catechism (Thursday from 1882 to 1972, then Wednesday), and required all teachers in public schools to have a formal certificate of competence (certificates of morality issued by the Church thus no longer sufficed, which excluded a number of congregationalist teachers). Then the law of 1886 stipulated the exclusion of clerics from the public schools within a period of five years and the exclusion of nuns as positions became vacant. The consequence was an extremely rapid fall in the number of teachers in public congregationalist schools, which often became entirely private congregationalist schools (see figure 3.8). These schools lost a great many students as a result of the end of public subsidies and the fact that the secular public schools were at the same time becoming entirely cost free, which attracted a growing number of families of modest and average incomes.

The second stage took place at the beginning of the 1900s. The law of 1904 totally prohibited educational congregations in both public and private education. Then the law of 1905 on the separation of church and state put an end to the public funding of religion from which ecclesiastical schools had benefited since 1790, once again depriving the Catholic camp of major financial resources and greatly reducing its ability to intervene in the social and educational spheres. The interdiction of educational congregations was finally suspended in 1914, and at that time, many religious, both male and female, who had left to teach abroad returned to France and to the private secular schools, though they were obliged to teach dressed in civilian clothes. Ultimately, between 1875 and 1914, congregationalist schools were absorbed into the private schools as they still exist today, and to top it all off, they suffered enormous losses in enrollment and social influence. Whereas in 1875, 70 percent of girls were enrolled in private religious schools, by 1914 no more than 25 percent were enrolled in these schools. As for boys, their share of enrollment in these schools fell from 30 percent to 15 percent. In a little more than three decades, the Third Republic completely transformed the structure of primary education. The motivations for this radical transformation are multiple. The most obvious is the defense of the republican regime, whose fate was far from assured in the 1870s. The Catholic camp and the religious congregations are closely associated with a possible restoration of the monarchy, and it was thus essential to put an end to the grip that the private and religious schools were thought have on young people, and particularly on girls and future mothers. It is important to emphasize that the transformations within primary education between 1875 and 1914 affected only marginally the extremely elitist and inegalitarian educational system in force at the time, with the continuation of a very strong concentration of resources to the benefit of the small minority who had access to secondary and higher education (which opened up only very slightly at that time). From this point of view, what was at stake can be seen more as aspects of a conflict between different elites for control of a generally inegalitarian system than as a genuine attempt to redistribute fortunes and opportunities among the social classes. The Third Republic's ruling classes—which often emerged from the urban bourgeoisie or business circles, and which were inclined to be freethinkers or Freemasons, and sometimes Protestants or Jews, or simply less staunchly Catholic than the traditional elites—wanted to build a new world and make a definitive break with the old ruling classes.

Conversely, in the laws of 1882 and 1886 the Catholic elites saw a violent and underhanded attack on the congregationalist schools, which, in the eyes of their partisans, had served the country and its children well and for so long. The most virulent of these partisans saw in this the mark of those who were against France, the hand of unscrupulous wheeler-dealers, freethinkers, and Freemasons seeking to divide the nation in the name of individuals without roots, at a time when the country had such a great need for unity after the debacle of 1870. The multiple politico-financial scandals that tarnished the elites in power (the failure of the Union Générale bank in 1882, the Panama Canal scandal in 1892) were abundantly cited to show the hypocrisy and venality of the republican leaders, who were said to be attempting to hold onto power by all means to ensure that they would grow still wealthier, even if that meant destroying social and educational institutions that had proved their value. *La Croix,* a newspaper created in 1883 to mobilize the Catholic camp against attacks on the congregations, thus presented itself in 1890 as "the most anti-Jewish newspaper in France." At the same time, Charles Maurras, who was getting ready to promote his doctrine of "integral nationalism" as the head of the Action française movement (1899), denounced the "four confederate states" (Protestants, Jews, Freemasons, and "Métèques"—that is, aliens), whom he said were seeking to destroy France and its Catholic heritage, the better to seize power and promote their private interests.[33] It was also in this context that the republican camp decided in 1904 to ban the congregations, who had made themselves infamous with their virulent anti-Dreyfus stance in 1898–1901, along with the Catholic press.

In addition to acknowledging this climate of extreme tension and these ultranationalist, anti-Semitic, and willingly conspiracy-minded reactions, it is important to take the measure of the upheaval that these educational transformations represented for a large sector of the country. For millions of parents who had experienced only religious schools, it was incomprehensible that those schools had been suddenly deprived of public subsidies and that their instructors were prevented from teaching their classes because the congregations had been banned.[34] When *La Croix* launched the Committee of Justice and Equality in 1896 in preparation for the elections of 1898, the first demand was justice in education and the end of the double taxation of Catholics, whose taxes helped to finance secular schools and who also had to pay the fees for religious schools for their own children. The Catholic camp saw this as an infamous injustice that was associated with all the forces

---

33. See C. Maurras, *Enquête sur la monarchie,* first published in 1900–1901 in *La Gazette de France,* definitive edition published in 1924 (Nouvelle imprimerie nationale).

34. It was also following the expulsion of the congregations and the "affair of the cards" that Dreyfusard intellectuals like Péguy decided to break with the Radical and Socialist Left, which in their eyes was guilty of dividing the country in order to ensure the success of their political careers. See C. Péguy, "Notre jeunesse," *Cahiers de la quinzaine,* 1910.

deemed to be anti-Christian (including Socialists, Freemasons, and Jews).[35] This demand was to play a structuring role in bonding together right-wing groups in the following decades. The group Action libérale populaire (ALP), founded in 1901 by the Catholics Albert de Mun and Jacques Piou to try to influence the Republic from the inside and to end its attacks on Catholics, gained the support of the Committee of Justice and Equality (renamed the Catholic Committee for Electoral Action in 1900) a few years later, thanks especially to the militant activism of Raymond de La Rocque, the father of Colonel François de La Rocque, who later founded the French Social Party (PSF) in the 1930s.

Life and Death of the State Budget for Churches

We must also emphasize the shock that the suppression of the budget for the churches and the law of 1905 separating church and state represented for Catholics. The trauma was comparable to that caused by the expropriation of the Church's assets in 1789 (and their privatization to the advantage of vile speculators, which was still being denounced by Balzac and the young Victor Hugo in 1830–1840) and the civil constitution of the clergy adopted by the National Assembly in July 1790 and validated, against his will, by Louis XVI in August 1790. All this was topped off by the establishment of a budget for the churches that allowed the state to pay priests. The legislation of 1790 also included a complete reorganization of church governance. The dioceses were modeled on the departments, and thousands of parishes were redrawn, combined, or suppressed (redistributions that villagers often saw as being to their disadvantage and to the advantage of the towns, even if the reality is more complex and variable from one territory to another). The curés and bishops were henceforth to be elected in the framework of cantonal and departmental electoral assemblies. In addition to the fact that these assemblies excluded poor peasants and were often dominated by the wealthiest electors (especially at the departmental level), the most striking aspect of the new system was that the religious authorities had completely lost control of the selection of the curés and bishops, and that because everyone had to contribute to the budget for the churches, the citizens who were the least religiously observant were judged to be just as qualified to participate in the vote as those who were more devout. For many believers and priests, this was too much, and in 1791 they refused to swear allegiance to the new constitution. These "refractory priests" represented about 46 percent of the clergy on the scale of the country as a whole, and they were to

---

35. See the Committee's manifesto published on the front page of *La Croix,* 11 November 1896.

play a central part in the opposition to the Paris authorities in the quasi civil war that broke out after the mass conscription of February 1793.[36] The concordat of 1801 between the Napoleonic government and the papacy did away with this audacious elective system (bishops were henceforth to be appointed by the minister of the interior after coming to an agreement with the apostolic nuncio, and then, in their turn, the bishops would appoint the curés, as in the past) but retained the church budget established in 1790. The law of 1905 subsequently canceled the state's appointment of the bishops (which had been a very theoretical power, since the nuncio's prior agreement was required, and which now returned entirely to the papacy) and above all, it put an end to the church budget.

In practice, this budget had already undergone many variations in the course of the nineteenth century. Between 1851 and 1872, censuses of the population had included questions on religion. The results obtained were in principle supposed to determine the division of the church budget among the three recognized religions (Catholicism, Protestantism, Judaism) objectively, but this experiment was tarnished by various manipulations of the results published at the local level concerning the Protestant Church.[37] In practice, the Catholic Church still represented about 97–98 percent of both the faithful and the budgets, and the setting of the overall amount allocated to the churches was a highly political exercise in negotiation between the state and the ecclesiastical authorities, under the watchful eye of the electors. During the Restoration and under the July Monarchy, the Church obtained a significant increase in its budget, and then again under the Second Empire. In all, between 1820 and 1870, the Church's budget amounted to about 0.3–0.5 percent of the national revenue. That sum may seem modest, and in fact, it is extraordinarily smaller than the level of resources available to the Church under the Old Regime,[38] but it nonetheless represented a considerable burden for the state.

In fact, we have to place ourselves in a general context of very weak state intervention in economic life, where the totality of receipts and public expenditures

36. An event that triggered the war in Vendée, the *levée en masse* of 300,000 men was approved by the Convention on 23 February 1793 in order to reinforce the armies.

37. See E. Poulat, "Les cultes dans les statistiques officielles en France au 19e siècle," *Archives de sociologie des religions,* 1956.

38. The Church's resources in 1789 are generally estimated to have been about 150 million livres (including 70 million in real estate incomes and 80 million in tithes), or about 4 percent of the national revenue at the time (around 4 billion livres). See C. Jourdain, *Le budget des cultes en France depuis le Concordat jusqu'à nos jours* (Hachette, 1859), 1–2. This is possibly an underestimate.

barely reached 8 to 9 percent of the national revenue, and where the quasi-totality of the resources was absorbed by sovereign expenditures (police, judicial system, general administration, the army), which left very little for the other positions.[39] Specifically, at the beginning of the 1870s the church budget was approximately the same size as the total budget for public education (all levels taken together, from primary school to university)—that is, about 0.3 percent of the national revenue in both cases. Then the two budgets cross: the church budget began to continuously erode at the end of the 1870s, to the point that in 1905, the last year before its definitive suppression, it represented barely more than 0.1 percent of the national revenue.[40] At the same time, the resources allocated for public education rose to 0.6 percent of the national revenue, essentially because the state undertook to remunerate public school teachers.[41] In public budgets that were on the whole small in comparison to present-day budgets, a complete upheaval took place between 1875 and 1905, to the detriment of the church budget and to the benefit of the budget for secular primary education.

The 1959 Compromise and the New Public-Private Balance

The interdiction of the teaching congregations and the suppression of the church budget in 1904–1905 did not put an end to public-private confrontations—far from it. In primary education, the share of private schools stabilized at around 20 percent during the interwar period, with a tendency to decrease, which is explained by both the slow movement of de-Christianization and cost-free public education. The Vichy regime multiplied measures favoring the private schools (the reestablishment of the teaching congregations, the development of municipal subsidies favoring private schools) that were then gaining ground,[42] but these decisions

---

39. See chapter 1, figure 1.7.
40. The church budget (pensions included) rose from about 20 million francs in 1810 (approximately 0.3 percent of the national revenue of about 7 billion) to 40 million in 1830 (almost 0.5 percent of the national revenue of around 9 billion), and to 60 million in 1872 (the nominal maximum reached, but only 0.3 percent of the national revenue, then close to 20 billion), and then fell to only 40 million in 1905 (0.1 percent of the national income of 40 billion). On the church budget, see Jourdain, *Le budget des cultes,* 291–324; J. M. Leniaud, *Le budget des cultes* (École des Chartes, 2007), 73–79.
41. In 1905, the budget for public education was about 240 million francs (including more than 150 million for the remuneration of school teachers, or 0.6 percent of a national income of 40 billion. See the Law establishing the expenditure and revenue budget for the financial year 1905, J.O. 23 April 1905, 2583–2584.
42. See Luc, Condette, and Verneuil, *Histoire de l'enseignement,* 200–214.

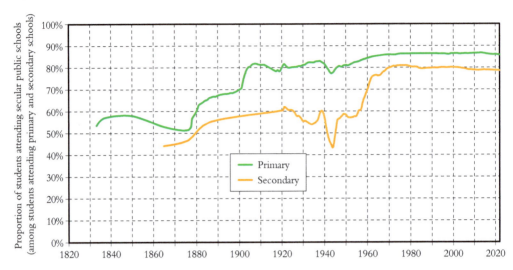

FIGURE 3.9. The share of the public schools in primary and secondary education

The proportion of students attending public schools has always been smaller in secondary educa-tion (*collèges* and lycées) than in primary education. After a decrease in attendance at public schools during the Vichy regime and several increases during the 1930s and 1950s when public secondary schools became free of charge, the development of private education under contract after the Debré law was adopted in 1959 led to a stabilization of public / private education starting in the 1960s, with a small decline in public schools in the recent period.

Sources and series: unehistoireduconflitpolitique.fr

were canceled when Liberation came, and the share of private education began to fall again after 1945. In the late 1950s, it was scarcely more than 15 percent (see figure 3.9).

But it was above all in secondary education that the battle was now being waged. Despite the attempts made by the governments of the Third Republic between 1875 and 1910 to create new public middle schools and high schools, the share of private education remained extremely high: private and religious schools enrolled between 40 and 50 percent of students in secondary education at the beginning of the twentieth century and during the interwar period, both for boys and for girls.[43] Starting in the 1920s, the central debate was about public secondary education, which was at that time not free of charge, and its cost was largely unaffordable for families of modest and average means. Since school attendance was obligatory until

---

43. Secondary education long remained something only for boys: girls represented little more than 1 percent of the students in middle schools and lycées in the early 1880s, about one-quarter on the eve of World War I, one-third around 1930, and half (or even a little more) since 1960.

the age of thirteen, children whose families could not afford secondary education generally bided their time in primary school classes that were dubbed "superior" and were conceived for this purpose. The Catholic camp was strongly opposed to the prospect of free public secondary schools, because it would constitute a new, unfair competition with the private schools, which would then be in danger of experiencing the same fate that befell primary education. Édouard Herriot—who was appointed minister of education in 1926, after having served as president of the Council of Ministers under the Cartel of the Left in 1924—maneuvered very cleverly. He multiplied the gateways that permitted pupils in superior primary schools to attend certain courses in the public middle schools, still free of charge because they remained officially pupils in primary school. The coexistence of students who paid fees and those who did not quickly proved impracticable, and free education was gradually extended to all public middle schools and high schools between 1927 and 1932.[44] Although private schools obtained favorable measures under the Vichy government and regained part of the terrain they had lost, the progress of cost-free secondary education resumed its course after 1945 and gradually threatened private secondary schools with marginalization.

Faced with this competition it deemed unfair, the Catholic camp mobilized to obtain subsidies under the iron rule of the MRP (Mouvement républicain populaire), a Catholic-social party that was neck and neck with the French Communist Party, and ahead of the SFIO (the French Section of the Workers' International). The Barangé law adopted in 1951 on the initiative of the MRP, with the support of the RPF (Rassemblement du peuple français, Charles de Gaulle's political party), instituted an allocation of 1,000 francs per trimester per child that parents could use to pay the fees of the public or private school of their choice. But the amount soon proved ridiculously inadequate, considering the inflation at the time.[45] Thanks to the fact that they were free of charge, middle schools and public lycées were tremendously successful in the 1950s and seemed to be about to eliminate private schools altogether (see figure 3.9). In the end, it was the Gaullist government, with the Debré law of 1959, that was to bring about the adoption of the new educational system that the French Right and the parents of pupils in private schools had been hoping for since *La Croix* created the Committee of Justice and Equality in 1896. The new legislation produced a permanent framework

---

44. Jean Zay, the Front populaire's minister of public education in 1936–1937, extended the age of compulsory school attendance from thirteen to fourteen, but he still did not succeed in imposing a single middle school that would take all children from the entire cohort. which would become effective only in 1975, after the Berthoin reform of 1959 went fully into force.

45. The national revenue per inhabitant exceeded 270,000 francs in 1951.

that made it possible to grant public subsidies to private schools that were under contract with the state. Concretely, teachers in private schools became public employees paid by the state, under the same conditions as the teachers in public schools. Private schools had to agree to follow the same academic programs. But they retained the right to choose their students individually, following their own procedures, on the condition that no student would be rejected solely on grounds of origin or belief. They could also continue to make families pay additional fees in addition to the public financing, which gave them supplementary funds that public schools did not have.

Facing this competition that had become unfair to public education, the Comité national d'action laïque (National Committee for Secular Action, an association founded in 1953) launched a vast petition (10.8 million signatures, the largest in French history up to that time) and organized a huge rally (400,000 persons) at the Bois de Vincennes in June 1960. It was not a success, because the Debré law had created a strong right-wing parliamentary majority: the Christian Democratic, liberal, and moderate deputies were now solidly allied with the Gaullists, although some people accused the latter of presidentialism and an authoritarian use of power. The Guermeur law of 1977 completed the Debré law by strengthening the powers of the principals of private schools to choose their teachers, who were now appointed on their recommendation rather than only their agreement. In 1984, the Socialist majority tried to constitute a "great unified public educational service." Concretely, this meant abrogating the right of private schools receiving public funds to choose their teachers and their students and subjecting them, on these two crucial points, to common rules. But this project was launched three years after the Socialists' victory in 1981, when the new government was already very unpopular, and it ended up being withdrawn in the face of an unprecedented uprising of the parents of children in private schools. After the first act that took place between 1875 and 1905, the second part of the battle between the public and the private was to be played out between 1959 and 1984, and it turned to the advantage of the private.

The Geography of Religion and Private Schools

Ultimately, the compromise of 1959 led to a stabilization of the public-private division, after more than a century of incessant variations. In primary education, the share of the private schools has stabilized at around 14 percent since the 1960s, with a slight rise since 2010. Girls and boys have been attending public and private schools in almost the same proportions since the early 1970s, thus putting an end to a tradition going back to the beginning of the nineteenth century (see figure 3.7). In secondary education, private schools' share has stabilized at about 20 percent since the end of the 1960s, though there has been an underlying increase during the recent period that is beginning to become significant, even more than in primary education (see figure 3.9). The proportion of students attending private schools has thus risen from about 19 percent in the 1970s to more than 21 percent in the 2010s and at the beginning of the 2020s, with a particularly marked progression in the richest territories.

Generally speaking, it is essential to draw a clear distinction between the geography of beliefs and religious practices on the one hand, and the geography of private education on the other. The two naturally intersect in part, but only in part, and the transformations of each of them often follow quite distinct logics and temporalities. Concretely, the general decline in religious practices today means that the recourse to private education has far more to do with educational competition than of a strictly religious logic. To be sure, the desire to find the best possible school for one's child, or simply the one most in conformity with one's values and personal, familial, and vocational experience, has always played a central role in educational choices. But the fact is that over time, the question of the Catholic religion (to which the immense majority of private schools continue to adhere by tradition) has lost much of its importance.[46]

In the study of religious geography, one of the oldest sources concerns the proportion of refractory priests in 1791. The data have been collected and studied at the level of the districts (groups of cantons) by the US historian Timothy Tackett.[47] This is not, strictly speaking, a source on faith or religious practice, because for a priest, the decision to refuse to swear allegiance to the constitution could be the result of a multitude of local factors, connected, for example, with changes in the boundaries of parishes or with the circumstances of the sale of national goods. It is often a matter of a complex compromise between a curé's personal engagement and the pressure exerted by the parishioners, who are themselves shot through with contradictory perceptions and experiences. The fact remains that the geography

---

46. We will return to this at the end of this chapter, but the recourse to private schools is increasingly one of the strategies of the most favored classes for avoiding contact with less privileged classes.

47. See T. Tackett, *Religion, Revolution, and Regional Culture in 18th-Century France: The Ecclesiastical Oath of 1791* (Princeton University Press, 1986). The district is an administrative unit intermediary between the canton and the department that was used between 1789 and 1799; at the time, the country had about 550 districts (generally, between five and six per department) and 3,000 cantons (between thirty and forty per department).

obtained is on the whole coherent in its main lines with the other sources available, such as the share of children attending private and religious schools, observed at the level of the cantons in 1894 and 2021.[48] We note, for instance, that it is the departments in the west of the country that have both the largest number of refractory priests in 1791 and the biggest share of private schools in primary education in 1894, a regularity that is found again if we examine attendance in private schools in 2021 (see map 3.2).[49]

It would, however, be a mistake to confine ourselves to these overall geographical similarities. To study the practice of religion properly, the most ambitious research project undertaken in France was developed in the 1950s by the canon Fernand Boulard and a team of historians and sociologists on the basis of ecclesiastical archives. The researchers discovered in the documents that the Church preserved at the parish level records of the number of children baptized and catechized, the number of believers attending Sunday mass (*messalisants*) or at least the Easter mass (*pascalisants*), the number who took communion, and so on. The lists covered almost the whole of the territory, for several dates spaced out over the periods 1800–1810 and 1950–1960, and they gave rise to the publication of numerous studies.[50] Although the departmental distributions of religious practice

48. The data on 1894 were preserved in the National Archives and are similar to those used by Siegfried for 1911 (not preserved, unfortunately). The data on 2021 come from the files of the Ministry of National Education, and they are also available at the level of the municipalities. Taking into account the large number of small municipalities without a primary school, we choose to use the data at the cantonal level, because that provides a better indication of the choices available and the practices at the local level. See unehistoireduconflitpolitique.fr, map C3.4, for the geography of private education in 2021 at the level of the municipalities (not the cantons). Let us also add that we limited ourselves to these two years, but these data could potentially be collected and digitized more systematically in order to study the detailed variations over the last two centuries (as we have done, for example, for the data on the wealth of the municipalities and the size of the agglomeration or the municipality).

49. See unehistoireduconflitpolitique.fr, maps C3.5–C3.7, for the geographical distributions of refractory priests in 1789 and of girls and boys attending private schools in 1894.

50. For detailed results emerging from this project, see F. Boulard, G. Cholvy, J. Gadille, and Y. M. Hilaire, *Matériaux pour l'histoire religieuse du peuple français*, 3 vols. (EHESS, 1982–1992). See also F. Boulard, *Premiers itinéraires en sociologie religieuse* (Ouvrières, 1954); G. Le Bras, *Études de sociologie religieuse* (Presses Universitaires de France, 1955); F. A. Isambert and J. P. Terrenoire, *Atlas de la pratique religieuse des catholiques en France* (Presses de la FNSP, 1980); J. P. Terrenoire, "Les pratiques cultuelles dans leur contexte social et historique," *Archives des sciences sociales des religions,* 1982; C. Sorrel, *Les "Matériaux Boulard" trente ans après. Des chiffres et des cartes: Approches sérielles et spatiales en histoire religieuse* (Larhra, 2013). This research program owes a great deal to the works launched during the interwar period by Gabriel Le Bras, who was himself strongly influenced by reading André Siegfried. See G. Le Bras, "Statistique et histoire religieuses. Pour un examen détaillé et pour une analyse historique de l'état du

At the primary level
At the secondary level

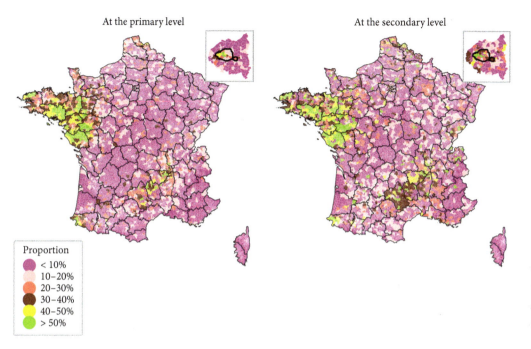

Proportion
- 🟣 < 10%
- 🔴 10–20%
- 🟠 20–30%
- 🟤 30–40%
- 🟡 40–50%
- 🟢 > 50%

MAP 3.2. The geography of private education, 2021

The maps above represent the proportion of students attending primary schools (left) and secondary schools (right) by canton (national average: 14% in primary, 21% in secondary).

Sources and series: unehistoireduconflitpolitique.fr

estimated in this way are on the whole quite close to those obtained on the basis of the number of refractory priests in 1791 or the enrollments in private schools in 1894 or 2021, one of the most striking results of this inquiry is the discovery of very large variations at the local level (which could reflect difficulties connected with the collection and preservation of the documents). Villages and towns not far from each other sometimes had very different practices related to different experiences with curés, monks, or bishops in the neighborhood in connection with various real property systems at the local level, and in accord with configurations that are difficult to study precisely on a case-by-case basis. In addition to numerous regional and local variations, we observe on average a relatively strong positive relation between religious practice, economic patrimony, and political

catholicisme dans les diverses régions de France," *Revue d'histoire de l'Église de France*, 1931; D. Julia, "Un passeur de frontières. Gabriel Le Bras et l'enquête sur la pratique religieuse en France," *Revue d'histoire de l'Église de France*, 2006.

positioning. In the counts made in Paris in 1903–1908, Boulard and his colleagues found, for example, that the proportion of *pascalisants* in the population was only 5 percent in the 20th arrondissement and 8 percent in the 19th arrondissement, whereas it reached 54 percent in the 8th and 57 percent in the 7th.[51] In the same period, all the right-wing parties taken together obtained, respectively, 64 percent and 87 percent of the votes in the 7th and 8th arrondissements in the first round of the legislative elections of 1906, as contrasted with only 17 percent and 21 percent in the 19th and 20th arrondissements.[52]

In a very rich inquiry (both qualitative and quantitative) conducted in 1966, Guy Michelat and Michel Simon clearly demonstrated the complexity of the relations between social class, religious identity, and political attitude. Based on dozens of detailed interviews with people of all social origins and beliefs, they describe how Catholics are characterized in particular by an absolute fear of communism. Of course, believers recognize a form of kinship on principles ("Christ was the first Communist," "Communists sometimes do good things at the local level for schools and dispensaries, whereas the others say there is never enough money"), but they absolutely reject the negation of the family, small property holding, the individual, and the role of the mother / housewife, which they perceive in communism. In addition, believers have a very negative view of Communist countries. On the basis of a national sample representing 1,800 persons, Michelat and Simon also show that there is a very strong statistical association between having a patrimony, religious belief, and voting for right-wing candidates, without any one factor completely overshadowing the others. In other words, religious belief always has an autonomous impact on political behavior, even when controlling for wealth, objective and subjective social class, income, and other factors, and vice versa.[53] This result is found in all the postelectoral surveys conducted from the 1960s up to the present; if today there is still a positive correlation between Catholic religious practice and the level of patrimony and income, the latter explains only part of the effect of religion on the right-wing vote (generally less than half).[54]

---

51. See Boulard et al., *Matériaux pour l'histoire religieuse,* 1:207, table 75.14.

52. We will return in chapter 9 to the connection between Catholicism and the right-wing vote, particularly during this pivotal period and in comparison with the current situation.

53. See G. Michelat and M. Simon, *Classe, religion et comportement politique* (Presses de la FNSP, 1977); G. Michelat and M. Simon, "Religion, classe sociale et comportement électoral: La dimension symbolique," in *Explication du vote. Un bilan des études électorales en France,* ed. D. Gaxie (Presses de la FNSP, 1985).

54. See T. Piketty, *Capital et idéologie* (Seuil, 2019), 901–903; T. Piketty, "Brahmin Left vs. Merchant Right. Rising Inequality and the Changing Structure of Political Conflict" (World Inequality Lab working paper 2018 / 07), figures 2.6b–2.6d.

From the point of view of the geography of the whole country, we must also note the complexity of the relations of religious proximity (such as the proportions of refractory priests, or children attending private schools) and indicators of educational and economic development. Among the most Catholic regions, there were some that were lagging historically in terms of educational and economic development in continental France in the eighteenth and nineteenth centuries (for example, western France, particularly Brittany and Vendée), but there were also others that on the contrary figure among the most advanced (such as Alsace). Above all, we must note the extent of the variations within each region, at the municipal level and at the individual level, particularly in relation to local and familial trajectories and collectivities' and families' experiences with the Church and its different institutions.

Private Education Overrepresented in Metropoles and Towns

We now return to the geography of private education. At the departmental level, the share of private schools corresponds to religious practice, for example in the west of the country. But as soon as we return to a more granular level, things get more complicated. In particular, in 1894, as in 2021, we see that private education is especially overrepresented in the metropoles, and to a lesser degree in the towns, whereas it is relatively scarce in villages and in the suburbs. In 2021, the position of the metropoles was particularly strong in private secondary education, even more than in private primary education, as well as in primary education for boys in 1894. The position of villages is especially weak in both cases (see figure 3.10). In comparison with the map of religious practice, the low level of private education in villages shows that other factors are involved.[55]

Two main explanations that are closely linked are pertinent here: the lesser availability of private schools in villages and suburbs, and the parents' income level. If we examine separately poor villages and rich ones (the 50 percent with the lowest and highest incomes), we find that the diffusion of private education is just as small in both types of villages, in 1894 and in 2021. This suggests an explanation based on supply. At the level of the towns, recourse to private education is only a little greater in the rich towns than in the poor towns. The effect of income is considerably

---

55. Religious practice is generally at least as assiduous in villages as it is in towns and metropoles, according to Fernand Boulard's materials. The proportion of refractory priests estimated on the basis of data by district is, moreover, just as great in villages as it is in towns, which may reflect conflicts between villages and towns within districts that include towns). See unehistoireduconflitpolitique.fr, figure B3.5c.

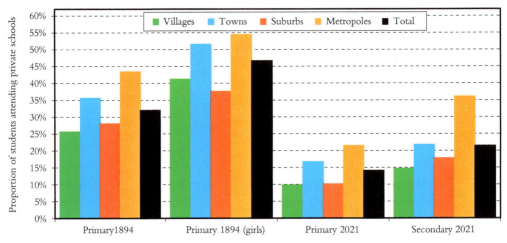

FIGURE 3.10. Villages, towns, suburbs, metropoles: The share of private education in 1894 and 2021

In 1894, as in 2021, the proportion of students enrolled in private schools (observed at the level of the cantons) was greater in the metropoles and towns than in the villages and suburbs. The gap between metropoles and towns is particularly large in the case of secondary education in 2021 (in comparison to primary education) and for boys in primary school in 1894 (in comparison to girls). Note: Villages, towns, suburbs, and metropoles are defined as they were in chapter 2 (conurbations of fewer than 2,000 inhabitants, conurbations with between 2,000 and 100,000 inhabitants, and secondary municipalities and principal municipalities of conurbations of more than 100,000 inhabitants, respectively).
Sources and series: unehistoireduconflitpolitique.fr

greater in the rich suburbs, and in 2021 it was even clearer than it was in 1894. This is especially the case for secondary education; in 2021 the recourse to private schools in rich suburbs was almost as great as it was in towns. Still, it is much smaller than it is in the metropoles, which are the leaders by far in terms of the number of private secondary schools.[56]

This reflects considerable territorial disparities in the availability of private education, as well as a major interaction with the level of wealth, which increases the demand for private schools and sometimes makes it possible to secure the opening up of supplementary classes (and more rarely, of additional private schools). In the Paris region, the spread of private education has always been historically greater in the upper-crust territories than in the others, and this disparity has grown over recent decades. In 2022, whereas on average 14 percent of the pupils in primary education

---

56. See unehistoireduconflitpolitique.fr, figures B3.5a–B3.5d. It will be noted that the effect of wealth (real estate capital or income) goes in the opposite direction so far as the refractory priests are concerned: their proportion is still a little higher in poor villages, towns, suburbs, and metropoles than it is in rich villages, towns, suburbs, and metropoles.

were enrolled in private schools, their share reached almost 26 percent in Paris and 6 percent in Hauts-de-Seine, as opposed to 6 percent in Seine-Saint-Denis, for example. In secondary schools, the share of private schools was 21 percent on average in country as a whole, but it reached 37 percent in Paris and 26 percent in Hauts-de-Seine, as opposed to 13 percent in Seine-Saint-Denis and 15 percent in Val-de-Marne.[57] We also note that the proportion of students attending private schools greatly increased in the capital between 2000 and 2022: it rose from 31 percent to 36 percent in middle schools, and from 37 percent to 40 percent in lycées. Recent research has shown that this development reflects a growing recourse to private education on the part of the most privileged social categories. Conversely, disadvantaged social categories are almost completely absent from the capital's middle schools and lycées. Because admission policies are not known and thus cannot be evaluated and discussed publicly, it is impossible to say to what extent this reflects just the choices by families of modest means to forgo private schools (because of the cost) or also the admission choices made by the schools themselves. In the end, the segregation prevailing in the capital's middle schools is partly explained by residential segregation and partly by recourse to private schools.[58]

The New Educational Inequalities and the Battle of the Algorithms

Let us conclude this chapter by emphasizing that questions of education have played a structuring role in political and electoral conflict over the past two centuries, and that along with questions of access to healthcare and other public services, they certainly will continue to do so in the future. The French educational system is still shot through with profound inequalities, in primary and secondary education as well as in higher education. In primary and secondary education, teachers who hold temporary positions and have little experience are overrepresented in the most disadvantaged territories, to the extent that the average salary of a teacher is in reality a growing function of the proportion of socially advantaged

---

57. See *Repères et références statistiques 2022,* Ministère de l'éducation nationale, 81.
58. See J. Grenet and Y. Souidi, *Renforcer la mixité sociale au collège: Une évaluation des secteurs multi-collèges à Paris* (IPP, 2021); J. Grenet, *"La tentation du privé." Situation et avenir de l'offre éducative à Paris* (IPP, 2022). Out of the ninety-one lycées in Paris (forty-two public lycées and thirty-nine public lycées), we note that the forty lycées with the smallest proportions of students from disadvantaged occupational backgrounds (less than 4 percent) are all private lycées, without exception, which reminds us that the sometimes excessive elitism of the best public schools never reaches the extreme level of social exclusion observed in private schools (which, it is true, does not set the bar very high). A similar situation prevails for middle schools.

pupils in the school. In higher education, three to four times as much public money is invested per student in the selective programs of study than in the least funded programs, where the most socially disadvantaged students are concentrated. If the system is struggling to reform itself, that is also because the educational options put at stake what is most precious and most private in families, and thus any change arouses considerable tensions between social classes and territories as well as within the latter. In the next chapters, we will see that the impact of education and diploma type on political behavior and the right-wing, center, and left-wing vote has undergone important changes over a long period— more than the impact of the level of wealth on the vote (which by comparison seems more stable)—and that these differentiated changes challenge specific views of the role of education in the long-term transformations of the socioeconomic system and the productive structure.[59]

A new actor has recently appeared in this long history of political conflicts over the educational system: the algorithms that govern the admission of students into secondary schools and institutions of higher education. In theory, replacing the system of individual admission decisions (which are sometimes subject to pressure from the families with the most social, cultural, and economic capital) with a centralized procedure that takes into account the pertinent social, educational, and geographic criteria, using a method that is objective and cannot be manipulated, could be a source of collective progress. In practice, however, there is a risk of promoting a generalized culture of competition and exacerbating inequalities. A recent experiment in Paris that assigned students to different public middle schools in order to rebalance the schools' social mixture showed that it is possible to significantly increase balance by changing the admission procedures.[60] The great limitation of this experiment was that the private schools—although they are well financed with public monies paid by all taxpayers—entirely escaped these common procedures and continued to recruit their students in accord with their own rules (as they did in recruiting their teachers). This greatly diminished the possibilities of reducing social segregation in schools, especially because such a policy limited to public institutions can also to an extent help fuel the departure of the most privileged students to private schools. In theory, it is absolutely possible to imagine a system in which a certain diversity of statuses would be retained—for example, that some schools would continue to be operated by diverse associative structures on a nonprofit basis—and at the same time, all schools would be subject to common

59. See, in particular, chapter 11.
60. See Grenet and Souidi, *Renforcer la mixité sociale au collège*.

procedures concerning admissions.[61] However, it's very likely that such a transformation would not be to the taste of some parents who are very committed to the educational options in private schools and who would think, for example, that such a change would unduly favor parents and pupils who are less committed and less meritorious. As always in the history of education, this type of transformation almost inevitably implies tense and conflictual processes.

In higher education, the development of centralized procedures for assigning young students to different tracks (Admission Post-Bac [APB] in 2009, then Parcoursup since 2017) has been central to the debate since the beginning of the 2010s. These procedures are on the verge of upending the structure of the system of higher education, particularly the borderlines between selective tracks and nonselective tracks. The question of the social and academic criteria to be used to share out the places in IUTs (university technical institutes) between candidates for vocational, technological, and general bachelor degrees, for example, raises highly political issues. To this day, however, the procedures of APB and Parcoursup have been characterized above all by a lack of transparency and by multiple misunderstandings and frustrations among lycée students and their parents. This has to do especially with the repeated refusal by the governments in place and by the administration to open up access to the data that is needed to nourish democratic debate on these essential questions. In addition, no assignment procedure will be able to resolve the fundamental contradiction in the educational policy of recent decades—namely, the fact that the considerable increase in the number of students in higher education has been accompanied by a stagnation in the public resources invested in education. Without a return to the forward movement of investment in education, which saw historic progress between 1900 and 1910 and between 1980 and 1990 (from 0.5 percent to almost 6 percent of the national income), and which has stagnated in recent decades,[62] it will be difficult to satisfactorily meet expectations. Obviously, the question of education is not about to stop playing a central role in the political and democratic confrontation.

---

61. Generally, the question of the governance of schools and the involvement of citizens in the organization of public services and the welfare state as a whole has always been a central question, and it ought to be more and more central in the framework of a welfare state whose cost reaches or exceeds 50 percent of the national income.

62. See chapter 1, figure 1.7.

CHAPTER 4

The New Diversity of Origins

We turn now to the new diversity of origins observed in Metropolitan France in recent decades. Since 1960–1970 we have seen the development of non-European immigration on a scale that can certainly be considered relatively modest in absolute terms, but which nonetheless constitutes a significant change with respect to earlier periods. Moreover, the decline of Catholicism and the rise in Islam have led to a new form of religious pluralism in the national territory, in proportions unprecedented for centuries. Starting in the 1980s and 1990s, these developments have helped sustain the emergence of new anti-immigrant political tendencies, even if one also thinks that the vote for the National Front (FN), and then for the National Rally (RN), expresses social and political concerns other than a simple obsession with migration and identity. In reality, one of the main results of our inquiry is that the socioeconomic variables connected with wealth, occupation, and diploma are determinants of voting far more important than the variables connected with origins (even for the FN-RN vote, which since 2000–2010 no longer has any relation to proximity to people of immigrant origin—or indeed, it may even have a negative relation).[1] The fact that public debate often focuses on identitarian questions testifies above all to an obliviousness to the social question and the abandonment of any ambitious prospect of transforming the economic system in a context of a worsening of territorial inequalities.

The fact remains that the question of the conflicts connected with the growing diversity of origins within the French people arises and deserves to be examined in detail. We will therefore begin by analyzing the evolution of populations of foreign origin in France on the national level since the nineteenth century, then turn to studying the geographical and spatial dimensions, and in particular how rich and poor villages, towns, suburbs, and metropoles have been exposed to significantly different experiences of the diversity of origins over recent decades. Finally, we will emphasize everything that brings the different categories of poor territories closer together.

---

1. See chapters 11, 12, and 13 (in particular, figures 11.18–11.19).

The Diversification of Origins in France since the Nineteenth Century

Let us begin by recalling the main lines of the evolution of the population of foreign nationality and its origins since the nineteenth century. The censuses include detailed information about nationality from 1851 on. For the preceding periods, the estimates can only be approximate.[2] We note that the proportion of foreigners (in the sense of nationality) within the metropolitan population underwent irregular growth over the course of the past two centuries, with a first peak in the interwar period (6.6 percent in 1931) and a second peak in the present period (7.4 percent in 2022) (see figure 4.1).

At the time of the 1851 census, there were very few persons of foreign nationality in France: scarcely 1.1 percent of the total population. The nationalities most highly represented were Belgians, followed by Italians and Spaniards. Foreigners from nearby countries were long the largest contingent, and they continued to occupy a central position. Thus, Belgians were the most numerous foreigners in the census of 1851 and they remained so until the census of 1896; then it was Italians from 1901 to 1962, Spaniards in the census of 1968, and finally Portuguese since the census of 1975.[3] The proportion of foreigners underwent an accelerated progression starting in 1850–1860, then stabilized at about 3 percent between the censuses of 1891 and 1911. The increase between 1851 and 1891 was accompanied by the first social and political tensions, leading to the massacre of Italian workers in the department of Gard in 1893.[4] The immigration question did not yet have the prominence that it later acquired, but these tensions nonetheless correspond to an initial hardening of attitudes with regard to foreign workers (soon to be called *métèques* by their detractors), even before World War I.[5]

In 1921, the proportion of foreigners reached 3.9 percent because of the multiple displacements of people connected with the war, and then it progressed very

2. The estimates for 1840 indicated below were calculated supposing that the evolution between 1840 and 1851 was of the same kind as the one seen between 1851 and 1856 (that is, a slow increase in the proportion of foreigners).
3. With the exception of the census of 1982, in which Algerians were more numerous than the Portuguese. Since the census of 1990, the Portuguese have been slightly ahead of the Algerians.
4. G. Noiriel, *Le massacre des Italiens, Aigues-Mortes, 17 août 1893* (Fayard, 2010).
5. The *"métèques"* in Charles Maurras's "four confederate states" ("Protestants, Jews, Free Masons, and *métèques*") refers to the foreigners living in France (especially the Italians), and they played a significant role in his overall schema seeking to denounce all those who were contributing to the dissolution of the nation, even if at that time foreigners did not have the same symbolic importance to nationalists that Freemasons, Protestants, and Jews did. See C. Maurras, *Enquête sur la monarchie* (1900–1901; Nouvelle imprimerie nationale,1924).

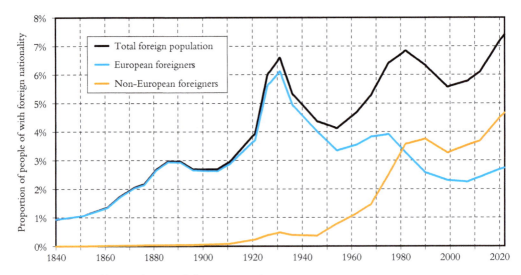

FIGURE 4.1. The population with foreign nationality, 1840–2022

The proportion of persons with foreign nationality rose from 1.1% of the total population in 1851 to 6.6% in 1931, and 7.4% in 2022. Foreigners with non-European nationalities constituted less than 0.1% of total population until 1911. They became more numerous than European foreigners in 1982 (3.5% vs. 3.3%) and represented almost two-thirds of the total in 2022 (4.7% vs. 2.7%). Sources and series: unehistoireduconflitpolitique.fr

rapidly during the 1920s to reach 6.6 percent of the total population in 1931. This first peak corresponds both to a great increase in the number of Italians and Spaniards arriving in France in the 1920s and to the development of new waves of migration from Poland and other countries of Eastern Europe (in particular, Jewish populations fleeing pogroms and conflicts) in a context in which the country was seeking to rebuild itself by calling on the help of foreign labor, and in which numerous age groups had been decimated by the war. Then the economic crisis of the 1930s led to a tight restriction of migratory movements and a hardening of the stipulations for taking in foreigners (whose share of the population fell to 5.3 percent in the 1936 census). It also helped nourish the virulent xenophobia and anti-Semitism that characterized the period, which ended with state anti-Semitism under Vichy and deportations to the death camps.[6]

6. Vichy also launched into a vast project of denaturalization, targeting hundreds of thousands of persons who had obtained French nationality during the interwar period (notably, after the law of 1927, which had established a relatively open regime, in a context in which the perceived priority was the growth of the national population). See C. Zalc, *Dénaturalisés. Les retraits de nationalité sous Vichy* (Seuil, 2016).

After World War II, the proportion of foreigners decreased to barely 4 percent before beginning to increase again starting in the 1960s and 1970s, first with Spanish and Portuguese immigration, then with North African and sub-Saharan immigration. In the 1982 census, foreigners from outside Europe reached 3.5 percent of the population and for the first time outnumbered European foreigners (3.3 percent). In 2022, non-Europeans represented almost two-thirds of the immigrant population—4.7 percent of France's total population, as compared to 2.7 percent for European foreigners (see figure 4.1). To be sure, it can be said that these figures remain relatively small in absolute terms, since non-Europeans still represented only a small percentage of the population. But it nonetheless constituted a significant change for a country whose population of non-Europeans on its soil had always been less than 0.1 percent up to World War I, and hardly more than 1 percent up to 1960–1970. In 1911, the last census conducted before the war, scarcely 33,000 non-Europeans were counted in all of continental France, including 10,000 Asians, 20,000 Americans (of North and South America), and only 3,000 Africans.[7] Naturally, France had had economic relations with Africa for centuries, but these relations were maintained through the intermediary of merchants, soldiers, and planters, and they led to encounters in metropolitan territory only in exceptional cases. Let us also recall that from the end of the nineteenth century to the middle of the twentieth, the French colonial empire had a total population in Africa and Indochina comparable to that of continental France (around 40–50 million inhabitants in both cases, or even a little more than 60 million for the empire at its apogee during the interwar period), including a very small fraction of colonists.[8] These were to a large extent two juxtaposed worlds, with major commercial and financial flows between them, of course, but with extremely limited human contacts, notably in continental France, to the point that most metropolitans probably had only a limited awareness of the existence of this other world.

---

7. The extra-European national categories themselves entered the census results only very gradually. The categories "Turks" and "Americans" appeared in 1861, then "Chinese, Indians, and other Asians" in 1872, "Turks and Egyptians" in 1876, "Turks and Africans" in 1881, and "Africans" in 1891. In 1946, "Algerians," "Moroccans," and "Tunisians" were separated from other "Africans," and further decompositions appeared later on.

8. The European colonists (mainly French) represented barely 2 percent of the empire's population, with very large variations: less than 0.1 percent in French West Africa and French Equatorial Africa and in Indochina, 0.5 percent in Madagascar, but as many as 10 percent in North Africa and especially in Algeria (about a million colonists out of a total population of 10 million at the time of the war of independence). See D. Cogneau, *Un empire bon marché. Histoire et économie politique de la colonisation française, 19e–21e siècles* (Seuil, 2023), table 7.1.

World War I marked the first rupture. In the 1920s, populations from Africa and Indochina on metropolitan soil reached a few hundred thousand (no longer just a few thousand) following mobilizations of colonial troops on European battlefields and new demands for labor. These new types of migratory flows (including coerced migrations, in the case of military flows) were developed essentially on the initiative of state authorities and businesses. After 1945, the needs of employers in Metropolitan France once again played a central role in gradually increasing the non-European population to 1 million in the 1970s, 2 million in the 1980s, and about 3 million in 2022. In comparison, at the end of the nineteenth century, the foreign population of European origin was already more than 1 million, and it was about 1.8 million or approximately the same proportion of the total population as it was a century earlier (between 2.5 and 3 percent). At the same time, the non-European population grew from barely 0.1 percent to almost 5 percent of the total population, a nearly fiftyfold increase—starting, it is true, from an infinitesimal level (see figure 4.1).

It will be noted that the composition of non-European foreigners, too, has undergone important transformations in recent decades. Between 1960 and 1980, North Africans (Algerians, Moroccans, Tunisians) alone still represented about 80 percent of the total of non-Europeans, versus sub-Saharan Africans (10 percent) and Asians and others (10 percent). Among the European foreigners, Italians, Spaniards, and Portuguese represented about 70–80 percent of the total between 1960 and 2000, and around 50 percent in 2022 (a level close to that at the beginning of the twentieth century and the interwar period).[9]

Foreigners, Naturalized Citizens, and Long-Term Immigrants

Censuses since 1851 allow us to follow the evolution of naturalized citizens (that is, people who did not have French nationality at birth but acquired it during their lives). The number of naturalized citizens increased considerably over the past two centuries, as some of those issuing from the various waves of immigration settled permanently in France and obtained access to French nationality for themselves and their children.[10] The number of naturalized citizens thus rose from less than

---

9. This is explained by the increasing numbers of Eastern Europeans, but also of Germans, Britons, Belgians, and others. See unehistoireduconflitpolitique.fr, figure B5.1a and appendix B5.

10. Let us recall that since the law of 1889, French law has been based on a twofold right to French nationality—that is, on its automatic nature for those who were born on French soil and / or have at least one parent who was born in France. Persons born in France of parents born outside France must wait until they reach majority (currently, the age of eighteen; before 1974, the

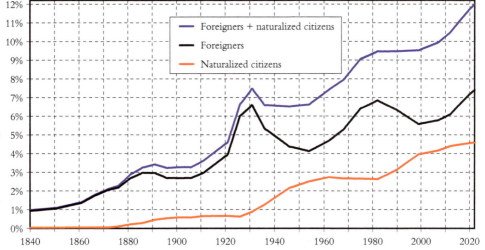

FIGURE 4.2. Foreigners and naturalized citizens, 1840–2022

The proportion of foreigners (persons with foreign nationality) rose from 1.1% of the total population in 1851 to 7.4% in 2022. The proportion of naturalized citizens (persons with French nationality who have acquired French nationality in the course of their lives) rose from less than 0.1% in 1851 to 4.6% in 2022, such that the total combined proportion of foreigners and naturalized French citizens rose from 1.1% to 12.0% between 1851 and 2022.

0.1 percent of the total population in 1851 to 4.6 percent in 2022, growing more regularly than the number of foreigners, who were affected more directly by the vicissitudes of immigration policy. If we take these two categories together, we see that the combined share of foreigners and naturalized citizens grew from 1.1 percent of the total population in 1851 to 4.6 percent in 1921 and 12.0 percent in 2022 (see figure 4.2).[11]

Thus, since the 1921 census it has been possible to follow the evolution of immigrants, who are currently defined by INSEE as persons born abroad who have a foreign nationality (though they can now have French nationality as well).[12] We

---

age of twenty-one) to have access to French nationality (which they obtain automatically if they have resided in France for at least five years between the ages of eleven and eighteen). In that case, they are counted among the naturalized citizens. See P. Weil, *Qu'est-ce qu'un Français? Histoire de la nationalité française depuis la Révolution* (Gallimard, 2002).

11. Note that the large waves of naturalizations in the late 1920s and the early 1930s (following the law of 10 August 1927 on nationality, which made naturalization easier to obtain) and then in the 1980s (following similar measures adopted in 1981–1982) partly explain the concomitant drop in the number of foreigners (hence the interest in looking at the evolution in its totality).

12. This complex definition makes it possible not to count as immigrants any persons born abroad who have French nationality (generally because both their parents are French—for the most

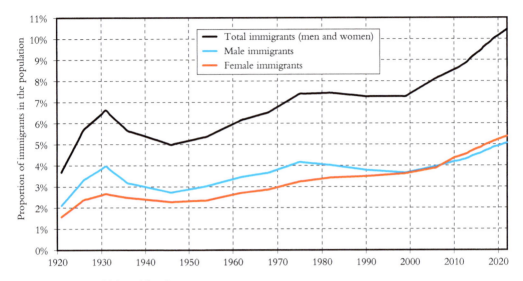

FIGURE 4.3. Male and female immigrants, 1921–2022

The proportion of immigrants (persons born outside France with foreign nationality, and who may now be of French or foreign nationality) rose from 3.7% of the population in 1921 to 10.4% in 2022. Since 2008, the majority of immigrants are female.

Sources and series: unehistoireduconflitpolitique.fr

note that the proportion of immigrants thus defined has risen from 4.1 percent of the population in 1921 to 10.4 percent in 2022. In 2022, immigrants were less numerous by two percentage points than the combined total of foreigners and naturalized citizens, a fact that is explained by the existence of a large number of foreigners and naturalized citizens born in France (who are thus not immigrants). We can also see that since 2008, more than half of immigrants have been women, and this reflects structural changes in the types of jobs occupied by immigrants (from industry to services), as well as the increased importance of the immigration of university students and degree holders.[13]

Over the long term, the most detailed data available concerns persons of foreign nationality, which is especially useful for studying inequalities on the spatial level. In particular, starting with the 1851 census, it is possible to follow the distribution of the foreign population among departments (as well as on the level of

part, these are children of French expatriates), who currently represent about 2.5 percent of the French population. Let us also add that binationals are usually counted as French (insofar as they declare themselves as such in censuses).

13. On these developments, see F. Héran, *Avec l'immigration. Mesurer, débattre, agir* (La Découverte, 2017); E. M. Mouhoud, *L'immigration en France. Mythes et réalités* (Fayard, 2017).

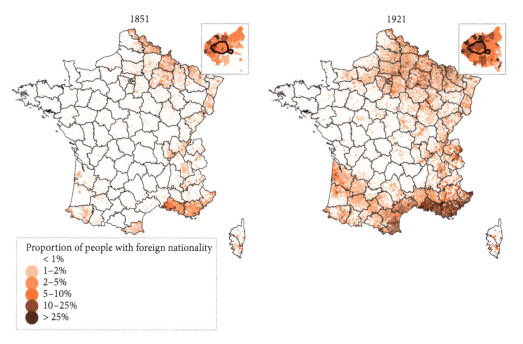

MAP 4.1. The geography of the foreign population in 1851 and 1921

The map represents for each municipality the proportion of persons of foreign nationality within the total population in 1851 (map on the left) and in 1921 (map on the right) (national average: 1.1% in 1851, 3.8% in 1921).

Sources and series: unehistoireduconflitpolitique.fr

the principal municipalities in each department).[14] If we examine geographical distributions, we find that foreign populations have always been heavily concentrated in certain parts of the territory (see maps 4.1 and 4.2). Although the share of the foreign population has risen from 1.1 percent to 7.4 percent on average, over the whole of the national territory, it rose from 3.8 percent to 12.2 percent in the twenty departments with the largest share of foreigners, and from 0.1 percent to 2.7 percent in the twenty departments with the smallest share of foreigners (see figure 4.4). Nonetheless, it should be noted that the internationalization of the

14. For nationality, as for most of the information figuring in the censuses conducted since 1851, the data are available at the level of the departments, municipalities that are the main towns of an arrondissement (corresponding to subprefectures), and municipalities of more than 10,000 inhabitants (which enables us to deduce the distributions in smaller municipalities from the difference to the departmental data). Starting with the 1962 census, the data are directly available at the level of the 36,000 municipalities. All the details concerning the sources used are available at unehistoireduconflitpolitique.fr.

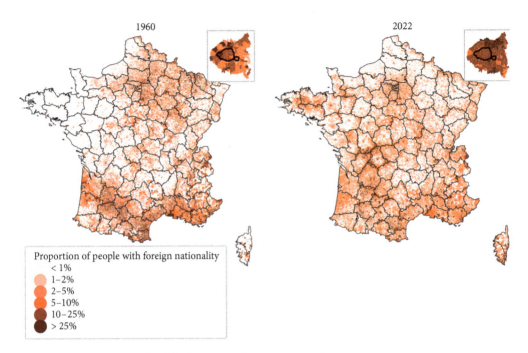

MAP 4.2. The geography of the foreign population in 1960 and 2022

The map represents for each municipality the proportion of persons of foreign nationality in the total population in 1960 (map on the left) and in 2022 (map on the right) (national average: 4.5% in 1960, 7.4% in 2022).

Sources and series: unehistoireduconflitpolitique.fr

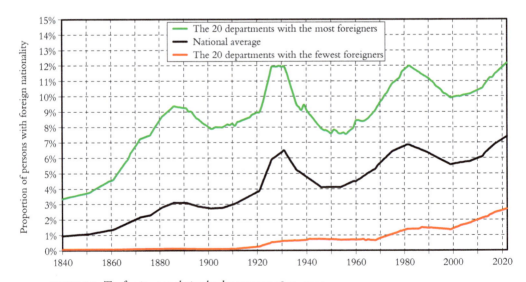

FIGURE 4.4. The foreign population by department, 1840–2022

The proportion of persons of foreign nationality has risen from 1.1% of the total population in 1851 to 7.4% in 2022. On average, it rose from 3.8% to 12.2% in the twenty departments with the largest proportion of foreigners, and from 0.1% to 2.7%.

Sources and series: unehistoireduconflitpolitique.fr

population has affected the entire country, in the sense that the twenty departments with the smallest foreign populations (which in the nineteenth century had
virtually no foreigners) now have a proportion of foreigners almost equivalent to
that of the twenty departments with the largest foreign population in the mid-
nineteenth century (but significantly lower than that of the twenty departments
with the largest foreign presence around 1900).

The Decline in Catholicism, the Rise in Islam: The New Religious Diversity

Perhaps even more than the diversification of foreign origins, one of the most
striking changes in recent decades is the appearance in the metropolitan territory
of a new form of religious diversity, with the acceleration of the decline in Catholicism and the emergence of a Muslim population of a significant size. This change
is partly linked to the preceding one, because the rise in Islam derives in large
measure from North African immigration, but only partly: whereas the evolution
of Catholic religious practices derives from transformations that have been
underway for several centuries, a large number of people with North African ancestry have no Muslim religious practice (whereas conversely, persons of sub-
Saharan or European ancestry may have one). Generally, we must emphasize that
the measure of the population's religious structure and its evolution over a long
period poses considerable difficulties, in France as in all countries. Identity and
religious practice correspond in fact to complex, plural, and changing realities,
and the conclusions drawn always depend in large measure on how the questions
were formulated and how the data were collected. But with the requisite care, we
can nonetheless rely on the research of Fernand Boulard on religious practice (to
which we already referred in chapter 3), the censuses by religion carried out between 1851 and 1872, and the surveys conducted starting in the 1960s to describe
the main lines of the evolution of the population's religious structure over the
past two centuries (see figure 4.5).

Several points must be clarified at the outset. First of all, the censuses conducted
between 1851 and 1872—which are the only censuses conducted in France that include questions on religion—limit themselves to asking "What is your religion?"
without probing for any details concerning the actual practice of religion or the
family's religious origins. In practice, almost 98 percent of the individuals questioned declared that they were "Catholic," 2 percent "Protestant," 0.2 percent "Is-
raelite" (following the terminology of the period), and less than 0.1 percent said

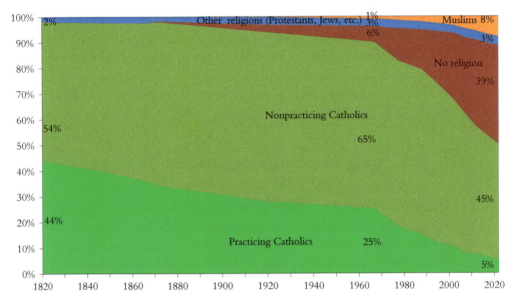

FIGURE 4.5. The religious structure of France, 1820–2022

Between 1820 and 2022, the number of Catholics decreased from 98% to 50% of the population, people who say they have no religion rose from 0.1 to 39%, Muslims from 0.1% to 8%, and other religions (mainly Protestants and Jews) have remained stable around 2–3%. Note: These estimates are based on Boulard's studies of religious practice (1820–1960), the censuses by religion (1851–1872), and studies based on polls (1960–2022). Practicing Catholics are defined as those who attend mass at least once a month.

Sources and series: unehistoireduconflitpolitique.fr

they were "without religion" or had "another religion."[15] However, Boulard's investigations in the ecclesiastical archives show that as early as the beginning of the nineteenth century, this crushing majority of Catholics practiced their religion very unequally in terms of attendance at Sunday mass or Easter mass. Starting in the 1950s and 1960s, we have numerous surveys on the practice of religion that were carried out with representative samples of the population. In particular, most of the exit polls conducted since the legislative elections of 1967 asked questions on the practice of religion that remained relatively homogeneous over time. By

15. "Protestants" were subdivided into approximately two-thirds "Reformed" and one-third "Lutherans." After the loss of Alsace-Moselle, the number of Protestants fell from about 800,000 to 600,000 between the censuses of 1866 and 1872 (from 2.1 to 1.6 percent of the population), and the number of Jews fell from 90,000 to 50,000 (from 0.2 to 0.1 percent of the population). See E. Poulat, "Les cultes dans les statistiques officielles en France au 19e siècle," *Archives de sociologie des religions,* 1956.

supplementing them for earlier periods using Boulard's surveys, we can estimate that the proportion of people who considered themselves Catholic fell from 98 percent at the beginning of the nineteenth century to 90 percent in the 1960s and 50 percent in 2022, whereas the proportion of those who practice their religion (defined here as those who went to mass at least once a month) dropped from a little more than 40 percent at the beginning of the nineteenth century to 25 percent in the 1960s and scarcely 5 percent in 2022 (see figure 4.5).

Over the same period, persons declaring they had no religion rose from barely 0.1 percent of the population in the nineteenth century censuses to 6 percent in the surveys of the 1960s and 39 percent in the early 2020s. Among young people, persons declaring themselves to be without religion clearly outnumbered the self-declared Catholics (whether they practiced or not) in the middle of the 2000s, and they have become three times more numerous than the latter in the most recent surveys available. Everything seems to indicate that these evolutions will continue and that in the coming decades, persons without religion will become a clear majority of the population as a whole.[16]

Concerning Protestants, we note that their share of the population has remained relatively stable at around 2 percent since the early nineteenth century. The available historical works on the question indicate that Protestants represented more than 12 percent of the French population at the beginning of the 1560s, shortly before the outbreak of the Wars of Religion, with a proportion reaching several tens of percent in some regions. At the time of the Edict of Nantes (1598), which marked the end of the hostilities and the beginning of a (relative) tolerance for the Protestant religion, their share in the population was no more than about 9 percent. The pressure to incite forced conversions or exile hardened again during the reign of Louis XIV, when the proportion of Protestants fell to about 4 percent

16. About 60–65 percent of people younger than thirty years old declared themselves to be without religion in the latest surveys, versus barely more than 20 percent saying they are Catholics. We should add that 50 percent of the population (all ages) now declare themselves to be Catholic when asked a question like "What is your religion?" or "Are you Catholic, without religion, [or something else]?" but this share drops to barely more than 30 percent when the question they are asked is "Do you identify with the Catholic religion?' or "Do you identify with a religion, and if so, which one?" This shows that the borderline between Catholics who don't practice their religion and persons without religion is relatively porous; many people answer "Catholic" as a matter of family tradition but do not really identify themselves with the Catholic religion as soon as the question is asked more directly. The data on the sacraments published by the Church of France concerning the numbers of Catholic marriages (about 80 percent of all marriages in the 1950s and 1960s, and 20 percent now) and baptisms (about 70 percent of births in 1980, 50 percent in 2000, and 25 percent today) indicate trends of the same order.

of the population in 1670, and then to around 2 percent in 1685 when the Edict of Nantes was revoked.[17] Starting in 1685, Protestantism was officially banned in the kingdom, except in Alsace, where a large part of the Protestants had taken refuge. The Revolution led to the establishment of freedom of religion and of movement, for Protestants and Jews alike. The Protestant population very slowly increased as a result of the return of the émigrés, but the main effect was to allow Alsatian Protestants to settle anywhere in the territory. The considerable increase in the number of Protestants living in the capital and the role that some of them were to play in finance (for example, Schlumberger) and politics under the Second Empire and the Third Republic would help sustain anti-Protestant nationalist discourses of the Maurassian type at the end of the nineteenth century and the beginning of the twentieth.

The Jewish population underwent a comparable evolution, but starting from a much lower base. In 1789, it was estimated to consist of about 40,000 persons (that is, a little more than 0.1 percent of the country's population), and it was concentrated in Alsace, one of the few regions where Jewish people had been tolerated since the expulsion of the Jews from the kingdom in 1394.[18]

The emancipation of the Jews under the Revolution allowed some of them to settle anywhere in the territory throughout the nineteenth century, and particularly in the capital, from which they had been almost completely absent up to that point. This greatly annoyed some of the traditional elites, especially nobles who had lost much of their former status. After the loss of Alsace-Moselle as a result of the Franco-Prussian War of 1870, a new emigration of Alsatian Jews who wanted to remain in France moved to the capital (including Captain Alfred Dreyfus, who lived in Paris during his high school studies and then at the École Polytechnique), which was to help nourish suspicions that they were guilty of Germanophilia and espionage.

In 1886, the journalist and polemicist Édouard Drumont published *La France juive,* in which he claimed that there were more than 500,000 Jews in the country (which would have represented 1.3 percent of the total population), or six times more than the actual number at that time (around 75,000 Jews, or 0.2 percent of the population). The anti-Semitic writer described a regime entirely corrupted by

---

17. See P. Cabanel, *Histoire des protestants en France 16e–21e siècles* (Fayard, 2012).
18. The Jewish population is thought to have reached 100,000 before the expulsion ordered by Charles VI in 1394 (or about 1 percent of the population at that time, versus about 0.7 percent in France today, and 1.8 percent in the United States). See E. Benbassa, *Histoire des Juifs de France de l'Antiquité à nos jours* (Seuil, 2000); M. Winock, *La France et les juifs de 1789 à nos jours* (Seuil, 2004).

Jews, who pulled all the strings of high finance and politics, such as the Rothschilds. Drumont was elected a deputy for Algiers in 1898 by capitalizing on the virulent discontent of some of the French colonists after the Crémieux Decree of 1870, which granted French citizenship to Algerian Jews. The fact that Adolphe Crémieux (who had already been minister of justice in 1848, and then again in the provisional government of 1870–1871) came from a Jewish family (as did the bankers Michel Goudchaux and Achille Fould, who succeeded each other as ministers of finance in 1848–1849 and then under the Second Empire) was cleverly exploited by Drumont, especially in light of rumors that the Rothschild family (which was to play an essential role in placing with savers the loan intended to finance the war indemnities paid to Prussia following the defeat of 1870) forced the maintenance of the Crémieux Decree after Thiers tried to have it annulled in 1871 to calm the fury of the Algerian colonists. The rise in anti-Semitism was also stoked by the Catholic camp, notably with the Mortara affair of 1858,[19] and then with their opposition to the republican government over its handling of the congregations in the early 1880s and the Dreyfus affair in the late 1890s.[20] Celebrated by *La Croix* and *Le Figaro*, *La France juive* was an immense bestseller.

Although Drumont relied in part on groundless figures, the fact is that at the end of the nineteenth and the beginning of the twentieth centuries an emigration of Jews fleeing pogroms in Russia and Central Europe was beginning to develop, such that the Jewish population residing in France reached about 180,000 people (0.5 percent of the total population) in 1914, according to the estimates available.

19. The Mortara affair took its name from a Jewish family of Bologna, one of whose children was claimed by the pope as Catholic because the family's Christian servant had had him baptized (even though in theory, Jews were not allowed to have servants in the Papal States). When he was six years old, little Edgardo Mortara was taken away from his family by the papal police and transported from Bologna to Rome. The affair had an immense impact in Europe, as demonstrated by Philibert Audebrand's article in the *Corsaire* on 8 November 1858: "Three months ago, all over Europe, six hundred pens of serious men covered half a kilometer of paper every day to talk about the little Jew from Bologna." He concludes, "The little Mortara is becoming a page of history"—especially in France, with the liberal and republican camp defending the Mortara family against the Church (in Italy, the affair was strengthened opinion against the Papal States and for Italian unity), while the Catholic camp attacked the Jews and their undue influence in Christian lands.

20. Moreover, on 17 January 1899, *La Croix* also drew a parallel between the Dreyfus affair and the Mortara affair, denouncing "the gossip in the newspapers" and emphasizing that "the most vital interests of France, society, and the Church itself are at stake." For this newspaper, it was the same men who had appeared on the stage forty years earlier, "but then there was a reason to insult and combat the papacy. Today, the army is insulted, the judicial system is ridiculed, in order to destroy these two social forces."

The arrival of new refugees in the 1920s and 1930s raised the Jewish population to almost 300,000 on the eve of World War II, or about 0.7 percent of the population, which is still very small in absolute terms, but nonetheless reflects a significant increase that was intensely exploited by the multiple anti-Semitic movements of the 1930s, starting with Action française. This group also emphasized the overrepresentation of Jews in certain occupations, a theme that was later taken up and put into practice under Vichy to impose quotas on Jewish lawyers.[21] Since 1945, the French Jewish population, as it can be gauged in the surveys with questions on religion, appears to have been relatively stable at about 0.6–0.7 percent of the population. However, we must add that the small size of the surveys available and the limitations of the questionnaires that were used do not allow us to go beyond this order of magnitude to study the multiple heterogeneities and evolutions that it covers, both on the temporal and spatial levels and in regard to beliefs, origins, and practices.[22]

A New War of Religion around French Islam?

Let us now take up the question of Islam. According to the available surveys, the proportion of the population that declares itself to be Muslim has risen from barely 1 percent in 1970 to about 3 percent in the 1990s and 8 percent at the beginning of the 2020s (see figure 4.5). Here again, we have to remember that these orders of magnitude cover multiple uncertainties and variations in practices. In exit polls, which are limited to the population of French nationals registered on the electoral lists, the proportion of Muslims is significantly smaller: scarcely more than 1 percent in the 1990s, and about 5 percent in the 2010s and at the beginning of the 2020s. Surveys relating to the whole of the population residing in France, independent of nationality and registration on electoral lists, indicate a proportion of Muslims

---

21. The decree of 16 July 1941 established a numerus clausus of 2 percent for Jewish lawyers in Paris, whereas, according to Robert Badinter, they then represented between 15 and 20 percent of the lawyers (that is, between 300 and 400 out of a total of 2,000 lawyers practicing in the capital in 1939). See R. Badinter, *Un antisémitisme ordinaire. Vichy et les avocats juifs (1940–1944)* (Fayard, 1997); Winock, *La France et les juifs.*

22. From collecting undertakers' statistics, Boulard concluded, for example, that Jewish funeral processions represent about 4 to 5 percent of the deaths in Paris in the 1950s–1960s, versus 2 to 3 percent in 1920–1930 and 1 to 2 percent in 1890–1910. Nothing allows us to separate what here pertains to changes in practices or origins. See F. Boulard, "La 'déchristianisation' de Paris. L'évolution historique du non-conformisme," *Archives de sociologie des religions,* 1971, 78–79.

close to 7–8 percent for recent years.[23] The evidence available shows, moreover, a religious practice just as uneven as that of Catholics, with about three-quarters of the self-declared Muslims indicating no practice, or a practice limited to observation of the major holy days and ceremonies (marriages and births, for example).[24] It is interesting to note that there is a considerable disparity between perceptions of the proportion of Muslims in France and reality (a little like the perception of the size of the Jewish population at the end of the nineteenth century and the beginning of the twentieth, but on a much larger scale). The gap is considerable in all Western countries, but the available data suggest that France is the country where it is greatest: on average, the people questioned answer that Muslims represent 31 percent of the population, or almost four times more than the reality (8 percent).[25] This is a considerable disparity, unrelated to anything that might be explained by uncertainties about the size of the foreign population and the existence of irregular immigration poorly recorded in official statistics (uncertainties that might account for, at most, only 1 percent of the total population).[26]

---

23. See H. El Karoui, *L'Islam, une religion française* (Gallimard, 2018), 20–26. See also C. Beauchemin, C. Hamel, and P. Simon, eds., *Trajectoires et origines. Enquête sur la diversité des populations en France* (INED éditions, 2015), 562, table 1.

24. In the most recent exit polls, the proportion indicating participation in religious practice at least once a month seems to be a little higher among Muslims than among Catholics, but the proportion indicating no participation in religious practice is also higher among Muslims.

25. See "Perils of Perception: A 14-Country Study" (IPSOS, 2018). Belgium comes immediately after France (with a perceived proportion of 29 percent versus a reality of 6 percent), followed by the United Kingdom (21 percent versus 6 percent), Italy (20 percent versus 4 percent), and Germany (19 percent versus 6 percent).

26. The highest figures brandished by the leaders of the Rassemblement National regarding foreigners whose papers are not in order refer to about 1 million people (or 1.5 percent of the population). In reality, the best documented estimates suggest 600,000, of which about half benefit from *aide médicale d'État* (AME, state medical aid), a mechanism that gives foreigners without documents access to healthcare. See F. Jusot, P. Dourgnon, J. Wittmer, and J. Sarhiri, *Le recours à l'Aide médicale de l'État des personnes en situation irrégulière en France: Premiers enseignements de l'enquête Premiers Pas* (IRDES, 2019). Moreover, everything indicates that most of these persons are already counted in the 4.8 million foreigners listed in the census (7.4 percent of the population), especially the majority of those living in ordinary housing. Adding up the official residence permits in force, we can estimate that the number of illegal residents taken into account in the censuses is about 400,000, which would leave about 200,000 illegal residents not taken into account (0.3 percent of the population). See P. Connor and J. Passel, *Europe's Unauthorized Migrant Population* (Pew Research Center, 2019). Furthermore, the homeless population is estimated to be around 300,000 persons, of which about half were born outside France, which is consistent with the first estimate. See *L'état du mal logement en France 2022*, Fondation Abbé Pierre.

Such disparities are disturbing, and it is tempting to interpret them as a sign of a fear of cultural and migratory submersion, of a "great replacement" to which no rational argument or attempt at conciliation could be opposed.[27] However, such a pessimistic interpretation would be excessive. The fact that the Muslim religion, which was virtually unknown in the national territory before 1914, and which included less that 1 percent of the population until the 1960s and 1970s, now approaches 10 percent, constitutes a significant transformation. In fact, this is the first time since the period of the Wars of Religion that a religion other than Catholicism has gained such importance. At that time, many Catholics allowed themselves to be persuaded that the Protestants were trying to seize power and radically challenge the religious, political, and territorial organization of the country (which was true, in a certain way, at least with regard to religious organization) and that it was urgent to stop them before it was too late. Regarding Arab-Muslim immigration, many political officials—and not only those in the Front national—have for decades helped to spread the idea that it would be structurally and irremediably foreign to France and unrelated to the preceding waves of immigrants, quickly forgetting the violent and ultimately surmounted indictments of the past immigrations of white Europeans (Italian, Jewish, and Portuguese immigrants). Naturally, one is reminded of the reference to "noise and odor" made by Jacques Chirac in Orléans in 1991.[28]

---

27. This fear of a "great replacement" is sustained by certain media outlets—we can cite the news magazine *Valeurs actuelles* and the television and radio networks of which Vincent Bolloré has taken control in recent years, beginning with CNews—which scorn their mission of providing information and seek instead to inflame public debate. See, for example, J. Cagé, *Pour une télé libre. Contre Bolloré* (Seuil, 2022), and C. Alduy, *La langue de Zemmour* (Seuil, 2022). On the media's impact on the perception of the immigration question, also see J. Valette and S. Schneider-Strawczynski, "Media Coverage of Immigration and the Polarization of Attitudes" (working paper, Paris School of Economics, 2021), 46.

28. "Our problem is not foreigners, it is that there is an overdose. It is perhaps true that there are no more foreigners than there were before the war, but these are not the same foreigners, and that makes a difference. It is certain that having Spaniards, Poles, and Portuguese working in our country raises fewer problems that having Muslims and Blacks.... How can you expect a French worker who lives in Goutte-d'or, where I walked with Alain Juppé a few days ago, who works with his wife and the two of them earn about 15,000 francs, and who sees on his landing in his HLM, jammed in together, a family with a father, three or four wives, and about twenty children, and who is paid 50,000 francs in welfare benefits, but of course without working! [prolonged applause] If you add to this the noise and the odor [sustained laughter], well, the French worker on the landing goes crazy. He goes crazy. That's how it is. And you have to understand him; if you were there, you'd have the same reaction. And it isn't racist to say that." Speech given on 19 June 1991 in Orléans; video extracts available on the website of the Institut national de l'audiovisuel, www.ina .fr. This speech inspired the song "Le bruit et l'odeur" by the Toulouse group Zebda in 1995.

Moreover, we have to remember the magnitude of the trauma caused by the rise in Muslim fundamentalism and jihadist terrorism during the last half century, both on a worldwide scale and specifically in France, from the Palestinians' first attempts to carry out terror attacks in the early 1970s to the virtual civil war in Algeria in the 1990s after the cancellation of the 1992 elections; the attacks of 11 September 2001; the war in Iraq in 2004–2005; the creation of the Islamic State in Syria and the Levant in 2014; and in France, the wave of attacks on the headquarters of *Charlie Hebdo,* at the Bataclan, and in Nice in 2015–2016, and the decapitation of the history teacher Samuel Paty in 2020. These were the bloodiest events to have occurred on French soil since 1945, and it would be very surprising it they had left people indifferent and had not been instrumentalized. This was also a radically new historical context, with unprecedented social, international, and geopolitical ramifications. Gravity and humility are needed here: no one can foresee the evolution of the situation.

A Conflict about Socioeconomic Origins and Resources

There are, however, many reasons for thinking that the immense majority of the population is aware that the 5 million or so French Muslims have nothing to do with the jihadist ultraminority. Everyone understands that it doesn't make much sense to suspect that everyone who wears a scarf over her hair or leggings at the beach is a terrorist sympathizer, at a time when the country should, on the contrary, be supporting its judicial system, police, and intelligence services in order to fight terrorism more effectively. The very high level of mixed marriages between people of different origins, to which we will return, suggests that a majority of French society has moved beyond these prejudices and is no longer threated by a new war of religion. The reality of the French uneasiness surrounding the diversity of origins is at once less disquieting and more profound: above all, it relates to socioeconomic stakes.

This observation—which could be seen as optimistic—must nonetheless be immediately qualified. Although the few small extremist groups who seek to stir up hatred and violence between communities represent, fortunately, only a tiny minority, there is also a more substantial minority of "people of genuine French origin" (or people who see themselves as such) who suffer from a veritable "cultural insecurity," in the sense that they perceive French Muslims as fundamentally foreign and incapable of being assimilated into the French national community, and who are wary of mixed origins and mixed families. This perception is found, for example, partly in the support for Éric Zemmour (7 percent of the vote) in the presidential elections of 2022. This was clearly a minority group, but a minority of significant size. We shall see that it was mainly an urban, wealthy electorate, diametrically opposed to the FN-RN electorate, which had become, in the years between 2000 and 2010, rural and popular and no longer connected with the presence of foreigners at the local level.[29]

Second, and most importantly, the fact that for the vast majority of voters, conflicts are primarily about socioeconomic rather than identity-related issues, does not mean that those conflicts are easy to resolve. The socioeconomic conflicts over origins are expressed in part in concerns about the size of the migratory flow and its perceived effects on access to jobs and resources (housing and welfare payments in particular). The discontent is also and especially animated by conflicts between territories over the stakes involved in local development and access to public services. Whatever one's origins and one's perception of other origins, everyone is in fact primarily concerned about their own conditions of housing and employment, about their children's futures and their friends, and about the future of their country and the planet. Contemporary French society is built around a very broad consensus regarding the state under the rule of law, electoral pluralism, social security, and free education and public services, regardless of origins, and it is usually within this consensus that legitimate conflicts arise. However, the difficulty is that socioeconomic conflicts have been redefined over time to directly connect them with the question of origins, in the sense that everyone suspects other groups of benefiting from preferential treatment, sometimes because of their origins, and particularly with regard to social benefits, public services, the education and healthcare systems, access to housing or employment, and so on.

These suspicions are shared by both a part of the immigrant population who are persuaded that they are victims of massive discrimination—not without some good reasons—and a part of the nonimmigrant population who are just as convinced that they and their territories are treated more poorly than the immigrants and the territories where they reside, and whether they are true or false, greatly exaggerated or partially justified, is of little importance here. Furthermore, the two opposing systems of perception may be proven to be partially true at the same time, depending on the public services or the territories in question. The fact is that the conflict is above all socioeconomic, and it can only admit of socioeconomic responses, including an overall improvement in the quality of public services, further investment in the welfare state, and much greater transparency about what the various social groups actually benefit from. We note, moreover, that Chiraq's famous speech of 1991 ultimately says much more about socioeconomic issues,

---

29. See chapters 11, 12, and 13.

living standards, and incomes (along with an assumed injustice in their distribution) than it does about noise, odor, or religion. In the end, France is involved more in a new class struggle than in a religious war. Or, more precisely, today France is suffering from the fact that its politicians refuse to come to grips with class conflict—and in particular, with the question of the growth of socioeconomic and territorial inequalities—preferring to focus, because it is easier, on the questions of origins and religions, and to exacerbate tensions that are in fact often less pronounced than they are said to be. We shall see that a great misunderstanding has thus been created in regard to the battle over *assistanat* and the question of identity, even though, all things being otherwise equal, foreign and immigrant populations in fact have relatively less recourse to the *revenu de solidarité active* (RSA). But since the universe of the wealthy has become invisible, often the only thing that remains is "inequalities of proximity," which a political actor has recently described, accurately, as "injustice with a minuscule."[30]

It will also be noted that this new class struggle is between geosocial classes, mixing major social and territorial dimensions in an advanced welfare state system and a globalized economy that is being reorganized. However, the question remains largely open whether and when the country will succeed in defining constructive socioeconomic and political outcomes to move beyond this malaise, instead of getting lost in identitarian conflicts that lead nowhere. Analysis of the transformations of long-term electoral cleavages can help us better understand these stakes. To move forward in this direction, it is useful to begin by studying how different territories have been exposed in recent decades to significantly different concrete, everyday experiences of the diversity of origins.

Villages, Towns, Suburbs, and Metropoles Facing Diversity

Let us begin by examining the proportions of foreigners in the populations of villages, towns, suburbs, and metropoles (defined in the same way as in the preceding chapters). The detailed results issuing from censuses, available at the level of France's 36,000 municipalities, enable us to analyze in a relatively granular way these transformations from 1960s to 2022. Unsurprisingly, we see first of all that the proportion of persons of foreign nationality has always been much larger in the metropoles and suburbs than in towns and villages. This reality (and more particularly, the concentration in the poorest suburbs) results from the interaction of family and occupational networks connected with migratory trajectories, and

---

30. F. Ruffin, *Je vous écris du fond de la Somme* (Les liens qui libèrent, 2022).

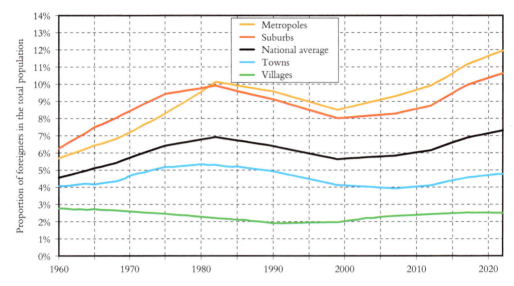

FIGURE 4.6. The foreign population in the territories, 1960–2022

The proportion of foreigners, which has risen from 4.6% in 1960 to 7.2% in 2022, has always been greater in the metropoles and suburbs than in the towns and villages, and the disparity between them is increasing. Note: The definition of villages, towns, suburbs, and metropoles is the same as the one introduced in chapter 2 (conurbations of fewer than 2,000 inhabitants, conurbations with between 2,000 and 100,000 inhabitants, and secondary municipalities and principal municipalities of conurbations of more than 100,000 inhabitants).

Sources and series: unehistoireduconflitpolitique.fr

also from the very strong residential segregation characterizing the structure of the locale in general (because of a lack of adequate policies favoring a genuine mixture). It will also be noted that the gap between the rural and urban worlds has become much larger over time. In towns and villages, the proportion of foreigners in the population was just as small in 2022 as it was in 1960: it has even decreased slightly in villages (from 2.8 percent to 2.6 percent), whereas it increased slightly in towns (from 4.1 percent to 4.9 percent). Over the same period, this proportion has almost doubled in metropoles and suburbs, rising in both cases from about 6 percent in 1960 to 11–12 percent in 2022 (see figure 4.6 and map 4.2). If we examine the available data by nationality, we find that this expansion of the gap, which took place at the time when the share of non-European foreigners overtook that of European foreigners, is for the most part explained by an inflow of North African and sub-Saharan foreigners, especially in the suburbs.[31] To sum up, the

31. See unehistoireduconflitpolitique.fr, figures B5.3m–B5.3n and appendix B5.

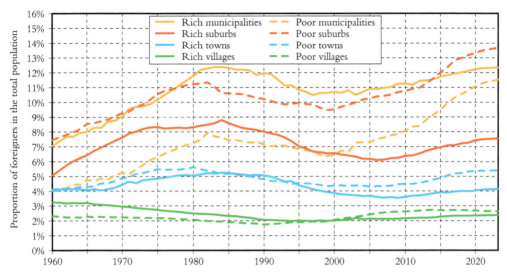

FIGURE 4.7. Foreigners in rich municipalities and poor municipalities, 1960–2022

The proportion of foreigners has always been greater in the metropoles and suburbs than in towns and villages, with an increasing gap between the two groups, particularly between the poor suburbs (and to a lesser degree, the poor metropoles) and the towns and villages.

Sources and series: unehistoireduconflitpolitique.fr

new experience of the diversity of origins in France from 1960 to 2022 is in reality an experience that concerns almost exclusively the metropoles and suburbs, and very little the towns and villages.

We must also emphasize the enormous diversity of experiences between rich and poor territories. So far as villages and towns are concerned, the question of wealth does not make much difference, whether we use the criterion of the value of housing (property per inhabitant) or the average income per inhabitant. Specifically, the proportion of foreigners is virtually the same in poor and rich villages (defined as the 50 percent of villages with the lowest and the highest incomes), as well as in poor and rich towns (see figure 4.7).[32] This has been the case throughout the period 1960–2022, even though since the late 1990s the proportion of foreigners has become a little larger in poor towns and villages than it has in rich

32. As we noted in chapter 2, the poorest 50 percent of villages designate the 50 percent of the population living in the poorest villages (and in the same way, for the poorest 20 percent or other indicators). This allows us to correct the potential biases connected with small municipalities, and in practice has no impact on the results presented here.

towns and villages, whereas the situation was the reverse at the beginning of the period.

By comparison, the criterion of wealth has a far greater impact in suburbs and metropoles. In particular, the proportion of foreigners has always been much greater in poor suburbs than in rich suburbs, and this disparity has become much larger in recent decades. In rich suburbs (defined as the 50 percent of suburbs with the highest income), the proportion of foreigners has oscillated between 6 and 8 percent during the period from 1960 to 2022; in the end, it has hardly risen at all in that time. In the poor suburbs, this proportion has almost doubled in the same period, rising from a little more than 7 percent in 1960 to almost 14 percent in 2022 (see figure 4.7). We note also that the proportion of foreigners has always been higher in the rich metropoles than in the poor metropoles (essentially because of non-Europeans) and is tending to approach the level observed in the rich metropoles (with a different composition), while remaining, however, clearly below that of poor suburbs.

We must also mention the very special case of the repatriates from Algeria— that is, the population of French colonists (*pieds noirs*) who arrived in Metropolitan France in 1962, and who were the object of a separate count at the level of the 36,000 municipalities during the 1968 census, when they represented about 1.5 percent of the total population (or almost 800,000 persons). The distribution over the territory was nonetheless very different from that of foreigners, and in particular "Algerian Muslims" (as they are still designated in the 1962 census), or persons of Algerian nationality (as they are called starting in 1968). Whereas Algerian nationals were overrepresented in the suburbs (and particularly in the poorest 50 percent of suburbs) and almost totally absent from villages and towns, the people repatriated from Algeria were more equally distributed: they were almost as numerous in the towns as in suburbs (in proportion to the population), and just as numerous in poor towns and rich towns, and in poor suburbs and rich suburbs.[33] We will return to this subject when we study electoral behaviors in this geography, which is very specific and very different from that of North African immigration (even if both are strongly present in the South of France, usually in separate territories) and has had lasting effects on voting patterns right down to the present day.[34]

---

33. See unehistoireduconflitpolitique.fr, map C4.1. Note also that repatriates are heavily represented in the least affluent middle-sized metropoles (see figures B5.3m–B5.3n and appendix B5).

34. See chapter 12 for an analysis of the vote for Tixier-Vignancour in 1965, and then for Jean-Marie Le Pen and his daughter Marine Le Pen from 1974 to 2022.

Foreigners and Immigrants Form Very Small Minorities, Including in the Suburbs

Thus, we see that the different territories have had very different experiences of the diversity of origins in recent decades, with a particularly marked contrast between metropoles and suburbs (and notably the poor suburbs) and between towns and villages (whose experience of diversity has progressed only a little over time). However, we must emphasize here an essential point that is sometimes neglected in public debate: populations of foreign origin are often more strongly represented in the suburbs than in the rest of the country, but they nonetheless remain clearly a minority, even in the suburbs. What characterizes the suburbs is above all not the fact that they are populated mainly by foreigners or immigrants—which is not the case—but rather the experience of a common sociability among persons with different origins. This is not to idealize the conditions or the reality of this sociability—a complex question to which we shall return when we study electoral behaviors—but simply to clarify orders of magnitude that are sometimes not well known.

It is true that in 2022, persons of foreign nationality represented almost 14 percent of the population in the poorest 50 percent of the suburbs, but it nonetheless remains that more than 86 percent of the individuals residing there had French nationality. If we now examine the immigrant population (born abroad with foreign nationality, but who may now be French or foreign), the levels observed are naturally higher than for the population of foreign nationality, while at the same time remaining more moderate than is sometimes imagined. Since the census of 2007, the data on the immigrant population have been available at the level of the 36,000 municipalities, and we are going to concentrate on the period 2007–2022. If we begin by considering the villages, towns, suburbs, and metropoles as a whole, we see the same general configuration for the immigrant population as for the population of foreign nationality. In other words, the share of the immigrant population in the total population has always been clearly higher in the metropoles and suburbs than in the towns and villages, and this disparity has had a tendency to grow in the recent period (see figure 4.8).

If we now decompose the different spaces into rich and poor territories (still defined in the same way), we see here as well the same configuration for the immigrant population as for the foreign population. In other words, the share of the immigrant population is not very different in the poor villages and the rich villages, or in the poor towns and the rich towns, whereas inversely, it is much higher in the poor suburbs than in the rich suburbs. In 2022, the immigrant population

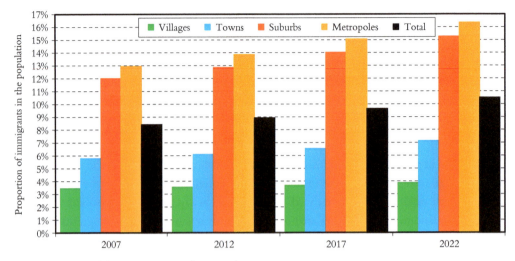

FIGURE 4.8. The immigrant population in the territories, 2007–2022

The proportion of immigrants in the total population has risen from 8.4% in 2007 to 10.4% in 2022. It has always been greater in the metropoles and suburbs than in the towns and villages, with an increasing gap between these two groups, particularly between the poor suburbs (the poorest 50% in terms of income) and the poor or rich towns and villages, defined in the same way.
Sources and series: unehistoireduconflitpolitique.fr

thus reached almost 19 percent in the poor suburbs versus less than 12 percent in the rich suburbs (see figure 4.9). However, it must be stressed that the nonimmigrant population represents more than 81 percent of the population of the poor suburbs (that is, 50 percent of the poorest suburbs in France), which constitutes a very large majority.

If we turn now to the very poor suburbs (defined as the poorest 20 percent of the suburbs), we find that in 2022 the share of the immigrant population reached 23 percent on average,[35] which is, to be sure, more than twice as high as the national average over the whole of the territory (10.4 percent), but it also means that more than three-quarters of the population is not immigrant. Of course, there are a small number of municipalities in the suburbs where the foreign and immigrant populations reached significantly higher levels. In 2022 in the department of Seine-Saint-Denis, the proportions of immigrants rose to 51 percent in Aubervilliers and 41 percent in Saint-Denis (see map 4.3). But the fact is that these municipalities represent only a small fraction of the overall population and are not representative

35. See unehistoireduconflitpolitique.fr, figure B5.3c.

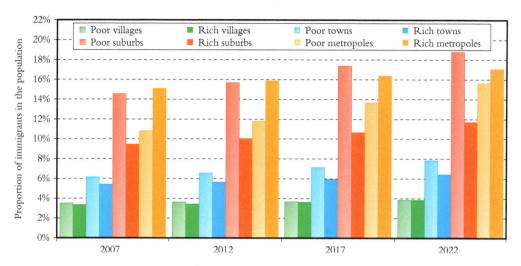

FIGURE 4.9. The immigrants in rich territories and poor territories, 2007–2022

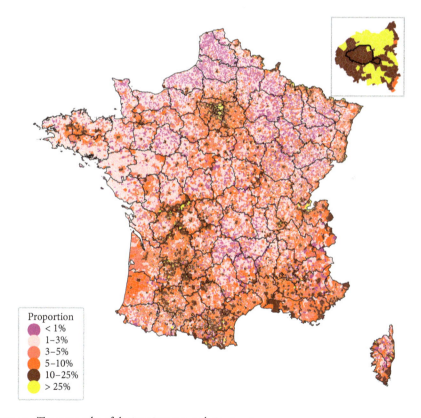

MAP 4.3. The geography of the immigrant population in 2022

This map represents for each municipality the proportion of persons who have immigrated (born abroad with foreign nationality) in the total population in 2022 (national average: 20.4%).

Sources and series: unehistoireduconflitpolitique.fr

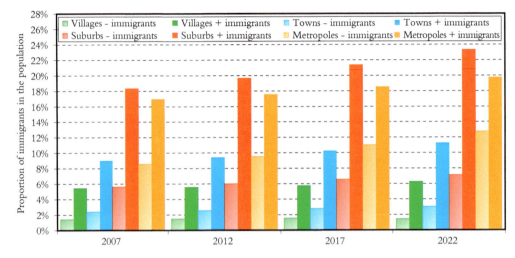

FIGURE 4.10. Immigrants in territories that have more or fewer immigrants

The disparity between the proportion of immigrants in the 50% of suburbs with the most or least immigrants has always been larger than the corresponding disparities for villages, towns, and metropoles.

Sources and series: unehistoireduconflitpolitique.fr

of the suburbs in general. To clarify this point, we can organize the municipalities in the suburbs and the various territories in relation not to their average level of income, but to their share of the immigrant population. Then we see that the proportion of immigrants is on average 23 percent in the 50 percent of the suburbs with the highest proportions of immigrants, and 7 percent in the 50 percent with the lowest proportion (see figure 4.10). This proportion rises to 31 percent on average in the 20 percent of the suburbs with the highest proportions of immigrants (a category that includes municipalities where more than 24 percent of the population consists of immigrants), which shows that cases like Aubervilliers or Saint-Denis correspond to only a limited, minority fraction of the population residing in the municipalities of the suburbs.[36]

It is also interesting to analyze the disparities between territories from the point of view of the proportion of naturalized citizens (that is, people who have acquired French nationality during their lives) among persons holding French nationality. This will be useful to us when we examine the impact on political behaviors on the basis of electoral data, which by definition concerns only persons with French nationality. We see the same overall configuration for foreign and immigrant

36. See unehistoireduconflitpolitique.fr, figures B5.3d–B5.3e.

populations. The share of naturalized persons in the population of persons holding French nationality is much greater in the suburbs and metropoles than it is in towns and villages, and the disparity has grown over time, with a particularly substantial increase in poor suburbs. Specifically, naturalized citizens represented almost 9 percent of the potential voters in the poor suburbs in 2022, versus scarcely 2–3 percent in towns and villages and 5 percent on average in France. The proportion of naturalized citizens in the population with French nationality reached 11 percent in the 50 percent of the suburbs with the largest proportions of naturalized citizens, and 15 percent in the 20 percent of the suburbs with the most naturalized citizens.[37] In the most extreme cases, it reached 19 percent in Saint-Denis and exceeded 20 percent in Aubervilliers, which reflects the fact that the majority of immigrants do not have French nationality. These are important figures that testify once again to large territorial disparities with respect to the experience of the diversity of origins over recent decades, but which can by themselves explain only a small number of the disparities in voting behavior that we will highlight, notably between suburbs and towns, and which in all probability can be better explained by differences in sociability (in the broad sense) than simply and mechanically by demography. We will return to this point when we present the results concerning the structure of votes.[38]

From Mixed, Ultramajority Origins to the Third Generation

If we take an interest not just in persons with foreign nationality and immigrants (born abroad, with foreign nationality) or naturalized (having acquired French nationality in the course of their lives) but in all persons who have "come from immigration" two, three, or four generations ago (or even more), then we can naturally find much lower proportions of this population in many territories. Taking into account the high level of mixed marriages and *métissage* (interbreeding), however, we can see that this kind of exercise raises multiple issues. Over the very long term, it is clear that the totality of the French population has immigrant ancestry. It is therefore essential to keep in mind that the process of *métissage* takes place much more rapidly than is sometimes imagined, in the sense that mixed origins become the ultramajority as soon as the third generation. Although this reality may upset a minority, it can legitimately be seen as a good thing from the point of

---

37. There is also a strong correlation between the territories with the largest proportions of foreigners and naturalized citizens. See unehistoireduconflitpolitique.fr, C4.2 and figures B5.3f–B5.31.
38. See in particular chapter 11.

view of the great majority of the population, in the sense that it points to a very rapid advance of integration and mixed marriages that is much more rapid than, for example, the historically observed integration of the Black and white populations in the United States (a country marked by an experience of segregation that is extreme and rarely taken as a model in France or in Europe). But this also implies that taking into account origins beyond the second generation would make little sense, because it would amount to assigning a single identity to persons whose origins are profoundly plural and multiple.

The most complete sources at our disposal for studying these questions in France are provided by the Trajectories and Origins survey (Trajectoires et origines, or TeO) organized periodically by the INED and INSEE. The TeO survey carried out in 2008–2009 made it possible for the first time to collect detailed information regarding familial and migratory trajectories using a very large sample. The survey established, for instance, that the proportion of intermarriage reached 30–35 percent for persons with a North African origin in the preceding generation—the same level as those with a second-generation Portuguese origin.[39] Such a level of intermarriage implies that mixed origins become clearly majority origins after a few generations. For example, with a 35 percent rate of intermarriage, three-quarters of persons with a grandparent of a given origin have at least one other grandparent of a different origin.[40]

The TeO survey conducted in 2019–2010 allowed us to dig deeper into this question and to note that mixed marriages are increasingly numerous as time goes on, such that mixed origins become preponderant even more rapidly than was earlier thought. If we consider, for example, all young people who were younger than eighteen years old in 2019–2020 and had at least one immigrant grandparent (that is, a grandparent who was born abroad, with foreign nationality, and who came to live in France), we see that only 9 percent have four immigrant grandparents, 5 percent have three immigrant grandparents, 38 percent have two immigrant grandparents, and 48 percent have only one immigrant grandparent. In other words, 91 percent of persons who have one immigrant grandparent have mixed origins. That is the case for 81 percent of individuals with one immigrant grandparent born in the Maghreb or Asia, for 93 percent of those

---

39. This rate reaches 60 percent for persons with Spanish or Italian origins. See C. Beauchemin, B. Lhommeau, and P. Simon, "Histoires migratoires et profils socioéconomiques," in Beauchemin, Hamel, and Simon, *Trajectoires et origines.*.

40. More precisely, with a rate of endogamy of 65 percent, only 27 percent of persons with a grandparent of a given origin have four grandparents of that same origin (0.65x0, 65x0, 65 = 0,27).

with an immigrant grandparent born in sub-Saharan Africa, and for 96 percent of those with an immigrant grandparent born in Spain, Italy, or Portugal.[41]

Considering this preponderance of mixed origins, we see to what extent a rigid system of ethnoracial categories of the type white / Black, Maghrebin / Asian, inspired by the system applied in the United States, can have perverse effects in the French context. It would oblige everyone to choose a principal identity to the detriment of others and could contribute in this way to rigidifying the borderlines between groups and exacerbating antagonisms, as it has been possible to see in multiple colonial and postcolonial contexts. In the United States, categories like white / Black used in censuses were developed in a very specific environment, in support of slavery and then the segregation system. In the early twentieth century, the rule most commonly applied in the states of the South was that every person who had at least one-eighth Black blood (that is, one Black great-grandparent out of eight, the infamous "one drop rule") was automatically considered Black and was subject to legal discrimination in access to schools, public transit, and so on. In addition, interracial marriages were prohibited by several states until 1967. But we find a considerable increase in intermarriage since then, even if the level observed remains lower than it is in France (or in Europe in general); currently, about 15 percent of mixed marriages in the United States involve persons declaring themselves to be Black (versus 2 percent in 1967).[42]

Although it seems that a rigid system of ethnoracial categories should be proscribed (a view that is, widely accepted in French society), it could still be useful to use censuses to collect information on the birth countries of parents and ascendants. In theory, that could make it possible to follow the evolution of occupational discrimination in hiring or promotion at a detailed geographic and sectorial level, and then to put in place jurisdictional actions and other suitable antidiscrimination

41. See J. Lê, P. Simon, and B. Coulmont, "La diversité des origines et la mixité des unions progressent au fil des générations" (INSEE Première, 2022), table 3. In all, regarding the most recent generations studied (children under four years old in 2019–2020), about 40 percent of these children have at least one immigrant ancestor at the level of a parent or grandparent, including about 10 percent with a European immigrant ancestor and 30 percent with a non-European immigrant ancestor (17 percent North African, 7 percent sub-Saharan, and 6 percent Asian or other), and also, in the great majority of cases, mixed origins that also imply nonimmigrant parents or grandparents.

42. The proportion of mixed marriages has reached 25–30 percent for Latinx and Asian minorities—that is, closer to the levels observed for immigrant populations in France and Europe. See G. Livingston and A. Brown, "Intermarriage in the U.S. 50 Years after *Loving v. Virginia*" (Pew Research Center, 2017).

mechanisms.[43] Nevertheless, this is a complex question, because such information could also be used to stigmatize certain origins and exacerbate conflicts between groups. In practice, such provisions can attract very strong opposition from both antiracist associations fearing increased stigmatization and nativist political movements concerned, on the contrary, that they might lead to undue advantages benefiting populations of immigrant origin.

Poor Towns and Poor Suburbs: Drawing Attention to Common Interests

Let us sum up. We have noted, in the course of the previous chapters, that the different territories bring together geosocial classes whose interests and aspirations may be sometimes convergent, sometimes clearly divergent. For example, we have seen that poor towns and poor suburbs were equally disadvantaged in terms of income and economic wealth; what brings them together on this terrain is in large measure much more considerable than what separates them from, for instance, rich suburbs and rich metropoles. However, poor towns and suburbs are distinguished by certain aspects of their productive specialization and their relation to property, by living in detached houses, by their modes of transportation, and to a certain extent, by their relation to education and to a diversity of origins. The fact remains that these different poor territories have common interests that would benefit from more attention.

We must also emphasize the fact that conflicts around origins have also, and perhaps especially, a socioeconomic dimension, such that the borderlines between these different points of friction are often porous. For example, a voter in a town casting his ballot for the FN or RN is not necessarily expressing first and foremost a racial or religious prejudice. He may also think (rightly or wrongly) that his territory has been abandoned in terms of public services and policies of economic development and territorial improvement. He may also think that the suburbs are treated much better than towns because the authorities in place and the dominant groups prefer the immigrants who reside there over the residents of the towns and villages (for example, because of what is sometimes presented as an excessive predilection for interracial families and social mixture shown by the globalized elite). These belief systems must be taken seriously, even though they sometimes seem

43. See T. Piketty, *Mesurer le racisme, vaincre les discriminations* (Seuil, 2022). Information on the birth countries of parents or ascendants is already available in certain surveys, like those conducted by TeO or employment surveys, but the size of the samples is insufficient to carry out detailed territorial or sectorial decompositions, which only a census would make possible.

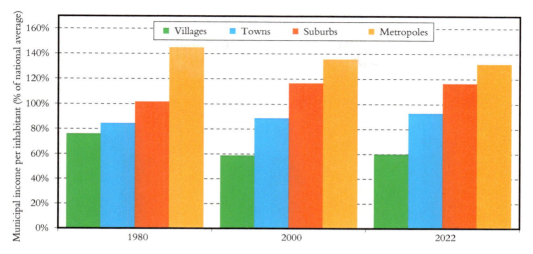

FIGURE 4.11. The average municipal income in the territories, 1980–2022

difficult to verify empirically. In practice, one has the impression that poor towns, like poor suburbs, are in a certain way abandoned, notably when compared with rich suburbs and rich metropoles. In other words, the dominant groups and favored classes seem preoccupied primarily with the territories where they live, which is, after all, not very surprising. Rather than contrasting towns and suburbs, it might be more pertinent to emphasize the inequalities within these spaces and imagine policies of redistribution that would benefit all poor territories. We have already mentioned this point in relation to education: the average salary per teacher is structurally higher in rich territories than in poor territories (because the latter have more teachers who either are on temporary contracts or lack experience), and this injustice affects the poor suburbs as much as it does the poor towns. But in fact, the reality of the injustice is broader than this. If, for example, we examine the budgetary resources at the disposal of the various categories of municipalities, it is striking to note that poor towns and villages, like the poorest suburbs, are all disadvantaged in comparison with the richest territories, contrary to what is often asserted in public debate. If we look first at the main fiscal incomes from which municipalities benefit (the property tax and the local residence tax), we see that the municipal income per inhabitant has always been considerably higher in the metropoles, followed by the suburbs, towns, and villages (see figure 4.11).

If we decompose these results in relation to the wealth of the territory, we observe that the municipal tax revenue per inhabitant is particularly high in the richest municipalities, especially in the richest metropoles and suburbs (see

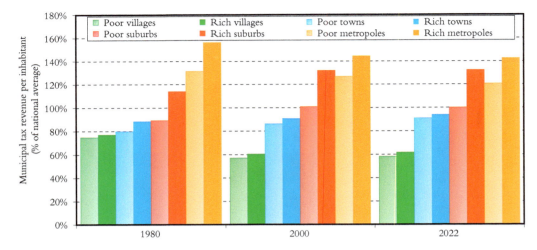

FIGURE 4.12. The municipal tax revenue in rich and poor territories

Between 1980 and 2022, the municipal tax revenue per inhabitant proceeding from the main local taxes (property tax, residence tax) is always higher in the metropoles, followed by the suburbs, then by the towns and villages. In the course of this period, the rich suburbs (defined as the 50% of the suburbs with the highest tax revenues per inhabitant) deepened the cleavage separating them from the poor suburbs and moved toward the rich metropoles.

Sources and series: unehistoireduconflitpolitique.fr

figure 4.12). This derives from the simple fact that these revenues depend on the municipalities' tax bases (in particular, the value of housing), which are significantly higher in the richest municipalities. However, it is worth noting that the rich metropoles have not increased their revenues as much as the rise in property values might have allowed; in view of the large increase in property values, they were able to lower their tax rates while at the same time maintaining a comfortable budgetary lead over the rest of the country. We can also note a fall in the municipal income per inhabitant in villages since the 1980s, on the same scale as the decline of their property tax base relative to other territories.[44] In the suburbs, the major phenomenon is the growing gap between the poor suburbs and the rich suburbs, with the latter rapidly catching up with the richest metropoles (with a municipal receipt per inhabitant around 30–40 percent above the national average in recent years). The income per inhabitant is a little higher in the poor suburbs than it is in the poor towns (about 5–10 percent higher), which can be explained by broader property tax bases as well as greater budgetary needs connected with

44. Contrary to their average income, which was maintained. See chapter 2, figures 2.13–2.15.

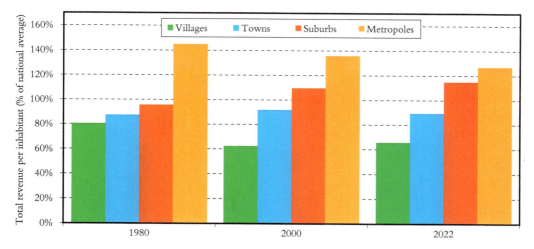

FIGURE 4.13. Total public revenue in the territories

Between 1980 and 2022, the total revenue per inhabitant (all receipts taken together, including tax revenues and allocations from the central government) was always higher in the metropoles, followed by the suburbs, then the towns and villages.

Sources and series: unehistoireduconflitpolitique.fr

the youth of the population. Considering the fact that the average income is just as low in the suburbs as it is in poor towns and villages, this also means greater fiscal pressure for inhabitants of the suburbs (if we express it as a percentage of income).

If we now examine the total income per inhabitant available to the municipalities to finance their expenses, including notably all the local taxes and fees (not just the property tax and the local residence tax), as well as the diverse allocations paid by the state (in particular, the overall operating allowance),[45] we see that the hierarchy between territories remains unchanged, and that the disparities in funding were only slightly affected (see figures 4.13–4.14). In particular, after taking into account the whole of the resources, the income per inhabitant is about 30–40 percent higher in rich metropoles and rich suburbs than it is in poor suburbs and towns, and almost twice as high as it is in villages. This observation is explained by the fact that state allocations represent only one, minor part of the municipalities' total resources (about a quarter), and by the fact that the other

---

45. The general operating allocation (DGF) is a complex system composed of twelve allocations, of which several are called "equalizing" allocations—that is, their objective is to reduce inequalities in resources among the collectivities.

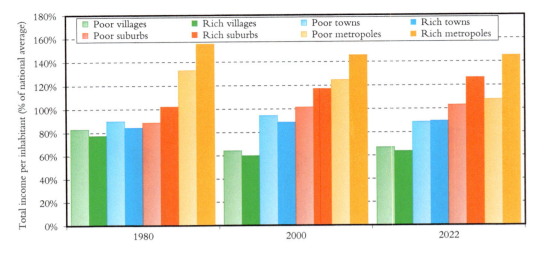

FIGURE 4.14. Total public revenue in rich and poor territories

Between 1980 and 2022, the total revenue per inhabitant (all receipts taken together, including tax revenue and allocations from the central government) was always higher in the metropoles, followed by the suburbs, then the towns and villages. In course of this period, the rich suburbs (defined as the 50% of the suburbs with the highest total revenues per inhabitant) deepened the cleavage separating them from the poor suburbs and moved toward the rich metropoles.
Sources and series: unehistoireduconflitpolitique.fr

municipal fiscal incomes are very unequally distributed, sometimes even more than the property tax and the local residence tax, which tends to compensate for the effect of the allocations. This is notably the case for the business tax (renamed the "territorial economic contribution" in 2010), which is particularly concentrated in metropoles where the headquarters of the great enterprises are located, which make it possible in some cases to lower local taxes weighing on households (as it does in Paris).[46]

If we examine the disparities in total income per inhabitant between very rich metropoles (the richest 20 percent) and very poor suburbs (the poorest 20 percent), we see that in the course of the last twenty years the income in very rich metropoles has been twice that in very poor suburbs, and that the income per inhabitant in the latter has even fallen (slightly) below that of very poor towns (defined in the same way).[47] Of course, we can feel reassured when we note that the disparities in

46. Let us recall here that—although they are still restricted by a set of complex rules defined in the general tax code—the rates of local direct taxes are voted on by the collectivities.

47. See unehistoireduconflitpolitique.fr, figures B8.1c and B8.1h.

budgetary funding separating the richest metropoles from the rest of the country were even greater at the end of the nineteenth century and the beginning of the twentieth.[48] However, these disparities are considerable, and not very compatible with contemporary talk about the equality of rights and opportunities, which can only contribute to exacerbating the tensions between territories and social groups.

Socioeconomic Common Interests Are More Important than Migratory Disagreements

From the point of view of budgetary resources and, more generally, of socioeconomic interests, we therefore see that poor suburbs and poor towns and villages are actually in rather similar situations. All these territories are disadvantaged in comparison with rich suburbs and rich metropoles, and they might have an interest in coalescing with one another and supporting a single political movement proposing to reduce social and territorial inequalities as a whole. That has already been seen in the past and is one of the possible trajectories for the future. We will return to this at length when we study electoral behaviors and their historical transformations. However, for several reasons, things are not so simple, beginning with the opacity and complexity of budgetary processes, which help nourish multiple uncertainties and arouse suspicions of favoritism between territories. Let us stress in particular that much financing is transferred through channels other than the municipal budgets examined earlier—for example, through the payroll for teachers, and investments in railways or in major equipment for universities and hospitals—so it is objectively very difficult to draw up a complete and transparent balance sheet. In addition, the needs for public services are not the same in the various territories, with the youth of the suburbs on the one hand, and the specific needs of towns and villages in terms of transportation on the other.[49] In theory, all these difficulties can be surmounted, but doing so requires appropriate

---

48. These disparities can be measured historically thanks to the archives of the Ministry of the Interior, which published annually, starting in 1878 and continuing until the end of the 1930s, a report on "La situation financière des communes" including, in particular, their annual revenues. The historical data issuing from the "États du montant des rôles généraux" (subsequently called "États des sommes imposées") provide another source of valuable information. See unehistoireduconflitpolitique.fr, figures B8.2a–B8.2p.

49. The fact that the average budget per inhabitant is so much smaller in villages also reflects the fact that the inhabitants of villages sometimes have access to certain collective resources (such as athletic or cultural facililties) in the towns, metropoles, or suburbs around them, and this complicates once again this type of comparison.

mobilizations and mediations that may be more complex to construct in a world in which the welfare state has become denser than it was in earlier periods when everything remained to be done, and all territories and social groups were starting out from near zero.

Assuming that these difficulties have been overcome and that a common platform regarding public services (in the broadest sense) helps unite towns and suburbs, or at least groups of voters that constitute a majority, we must also emphasize that disagreements may persist regarding migration policy properly so called. For example, people living in poor suburbs may want to maintain or extend the possibilities of reuniting members of families, either because the issue affects their own families or persons they know who share their origins, or because it affects people they know socially with whom they do not share common origins. Conversely, the inhabitants of towns and villages are less likely to have been directly exposed to the concrete consequences of these policies for the individual and may choose to put the emphasis on a general objective of restricting migratory flows (and thus of grouping together family members, which generally constitutes the principal component). Let us add that these disagreements are never settled and are constantly being renewed, notably in relation to the social relations of various people and individual experiences. They may also take more complex forms, when, for example, people issuing from earlier waves of migration in the relatively distant past (such as the first waves migrating from North Africa) maintain that the new flows of Maghrebin or sub-Saharan immigrants are less capable of integrating or might harm them in some way or another.

In practice, conflicts also concern multiple dimensions of integration policies and access to French citizenship and residence permits. For example, the Pasqua-Debré law of 1993 established, for young people born in France whose parents are immigrants, the principle of an obligatory demonstration of a will to be French, which must be solemnly expressed between the ages of sixteen and twenty-one, in order to ensure that these young people are sufficiently motivated to acquire French nationality. Pointing out the unfairness of subjecting them to an unfounded suspicion, when no one dreams requiring such a thing from young people who were born in France, in 1998 the Chevènement-Guigou law put an end to this requirement and returned to the rules that were applied before 1993 (namely, automatic acquisition of French nationality at the age of eighteen), which are still in force today. In other cases, conflict can arise over the conditions for naturalization. For example, the Sarkozy law of 2006 raises from two to four years the length of residence in France required to apply for naturalization following a marriage with a person of French nationality, a requirement that is still applicable today. The ostensible goal of the reform was to deter marriages of convenience. Research showed that the main effect was to complicate considerably young married couples' access to jobs (since employers prefer people with French nationality to those who have only a temporary residence permit), without reducing the frequency or duration of marriages (which contradicts the idea of marriages of convenience).[50] Considering the limited information that everyone has regarding these complex questions, it is nonetheless hardly surprising that people's opinions are strongly influenced by whether or not they have been in contact with persons affected by these situations, which again leads to drawing distinctions between towns and suburbs, whose experiences in terms of social contacts with immigrant populations are extremely different.[51]

Another subject of conflict concerns access to housing. Many studies based on random testing have demonstrated the existence of major cases of discrimination in France in the last ten years against persons with family or given names that sound non-European, especially in regard to accessing job interviews, temporary employment agencies, and private rental housing.[52] Partly for that reason—and also partly because of the low incomes and the geographical localization of populations of immigrant origins—these populations are often strongly represented in the low-income rental stock. This can contribute to making the allocation of housing more complex; while it is primarily based on the incomes and needs of the applicants, in fact, it often also takes nationalities into account in order to avoid concentrations of people of a certain origin in one part of a housing development, which can lead to tensions in other parts where people who are not foreign may feel they are being treated as second class. In addition, the very existence of low-cost housing in the suburbs and the peripheries of large cities can also feed jealousies in towns and villages, whose inhabitants often have to shift for themselves to find housing. These feelings are not without contradictions, because a large segment of the residents and officials of towns and villages (in particular, in the territories where the FN or RN is strongest) are wary of collective housing projects and prefer to rely on neighborhoods made of individual houses, which

---

50. See Y. Govind, "Is Naturalization a Passport for Better Labor Market Integration? Evidence from a Quasi-experimental Setting" (working paper, Paris School of Economics, 2021).

51. On the way in which personal experiences of discrimination and contacts with the persons concerned influence (or fail to influence) political trajectories, see, for example, the fascinating interviews collected in E. Agrikoliansky, P. Aldrin, and S. Lévêque, *Voter par temps de crise. Portraits d'électrices et d'électeurs ordinaires* (Presses Universitaires de France / Irisso, 2021), esp. 260–280, 309–346.

52. See Piketty, *Mesurer le racisme*, 25–33.

municipal officials partly control through construction permits, thus guaranteeing a population that is more homogeneous and more in conformity with the aspirations of a majority of the inhabitants.[53]

There again, it would in theory be possible to improve housing both in poor suburbs and in poor towns and villages, and this would no doubt entail raising taxes on the inhabitants of the richest metropoles and suburbs. The SRU (solidarity and urban renewal) law, passed in 2000, has established an obligation for all municipalities of more than 50,000 inhabitants to attain a level of 20 percent low-cost housing. The law of 2013 raised the low-cost housing target to 25 percent, without setting up the automatic and dissuasive sanctions necessary to guarantee its actual application in the richest municipalities, which instead seek first of all to preserve the feeling of living among people like oneself and refuse to meet the threshold.[54] Another limitation of the law is that it puts the emphasis chiefly on the stock of rental housing, when it could involve to a greater extent those who aspire to individual property ownership, and still maintain the binding and universal objectives of social mixture.[55]

The Illusions of the Battle over the *Assistanat* and Insecurity

Take the case of the conflict over the so-called *assistanat*. This pejorative term is often used by the right wing to refer to the Left's allegedly excessive reliance on social transfers and allocations of all kinds that discourage effort and merit in order to win the votes of groups that are not inclined to work. On the contrary, in the twentieth century, the construction of the welfare state has had a tendency over the long term to accompany an unprecedented increase in productivity and collective prosperity, thanks in particular to investments in social programs and education and to the income guarantees made during periods of recession, which decrease the force of the criticism. Still, the precise organization of a system of social transfers naturally raises issues that have become all the more legitimate as the system has grown considerably over time. The difficulty is twofold. First, the de-

---

53. See V. Girard, *Le vote FN au village. Trajectoires de ménages populaires du périurbain* (Éditions du Croquant, 2017).

54. Article 55 of the SRU law foresees financial sanctions for municipalities that do not respect their commitments, but in fact these sanctions seem to be insufficient, because many municipalities prefer to pay a levy on their fiscal resources instead of producing the legal required level of low-cost housing.

55. We will return at length to this question of access to property. See, in particular, chapter 13.

bate about the *assistanat* tends to make the poor the enemy of wage earners with modest salaries, and the working classes the enemy of the middle classes, whereas a different solution might involve also raising the incomes received by the working and middle classes, to the detriment of the upper classes. Second, the stigmatization of people who are allegedly disinclined to work disregards the complexity of individuals' life trajectories and is often accompanied by an implicit or explicit allegation that people of immigrant origin are particularly likely to sponge off society (as is shown by Chirac's famous 1991 speech). So, the Left supposedly distributes transfers to immigrants in order to win votes, at the price of undoing the meaning of work and dignity in the country. This accusation has often been made in the United States, notably by Republicans seeking to denounce the Democrats' supposed giveaways to African American voters, and the success of this discourse no doubt explains, to a non-negligible extent, why the welfare state is less developed in the United States than it is in Europe.[56]

In the French context, the accusation is all the more problematic because the available studies suggest a quite different reality. For given social origins, especially in terms of the parents' occupations, persons of immigrant origins make particularly great efforts to invest in their educations and to obtain unusually advanced diplomas, even if this major educational investment does not always result in job interviews and employment.[57] We must also emphasize that the geography of social transfers, and especially of the RSA, hardly seems consistent with its often anti-immigrant political instrumentalization. In practice, the rate of recourse to the RSA, defined here as the proportion of the population of the municipality (including spouses and children) benefiting from the RSA, has always been considerably higher in the metropoles, followed by the suburbs and the towns, and then the villages (see figure 4.15). Within these territories, the level of the municipality's average income has a massive effect on the rate of recourse to the RSA (see figure 4.16). In comparison, we see a significantly smaller effect of the foreign or immigrant population, an effect that even becomes slightly negative when we control for income (that is, when we look at the effect of foreign or immigrant population for a given average income level), reflecting a lower take-up of the RSA among immigrants with given socioeconomic characteristics, perhaps because they

---

56. See, for example, Beauchemin, Lhommeau, and Simon, "Histoires migratoires et profils socioéconomiques."

57. See unehistoireduconflitpolitique.fr, figures B8.3b–B8.3e. Data on those who benefit from the RSA at the municipal level are not available before April 2016, and do not allow us to make a long-term analysis.

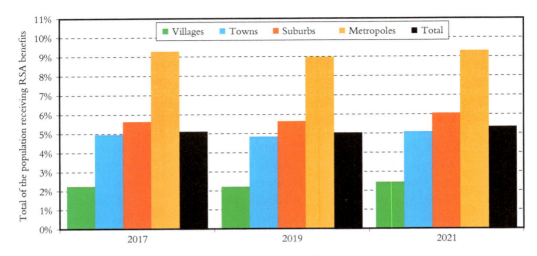

FIGURE 4.15. Recourse to the RSA (minimum income) in the territories

The proportion of the population receiving RSA benefits (defined as the number of persons living in RSA housing) moved from 5.1% in 2017 to 5.0% in 2019, and 5.03% in 2021. This proportion has always been greater in the metropoles, followed by suburbs, then towns and villages.

Sources and series: unehistoireduconflitpolitique.fr

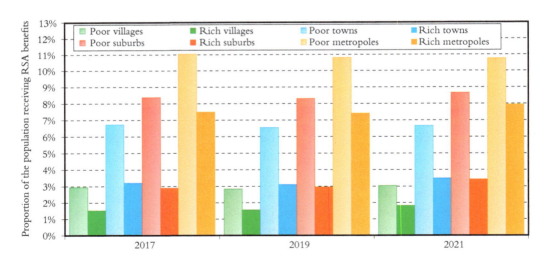

FIGURE 4.16. The RSA (minimum income) in rich and poor territories

The proportion of the population receiving RSA benefits (defined as the number of persons living in RSA housing divided by the total population) moved from 5.1% in 2017 to 5.0% in 2019 and 5.3% in 2021. This proportion has always been greater in the poor metropoles, followed by the poor suburbs, and then the rich metropoles.

Sources and series: unehistoireduconflitpolitique.fr

are less familiar with entitlements, have less knowledge of their rights, or have a greater perception of the stigma associated with it.[58]

We note in addition that the heaviest recourse to the RSA in metropoles is almost perfectly correlated with the unemployment rate, which during the period 1960–2022 has always been far higher in the metropoles, followed at a considerable distance by the suburbs and towns, and then by the villages.[59] In other words, the metropoles have always been marked by inequalities, with high concentrations of the wealthy (the proportion of managers there is always maximal, and so are the average incomes and the average property prices) as well as people seeking jobs (who may have moved to the capital for that reason, considering the large number of employers located there).

Let us now take up the question of insecurity, which rightly constitutes an extremely important political issue in France, as it does in all countries. It is no doubt the central question that provides the foundation for anti-immigrant discourses and perceptions, especially regarding the overrepresentation of foreign nationals in the prison population. In fact, and even though it has decreased significantly over the last few decades, the proportion of foreigners among prisoners is currently more than 20 percent, which remains significantly higher than the share of foreigners in the population (between 7 and 8 percent) or even among the unemployed (about 15 percent).[60] As for the rate of unemployment among foreigners, it is about twice as high as it is in the general population. This overrepresentation of foreigners can be explained in different ways, especially in connection with the proven job discrimination to which foreigners and immigrants are subjected in the legal labor market, which can lead to resorting to illegal activities (such as drug trafficking) that are more frequent than for populations against which there is less discrimination, as well as, in certain cases, discrimination within the police and

---

58. See J. Roemer, W. Lee, and K. Van der Straeten, *Racism, Xenophobia, and Distribution. Multi-Issue Politics in Advanced Democracies* (Harvard University Press, 2007). See also A. Alesina, E. Galeser, and B. Sacredote, "Why Doesn't the United States Have a European-Style Welfare State?" (Brookings Papers on Economic Activity, 2001); A. Alesina and E. Galeser, *Fighting Poverty in the U.S. and Europe: A World of Difference* (Oxford University Press, 2004).

59. See, for example, Beauchemin, Lhommeau, and Simon, "Histoires migratoires et profils socioéconomiques."

60. Among prisoners, this share was 15 percent in 1970, 20 percent in 1980, and 30–32 percent in 1990, then it fell back to 23–24 percent in 2020–2021. *Annuaire rétrospectif de la France* (INSEE, 1990), 639; *Statistique trimestrielle des personnes écrouées en France* (Ministère de la Justice, 2022), 13, table 9; *Tableau de l'économie française* (INSEE, 2019), 37. The share of foreigners among the unemployed is thus about 15 percent.

judicial systems.[61] From the point of view of antiforeigner discourses, such considerations seem insufficient. Without necessarily going so far as to mention explicitly racial or cultural considerations, the overrepresentation of foreigners in prison is said to be proof that migratory flows exceed the country's capacity to receive and integrate them. According to this way of seeing things, this conclusion should take priority over any other consideration and consequently lead to a decision to drastically reduce migratory flows, no matter what the restrictive consequences for family life or economic activity might be. As always in such cases, individual opinions are likely to be influenced by personal experiences with insecurity, as well as by each individual's experience and sociability in relation to immigration.

Nonetheless, it is useful to stress the following point: whatever conclusions we might draw regarding migration policy, it must be made clear that the prison population represents about 0.1 percent of the total population (about 65,000 detainees for 66 million inhabitants in Metropolitan France). In other words, the immense majority of foreigners and immigrants residing in France are above all likely to be victims of insecurity (and not the perpetrators of crimes or offenses). Generally speaking, if we examine the geographic distribution of insecurity, we note that the rate of infraction (defined here as the number of crimes and offenses recorded by the police or by gendarmes, divided by the population of the municipality) is particularly high in the metropoles, followed, again, by the suburbs and towns, then by the villages (see figures 4.17–4.18). We find the same gradation for all infractions (violence against persons, burglaries, car thefts, other thefts) with the exception of burglaries, which are more numerous in villages than in towns. In comparison with the geography of the RSA, we observe that infractions are still more numerous in rich metropoles than in poor metropoles, which testifies to the fact that metropoles are stopping-off places, and that the data pertain to the places where the infractions are committed and recorded (and not the places where the perpetrators or their victims reside). On the other hand, the rate of infraction is significantly higher in poor towns than in rich suburbs, and to a lesser degree higher in poor suburbs than in rich suburbs. There again, the level of income seems to play a more important role than the proportion of immigrants or foreigners, whose effect disappears when we control for income.[62]

---

61. The available studies also indicate that foreign delinquents are sent to prison more often and for longer periods than the equivalent French delinquents (for the same crimes and similar characteristics). See A. Philippe, J. Valette, "Immigration et délinquance: Réalités et perceptions" (CEPII, 2023).

62. See unehistoireduconflitpolitique.fr, figures B8.4a–B8.4y and appendix B8. Unfortunately, the data concerning the infractions registered at the municipal level are not available for the period before 2017 and thus do not allow us to make a long-term analysis.

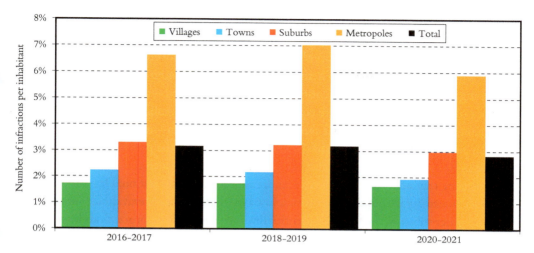

FIGURE 4.17. Infractions in the territories

The number of infractions per annum (all crimes and misdemeanors registered by the police) moved from 3.1% in 2016–2017 to 3.2% in 2018–2019 and 2.8% in 2020–2021 (this latter decrease is partly explained by COVID). This rate of infraction has always been greater in the metropoles, followed by the suburbs, and then the towns and villages.

Sources and series: unehistoireduconflitpolitique.fr

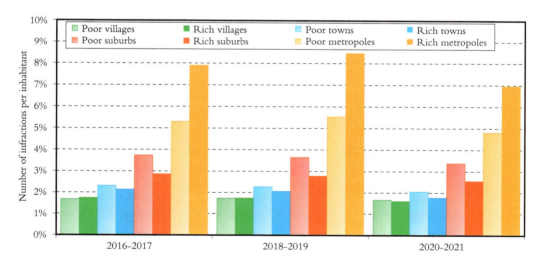

FIGURE 4.18. Infractions in rich and poor territories

The rate of infractions (i.e., the total number of infractions registered by the police, all crimes and misdemeanors taken together, expressed in proportion of the population) has always been greater in the metropoles (particularly in rich metropoles, defined here as the richest 50% in terms of per capita income), followed by the suburbs (particularly the poor suburbs), then towns and villages (where wealth doesn't make much difference).

Sources and series: unehistoireduconflitpolitique.fr

To sum up, there is something strange about the fact that voters in towns and suburbs disagree on the question of the policies to be followed in matters of security, or at least they vote—as we shall see—for political movements that seem to be opposed on this subject. Whether there is a conflict on migratory policy is one thing, but when it comes to security policy properly so called—that is, the number of police officers, how they are equipped and the most suitable way to organize them, as well as the funds that should be allocated to them—it is difficult to understand why the inhabitants of the poor suburbs and of the poor towns should be in disagreement. In particular, all poor territories have a common interest in ensuring that adequate fiscal resources are mobilized at the national level to reduce insecurity within their territories. Just as with the debate about the *assistanat* and other subjects, the focus on identity limits the democratic process's ability to produce concrete socioeconomic solutions to the problems that arise. Furthermore, we will see that voters are not dupes: even though political officials try to focus their fight on security questions, voters' choices are determined above all by socioeconomic considerations. Having been personally confronted by insecurity in one's immediate environment has a relatively limited effect on voting—and in addition, it is more complex and less right-wing than some people might think.[63]

The Obsession with Origins: A Consequence of Forgetting the Social Question?

It is time to conclude this chapter and this first part devoted to the transformations of sociospatial inequalities in France over the past two centuries. To sum up, one might be tempted to say that identitarian conflicts prosper when the social question is allowed to lie fallow. To put it another way, if ambitious programs of social and economic transformation do not succeed in convincing the working classes of different origins that what unites them is more important than what divides them, then conflicts connected with origins and identities will have a tendency to gain the upper hand—if need be, through the intermediary of political entrepreneurs who have a vested interest in stirring them up. To that end, they will bet everything on policies such as the religious policies of the eighteenth and nineteenth centuries or the migration policies in the twentieth and twenty-first centuries, which are, to be sure, important and complex, and may be the object of legitimate political disagreements and confrontations, but which by themselves are hardly capable of responding to the great socioeconomic stakes involved, which

---

63. See in particular chapter 14, figures 14.28–14.29.

usually require universalist approaches that disregard differences in origin or religion: public, cost-free education, social security, a progressive income tax, the right to housing, and so on.

This way of seeing things is in large part justified, but it must not lead us to forget that identitarian and socioeconomic issues are often closely intertwined, and that untangling them requires patient efforts to understand different points of view. At the end of the eighteenth century and during the nineteenth, religious conflict was intimately connected with the question of the redistribution of the Church's lands and their seizure by the urban elites, and then with the question of the educational system and particularly the schooling of girls, who had been largely forgotten by the state public system. At the end of the twentieth century and the beginning of the twenty-first, the migration conflict was closely associated with the question of territories and public services and with the intersecting perceptions of abandonment and favoritism that developed on this subject, notably between towns and suburbs. That takes nothing away from the fact that the solutions are above all socioeconomic—quite the contrary. But tackling this complexity and multidimensionality of the conflicts between the different geosocial classes involved is essential for better understanding the possible solutions and evolutions. To move forward with this analysis, we now need to turn to a detailed study of electoral behaviors and their transformations over long periods.

PART II

The Rise and Fall of Democratic Mobilization

ELECTORAL TURNOUT IN FRANCE, 1789-2022

CHAPTER 5

The General Evolution of Turnout since 1789

After studying in the first part of this work the main lines of the evolution of socio-spatial inequalities in France since the Revolution, we can now consider the heart of the matter and analyze the factors that determine electoral behaviors. In the second part of the book we will focus on the study of electoral turnout in the different kinds of elections studied (legislative, presidential, referenda). We will examine the votes for the various political tendencies in legislative elections in part 3, and in presidential elections and referenda in part 4. In this chapter we will begin by describing the main lines of the evolution of electoral turnout since 1789, and then in the two following chapters we will examine in greater detail the socioeconomic determinants of turnout and its transformations.

How Should the Rise and Then the Decline of Turnout Be Described?

If we examine voting behaviors over the long term, one of the most striking facts is the boom in electoral turnout in the nineteenth century, its continuation at a high level during the second half of the nineteenth century and most of the twentieth, and then the rapid decline in turnout at the end of the twentieth century and the beginning of the twenty-first. Specifically, the rate of turnout in national elections reached about 30 to 40 percent under the Revolution before rising to around 70 to 80 percent in 1848–1849 and stabilizing at that level until 1980–1990, and then undergoing a marked decline since 1990–2000, with less than 50 percent turnout among voters registered during the legislative elections of 2022—the lowest level registered for two centuries (see figure 5.1).[1] This is a form of democratic regression that is particularly disturbing. Democracy is in fact founded on a promise that the majority will participate in public decisions, but two centuries after the French Revolution, the working classes seem to be withdrawing from the

---

1. Turnout is defined here in relation to the number of registered voters, which also varies during the period—as we mentioned in chapter 1—notably because of the gradual extension of the right to vote first to the poorest men and then to women. The rate of registration also fluctuates over time, but to a far smaller degree than turnout does,.

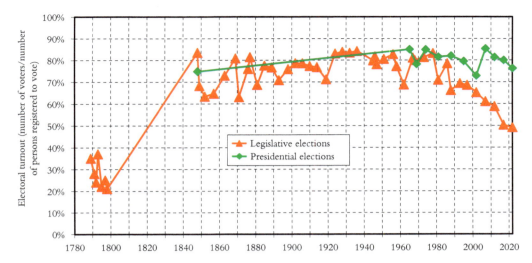

FIGURE 5.1. Electoral turnout, 1789–2022

Turnout in legislative elections was around 30–40% under the Revolution (indirect election). With the establishment of direct election, it oscillated around 70–80% from 1848 to 1980–1990, and has clearly decreased since 2000; it fell below 50% in 2022. Turnout for presidential elections was around 70–80% in 1848, as it was from 1965 to 2022. Note: The turnout indicated here is still the one observed in Metropolitan France for the first round of legislative and presidential elections.

Sources and series: unehistoireduconflitpolitique.fr

electoral game in unprecedented proportions.[2] We defend the thesis that this withdrawal has complex and multiple causes, but that the most important of them is probably the working classes' growing feeling of abandonment when they are confronted by the political and socioeconomic programs that have been proposed to them since 1990–2000, in connection with the gradual crumbling of the Left-Right two-party system and the gradual rise of a three-party system. In theory, we could, of course, imagine that a three-party system and the appearance of new political options would make it possible to increase turnout. But in practice, we are witnessing the fall of the two-party system and the increasing division of the working classes into several blocs, perhaps because they sense that the new, partisan

2. In the context of this research, the notion of "working classes" (*classes populaires*) will be defined in a flexible, multidimensional way, by correlating income, wealth (in particular, real estate assets), occupation, diplomas, and other factors. In this case, all these dimensions are associated with a deepening of the gaps in turnout, but we will see that the same is not true when it is a question of explaining the votes for the Left and the Right. It is therefore particularly important to distinguish very precisely between these different dimensions.

and ideological structure no longer allows a genuine alternation of power at the head of the state.

However, several points must be clarified. First of all, the previously unpublished sources that we have collected to analyze the transformations of electoral behaviors over more than two centuries remain imperfect and incomplete, and they do not allow us to account for the whole of the observed developments in a thoroughly satisfactory way. Our first objective regarding electoral turnout and the votes cast for the different political tendencies is to shed light on certain facts and historical transformations and to draw up a list of the most plausible interpretive hypotheses. To have any hope of understanding recent trends, it seems to us essential to begin by adopting a long-term view. Regarding turnout in voting, before analyzing the current decline, it is necessary to understand how it was possible to achieve a large mobilization historically—particularly at a time when the sources of information were much less numerous and more difficult to access—and how it was sustained for such a long time. In each case, we will explain what seems to us the most convincing interpretation to explain the observed developments, taking into account the data at our disposal, but the objective is certainly not to put an end to debate; instead, we seek to open it up in a transparent way and in all its complexity.

Among the many limitations of the available sources, it is truly only starting with the legislative and presidential elections of 1848 that it is possible to study rigorously the structure of the electoral turnout and the votes for the different political tendencies. The Revolution of February 1848 marks the definitive advent of universal male suffrage, and it is only since that date that the electoral records kept at the level of the cantons and municipalities take a relatively homogeneous form all over the territory and indicate (almost) systematically the number of registered voters, the number of blank and null ballots, the total number of votes cast (minus blank or null votes), and the detailed breakdown of the votes among the different candidates. These records have been preserved in the National Archives, and it is thanks to the digitization of these documents that we have carried out for the whole of Metropolitan France that we are able to study electoral behaviors. In particular, it is starting in 1848 that we can measure both the rate of registration on electoral lists (that is, the number of registered voters divided by the number of persons with the right to vote, as estimated using the censuses) and the rate of turnout (that is, the number of voters divided by the number of registered voters).

Regarding the elections of the revolutionary and Napoleonic periods (1789–1815), the records established by the electoral assemblies at the local level were preserved much more unevenly, and above all, these documents take forms that are extremely variable and heterogeneous over the territory. They generally enable us to estimate the number of registered voters and the voters who cast ballots, and the rate of turnout at the local level, but it is often difficult to go much further. In particular, it is hard to measure precisely the rate of registration, given the incomplete demographic data for this period as well as the absence of any centralized procedure for registering on the electoral lists, in a context where the rules about the extent of the right to vote were frequently modified and were also the subject of numerous conflicts of interpretation among the different social groups present at the local level.[3] It is also very difficult (if not impossible) to use these documents to study the votes for the different candidates in the legislative elections (we will come back to this in part 3). Generally speaking, the records of the electoral assemblies of the revolutionary period constitute an extremely rich body of material for studying the political conflicts of this foundational moment, but they do not allow us to envisage the constitution of a systematic database that is comparable to what we can do for the post-1848 period. That is why we have limited ourselves, for the revolutionary period, to making use of the data on turnout already collected by other authors (in particular, Serge Aberdam for the referenda of 1793 and 1795, and Marvin Edelstein for the legislative elections of the decade 1789–1799).[4] Concerning the electoral data issuing from the period of the censitary monarchies (1815–1848), when only 1–2 percent of adult males had the right to vote—so that electoral conflict was by definition reduced to a conflict among the elites (a fascinating subject in itself, but one that involves questions different from those that we will concentrate on here)—we have chosen not to pursue it in the framework of this research project.[5]

3. The works of Edelstein and Aberdam on the basis of the records of the electoral assemblies indicate the existence of numerous conflicts of this kind, particularly when city dwellers or well-off peasants challenged the right to vote of persons situated at the borders of the world of day laborers and domestic servants. See chapter 1.

4. The results obtained for the legislative elections are summed up in the tables reproduced in the works in question (see references below) and are unfortunately not available in the form of a homogeneous and reusable database. On the other hand, the data concerning the referenda of 1793 and 1795 are available in the form of a database at the level of the districts and cantons; we will use them below.

5. On the evolution of the right to vote since 1789, see chapter 1, figures 1.1–1.3. The systematic study of the period from 1815 to 1848 would be all the more interesting because the nominative lists of the electors indicating the amount of taxes they paid to secure the right to vote have been preserved and can be used for studying the votes at the local level. On the elections of the censitary period, see A. Jardin and A. J. Tudesq, *La France des notables (1815–1848)* (Seuil, 1973).

Three Forms of Electoral Democracy:
Legislative, Presidential, Referenda-Based

It is also pertinent to emphasize here the fact that the evolution of electoral turnout depends on numerous factors connected with the different material and collective forms of political mobilization (such as means of transportation, pamphlets and newspapers, and clubs and parties), which may vary greatly with the type of election concerned. Generally speaking, in this book we will be interested in three types of elections organized at the national level: legislative elections, presidential elections, and referenda. These are the three grand forms taken by electoral democracy on the national scale since the Revolution.

In theory, we could also have taken an interest in municipal and departmental elections, which, in their choosing of municipal councils and general councils (departmental parliaments), have constituted the leading elections of electoral democracy on the local scale. However, these elections raise questions rather different from those raised by national elections, insofar as they propose many candidates without a clear political label on the national level (particularly in municipal elections). We could also have studied the European elections organized since the establishment in 1979 of a European parliament elected by universal suffrage, or the regional elections carried out since the creation in 1986 of regional councils elected by universal suffrage. However, these elections have existed for only a few decades. Taking into account the long-term historical perspective that we have adopted here, we have chosen to concentrate on the legislative and presidential elections and the referenda. However, it will be noted that turnout in municipal and regional elections has gradually declined from about 70 to 80 percent in the 1980s to barely 40 to 50 percent in the early 2020s—a decline comparable to the one observed in the legislative elections (see figure 5.2).[6] Concerning European elections, turnout has always been relatively low since 1979, but with a significant increase in 2019 that ran against the trend. Naturally, it is too early to say whether this might be an enduring phenomenon—perhaps linked to the growing importance of the European stake and of the public policies established at this level—or a result of the change in the mode of election, with the transition from eight interregional districts to a single national district in

---

6. We have not sought to collect complete historical data on municipal elections since the nineteenth century, and we have limited ourselves here to indicating the levels of turnout observed since the 1947 municipal elections, based chiefly on the data collected in A. Lancelot's classic work *L'abstention électorale en France* (Presses de Sciences Po, 1968).

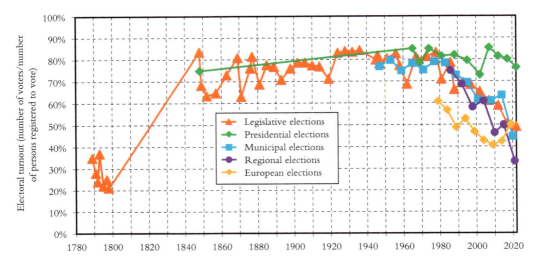

FIGURE 5.2. National, local, and European turnout

Recently, turnout for municipal and regional elections has suffered a decrease similar to that of turnout for legislative elections: it fell from about 70–80% in the 1980s to about 40–50% at the beginning of the 2020s. Turnout for European elections has always been rather low ever since they were introduced in 1979, it but rose slightly in 2019. Note: The turnout indicated here is always that observed in Metropolitan France for the first round of the various elections.

Sources and series: unehistoireduconflitpolitique.fr

continental France, or whether there is some other explanation that will be apparent only with greater historical distance.[7]

Of the three forms of electoral democracy organized at the national level over the past two centuries (legislative elections, presidential elections, and referenda), legislative elections constitute, from our point of view, the most significant, because it is elections that allow the greatest number of political families and tendencies to express themselves (generally, we will distinguish between eight and fifteen tendencies, depending on the election), and because they are the only elections that have taken place repeatedly and regularly over the course of the last two centuries. In addition to the legislative elections in the revolutionary period, we count no fewer than forty-five legislative elections conducted between 1848 and 2022,

---

7. International comparisons are of little help here. Whereas, as in France, turnout has increased in Germany (from 48 to 61 percent) and in Spain (from 43 to 61 percent) between the elections of 2014 and 2019, it decreased in Italy (from 57 to 54 percent) and Portugal (from 34 to 31 percent).

or one election every four years, on average (see figure 5.1).[8] Of these forty-five elections, twenty-four were held within the framework of universal male suffrage (from 1848 to 1936) and twenty-one under universal female and male suffrage (from 1945 to 2022). We note that the extension of the vote to women did not have a major effect on turnout: the number of registered voters leaped from 11.8 million voters in 1936 to 24.6 million voters in 1945, but the percentage of voters remained virtually the same (84 percent in 1936, 80 percent in 1945), or a variation of the same order as those frequently observed from one election to another.[9]

Generally, it is striking to see that the rate of turnout in legislative elections shows no clear trend from the 1840s to the 1980s: for almost a century and a half, turnout has always been around 70 to 80 percent, without any obvious development in one direction or another, neither increasing nor decreasing. This makes all the more spectacular the decline that began to appear in the 1990s and 2000s and accelerated in the 2010s and at the beginning of the 2020s, with turnouts of scarcely 50 percent in the legislative elections of 2017 and 2022. Let us add that we have indicated, for each legislative election, the moderate turnout in the first round of voting in Metropolitan France, in order to ensure a maximal comparability over time.[10]

---

8. We refer to the legislative elections of 1848, 1849, 1852, 1857, 1863, 1869, 1871 (two elections), 1876, 1877, 1881, 1885, 1889, 1893, 1898, 1902, 1906, 1910, 1914, 1919, 1924, 1928, 1932, 1936, 1945, 1946 (two elections), 1951, 1956, 1958, 1962, 1967, 1968, 1973, 1978, 1981, 1986, 1988, 1993, 1997, 2002, 2007, 2012, 2017, and 2022. Two elections were organized in 1946 (the constitutive assembly in June and the legislative assembly in November). Strictly speaking, there was only one election in 1871, but in practice, the partial elections held in July concerned more than half of the departments (taking the multiple withdrawals into account), and we treat them as an election distinct from that of February (see below). For the overall study of the evolution of turnout, we have included in figure 5.1 the four legislative elections of the Second Empire (1852, 1857, 1863, and 1869). On the other hand, these elections were not taken into account in either the analysis of turnout at the level of the municipalities or the analysis of political tendencies that was conducted (which was thus limited to forty-one elections).

9. However, it is possible that one important part of this decrease might in this case be attributed to the disparity between female and male abstentions that existed at that time, a disparity of between five and ten percentage points in the surveys carried out after the elections of 1951, 1956, and 1962 (no similar survey seems to have been made in 1945). See Lancelot, *L'abstention électorale*. We will later return to the evolution of gender gaps in electoral behaviors.

10. The evolution of turnout is rigorously the same over the long term in the second round of voting (the turnout figures are usually very close in the two rounds). However, the second round raises problems of comparability in time, insofar as only the electors from districts whose seats have not been filled in the first round are eligible to vote in the second round, which excludes a variable part of the electorate, depending on the periods and the elections. In part 3, we will also return to the changes in the modes of voting in legislative elections and their possible impact on the votes.

The legislative elections will thus constitute in this work our main observation post for studying electoral behaviors in France over a long period. However, we must not underestimate the importance of presidential elections and referenda, which over the course of the last two centuries have been two fundamental and complementary ways of expressing universal suffrage on the national scale. We will see that both of them have had decisive impacts on the structuring of political conflict since the Revolution. In particular, the presidential election of 1848 played an essential role in the formation of partisan affiliations in the middle of the nineteenth century, and it also helped fuel a certain skepticism regarding direct democracy and presidentialism, to the extent that it was not until 1965 that the election of the president of the Republic by universal suffrage returned, and not without passionate disagreements.[11] It is generally thought that the reintroduction in 1965 of universal direct suffrage for presidential elections also had a major impact on the consolidation of the two-party system (henceforth, each camp has had to unite in the second round at the national level), although the crumbling of this system since the 1990s and the rise of the three-party system in 2017 and 2022 remind us that the effect of the electoral system on political-ideological structures must not be exaggerated. Referenda have also played a fundamental role in French political history, from the 1793 referendum on the republican constitution (the vote with the highest turnout of the period) to the 1992 and 2005 referenda on the Maastricht Treaty and the European constitutional treaty, which had a crucial impact on the political reconfigurations of recent decades, as we shall see.

The main limitation of presidential elections and referenda is that they are relatively irregular in comparison to legislative elections. Whereas from 1848 to 2022 there were forty-five legislative elections at regular intervals, there was only one presidential election in 1848, followed by an interruption of more than a century, and then eleven elections between 1965 and 2022. In addition, the nature of the electoral choice is far more unstable for presidential elections (which are often very personalized and raise serious problems in comparing candidacies and the meaning of the votes over time) than for legislative elections (during which the main political tendencies are constantly reshaped, to be sure, but generally in a more gradual way than the individual personalities involved in presidential elections are). We also note that the decline in turnout observed in legislative elections during the period between 1990 and 2022 is not found in presidential elections, which continue to be characterized by a turnout on the order of 70 to 80 percent, with a slight decrease, of course, during the last elections, but with no very strong,

---

11. See chapter 1.

clear trend to date (see figure 5.1).[12] We will come back to this decoupling and its interpretation.

The Four Ages of the Referendum in France

Like legislative elections, referendum elections also are characterized by their occurrences at irregular intervals and by the fact that the questions the electors are asked are constantly changing. To sum up, we can distinguish four major periods in the history of the referendum in France: the referenda of the revolutionary period, conducted from 1793 to 1815; the referenda of the Second Empire, conducted from 1851 to 1870; the referenda of the Liberation and of Gaullism, from 1945 to 1969; and finally, the referenda of the contemporary period, dominated by the two European referenda of 1992 and 2005, as well as several elections of lesser importance. If we examine the evolution of the turnout in referenda over a long term, we see an overall movement that is in some respects comparable to the curve noted for legislative elections: a relatively modest turnout at the end of the eighteenth century and the beginning of the nineteenth, then a stabilization at a high level from the middle of the nineteenth century to the second half of the twentieth century, and a tendency to decrease starting in the end of the twentieth century (see figure 5.3).

The comparison with the legislative elections must not be pushed too far, though: referenda have a specific history connected with the diversity of the political uses to which they have been put. Historically, referenda were at first used not to settle a disputed or unclear question, but rather to demonstrate overtly the public's strong support for a change in the regime or the constitution. Usually, what was at stake was not so much the number of Yes votes as how many people voted. It was only later on, starting in the middle of the twentieth century, that referenda ceased to be seen as plebiscites, and some were decided by relatively close votes. Of the twenty-one national referenda organized in France since 1793, only three resulted in victories for No voters: the first constitutional referendum in 1946, the referendum of 1969 regarding the Senate (when what was at stake was especially

---

12. In order to facilitate the comparison with turnout in legislative elections, we have indicated here the turnout in the first round of presidential elections. In 1848, Louis-Napoléon Bonaparte was elected in the first round. Between 1965 and 2012, turnout was generally slightly higher in the second round than in the first (notably in 2002, after the low turnout in the first round). On the other hand, in 2017 and 2022 turnout was lower in the second round than in the first, which accentuated the underlying decline turnout in the voting for president in the most recent elections.

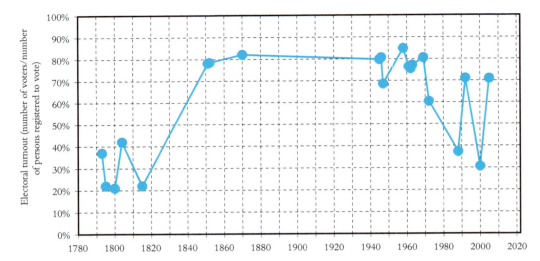

FIGURE 5.3. Turnout for referenda, 1793–2005

Four phases can be distinguished in the history of referenda in France: the Revolution (constitutions of 1793 and 1795, referenda in 1800, 1804, 1815), with turnout of 20–40%; the Second Empire (referenda in 1851, 1852, and 1870); Liberation and Gaullism (referenda of 1945–1946, 1958, 1961, 1962, and 1969 with turnout of 70–80%; and the post-Gaullist period, with varying turnout—more than 70% for the European referenda of 1992 and 2005, barely 60% for that on the United Kingdom (1972), and 30–40% for Nouvelle-Calédonie (1988) and the five-year presidential term (2000).

Sources and series: unehistoireduconflitpolitique.fr

the anticipated departure of General de Gaulle), and the European referendum of 2005, where the No vote won most clearly, with 55 percent of the vote, despite the fact that all the government parties supported the Yes side. This experience was so traumatizing for the parties and the officials that no referenda have been organized since then.[13]

Conversely, the first two referenda in French electoral history, conducted in July 1793 and September 1795 to ratify the new republican constitutions, both registered around 99.5 percent Yes votes and barely 0.5 percent No votes. Nonetheless, we must add that the notion of a No vote is itself complex and hard to define in

---

13. The constitutional reform of 2008 introduced the possibility of a referendum initiated by the parliament in conjunction with citizens at large, but the conditions set for it are so restrictive that it has never been used (see chapter 1). Let us note, moreover, that the experience of the referendum of 2005 was also traumatizing for the citizens themselves because their massive No did not prevent the subsequent adoption of the Treaty of Lisbon, which was ratified in France by the parliament in 2008 and went into force in 2009.

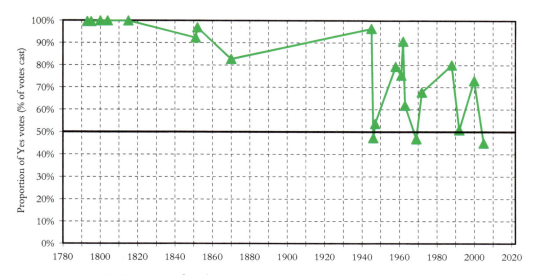

FIGURE 5.4. The Yes vote in referenda, 1793–2005

The result obtained by the Yes voters exceeded 99% in the referenda of the Revolutionary period (with barely 0.5% of No votes in 1793 and 1795 and less than 0.1% in 1800, 1804, and 1815) and was about 80–95% in the referenda conducted under the Second Empire (1851, 1852, and 1870). Conversely, the referenda conducted since 1945 have often led to much closer results and even defeats for the Yes camp (47% in 1946 in the first referendum on the constitution, 54% in the second; 47% Yes in the referendum of 1769; 51% and 45% in the referenda of 1992 and 2005).

Sources and series: unehistoireduconflitpolitique.fr

the institutional context of the period. In the framework of the electoral assemblies of the revolutionary period, which were strongly inclined to vote Yes, it was not very easy for a dissenting voice to make itself heard. In this case, the 0.5 percent corresponds to the individual negative votes that were explicitly recorded as such in the minutes of the electoral assemblies collected by researchers.[14] But that does not mean that there were no other dissenting voices during these assemblies held in the canton's main town.

One way to proceed would be to take into account the multiple petitions, declarations, and other amendments to the constitution that were sometimes adopted by primary assemblies, particularly in 1793, even if these assemblies decided to send

---

14. For the referenda of 1793 and 1795, we use the databases constituted at the level of the districts and cantons by Serge Aberdam, on the basis of electoral reports. See Aberdam, *L'élargissement du droit de vote entre 1792 et 1795 au travers du dénombrement du comité de division et des votes populaires sur les constitutions de 1793 et 1795* (Paris I, 2001.

to Paris a delegate who was in favor of the constitution. For example, if we choose to count as negative votes all the votes of the assemblies that adopted a petition or a modification of one kind or another to the text of the constitution, then we would obtain about 10 percent No, not just 0.5 percent. The problem, as Serge Aberdam has shown, is that these petitions and amendments can be of very different kinds, some of them requiring more egalitarian socioeconomic measures (such as a maximum price for bread, or redistribution of land in favor of poor peasants) and others defending refractory priests or denouncing those who seized national goods, and still others making alternative institutional propositions.[15] Under these conditions, it is undoubtedly preferable to limit oneself to the No votes duly recorded as such, and to use the variations in the rate of turnout (or rather of the rate of approval—that is, the number of Yes votes divided by the number of registered voters, which is virtually identical with turnout) as an imperfect but significant indicator of the support enjoyed by the proposed constitution and its variations, depending on the territories concerned.

During the referendum of 1793, the average rate of turnout was 37 percent,[16] which could seem small compared with modern standards of turnout, but it represents the largest mobilization of the period. We must also emphasize the fact that the material conditions of voting were extremely difficult at that time. The election took place in the canton's main town, which could mean several hours of walking for villagers, on poor roads and in challenging weather. It also entailed leaving one's village and goods without male surveillance, which raised fears about security. Furthermore, the means of information and the diffusion of leaflets were very limited. Political clubs and movements were few, and mainly established in cities. Under these conditions, such a mobilization is impressive and can be interpreted as a sign of the strong demand for democratic participation in the revolutionary period, especially in connection with the approval of a constitution that established universal male suffrage, the direct election of deputies, and the possi-

---

15. See Aberdam, *L'élargissement du droit de vote.* For the attempts to gauge the size of the No vote on the basis of petitions and amendments, see R. Baticle, "Le plébiscite sur la constitution de 1793," *La Révolution française,* 1909; M. Vovelle, *La découverte de la politique. Géopolitique de la Révolution française* (La Découverte, 1992), 202.

16. This estimate is based on the data collected by Aberdam and Edelstein over the whole of the territory. Taking into account the limitations of the sources available for that time, it is nevertheless more prudent to stick to an order of magnitude—around 35–40 percent—rather than an exact figure.

bilities of a participative referendum.[17] During the referendum on the conservative constitution of 1795, which reestablished censitary suffrage and the election of deputies in several stages, turnout fell to little more than 20 percent (see figure 5.3). We find a similar mobilization (or a slightly smaller one) in the case of the referendum organized in January 1800 by Napoleon Bonaparte to ratify the constitution of the Consulate after the coup d'état of 18 Brumaire (November 1799), despite the proven attempts of the minister of the interior, Lucien Bonaparte—one is never so well served as by one's brother—to falsify the results to double the score in favor of the referendum and lift it above the level of 1793 (which was already being hailed as the peak of the mobilization, despite the very approximate character of the electoral statistics at the time).[18] The authoritarian turn taken by the Napoleonic regime and the lack of voting secrecy (the obligatory use of a voting booth was introduced only in 1913) accentuated the referenda's similarity to plebiscites. In the referenda of 1800 (establishing the Consulate), 1804 (establishing the Empire), and 1815 (reestablishing the Empire during the "Hundred Days"), the No votes represented barely 0.1 percent of the ballots counted. Turnout reached 40 percent, according to the results of the 1804 election (apparently not falsified), and fell back to about 20 percent in 1815.

The referenda conducted several decades later, under the Second Empire, took place in a transformed context. The definitive institution of universal male suffrage in 1848 and the disputed legislative and presidential elections of 1848 and 1849 were accompanied by an unprecedented rate of turnout, 70 to 80 percent, a level that was reached again in the referenda of 1851 (establishing a strong presidency), and in 1852 (reestablishing the imperial regime), though with levels of No votes that were increasingly significant: around 5 to 10 percent of the voters in 1851 and 1852, and almost 20 percent in 1870, with a rapidly expanding republican opposition. The establishment of the Third Republic was accompanied by a rejection of the plebiscite-like practices associated with Bonapartism, as the disgraced referendum was banished from democratic practices for seventy-five years.

---

17. See chapter 1. See also S. Aberdam, *L'élargissement du droit de vote entre 1792 et 1795 au travers du dénombrement du comité de division et des votes populaires sur les constitutions de 1793 et 1795* (Paris I, 2001); S. Aberdam, *Démographes et démocrates. L'oeuvre du comité de division de la Convention nationale* (SER, 2004); S. Aberdam et al., *Voter, élire pendant la Révolution française 1789–1799. Guide pour la recherche* (CTHS, 2006); and M. Edelstein, *La Révolution française et la naissance de la démocratie électorale* (PUR, 2013).

18. See C. Langlois, "Le plébiscite de l'an VII, ou le coup d'État du 18 pluviôse an VIII," *Annales historiques de la Révolution française*, 1972.

From Referenda-Plebiscites to the Disputed
Votes of 1946, 1992, and 2005

The referendum made its comeback in October 1945, with the approval, by 96 percent of the votes, of the establishment of a constitutive assembly entrusted with writing a new constitution for the Fourth Republic. It was then that the referendum was to become for the first time in France the object of fiercely disputed elections. A first constitutive assembly (which also had, equally and temporarily, legislative powers) was elected in December 1945. These were the first parliamentary elections since 1936, and they saw a strong surge by the Communist and Socialist Parties. The constitution written under their influence was contested by the Gaullists and the right-wing parties, who denounced the return of an assembly regime and especially the suppression of the senatorial veto, which they warned might lead to an omnipotent National Assembly controlled by the Left, without a counterweight. The draft constitution was rejected in May 1946 with 53 percent voting No, which led to the election in June 1946 of a second constitutive assembly (which also had legislative power and leaned markedly to the left). The new draft constitution was not very different from the first one, and in particular it confirmed the suppression of the senatorial veto.[19] In the end, it was adopted in October 1946 with 54 percent of the vote and led to the establishment of the Fourth Republic and to legislative elections in November 1946.

General de Gaulle's return to power in 1958 was to lead to a new series of referenda, first in 1958 to approve the new constitution; then in 1961 and 1962 regarding the Évian Accords and Algerian independence; again in 1962 for the election of the president with universal male suffrage (approved by 62 percent of the votes); and finally in 1969 for the reform of the Senate (rejected by 53 percent of the votes, which led to the anticipated departure of de Gaulle). About 70 to 80 percent of registered voters participated in each of these referenda. This was not the case in the 1972 referendum on the entry of the United Kingdom into the European Economic Community, when turnout fell to 60 percent, and especially not in the 1988 and 2000 elections on New Caledonia and the five-year term for the president, when turnout fell to about 30 to 40 percent (see figure 5.3). Contrary to what people might have assumed from the 1840s to the 1960s, the systematic mobilization of 70 to 80 percent of the voters for national elections is not set in stone. When voters think the election is not interesting enough, turnout may be much lower (at least, that is what we have seen since the 1970s).

---

19. We will return to the differences between the two drafts in chapter 14.

In this book, we will concentrate on five referenda that are among the most significant organized since the Revolution: the referenda of 1793 and 1795, the constitutional referendum of 1946,[20] and the two European referenda of 1992 and 2005. The latter two elections were the first to put at stake in referenda major economic and international choices that were, moreover, formulated in the context of European integration and the debates centering on globalization and commercial and financial liberalization. The referendum of 1992 led to the approval, by a hair's breadth, of the creation of the euro (51 percent Yes), whereas the referendum of 1992, conducted in the context of a perceived social and salarial competition with Eastern Europe (made famous by the debate over "Polish plumbers"), was rejected by a 55 percent No vote. Both of these referenda attracted the participation of about 70 percent of the voters (see figures 5.3–5.4). We will have more to say about these elections, which have played a central role in the restructuring of the political field around the question of globalization and economic and commercial liberalization, as well as the national question.

Turnout during the Revolution: A Strong Rural Mobilization

Let us return to a chronological approach and start to examine the structure of electoral turnout in the various elections held during the Revolution. The available sources are less complete than those for the post-1848 period, but they nonetheless allow us to sketch an overall panorama of the variations in the rates of turnout. We will base our remarks chiefly on the works of Marvin Edelstein, which are in turn based on the most complete collections of data currently available to us, the minutes of the electoral assemblies.[21] The most striking result emerging from these studies is the very strong electoral mobilization seen in rural areas and villages, which generally was greater than in the large cities. This is notably the case in the municipal elections of February 1790, which are the first elections organized in the framework of the new electoral system set up in the autumn of 1789. According to the lists drawn up by Edelstein, turnout reached about 55 to 60 percent in the villages, compared to 30 to 40 percent in the cities. We find the same enthusiasm in

---

20. Whence the existence of two legislative elections in 1946 (one in May, the other in November), taking into account the fact that elections to the Constituent Assembly in December 1945 and May 1946 were also legislative elections (with the constituent assemblies exercising legislative power while awaiting the creation of new institutions).
21. See M. Edelstein, *La Révolution française et la naissance de la démocratie électorale* (Presses Universitaires de Rennes, 2013). See also M. Crook, *Elections in the French Revolution: An Apprenticeship in Democracy, 1789–1799* (Cambridge University Press, 1996).

working classes were able to rely more on the weight of numbers and their experience with shared anti-aristocratic mobilizations in order to assert themselves (or at least to go vote).[26] In any case, these results demolish the idea of a rural world that is structurally conservative and averse to democracy. The results that we obtain for later periods confirm the existence, since the Revolution, of a turnout structurally greater in the rural world than in the urban world, as well as the importance of the processes of collective mobilization in accounting for the historical variations around this central schema.

The Rise in Turnout and Registration to Vote in the Nineteenth Century

We come now to the electoral turnout for the period from the elections of the post-1848 period to those of 2022. The sources we have collected for the post-1848 period allow an analysis of the participation and the vote that is much more detailed and systematic than for the period from 1789 to 1815. In particular, we can study both the rate of electoral turnout (classically defined as the number of voters divided by the number of names on registration lists) and the rate of registration to vote (defined as the number of registered voters divided by the number of people with the right to vote, as they can be estimated on the basis of censuses), starting in 1848. If we examine first the evolution of the rate of registration at the national level, we see relative stability over the long term. The rate of electoral registration is about 90 percent throughout the period between 1848 and 2022, with slight variations, generally between 88–89 percent and 93–94 percent, but with no clear trend over the course of the last two centuries (see figure 5.5). Even if it is a relatively high rate, it implies that from 1848 to 2022 almost 10 percent of the population has always had the right to vote but does not appear on any electoral list. In addition, it implies that electoral turnout as it has traditionally been measured tends to overestimate the actual turnout by about 10 percent. We will see that this average rate of electoral registration at the national level is also characterized by major variations between territories.

Several points are worth clarifying here. First of all, we have estimated the population with the right to vote on the basis of censuses; this includes the male

---

26. Some authors also trace the stronger rural than urban turnout to the Estates General of 1561 and 1614, in connection with the strategies of the Old Regime's administrative elites to mobilize the countryside and establish their own legitimacy with respect to the nobility and the urban bourgeoisie. See R. Halevi, "Modalités, turnouts et luttes électorales dans la France d'Ancien régime," in *Explication du vote. Un bilan des études électorales en France,* ed. D. Gaxie (Presses de la FNSP, 1985).

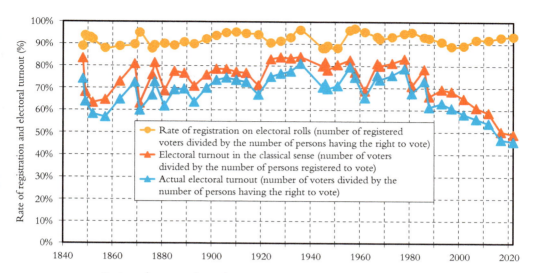

FIGURE 5.5. Registered voters and actual turnout

The rate of registration on electoral rolls (i.e., the number of registered voters divided by the number of persons with the right to vote) has generally been about 90% in Metropolitan France from 1848 to the beginning of the twenty-first century. Consequently, the actual electoral turnout (the number of voters divided by the number of persons with the right to vote) has always been about 10% less than electoral turnout in the classic sense (the number of voters divided by the number of registered voters).

Sources and series: unehistoireduconflitpolitique.fr

population that had French nationality and was twenty-one or older (from 1848 to 1936) and the male and female population that had French nationality and was twenty-one or older (from 1945 to 1974) or eighteen or older (from 1974 to 2022). The orders of magnitude obtained for the calculation of the rate of registration can be considered broadly valid, but the data are imprecise and must be interpreted with caution. In particular, the results of the censuses available at the level of the departments and municipalities do not always indicate the breakdown by the men's exact ages in accordance with their nationalities, which forces us to make diverse hypotheses and approximations.[27] More fundamentally, the notion of residence as it is used in censuses does not always coincide with residence in the electoral sense; for instance, people who move can be living in a municipality at the time of the census while continuing to be registered to vote in their former municipality. Surveys conducted in France starting in the late 1970s show that "misregistration"—

---

27. For example, the results are sometimes organized into quinquennial age groups, which obliges us to make hypotheses regarding the distribution of the population within a cohort.

that is, being registered in a municipality other than one's municipality of residence—might affect almost 10 percent of the people registered on electoral lists, with levels below 4 percent for older populations in rural areas and exceeding 20 percent for young populations in the metropoles.[28] Although that does not, of course, affect the rate of registration as a whole, it may help explain an important part of abstention, and it suggests that simplified and automated registration procedures might help reduce it.[29] However, the sources available over the long term do not allow us to measure rigorously the development of misregistration, and we will therefore concentrate here on nonregistration. But it is important to keep in mind that the former is potentially just as important as the latter.

Let us also add that according to the available estimates, the average rate of registration was around 90 percent under the French Revolution.[30] Nevertheless, there is a difference in the nature of electoral registration during the revolutionary period versus after 1848. Under the Revolution, the process of registration on the electoral lists was organized wholly on the local level. No information on the numbers of registered voters or the population with the right to vote was centralized at the national level. In addition, between 1789 and 1799, a significant portion of the adult males was excluded from voting (generally between a fourth and half, depending on the years), with the incessant variations of the rules on the national scale and multiple sources of conflict at the municipal and cantonal level. The institutional context was entirely different in 1848. Starting in 1801, censuses were organized at the national level and became increasingly regular and uniform in the 1820s and 1830s until the censuses of 1841 and 1846. By the time of the elections of 1848, the municipal populations were well registered and known by everyone, which was absolutely not the case in the 1790s.[31]

---

28. See F. Subileau and M. F. Toinet, "L'abstentionnisme en France et aux États-Unis: Méthodes et interprétations," in Gaxie, *Explication du vote*.

29. For what concerns us here, the hypotheses we have to make can lead us to underestimate or overestimate the actual rate of registration on the electoral lists in certain municipalities with respect to others; we will return to this.

30. See unehistoireduconflitpolitique.fr, figure A1.1e and appendix A1.

31. As Aberdam has shown, the development of a system of registering municipal populations was inseparable from the chaotic and conflictual process of extending the right to vote in the 1790s. In particular, the central article of the constitution of 1793 (never applied) is article 23, which stipulates that each deputy is elected by a district with exactly 40,000 inhabitants ("between 39,000 and 41,000 souls"), in order to avoid the manipulations and circumventions of universal suffrage. That implies the development of an extremely reliable system of registering populations that was entirely established only in the course of the following decades. See Aberdam, *L'élargissement du droit de vote;* Aberdam, *Démographes et démocrates.* On the organization of

Above all, men's universal right to vote was now no longer contested: the decree issued after the revolutionary days of February 1848 foresaw a condition of residency in the canton of only six months (and all the modes of proof thereof) to be able to register on the electoral lists. In May 1850, with the so-called Burgraves' law, the conservative Assembly elected in 1849 attempted to exclude a third of those registered by instituting a residence requirement of three years and obliging voters to produce a fiscal certificate, which outraged the population and allowed Louis-Napoléon Bonaparte to launch his coup d'état in December 1851 in the name of the reestablishment of universal suffrage. In addition, the prince-president decided in 1852 to generalize the establishment of voting stations in municipalities (and not just in cantons or sections of cantons, as had been the case in 1848 and 1849), a measure that was very popular in the rural world and considerably reduced the travel time for inhabitants of the countryside. After this crisis, no significant political movement sought to contest universal suffrage in France again, no matter how authoritarian the regimes in place might be in other respects (starting with the imperial regime itself).[32]

Although universal suffrage was no longer contested after 1848, and turnout stabilized for the first time at about 70–80 percent during the legislative elections of April 1848 and May 1849 and also in the presidential election of December 1848, that was also because in the course of the preceding half century the republican, democratic conception had made its way into people's consciousnesses, the newspapers, and the practices of mobilization (such as the republican banquets). Works by Bois, Tilly, Aberdam, and Edelstein clearly show the strength of the demand for democracy that was already being expressed in the electoral assemblies of the revolutionary period. The turnout for these assemblies nevertheless remained less than half of the registered voters (30–40 percent, not 70–80 percent). Other studies, like those of Maurice Agulhon on the rise in republican feeling in the campaigns in the department of Var between 1815 and 1848, have examined the stages in this long process of spreading the democratic idea and the legitimacy

---

the vote in 1848, see A. Garrigou, *Le vote et la vertu. Comment les Français sont devenus électeurs* (Presses de la FNSP, 1992), 30–48.

32. The draft constitution presented by Marshal Pétain on 30 January 1944 foresaw a double vote for fathers with three children (a measure defended by Jean-Marie Le Pen in the 1980s and 1990s), as well as a president elected for ten years by the Chamber of Deputies and the Senate in plenary session (including fifty members named by the head of state "among the elites of the country" and among the professional associations) but without directly challenging universal suffrage. The suffrage was even extended to women: on this point, Pétain felt obliged to follow through on the announcement made by General de Gaulle in 1942, which was finally applied for the first time in 1945.

of voting as a way of expressing disagreements and settling conflicts, notably in connection with fiscal questions, access to land and wood, and rural mobilizations concerning local and municipal issues.[33] Let us also recall that the cens (the tax quota for voting rights) was much smaller for municipal elections than for the legislative elections between 1831 and 1848; between 2 and 3 million persons could vote in the municipal elections—that is, between 20 percent and 30 percent of adult men—whereas less than 2 percent could vote in the legislative elections.[34] These municipal elections were to constitute an important stage in learning about electoral democracy and fuel the demands for a return to universal suffrage as the revolutionary days of 1848 approached, in the context of the agricultural and industrial crisis of 1846–1847.[35]

To sum up, the transition from an electoral turnout of 30–40 percent in the 1790s to a turnout of 70–80 percent starting in 1848 (and continuing until the 1980s), and all of this with a well-established electoral registration (around 90 percent), can be seen as the outcome of a complex process of collective mobilization and of institutional, sociohistorical, and cultural change. In other words, there is nothing particularly natural about the social construction of a turnout of 70–80 percent; decreeing the right to vote does not suffice to make the population join in the game and rush to the voting booth. In addition, and above all, voters have to be convinced that the electoral process is useful, equitable, and legitimate. The historical circumstances permitting such a construction are far from being completely understood, but everything indicates that it is a fragile process responding to specific conditions. This also implies that what has been done can be undone, and consequently, that we must give the greatest attention to the unprecedented decline in electoral turnout in recent decades.

Turnout, Registration, and Effective Turnout

Let us now return to the rate of voter registration of about 90 percent observed from 1848 to 2022 and to its consequences for the analysis of voter turnout in France. The first consequence is naturally that effective turnout (which we can define as the number of voters divided by the number of people who have the right to vote) is considerably smaller than turnout in the classic sense (defined as the

33.   See M. Agulhon, *La République au village. Les populations du Var de la Révolution à la Seconde République* (Plon, 1970).

34.   See A. J. Tudesq, "Les comportements électoraux sous les régimes censitaires," in Gaxie, *Explication du vote.*

35.   We will return to this subject in chapter 9, on the context of the elections of 1848.

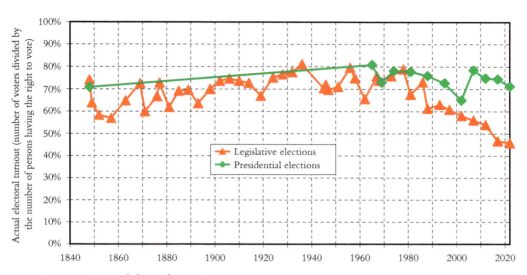

FIGURE 5.6. Actual electoral turnout

If we examine the actual electoral turnout (number of voters divided by the number of persons with the right to vote) and not electoral turnout in the classic sense (number of voters divided by the number of registered voters), we see that the maximal turnout was reached for the legislative elections of 1936, with 81% turnout (followed by those of 1956 and 1978, with 7% turnout), and for the presidential election of 1965 with 81% turnout (followed by that of 1974 with 78%).

Sources and series: unehistoireduconflitpolitique.fr

number of voters divided by the number of registered voters). In the rest of this book, we will continue to use the classic definition, which has the twofold advantage of emphasizing what is commonly used in France, and of avoiding the difficulties of estimating the population that has the right to vote in legislative elections, presidential elections, and other elections (see figures 5.5–5.6). In particular, effective turnout was barely 45 percent during in the legislative elections of 2022, not 50 percent, as turnout in the classic sense suggests. In other words, less than one French person out of two who had the right to vote actually exercised it.

These questions are all the more important because different countries do not necessarily adopt the same definition of electoral turnout. In France, a country where the system of electoral registration covers the immense majority of the population (without being completely universal), turnout is usually measured by comparing the number of voters to the number of registered voters. Electoral lists are documents of great political and symbolic importance, and they can be consulted publicly by anyone in the days following an election in order to guarantee its validity. This has given rise to fascinating research on turnout at the individual level: for example, by collecting data taken from tally sheets (indicating the signatures of voters taking part in the voting) for a sample of voting stations, researchers have shown that there are very few permanent abstentionists. Out of the totality of the local and national elections conducted between 1978 and 1992 (about ten elections in all), in a period when the average percentage of abstentions was about 20–25 percent in each election, scarcely 1 to 2 percent of registered voters abstained systematically in all the elections. To put it another way, most of those who abstained voted at one time or another in elections, even though they sometimes abstained (because they were out of town or had a scheduling conflict, for example).[36] It would be interesting to analyze the historical evolution of this type of behavior, but unfortunately it is impossible to gain access to such data on the national scale and over the long term, which it what interests us here.

Conversely, there are other countries where registration on electoral lists is much less widespread and standardized than it is in France. This is notably the case in the United States, where the rates of registration are often rather low, with very great variations between the individual states. In many cases, it is also impossible to register on the day of the election (so that the notion of registration virtually coincides with the act of voting). That is why most of the studies of voter turnout in the United States define turnout by dividing the number of voters by an estimate of the population that has the right to vote (calculated on the basis of censuses). This is, de facto, the only method that allows us to compare the levels of turnout over time and between states, and for decades the US Census Bureau has been publishing official estimates of voter turnout based on this method. This difference in the mode of approach has long fueled a recurrent polemic between US and French researchers, with the former accusing the latter of exaggerating in this way the disparity between turnout in the two countries. French researchers

---

36. On the other hand, people who were not registered to vote—who in fact also "abstained"—can abstain in a much more lasting way. See F. Subileau and M. F. Toinet, *Les chemins de l'abstention. Une comparaison franco américaine* (La Découverte, 1993), 155–157. Since 1988, INSEE has organized surveys on electoral turnout based on the study of attendance sheets for a representative sample of the population in the days following the elections, which makes it possible to establish the same type of breakdown between permanent and intermittent abstentionists. See C. Braconnier, B. Coulmont, and J.-Y. Dormagen, "Toujours pas de chrysanthèmes pour les variables lourdes de la participation électorale," *Revue française de science politique,* 2017; E. Algava and K. Bloch, "Vingt ans de participation électorale," *INSEE première,* 2022. See M. Dogan and J. Narbonne, "L'abstentionnisme électoral en France," *Revue française de science politique,* 1954, for a pioneering survey carried out during the legislative elections of 1951 on the basis of attendance sheets analyzed in about ten cities.

have long replied that the historical disparity in turnout in favor of France was large in any case (even when applying to both countries the same measure of actual turnout—that is, dividing the number of registered voters by the population that has the right to vote). Although that response was valid up to 1990–2000,[37] we are obliged to note that it no longer really is if we examine the matter with the data available in the early 2020s. The turnout in France has in fact declined in recent elections, whereas it has increased significantly in the United States, with a number of voters equal to 59 percent of the population who have the right to vote in 2000, 64 percent in 2008, and 68 percent in 2020, according to the official estimates, even if it is still too early to say whether this is an enduring increase or a flash in the pan connected with elections that have been particularly disputed.[38]

In any case, with equivalent definitions—that is, when voters are defined simply as individuals who have the right to vote—the actual turnout was almost exactly the same in the US presidential election of 2020 and the French presidential election of 2022: about 70 percent in both cases. Taking into account that the elections to the House of Representatives took place on the same day as the presidential election in the United States (with an only slightly lower turnout than in France), that means that turnout for the recent legislative elections was clearly higher in the United States than in France.[39] This comparison is important, because the notion of a structurally greater turnout in France than in the United States (which was valid until 1990–2000, but is definitely not valid in the early 2020s) has long played a central role in the French belief that electoral mobilization was greater in France because of a system of political parties that made more room for the aspirations of the working classes (whereas conversely, the parties in the United States, which were more closely linked historically with the great economic actors and big business

37. See, for instance, Subileau and Toinet, *Les chemins de l'abstention.*
38. See "2020 Presidential Election Voting and Registration Tables" (US Census Bureau, 2021). According to these estimates and those made by researchers involved in the electproject.org program, the rate of turnout in the presidential elections (still expressed as a percentage of the population with the right to vote, hence people eighteen years old or older with US nationality) fluctuated between 10 and 30 percent in 1790–1810, then rose steeply between 1810 and 1840, reaching 60–70 percent in 1840–1890, fell significantly between 1890 and 1920 (in connection, no doubt, with the restrictions on the African American vote), and stabilized at about 50–60 percent in 1920–2020 (40–50 percent for midterm elections), though with a perceptible increase in recent elections.
39. The disparity between the United States and France in the latest elections is much smaller if we consider the turnout for the midterm legislative elections.

interests, would never have been able to mobilize the working classes so powerfully). This perception is clearly no longer valid in view of the most recent elections, and this illustrates the gravity and historical character of the current developments and the necessity of understanding them better. It will also be noted that a decline in turnout can be observed in other European electoral democracies (in particular, in the United Kingdom and Germany), but the decline seen in the most recent French legislative elections seems particularly marked.[40]

An Electoral Registration Structurally Greater in Villages

Let us now turn to the question of the variations in the rate of registration according to the types of territories. Do people register at higher rates on the electoral lists in wealthy or in poor municipalities, in urban or in rural municipalities, in suburbs or in metropoles, and how have these realities evolved from the elections of 1848 to those of 2022? The results obtained on the basis of the data that we have collected at the municipal and cantonal levels are particularly clear. During the last two centuries, the registration rate has usually been higher in the villages (about 5 to 10 percent above the national average), followed by the towns and suburbs (about the national average), and then the metropoles (about 10 to 15 percent below the national average) (see figure 5.7). Concretely, that means, for example, that if the registration rate on the electoral lists is on average 90 to 92 percent in the country, then it reaches 95 to 98 percent in the villages and is barely 80 percent in the metropoles. It is a matter of very significant variations, which it will be important to keep in mind when we study the disparities in turnout between rural and urban territories. The only exception concerns the elections of 1848–1849 (for which the registration rates appear to be slightly higher in the metropoles than in the towns and villages).[41] After that, the noted pattern was established in the elections of 1871, with an appreciably higher registration rate in the villages, followed

---

40. See T. Piketty, "Brahmin Left vs. Merchant Right. Rising Inequality and the Changing Structure of Political Conflict" (World Inequality Lab working paper 2018 / 07), figure A1.

41. One explanation might be that the elections of 1848–1849 took place in the cantons' main towns, which hindered inhabitants of the villages. However, these results must be interpreted cautiously, as the data taken from the censuses for this period are by nature imprecise. Later, under the Second Empire, voting was to take place in the municipalities, which may have altered registration rates; voting in the cantons' main towns was briefly reintroduced in February 1871, and then voting was definitively located in the municipalities starting with the election of July 1871.

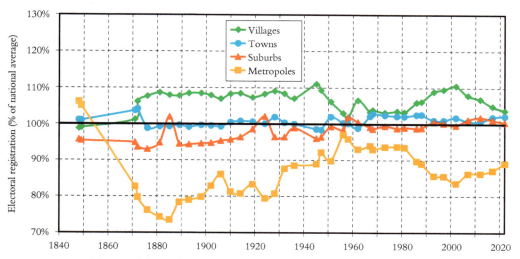

FIGURE 5.7. The rate of electoral registration in the territories, 1848–2022

From the legislative elections of 1848 to those of 2022, the rate of electoral registration (number of registered voters divided by the number of persons with the right to vote) has generally been higher in villages (about 5–10% above the national average), followed by towns and suburbs (about 10–20% below the national average). Note: The definition of villages, towns, suburbs, and metropoles is the same as the one introduced in chapter 2 (conurbations of less than 2,000 inhabitants, conurbations of between 2,000 and 100,000 inhabitants, and secondary municipalities and principal municipalities of conurbations of more than 100,000 inhabitants).
Sources and series: unehistoireduconflitpolitique.fr

by the towns and the suburbs, with the metropoles clearly lagging behind.[42] We should also note that there is no meaningful evolution over the long term: these

42. The elections of February 1871 and July 1871 are treated in figure 5.7 and in all the figures here that follow as two distinct elections. Even if, strictly speaking, they are the same election, this choice is justified by the context of war (which made the organization of the vote very difficult in certain departments in February), the change of the place where the vote took place (the main town of the municipality), the very rapid evolution of the political situation (the monarchists did very well in the February elections, considering the poor military situation they inherited from the provisional republican government that had held power since September 1870, but then the republicans recouped some of their losses in July), and especially the multiple partial elections (it sufficed that only a single seat fall vacant—by, for example, Thiers and Gambetta being elected in several departments—for the whole department to be called back to the ballot box to fill the vacancy), with the result that more than half the electors voted in July. Specifically, we have been able to identify and digitize the electoral reports corresponding to 77 percent of the registered voters in February (7.5 million out of 9.7 million) and 52 percent of the registered voters in July (5.2 million).

disparities between territories manifest no clear trend between 1871 and 2022.[43] We will see that things are very different in regard to the structure of the turnout, which has undergone significant transformations since the nineteenth century, despite several important regularities.

The definition of villages, towns, suburbs, and metropoles used here is the same as the one introduced in chapter 2, and it has the merit of simplicity: it always refers to conurbations of less than 2,000 inhabitants, those comprising between 2,000 and 100,000 inhabitants, and secondary and principal municipalities of conurbations of more than 100,000 inhabitants. We have also examined the disparities in the rates of registration between different groups of municipalities and conurbations combining portions of the total population that are stable over time, which allows more satisfying temporal comparisons to be made. For example, at any time, we can divide the population of the approximately 36,000 municipalities in Metropolitan France into two equal halves: the 50 percent of the population living in the smallest conurbations and the 50 percent living in the largest conurbations. We note that in 1871 the registration rate was 1.11 times higher in the former than in the latter,[44] and that this ratio was 1.06 in 2022, with ratios generally ranging from 1.05 to 1.15 and 1.15 to 120 from 1871 to 2022. If we now compare the 20 percent of the population living in the smallest conurbations and the 20 percent living in the largest conurbations, we usually observe higher ratios (1.24 in 1871 and 1.07 in 2022). More generally, we note that the ratios between the registration rates in the 50 percent of the smallest and largest conurbations and in the 20 percent of the

---

43. For the elections for which we have electoral data only at the level of the 3,000 cantons and not the 35,000 municipalities, in particular for 1848–1849 and February 1871 elections (which were organized at the level of the main towns of the cantons and not the municipalities), the results indicated in figure 5.7 (and the figures that follow) were obtained by attributing to all the municipalities in a given canton the average registration rate of the canton. We have proceeded in the same way with the results pertaining to the turnout and the vote. The estimates thus produced are less granular than those obtained on the basis of July 1871 with the municipal data (which tends to artificially merge the results in the towns and villages), but in practice, the differences remain limited, considering the fact that most of the cantons are almost entirely rural or urban. For all the results presented in this book, we have taken care to verify that no significant evolution was biased by the shift from cantonal to municipal data.

44. It will be noted that this ratio rises from 1.03 to 1.11 between February and July 1871, which may be explained by the move to voting by municipality, but also by the fact that it was not exactly the same parts of the country that voted on these two dates. However, the results are qualitatively similar, with greater registration in villages and small conurbations in both cases.

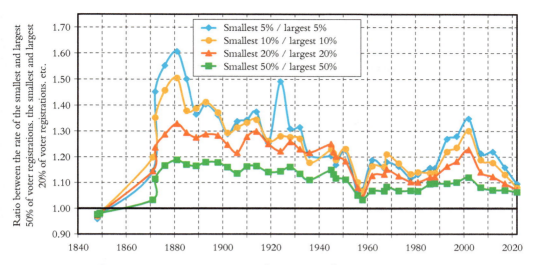

FIGURE 5.8. Disparities in voter registration rates between conurbations, 1848–2022

The rate of electoral registration (the number of registered voters divided by the number of persons with the right to vote, as it can be estimated on the basis of census data) has generally been higher in the smallest conurbations than in the largest conurbations.

Sources and series: unehistoireduconflitpolitique.fr

smallest and largest conurbations were systematically greater than 1 between 1871 and 2022 (in other words, the registration rates have always been greater in the smallest conurbations), and they have not changed much over a long period, although there were particularly large disparities between the rural world and the urban world at the end of the nineteenth century and the beginning of the twentieth (see figure 5.8).[45]

We obtain the same results by comparing the 10 percent of the smallest and the largest conurbations, and the 5 percent of the smallest and the largest conurbations. We see, however, that the ratios involving the 10 percent or the 5 percent of the largest conurbations are more volatile, which may be explained in part by the difficulty of estimating with precision the population with the right to vote in the great

45. In order to avoid the biases connected with small municipalities and to allow maximal comparability of changes over time, these definitions take into account, as before, the size of the municipalities. In other words, the 50 percent of the smallest conurbations designate the 50 percent of the population living in the smallest conurbations, and so on.

metropoles (notably, Paris).[46] This volatility also seems to be due to more erratic registration behaviors in the metropoles in comparison to the rest of the country. The registrations on the electoral lists are thus particularly low in Paris in the 1870s and until 1881, then they accelerate in the 1880s and 1890s at the time of Boulangism and then the Dreyfus affair. They are once again unusually low in the capital in the 1990s and until 2002 (when Jean-Marie Le Pen qualified for the second round of the presidential election), then they accelerate and reach their previous level again in 2007. In any case, the registration rates in the large conurbations (and notably in Paris) are systematically lower than in the rest of the country, all through the period from 1871 to 2022.[47]

Our results agree with and confirm the conclusions drawn by other researchers like Alain Lancelot and Michel Offerlé, who had already noted that the rates of electoral registration were as a rule higher in the rural world than in the urban world. Thus, Lancelot drew maps showing the rates of registration in 1877, 1946, and 1962 for the different departments, which allowed him to observe the higher rates in rural departments.[48] By comparing the numbers of registered voters in the legislative elections of 1876 and 1889 to the populations measured by the censuses for several municipalities of different sizes, Offerlé shows particularly low rates of registration in Paris in comparison to those observed in middle-sized cities (Roubaix and Le Creusot, for example).[49] Offerlé also noted that within the capital, the relationship between wealth and political mobilizations was much more complex than is sometimes thought. Registration rates were particularly low in the richest arrondissements (the 7th, 8th, and 16th), where the *grande bourgeoisie* was also characterized by a fashionable abstentionism and seems to have been little concerned initially by the increasing strength of universal suffrage and the republican regime.[50] Although

---

46. The volatility issues entirely from the largest 5 percent and 10 percent of conurbations, and not from the smallest 5 percent and 10 percent of the conurbations. See unehistoireduconflitpolitique. fr, figures C3.3b–C3.3c and appendix C3. The Parisian conurbation grew from 5 percent of the national population in 1848 to 10 percent in 1920 and 15 percent in 2022 (and the city of Paris from 3.5 percent in 1848 to 7 percent in 1920, and then 3.5 percent in 2022; see figure B1.4g), then 5 percent and 10 percent of the population living in the largest conurbations merge in large measure with the latter. Within a single conurbation, the municipalities have been ranked by population.

47. See unehistoireduconflitpolitique.fr, figures C3.3b–C3.3c.

48. See Lancelot, *L'abstention électorale,* 33–35.

49. M. Offerlé, "Mobilisation électorale et invention du citoyen: Le cas du milieu urbain français à la fin du 19e siècle," in Gaxie, *Explication du vote.*

50. This weak mobilization can also be explained in part by the feeling that the outcome of an election is generally decided in advance in these bourgeois arrondissements (where conservative deputies often win very easily). We will return to this in part 3.

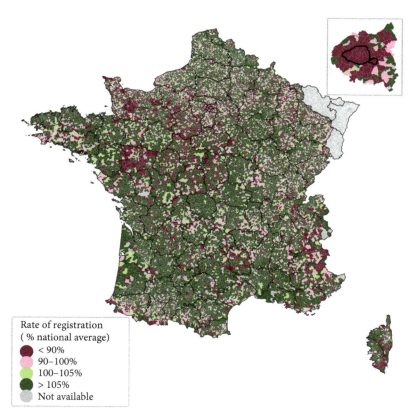

MAP 5.1. The geography of the rate of electoral registration in 1893
The map represents the rate of a municipality's registration as a ratio of the national average.
Sources and series: unehistoireduconflitpolitique.fr

the rates of registration and turnout in the 1870s and 1880s were also very low in the working-class neighborhoods (the 18th and 19th), many of whose inhabitants had recently migrated to the capital from the provinces, they were considerably higher in the neighborhoods populated by skilled Parisian workers (the 3rd, 11th, and 20th), even though these workers remained much less numerous than they were in the middle-sized cities and in the countryside. In comparison with these studies, the advantage of the data that we have assembled is that we can examine these questions for the whole of the period 1848–2022 and, moreover, on the scale of the whole national territory and its 36,000 municipalities (see maps 5.1 and 5.2 for illustrations of the elections of 1893 and

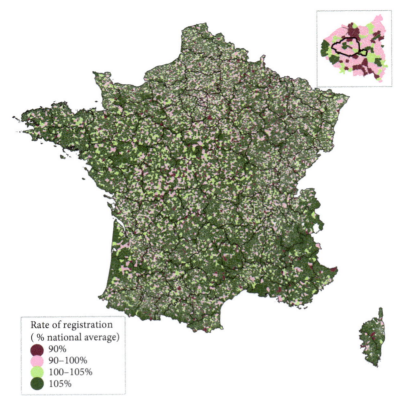

MAP 5.2. The geography of the rate of electoral registration in 2022

The map represents the rate of a municipality's registration as a ratio of the national average.

Sources and series: unehistoireduconflitpolitique.fr

2022).[51] From this point of view, the most striking result is the maintenance at a relatively stable level since the last third of the nineteenth century of a registration rate that is structurally higher than the national average in villages, whereas towns and suburbs are close to the national average and metropoles are clearly below it, perhaps with a slight narrowing of the gaps between these different territories at the end of the twentieth century and the beginning of the twenty-first in comparison to earlier periods (see figures 5.7–5.8).

---

51. In maps 5.1–5.2 we have represented the registration rates of each municipality as a ratio of the national average. We have done this so that comparisons between municipalities over time will not be affected by the evolution of this rate at the national level. For the geography of the registration rates themselves, see unehistoireduconflitpolitique.fr, maps C5.1–C5.2.

A Modest Effect of Wealth on Electoral Registration
at the End of the Period

The data collected also allow us to note that the size of the conurbation and the municipality is the only variable that has a clear and systematic impact on registration rates.[52] In particular, neither the level of wealth (measured by, for example, the average income or the average real estate assets) nor the diploma held seems to have a major autonomous effect on registration rates, with the exception of a slight negative effect from 1871 to the 1990s and a slight positive effect since 2000–2010. If we compare the richest and poorest 50 percent of the municipalities, the richest and poorest 20 percent, the richest and poorest 10 percent, and so on, we see that from 1871 to the early 2000s, registration rates have usually been higher in the poor municipalities than in the richest metropoles, but this effect is explained principally by the fact that the rate of registration is higher in villages and small conurbations than in metropoles and large conurbations, and that the average income is lower in the former than in the latter (see figure 5.9).

If we examine the disparities within the villages, towns, suburbs, and metropoles, comparing the richest and the poorest 50 percent of the villages, the richest and poorest 50 percent of the towns, and so on, we see in fact that the average income has only a limited effect on the registration rate between 1848 and 2000 (and generally a slightly negative effect, particularly between the rich and poor suburbs and the rich and poor metropoles between 1880 and 1980). Since the beginning of the twenty-first century we see a slight positive effect of income (and more generally of wealth or a diploma) on the registration rate within each category of territory. However, this effect remains rather small in comparison with the disparities between territories. In 2022, the rate of registration was 1.01 times higher in rich suburbs than in poor suburbs.[53] Nonetheless, this was the first time in the last two centuries that such a differential has appeared.

More generally, it is possible to distinguish more systematically between the effects of income and those of the size of the conurbation by reasoning on a ceteris paribus basis, which can be done by introducing the "control variables" method that we will often use subsequently. This is relatively easy, considering the large body of observations at the municipal level available to us; for example, in the smallest 5 percent of conurbations, the next smallest 5 percent, and so on, there are always

---

52. See unehistoireduconflitpolitique.fr, appendix C3 for a complete presentation of the results concerning the socioeconomic determinants of electoral registration.
53. See unehistoireduconflitpolitique.fr, figures C3.1g–C3.1h.

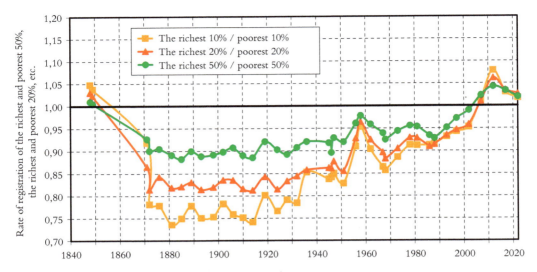

FIGURE 5.9. Registration in rich and poor municipalities

The rate of voter registration (the number of registered voters divided by the number of persons with the right to vote, as it can be estimated on the basis of census data) has generally been higher in poor municipalities (in the sense of the average income per inhabitant) than in rich municipalities, mainly because registration is higher in small municipalities (which are, moreover, poorer). Sources and series: unehistoireduconflitpolitique.fr

hundreds of municipalities that have very different levels of income, which makes it possible to observe the pure effect of income (that is, for a conurbation of a given size). If we proceed in this way, we note, for instance, that the ratio between the registration rate in the richest 20 percent of the municipalities and the poorest 20 percent becomes much closer to 1 as soon as we introduce the size of a conurbation as a control variable (see figure 5.10).[54] In other words, the essence of the apparent effect of income is in reality due to the size of the conurbation. We have also indicated in figure 5.10 the results obtained by introducing as controls the set of the available sociodemographic variables (including age, sex, real estate assets, occupations, diplomas, and origins),, and the general shape of the curve is

54. All the technical details concerning the multifactorial regressions carried out, as well as all the computer codes allowing these results to be reproduced, are available online at unehistoireduconflitpolitique.fr. In order to take into account the effects in a manner as flexible and non-linear as possible, the control variables have generally been introduced in the form of categorical variables, taking twenty values corresponding to the ventiles of the distribution in question (for instance, the twenty ventiles of the distribution of the sizes of conurbation, from the smallest 5 percent to the largest 5 percent).

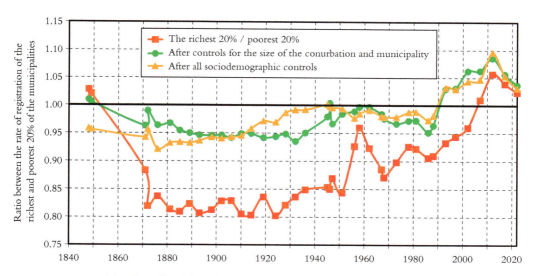

FIGURE 5.10. The effect of wealth on the rate of registration

From the legislative elections of 1848 to those of 2022, registration on electoral rolls has generally been higher in poor municipalities (in the sense of the average income per inhabitant) than in rich municipalities, except during the recent period, when this relation was inverted, with or without taking control variables into account.

Sources and series: unehistoireduconflitpolitique.fr

not much affected; income still has a residual effect on the rate of registration (slightly negative until the 1980s, then slightly positive since 1990–2000), but it is small. We find the same results if we examine the disparities in the rate of registration between the richest and the poorest 50 percent of the municipalities, the richest and the poorest 10 percent, and so on.[55]

Finally, let us explain that these disparities seem to be determined more by voters' income or wealth than by their origins.[56] The registration rates on the electoral lists are generally very close in towns and suburbs, despite the fact that the suburbs are composed of people from very different foreign origins. A disparity appeared in recent decades between the suburbs most closely linked to immigration (the

---

55. See unehistoireduconflitpolitique.fr, figures C3.2a–C3.2e.

56. On the other hand, taking into account the weakness of the effects involved and the imprecisions connected with the measurement of the population with the right to vote at the municipal level, it is difficult to say whether this effect of wealth is linked more to income, real estate assets, or diploma (each of these dimensions seems to have an autonomous impact, but the differences between the coefficients are not significant). See also the results presented by J. L. Pan Ké Shon, "Déterminants de la non-inscription électorale et quartiers sensibles en France," *Population*, 2004.

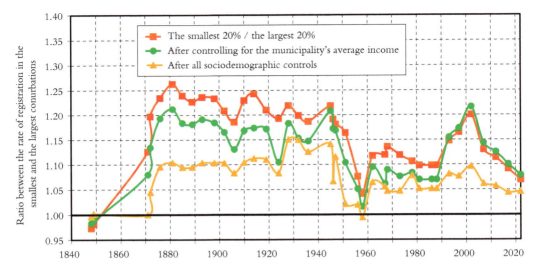

FIGURE 5.11. The effect of the size of the conurbation on registration

From the legislative elections of 1848 to those of 2022, registration on electoral rolls has generally been higher in small conurbations than in rich conurbations, with or without controlling for control variables.

Sources and series: unehistoireduconflitpolitique.fr

is, the difference between the smallest and the largest municipalities becomes less marked (see figure 5.1).

Examining things in greater detail, we note that this result is explained mainly by the structure by age. In other words, villages and small conurbations tend to have older populations, and generally speaking, municipalities that have older populations tend to have higher registration rates, regardless of the size of the municipality or conurbation, and perhaps in connection with how long their residents have lived there (even if that can never be measured perfectly).[60] However, we

60. Let us also note that, even in the absence of any mobility, we can logically expect the registration rates of the oldest residents to be higher than those of the younger residents. Contrary to turnout, registration is in fact a phenomenon that most often occurs "once and for all." Thus, a single election in which something important is at stake, or an election that results in a major political upheaval, may suffice to make some citizens decide to register—and stay registered for the rest of their lives. We mentioned earlier the very high level of registration in Clichy-sous-Bois, compared to Saint-Denis, for example. It is interesting to note that the rate of registration in Clichy-sous-Bois was only 77 percent in 2012 and that it rose to 93 percent five years later, in 2017, which we might be tempted to associate with the politicization of a younger generation shaped by the riots of 2005.

note that in every case, this is only part of the explanation. The addition of the whole set of the sociodemographic variables (and in particular the structure by age) merely divides by approximately two the effect of the size of the conurbation on the registration rate, which is important, but nonetheless leaves a non-negligible, autonomous role for rurality as such (see figure 5.11).[61] Before going further in the interpretation of the results obtained, we must now leave the analysis of registration rates (defined by the number of people with the right to vote) and study the socioeconomic determinants of the rate of turnout (defined by the number of voters divided by the number of those registered to vote) and their transformations over the past two centuries.

---

61. We find the same results if we examine the disparities in the registration rates between the smallest and the largest 50 percent of the municipalities, the smallest and largest 10 percent, and so on. See unehistoireduconflitpolitique.fr, figures C3.2a–C3.2e and appendix C3.

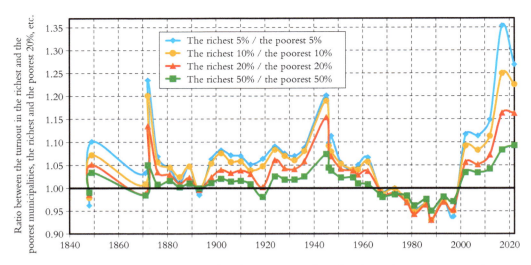

FIGURE 6.1. Disparities in turnout: Rich and poor municipalities (legislative elections, 1848–2022)

In the legislative elections of 2022, the turnout was 1.27 times higher in the richest 5% municipalities than in the poorest 5%. From the legislative elections of 1848 to those of 2022, the turnout has been in general higher in rich municipalities than in poor municipalities, with a very clear broadening of the gap over recent decades.

Sources and series: unehistoireduconflitpolitique.fr

If we make our analysis more detailed and compare the richest 1 percent of municipalities to the poorest 1 percent, we see that in the most recent legislative elections, the turnout ratio was 1.4–1.5 (that is, it was almost twice as large as it was during the earlier historical highs).[4] To put it another way, the municipalities whose average annual income was between 60,000 and 70,000 euros per inhabitant voted on average 40 to 50 percent more often (for the same number of registered voters on the electoral lists) than did those where the average annual income was only 6,000 to 7,000 euros. Although in this chapter we will concentrate essentially on the determinants of these disparities in turnout, it is important to stress here what this implies for democratic debate. Within a single electoral district, because they turn out more often, the electors in the wealthiest municipalities can swing an election to their way, even where the result would have been different without the disparity in turnout (supposing that the poorest electors would have voted, on average, the same way as their peers who took the trouble to go to the polls—which is usually the case, at least on a first approximation).

---

4. See unehistoireduconflitpolitique.fr, appendix C1.1c–C1.1d. Let us remember that in all our analyses we are treating the twenty Paris arrondissements as if they were separate municipalities.

It is tempting to connect the emergence of these very great disparities in turnout between rich and poor municipalities and the rising disparities in incomes between municipalities observed in recent decades (see chapter 2). For example, the increase in inequalities may have helped feed feelings of abandonment and political discouragement in the poorest municipalities. In the following chapters we will return to this complex question and to the intersecting socioeconomic interactions and political mobilization. At this stage, we will limit ourselves to noting that this explanation is not sufficient on its own—the gaps in wealth between municipalities were even greater during the nineteenth century and at the beginning of the twentieth, and yet the disparities in the rate of turnout were not as large as they are today. The perception of a gross injustice does not necessarily lead to abstention; in theory, it can just as well fuel a powerful mobilization, depending on the nature of the political options that are proposed. The second half of the nineteenth century and most of the twentieth can also be seen as a period of learning about representative democracy; even the humblest citizens continued to believe in the virtues of elections, despite the economic inequalities, or perhaps even as a result of them, because the political forces on hand seemed to be the bearers of profound change. At the end of the twentieth century and the beginning of the twenty-first, the rise in injustices and the perception of a very broad uniformity in programs may explain in part their lost illusions. It is true that this might not last forever, but it is the present situation.

If we examine separately the levels of turnout in the richest and the poorest municipalities over the past decades, we see relatively regular and symmetrical developments in recent decades. In other words, the richest municipalities have gradually started voting in greater numbers in comparison with the national average, whereas the poorest municipalities have followed a rigorously inverse trajectory (see figure 6.2). We will also see a slight increase in the turnout in the poorest municipalities in 2022 as compared to 2017. We will return to this when we study the development of the political options proposed in the various elections.

It will also be noted that although the disparity in turnout between rich municipalities and poor ones has never been as great as it currently is, the fact is that since 1848 it has almost always been positive. There is a striking contrast with what we have seen in chapter 5 regarding the rate of registration on the electoral lists, which has generally been lower in rich municipalities than in poor ones (except at the very end of a period, when the relation is slightly reversed).[5]

---

5. See chapter 5, figures 5.8–5.11.

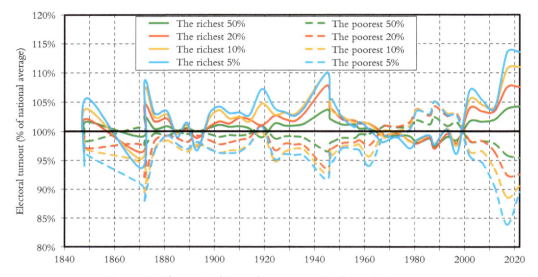

FIGURE 6.2. Turnout in rich municipalities and in poor municipalities, 1848–2022

In 2022, turnout for legislative elections was 14% higher than the national average in the richest 5% of the municipalities (in the sense of income), and 11% lower than the national average in the poorest 5%. Over recent decades, turnout has become clearly higher in the rich municipalities than in poor municipalities, which was not the case earlier.

Sources and series: unehistoireduconflitpolitique.fr

Rural Turnout Greater from 1848 to 2022, Except between 1920 and 1970

Let us turn now to the second important result concerning electoral turnout—namely, the fact that it has generally been greater in the rural world than in the urban world, but with an important exception during the period between 1920 and 1970 (particularly between 1930 and 1960). Here again, this involves a significant difference from the results regarding the rate of registration, which we have shown to have been high in the rural world all through the 1871–2022 period. Specifically, if we examine the ratios between average electoral turnout in the smallest 50 percent of the conurbations and the largest 50 percent, or between the smallest 20 percent and the largest 20 percent, and so on, we see that these ratios were generally higher than 1 in the nineteenth century and until 1920–1930, and then again clearly higher than 1 since 1960–1970. It was really only between 1930 and 1960 that these ratios fell below 1—that is, it was only in that period that the largest conurbations had a turnout higher than the smallest ones (see figure 6.3).

If we examine this parenthesis in greater detail, we see that it was the suburbs that drove this development. During this period, the turnout in the suburbs (and

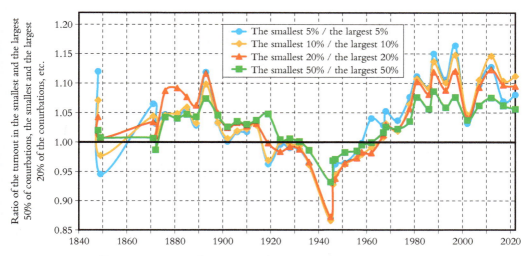

FIGURE 6.3. Disparities in turnout between conurbations, 1848–2022

In 2022, turnout for legislative elections was 1.11 times higher in the smallest 10% of the conurbations than in the largest 10% of the conurbations. From the legislative elections of 1848 to those of 2022, turnout has generally been higher in the smallest conurbations, except in the period 1920–1970.

Sources and series: unehistoireduconflitpolitique.fr

especially in the working-class suburbs) was clearly higher than the national average, whereas the turnout in the metropoles, villages, and towns was situated around the national average (or slightly below it). Then, during the 1970s and 1980s, the suburbs fell back below the national average so that since then we find the same configuration that was seen up to 1920–1930: a maximal turnout in the villages, followed by the towns, the suburbs, and the metropoles (see figure 6.4). When we study the structure of the votes for the different political tendencies, we see that this high turnout in the working-class suburbs between 1930 and 1960 is explained mainly by the Communist vote.

In distinguishing the effects connected with the type of territory from those connected to wealth, it is also interesting to examine the evolution of disparities in turnout between rich and poor municipalities within each territory. Then we can see that the disparities between rich and poor suburbs (based on average income) have shot up since the end of the 1990s.I In the late 2010s and at the beginning of the 2020s, the richest 50 percent of the suburbs voted between 20 and 25 percent more than the poorest 50 percent, whereas the disparity was insignificant (or negative) until the 1980s–1990s. We also see only a slightly larger gap since

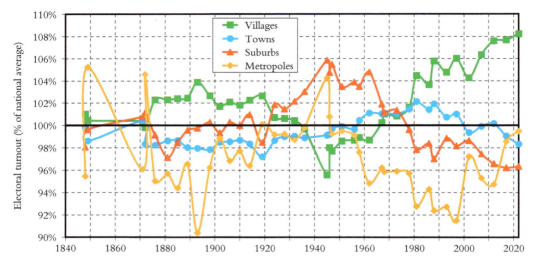

FIGURE 6.4. Disparities in turnout between territories, 1848–2022

In 2022, turnout for legislative elections was 8% higher than the national average in villages, and about 4% lower than the national average in the suburbs. With the exception of the period 1930–1966, when it was higher in the suburbs, turnout has generally been higher in villages than in towns, suburbs, and metropoles.

Sources and series: unehistoireduconflitpolitique.fr

the end of the 1990s between rich and poor metropoles, and to a lesser degree, between rich and poor towns. Finally, let us note that in the nineteenth century there was already a very large disparity in turnout between rich and poor metropoles that just reappeared, in a way, at the beginning of the twenty-first century, with the difference that this phenomenon is also seen today in towns and suburbs, and it is particularly massive in the latter (see figure 6.5).

The largest turnout observed in the rural world in the last two decades (with the exception of the 1930–1960 period) is all the more striking because as a rule, rural municipalities have lower incomes than the rest of the country, and higher incomes have led, on average, to larger turnouts, notably at the end of the period. In other words, the positive effect of rurality on turnout is in reality even greater than it seems, if we reason on the basis of ceteris paribus and introduce control variables. In the same way as for the analysis of registration rates, this type of method is relatively easy to apply here, because of the large number of municipal observations at our disposal: for a given level of income, there are always hundreds of localized municipalities in small or large conurbations, which makes it possible to observe the pure effect of the size of the conurbation (that is, for a given

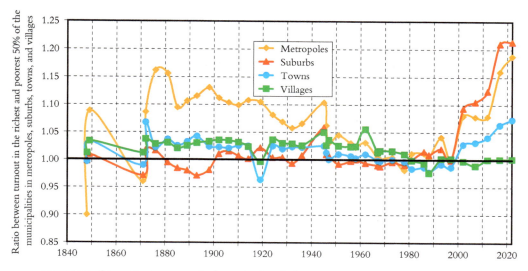

FIGURE 6.5. Disparities in turnout in the territories, 1848–2022

During the legislative elections of 2022, turnout was 1.21 times higher in rich suburbs (the richest 50% of the suburbs) than in the poor suburbs. From the legislative elections of 1848 to those of 2022, turnout has generally been higher in rich territories than in poor territories, with a clear broadening of the gap over recent decades.

Sources and series: unehistoireduconflitpolitique.fr

municipal income). If we proceed in this way, we note, for instance, that the ratio between the registration rate of the smallest and the largest 20 percent of conurbations is even higher after the average municipal income has been introduced as a control variable: it rises from scarcely 1.10 to more than 1.17 in 2022 (see figure 6.6).[6]

If we control for the set of sociodemographic variables that is available to us at the municipal level (including age, sex, income, real estate assets, occupations, diploma, and origins), we note that the general shape of the curve is little affected. However, its level is lower toward the end of the period, which is explained chiefly by the fact that small conurbations have populations that are particularly

---

6. As we have already noted, the technical details of the statistical regressions carried out, as well as all the computer codes allowing us to reproduce these results, from raw data to the graphs presented here, are available online. In order to take the effects into account as flexibly as possible, the control variables have generally been introduced in the form of categorial variables taking twenty values corresponding to the ventiles of the distribution in question (for example, the twenty ventiles of the distribution of the incomes among the municipalities, from the poorest 5 percent to the richest 5 percent).

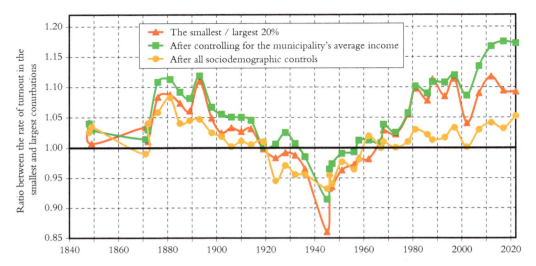

FIGURE 6.6. Size of conurbation and turnout

From the legislative elections of 1848 to those of 2022, turnout has generally been slightly higher in small conurbations than in large conurbations, with or without taking control variables into account, with the exception of the period 1930–1960.

Sources and series: unehistoireduconflitpolitique.fr

elderly in comparison with the rest of the country, and by the fact that elderly municipalities have tended to vote in great numbers during the recent period, regardless of the size of the conurbation. All in all, taking control variables into account has only a small impact on the general conclusion that turnout has been greater in small conurbations than in large ones throughout the period 1848–2022, with the exception of the period 1930–1960, both before and after taking into account other explanatory variables.[7]

A Disparity in Turnout Connected with Wealth, Diploma, and Occupation

We come now to a more complex question: Is the development of a very large disparity in turnout between rich and poor municipalities in recent decades more connected with income, real estate assets, diplomas, or occupations? It is not easy to give a simple answer to this question because the different dimensions of economic

7. We obtain the same results for the gap between the smallest 50 percent of the conurbations and the largest 50 percent, the smallest and largest 10 percent, and so on. See unehistoireduconflitpolitique.fr, figures C1.10a–C1.10e.

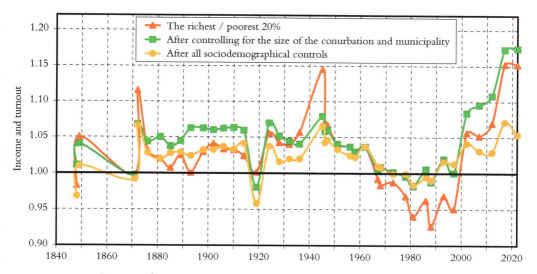

FIGURE 6.7. Income and turnout

From the legislative elections of 1848 to those of 2022, turnout was generally higher in rich munici-palities than poor municipalities, with a very clear increase in the gap between the two over recent decades, whether or not control variables are taken into account.

Sources and series: unehistoireduconflitpolitique.fr

wealth, occupational status, and school and university capital are closely correlated with one another at the municipal level (as well as at the individual level), and also, and especially, because each of them seems to have contributed to this growth in disparities in terms of turnout. In other words, new inequalities surrounding turnout are connected with disparities in economic and financial capital, educa-tional and cultural capital, and productive and professional specialization.

Let us begin with the effect of income. In practice, municipalities that have the highest average incomes also tend to have the highest average real estate capital (total value of housing), and the highest proportions of managers and people with advanced degrees. However, these different correlations are far from perfect, which, given the very large number of municipalities, makes it possible to reason ceteris paribus and to identify, as before, the peculiar effects of the different variables. In this case, after introducing all the available control variables, we note that the very positive effect of income on turnout observed in the preceding period diminishes in size but remains extremely significant (see figure 6.7).[8] In other words, the

8.   In order to avoid overloading the graphs, we have not indicated the disparity types, but they are always lower than 0.05 (and generally lower than 0.02–0.03). In other words, a ratio greater

positive effect of income is explained in part by the correlation with other variables (for example, by the fact that the municipalities with high incomes also tend to have a relatively high level of real estate assets per inhabitant, and by the fact that the latter are associated with large turnout), but not by it alone; even after the set of these control variables has been taken into account, the "pure" effect of income remains considerable.

In comparison, real estate assets per inhabitant seems to play a less important role, in the sense that its positive effect on turnout disappears almost completely as soon as the other control variables (particularly the average municipal income) are introduced.[9] Generally, one of the most significant variables for explaining the differentials of turnout since 1990–2000 is the proportion of households that own their own homes. After taking into account the set of control variables, in particular income and real estate assets per inhabitant, the proportion of homeowners appears to have been a very significant determinant of the rate of turnout at the end of the twentieth century and in the first two decades of the twenty-first (see figure 6.8). It is striking to note that as in the case of income and real estate assets, there was no significant effect of this type (or at least not of the same magnitude) on turnout in the earlier periods.[10] This is an interesting result, to which we will return when we study the impact of the proportion of homeowners on the vote for the various political trends—in this case, there has been an increasingly clear effect on the FN-RN (Front national–Rassemblement national) vote since 2000–2010.[11] Generally speaking, the heavy turnout observed among homeowners (including those with average or modest incomes, particularly in the villages and towns) can be explained by the fact that these voters, more than other social groups, have identified a political option sensitive to their aspirations.[12]

We find the same phenomenon with the level of education or diplomas, whether we use the proportion of literate people, secondary school graduates, or holders of advanced degrees.[13] Until 1980–1990, educational capital had a relatively weak, unstable (and generally negative) effect on electoral turnout. In 1990–2000, the disparity in turnout between the most educated and the least educated 20 percent

than 1.05 or lower than 0.95 is still significant from a statistical point of view. All the detailed results of the regressions are available online, as are the corresponding computer codes.

9. See unehistoireduconflitpolitique.fr, figures C1.3a–C1.3d.

10. Concerning income, there was a positive effect on turnout from 1848 to 1960–1970, but this effect largely disappears after the control variables have been taken into account (see figure 6.7).

11. See chapter 11, figure 11.22.

12. We can also conclude that the reservoir of votes is smaller in this electoral segment.

13. See chapter 3.

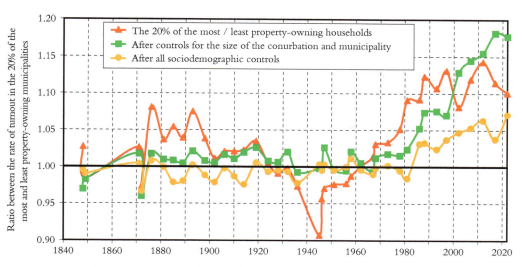

FIGURE 6.8. Property-owning households and turnout

In the course of recent decades, a very clear disparity in turnout has appeared between the municipalities with the largest proportions of homeowners (the "most property-owning municipalities")
and municipalities with the smallest proportions of homeowners, whether or not control variables
are taken into account.

Sources and series: unehistoireduconflitpolitique.fr

of the municipalities began to shoot up, and at the beginning of the 2020s it
reached an unprecedented level (see figure 6.9). As in the cases of the average income per inhabitant and the proportion of homeowners, these conclusions are
valid whether we examine the ratio between the most and the least educated
20 percent of the municipalities, the most and the least educated 50 percent of
the municipalities, the most and the least educated 20 percent of the municipalities, the most and the least educated 10 percent of the municipalities, and so on.
If we compare the explanatory power of the different variables on the statistical
level, then the proportion of homeowners and the proportion of people with university degrees both seem to play particularly important roles.[14]

We also observe an important role played by the proportion of managers and
advanced intellectual professions. Whereas the latter had no significant impact (or
a negative impact) on turnout until 1980–1990, in most recent decades it has
become strongly associated with a higher turnout (see figure 6.10).

14. See unehistoireduconflitpolitique.fr, figures C1.1a–C1.12n and appendix C1.

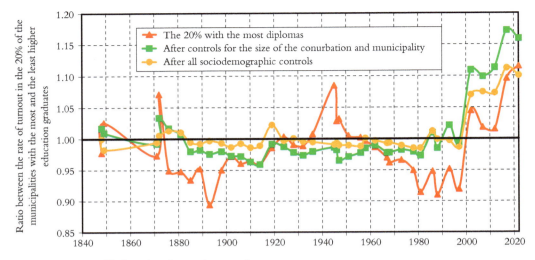

FIGURE 6.9. Higher education graduates and turnout

In recent decades, a very clear disparity in turnout has appeared between the municipalities with the greatest proportions of higher education graduates (the municipalities with the most graduates") and municipalities with the smallest proportions of graduates ("municipalities with the fewest graduates"), whether or not control variables are taken into account.

Sources and series: unehistoireduconflitpolitique.fr

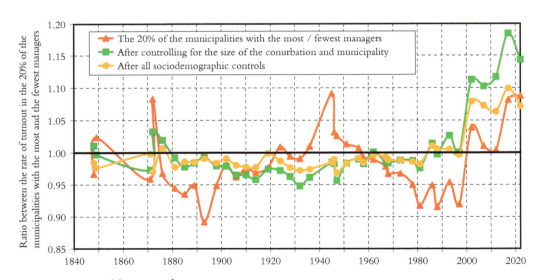

FIGURE 6.10. Managers and turnout

Over recent decades, a very clear disparity in turnout has appeared between the municipalities with the greatest proportions of managers and intellectual professionals and those with the smallest proportions, whether or not control variables are taken into account.

Sources and series: unehistoireduconflitpolitique.fr

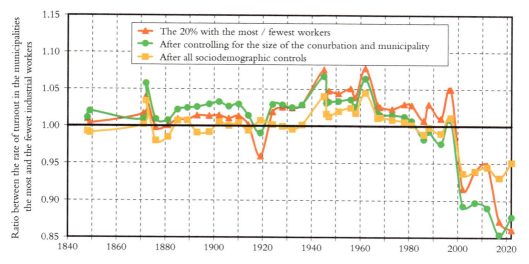

FIGURE 6.11. Blue-collar industrial workers and turnout

From 1848 to 1980–1990, turnout has generally been slightly higher in working-class municipalities than those that are not working class, but it has clearly fallen since 1990–2000, with or without taking control variables into account.

Sources and series: unehistoireduconflitpolitique.fr

Conversely, it is striking to note the particularly spectacular decline of turnout in the most working-class municipalities. In the nineteenth century, as in the twentieth, the most working-class municipalities were characterized, as a rule, by a larger turnout than the least working-class municipalities. This was notably the case during the interwar period and in the 1950s, 1960s, and 1970s. It was also true in the 1980s and 1990s, although less and less clearly, and more in relation to the smaller towns and conurbations, where workers were starting to be increasingly concentrated (and where turnout was becoming relatively high again). Then, beginning at the end of the 1990s, and especially in the 2000s and 2010s, there was a genuine collapse in turnout in the most working-class municipalities relative to the others (see figure 6.11). This collapse, unprecedented in French electoral history, is observed before and after the control variables were taken into account, and in all the territories and categories of municipalities. Specifically, it affected not only the most working-class villages and towns, but also the most working-class suburbs and metropoles.

To be sure, it is no surprise that blue-collar workers and those without diplomas participate relatively less in elections; that was already established for the recent elections thanks to the analysis of postelectoral survey data.[15] What is striking here—and what allows us to update this historical approach over more than two centuries—is the novelty of this phenomenon and its recent exacerbation: the disparities in turnout owing to income and wealth or to socio-occupational category have never been so great since the French Revolution and the first legislative election. In particular, these disparities did not exist in the middle of the twentieth century or in the first decades after World War II, and sometimes they even moved in the opposite direction.[16] This relatively recent deterioration over the long term apparently testifies to a crisis of a magnitude unparalleled in our democratic system; at the end of this chapter we will try to understand the reasons for it.

A Decreasing Turnout among Electors of Foreign Origin

The divergence in the turnout observed between rich municipalities and poor ones over recent decades is above all a phenomenon connected with the social and economic characteristics of the municipalities: economic capital (income, real estate capital, the proportion of homeowners), educational capital (university-level degrees), and socio-occupational structure (the proportions of managers and workers). It affects all the territories, independently of the populations' origins. It must nonetheless be emphasized that in the municipal data of the most recent decades we also observe, in addition this overall socioeconomic schema (which is by far the largest quantitatively) another negative effect on turnout which is connected with the influence of voters of foreign origin. Generally, we have already noted a particularly large increase in the disparity in turnout between rich and poor suburbs (the richest 50 percent and the poorest 50 percent of the suburbs, in terms of average income), which is considerably bigger than the disparities between rich and poor metropoles and rich and poor towns (see figure 6.5). The divergence seen in recent decades is even more spectacular if we examine the case of very rich

---

15. See, for example, C. Peugny, "Pour une prise en compte des clivages au sein des classes populaires. La participation politique des ouvriers et des employés," *Revue française de science politique,* 2015; T. Piketty, "Brahmin Left vs. Merchant Right. Rising Inequality and the Changing Structure of Political Conflict" (World Inequality Lab working paper 2018 / 07).

16. In his book on the "hidden census," Gaxie notes with astonishment that the first surveys carried out after the legislative elections of 1951 indicate a bigger turnout by the least educated than by the most educated, and he wonders what meaning should be given to this "aberrant" result. See D. Gaxie, *Le cens caché. Inégalités culturelles et ségrégation politique* (Seuil, 1978), 208–210. Our results over a longer period show that this observation is in no way abnormal and must be resituated in a long-term historical perspective.

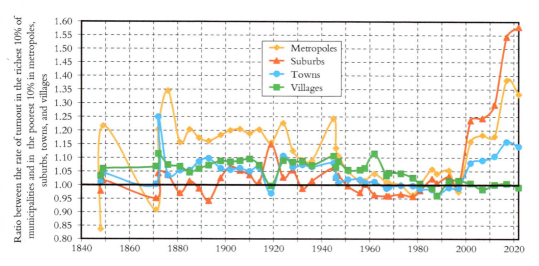

FIGURE 6.12. The divergence of turnout in the suburbs

In 2022, turnout was 1.58 times higher in the very rich suburbs (the richest 10% of the suburbs) than in very poor suburbs. From the legislative elections of 1848 to those of 2022, turnout has generally been higher in rich territories than in poor territories, with a clear broadening of the gap in the course of recent decades, particularly in the suburbs.

Sources and series: unehistoireduconflitpolitique.fr

suburbs (the richest 10 percent), which during the 2022 legislative elections had a turnout almost 60 percent higher than the one seen in the very poor suburbs (the poorest 10 percent). Never in French electoral history has such a large divergence been observed (see figure 6.12).

If we examine these matters in greater detail, we see that this divergence is connected mainly with socioeconomic characteristics, but it also depends on the proportion of inhabitants with foreign origins in the municipal population. For example, if we look at the ratio between the rate of turnout in the 10 percent of the municipalities that have the biggest proportions of inhabitants of foreign nationality and the 90 percent of the municipalities that have the smallest proportions, we find that this ratio was relatively close to 1 from 1848 to 1970–1980, before and after taking sociodemographic controls into account, and that since 1980–1990 it has fallen very steeply, finally standing at 0.82 in 2022 (before taking controls into account). In other words, there was no historical differential in turnout connected with foreign origins in the population, and then a major disparity appeared in recent decades, to the point that the 10 percent of the

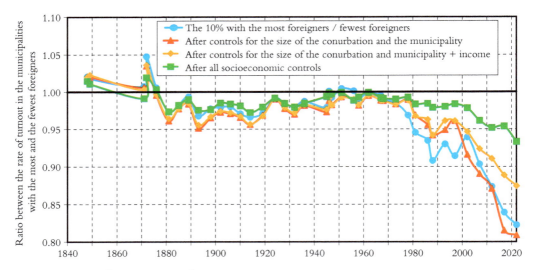

FIGURE 6.13. Foreign origins and turnout

In recent decades, a very clear disparity in turnout has appeared between the municipalities with the greatest proportions of inhabitants with foreign nationality (the "municipalities with the most foreigners") and the municipalities with the smallest proportions of foreigners (the "municipalities with least foreigners"), with or without taking control variables into account.

Sources and series: unehistoireduconflitpolitique.fr

municipalities with the largest foreign populations voted 18 percent less often than other municipalities (as a percentage of registered voters) during the last legislative elections. This is certainly explained in large part by the fact that these municipalities are poorer than the others—and that poor and working-class municipalities now vote less than the others, regardless of the foreign origins of the population—but that is not the only reason. Once the effect of the other sociodemocratic variables is taken into account, we see that in 2022 the ratio of the rates of turnout remains 0.94. That is, the 10 percent of the municipalities with the largest proportions of electors of foreign origin votes, ceteris paribus, 6 percent less than the 90 percent with the smallest proportions of electors of foreign origin (see figure 6.13).

To put it another way, if the disparity in rates of turnout is two-thirds explained by other characteristics of municipalities, a significant effect connected with the population's origins still remains. We can imagine various explanations for this additional decrease in turnout, in particular a strong feeling of abandonment when confronted with the available political options; we will return to this. At this point, let us simply add that we obtain the same results when we examine the ratio between the turnout in the 20 percent of the municipalities with the greatest number of foreigners and in the 80 percent with the fewest, and so on, or if we use the proportion of immigrants or naturalized citizens as an indicator.[17]

The Divergence of Turnout, from Neuilly-sur-Seine to Liéven and Aubervilliers

We can also illustrate this result by taking as examples municipalities chosen from different parts of the territory (see figure 6.14). Generally speaking, as soon as we begin to examine particular municipalities that are representative of different levels of wealth, it is striking to note the extent to which the disparities in turnout between rich and poor municipalities were relatively small and not very systematic in the legislative elections from 1848 to the 1980s and 1990s. Conversely, since 1990–2000, turnout has risen sharply in the richest municipalities (relative to the national average) and fallen in the poorest municipalities. The big increase observed in rich municipalities is found, for example, in the 6th arrondissement in Paris (a typical example of a very rich municipality, with an average income of 79,000 euros per annum in 2022, children included), in Neuilly-sur-Seine (a very rich suburb in Hauts-de-Seine, with an average income of 78,000 euros, and very well placed in the richest 1 percent of municipalities), and in Marcq-en-Baroeul (a well-off residential suburb of Lille, with "only" 31,000 euros in average income, which still situates it in the richest 6 percent of municipalities).[18] These municipalities had turnouts that were generally close to the national average in the past (or manifested erratic variations) before beginning to steadily increase in 1990–2000.

At the same time, turnout fell in poor municipalities such as Hénin-Beaumont (a poor town in Pas-de-Calais with an average income of 14,000 euros, making it one of the poorest 18 percent of municipalities), and it fell even more in Liévin (a very poor suburb of Lens, also in Pas-de-Calais, with an average income of 11,000 euros, figuring among the poorest 5 percent of the municipalities) and in Aubervilliers (a very poor suburb of Seine-Saint-Denis with an average income of barely 9,000 euros, one of the poorest 2 percent of municipalities). In this

---

17. See unehistoireduconflitpolitique.fr, figures C1.9a–C1.9d and appendix C1. Here, we concentrate on the proportion of foreigners, because we have access to municipal data on immigrants and naturalized citizens only for recent decades. In practice, the proportion of foreigners is strongly correlated with the presence of immigrants and naturalized citizens. See chapter 3.

18. As before, the richest 6 percent of municipalities designates the 6 percent of the population living in the richest municipalities in the country, and so on. This allows us to avoid the biases connected with small municipalities and ensure maximal comparability over time.

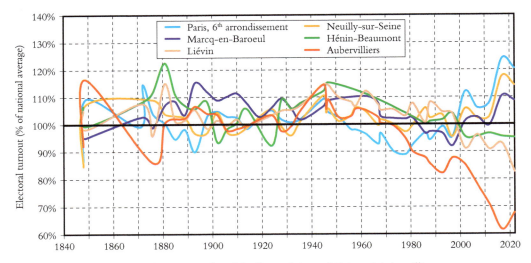

FIGURE 6.14. Disparities in turnout, from Neuilly-sur-Seine to Liévin and Aubervilliers

From 1848 to 1980–1990, the disparities in turnout between rich metropoles (e.g., Paris 16th arrondissement), rich suburbs (Neuilly-sur-Seine, Marcq-en-Baroeul), poor suburbs (Liévin, Aubervilliers) and poor towns (Hénin-Beaumont) have been small and not very systematic. Since 1990–2000, turnout has risen greatly in the richest municipalities (relative to the national average) and fallen in the poorest municipalities, particularly in the poorest municipalities with large populations of foreign origin (Aubervilliers).
Sources and series: unehistoireduconflitpolitique.fr

case, Aubervilliers is also one of the French municipalities with the highest proportions of foreigners, and the particularly steep fall in turnout illustrates in an extreme way the more general result observed at the national level. However, we note that the decrease in turnout is also very significant in Hénin-Beaumont and especially in Liévin, two municipalities that have foreign populations that are among the smallest in the country (hardly more than 2 percent of the population). This illustrates again a more general result: the poor municipalities saw their turnouts fall relative to the rich municipalities, regardless of the origins of their populations, but the fact that that the population has foreign origins emphasizes this more general phenomenon.

We could multiply the examples of municipalities that illustrate these results.[19] For almost a century and a half, from 1848 to 1980–1990, turnout in municipalities like Aubervilliers, Liévin, and Hénin-Beaumont was no smaller than it was in

19. See unehistoireduconflitpolitique.fr for detailed data, municipality by municipality, which anyone can visualize very simply thanks to the tools available online.

Neuilly-sur-Seine or Marcq-en-Baroeul—quite the contrary: it was often higher, subject to modalities that varied depending on the periods and the territories, particularly in relation to strategies of political mobilization. In the capital, it is only very recently that turnout in the most bourgeois arrondissements (especially the 6th, 7th, 8th, and 16th) has become structurally greater than in the more working-class arrondissements (in particular, the 18th, 19th, and 20th), whereas that was not the case in the nineteenth and twentieth centuries. We reach the same general conclusion if we examine the rich and poor municipalities of the conurbations of Lyon, Marseille, and Toulouse, for example, or the towns and villages in different parts of the country.

Beyond General Tendencies: The Geography of Turnout

Let's sum up. We have presented three general tendencies characterizing the structure of turnout in legislative elections from 1848 to 2022 (see figures 6.1–6.13). First, turnout has generally been higher in the rural world and in small conurbations than in the urban world and the large conurbations in the last two centuries, with the exception of the period 1920–1970 (and particularly 1930–1960), when turnout was highest in the major conurbations (particularly, the working-class suburbs). Second, the wealth of municipalities has usually had a relatively small effect on turnout, except in the period 1990–2022, when a disparity in turnout of an unprecedented magnitude developed between rich and poor municipalities, in connection with economic capital (income, real estate capital, the proportion of homeowners), educational and cultural capital (the proportion of people with higher education degrees), and the socio-occupational structure (the proportions of managers and workers). Finally, in poor municipalities, the existence of a large population of foreign origin has had, over recent decades, an additional negative impact on turnout, whereas this kind of effect did not exist in the preceding periods.

It would obviously be a mistake to reduce the whole history of electoral turnout at the municipal level over the past two centuries to these three general tendencies. In addition to these overall regularities, there is a multitude of singular histories and specific reasons enabling us to understand why the turnout in this or that municipality is particularly influenced by various national or local factors. For example, the electoral turnout in the city of Paris, taken as a whole, is generally slightly higher than the average of the country from 1848 to 1956, largely running counter to national tendencies, because in the nineteenth century and at beginning of the twentieth turnout was on average higher in the small conurbations than

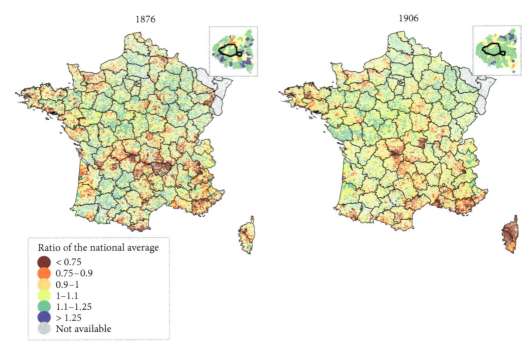

MAP 6.1. The geography of electoral turnout in 1876 and 1906

In 1876 as in 1906, we find great variations in turnout between departments as well as within departments. Despite a rather good turnout in Paris, turnout in the rural world has generally been greater than turnout in the urban world.

Sources and series: unehistoireduconflitpolitique.fr

in the large ones. This testifies to the intense politicization observed in the capital during that period, on the left as well as on the right, as we will see when we study the structure of the votes for the various political tendencies. Then turnout in Paris fell slightly below the national average from 1958 to 1997, before finally rising above the average from 2002 to 2022, following the surge in turnout noted in the rich municipalities in the recent period.[20] Besides the case of Paris, there is a very great diversity of situations in the 36,000 municipalities, and the general tendencies we have brought to light at the national level are in no way intended to underestimate them; on the contrary, they deserve to be studied in detail at the local and regional levels (see maps 6.1 and 6.2).

---

20. See unehistoireduconflitpolitique.fr, figures C6.2a–C6.2b. We have also noted above the erratic variations of the turnout in Paris in 1848–1849 and in 1871.

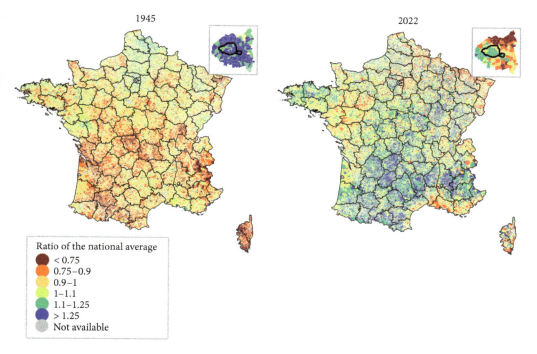

MAP 6.2. The geography of electoral turnout in 1945 and 2022

In 1945 and generally between 1920 and 1970, political participation in the legislative elections was greater in the urban world than in the rural world. In 2022, once again the urban world voted less than the rural world, and we also note an explosion of inequalities in turnout between rich and poor suburbs.

Sources and series: unehistoireduconflitpolitique.fr

Still, it is worth emphasizing the weight of the social determinants of electoral turnout on the national scale, a weight that has always been relatively great and which has had a clear tendency to grow over the last two centuries. Technically, it is possible to calculate for each legislative election the share of the variations observed in electoral turnout at the municipal level that can be explained by sociodemographic variables (the size of the conurbation or the municipality, age, sex, income, real estate assets, education, diplomas, occupations, origins, and so on). We note that the share of the variance explained by sociodemographic characteristics has risen from about 30 percent in 1848 to almost 70 percent in 2022. Among the explanatory variables, the most important ones are the sizes of the conurbation and the municipality, income, and real estate capital—alone, they represent between half and two-thirds of the total explanatory power (see figure 6.15).

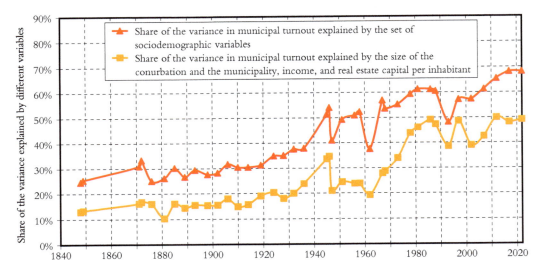

FIGURE 6.15. The social determinants of electoral turnout

From the legislative elections of 1848 to those of 2022, the share of the variance of municipal turnout explained by the sociodemographic variables (in the sense of the R2 and the multifactorial regression) rose from less than 30% to almost 70%. The size of the conurbation and the municipality, income, and real estate capital (the total value of housing) generally represent by themselves alone between half and three-quarters of the total explanatory power. The other sociodemographic variables are age and sex, occupation, higher education, origins, etc.

Sources and series: unehistoireduconflitpolitique.fr

Several points regarding these results must be clarified. First, it is relatively surprising that the sociodemographic variables can explain almost 70 percent of the disparities in municipal turnout during recent elections (68 percent in 2017 and 2022, the highest level ever observed), independent of any properly geographic information connected with the localization on the national territory. The fact that only four variables (the sizes of the conurbation and the municipality, income, and real estate assets) alone explain 43 percent of the variance in 2017 and 2022 is particularly striking. We should stress that the sociodemographic variables available to us are rather crude; if we used finer measures—for example, the distribution of incomes by category within the municipalities (and not simply the average income per municipality), the type of diplomas obtained (and not solely the fact of having or not having a university-level degree), details about occupations (and not just the proportions of managers and workers), and so on—then by definition, the share of the variance in turnout that could be explained in this way would be even larger than what we obtain here.

The Growing Explanatory Power of Geosocial Class

Of course, the great increase in the explanatory power of sociodemographic variables over time must be interpreted with care. It is possible that this increase is explained in part by the fact that the quality of the sociodemographic variables at our disposal has itself improved over the long term. However, it will be noted that we find the same growth in the explanatory power of the social determinants of the vote if we limit ourselves to characteristics that are in theory measured with the same precision from the nineteenth century to the twenty-first, such as the size of the conurbation and the municipality, or the municipal real estate assets per inhabitant. It will also be noted that the quality of the available data at the municipal level (issuing in particular from censuses) has hardly changed since the early 1960s, and that it was over the course of the period 1960–2022 that the explanatory power of sociodemographic variables grew the most. This structural increase in the power of the social determinants of turnout thus seems to correspond to a reality and not to a statistical bias, at least in large part.[21]

If we add the department (*département*) as a variable explaining voting behavior, the share of the variance that it is possible to explain naturally increases. It will be noted, however, that the importance of the properly geographic determinants of the vote (and in this case, the importance of departmental determinants) has greatly changed relative to social determinants. Regarding 1848–1849, the share of the variance in turnout that it is possible to explain rises from 25 percent to 48 percent when the department is included as an explanatory variable. In other words, the department has an explanatory power almost as great as that of all the sociodemographic variables taken together, which is considerable. At the end of the nineteenth century and at the beginning of the twentieth, the explanatory power of the department is between one-third and half of that of sociodemographic variables. Conversely, in 2022, adding the department causes the share of the variance that is explained to rise from 68 percent to 75 percent. The department's explanatory power is thus equivalent to barely a tenth of that of the sociodemographic

---

21. In theory, the rise in the predictive power of sociodemographic variables could also be explained—at least in part—by a structural growth of residential segregation (both directly and indirectly, through the effects of socialization). However, the available estimates regarding segregation suggest underlying increases that are relatively slow and probably insufficient to explain a substantial part of the very strong increase in the predictive power of sociodemographic variables (more than 50 percent between 1960 and 2020), which seems to be due above all to directly political processes connected with the transformations of electoral options.

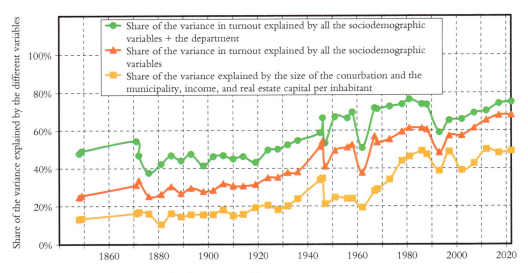

FIGURE 6.16. Turnout: Social and geographical determinants

From the legislative elections of 1848 to those of 2022, the share of the variance explained by the sociodemographic variables (in the sense of the R2 of the multifactorial regression) rose from less than 30% to almost 70%. The department has an additional explanatory power equivalent to all the sociodemographic variables in 1848, but only one-tenth of their explanatory power in 2022.
Sources and series: unehistoireduconflitpolitique.fr

variables (see figure 6.16). Let us further note that over a long period, the explanatory power of the department has decreased, particularly since the 1970s, and it is the explanatory power of the sociodemographic variables that has greatly increased.

In theory, we can imagine several explanations that could account for this relative decline of geographic factors. The most obvious is the development of means of transportation and communication, and particularly the audiovisual media available on the level of the whole country, which have made it possible to give electoral campaigns a more clearly national character, and consequently to bring together electoral behaviors that used to depend more on the local press and other territorial processes of political mobilization. It should be noted that the magnitude of the variations in the rate of turnout at the national level has tended to decline over the last two centuries, at the level of the municipalities as well as the cantons and departments, which can be interpreted as a sign of the country's political unification.[22]

_____

22. See unehistoireduconflitpolitique.fr, figures A1.2f–A1.2g and appendix A1. These disparities greatly diminished between 1900 and 1980, but they have risen slightly since 1980–1990.

Whatever the reason for the relative decline of geographic and departmental factors, we must stress above all the sharp increase in the weight of the social determinants of turnout. Social class has never played such an important role in predicting turnout as it has in the course of the last decades. Moreover, it is a matter of geosocial class rather than social class in the traditional sense, because we have seen that the sizes of the conurbation and the municipality (independent of the department) have always been important factors in turnout, in addition to economic and educational capital and occupation, whose roles have increased greatly in the recent period. We will return at length to these questions when we study the social and territorial determinants of the vote for the various political tendencies.

Territories and Electors: The Question of the "Ecological Fallacy"

It is useful to pause here to examine one of the important limitations of our approach and of the data that we have collected. Although it is always tempting to interpret the results in terms of individual political behaviors, the fact is that we observe electoral data solely at the levels of the municipalities and territories, and not at the level of individual voters. We must therefore be cautious with our interpretations.[23] For example, if we observe a growing disparity in turnout between rich and poor municipalities, as has been the case over the last few decades, that does not necessarily imply a growing disparity in turnout between rich and poor voters. In theory, we could, for example, imagine that it is the poorest voters in the richest municipalities who started turning out for elections more regularly—so much so that they succeeded in increasing the average turnout in the municipalities without the richest voters increasing their own turnout. Such a hypothesis seems in this case relatively far-fetched, but it cannot be completely excluded.

Fortunately, we have another source and another method for studying the structure of voting: since the 1950s there have been, in most electoral democracies (and in particular in France), postelectoral surveys that enable us to study political

---

23. Another limitation of our historical approach issues from the fact that at the level of the municipalities and because of the available data, we cannot control directly for a certain number of factors—for example, social mobility—even though we know that they may influence perceptions and voting behaviors. From this point of view, fieldwork on-site remains indispensable. See, for instance, M. Cartier, I. Coutant, O. Masclet, and Y. Siblot, *La France des "petits-moyens."* *Enquête sur la banlieue pavillonnaire* (La Découverte, 2008), for a study of the itinerary of social ascension in a suburb of individual homeowners and an analysis of the electoral behaviors that flow from it.

behaviors at the level of the individual. These surveys have recently been collected and utilized on a basis that is homogeneous and comparable in time and space, and one of the striking results is precisely that the disparity between the rate of turnout of the richest and the poorest 50 percent of voters (in terms of individual income) has sharply increased in France since the 1980s–1990s. This disparity was virtually zero (or only very slightly positive) throughout the period between 1950 and 1980. Then in 1980–1990 it began a gradual ascent and eventually reached, in the early 2020s, almost the same level seen in the United States since the 1950s. The development observed in the United Kingdom is identical to that observed in France: no significant disparity in turnout between rich and poor voters from the 1950s to the 1980s (or a very slight positive gap), then an increasing divergence since 1980–1990 that led, during the most recent elections, to an inequality in turnout at a level long observed in the United States.[24]

In other words, over the course of the period 1950–2022 disparities in turnout between rich and poor voters seem to have followed exactly the same evolution as the disparities between rich and poor municipalities (see figures 6.1 and 6.7). Unfortunately, we do not have representative national surveys before the 1950s, and it is therefore not possible to conduct these comparisons systematically over the long term—whence the advantage of our historical approach based on municipal variations. Let us simply say that whenever it was possible, we have conducted comparisons between the results obtained on the basis of municipal data and on the basis of national surveys at the level of the individual for the turnout and for the vote, and we have found systematically that the results were coherent.[25] When these comparisons are impossible, we have to be cautious in interpreting the results, which have to do above all with territories and not individuals. Keeping these limits in mind, and proceeding methodically, it is nonetheless possible to better understand the sociodemographic characteristics associated with the different kinds of voting behavior.[26]

---

24. See A. Gethin, C. Martinez-Toledano, and T. Piketty, eds., *Clivages politiques et inégalités sociales. Une étude de 50 démocraties, 1948–2020* (EHESS / Gallimard / Seuil, 2021); Piketty, "Brahmin Left vs. Merchant Right," figure A2.

25. Let us note, in addition, that the individual sociodemographic characteristics play a much smaller part in explaining electoral choices (around 6 percent in France between 1988 and 2007) than the characteristics of the municipalities do. See E. Belanger, B. Cautrès, M. Foucault, M. S. Lewis-Beck, and R. Nadeau, *Le vote des Français de Mitterrand à Sarkozy* (Presses de Sciences Po, 2012).

26. Different methods founded on multifactorial analyses have also been developed in order to estimate the statistical form of individual behavior on the basis of spatial data. See, for example, G. King, *A Solution to the Ecological Problem: Reconstructing Individual Behavior from Aggre-*

Nevertheless, we emphasize that no statistical method can totally eliminate the diverse ambiguities connected with the use of territorial data, particularly when it is a matter of the effects of a sociodemographic variable concerning a minority of the inhabitants of the territories in question. Take, for example, the result indicating that a greater proportion of inhabitants of foreign origin is associated with a negative effect on turnout in recent decades. Taking into account that the proportion of voters of foreign origin is relatively small in most cases, it is not certain that this effect can be explained solely (or even principally) by the behavior of these voters. It is also possible that voters who do not have foreign origins but reside in municipalities with a large population of foreign origin have reduced their own turnout as well, for example because they sense that their territory has been abandoned and that their vote counts for little. In this case, national surveys cannot settle this question because the insufficient size of the samples prevents us from combining the different sociodemographic and territorial variables at such a detailed level. To have any hope of making progress in interpreting the results, the only available method consists in introducing the control values patiently, and in this case, such a method does not allow us to eliminate all the uncertainties.

There are also cases in which the effect observed at the territorial level, on the basis of a minority characteristic, runs counter to the individual effect. That is the case if we observe a larger vote for the antimigrant parties in municipalities with the largest proportions of immigrants (as was the situation with the FN vote in the 1980s and 1990s, before this relation disappeared completely and ended up being inverted in the 2000s and 2020s). It seems obvious that this result is more likely to be explained by the votes of nonimmigrants in these municipalities; in any case, the voters of immigrant origin very seldom vote for the parties in question. This is the typical example of what is conventionally called an "ecological fallacy," which refers to the fact that we sometimes attribute to individuals with a given characteristic something that is in reality connected with the social environment associated with that characteristic.[27] We will return to these

---

gate Data (Princeton University Press, 1997). We choose to concentrate on the results obtained by introducing the control variables gradually, which makes it possible to arrive at simpler, more intuitive interpretations that are less dependent on statistical and parametric hypotheses. All our data are nonetheless freely available online if an interested reader wishes to consider more complex models.

27. On the "ecological fallacy," see the classic article by W. Robinson, "Ecological Correlations and the Behavior of Individuals," *American Sociological Review*, 1950, which notes a positive correlation between the proportion of immigrants and the level of education in states in the United States census of 1930, whereas the surveys conducted at the individual level indicate that immigrants have a more established level of education mainly in the more urban and educated

questions when we study the evolution of the structure of the votes for the different political tendencies in the legislative elections (and in particular, for the FN and the RN).[28] We will also see that the transformations of residential segregation play an important role in explaining certain important developments (such as the presence or lack of a significant left-wing vote in the wealthiest municipalities).[29]

The Social Geography of the Blank or Null Vote, from 1848 to 2022

Before we come to the various possible interpretations of the developments obtained regarding turnout, it is useful to examine what can be said about the structure of blank or null voting and how it has changed from the legislative elections of 1848 to those of 2022. Let us begin by clarifying that blank or null voting has always been relatively rare and shows no long-term trend. The proportion of blank or null votes has generally oscillated around 1 to 2 percent of registered voters over the last two centuries, with a few short-lived peaks around 3–4 percent during, for example, the legislative elections of 1910, 1986, 1993, and 1997 (see figure 6.17).

Several comments must be made about these results. First, the vote counts available in the electoral reports preserved at the municipal level do not always allow us to distinguish between a blank vote (a blank ballot placed in the voting envelope) and a null vote (a ballot crossed out or including various remarks or the names of persons who are not candidates) in a way that is rigorously homogeneous and comparable over a long period. That is why we have been obliged to group "blank or null votes" in one and the same category. Next, we note that the historical variations in the blank or null vote are very small in scope compared with those in the rate of abstention, which oscillated around 20–30 percent of the number of registered voters from 1848 to 1980–1990, and then shot up in recent decades and was more than 50 percent in the last elections. Specifically, if we add the blank or null vote to the curve of abstention, it has virtually no effect on the appearance of the latter (see figure 6.17).

If we now examine the social characteristics of the municipalities most closely associated with blank or null votes, we find a particular structure and a specific history that correspond neither to the profile of the rate of electoral registration

---

states. Generally speaking, the ecological fallacy tends naturally to disappear if more specific geographical levels are used (the county or the municipality instead of the state), hence the interest in working at the level of France's 36,000 municipalities, many of which have a relatively small population at all levels of wealth and sizes of conurbation.

28. See chapter 11, figures 11.18–11.19.

29. See chapter 9, figures 9.5–9.10.

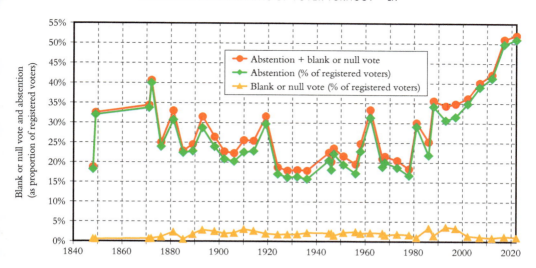

FIGURE 6.17. The blank or null vote in France, 1848–2022

The blank or null vote has always represented about 1–2% of the registered voters in France in the legislative elections from 1848 to 2022, except in 1910, when it reached 3%, and in 1986, 1993, and 1997, when it was 3–4%. Generally speaking, the temporal variations in the blank or null vote are relatively small in comparison to the variations in the rate of abstention. Note: The results indicated here are still those for Metropolitan France and for the first round.
Sources and series: unehistoireduconflitpolitique.fr

nor to that of electoral turnout. Since 1960–1970, the number of blank or null votes has been higher in small conurbations than in large ones, before and after taking control variables into account (see figure 6.18). We generally find this relation in the course of earlier periods, though with important exceptions for the years 1880–1900 and 1920–1960, when the relation sometimes runs in the opposite direction.[30]

Given the relatively low level of blank or null votes in general, the importance of these variations should not be exaggerated. Specifically, electoral turnout was about 10–15 percent higher in small conurbations than in large ones in the most recent elections (see figure 6.6), which, with an average turnout on the order of 50 percent, corresponds to a supplementary motivation of about 5–7 percent of the registered voters. The fact that blank or null votes were 20–30 percent

---

30. We find the same results if we compare not the 20 percent of the smallest and largest of the conurbations, but rather the 50 percent of the smallest and the largest, the 10 percent of the smallest and the largest, and so on. See unehistoireduconflitpolitique.fr, figures C4.1a–C4.10e and appendix C4.

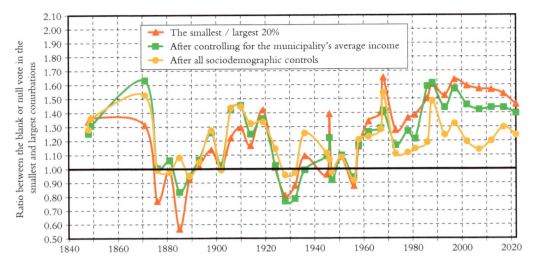

FIGURE 6.18. Size of the conurbation and the blank or null vote, 1848–2022

Since the 1960s, the rate of blank or null votes (as a proportion of registered voters) has been higher in small conurbations than in large ones, before and after control variables. We generally observe a similar relation from the legislative elections of 1848 to those of 2022, though with some important variations.

Sources and series: unehistoireduconflitpolitique.fr

more numerous in small conurbations than in large ones during the last elections (see figure 6.18) is comparatively unimportant; since blank or null votes represented only about 1 percent of the registered voters in 2017–2022, the differential with voting blank or null observed in small conurbations concerns only 0.2– 0.3 percent of the registered voters. To sum up, the major phenomenon is that electoral turnout is considerably greater in the rural world; the fact that a small fraction of this supplementary mobilization is found in a larger blank or null vote has only a marginal impact on this primary reality. Regarding the level of wealth, we also find a structural change over the course of the last two centuries: at the end of the nineteenth century, the blank or null vote was larger in rich municipalities; then, beginning in the early twentieth century, they became somewhat more widespread in poor municipalities, and this phenomenon increased slightly at the end of the twentieth century and at the beginning of the twenty-first, before and after taking into account other municipal characteristics (see figure 6.19).

In other words, in recent decades, the poorest municipalities have been characterized by both a smaller turnout and larger blank or null vote, with the two

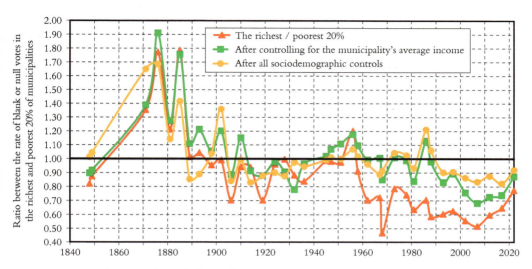

FIGURE 6.19. Income and the blank or null vote

In the elections conducted in the 1870s and 1880s, the rate of blank or null votes (as a proportion of registered voters) tended to be higher in the richest municipalities than in the poorest munici- palities. Since the 1960s, the converse has been true, even if the disparities are much smaller after taking control variables into account.

Sources and series: unehistoireduconflitpolitique.fr

effects combining to produce a smaller number of votes in proportion to the number of registered voters. This configuration is the inverse of the one seen in small conurbations, where the two effects run in the opposite direction: the turnout is higher and blank or null voting is greater. In both cases, however, we see that the effect of blank or null voting is quantitatively relatively marginal in compar- ison to the effect of turnout. Specifically, if poor municipalities expressed them- selves much less than rich municipalities did in the last elections, that is almost entirely because of a far smaller turnout (see figure 6.7) and only secondarily because of more frequent blank or null votes.[31]

---

31. Let us stress here that we are well aware of the fact that blank voting can be seen as a form of political expression; however, despite the fact that it is highly controversial, this form of expression is not taken into account in France because the choice has been made not to count blank votes. It is an open question whether taking it into account (for example, by cancelling the election and convoking a new election if the blank vote exceeds a certain threshold) would lead to an increase in turnout and in blank voting, or whether blank voting would remain at relatively low levels in any case.

Registration and Turnout: Two Distinct Logics

Let us now take up the question of the interpretation of results. How can we explain the different developments regarding turnout in legislative elections from 1848 to 2022? At this point, we can offer only relatively piecemeal and incomplete fragments of an answer, which we will try to clarify after we have examined the structure of turnout in presidential elections and referenda in chapter 7, and especially the structure of voting for the different political tendencies presented in the rest of this work. As we have already noted, abstention, as well as feelings of abandonment and the uselessness of voting, cannot in fact be analyzed independently of the political options and their transformations. In particular, because turnout has collapsed so massively in recent decades, especially in poor municipalities, the explanation must be sought first in the evolution of the different political movements on offer.

At this stage, we are going to limit ourselves to emphasizing that the behaviors of registering on the electoral lists and turning out for the elections (once registered on the lists) belong to different logics, and comparing them can allow us to define better the social processes involved. To be sure, there are common points in the results obtained for registration and turnout. In particular, we have shown that the rates of registration and turnout were generally higher in villages and small conurbations than in the metropoles and large conurbations. This result, observed for the most part in the period 1848–2022, is in line with Marvin Edelstein's conclusions concerning the higher turnout in the rural world during the French Revolution. Finally, if we consider the whole of the period 1789–2022, the most striking result is probably the revelation of a rural world more politically mobilized than the urban world, in terms of both registration and turnout. This runs counter to relatively widespread prejudices about the rural world, which is supposed to be structurally conservative and disinclined to participate in collective, democratic mobilization. If we follow the interpretation developed by Edelstein (with great prudence) on the period of the Revolution, we might on the contrary emphasize the idea that the stronger rootedness peculiar to the rural world is accompanied by a greater social consciousness and more involvement in the collectivity and the community, in contrast to an urban world that is more atomized and rootless.

But such a view would be too deterministic and would amount to replacing one normalization with another. The fact is that there is an essential difference between the results obtained for electoral registration and those obtained for turnout. Whereas throughout the period 1871–2022 registration is systematically greater in villages than it is in metropoles,[32] the same does not hold for turnout. Generally speaking, while over the long term, registration seems to follow relatively stable social processes, probably in connection with seniority in the municipality and the structure of the population by age groups, the behavior of turnout involves social and political forces that can vary far more, depending on the periods. In this case, although turnout has usually been greater in the rural world between 1848 and 2002, there is an important exception between 1920 and 1970 (and particularly between 1930 and 1960), in which turnout was on the contrary higher in large conurbations, and especially in the suburbs (see figures 6.3, 6.4, and 6.6). The fact is that this higher turnout in the suburbs is explained essentially by a specific set of political options and particular processes of mobilization, especially in connection with the workers' vote and the Communist Party. This clearly shows that there is no general, deterministic mechanism that explains why the rural world would be more mobilized than the urban world (or vice versa); everything depends on the political options and the processes through which political actors mobilize networks and organizations, pamphlets and newspapers, programs and activists, and symbolic and financial capital. Naturally, the forms of mobilization might change over time; they will not be the same in the twenty-first century as they were in the twentieth or the nineteenth. But this general conclusion remains: electoral turnout is the result of a complex social and historical construct involving numerous actors, and its contours are capable of changing radically in one direction or another relatively quickly (on the scale of a few decades).

Explaining the Historical Decline of Electoral Turnout, 1990–2022

We come now to the factors that can explain the historical decline of turnout in legislative elections during the period 1990–2022. We can distinguish three main explanations, which are, moreover, connected with each other, and each of them has probably played an important role. The first explanation, and in our view the most decisive one, involves the feeling of abandonment among the working class since 1980–1990, in relation to the weakening of the Left-Right bipolarization. This feeling of abandonment is closely linked to the perception of a convergence of the economic programs of the main political formations. From the moment that citizens have the impression that all the parties are proposing more or less the same program—that they have been won over to free market ideology and have surren-

---

32. See chapter 5, figure 5.11.

dered any prospect of a general transformation of the economic system—a large part of the earlier motivations to vote disappears. We will return to this hypothesis in detail when we study the transformations of the political options and the structure of the vote for the different tendencies in the third and fourth parts of this book. At this stage, let us simply say that it seems to us the most plausible explanation, considering that the decline in turnout was accompanied over the past two centuries by an unprecedented growth of the gap between rich and poor municipalities, based on income, property, education, and occupation, along with a collapse in turnout in working-class municipalities. We might add the fact that the working class is increasingly suffering from a deficit in descriptive representivity, since we see a decline in the proportion of workers among the deputies (and the candidates).[33] Several studies have shown that the deficit of representivity is positively correlated with a higher rate of abstention.[34]

The second explanation for the decline of turnout in legislative elections is connected with the presidentialization of the regime, and in particular with the fact that since 2002 the legislative elections have been held after the presidential elections. This explanation must not be neglected, insofar as the decline in turnout has actually grown since 2002, and insofar as this decline has clearly been smaller for the presidential elections.[35] The fact that turnout can decrease sharply in the event that consecutive elections take place in rapid succession—which is no doubt due to fatigue or to the fact that stakes in the second election are not made sufficiently clear—is moreover an old phenomenon that is already clearly perceptible in the electoral sequence of 1848–1849. Turnout thus reached 83 percent in the elections of April 1848 for the National Constituent Assembly—the first genuine elections by universal male suffrage in French electoral history—then fell to 78 percent in the presidential election of December 1848 and then to only 69 percent in the elections of May 1849 for the National Legislative Assembly, an assembly created by applying the new constitution that would play a crucial role in subsequent years, but which took its place in a long electoral sequence in which

33. With the exception of the legislative elections of 2022, in which the proportion of workers among the deputies elected increased very slightly. See chapter 11. Let us note that this decrease in the proportion of the working classes among the deputies elected is incommensurate with their decline in the active population. See J. Cagé, *Le prix de la démocratie* (Fayard, 2018), chap. 11.

34. See, for example, on the case of the United Kingdom, J. Cagé and E. Dewitte, "The Rising Demand for Representation: Lessons from 100 Years of Political Selection in the UK" (working paper, Sciences Po Paris, 2023), and on the case of Sweden, E. Dal Bo, F. Finan, O. Folke, T. Persson, and J. Rickne, "Economic and Social Outsiders but Political Insiders: Sweden's Populist Radical Right," *Review of Economic Studies,* 2023.

35. See chapter 5, figure 5.1.

fatigue clearly set in. In the same way, turnout rose to 81 percent in the first round of the presidential election in April 1981 before falling to 71 percent in the first round of the legislative elections in June 1981 (probably because many voters felt that the decisive battle had already taken place), then rose again to more than 78 percent during the legislative elections of 1986 (which were conducted independent of any presidential election, and thus had much clearer stakes).[36]

In a certain way, the new organization of French electoral temporality, which since 2002 has caused legislative elections to be held systematically after presidential elections, merely accentuated this general feature, and finally it led to a disparity in turnout of an unprecedented magnitude in 2022: 76 percent in the first round of the presidential election and only 49 percent in the first round of the legislative elections, a difference of thirty percentage points. But for all that, this impressive disconnect does not explain why the gap in legislative elections turnout between rich and poor municipalities has reached unprecedented levels in recent decades, unless we assume that working-class voters have a particularly high level of interest in presidential elections as compared with legislative elections (which was not the case before). We may also note that the disconnect between working-class turnout for legislative elections seems to begin in 1980–1990, considerably before the installation of the presidential five-year term and the new electoral schedule in 2002 (see figures 6.1 and 6.7–6.10). So although the presidentialization of the regime and the new electoral calendar help to explain in part the decline in turnout for legislative elections since 2002, this factor alone cannot constitute the sole explanation for all the observed developments. We will return to this question in chapter 7 when we study the evolution of the social structure of the turnout for presidential elections, which has also recently been transformed.

The third possible explanation for the decline in turnout for legislative elections is the appearance in 2017–2022 of a new party system founded on the tripartition of the political space. More precisely, we note the advent and then the continuation in power in 2017 and 2022 of a new centrist-liberal bloc that presents itself as more capable of governing than the Left and Right blocs, which are often described by the bloc in power as extremist and incapable of guiding the country. In theory, such a diversification of the political options could have led to an increase in turnout. In practice, turnout for the legislative elections has fallen to unprecedented levels,

36. Examples could be multiplied: turnout reached 82 percent in the presidential election of April 1988, then fell to 66 percent in the legislative elections of June 1988, before rising again (this time more modestly) to 69 percent and 68 percent in the legislative elections of 1993 and 1997, respectively, which were held separately from any presidential election. See chapter 5, figure 5.1.

declining from 61 percent in 2007 and 59 percent in 2012 to only 50 percent in 2017 and 49 percent in 2022.[37] That could be due to the fact that presidentialization has gradually become ordinary and has given rise to a previously unknown level of indifference to the legislative elections. It is also possible that the coming to power of this new central bloc, which, as we have already said, was financed more amply and more openly than in the past by the world of business and the most wealthy,[38] and which brings together an electorate that is socially very favored (probably even the most favored in French electoral history), has helped aggravate the electoral discouragement of the part of the working classes, who are confronted by a situation in which the possibility of genuine democratic alternations in power seems to many people even more improbable than in the past. No matter how great this discouragement and these perceptions might be, we must nonetheless make it clear that tripartition's rise to power in 2017–2022 is at most an additional factor accounting for the decrease in turnout; in no way can it be the central explanation. The decline in average turnout and the growth of the gap between rich and poor municipalities are phenomena that arose in the 1980s and 1990s and developed over several decades. Thus, it is instead in the more general process of political discouragement and the working classes' feelings of being abandoned that we must seek the principal explanatory factors. Moreover, we can think of tripartition itself as just the outcome of a deeper process connected with the gradual crumbling of the Left-Right bipolarization, which is the true cause of political demobilization.

Political demobilization among the poorest citizens can also be explained in part by the rise in inequalities insofar as access to and consumption of high-quality information—particularly political information—is concerned. With the emergence of cable television and then the development of the internet and social networks, recent decades have been marked by both an explosion of the supply of information and a decline in the quantity (and sometimes the quality) of the information consumed by the youngest, the least educated, and the poorest. According to some people, these groups spend less time informing themselves than they used to, while others say they are imprisoned in "filter bubbles" in the sense that they are exposed only to a homogeneous flow of information selected by commercial algorithms on the basis of their initial preferences and advertising

---

37. We refer in each case to the turnout observed in the first round of the election in Metropolitan France. See chapter 5, figure 5.1.

38. See chapter 1.

income, and in practice they are seldom likely to sharpen their critical senses.[39] Many works of political science and economics have documented the effect of the consumption of quality information on political turnout.[40]

Finally, let us add that the additional decline in turnout observed in recent decades in municipalities with large populations of foreign origin (on top of the decline observed in poor municipalities in general) also constitutes a complex phenomenon that admits of several possible explanations. The citizens most negative on the subject of extra-European immigration and the most skeptical of the possibility of creating a single human and political community comprising people with different cultural and civilizational origins could be tempted to see in this a lack of interest in national democratic life on the part of voters of North African or sub-Saharan origins (in contrast to preceding waves of immigration). But interpreting it as demonstrating their lack of interest or involvement raises multiple difficulties, because we would still have to explain the electoral demobilization of the working classes in general, and because we observe, for example, no significant decline in the rate of registration to vote in municipalities and territories that include large populations of foreign origin (particularly in the poorest suburbs). The outstanding educational performance of students from immigrant backgrounds (for a given parental social origin) also testifies to a desire to integrate socially that does not fit well with this interpretation.[41] As for the decline in working-class turnout in general, and the additional decline connected with origins, it seems to us more promising to ascribe it to a feeling of abandonment and discouragement linked to the political options on offer. We will return to this.

---

39. On the multiplication of the supply of information, but also of amusements, and for that reason, on the decline of the consumption of information by certain segments of the population and the increase of informational inequalities, see, in particular, on cable television, M. Prior, *Post-broadcast Democracy: How Media Choice Increases Inequality in Political Involvement and Polarizes Elections* (Cambridge University Press, 2007), and on the internet, A. Gavazza, M. Nardotto, and T. Valletti, "Internet and Politics: Evidence from U.K. Local Elections and Local Government Policies," *Review of Economic Studies,* 2019. The phenomenon of filter bubbles has been particularly well documented by E. Pariser, *The Filter Bubble: How the New Personalized Web Is Changing What We Read and How We Think* (Penguin, 2011).

40. See, for example, M. Gentzkow, J. Shapiro, and M. Sinkinson, "The Effect of Newspaper Entry and Exit on Electoral Politics," *American Economic Review,* 2011; and J. Cagé, "Media Competition, Information Provision, and Political Participation: Evidence from French Local Newspapers and Elections, 1944–2014," *Journal of Public Economics,* 2020.

41. See chapter 3.

CHAPTER 7

Turnout for Presidential Elections and Referenda, 1793–2022

We now turn to the structure of electoral turnout for presidential elections and referenda. To what extent are the results obtained regarding the social structure of legislative elections since the Revolution also applicable to presidential elections and referenda, and what lessons can we learn from them? Let us begin with the case of presidential elections held in 1848, and then those from 1965 to 2022. Next, we will take up the case of referenda, starting with those of 1793 and 1795, and then turn to the constitutional election of 1946 and the European referenda of 1992 and 2005. Generally speaking, we note for the presidential elections and referenda a growing disparity in turnout between rich and poor municipalities comparable to the disparity we found for legislative elections over recent decades, but with subtle differences of varying importance depending on the case. In particular, we will see that disparities in turnout between rich and poor municipalities grew less massively for presidential elections than for legislative elections. The study of turnout for the referenda of 1793 and 1795 (the only elections of the revolutionary period that lend themselves to a detailed statistical analysis) also allows us to show the sociospatial determinants of the vote and how they bear the seed of an important part of future electoral conflicts, together with the distribution of land and the sale of church property.

A Disparity in Turnout That Also Increases for Presidential Elections

As we have already observed, there is an impressive disconnect between the evolutions of turnout for legislative and presidential elections over the course of recent decades. Turnout for legislative elections oscillated around 70–80 percent for almost a century and a half, from 1848 to 1980–1990, before suddenly falling since 1990–2000 and barely reaching 50 percent in 2017 and 2022. In comparison, turnout for presidential elections has decreased relatively little: it has continued to be around 70–80 percent during the period 1990–2022.[1] Considering that

---

1. See chapter 5, figure 5.1.

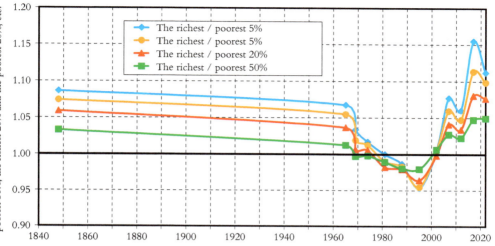

Ratio between the rates of turnout in the richest 50% and the poorest 50%, the richest 20% and the poorest 20%, etc.

FIGURE 7.1. Disparities in turnout between rich and poor municipalities (presidential elections of 1848 and 1965–2022)

In the presidential election of 2022, turnout was 1.11 times higher in the richest 5% municipalities than in the poorest 5%. We note a greater turnout in rich municipalities in 1848, 1965, and since 2002, whereas turnout was more balanced or slightly greater in poor municipalities from 1974 to 1995.

Sources and series: unehistoireduconflitpolitique.fr

turnout for the presidential election changed little, we might have expected its social structure to have remained unaltered as well. But it is striking to see that the disparities in turnout between rich and poor municipalities were completely transformed over recent decades. Whereas poor municipalities cast as many or more votes than the rich municipalities did in the presidential elections of 1974, 1981, 1988, and 1995, it was on the contrary the rich municipalities that began to vote more heavily beginning with the presidential elections of 2002, creating a gap that has not stopped growing since that time and that reached unprecedented levels in 2017 and 2022 (see figure 7.1).

Several points must be clarified here. First of all, we note that turnout was a little higher in rich municipalities than it was in poor ones in the presidential elections of 1848 and 1965, before the relation was reversed between 1974 and 1995, and then changed again starting in 2002. We note that in the same way as for the legislative elections, the ratio between the rate of turnout in very rich and very poor municipalities (the richest and the poorest 10 percent, or the richest and the poorest 5 percent) increased particularly rapidly between 1995 and 2022, still more clearly

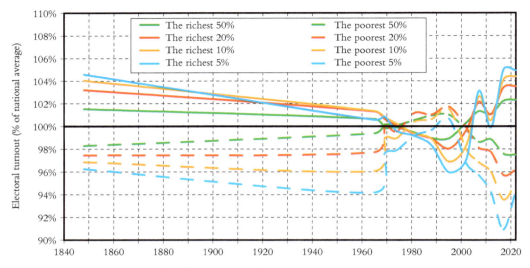

FIGURE 7.2. Turnout in rich and poor municipalities

In 2022, turnout for the presidential election was 5% higher than the national average in the richest 5% of the municipalities (in the sense of income), and 6% lower than the national average in the poorest 5% of the municipalities. In recent decades, turnout has clearly become higher in rich municipalities than in poor municipalities, which was not the case earlier.

Sources and series: unehistoireduconflitpolitique.fr

than the ratio between the richest and the poorest 50 percent of the municipalities (see figure 7.1). If we examine separately the levels of turnout in the richest and the poorest municipalities, we note, as for the legislative elections, relatively regular and systematic changes over the course of recent decades. In other words, the richest municipalities started gradually voting more and more often relative to the national average, whereas the poorest municipalities followed the inverse trajectory (see figure 7.2).[2] Note also a slight rise in the turnout of the poorest municipalities during the presidential election of 2002 in comparison with 2017, again in the same way as for the legislative elections (see figure 7.3).

It will also be noted that turnout was highest in the suburbs during the presidential elections of 1965, 1965, and 1974 (see figure 7.4). Since 1980–1990, turnout has been highest in villages, followed by towns, suburbs, and metropoles—again, as in the legislative elections.[3] Moreover, there was a great increase in disparities

---

2. However, as in the legislative elections, the absolute turnout rate of rich municipalities followed the national trend, with a gradual decline from 1965 to 2002, followed by a rebound in 2007 and a decline since then.

3. See chapter 6, figure 6.4.

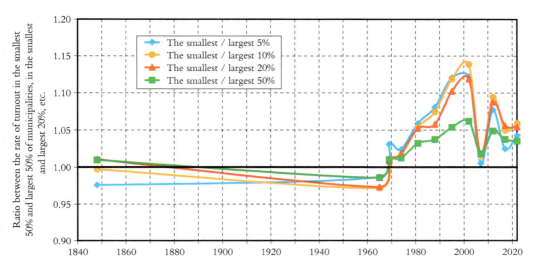

FIGURE 7.3. Disparities in turnout between conurbations

In 2002, the turnout for the presidential election was 1.06 times higher in the smallest 10% of the conurbations than it was in the largest 10%. From the presidential election of 1848 to that of 2022, turnout has generally been higher in the smallest conurbations, except for 1965 and 1974.

Sources and series: unehistoireduconflitpolitique.fr

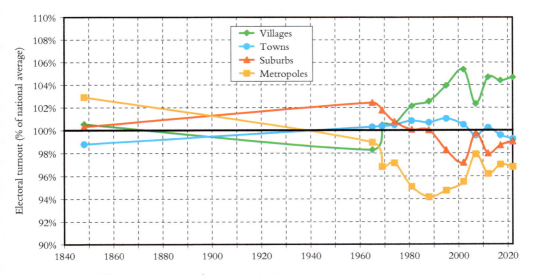

FIGURE 7.4. Disparities in turnout between territories

In 2022, turnout for the presidential election was 5% higher than the national average in villages, and about 3% lower than the national average in the metropoles. Since the presidential election of 1981, turnout has generally been greater in villages than in towns, suburbs, and metropoles.

Sources and series: unehistoireduconflitpolitique.fr

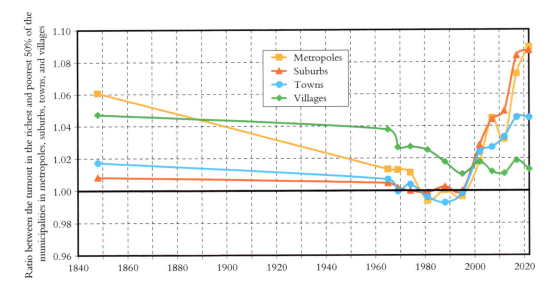

FIGURE 7.5. Disparities in turnout in the territories
In the presidential election of 2022, the turnout was 1.09 time higher in the rich suburbs (the richest 50% of the suburbs) than in the poorest 50%. From the presidential election of 1848 to that of 2022, turnout was generally higher in the richest territories than in the poor territories, with a clear broadening of the disparity in recent decades.
Sources and series: unehistoireduconflitpolitique.fr

in turnout within each of these categories of territory in the course of the period 1995–2022, particularly between the rich and the poor suburbs (the richest and the poorest 50 percent) and the rich and poor metropoles (see figure 7.5).

The Importance of Economic Capital, Education, and Occupation

If we now seek to clarify the role of the various explanatory factors by introducing control variables and reasoning on a ceteris paribus basis, we once again get results for the turnout for the presidential elections that are quite close to those observed in the legislative elections.[4] The turnout for the presidential elections was greater in small conurbations in 1848 and since 1980–1990 (and it continues to increase), before and after taking control variables into account, whereas the

4. See chapter 6, figures 6.6–6.11.

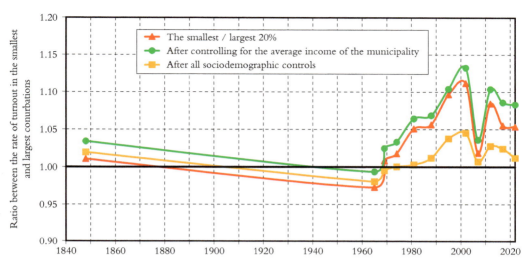

FIGURE 7.6. The size of the conurbation and turnout for presidential elections

From the presidential election of 1848, turnout has generally been slightly higher in small conurbations than in large ones, with or without taking control variables into account, with the exception of the presidential election of 1965.

Sources and series: unehistoireduconflitpolitique.fr

inverse relation prevailed in 1965 (see figure 7.6).[5] Concerning the effect of revenue, we also observe a growing gap between rich and poor municipalities since 1980–1990, before and after taking control variables into account (see figure 7.7).

Just as for legislative elections, we must also explain that it is not only revenue that becomes more and more closely associated with a large turnout in recent decades; there is also a set of variables connected both with economic and educational capital and with the socio-occupational structure. It is particularly striking to note the extent to which the proportion of home-owning households has become very closely associated (far more closely than the value of real estate assets per inhabitant, for example) with a high rate of turnout since 1980–1990, whereas that was not the case earlier (see figure 7.8). The proportion of persons with advanced degrees has also become a major indicator of

---

5. It is clear that this cannot be imputed to the specificity of the 1965 election—the Fifth Republic's first presidential election with direct universal suffrage—because a similar tendency is seen in the legislative elections of the years 1950–1960 (see chapter 6, figure 6.3).

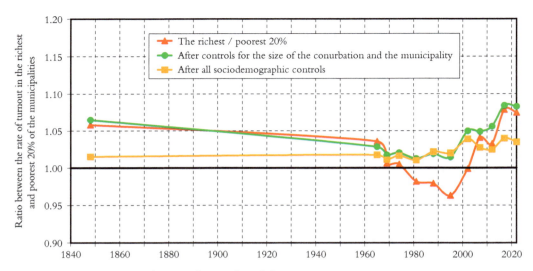

FIGURE 7.7. Income and turnout for presidential elections

Since 1990–2000, turnout for presidential elections has become higher and higher in rich municipalities relative to poor municipalities, with or without taking control variables into account.

Sources and series: unehistoireduconflitpolitique.fr

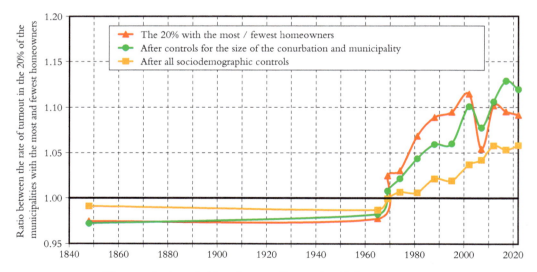

FIGURE 7.8. Homeowning households and turnout for presidential elections

In recent decades, a very clear disparity in turnout for presidential elections has appeared between
the municipalities with the largest proportions of homeowners and the municipalities with the
smallest proportions of homeowners, with or without taking control variables into account.

Sources and series: unehistoireduconflitpolitique.fr

voting, which was also not the case during the preceding decades.[6] The results regarding the socio-occupational structure also trend in the same direction as the legislative elections. We note in particular a significant decline in turnout in the most working-class municipalities relative to the least working-class municipalities since 1980–1990, whereas the turnout was greater in the latter during the presidential election of 1848 as well as during the presidential elections of the 1960s and 1970s.[7]

Finally, the recent period is also characterized by an additional crumbling of the turnout for presidential elections in municipalities with the largest populations of foreign origin in comparison to other working-class municipalities. Sometimes we also note very important variations from one election to another, which may be explained in part by the strong personalization of the presidential election. For example, during the 2007 election, we find a major reestablishment of turnout in municipalities with a large population of people of foreign extraction, which we could be tempted to interpret as a mobilization in opposition to Nicolas Sarkozy and his incendiary remarks about the suburbs. However, we note that this rebound disappears almost completely as soon as we control for the size of the conurbation and the municipality (see figure 7.9). In other words, it is the suburban municipalities as a whole (and to a certain, only slightly smaller degree, the metropoles) that experience a surge in turnout in 2007 (see figures 7.4 and 7.6), and not especially those with the greatest populations of foreign origin. We should point out as well that the disparity in turnout between rich and poor municipalities continued to grow in 2007. We will come back to this chronology in more detail when we study the votes for the different political tendencies and candidates in the later parts of this book.

In addition to these general tendencies, there exists, for presidential elections as for legislative elections, a great diversity of situations in the 36,000 municipalities, which deserve detailed local studies (see, for example, map 7.1).[8] But for the legislative elections, it is advisable to stress the importance of the social determinants of the turnout as well.

---

6. See unehistoireduconflitpolitique.fr, figure E1.7e.

7. See unehistoireduconflitpolitique.fr, figure E1.8e.

8. For better comparability over time, map 7.1 represents the turnout rate for each municipality in relation to the national average. For the absolute turnout rate for all the presidential elections from 1965 to 2022, see map C7.1j online.

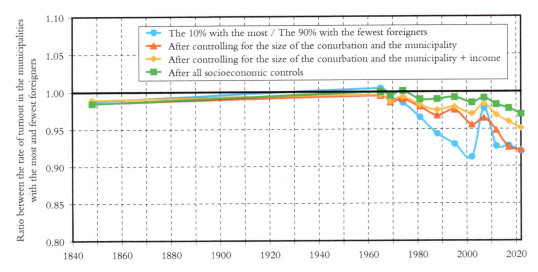

FIGURE 7.9. Foreign origins and turnout for presidential elections

In recent decades, a very clear disparity in turnout for presidential elections has appeared between the municipalities with the largest proportions of inhabitants of foreign nationality and those with the smallest. However, this disparity disappears to a great extent after taking into account sociodemographic control variables.

Sources and series: unehistoireduconflitpolitique.fr

Turnout for Presidential Elections: The Increasing Importance of Social Determinants

If we combine the set of explanatory factors with the sociodemographic variables in order to measure their overall explanatory power, we find for turnout in the presidential elections the same results as in legislative elections. The overall importance of the social determinants of turnout has always been relatively great, and it has progressed considerably over the long term, particularly over the course of recent decades (see figure 7.10).

We note that as for legislative elections, the additional explanatory power provided by taking the department into account in order to predict turnout for a presidential election has greatly diminished over time relative to social determinants. Specifically, the explanatory power of the department represents the equivalent of scarcely a tenth of that of all the sociodemographic variables taken together in the elections of 2022, whereas it was almost as great as the latter during the election of 1848 and still represented the equivalent of almost a third of the social determinants in 1965 (see figure 7.11).

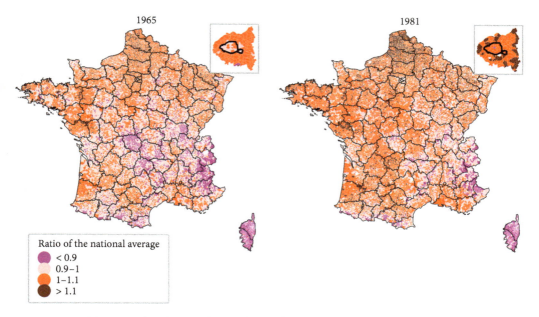

1965   1981

Ratio of the national average
● < 0.9
● 0.9−1
● 1−1.1
● > 1.1

MAP 7.1. The geography of turnout for presidential elections, 1965 and 1981

In 1965, as in 1981, turnout varied greatly, both between departments and within them. If we examine things in more detail, we see that the poor municipalities voted a little more than the rich municipalities in 1981, whereas the inverse was true in 1965.

Sources and series: unehistoireduconflitpolitique.fr

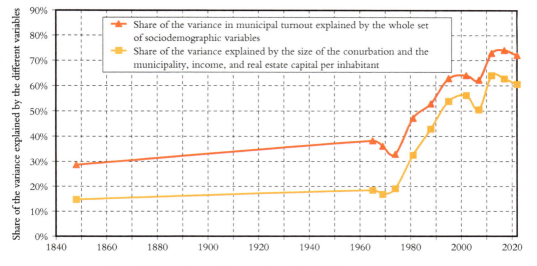

FIGURE 7.10. The social determinants of turnout in presidential elections

From the presidential election of 1848 to that of 2022, the share of the variance of the municipal turnout (in the sense of the R2 of the multifactorial regression) has risen from about 30% to more than 70%. The size of the conurbation and of the municipality, income, and real estate capital (the total value of housing) generally represent, by themselves, between half and three-quarters of the total explanatory power. The other sociodemographic variables are age, sex, occupation, higher education, foreign origins, etc.

Sources and series: unehistoireduconflitpolitique.fr

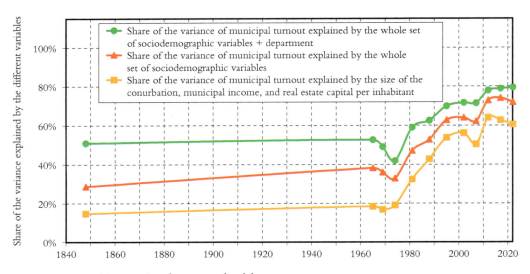

FIGURE 7.11. Turnout: Social vs. geographical determinants

From the presidential election of 1848 to that of 2022, the share of the variance of the turnout explained by sociodemographic variables (in the sense of the R2 of the multifactorial regression) has risen from about 30% to more than 70%. The department has an additional explanatory power equivalent to the whole set of sociodemographic variables in 1848, but only one-tenth in 2022. Sources and series: unehistoireduconflitpolitique.fr

Despite all the similarities between the evolutions of the turnout for presidential and legislative elections in recent decades, there remains an essential difference. In addition to the fact that the decrease of overall turnout has been very limited for presidential elections in comparison with the collapse observed in the legislative elections, the disparities in turnout between rich and poor municipalities have developed less massively for the presidential elections than for the legislative elections. This much is certain: the reversal of the effect of wealth on turnout has been very clear for presidential elections as well. The poorest municipalities voted as much or more than the richest in the presidential elections of the 1960s, 1970s, and 1980s, and a significant disparity has appeared in favor the rich municipalities since 1990–2000. The fact remains that the phenomenon is less marked for the presidential elections than for the legislative elections. For example, the ratio between the average turnout in the richest and the poorest 10 percent of the municipalities reached 1.2–1.3 in the legislative elections of 2017–2022 (see chapter 6, figure 6.1), whereas it was "only" 1.1–1.5 during the last presidential elections (see figure 7.1).

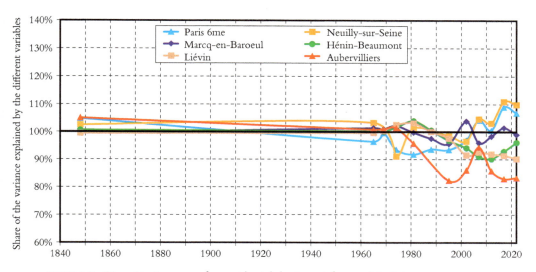

FIGURE 7.12. Disparities in turnout for presidential elections: A few municipalities

From the presidential election of 1848 to that of 2022, the disparities in the turnout for presidential elections between rich metropoles (Paris 6th), rich banlieues (Neuilly-sur-Seine, Marcq-en-Baroeul), poor suburbs (Hénin-Beaumont), and poor towns (Liévin, Aubervilliers), are small and unsystematic. Since 1990–2000, turnout has risen sharply in the richest municipalities (relative to the national average) and has fallen in the poorest municipalities, particularly in those with large populations of persons with foreign origins (Aubervilliers).

Sources and series: unehistoireduconflitpolitique.fr

We arrive at the same conclusion if we compare the magnitude of the different explanatory variables (the proportion of home-owning households, diploma holders, industrial workers, and so on) or if we examine, as an illustration, the evolution of turnout in a certain number of specific municipalities. For example, since 1990–2000, turnout in presidential elections has become structurally greater than the national average in Paris's 6th arrondissement and in Neuilly-sur-Seine, whereas it has fallen far below the national average in municipalities like Liévin in Pas-de-Calais and Aubervilliers in Seine-Saint-Denis (see figure 7.12). The gap observed is nonetheless clearly smaller than that seen in the legislative elections (see chapter 6, figure 6.13). Thus, the turnout rate for the presidential election of 2022 rose to 69 percent in Liévin, or twelve points less than the rate observed in Paris's 6th arrondissement (81 percent), whereas the gap between these two municipalities reached eighteen points in the legislative elections (with 41 percent and 59 percent turnout, respectively).

A French Electoral Calendar That Should Be Revised?

To sum up: a social bias in turnout has appeared in both legislative and presidential elections during recent decades, but considerably less massively in the latter than in the former. In other words, the population that took the trouble to go vote in presidential elections has become socially more favored than the national average, but it nevertheless remains closer to the national average than the population turning out for legislative elections. Insofar as electoral democracy is based on the promise of a political turnout as large and as representative as possible, it is natural to wonder what can be done to make turnout for legislative elections closer to that for presidential elections (and ideally, to also make the latter larger and more representative). The answer to this question is naturally complex. It involves numerous institutional factors, such as the organization of electoral campaigns and the system for financing political life that can influence the transformations of the political options, as well as other elements, such as informational practices. The results obtained also raise the question of the electoral calendar. When the five-year presidential term was adopted in 2002, there was a debate regarding the electoral calendar and it was finally decided to hold the presidential election first, which has certainly contributed to the disconnect between turnout for presidential elections and turnout for legislative elections (even if the growing gap between rich and poor municipalities began long before, as we have already seen in chapter 6). Faced with this observation, a recurrent question in French public debate is whether we should invert the electoral calendar once again, placing legislative elections before presidential elections.

On the basis of the results obtained and experiences in other countries, it seems to us that a better solution would be to hold presidential and legislative elections on the same date. The experience of the United States shows that simultaneous elections make it possible to obtain virtually the same turnout for the presidential and the legislative elections. In the French context, everything seems to indicate that a simultaneous vote would enable us to make the turnout for legislative elections rise to the level of the turnout for presidential elections, and perhaps even to increase the turnout for both elections, considering the interest that would be aroused by a public debate on personalities, political movements, and programs all at once. This might also prompt candidates for president to define more precisely the content of their legislative programs and the contours of the parliamentary majorities whose support they count on having. Such a reform of the electoral calendar could not, of course, check all the ills that plague French electoral democracy. The decline in turnout for legislative elections began in the 1980s and 1990s, the growth of a very large disparity in turnout between rich and poor municipalities concerns the presidential election as well, and only a very profound transformation of the political options could enable us to respond fully to the feelings of abandonment that are the source of these changes. Still, such a reform could make it possible to increase considerably the turnout for legislative elections and bring the social structure of the population of voters significantly closer to that of the French population in general, which would in itself be a positive change important for good democratic functioning.

The Referenda of 1793 and 1795: Electoral Conflict during the Revolution

We come now to the question of the social structure of turnout for referenda. As we have already noted, we are going to concentrate on the five most significant referenda in France since 1789: the polls of 1793 and 1795, the constitutional referendum of 1946, and the European referenda of 1992 and 2005. Within this set, the referenda of 1793 and 1795 have particular importance for two reasons: because the turnout for these elections constitutes a measure of the approval of the proposed constitutional changes (taking into account the infinitesimal number of No votes),[9] and because they are the only polls of the revolutionary period for which we have data solid enough to carry out a relatively systematic analysis. Concerning legislative elections and other elections held during the period 1789–1799, the data collected by Melvin Edelstein and other researchers relate to samples from departments, cities, and rural cantons. These data are sufficient to bring out general tendencies (in particular, the larger turnout observed in the rural world), but do not allow us to envisage a detailed analysis at the national level. In addition, the absence of previous candidacies implies that it is extremely complex to identify the candidates and to analyze the political significance of the votes when the deputies were chosen; only the turnout can really be used for the legislative elections of the revolutionary period.[10]

In comparison, the political meaning of the polls of 1793 and 1795 is relatively clear. The referendum of July 1793 concerned the adoption of a republican constitution that abolished the monarchy and instituted, for the first time in France, universal male suffrage and the direct election of deputies, and in certain cases, it allowed local electoral assemblies to intervene directly in the national legislative process. Moreover, it was the only election in the revolutionary period conducted

---

9. See chapter 5, figures 5.3–5.4 and discussion.
10. We will return to this question in chapter 8.

in the framework of quasi-universal male suffrage, and also the one that mobilized the greatest turnout (as a percentage of people with the right to vote, and even more in absolute terms). According to the available sources, turnout reached 37 percent in the referendum of 1793, then fell to 22 percent in the referendum of 1795, a decrease of more than 40 percent. Generally speaking, the referendum of September 1795 can be seen as a moment of conservative reaction: the new constitution sought to deprive a segment of the poorest electors of the right to vote during the primary assemblies, and especially to reestablish censitary suffrage with several steps in the selection of deputies, , a system that had applied from 1789 to 1793 and that limited the opportunity to become a deputy to the richest 10 percent of electors.[11] Ultimately, the referendum of 1795 can be seen as a stage in the process of establishing an authoritarian regime in 1799. The two votes thus have very different significances. The strong electoral mobilization during the referendum of 1793 reflects support for ending the monarchy and for a political system based on a participatory logic and universal suffrage, including for poorer voters, particularly among the most impoverished rural and peasant classes. Conversely, the vote in 1795 expresses a preference for a censitary system based on the exclusion of the poorest citizens, and for concentrating political power in working citizens who pay enough in taxes (in particular, for the selection of deputies), all while retaining a republican framework. It is therefore particularly interesting to compare the socioeconomic and geographic determinants of these two votes, which present a unique opportunity to analyze the structure of electoral and political conflict under the French Revolution.

Before presenting the results we have obtained, let us underline the limits and weaknesses of the available sources. The data collected by Serge Aberdam in the records of the electoral assemblies of 1793 and 1795, on which we have relied, are available at the level of the districts (groups of cantons), so the analysis it is possible

---

11. On the system with two steps, see chapter 1. In theory, the population that had the right to vote in the referendum of 1795 was the same as for the referendum of 1793 (about 82 percent of the adult male population), and it was only after the adoption of the new constitution of 1795 that it fell to 64 percent (that is, a level close to that of 1789–1792). See figures 1.1–1.3. The records of the electoral assemblies analyzed by Aberdam indicate that in practice, the power relationships at the local level were inverted even before the vote of 1795, such that it can be concluded that the decrease in the population allowed to vote (about 6.2 million registered voters in 1793–1794, as opposed to 5.1 million under the Directory in 1795–1799) was applied immediately after the referendum—that is the hypothesis we have adopted to calculate the turnout rate in 1795 (without which the latter would fall to 18 percent and not 22 percent; the number of voters decreased by more than half, sinking from about 2.3 million in 1793 to 1.1 million in 1795).

to make is less detailed than if we had municipal data.[12] Furthermore, the explanatory variables at our disposition are less rich for the revolutionary period than for later years. We have mainly information about the sizes of the municipalities and conurbations, along with information about the wealth of the municipalities, such that it can be gauged on the basis of the fiscal data issuing from land taxes and personal property taxes on the value of land, houses, and buildings.[13] We also have various sources connected with religious beliefs, such as the proportion of refractory priests in 1791 and the proportion of children attending private schools at different points in time during the nineteenth century (and also in the contemporary period). Finally, we must emphasize that the rate of turnout or approval noted during the referenda of 1793 and 1795 constitutes a relatively crude indicator of the genuine support for the constitutional changes being made.[14] In neither case was there any doubt that the new constitution would be adopted, and the local variations in the turnout rate may have reflected a multitude of factors unrelated to political opinions, such as the need to work in the fields at the time of the election, the weather and the condition of the roads, the military situation both domestic and foreign, and so on. More generally, the means of communication and transportation were at the time extremely rudimentary, and the knowledge that the various social groups in the territories had of the election being held should not be exaggerated. Moreover, this probably explains in large measure why

12. Specifically, the results indicated here have been obtained by attributing to each municipality the average result of the district to which it belongs (in proportion to the different municipal populations of the district). For the technical details connected with these estimates, see unehistoireduconflitpolitique.fr, appendix F. The sources meticulously gathered by Aberdam (whom we warmly thank for giving us access to these data) are also available in some cases at the level of the cantons, but the uneven preservation of the archived materials indicates that it is preferable to limit ourselves to the district level.

13. The fiscal data are available mainly at the departmental level for the end of the eighteenth century and the beginning of the nineteenth, and it was only in the course of the nineteenth century that the municipal data became systematically available (thanks to better preserved archives and to the volumes titled *Financial situation of the municipalities,* (Situation financière des communes), which were put together by the administration on the basis of the main fiscal and financial indicators of the 36,000 municipalities). Since the position of the municipalities within the departments evolved relatively slowly, these sources provide a good indication of the relative wealth of the municipalities at the time of the Revolution.

14. The results given here concern the rate of turnout (the number of voters divided by the number registered to vote). Considering the infinitesimal proportion of No votes (less than 0.5 percent of voters), the estimates obtained with the rate of approval (the number of Yes votes divided by the number registered to vote) are almost identical. See unehistoireduconflitpolitique.fr, appendix F.

the turnout rates observed were relatively low in comparison to contemporary standards.

The Referendum of 1793: A Rural and Anti-aristocratic Vote

Despite these difficulties, several results appear quite clearly. In sum, the vote of 1793 was first of all a rural, anti-aristocratic vote, in the sense that turnout was maximal in the rural world, and particularly in the rural territories where the concentration of agricultural land in the hands of the large landowners (who were often noble, but sometimes bourgeois) was the greatest, and where the landless peasants seem to have been very mobilized in support of the extension of suffrage to include them. The characteristics of the 1795 vote were strictly the reverse: it reached its lowest level in the rural world, and particularly in territories where the concentration of land in a few hands was the most extreme, and where poor peasants were obviously not very enthusiastic about the prospect of a return to censitary suffrage.

Let us begin with the effects of the size of the conurbation. Generally speaking, aside from very important regional variations (see map 7.2),[15] we see that the mobilization in favor of the constitution of 1793 was considerably greater in the rural world than it was in the urban world. In particular, turnout was highest among the 20 percent of the population living in the smallest conurbations, and it diminished regularly with the size of the conurbation, except for a rise to the level of the 20 percent of the population living in the largest conurbations (see map 7.2).

Several points must be clarified regarding this result. First of all, this conclusion confirms Edelstein's results concerning the greater mobilization of the rural world in general during the French Revolution. Considered as a whole, the rural world has always been poorer than the urban world, under the Revolution and as it is today.[16] It thus seems logical that rural voters lent greater support than urban voters to a constitutional transformation that extended the right to vote to the poorest rural classes. In comparison to the results obtained by Edelstein, who noted in the first elections of 1790 and 1791 a regular decline in turnout as a function of the size of the conurbation (with turnout that was highest in villages and rural cantons, lower in towns and middle-sized cities, and still lower in large

---

15. As before, map 7.2 presents electoral turnout by municipality in ratio to the national average; for the turnout rates actually observed for the referenda of 1793, 1795, 1946, 2002, and 2005, see unehistoireduconflitpolitique.fr, appendix C, maps C7.2a–C7.2e.

16. See chapter 2, figures 2.13–2.14.

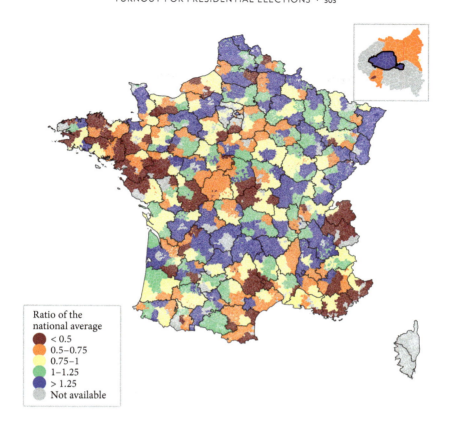

MAP 7.2. The geography of turnout for the referendum in 1793

The map represents the rate of turnout in the municipality as a ratio of the national average. In 1793, turnout varied greatly depending on the territories; it was maximal in rural territories with large concentrations of real estate.

Sources and series: unehistoireduconflitpolitique.fr

cities), our conclusions nonetheless seem more nuanced, with a slope that is less steep than the one shown by Edelstein, and a rebound of the turnout at the level of the largest conurbations. This can be interpreted in light of the fact that a significant part of the rural population had already been disappointed in 1793 by the Revolution's action. Their hopes for more fiscal justice and better access to land had not been fulfilled, and many of them blamed the new urban elites who had taken control of the Revolution and served themselves first, notably when the Church's property was sold off. The relatively high turnout observed in 1793 in the largest conurbations (especially in Paris, but not only there) also contrasts with the preceding years and reflects the existence of a specifically metropolitan

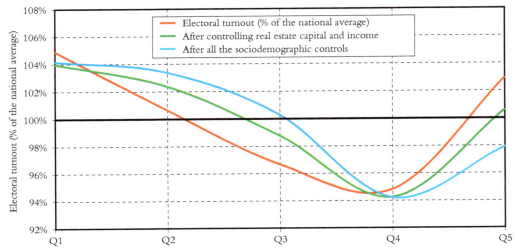

Distribution of the population by quintile as a function of the size of the conurbation

FIGURE 7.13. Turnout and the size of the conurbation in 1793

In the referendum of 1793, turnout was maximal among the 20% of the population living in the smallest conurbations, and diminished regularly with the size of the conurbation, if we except a rise at the level of the 20% of the population living in the largest conurbations, before and after taking control variables into account.

Sources and series: unehistoireduconflitpolitique.fr

dynamic at this point when political events and the revolutionary calendar were accelerating.

To properly interpret these results, it is important to put oneself in the context of the sociospatial geography of the period. In the 1790s, 54 percent of the population lived in villages (as defined in chapter 2—that is, conurbations of less than 2,000 inhabitants), 38 percent lived in towns conurbations with 2,000 to 100,000 inhabitants), and only 8 percent in metropoles and their suburbs (the principal and secondary municipalities of conurbations of more than 100,000 inhabitants).[17] In other words, the relation observed between turnout and the size of a conurbation during the referendum of 1793 reflects the fact that the villages were mobilized more than the towns (with a regular decline in participation in function of the size of the conurbation in the 80 percent of the population living in the least populated conurbations), but that turnout rises to the level of the metropoles while remaining lower than in villages (see figure 7.13).[18] From this point of view, the contrast with

17. See chapter 2, figure 2.6.

18. We will return later in this chapter to the geography of the turnout for referenda.

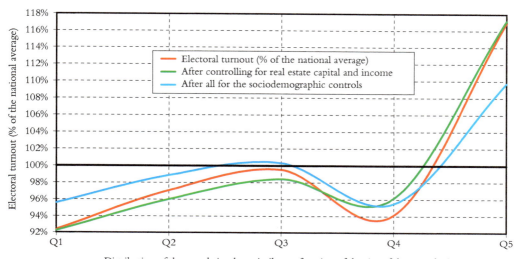

Distribution of the population by quintile as a function of the size of the conurbation

FIGURE 7.14. Turnout and size of the conurbation in 1795

In the referendum of 1795, conversely to that of 1793, turnout grew relatively regularly with the size of the conurbation and reached its maximal level in the 20% of the population living in the largest conurbations, before and after taking the control variables into account.

Sources and series: unehistoireduconflitpolitique.fr

the results obtained for the constitutional referendum of 1795 is particularly striking. The election of 1795 was a mirror image of the election of 1793: turnout grew in a relatively regular way along with the size of the conurbation, from the smallest conurbations to the largest (see figure 7.14). In particular, villages voted in smaller numbers than towns and metropoles, whereas the contrary had been true in 1793. A natural interpretation is that the poorest rural classes were particularly hostile to the return of censitary suffrage in several steps, which was synonymous with the disenfranchisement of poor voters and the control of political power by the dominant classes of the towns and metropoles. However—and we will return to this—the poorest classes lacked sufficient organizational capital to mobilize for the No vote, which was heavily stigmatized in the context of the period in most of the primary assemblies, which therefore preferred to abstain.

Proximity to the Catholic Church, Defiance of the Republican Regime

In addition to these effects of the size of a conurbation, several supplementary results deserve to be pointed out. We see in 1795 a slight positive effect of wealth

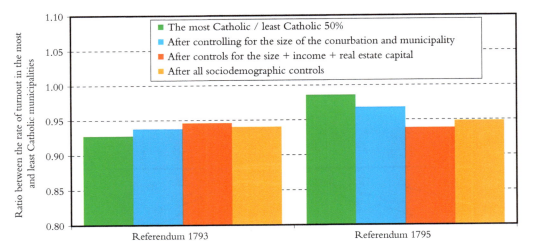

FIGURE 7.15. Turnout and religion in 1793–1795

In 1793, as in 1795, turnout was smaller in the most Catholic municipalities than it was in the least Catholic municipalities, before and after taking control variables into account. The indicator used here to measure the proximity of voters to the Catholic Church is the proportion of girls enrolled in private schools in 1795. Similar results are obtained with other indicators, such as the proportion of refractory priests in 1791 or the proportion of children attending private schools in 2021. Sources and series: unehistoireduconflitpolitique.fr

(measured by average real estate capital or average income) on turnout, particularly in metropoles, and to a lesser degree in town and villages.[19] Next, and especially, we see in 1793, as in 1795, a major, negative impact of religious values on electoral mobilization. In other words, turnout was smaller in territories where electors were characterized by a greater proximity to the Catholic Church, whether that proximity was measured by directly contemporary variables, such as the proportion of refractory priests in 1791, or by variables observed later on, such as the proportion of children attending private schools, especially during the nineteenth century. This is notably the case with the proportion of girls attending private schools in 1894 (see figure 7.15), a variable that everything suggests is strongly correlated with the presence of Catholic schools during the preceding periods.[20]

The most natural interpretation of these results is that the electors who felt closest to Catholic institutions and had the most confidence in them were also

---

19. See unehistoireduconflitpolitique.fr, figure F1.11 and appendix F.
20. See chapter 3 and unehistoireduconflitpolitique.fr, appendix B3.

those who were the most hostile to the privatization of ecclesiastical property that began between 1789 and 1793, and who consequently most distrusted the end of the monarchy and the arrest of Louis XVI (who had tried, unsuccessfully, to prevent the civil constitution of the clergy) and the establishment of a republican regime. The proportion of children attending private schools seems to have had a quantitatively greater systematic effect than the proportion of refractory priests, perhaps because families' experiences in school were ultimately the most decisive factor in their attitudes toward Catholic institutions, more than the clergy's oath of fidelity to the constitution, which might depend on individual and local factors connected with the priests in question.[21]

It will also be noted that we obtain a comparable impact of religious values on turnout, no matter what the size of the conurbation or the type of territory (village, town, suburb, or metropole), and more generally, that the effect is approximately the same before and after taking control variables into account. The negative effect of religion on turnout was quantitatively a little greater in 1793 than it was in 1795, but it is interesting to see that it was definitely present at the time of the two elections (see figure 7.15). In other words, the republican constitution of 1795 reestablished censitary suffrage with several steps, but it was nonetheless a republican regime, turning its back on the monarchy and basing itself on the civil constitution of the clergy and the privatization of ecclesiastical property to the benefit of urban elites, who had more power than ever. In the territories where the proximity to Catholic institutions was greatest, electoral mobilization remained weaker than elsewhere. This effect is seen again, no matter what the size of the conurbation.

The Concentration of Land Ownership, a Factor of Mobilization and Not of Submission to Landowners

Two criteria allow us to differentiate the vote of 1793 from that of 1795: first, the size of the conurbation (we have just seen that turnout was highest in the rural world in 1793, whereas the contrary is true in 1795), and second, the concentration of real estate ownership. The indicator used here is the proportion of agricultural lands held in farms of more than fifty hectares. This is an indicator very

---

21. In practice, these two indicators (the proportion of children attending private schools in 1894 and the proportion of refractory priests in 1791) are strongly correlated, but when they are not, it is the proportion of children (and in particular, girls) in private schools that seems to be connected the most strongly with the low rate of turnout in 1793–1795. See unehistoireduconflit-politique.fr, appendix F.

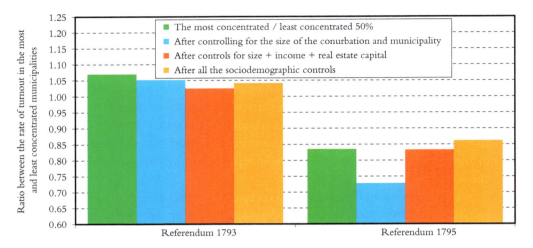

FIGURE 7.16. Turnout and the concentration of real estate capital, 1793–1795

In 1793, the turnout was higher in municipalities where real estate was most concentrated, before and after taking control variables into account. The converse was true in 1795. The indicator used here is the proportion of agricultural land owned in the framework of farms of more than fifty hectares, as it is measured in the 1962 census. Similar results are obtained with other indicators such the classification of real estate value per surface area in 1883.

Sources and series: unehistoireduconflitpolitique.fr

similar to the one Siegfried used in 1913 in his work on western France, which relied on property tax data on the cantonal distribution of agricultural land in 1883.[22] In this case, we are using data issuing from the 1962 census, which have the advantage of being available at the municipal level and for the whole of the national territory. They also yield results extremely close to those for the departments in the west of France obtained using the data for 1883, which show a high degree of persistence of rural real estate structures. However, contrary to Siegfried—who concluded, using a cartographic analysis conducted on the basis of the cantons of western France, that a strong concentration of land ownership was associated with a large monarchist or conservative vote in the legislative elections held from 1871 to 1910 (we will return to this when we study these elections)—we find that on the national scale, a strong concentration of land ownership led to a greater mobilization in favor of the constitution of 1793, and, conversely, to an extremely limited mobilization in the referendum of 1795 (see figure 7.16).

22. See the introduction.

Put another way, when there were large landowners, the effect of mobilization seemed to prevail over the effect of submission. In territories where almost all the land was in the hands of large landowners, the reaction of the peasant classes seems to have been to mobilize even more in order to support the constitution of 1793 and the establishment of universal suffrage, including for landless peasants and farmworkers who were often excluded from the right to vote in the framework of the censitary rules applied previously. Conversely, these same territories seem to have been very little mobilized in 1795, when it was a question of reestablishing the electoral cens. The results are even more striking if we compare the 20 percent of the municipalities with the greatest and the smallest concentrations of land ownership, rather than the 50 percent.[23] It will be noted that the indicator used is all the more interesting because it enables us to show the striking differences in the concentration of land ownership: farms of more than fifty hectares comprised the quasi-totality of agricultural land in the municipalities with the greatest concentrations (leaving virtually no space for the peasant population), and were almost absent in the municipalities with the smallest concentrations (which had de facto passed into the hands of small landowners).[24] Nonetheless, we must emphasize that the limitations of the available sources prevent us from offering a perfectly satisfactory analysis of these complex questions, and that the effects of mobilization and submission are not necessarily contradictory or mutually exclusive. There may be territories and historical periods in which the effect of mobilization prevails, and others, on the contrary, where the pressure exercised by the landowners, along with the interests and worldviews they defended, play a decisive role. However, on the scale of the national territory, the data we have seem to show rather clearly that the effect of mobilization prevailed, at least during the referendum of 1793. These results seem consistent with the analyses proposed by Paul Bois, Charles Tilly, and Serge Aberdam, who, on the basis of a study of the *Cahiers de doléance* and the records of the electoral assemblies, have demonstrated the importance of the peasant fighting spirit, especially regarding the question of access to land, and among the

23. See unehistoireduconflitpolitique.fr, figure F1.1i and appendix F.
24. In the 1962 census, farms of more than fifty hectares represented scarcely 4 percent of the approximately 1.7 million farms, but they comprised 26 percent of the land under cultivation (about 28 million hectares). This proportion of the land held in the framework of farms of more than fifty hectares reached 74 percent in the 10 percent of municipalities with the greatest concentration of land ownership, and it was only 8 percent in the 50 percent of the municipalities with the smallest concentration of land ownership.

poorest classes, particularly in territories where nobles held large amounts of real estate.[25]

Let us also note that our results reveal the limits and the ambiguities of this mobilization. In 1793, the peasant classes in the territories dominated by large landowners mobilized more than others to support the new constitution, but in the end, national turnout was only 37 percent, which remained modest in comparison with contemporary levels, especially for lack of adequate means of transportation and communication. In 1795, these same peasant classes refused to turn out to ratify the return of censitary suffrage, but in any case, they lacked the organizational capital, both material and symbolic, that in other contexts might have allowed them to go vote No. We should also note that relatively similar rural territories could find themselves opting for conflicting political choices, depending on their experiences with regard to the question of property and redistribution. When property was chiefly ecclesiastical and (before 1789) made possible the development of charitable works and major educational institutions, at least in part, the privatization of the Church's property to the benefit of the new urban elites could arouse strong negative sentiment against the Revolution and the republican regime. But when property was chiefly private and held by nobles, the revolutionary mobilization remained strong. Ultimately, our results illustrate above all the complexity of the heritage of 1789 and the multidimensionality of the political and electoral conflict that emerged from the French Revolution.

The Declining Influence of Geography and Religious Variables

It is equally interesting to analyze the overall influence of the social and geographic determinants of electoral turnout and the evolution of referenda, from those of 1793–1795 to those of 1992–2005. Several results stand out clearly. First of all, we see that in the same way as for the legislative and presidential elections (see figures 6.15–6.16 and 7.10–7.11), the influence of sociodemographic factors has increased over the long term, whereas the influence of strictly geographic factors has diminished (see figure 7.17).

In the referenda of 1793 and 1795, the sociodemographic variables thus explain about 30 percent of the variance in turnout, and adding the department as an explanatory variable increases the share of the variance to about 60 percent. In

---

25. See the introduction and chapter 1. More detailed historical data concerning the transformations of real estate structures on the local level since the Revolution could no doubt make it possible to produce results more detailed and more differentiated than those presented here.

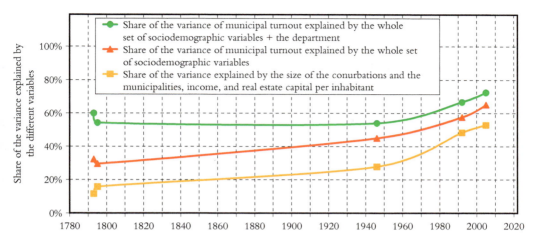

FIGURE 7.17. Social and geographical determinants of turnout (referenda, 1793–2005)

From the referendum of 1793 to that of 2005, the share of the variance in turnout explained by so-ciodemographic variables (in the sense of the R2 of the multifactorial regression) rose from about 30% to more than 60%. The size of the conurbation and the municipality, income, and real estate capital (the total value of housing) generally represent between half and three-quarters of the total explanatory power. The other sociodemographic variables are age, sex, occupation, higher educa-tion, origins, etc. The department has an additional explanatory power comparable the whole set of sociodemographic variables in 1793–1795, but only one-tenth of the explanatory power of these variables in 1992–2005.

Sources and series: unehistoireduconflitpolitique.fr

other words, the department has an explanatory power about equivalent to all the sociodemocratic determinants taken together. Inversely, during the referenda of 1992 and 2005, the social determinants explain about 60 percent of the dispari-ties in turnout between municipalities, and adding the department causes this figure to rise to about 65–70 percent, for an additional explanatory power equiv-alent to about one-tenth of that of the sociodemographic variables. Just as for the legislative and presidential elections, this result can be interpreted as the effect of a form of political unification of the country. In the 1970s, the perceptions of the political situation could be very different depending on the department, as is il-lustrated by the particularly low turnout in western France. Two centuries later, modern means of transportation and communication, the increased organizational capacity of political movements and parties, the greater power of audiovisual media, and other factors have helped bring together the different parts of the country in their view of the stakes involved in elections. On the other hand, the social and economic differentiations within each territory have become

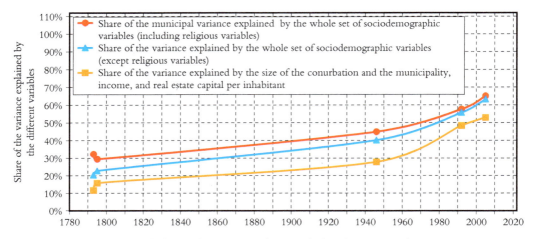

FIGURE 7.18. Social and religious determinants of turnout (referenda, 1793–2005)

The inclusion among the explanatory variables of variables connected with the Catholic religion (the proportion of refractory priests in 1791, the proportion of students enrolled in private schools in 1894 and 2021, etc.) causes the share of the explained disparities in turnout for the referenda to rise from 20% to 32% in 1793, from 40% to 45% in 1946, and from 63% to 65% in 2005. In other words, the explanatory power of the religious variables has diminished over time and was gradually absorbed by other sociodemographic variables (particularly economic variables).

Sources and series: unehistoireduconflitpolitique.fr

much stronger over the course of time, at least concerning disparities in electoral turnout. However, it must be stressed that the social determinants of voting were already very important in 1793 and 1795. The fact that 30 percent of the disparities in turnout can be explained simply on the basis of the relatively crude sociodemographic variables that we have for this period is striking in itself.

It is also interesting to isolate, in the set of sociodemographic variables at our disposal (such as the size of the conurbation and of the municipality, age and sex, real estate capital and revenue, education, occupation, and origins) the specific weight of the variables that can be qualified as "religious," in the sense that they allow us to grasp the degree of proximity to Catholicism and Catholic institutions. This is a matter of the proportion of refractory priests in 1791, as well as the proportion of girls and boys enrolled in private schools in different periods (in particular, in the 1894 and 2021) and at the levels of education (primary and secondary) for which we have collected the available data. We note that the weight of these religious variables was much greater during the referenda of 1793 and 1795 than in the referenda of 1946, 1992, and 2005 (see figure 7.18).

In 1793, the sociodemographic variables (not including religious variables) explain 20 percent of the disparities in turnout, and this figure rises to 32 percent when we introduce religious variables, which thus have an explanatory power equivalent to more than half the combined weight of the other variables (in particular, the size of the conurbation and the concentration of real estate ownership). In comparison, in 2005 the sociodemographic variables (excluding religious variables) explain 63 percent of the disparities, a figure that rises to 65 percent when we include religious variables, which now play only a secondary role in relation to the others. We note also that the influence of religious variables continued to decline between the 1946 referendum and that of 1992, and then declined again between the 1992 and 2005 referenda.

Religious Variables Absorbed by Socioeconomic Variables

In analyzing this phenomenon in greater detail, it is interesting to examine the explanatory power of religious variables also with regard to turnout for the legislative and presidential elections from 1848 to 2022. In the same way as for referenda, there is in both cases a very clear decrease in the importance of religious determinants over the past two centuries. In the legislative elections of 1848, the share of the variance of turnout explained by sociodemographic variables (not including religious variables) is 21 percent, which rises to 26 percent after the inclusion of religious variables, whose weight is thus equivalent to about one-quarter of all the other socioeconomic determinants. That is less than in 1793, but it remains very substantial. In 1962, the share of the disparities in turnout that can be explained by the different variables rises from 32 to 38 percent when religious variables are included, or an increase of about one-fifth of the explanatory power, which is far from negligible. In the legislative elections of 2022, on the other hand, the share of disparities in turnout hardly changes when religious variables are included: it rises from 66 to 68 percent (see figure 7.19). We find results of the same order in the presidential elections conducted from 1848 to 2022 (see figure 7.20).

Several points should be clarified. First, for reasons that are historical and concern the coherence of the analysis over time, the religious variables considered here are limited to variables connected with the Catholic religion, and therefore they do not take into account the recent rise in Islam, which has led to a new form of religious pluralism in France,[26] and which we include indirectly in the analysis a little further on, through variables pertaining to foreign origins (we will see that

---

26. See chapter 4.

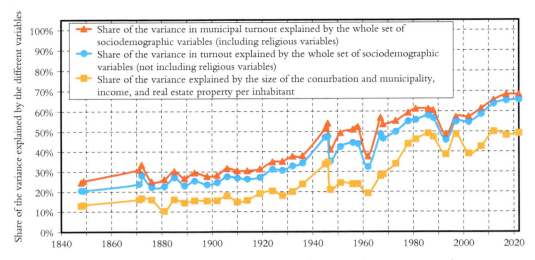

FIGURE 7.19. Social and religious determinants of turnout (legislative elections, 1848–2022)

The inclusion among the explanatory variables of variables connected with the Catholic religion (proportion of refractory priests in 1791, the proportions of students enrolled in private schools in 1894 and 2021, etc.) causes the share of the explained disparities in turnout for the legislative election to rise from 22% to 29% in 1848, from 29% to 35% in 1962, and from 66% to 68% in 2022. In other words, the explanatory power of religious variables has diminished over time and was gradually absorbed by other sociodemographic variables (particularly economic variables).

Sources and series: unehistoireduconflitpolitique.fr

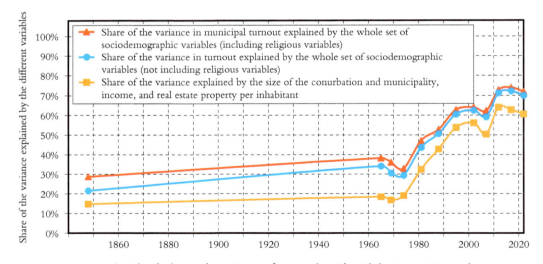

FIGURE 7.20. Social and religious determinants of turnout (presidential elections, 1848–2022)

The inclusion among the explanatory variables of variables connected with the Catholic religion (proportion of refractory priests in 1791, the proportions of students enrolled in private schools in 1894 and 2021, etc.) causes the share of the explained disparities in turnout for the presidential election to rise from 22% to 29% in 1848, from 36% to 39% in 1962, and from 70% to 72% in 2022. In other words, the explanatory power of religious variables has diminished over time, and was gradually absorbed by other sociodemographic variables (particularly economic variables).

Sources and series: unehistoireduconflitpolitique.fr

they, too, have a relatively limited influence). Second, the decline in the weight of religious variables in explaining turnout is a very long-term phenomenon that is spread over more than two centuries. The explanatory power of religious variables diminishes between 1793 and 1962, and again between 1962 and 2022. Within this long-term movement, we note a clear acceleration in the period 1962–2022—the explanatory power of socioeconomic variables is in free fall. Naturally, this observation can be connected with the concomitant acceleration of dechristianization since the 1960s.[27] In a France where Catholic religious practice is collapsing very rapidly, it is therefore not very surprising to note that the influence of variables connected with the Catholic religion is also collapsing. From this point of view, it is interesting to note that the proportion of students enrolled in private schools continues to have a significant predictive power over turnout if it is examined separately. We even observe that this raw predictive power (in this case, a strongly positive effect on turnout) has grown since 1980–1990. But as soon as we reason on a ceteris paribus basis—that is, as soon as we examine the weight of these variables while controlling for other determinants, and in particular, introduce socioeconomic controls measuring the territories' wealth (such as average income, real estate assets, or the proportion of property owners)—the influence of religious variables is absorbed by these controls and is reduced to very little.[28] In other words, over time, attending private schools has become increasingly closely correlated with economic wealth and has ultimately lost virtually all of its formerly autonomous role.

It is interesting to note that the meaning of the association between Catholic religious variables and turnout has changed since 1789. During the referenda of 1793 and 1795, the territories most closely linked with Catholic institutions had lower turnouts than the others, which reflected their distrust of the republican regime and the privatization of ecclesiastical property. The effect of religious variables on turnout becomes slightly positive in 1848 and increasingly clear between 1871 and 1914, expressing the Catholic electorate's desire to gain influence in republican and parliamentary political life, as did the Justice-Equality Committee (Comité Justice-Égalité, 1896–1900) promoted by the Catholic newspaper *La Croix*.[29] This effect was weak during the interwar period, but it increased in the 1950s and at the beginning of the 1960s, when a decisive battle for private education was fought. The raw effect gains an unprecedented importance starting in the

27. See chapter 4, figure 4.5.
28. See unehistoireduconflitpolitique.fr, figures C1.17a–C1.18e.
29. See chapter 4.

period 1980–1990, but for the most part it disappears when we introduce control variables (which are connected especially with economic wealth), which was much less the case in earlier periods.[30] Naturally, we will return to this question of the Catholic vote when we study the structure of voting for the various political tendencies.

As the variables connected with the Catholic religion lost importance over time, those connected with foreign origins evolved in the opposite direction. Since 1980–1990, the presence of a large population of foreign origin has been associated with a smaller turnout. However, it must be emphasized that this effect remains relatively modest if one is looking for a way to explain all the disparities in turnout and compares it with the weight of other sociodemographic variables. For example, during the legislative elections of 2022, sociodemographic variables (excluding variables linked to origins) explain 66 percent of the variance in the rate of turnout at the municipal level, and this figure rises to 68 percent when variables connected with origins (the proportion of people with foreign nationality, the proportion of immigrants, and the proportion of naturalized citizens) are included.[31] An effect of the same order is obtained for presidential elections.[32] Although the effect is significant, it will be noted that this additional explanatory power is of the same order as that observed for Catholic religious variables during the last elections, and considerably smaller than for religious variables up to 1960–1970, not to mention the explanatory power they had in 1848 or 1793.

From the Referendum of 1946 to the European Referenda of 1992 and 2005

Let us return to the social structure of the turnout during the referenda and examine its evolution from the constitutional referendum of 1946 to the European referenda of 1992 and 2005. Generally speaking, turnout for referenda between 1946 and 2005 resembles that of legislative and presidential elections during the same period. In particular, while turnout was higher in large conurbations (and especially in the suburbs) during the referendum of 1946, as it was in the legislative elections held at the same time, in the referenda of 1992 and 2005 it was higher in small conurbations, both before and after the control variables were taken into

---

30. See unehistoireduconflitpolitique.fr, figures C1.14a–C1.18e and E1.14a–E1.18e.
31. See unehistoireduconflitpolitique.fr, figure C1.2i. As for the set of the explanatory variables, the controls connected with origins are introduced in regressions in the form of categorial variables taking twenty values corresponding to the ventiles of the distribution in question.
32. See unehistoireduconflitpolitique.fr, figure E1.2i.

account,[33] just as it had been in legislative and presidential elections since the 1970s and 1980s.[34] Concerning the effect of municipal revenue, we note that the disparity in turnout between rich municipalities and poor ones diminished between the constitutional referendum of 1946 and the European referendum of 1992, then increased between the European referenda of 1992 and 2005, with or without control variables being taken into account.[35] Here again, it is a matter of changes similar to those observed for the legislative and presidential elections since 1945.[36]

Considering that no referendum has taken place since 2005, it is nonetheless impossible to say whether the growing disparity between rich and poor municipalities in turnout for referenda is closer in its magnitude to the change in turnout for legislative or presidential elections. In the fourth part of this book we will return to the powerful social cleavages that have divided the Yes camp from the No camp during the European referenda of 1992 and 2005, as they did in the constitutional referendum of 1946, though with very different political interpretations and parliamentary translations in the two cases. First, we must study the social structure of the vote for the different political tendencies that followed one another during the legislative elections held from 1848 to 2022, which we will do in the third part of this work.

---

33. See unehistoireduconflitpolitique.fr, figure F1.10f.
34. See chapter 6, figure 6.6, and figure 7.6.
35. See unehistoireduconflitpolitique.fr, figure F1.2f.
36. See chapter 6, figure 6.7, and figure 7.7.

PART III

Between Bipolarization and Tripartition

TWO CENTURIES OF LEGISLATIVE ELECTIONS IN FRANCE

CHAPTER 8

Coalitions and Political Families, 1848–2022

After studying in the first two parts of this book the evolution of sociospatial inequalities and the evolution of electoral turnout, it is now time to take up the study of voting for the different political tendencies and the analysis of the social structure of electorates. In this, the third part of this work, we will begin by exploring the determinants of voting in the framework of the legislative elections held in France from 1848 to 2022, and in the fourth and last part we will turn to the case of presidential elections and referenda.

This chapter presents the main outlines of the evolution of voting for the different political tendencies represented during the legislative elections from 1848 to 2022, taking a broad view of the period and stressing both the most important transformations and the principal regularities that we have brought to light. We will emphasize in particular two regularities that may seem paradoxical and contradictory, but which in reality constitute the foundational framework of the subject we are studying. On the one hand, left-wing political movements have always tended to realize their best results in the urban world (where the great majority of wealth has always been concentrated, moreover), whereas comparatively right-wing political movements have always won more votes in the rural world (which is on average poorer than the urban world), in connection with its persistent distrust of the Left with regard to the perceived hypocrisies of the world of cities since the Revolution. On the other hand, within the rural world, as in the urban world, we generally see an increasingly marked trend running in the opposite direction as the Left-Right bipolarization gained ground over the course of the twentieth century. We then see higher results for the Left in the poorest municipalities, and most importantly, we observe systematically higher results for the Right in the richest municipalities. Generally speaking, since the nineteenth century, left-wing trends have tended to rack up their best results in territories marked by particular social characteristics (such as a greater presence of workers or a greater concentration of land ownership in a few hands) in connection with the multifaceted and evolving program of redistribution carried out by these political movements. These two structural realities, which move partly in opposite directions—the rural-urban cleavage, the cleavage related to wealth—have changed in magnitude and strength over the past two centuries. These transformations can in turn be related to the changing strategies and programs of the various political movements, as well as to the socioeconomic and political context.

We will defend the idea that these variations determine in large measure the tendency of the electoral system to orient itself toward bipartition or tripartition. In short, when the cleavage connected with wealth wins out over the rural-urban cleavage, then the most working-class territories of the rural world and the urban world converge politically and tend to vote together in favor of the Left bloc, such that the system is oriented toward the Left-Right bipolarization. This corresponds, grosso modo, to the period 1910–1992. Conversely, when the rural-urban cleavage is stronger than the cleavage related to wealth, then the system is oriented toward tripartition, with a central bloc playing an autonomous role that is essential and often dominant between the two irreconcilable Left and Right blocs. This corresponds in large measure to what is observed in the period 1848–1910, and particularly in the 1880s and 1890s, when the Moderate and Opportunistic Republicans succeeded in taking power by exploiting the divisions of the urban and rural working classes between the Socialists and Radical-Socialists on the left and the conservatives, Catholics, and monarchists on the right. A trend of this kind also seems to be at work during the period 1992–2022, but with multiple contradictory elements that could lead the system back toward bipartition in the coming years. In this chapter, we will present these initial general results, taking a general view of the period 1848–2022, and then we will return in the next chapters to the three subperiods 1848–1910, 1910–1992, and 1992–2022. This will allow us to study in a more refined and precise way the diversity of the political tendencies and electoral affiliations present in the different periods and to better understand the socioeconomic and politico-ideological evolutions that might account for these two regularities and their transformations.

Political Tendencies and Coalitions: The Concept of Party System in French Context

Before presenting these results, we have to clarify several points concerning the sources we have collected, in particular the electoral records at the municipal level. We will discuss how we proceeded to characterize the political tendencies of the tens of thousands of candidates who stood for office in legislative elections held from 1848 to 2022, and regroup the different tendencies involved. We are not concerned with purely technical details or general methodological considerations (all of which can be found online). Instead, we aim to better understand the evolution of the structuration of political conflict, the way in which it is possible to measure and categorize it, and the meaning of the results that we will subsequently present.

In general, we must emphasize that the political and electoral landscape always involves a great diversity of political tendencies and subtle differences, and it can never be reduced to a binary confrontation between two monolithic blocs, or even to a ternary confrontation between three homogeneous blocs. The categories of Lefts, Rights, and Centers used by political actors (parties, voters, the media) in different historical periods—categories that we will use in turn—must be seen for what they are: flexible, unstable, and shifting notions mobilized by various actors to describe and simplify a complex and multidimensional reality. This operation may make it possible to facilitate partisan identifications and regroupings in coalitions, which are indispensable for rallying disparate electorates around common points of reference and for passing laws and governing in a way that is not merely piecemeal—which is not nothing. But although this need for simplification, intelligibility, and unification corresponds to an essential reality, it must not lead us to forget that the electoral scene usually includes a much larger diversity of political families in connection with the complexity and multiplicity of the stakes involved. This is particularly true in France, a country that has been characterized since the nineteenth century by a large number of political tendencies (about ten to fifteen significant ones in most of the legislative elections from 1848 to 2022), as well as by a rapid renewal of political organizations and partisan structures—a process that continued at top speed during the last elections.

Let us also note that while from this point of view the situation in France may seem to be different from what it is in countries characterized by a great durability of partisan structures—beginning with the United Kingdom and the United States—that is true only in part. In countries where there is a small number of large parties that are relatively stable over time, like the Conservatives and the Labour Party in the United Kingdom and the Republicans and Democrats in the United States, within each party there is usually a relatively large number of tendencies and lines of thought, organized more or less formally or informally (like, for example, the Tea Party movement and the MAGA movement[1] recently within the Republican Party), but it is in any case essential to take them into account to correctly analyze the ongoing transformations. Each major party often includes at least

---

1. The acronym MAGA stands for "Make America Great Again," a slogan that was used for the first time by Ronald Reagan in 1980 and that in recent years has become the rallying cry of Donald Trump's supporters.

three or four significant tendencies, so the underlying reality in terms of the number and diversity of elementary political families is not necessarily very different from the French situation, even if the institutional modalities of electoral competition are in fact very distinct (with, for example, the role of the intraparty primaries in the United States). Let us also remember that the British system is closer to tripartism than it is to bipartism. It took half a century (from 1900 to 1950) for Labour to replace the Liberals as the Conservatives' principal adversaries, and still today, the Liberal Democrats (distant heirs of the nineteenth-century Liberals) from time to time continue to play a significant role in the country's political life.[2] In the United States, it was not until the election of the Republican Lincoln in 1860, the Civil War, and the end of slavery that the institutional system was stabilized around the Democrats-Republicans pair.

Political scientists have also emphasized that the apparent stability of the formal party structures in the United States must not lead us to forget that the substance of the electoral confrontation on the political, socioeconomic, and ideological level has itself evolved profoundly since 1860. To describe the state of the political conflict, US political scientists have stressed particularly the notion of the "party system" or "partisan system"—which designates a set of relations that are relatively stable in their main lines between the principal parties or tendencies within the parties, enabling individuals to define themselves simply and effectively and to situate themselves with respect to one another.[3] The important point is that a party does not exist as such, as a pure ideology; instead, it is inserted into a system characterized by conflictual relationships and power struggles, with each party or tendency seeking to offer voters more convincing responses to the main social, economic, and political challenges of the moment, and mobilizing for that purpose multiple resources—human and material, organizational and logistical, symbolic and financial.

Researchers have thus acquired the habit of numbering the regimes that have succeeded each other since the foundation of the United States. From 1790 to about 1830, the "first party system" opposed the Federalists to the Democratic-Republicans (who were renamed "Democrats" in 1828 and were particularly active in the South and the plantation economy). In the 1830s, the Federalists (who were closer to the large cities of the Northeast and financial and industrial milieus) were replaced by the Whigs, thus giving rise to the "second party system" that opposed

2. It is even a system with four or five parties if we add new actors like the Scottish National Party and the UK Independence Party, which sometimes make things still more complex.

3. See, for example, P. Mair, *Party System Change: Approaches and Interpretations* (Oxford University Press, 1997).

Democrats and Whigs. The "third system" began with the election of Lincoln in 1860 and opposed Democrats and Republicans (who had replaced the Whigs in the late 1850s). The most widely accepted analysis maintains that the "third party system" was transformed into a "fourth system" around 1896–1900, with the arrival of the "populist" movement and the demand for redistribution, particularly within the Democratic Party (which formerly had been in favor of slaveholding), and then became a "fifth system" in 1932 with the crisis of the 1930s, the victory of Roosevelt's coalition, and the New Deal agenda, and finally a "sixth system" starting in the 1960s with the civil rights movement. According to some analysts, a "seventh system" was formed after Barack Obama's election in 2008, and especially after Donald Trump's election in 2016, in connection with the new territorial and ethnoracial cleavages in the country.[4] All this may seem distant from France, but it reminds us of the extent to which the substance of the electoral confrontation is variable and must always be resituated in its sociohistorical context.

The Institutional Question, the Social Question, the National Question

To analyze the evolution of political tendencies in France, it is clear that we must start from the specifics of the country's history and the challenges to which the forces involved have had to respond since 1789, which are considerably different from those with which the British or US parties have had to cope (even if there are common points, particularly in the recent period). Although French historians and political scientists may have resorted to the notion of a party system less than their colleagues in the United Kingdom and United States, they have also stressed the succession of several major phases in the political and electoral history of their country over the past two centuries, in connection with the updating of the questions that have defined public debate.

According to some authors, in France, the three great dimensions that have structured political conflict since the Revolution are, in chronological order, the institutional question from 1789 to 1890–1900, the social question from 1900–1910 until 1980–1990, and the national question since 1980–1990.[5] From

---

4. See, for example, S. Maisel and M. Brewer, *Parties and Elections in America* (Rowman and Littlefield, 2021).
5. See, in particular, G. Richard, *Histoire des droites en France de 1815 à nos jours* (Perrin, 2017). Earlier works like those of R. Rémond stressed the perennial nature of political tendencies and families, whereas G. Richard (rightly, in our view) puts the emphasis more on the updating of the stakes and the divisions in a sociohistorical perspective. See also the other references on the history of political trends on the right and on the left cited in the introduction.

the revolutionary period to the definitive acceptance of the Republic around 1890–1900, the central conflict thus sets supporters of a republican regime against supporters of a monarchical regime. The Left and gradually the Center of the political chessboard were composed of republicans of various tendencies, whereas the Right grouped together the monarchists who supported the existing dynasties (Legitimists and Orléanists), along with the Bonapartists defending an imperial dynasty. The institutional question sometimes tended to eclipse the social question, to the point that the central conflict could sometimes seem to resemble a conflict between republican elites and monarchist elites.[6]

Starting around 1900–1910, the consolidation of the republican regime and the increasing power of the labor movement foregrounded the social question and the opposition between proletarians and property owners, with a political conflict opposing, on the one hand, the Socialist and Communist Parties, and on the other hand, a group of parties and conservative and liberal trends defined in large measure by their rejection of the Socialist-Communist agenda (which was itself multifaceted, sometimes incoherent, and constantly evolving). Then, starting in 1980–1990, with the collapse of the Communist bloc and the loss of hope in the possibility of a social and economic system radically different from capitalism (at least for a time), new issues such as the migrant question, the European question, and more generally, the question of globalization and international economic integration, took on more and more importance. The party system underwent a new transformation with the weakening of the left- and right-wing parties that had characterized the preceding period and the emergence on the right side of the political chessboard of the Front national (FN) and then the Rassemblement national (RN), a new power putting at the heart of its program opposition to immigration, "globalism," and European integration.[7]

---

6. Or else between different monarchist elites (Legitimists and Orléanists, rural and urban, agrarian and industrial) during the period of censitary monarchies (1815–1848), when only 1–2 percent of adult men had the right to vote; we chose not to study it in the context of this work. This institutional conflict is found in the names of the nuances to which the candidates involved were attached during the elections, "monarchist" and "republican" being the principal labels used during the legislative elections of 1877, and "Bonapartist," "republican," "constitutional," and "Legitimist," during those of 1876.

7. Other dimensions of political conflict have gained new power in recent years, particularly the question of gender and that of environmental inequalities, and they too, along with the national question, have contributed to a redefinition of the connection with electoral conflict. We will return to this in the following chapters.

The Primacy of the Social Question, the Intertwining of the Issues

This view centered on the succession of three phases is valuable and pertinent to our investigation, but on the condition that several points are clarified. In particular, we must emphasize that the social question is omnipresent, and that it is often closely intertwined with the institutional question and the national question. During the revolutionary period, the discussions concerning the royal veto and the monarchical or republican regime were intimately connected with the question of the redistribution of wealth and social power. The conflicts over land reform and the privatization of ecclesiastical property played a foundational role.[8] The memory of the bourgeois hoarders who bought up the national properties and the question of the Church's role in social work and education continued to occupy people's minds until the end of the nineteenth century and beyond, independent of the question of the regime. Within the republican camp, profound divisions appeared as early as the revolutionary period and grew deeper in 1848–1852, and then again in the 1870s, 1880s, and 1890s, over the question of redistribution, property, and social hierarchies. To sum up, the social question already had fundamental importance during the period between 1789 and 1900, which could not be reduced to a purely institutional conflict between republicans and monarchists.

Similarly, the rising power of the national question since 1980–1990 is closely linked to socioeconomic issues. Beyond the complex question of the transcendence of the nation-state and the constitution of a transnational public power capable of regulating the world economy, it was above all, the content of transnational policies that was being debated. The feeling of having been abandoned by French and European policies of economic and commercial deregulation and the free circulation of goods, persons, and capital, a perception that was widespread in the most disadvantaged territories and social classes, thus played an essential role in weakening the old parties and constituting a new bloc of the nationalist, nationalist-patriotic, or social-nationalist type over the course of recent years. This bloc presents itself as being better able to defend the national interests than those who have governed before it, and in particular, as defending the interests of the most vulnerable, who have been abandoned by the elites who have succeeded one another in power—a claim that is difficult to contest effectively because so far, the bloc in question has never had to govern.

---

8. See the introduction, chapter 1, and chapter 3.

It will also be noted that the national question naturally played an essential (though less central) role long before 1980–1990. As early as the 1880s–1890s, protests against the allegedly unfair competition of immigrant workers led to an initial hardening of immigration policies.[9] Following the defeat of 1870 and during the first years of the Third Republic, the monarchist and conservative Right increasingly appropriated the theme of nationalism and patriotism, a theme originally seen as left-wing during the revolutionary period, at the time of the Battle of Valmy and republican protests against the exiled nobles and the monarchies who had formed coalitions against the Revolution of 1789. It was presented more and more often as the power best suited to defend the country's frontiers and interests against republicans accused of undermining national unity by attacking Catholics and the institutions that had been the pride of France, even as it awarded positions to Jews, Protestants, and *métèques,* not to mention Socialists and their current internationalist favorites. These themes were also to play an essential role during the interwar period and the economic crisis of the 1930s, as well as during the period of decolonization and the historic conflicts that resulted from it (in particular, conflicts between "people repatriated from Algeria" and immigrants of North African origin).

Political Trends and Party Systems in France: The First Reference Points

Let us first examine more closely the main trends that have embodied electoral and political conflict in these different phases. Simplifying, we can distinguish five party systems that have succeeded one another in France since the Revolution (see table 8.1).

Throughout the revolutionary period, the first party system opposed the Jacobins and Montagnards on the left against the Girondins in the center and the Feuillants and other monarchists on the right. These cleavages were formed during the constitutional monarchy (1789–1792) and the first years of the First Republic (1792–1795), particularly in the clubs where deputies of differing persuasions met. They had an obvious institutional dimension (the Jacobins and Girondins were republicans, the Feuillants were monarchists), but they also had a socioeconomic component that played an essential role in the development of events. Within the Jacobins, the Montagnards represented themselves as the primary defenders of the *sans culottes,* of the urban little people and poor peasants. They supported voluntarist economic measures such as a maximal price for grain and a compul-

---

9. See chapter 4.

Table 8.1   Political tendencies and party systems in France: First points of reference

	Left	Center	Right
1789–1799 Revolution and First Republic	Jacobins, Montagnards	Girondins	Feuillants, monarchistes
1848–1852 Second Republic (tripartition)	Démocrates-socialistes, Montagnards, Républicains avancés	Républicains modérés, Républicains constitutionnels	conservateurs, Parti de l'ordre, monarchistes, Bonapartistes
1871–1910 Beginning of Third Republic	Socialistes, Radicaux, Radicaux-socialistes, Républicains avancés	Républicains modérés, Républicains constitutionnels, Républicains opportunists	conservateurs, monarchistes, Bonapartistes, libéraux, Catholiques
1910–1992 Bipartition Left-Right	Communistes (PCF), Socialistes (SFIO-PS), various Left parties	Radicaux, various Center parties	conservateurs, libéraux, Catholiques, Gaullistes, etc. (FR, URD, ARD, MRP, RPF, UNR, UDR, RPR, UDF, etc.)
1992–2022 Toward a new tripartition?	Communistes (PCF), Socialistes (PS), LFI, EELV, various Left and ecologist parties	Modem, LREM, Ensemble, UDI, various Center parties	Gaullistes, libéraux, nationalistes, etc. (RPR, UDF, UMP, LR, FN, RN, etc.)

Note. We can distinguish five main party systems in French electoral history, sometimes characterized by tripartition (with three poles of comparable strength on the left, center, and right, notably between 1848 and 1910) and sometimes by a marked tendency to the two-party system (with two dominant poles on the left and the right, notably between 1910 and 1992). The period 1992–2022 seems to be marked by the return to a new form of tripartition.

Acronyms. SFIO: Section française de l'internationale ouvrière. PS: Parti socialiste. PCF: Parti communiste français. FR: Fédération républicaine. URD: Union républicaine et démocratique. ARD: Alliance républicaine démocratique. MRP: Mouvement républicain populaire. RPF: Rassemblement du peuple français. UNR: Union pour la nouvelle République. UDR: Union de défense de la République. RPR: Rassemblement pour la République. UDF: Union pour la démocratie française. UMP: Union pour une majorité populaire. LR: Les républicains. FN: Front national. RN: Rassemblement national. LFI: La France insoumise. EELV: Europe écologie–Les verts. Modem: Mouvement démocrate. LREM: La République en marche. UDI: Union des démocrates et indépendants.

Source. See unehistoireduconflitpolitique.fr, table A2, for election-by-election ranking of all nuances and parties into Left, Center-Left, Center, Center-Right, and Right.

sory loan imposed on the richest taxpayers (a form of progressive tax), to which the Girondins were opposed, finding liberal theses more persuasive. The Montagnards were also more aggressive on the issue of the abolition of forced labor (*les corvées*) and feudal rents, without compensation for property owners, and more generally on everything that could facilitate the redistribution of land and wealth, whereas the Girondins and the Feuillants were worried about the harmful consequences of occupying plots of land and an unlimited challenge to property rights.[10]

Nonetheless, let us make it clear that this first party system corresponds primarily to a parliamentary reality (which was itself very chaotic) and not an electoral reality.[11] Considering the mode of the election in two rounds that was in force at the time (with primary assemblies open to 60–70 percent of adult males to choose departmental electors among the 10–20 percent of the richest taxpayers, then departmental assemblies of those electors to choose the deputies), and given also the interdiction of candidacies preceding the meetings of the assemblies (a rule that was supposed to prevent manipulations and corruption, but which in practice also made any public debate before the election difficult, with the result that defeated candidates generally left no mark in the press),[12] it is impossible to use electoral reports and the available sources to attribute political labels to defeated candidates and thus to interpret the votes won by each of them. Although one could set out to study the labels of the elected deputies on the basis of their departments of origin—which some authors have attempted to do (not without difficulty, taking into account that the individual positions frequently vary over the course of a legislature)[13]—the materials at our disposition do not, unfortunately, allow us to go further and directly study the electors' votes (except for

---

10. See chapter 1 and R. Blaufarb, *The Great Demarcation: The French Revolution and the Invention of Modern Property* (Oxford University Press, 2016).

11. On the evolution of the positioning of the deputies from the Estates General to the Constitutive Assembly, see C. Le Digol, "Du côté gauche et du côté droit à la Constituante. Retour sur les 'origines' d'un clivage (1789–1791)," in *Gauche-Droite. Genèse d'un clivage politique,* ed. J. Le Bohec and C. Le Digol (Presses Universitaire de France, 2012).

12. See chapter 1. Only the names of the candidates were reported in the minutes, sometimes along with their titles and / or occupations. Thus, there was nothing that made it possible to study electoral programs and commitments; in contrast, in the second half of the nineteenth century, the press—which openly took sides—was full of information on the powers involved and their victories or defeats.

13. See, for example, M. Vovelle, *La découverte de la politique. Géopolitique de la Révolution française* (La Découverte, 1992), 210–218. See also L. Hunt, *Politics, Culture and Class in the French Revolution* (University of California Press, 1984); and J. R. Suratteau, "Heurs et malheurs de la sociologie électorale pour la période de la Révolution française," *Annales E.S.C.,* 1968.

turnout).[14] That is why our analysis of the legislative elections and party systems really begins only with the elections of 1848.

In fact, it was truly the Revolution of February 1848, followed by a legislative election in April 1848 (the election of a constitutive assembly) and presidential elections in December 1848 and May 1849 (conducted in accord with the new constitution), that led to the establishment, for the first time in France, of a party system corresponding to an electoral reality. Although there were still no political parties in the modern sense (they would appear and be officially authorized only after the implementation of the 1901 law on associations), the main blocs were rather clearly defined and organized by means of "electoral committees" entrusted with coordinating candidacies in the various departments and making them known by disseminating their arguments and programs in the press and in leaflets. During the election of May 1849, the three main committees were, on the left, the Democratic Socialist Committee, which supported the democratic socialist lists and those of the Montagnards (both terms were used) and sought to succeed the Montagnards of 1792 as the defenders of the *sans culottes,* landless peasants, workers, and the new urban proletarians; in the center, the Democratic Committee of the Friends of the Constitution, which brought together Moderate Republicans defending the application of the new constitution and universal suffrage, while at the same time remaining wary of attempts to challenge the social order and the property system of groups situated to their left; and on the right, the Committee of the rue de Poitiers, the spearhead of the "Party of Order" (as it was called at the time) bringing together the conservatives and former monarchists of various tendencies, united above all by their fear of the "Reds" and the tolerance of them by the Moderate Republicans and constitutionalists. The Committee of the rue de Poitiers, organized chiefly by Thiers and supported by Montalembert's Committee for the Defense of Religious Freedom (in the vanguard particularly for the defense of Catholic schools and the influence of religious schools in educational matters), was by far the best endowed financially and the most active in distributing pamphlets and arguments. In practice, the elected officials of the Party of Order were prepared to challenge the republican regime and universal suffrage if that proved necessary to counter the Red threat. It was they who voted in May 1850 for the Burgraves' law seeking to remove from the electoral lists the poorest 30 percent of voters (including more than half of the urban voters).[15]

---

14. See chapter 5.
15. See chapter 1.

The coup d'état of December 1851 and the establishment in 1852 of an authoritarian regime left little room for nonofficial candidacies put an abrupt end to the second party system. It was not until the advent of the Third Republic that a new party system was developed. From 1871 to about 1910 it was organized around three poles of comparable importance, with the Socialists, Radicals, and Radical-Socialists and other "advanced republicans" on the left, diverse groups of Moderate Republicans, constitutional Republicans, and Opportunistic Republicans (with names that changed with the subperiods) in the center, and several varieties of conservatives, monarchists, Bonapartists, and Catholics on the right (see table 8.1). Within the Left, the specifically socialist trends were relatively weak during this period, which is explained chiefly by the suppression of the workers' movement, which had already been massive and brutal in 1848–1849 and under the Second Empire, and which became blood-soaked during the crushing of the Paris Commune in May 1871, culminating in tens of thousands of deaths and deportations.[16] The violence of the fighting was such that the new regime waited until 1879 to return the capital from Versailles to Paris. This profound history of the Republic and the workers' movement no doubt explains in part the vigor of the syndical-autonomist tradition in France as well as a lasting break with republican and parliamentary socialism. On the electoral level, the socialist trends regained strength beginning with the legislative elections of 1893 and united in 1905 to form the Parti socialiste (PS) that still exists today, and which became at the same time the Section française de l'internationale ouvrière (SFIO, the French Section of the Workers' International). They were also known by the dual name PS-SFIO until the Epinay Congress of 1971, after which the name PS became the norm again.

The increasing power of the socialist and labor movement was to constitute one of the main forces driving the system toward bipolarization between 1910 and 1992. During this period, the Left was composed essentially of Socialists and Communists, united in principle around a program of socioeconomic transformation oriented toward collective ownership of the means of production. The Right amalgamated trends whose most powerful common denominator was opposition to this program and the defense of private property. This bipolar confrontation tended to reduce the Center to the smallest share: everyone had to

---

16. Between 10,000 and 20,000 dead during "Bloody Week" (21–28 May 1871), according to the most common estimates (as many as 40,000–50,000 dead according to other calculations), to which we must add almost 10,000 deportees. See Q. Deluermoz, "Les morts de la Semaine sanglante," in *La Commune de Paris, 1871. Les acteurs, les évènements, les lieux,* ed. M. Cordillot (Éditions de l'Atelier, 2021), 999–1101.

choose sides. However, this tendency should not be exaggerated. The divisions within each bloc remained considerable, particularly on the left, marked by the split at the Tours Congress in 1920 between Socialists and Communists over the question of support for the USSR. It was not until the new constitution of 1958 and the establishment of the presidential election by universal suffrage in 1962, along with its first application in 1965, that the logic of the union in the second round saw its full effects and reduced the Center to next to nothing (at least for a few decades). Between 1910 and 1958, the fractures within both the Left and the Right provided considerable room for centrist parties, especially the Radicals, who during the interwar period occupied a major place on the political chessboard, steering sometimes to the left, sometimes to the right, depending on the circumstances.

The Renewal of the Parties and the Drift toward the Left

Generally, over the long term, we see political movements drifting toward the left in the context of a substantial renewal of structures and parties. This drift toward the left can be interpreted as a partisan and electoral version of the long-term movement toward greater equality mentioned earlier.[17] Today, no significant political force challenges the existence of a welfare state based on the pooling of approximately half the national income in the form of contributions and taxes (value-added taxes, income taxes, and so on), making it possible to finance a diversified set of public services and social welfare transfers. The chief issue is whether this movement should be continued or consolidated; no one is proposing a grand return to the past. However, in the nineteenth century and the beginning of the twentieth, such a prospect would have seemed unimaginable to most political actors.

The political power that best incarnates this gradual drift to the left was no doubt the Radical Party. In the context of the 1870s and 1880s, the Radicals constituted the parliamentary force furthest to the left, though in a context in which the socialist and labor movement had just been decapitated. They were the most "radical" of the republicans, but their program of economic and social transformation remained moderate: they concentrated above all on the defense of the republican regime, the school question, and the battle against the Church's grip on education. They nonetheless retained the word "socialist" when in 1901 they constituted themselves as a political party with an endless name; the Parti républicain,

---

17. See chapter 1.

radical et radical-socialiste (PRRRS) was then the central political power behind the establishment of a progressive tax on inheritances (1901), and then a progressive tax on income (1914). But the radicals saw themselves as being primarily the defenders of small private property, and they were worried about the collectivist projects of parties situated to their left (the PS-SFIO, created in 1905, then the PCF in 1920), which were pushing them further toward the center. During the interwar period and after World War II, the "Rad-Socs" were often mocked for their centrism and their feebleness. They became less and less radical and never really socialist, but they were always ready to join coalitions in power.

The drift to the left is also found in the evolution of the "republican" label, which was located historically on the left when the Right was chiefly monarchist or Bonapartist, but which became, over time, the prerogative of right-wing parties. At the time of the creation of the PRRRS (1901) and the SFIO (1905), several new parties were established on the right half of the political chessboard, often on the basis of conservative, liberal, and Catholic deputies who had recently rallied to the republican regime and who realized that the monarchist label was no longer really current and did not allow them to effectively defend the program of action to which they were attached—concerning, for example, the defense of private schools and the values of economic liberalism. Founded in 1901, the Alliance républicaine démocratique (ARD) thus brought together deputies situated right of center but advocating an alliance with the Radicals in order to lead them away from the deputies furthest to the left, particularly the Socialists. Renamed Alliance démocratique (AD) in 1926, it was one of the main powers of the Center-Right during the interwar period.[18] At that time, the other major component of the parliamentary Right was the Fédération républicaine (FR). Founded in 1903, it was also based on the groups that had rallied to the Republic, but it rejected the coalition with the Radicals advocated by the ARD and was generally situated to the right of the ARD (though with a certain flexibility depending on the subject).[19] Starting in 1928, the FR's elected officials joined the parliamentary

18. The ARD frequently changed its name during this period: it was renamed Parti républicain démocratique from 1911 to 1917, then again was the Alliance républicaine démocratique from 1917 to 1920, then Parti républicain démocratique et social from 1920 to 1926, and finally Alliance démocratique from 1926 on.

19. Let us also mention the Action libérale populaire (ALP, also called Action libérale), which included, starting in 1901, some of the Catholics who had rallied to the Republic (formerly brought together in the Comité électoral catholique et anti-collectiviste), who for the most part rejoined the FR in 1919.

group of the Union républicaine et démocratique (URD).[20] The vice president of the FR in the 1930s, Xavier Vallat, remains sadly famous for his attack on Léon Blum from the rostrum of the Chamber of Deputies on 6 June 1936, to protesting whistles from the Left and applause from some of the Right: "For the first time, this old Gallo-Roman country will be governed by a Jew." He became commissioner for Jewish questions in 1941–1942, under the Vichy regime.

Discredited by their attitude under the Occupation, during the Liberation the parties situated to the right of the Radicals were restructured, with the creation of the MRP (Mouvement républicain populaire), which brought together the Christian Democrats, and the RPF (Rassemblement pour le peuple français), which united the Gaullists. Later on, the term *républicain* was used again and again by the Gaullist parties, who from 1958 and during the 1960s and 1970s regularly changed their names on the grounds that they needed to unify and defend the Republic (UNR, UDR, RPR).[21] After going by the title UMP (Union pour un mouvement populaire), in 2002 the principal party of the Gaullist Right became Les Républicains in 2015. The non-Gaullist Right, gathered particularly from the Républicains indépendants in 1962, regrouped in the framework of the UDF (Union pour la démocratie française) starting in the 1970s. Although the list of acronyms may be tiresome, still we must note that there is a real continuity in the social structure of the electorates, as we will see below, and this shows that at least to a certain extent, voters found what they were looking for. That is why we have

---

20. We also find, in the interwar period and under the Fourth Republic, denominations like "Républicains de gauche," "Gauche républicaine," and "Rassemblement des gauches républicaines" to designate groups of deputies or senators situated to the right of the Radicals and thus very clearly on the right side of the parliamentary hemicycle of the time. This habit, issuing from the period when the only true Right acknowledged as such was monarchical, ended up disappearing under the Fifth Republic, when only the Socialists, Communists, and similar groups described themselves as forming the Left. We note also that from 1898 on, the term "progressive Republicans" was used to designate the fringe furthest to the right of the former Moderate and Opportunistic Republicans, before the latter joined the Republican Federation.

21. Respectively, Union pour la nouvelle République, Union de défense de la République, and Rassemblement pour la République. Let us note that the "Republic" no longer has to be defended against a possible counterattack by an empire or a monarchy, which have become phantoms, but rather against the threat of the FN and other movements considered by the Right (and by the forces of the Left that also appeal to the "Republican front") to be opposed to the republican system. With the return of tripartition and because of a curious semantic slippage, the term *arc républicain* (republican arc) is becoming established, little by little, in the dialectic of the new centrist bloc, in order to dismiss the forces furthest to the left and to the right on the political chessboard.

placed all these parties and political movements within the Right and Center-Right in the framework of the party system in force from 1910 to 1992 (see table 8.1).

In addition to "republican," the other word most often used to designate parties and electoral alliances on the right side of the political chessboard is "national," from the "Bloc national" that grouped together all the forces of the Right and Center-Right during the legislative elections in 1919 to the Front national (FN), which was created in 1972 and replaced in 2018 by the Rassemblement national (RN). The rise of the FN and then the RN since the 1980s and 1990s has been impressive: the party has reached the second round in three of the five presidential elections conducted during the last twenty years (in 2002, 2017, and 2022), and its parliamentary group gained ascendancy over the other right-wing parties in the legislative elections of 2022. The emergence of the new nationalist-patriotic bloc (as it often calls itself) constitutes the principal innovation in the party system in the last decades and one of the most powerful forces weakening the Left-Right bipartition and pushing the system toward tripartition.

We will also note that this is virtually the first time in centuries that novelty has issued not from a new left-wing party pushing the old forces toward the center and the right (as the Radicals and then the Socialists and Communists did), but, on the contrary, from the Right.[22] This swing of the historical pendulum must, of course, be set alongside the collapse of the Communist countermodel, which marked an epochal change and a profound disappointment within the Socialist and Communist Left (at least for a time).

We will see, however, that rise of the FN-RN should not be interpreted solely as the consequence of a process of moving to the right, in a context of the hardening of attitudes on identitarian and security-related issues. In the towns and villages, this vote may also express a feeling of being abandoned, perhaps especially during the most recent period, in connection with a demand for social equality and broader access to public services and property. It will be noted that partisan innovation has also resumed in other segments of the political landscape. That is the case with the Center, which has been under reconstruction during recent decades, especially with the candidacy of François Bayrou for the presidency in 2007 and the transformation of the UDF into Modem (Mouvement démocrate), then the candidacies of Emmanuel Macron in 2017 and 2022, and the emergence of new parties—LRM, Ensemble, and UDI (see table 8.1). It is also the case with

---

22. We say virtually because Bonapartism and Gaullism, which were radical innovations in their own time, particularly on the institutional level and on the questions of the direct election of the president of the Republic and the use of the referendum, also came from the Right.

the Left, with the development of several ecology-oriented parties (notably, Europe écologie–Les verts in 2010) and new movements challenging the historical duopoly PCF-PS, beginning with the Parti de gauche (PG) in 2009 and La France insoumise (LFI) in 2017.[23] The various left-wing and ecological parties subsequently came together in the framework of the NUPES (Nouvelle union populaire écologique et sociale) in 2022, a structure whose staying power is, of course, still too early to determine, but which testifies to the fact that the renewal of structures affects all political sides.

Attributing Political Labels to Candidates: Methodological Elements

How did we proceed in attributing political labels to the tens of thousands of candidates who succeeded one another in the legislative elections from 1848 to 2022? Let us begin with the most recent elections (which are also the easiest to deal with) and move backward in time. For elections in recent decades, the situation is relatively simple. Since the legislative elections of 1993, the Ministry of the Interior has digitized the electoral registers at the municipal level and also classified the various parties and labels to draw up an official list of "political labels" for presenting the results. For the period 1993–2022, we have therefore simply reproduced the official files, with minor corrections to the distinctions drawn, which we have fine-tuned based in particular on the classifications and electoral results published by the newspaper *Le Monde* (which are sometimes more precise and relevant than the official classifications).[24]

Concerning the legislative elections held before 1993, before now there had been no digitization and complete online presentation of the electoral results at the municipal level, so we have therefore digitized the electoral registers preserved in the National Archives. These documents give the names of all the candidates (and sometimes the names of their proxies), and in order to determine the precise position of these candidates, we have completed them using the labels indi-

---

23. Starting in the 1970s, attempts to break up the PCF-PS duopoly were made by other left-wing parties, notably the Trotskyist parties (anti-Stalinist and anti-Soviet Communists), LO (Lutte ouvrière), and LCR (Ligne communistse révolutionnaire, which later became the NPA [Nouveau parti anticapitaliste]), but they were not able to overtake the PCF and the PS, contrary to what happened with LFI in 2017 and 2022.

24. Assigning political labels is always complex and potentially contentious, and it generally admits of several solutions, as shown in 2022 in the case of the NUPES, which the Ministry of the Interior refused to count as a distinct group in the official presentations of the results until it was forced to do so by the courts.

cated by the electoral results published by *Le Monde* since 1945, as well as by the *Livres blancs* published by the Ministry of the Interior since the elections of 1951,[25] as illustrated in reproduction 8.1 for the legislative elections of 1962 in the case of the department of Ain's first district.

The situation is even more complicated for elections held before World War II. The records preserved in the National Archives only sporadically mention the political parties of the interwar period (and only for the list-system elections of 1919 and 1924, unsystematically), and almost never for elections before World War I. Furthermore, the Ministry of the Interior published no report systematically presenting the results of these elections. The official volumes published by the Chamber of Deputies regarding electoral results before 1945 are valuable but very incomplete, since they include only information about the political labels of the deputies elected,[26] and nothing about the other candidates. Generally speaking, the only systematic information we have in electoral reports before World War I consists solely of the names of the various candidates and the total votes they won. Given these conditions, the only way to proceed is to rely on the press of the time, which has constituted our principal source for assigning political labels to candidates in legislative elections from 1848 to 1946. This method must be used with caution, however, because the various press headlines sometimes suffer from diverse political biases. Although their objective is usually to inform their readers as precisely as possible about the candidate options, they may have a tendency to group the candidates in more or less debatable or slanted ways, particularly when it is a question of the candidates most distant from their own preferences. We have

---

25. The *Livres blancs* are official publications compiling the results of legislative elections at the level of cantons and districts. These are valuable documents for clarifying certain political labels and for completing partial electoral reports, but unfortunately, they do not include the results at the municipal level, and thus do not obviate the need to go back to the municipal reports, which constitute the true primary source and our principal source for elections as a whole (and which we have put online in full for interested readers, at unehistoireduconflitpolitique.fr).

26. Or more precisely, concerning their parliamentary groups, which is not exactly the same thing, but nonetheless it constitutes valuable information in certain controversial cases. Let us add that the candidates' statements of their positions are collected in a very useful parliamentary document (commonly called "the Barodet") that has been published after each election since 1881. However, the statements of unsuccessful candidates are found hardly anywhere other than in the local press—but even there, not systematically, alas! (Since 1958 they have been collected and put online by the Centre de recherches politiques de Sciences Po CEVIPOF], relatively comprehensively.) We have also drawn on these documents (which were also used by Siegfried in his work published in 1913) in certain controversial cases, without seeking to collect all of them.

Reproduction 8.1: Attribution of political tendencies to candidates for the legislative elections from 1945 to 1988: The example of the first district of the department of Ain, 1962

Report of the general vote count issued in the electoral colleges of the department of Ain, 1st district, 1st round of the legislative elections of 1962

Ministry of the Interior. List of candidates in the legislative elections, 18–25 November 1962

The top photo reproduces the report of the vote count issued in the two cantons of Ain in first round of the legislative elections of 1962. The number of votes received by each of the candidates in each of the municipalities of the cantons is indicated, along with the candidates' names. The information about the party of each of these candidates is shown in the bottom photo, which reproduces a page from the *Livres blancs* (white papers) published by the Ministry of the Interior.

therefore always taken care to compare the information contained in the head-lines in different newspapers representing the plurality of trends involved in the various elections. Used in this way, press headlines have also constituted an extremely valuable source for arriving at a better understanding of the political context and the various points of view on the elections, apart from the question of political labels.

This need to compare different newspapers was noted by several of our predecessors, in particular Gaston Génique, who in an innovative study published in 1921 used newspapers from 1848 to assign political labels to the candidates and thus distribute the votes won by the different blocs on the departmental scale. Specifically, Génique based his work on the newspapers *L'Univers, Le Constitutionnel,* and *L'Ordre* to identify the candidates of the Party of Order supported by the Committee of the rue de Poitiers; on *Le National* and *Le Temps* for the Moderate Republicans and constitutional Republicans backed by the Committee of the Friends of the Constitution; and on *Le Peuple* for the Montagnards and the Democratic Socialists backed by the Democratic Socialist Committee.[27] We have proceeded in the same way as Génique, with the differences that we have collected the data from the electoral registers at the municipal and cantonal levels (and not solely at the departmental level) and we have applied this method to all the legislative elections conducted from 1848 to 1946 (and not solely for the elections of 1849).[28]

Political Labels, the Plurality of the Press, and Electoral Modes

For the elections of the period 1871–1936, we have used in particular the classifications published by *Le Temps* (a distant ancestor of the newspaper *Le Monde*),

---

27. See G. Génique, *L'élection de l'Assemblée législative en 1849. Essai d'une répartition géographique des partis en France* (Rieder, 1921). See also J. Bouillon, "Les démocrates-socialistes aux élections de 1849," *Revue française de science politique,* 1956; R. Huard, "Le 'suffrage universel' sous la Seconde République. État des travaux, questions en attente," *Revue d'histoire du 19e siècle,* 1997. On the highly political dimension of the process of attributing labels to the candidates, and in particular the collective construction of the notion of the Socialist vote at the end of the nineteenth century, see M. Offerlé, "Le nombre de voix. Électeurs, partis et électorats socialistes à la fin du 19e siècle en France," *Actes de la recherche en sciences sociales,* 1988.

28. Let us also note that although the big headlines in the national press proved to be sufficient for most of the elections, that was not the case for the legislative elections of 1849, for which the information regarding the minor candidates (not elected) was available only in the local press (for example, *Le Courrier de l'Ain, Le Journal de l'Ain,* and *L'Écho de la République* for the department of Ain; *L'Écho de l'Allier* and *Le Républicain démocrate de l'Allier* for Allier), which we examined systematically.

Reproduction 8.2: Attribution of political tendencies to candidates for the legislative elections of the Third Republic. The example of the 1st arrondissement of Paris (Seine), 1881

Report of the general vote count Seine, Paris, 1st arrondissement, legislative elections of 1881

List and party of the candidates for the legislative elections, *Le Temps*, 23 August 1881

The top photo reproduces the report of the vote count in the 1st arrondissement of Paris in the legislative elections of 1881. The number of votes received by each of these candidates is available in the bottom photo, which reproduces a page from the newspaper *Le Temps*.

which was the great newspaper of record before World War I and during the interwar period (see, for example, reproduction 8.2 for an illustration of the method for the elections of 1881).

For the elections of the period 1910–1936, we have also made use of the valuable works of Georges Lachapelle, who collected and published at the time, and with the support of the newspaper *Le Temps,* compilations of political labels and results at the cantonal level, in much the same way as the *Livres blancs* were published by the Ministry of the Interior beginning in 1951.[29] It is nonetheless essential to compare the information provided by *Le Temps* with that provided by other papers situated to its right (particularly the conservative and monarchical dailies) and to its left (notably, the Radical and Socialist newspapers), especially for elections before 1910.[30] For example, in the framework of the legislative elections conducted from the 1870s to the 1890s, *Le Temps* had a tendency to present the results in such a way as to make a central republican bloc appear to be as large as possible, even if it meant including candidates that other newspapers situated to its right or its left considered to be closer to their own preferences. The classifications that we arrived at by comparing the different points of view remain by nature imprecise and imperfect. They could doubtless be improved by making more use of the local press, particularly for a number of controversial candidates situated on the borderlines separating different tendencies, and for particularly sensitive elections like those organized in February and July 1871.[31] All the materials we used (such as electoral records, press clippings, compilations of results, and official publications) and all the methodological clarifications are available at unehistoireduconflitpolitique.fr, so that interested persons can access these sources and questions and let us know their reactions and proposals for improvement or expansion.[32]

29. These compilations of results were collected by Lachapelle for the elections from 1910 to 1936 and continued by Raoul Husson for the elections of 1945–1946. Like the *Livres blancs,* these publications concerned only the cantonal level, so it is essential to go back to the electoral records available at the municipal level in the National Archives. See unehistoireduconflitpolitique.fr for detailed references and digital copies of all these publications.

30. *Le Temps,* like the other publications on which we have based our work here (*Le mot d'ordre, Le Gaulois, L'Union, La Gazette de France, La Lanterne, Le Rappel,* and others) are for the most part available online at Gallica, the digital library of the Bibliothèque nationale de France (BNF); another resource is *Retronews.* When these newspapers (especially the local press) are not available online, they can in many cases be consulted directly at the BNF (on paper or microfilm).

31. In particular, although we succeeded in classifying most of the candidates for election in July 1871 on the basis of the national press, this is more difficult for the elections organized in record time for February 1871, after a particularly short campaign in a country that was largely occupied; a more systematic use of the local press would permit a better classification of the candidates.

32. Here there is an essential difference from the works of Génique, Bouillon, and Siegfried, who unfortunately have left no trace in terms of a database, so all their collecting of records and press headlines must be done all over from scratch. We have had the good luck to be working in a period when it is possible to digitize all the sources and data collected and to put them online, at the disposal of everyone, which makes it possible to begin a cumulative process. This will also enable interested readers to challenge our classification choices, since we report for all

Finally, let us add that the form of the electoral registers varies somewhat with the electoral system used. When the electoral system is a uninominal, first-past-the-post system with two rounds—that is, when each constituency comprises a single deputy's seat, so each voter has to vote for a single name, on pain of nullity (the electoral system currently in force, and the one most frequently used in France for the past two centuries)—then electoral reports consist solely of a list of names and the number of votes won by each candidate. But since 1848, some legislative elections have been conducted by applying a mode of plurinominal election (with one or two rounds)—that is, with districts including several deputy's seats, generally at the level of the department, or of departmental sections in the case of the most heavily populated departments. In the latter case, the political trends present lists including as many names as there are seats to be filled, and these lists usually have titles that are mentioned in the electoral record in addition to the names of the candidates (for example, "List of the Popular and Social Union," or "List of the Democratic and Republican Rally").[33]

During the Revolution of 1848, the plurinominal (or "multimandate") mode of election was considered the most democratic system, because it made it possible to present to the voters a collective of candidates characterized by a common program and to bypass the power of individual notables associated with a uninominal election. In practice, the plurinominal election led to other dissatisfactions, and after having been applied several times, from the legislative elections of 1848 to those of 1986, it was gradually abandoned and replaced by the uninominal election (introduced for the first time under the Second Empire during the legislative elections of 1852).[34] However, the changes in the electoral mode had little effect on our subject insofar as the titles of the plurinominal lists were often not very explicit, so in all cases we drew on other sources (in particular, press

---

candidates not only the nuances that seem to us the most appropriate to attribute to them but also their trends as they are indicated in the press headlines we analyzed.

33. See unehistoireduconflitpolitique.fr, reproduction R8.1, for an illustration using the legislative elections of 1924.

34. The list-system (or plurinominal) election mode was applied in 1848, 1849, 1871, 1885, 1919, 1924, 1945, 1946, 1951, 1956, and 1986, with extremely variable rules for distributing the seats within departmental districts (which were more or less proportional or majoritarian, with closed lists or with possibilities for voters to mix the lists). The Republicans' support for the uninominal mode in 1889 owed much to the fear that the list system would favor the Boulangists. However, the Left's adoption of the list system in 1986 shows the persistence of this historical tradition. For a history of electoral modes, electoral redistricting, and detailed maps of the districts and cantons since 1815, see B. Gaudillère, *Atlas historique des circonscriptions électorales françaises* (Droz, 1995).

headlines) in attributing political labels. Moreover, no matter what the electoral mode was, we concentrated on the analysis of the votes cast during the first round because it is the only one for which the whole of the country is called on to vote simultaneously.[35]

Political Labels and Political Trends, from the Left to the Right

In the end, the database we have constituted includes, for all the legislative elections held from 1848 to 2022, the votes won by each of the candidates at the most detailed spatial level available in the electoral registers (generally, at the level of the 36,000 municipalities, and more rarely at the level of sections of the municipality, or even polling stations). All the candidates have been categorized under about ten political labels (usually between eight and fifteen, depending on the election). Some labels were involved in many elections (the PS-SFIO, for example), others appeared at the beginning of the Third Republic and then disappeared (like the various monarchist, Legitimist or Orléanist, Bonapartist, and Boulangist nuances), and still others were present only once, like the French Union and Fraternity–Union for the Defense of Merchants and Artisans (Union et fraternité française–Union de défense des commerçants et artisans, UFF-UDCA), which brought together the candidates supported by Pierre Poujade in 1956, who were united around a program of defending the self-employed against taxation. Over the whole period 1848–2022, or about forty legislative elections, we counted more than one hundred political labels.

Each of these labels has its own political identity and would be worth studying in depth, examining both its program and the social structure of its electorate, which we will do in a number of cases. However, in order to carry out long-term, overall comparisons, it is essential to make supplementary classifications. We have therefore classified all the political nuances in five principal trends: Left, Center-Left, Center, Center-Right, and Right. When we speak of "left-wing political trends," "Left bloc," or "vote for the Left," without further qualification, we always regroup the nuances classified as the Left or Center-Left, and the same goes for the right wing. In general, we will study separately the nuances classified as the

---

35. That is not the case for the second round, given the seats already filled in the first round, as well as the variable rules depending on the period. The data collected could also be used to study the votes reported for the second round, as well as the effects of the changes in the electoral mode on voting behavior. At first glance, however, the multiple electoral reforms seem not to have had any significant impact on the evolution of the overall distribution of the votes among political persuasions, which is the main focus of our study in the framework of this research.

Center. Let us add that this classification entails no value judgment, normalization, or essentialization of the notions of Left, Center, and Right. In our view, there is neither a "true Left" nor a "false Right," but simply a shifting and multidimensional plurality of political trends. We will return at length to the programs of action put forward by the different nuances, which have, of course, undergone radical transformations over time, and which must always be understood in a pluridimensional and sociohistorical sense. In order to avoid any a priori stigmatization, we have also opted not to resort to the terms "extreme Left" and "extreme Right," which candidates seldom use to describe themselves, and which are generally used to disqualify opponents and to discredit in advance any possibility of a peaceful democratic transfer of power (notably by groups that seek to present themselves as centrists or as reasonable and moderate).[36]

Generally, we have tried as much as possible to describe each political family using terms by which the partisans of each family can recognize themselves. The notions of Lefts, Centers, and Rights are conceived here as eminently relative, peculiar to each period and to the party systems that have succeeded one another for two centuries, as we have described them succinctly (see table 8.1).[37] We have always classified as Left the political trends generally considered by the various actors of the time in question to be situated furthest to the left within the Left bloc (like the PCF when it was created in 1920 and made its first appearance during the legislative elections of 1924), and as Center-Left the trends less far to the left than the former (like the PS-SFIO during periods when the PCF was present). Similarly, the trends classified as Right are those that are generally considered as the furthest to the right within the Right bloc, like the different conservative or monarchist groups at the beginning of the Third Republic, or the FN and RN since their first significant appearance during the legislative elections of 1986. We have also followed a coalition logic. Thus, we classified as part of the Center the political forces planning to govern without the Left and without the Right, or else by

---

36. The notions of extreme Right and extreme Left have sometimes been used in a nonpejorative way in parliamentary precincts under the censitarian monarchies, and at the beginning of the Third Republic in a purely topographic and descriptive way. But after the experience of totalitarianisms in the twentieth century (Stalinism and Nazism) the weight of these terms has become considerable, and now they are used in a positive sense much more rarely than they are instrumentalized to stigmatize a priori a political trend (and its electorate). We will return to this discussion in our analysis of the recent period (see, in particular, chapter 11).

37. For a complete description of the way we have classified the approximately one hundred political nuances of the period 1848–2022 in five political trends (Left, Center-Left, Center, Center-Right, Right), as well as an analysis of the diverse variants, see unehistoireduconflitpolitique.fr, appendix A2, table A2.

relying exclusively on the Center-Left and the Center-Right. That was the case with, for instance, the Moderate and Opportunist Republicans at the beginning of the Third Republic and the LRM, Ensemble, and Modem parties in the early 2020s. Inversely, the Center-Left parties are generally those that are prepared to govern with the whole of the Left in a logic of a unified Left, at least on the level of principles. However, there are numerous exceptions to this general rule, insofar as there are many historical periods when the Center-Left preferred to ally itself with the Center (or even with the Center-Right) rather than with the rest of the Left—under the Fourth Republic, for example. The same goes for the Center-Right in the early Third Republic or since the appearance of the FN-RN.

To reiterate, these are continuous, flexible, and shifting categories, whose sole interest is to enable us to make long-term historical comparisons. As always with categorizations of this type, they can be judged only on the basis of the results and the historical evolutions that they allow us to reveal or illuminate. These categories are above all simplifications that make it possible to reclassify and analyze historical evolutions within an electoral landscape generally including about ten elementary political families that are perpetually renewing themselves. If we really want to understand as best as possible the political confrontations that occur during a given election, we have to study these elementary political families (or a total of more than a hundred political labels between 1848 and 2022). But if we also want to be able to study evolutions over a long period, then such reclassifications can be justified. We apologize in advance to readers and voters who might be offended by this or that classification, and we ask them to examine the results obtained before drawing their own conclusions regarding the utility of such reclassifications.[38]

---

38. For example, today it is clear that there are RN voters who do not see themselves as being on the right (and also, though they are probably rarer, LFI voters who do not see themselves as being on the left). We nonetheless see in every survey that a large majority of the RN voters who accept being situated on a Left-Right axis more often classify themselves as being on the right than on the left (and vice versa for LFI voters), which provides an objective—if not wholly convincing—basis for such operations. Thus, during the ninth wave of the French electoral survey conducted on 2 or 4 April 2022, among the 12 percent of individuals surveyed who said they felt close to the RN (12,600 people in all were questioned, of which 71 percent responded to the question about "the party that you feel yourself close to or less distant from than the others"), almost 82 percent placed themselves on the right (between 6 and 10 on a scale from 1 (very left-wing) to 10 (very right-wing), and of them, 30 percent placed themselves on the "far right." Only 5 percent situated themselves between 0 and 4, as opposed to 88 percent among those surveyed who declared themselves close to LFI (8 percent of those surveyed) (calculations made by the authors on the basis of the survey files).

Between Bipolarization and Tripartition: The Three Periods of French Electoral History

Let us turn now to the results. Before presenting the principal regularities characterizing the social structure of the electorates, we will first examine the general evolution of the number of votes won by the main political families from 1848 to 2022 (see figure 8.1).

First of all, we note that from 1848 to 2022, the French political system oscillated between phases marked by tripartition, with three poles of comparable size on the left, in the center, and on the right, notably between 1848 and 1910, and phases marked by a pronounced movement toward bipartition, with one main pole on the left, another on the right, and a Center reduced to the smallest share, particularly between 1910 and 1992. Conversely, the period 1992–2022 seems to be characterized by a return to a new form of tripartition.

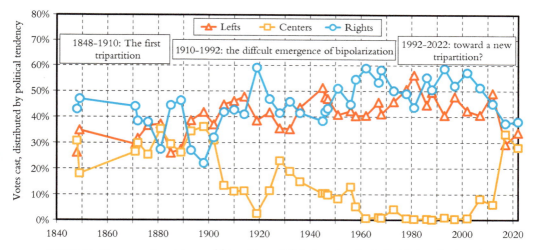

FIGURE 8.1. Between tripartition and bipartition: Political tendencies in legislative elections in France, 1848–2022

Between 1848 and 2022 the political system oscillated between tripartition (with three poles comparable to Left, Center, and Right), and bipartition (with two dominant poles, Left and Right). The tendencies classified as Center include the Moderate and Opportunistic Republicans in 1848 and Modem and LREM in 2017–2022. Those classified as Left include the Socialists and Radicals in 1848 and the PCF, PS, LFI, etc. in 2017–2022. Those classified as Right include the conservatives, monarchists, and liberals, etc. in 1848 to 1910, and the RN, LR, etc. in 2017–2022. See table 8.1 on the party regimes. On average, during the period 2017–2022, the Left bloc received 41% of the votes, the Center bloc 14%, and the Right bloc 45%.

Sources and series: unehistoireduconflitpolitique.fr

Several points must be clarified. First, the overall equilibrium between two or three poles is always only approximate and perceptible only over time. During the foundational elections of April 1848, the conservative bloc won about 43 percent of the votes cast, according to our count, as compared with 31 percent for the centrist bloc of the Moderate Republicans and 26 percent for the Democratic Socialist and Montagnard bloc.[39] In practice, with the support of part of the Moderate Republicans, the conservatives had a solid majority of seats, but it nonetheless remains that the balance of power was precarious and could potentially disintegrate rather suddenly. During the elections of May 1849, the conservatives consolidated their result with 47 percent of the votes, but the Moderate Republicans (who, with the very unpopular General Cavaignac, had taken power during the second half of 1848) collapsed with 18 percent of the votes, whereas the Democratic Socialists shot up with 35 percent of the votes cast. That was all it took for the fear of the Reds to grip the conservative bloc, especially since the partial elections held at the end of 1849 and the beginning of 1850 led to new victories by the Democratic Socialists, not only within the urban proletariat but also in several rural territories, which sowed terror among the large landowners. The prospect of an impending victory by the Reds led the Party of Order to restrict the right to vote with the law of May 1850, and the whole sequence of events concluded with the coup d'état of December 1851. We see at once how tripartition can be related to an unstable system, which is frightening for the groups in power and rich in potentialities for opposition groups, but in the end, it is unlikely to allow for peaceful alternations in power, especially in a context in which what is at stake is the legitimacy of both universal suffrage itself and a possible democratic redistribution of wealth.

Over the course of the first decades of the Third Republic, the system seemed to have been stabilized. The central bloc of the Moderate, constitutional, and Opportunistic Republicans won between 30 and 40 percent of the votes in the 1880s and 1890s. With the help of some of the Radicals in the Left bloc, it succeeded in prevailing over the conservatives and monarchists of the Right bloc. But as soon as the foundations of the republican regime and of the new education policy were laid, the head of the Opportunistic Republicans, Jules Ferry, did not hesitate to declare, in 1883, that the principal danger was no longer on the right (the monarchists had been defeated), but on the left (where the Socialists were gradu-

39. The votes won by the small lists and by unclassifiable candidates (in general, only a very small percentage of the votes) have been equally divided among the five principal political trends (Left, Center-Left, Center, Center-Right, Right), such that by construction the three blocs always add up to 100 percent.

ally regaining strength, worrying wheeler-dealers and moderates like Ferry). In fact, the rising power of the Socialists allied with the Radical-Socialists was to lead to a very clear crumbling of the Center and to a movement toward bipolarization as early as the elections of 1906 and 1910 (see figure 8.1). The system remained very unstable, however. In the interwar period, the divisions within the Left between the SFIO and the PCF were considerable, and the Radicals (whom we classify in the Center starting in 1924) constituted a non-negligible central bloc (about 20 percent of the votes), but it was less powerful than the Moderate and Opportunistic Republicans of the early years of the Third Republic, whence the very fragile coalitions in which the Radicals steered alternately left and right.[40]

The central bloc was weakened again under the Fourth Republic, due to the power of the Socialists and especially the Communists, and then the bipolarization introduced by the Fifth Republic and the election of the president took the Center to near-zero levels; each party had to choose a side. The Center's recovery took place gradually during the period 1992–2022 and accelerated in the most recent elections, with strong increases by Modem, the UDI, and especially LRM and Ensemble. During the legislative elections of 2017 and 2022, the three blocs—which can be qualified as the social-ecological bloc (PS, PCF, LFI, EELV, and so on), the liberal-progressive bloc (LRM, Ensemble, Modem, UDI), and the nationalist-patriotic bloc (FN-RN, LR, DLF, Reconquête)—each won around a third of the votes.[41] We are not far from the situation observed between 1848 and 1910, and particularly in the 1880s and 1890s, with the three blocs constituted on the left by the Socialists and Radical-Socialists, in the center by the Moderate and Opportunistic Republicans, and on the right by the conservatives, Catholics, and monarchists (see figure 8.1).

Over the whole of the period 1848–2022 and with the classifications chosen, we see that the Left won on average 41 percent of the votes cast, compared with 14 percent for the Center and 45 percent for the Right. Other definitions would,

---

40. It is logical to classify the Radicals as being in the center beginning in 1924, insofar as the PCF henceforth occupied the Left and the SFIO occupied the Center-Left. The Radicals ultimately split into several factions in the 1960s and 1970s, and then we move the Radicals from the Left to the Center-Left, and the so-called Valoisian Radicals (who retained the party's historic headquarters on the rue de Valois) to the Center-Right.

41. We will return to this new tripartition and this terminology in chapter 11. We have brought together here in the social-ecological bloc all the trends classified as Left and Center-Left, in the liberal-progressive bloc all the trends classified as Central, and in the nationalist-patriotic bloc all the trends classified as Right and Center-Right (including LR, which in reality occupies a place intermediary between the liberal-progressive bloc and the nationalist-patriotic bloc, which we will discuss in considerable detail).

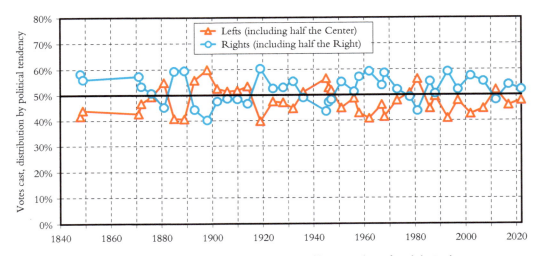

FIGURE 8.2. Permanent bipartition: The Center distributed between the Left and the Right

If we distribute the votes for the Center fifty-fifty between Left and Right, then by construction bipartition appears to be permanent, with highs for the Right in 1848, 1871, 1919, 1968, and 1993 (around 58–59% of the votes, against 41–42% for the Left), and highs for the Left in 1881, 1898, 1945, and 1981 (around 56–57% of the votes, against 43–44% for the Right). On average, during the period 1848–2022, the Left and the Right defined in this way received 48% and 52% of the votes, respectively. However, this view centered on Left-Right bipartition overlooks the importance of the Center bloc as an autonomous actor during certain periods, and the considerable, quasi-permanent contradictions within the Left and Right blocs.

Sources and series: unehistoireduconflitpolitique.fr

of course, have led to different results. For example, if we chose to evacuate the Center and distribute its votes fifty-fifty to the Left and the Right, then by construction we would obtain a different view of the electoral system, characterized by a permanent bipartition, with on average 48 percent of the votes for the Left and 52 percent for the Right between 1848 and 2022 (see figure 8.2).[42]

With such a view of things (which is not the one we have chosen here), electoral history would be reduced to an eternal struggle between the Left and the Right, with high points for the Right found especially in 1848, 1871, 1919, 1962, 1968, and 1993 (when the Right, defined in this way, won 58–59 percent of the votes, as compared with 41–42 percent for the Left), and the high points for the Left in 1881, 1893, 1898, 1945, and 1981 (with 56–57 percent of the votes for the Left and 43–44 percent for the Right), and a quasi-permanent return to a form

42. By definition, we would obtain the same average Left-Right distribution, 48–52 percent, and the same figure 8.2 by excluding the votes from the Center and calculating the percentages as a fraction of the Left-Right total.

of 50–50 balance. This is in part the view developed by François Goguel in his classic work on party politics under the Third Republic, published in 1946, in which the author develops the idea of an irrepressible tendency of the political system to divide itself into two blocs, Order and Movement, each one fulfilling an essential role to preserve what has to be preserved in the social and institutional order handed down by the past (at the risk of resisting necessary changes for too long) or, on the contrary, to radically transform existing structures (even if it means underestimating the difficulties and risks involved).[43] Goguel naturally takes the trouble to describe the many subfamilies within the two blocs, and we must keep in mind that his analysis is embedded in the time when he was writing and in the period he was studying (which was in fact characterized by the rise of bipolarization). Raising these questions anew on the basis of the materials and the historical distance available to us at the beginning of the 2020s, it seems to us richer and more pertinent to describe the changes observed between 1848 and 2022, distinguishing three blocs rather than two and avoiding excessive rigidification of the ideological and programmatic contours of the various blocs. However, we share with Goguel the conclusion that the tendency to bipolarization corresponds to a deep logic that is probably desirable, even if uncertain.[44]

Competition between Blocs, Competition inside Blocs

The presentation in three blocs (Left, Center, Right) and not two seems to us to be better suited for our purposes because within the Left and Right blocs the forces that we have classified as Center-Left and Center-Right often occupy an essential place and sometimes feel themselves to be closer to the Center than to the rest of the Left or the Right.

On average, throughout the period 1848–2022, within the 41 percent of the votes going to the Left bloc, according to our count, 24 percent thus correspond to

---

43. See F. Goguel, *La politique des partis sous la IIIe République.* (Seuil, 1946).

44. Let us note that Goguel himself favored a form of clarification-rationalization of parliamentary bipolarization that he had studied in its unstable form under the Third Republic, as his intense Gaullist and Pompidolian engagement shows. We find a comparable positioning in the work of Odile Rudelle, who was very committed in her support for Gaullist presidentialism and against the excesses of parliamentarism, and who was delighted after the presidential election of 1981 that the electors had finally been able to decide clearly and for the first time since 1789 that there would be a political transfer of power that was democratic, clear, and irrevocable. Conversely, she considered the parliamentary system that was set up at the beginning of the Third Republic to be a way of confiscating power and a rejection of the democratic alternations in power borne by popular choices. See O. Rudelle, *La République absolue, 1870–1889* (Éditions de la Sorbonne, 1982).

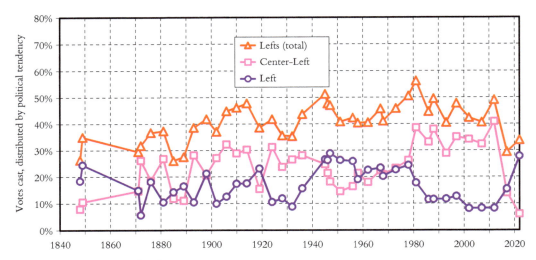

FIGURE 8.3. The Left and its components, 1848–2022

For all the legislative elections from 1848 to 2022, the candidates' political tendencies (generally eight to fifteen, depending on the election) have been classified as Left, Center-Left, Center, Center-Right, and Right. The Left bloc includes the Left and the Center-Left, and the Right bloc includes the Right and the Center-Right. According to our counts, on average, for the whole of the period 1848–2022, within the 41% of the votes going to the Left bloc, 24% correspond to the Center-Left and 17% to the Left, with a balance between the two poles that varies greatly over time. Sources and series: unehistoireduconflitpolitique.fr

the Center-Left and 17 percent to the Left properly so called, with a balance between the two poles that varies considerably over time (see figure 8.3). The borderline is sometimes porous and imprecise, but we will see that it nonetheless corresponds to lasting and meaningful divisions in the social structure of the electorates. It will be noted that the Center-Left was dominant at the end of the nineteenth century and at the beginning of the twentieth (when the Radicals still outnumbered the Social-ists), and during the interwar period, when the Socialists outnumbered the Com-munists, a situation that was reproduced from the 1980s to the early 2010s. Con-versely, the Left dominated the Center-Left after World War I (when the Socialists outnumbered the Radicals), and then after World War II and in the 1950s and 1960s, when the Communists outnumbered the Socialists for a long time. The same was true, more briefly, in 1848–1849 with the Democratic Socialists,[45] as well as in 2017–

---

45. The available sources are imprecise, but they suggest that the candidates furthest to the left (Democratic Socialists and Montagnards) won significantly more votes than the "advanced republicans" we have placed in the Center-Left for these elections.

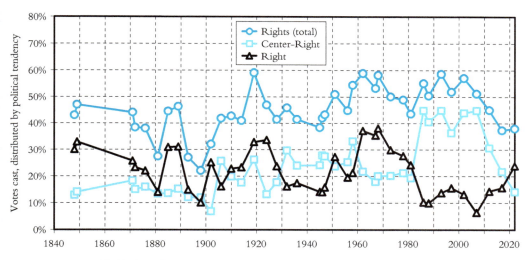

FIGURE 8.4. The Right and its components, 1848–2022

For all the legislative elections from 1848 to 2022, the candidates' political tendencies (generally eight to fifteen, depending on the election) have been classified as Left, Center-Left, Center, Center-Right, and Right. The Left bloc includes the Left and the Center-Left, and the Right bloc includes the Right and the Center-Right. According to our counts, on average, for the whole of the period 1848–2022, within the 45% of the votes going to the Right bloc, 23% correspond to the Center-Right and 22% to the Right, with a balance between the two poles that varies greatly over time.

Sources and series: unehistoireduconflitpolitique.fr

2022, with the rise of LFI and the constitution of NUPES.[46] This logic of the drift toward the Left and the competition internal to the Left bloc plays a driving role in the electoral dynamics of the whole from the nineteenth century to the beginning of the twenty-first.

Within the Right bloc, the situation is often more confused. On average during the period 1848–2022, among the 45 percent of the votes that went to the Right bloc, 23 percent corresponded to the Center-Right and 22 percent to the Right properly so called, with a balance between the two poles that also varied greatly over time (see figure 8.4). The difference with the Left is that on the right, there is sometimes a rather great uncertainty concerning who must be placed to the right of whom. Within the Left, there is a general consensus regarding the trends and

---

46. For the elections of 2202, we classified as Left all the NUPES candidates, and as Center-Left the dissident candidates of NUPES who had come from the ranks of the Socialists, ecologists, or various left-wing persuasions. This example shows how porous these borderlines are, as they are redefined in relation to the context peculiar to each election.

parties that have to be considered as a whole to be the furthest left or the least far left, even if there can sometimes be disagreements about the classification chosen as a function of the dimension considered (such as salary scales, social and syndical rights, tax reform, direct democracy, migratory policy, or energy system). By definition, a political conflict that is structurally multidimensional cannot be easily limited to a single axis. Within the Right, the confusion is much greater still, in part for the same reasons, and perhaps also because contrary to the Left—which has been historically dominated by the social question—the Right has been defined in relation to more diverse stakes, mixing the institutional question, the national question, and, of course, the social question.[47]

In practice, and in accord with the most common usage, we have placed in the Right the monarchist trends and the most conservative trends of the nineteenth century, and in the Center-Right the liberal, Orléanist, and Bonapartist trends. At the beginning of the twentieth century and during the interwar period, we have classified in the Center-Right the trends that rallied to the Republic and that were the closest to the Center (like the Democratic Alliance), and in the Right the trends that were more conservative or more resistant to the alliance with the Center, like the Republican Federation, as well as nationalist movements like Action française (which was, however, not much involved in elections). After World War II, and up to the 1980s, we place in the Center-Right the Christian democrats of the MRP, the liberals, the independent republicans, the UDF, and others, and in the Right the Gaullist parties (from the RPF to the RPR) and the parties situating themselves furthest from the Center, like the PRL (Parti républicain de la liberté) in 1946 and the Poujadists in 1956. Starting with the legislative elections of 1986 and the FN's first electoral successes, we classify as right-wing the FN, the RN, and the other parties that situate themselves to the Right of the Right (like Reconquête in 2022), and we put in the Center-Right all the other forces situated to the right of Center (particularly the formerly Gaullist and liberal parties such as UMP and LR).[48]

47. This is no doubt also explained in part by the fact that the very term "right" is historically associated with causes that have fallen silent today (the defense of the monarchical regime in the nineteenth century, support for the Vichy regime in the twentieth century), so its positive use is much less widespread than for the word "left." For example, René Rémond notes in his preface to the first edition of *Le Front national à découvert* that before 1981, at a time "when everyone denied being on the right and resorted to circumlocutions to define himself," the FN was "the only formation that had not contested its assignment to the right." R. Rémond, preface to *Le Front national à découvert*, ed. N. Mayer and P. Perrineau (Presses de Sciences Po, 1989).

48. See unehistoireduconflitpolitique.fr, table A2.1, for the detailed classification. In practice, the details of the classification have only limited importance for our subject, insofar as we are

With these classifications, we see that between 1848 and 1981 the distribution of votes has varied greatly between the Center-Right and the Right, and has in general been rather well balanced. Starting in 1986, the Center-Right takes a strong advantage, for the good and simple reason that only the FN and its allies are now classified as being on the right. The balance was gradually inverted during the recent period, and the nationalist-patriotic Right clearly dominated the Center-Right during the legislative elections of 2022 (see figure 8.4). In the same way as for the Left, we will see that the internal competition in the Right has played and continues to play a central role in the evolution of the French electoral and political system.

The Foundational Regularity: The Rural World on the Right, the Urban World on the Left

Let us now come to the analysis of the social structure of the electorates. In the following chapters we will return to the detailed analysis of the major subperiods (1848–1910, 1910–1992, 1992–2022), usually going back to the elementary political families. At this stage, we want to know whether there are general regularities that apply to the whole period from 1848 to 2022, which is also a way of wondering whether the categories of the Lefts, the Centers, and Rights that we have just presented correspond to social cleavages that are lasting and coherent over the long term. In other words, it is a question of knowing whether these categories are pertinent from the point of view of the social history of the electorates, and not just ideological, cultural, and linguistic history. In this case, our conclusion is that these categories refer to lasting and coherent socioeconomic cleavages, and that analyzing them can make it possible to better understand the most significant politico-ideological and programmatic characteristics of the various political families involved, as they have been perceived by voters over the course of the last two centuries.

We will begin with what is no doubt the most general regularity and the most striking one—namely, the fact that the political movements on the right have always had a tendency to achieve their best results in the rural world, whereas the movements on the left have always won more votes in the urban world. Then we will move on to the second regularity, which concerns the social characteristics

going to study especially the structure of the electorates of the Left and Right blocs considered as wholes so far as long-term evolutions are concerned, and the elementary political families for short- and middle-term analyses.

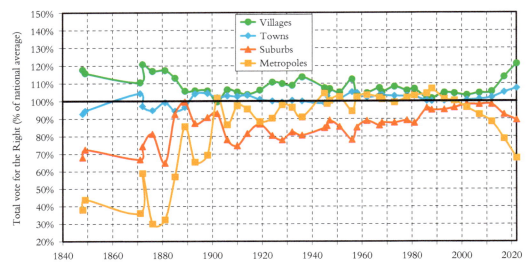

FIGURE 8.5. The vote for the Right according to the territories, 1848–2022

From the legislative elections of 1848 to those of 2022, the total vote for the Right has generally been highest in villages, then in the towns, suburbs, and metropoles. The disparity was particularly was particularly high from 1848 to 1910, more moderate from 1910 to 1990, and has been increasing since 2000–2010. In 2022, the total vote for the Right was 21% higher than the national average in the villages and 33% lower in the metropoles.

Sources and series: unehistoireduconflitpolitique.fr

(particularly, in terms of wealth) most closely associated with voting for the Left and voting for the Right within the rural world and within the urban world. The combination of these two cleavages—the rural-urban cleavage and the cleavage related to wealth—will allow us to better understand some of the forces pushing toward tripartition or bipartition.

Let us first examine the way in which the vote for the Right (as we have defined it above, by combining the Right and the Center-Right) varies according to the type of territories, using the notions of villages, towns, suburbs, and metropoles introduced earlier.[49]

Several points must be clarified regarding this regularity. First, the disparities in electoral behavior between territories can be considerable. Under the Second

49. See chapter 2. Villages group together conurbations of fewer than 2,000 inhabitants, towns comprise conurbations of between 2,000 and 100,000 inhabitants, suburbs the secondary municipalities of conurbations of more than 100,000 inhabitants, and metropoles the principal municipalities of these conurbations.

Republic, in 1848–1849, and then again at the beginning of the Third Republic, in the 1870s and 1880s, the vote for the Right was almost 20 percent higher than the national average in villages, almost 10 percent lower than in suburbs, and more than 50 percent lower than in the metropoles. These average disparities are all the more considerable because within villages, towns, suburbs, and metropoles there are very marked differences in terms of wealth as well as in terms of voting, as we will see later on. The disparities between territories are smaller between 1910 and 1990—though they remain substantial—and then they increase notice-ably in the last few decades and the most recent elections. During the legislative elections of 2022, the right-wing vote in villages was thus more than 20 percent higher than the national average (a gap even larger than it was in the nineteenth century); this time, it was almost 10 percent greater than the national average in towns, almost 10 percent smaller in the suburbs, and more than 30 percent smaller in the metropoles. Again, this result is all the more striking because here we are examining the average gaps between territories, and because within each of these categories of municipalities there are immense disparities, particularly between poor villages and rich ones, poor towns and rich ones, and so on, and because these inequalities within each category have greatly increased over recent decades (see chapter 2).

Next, and especially, we must stress that this regularity observed over almost two centuries—though it may be relatively well-known (everyone has heard that "people in the countryside vote for the Right" and that "cities vote for the Left")—seems to us to be actually underestimated in its fundamental impor-tance, and above all, poorly understood. Too often, observers are content to explain this regularity by referring to rural people's supposed spontaneous con-servatism, or even their natural backwardness. But this is an explanation that explains nothing; it merely reflects the negative prejudices of urban people re-garding rural people—prejudices that can be found, moreover, not only among liberal and bourgeois elites but also within some working-class and socialist organizations. To understand rural voters and urban voters, in 1848 as in 2022, we have to begin by taking seriously the choices made by both of these groups and trying to discern what they express. In particular, we have to start from the principle that the different geosocial classes have contradictory interests and aspirations, to which the multiple political trends involved try to respond by proposing worldviews and programs for action to move beyond these differ-ences, but which in practice frequently correspond more to some aspirations than to others.

The Rural-Urban Cleavage in the Twenty-First Century:
A Return to the Nineteenth Century?

To begin, we must emphasize that the rural-urban cleavage in favor of the Right is not constant over time: it was particularly pronounced in the nineteenth century and less so in the twentieth, then it increased greatly again during the first decades of the twenty-first century. We must find explanations and understand what this tells us about the different kinds of the Rights, Lefts, and Centers that expressed themselves during these various periods. An explanation based on the eternal backwardness of the countryside will not do the trick, nor will a theory that stresses the importance of the agricultural sector, which has only declined for the past two centuries. For our part, we will emphasize the key role of political factors, and in particular the left-wing trends that over the course of the twentieth century succeeded in developing a redistributive platform that is more ambitious and attractive for the whole of the country (including the rural world) than in other periods, while at the same time stressing the multiplicity of factors involved.

But for gauging the magnitude of the rural-urban cleavage and its development over time, the comparisons between territories indicated in figure 8.5 are unsatisfactory, insofar as the distribution of the population among villages, towns, suburbs, and metropoles has been completely transformed over the last two centuries. Therefore, we have to begin by clarifying things. In 1848, 48 percent of the country's population lived in villages and 40 percent in towns, while the suburbs and metropoles accounted for 5 percent and 7 percent, respectively. In 2022, the distribution of the population was much more balanced, with 19 percent in villages, 34 percent in towns, 31 percent in suburbs, and 16 percent in metropoles.[50] In order to compare the magnitude of the rural-urban cleavage over time, it is preferable to analyze the disparities between fixed fractions of the population. For example, we can begin by dividing the population of the country into two equal parts at each point in time: the 50 percent living in smaller conurbations (the rural world) and the 50 percent living in larger conurbations (the urban world). If we proceed in this way, we see that in the legislative elections conducted from 1848 to 2022 the rural world voted more for the Right than the urban world, without exception (see figure 8.6).

If we examine the ratio between the vote for the Right within the most rural and the most urban 5 percent of the population, we see that it sometimes sinks slightly below 1, as in the 1951 election, in which the RPF achieved an excellent

---

50. See chapter 2, figure 2.6.

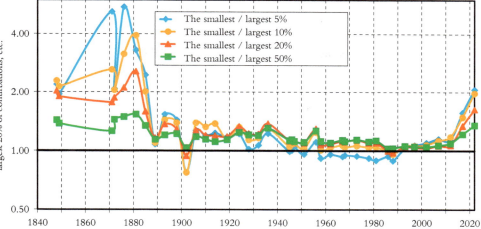

FIGURE 8.6. Disparities in the vote for the Right according to the size of the conurbation

From the legislative elections of 1848 to those of 2022, the total vote for the Right has generally been higher in small conurbations than in large ones. The disparity was particularly great in the nineteenth century and is again at the beginning of the twenty-first century. In 2022, as in 1848, the vote for the Right was thus about 1.4 times higher in the rural world (the 50% of the population living in the smallest conurbations) than in the urban world, and twice as high in the most rural 10% of the population than it was among the most urban 10%,

Sources and series: unehistoireduconflitpolitique.fr

result in Paris, and more generally from the 1950s to the 1980s, when Paris voted more for the Right than the rest of the country (whereas on the whole, the inverse is true before and after that period).[51] But if we observe the ratio between the vote for the Right within the 50 percent of the most rural and the 50 percent of the most urban populations, then we find that it is systematically higher than 1 in the last two centuries. Generally speaking, the middle of the twentieth century is the moment when the territorial cleavage is at its smallest. We can also note that in 2022 the magnitude of the electoral gap between the rural and the urban worlds returned to the level observed in 1848–1849 and in the 1870s and 1880s. In both cases, the vote for the Right is about 1.35 to 1.4 times higher in the rural world than it is in the urban world, which constitutes a considerable disparity when we compare the two halves of the population (within which there exist, moreover, very large inequalities). If we now compare the most rural and the most urban 10 percent

51. See unehistoireduconflitpolitique.fr, figure D1.1e.

of the population, we see that the vote for the Right is about twice as high in 1848–1849 as it was in 2022, whereas this ratio was most often more moderate between 1910 and 1990 (between 1 and 1.5, and sometimes even slightly less than 1).[52] The fact that the rural-urban cleavage was particularly great between 1848 and 1900 and then again in the 2010s and 2020s (in both cases, during periods marked by tripartition) is a result that demands a response. De facto, the existence of a particularly marked rural-urban cleavage between the Right and the Left seems to help open up a space for a central bloc capable of governing by circumventing this cleavage, even if it sometimes means perpetuating or even exacerbating the cleavage in order to remain in power. This possibility deserves to be clarified and compared with other interpretations. We will return to this at length.

Turning now to the vote for the Left, we see, grosso modo, the mirror image of the vote for the Right. From 1848 to 2022, the vote for the Left has generally been greater in metropoles and suburbs, followed by towns and villages (see figure 8.7). The ratio between the vote for the Left in the smallest and the largest conurbations was particularly low between 1848 and 1900 (generally between 0.5 and 0.7), and then rose again to levels closer to 1 over the course of the twentieth century, especially between 1950 and 1990 (when it sometimes slightly exceeded 1, which means that the Left's result was a little higher in the smallest conurbations than in the largest ones, thus running counter to the usual regularity), then fell again to around 0.6–0.8 in 2022 (see figure 8.8).

It is also striking to see that the vote for the Center bloc, in periods when it is strong, and especially between 1848 and 1900 (the bloc of the Moderate and Opportunistic Republicans) and in 2017–2022 (the bloc of the liberal-progressive LRM-Modem-Ensemble), does not seem to follow a very marked regularity from the point of view of the rural-urban cleavage. The vote for the Center bloc is sometimes slightly stronger in the urban world than in the rural world, in particular in 1848–1849, 1871, 1885, and 2017–2022, and sometimes a little stronger in the rural world, particularly in 1876–1881 and 1889–1893, but in all cases the disparities are small in comparison with those observed for the vote for the Right and the vote

---

52. In order to avoid the biases connected with small municipalities and to make possible a maximal comparability of evolutions over time, the definitions used in figure 8.6 and the next ones take into account, as before, the size of the municipalities. In other words, the 50 percent of the smallest conurbations designates the 50 percent of the population living in the smallest conurbations, and so on.

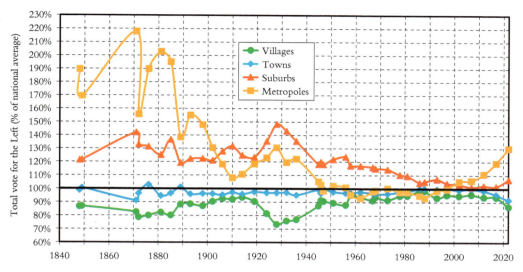

FIGURE 8.7. The vote for the Left according to the territories

From the legislative elections of 1848 to those of 2022, the total vote for the Left has generally been highest in the metropoles and suburbs, followed by towns and villages. The disparity was particularly was particularly high from 1848 to 1910 and more moderate from 1910 to 1990, and has been increasing since 2000–2010. In 2022, the total vote for the Left was 31% higher than the national average in the metropoles and 14% lower in villages.

Sources and series: unehistoireduconflitpolitique.fr

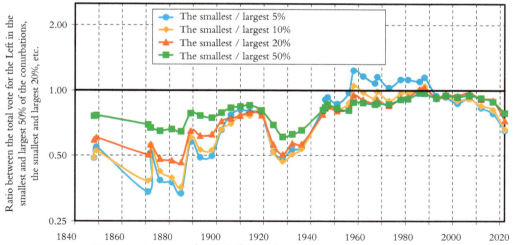

FIGURE 8.8. Disparities in the vote for the Left according to the size of the conurbation

From the legislative elections of 1848 to those of 2022, the vote for the Left has generally been smaller in small conurbations than in large ones. The disparity was particularly high in the nineteenth century and at the beginning of the twentieth century, and is increasing again at the beginning of the twenty-first century.

Sources and series: unehistoireduconflitpolitique.fr

for the Left.[53] Although it is little affected by the rural-urban dimension, as we will see, the vote for the Center bloc is strongly determined by the level of wealth, particularly in 2017–2022.

The Rural Vote for the Right: The Great Disappointment with the Revolution and the Left

How do we explain the fact that the rural world has voted more for the Right for the past two centuries, and that at the beginning of the twenty-first century this serious structural tendency seems to be regaining the same magnitude it had in the nineteenth century, after a period of more moderate disparities during much of the twentieth? The general explanation that we will propose is that these structural disparities tend to diminish when the question of wealth and the reduction of inequalities (regardless of the territory) is at the heart of political conflict, and that inversely, the rural-urban cleavage regains the upper hand when programs of redistribution are less ambitious or less suited to the various territories.

But before drawing this conclusion, it is important to understand the reasons for this structural and foundational regularity, which must in no way be discussed as if it were self-evident ("the rural world is conservative, that's just how it is"); on the contrary, we must emphasize from the outset its paradoxical side. The rural world has in fact always been poorer on average than the urban world, with disparities in wealth between the two types of territories that have on the whole remained at a high level for two centuries, in terms of both average income per inhabitant and real estate assets per inhabitant.[54] Considering that the Left has usually presented itself as the political camp most attached to equality and the redistribution of wealth, one might have thought that it would achieve its best results in the territories most likely to benefit from such a policy. But for the past two centuries, we always find exactly the opposite over the course of some forty consecutive legislative elections. There is food for thought here.

As we have already noted, the claim that the countryside is structurally conservative does not hold water, because it was to a large extent the peasant revolts and occupations of parcels of land in protest of property owners and their

---

53. With ratios generally ranging between 0.9 and 1.1 when compared with the vote for the Center bloc among the most rural and most urban 50 percent of the population.

54. On the other hand, the disparities in wealth between municipalities in both the rural world and the urban world clearly decreased during the twentieth century and then shot up over recent decades. See chapter 2. See also unehistoireduconflitpolitique.fr, figures B1.5n–B1.5w, B6.5f, and B7.4g.

privileges that led to the French Revolution. Many studies, particularly those by Paul Bois and Charles Tilly,[55] have shown convincingly, on the basis of the minutes of the electoral assemblies of the revolutionary period, that voters from the countryside were often ahead on the question of fiscal justice, and more generally in challenging the social order, especially so far as the key question of land reform was concerned. The disappointment was immense when rural people realized that no agrarian redistribution was really on the agenda and that lands owned by the Church were going to be privatized to the benefit of rich city dwellers. The auctioning off of the Church's property served in part to pay back the public debt, which was itself held by rich urban investors, who were to become the owners of a large part of the rural world in exchange for their debt securities, whereas the rural poor expected something quite different from the revolutionary process. As Bois and Tilly show, it was often the cantons that were the most in revolt against authority under the Old Regime that became the most resistant to the new revolutionary authorities when they discovered that they had been deceived. The exemptions from military service that some of the urban bourgeois and their children were to enjoy in early 1793 convinced many poor peasants of the iniquity of the established power, and this would hasten the descent of part of the country into counterrevolutionary uprising (*chouannerie*).[56] More generally, these events were to lead to a profound distrust among the peasant classes regarding the new urban and republican elites in almost all of the territory.

Although of course it is impossible to replay history in an alternative scenario (for example, if the ecclesiastical lands had been massively redistributed to poor peasants instead of being sold to rich city dwellers in the 1790s and the public debt had been cancelled or paid it off by imposing an exceptional levy on the patrimonies of the owners, whether nobles or bourgeois), everything seems to indicate that these events played a fundamental role in provoking the rural distrust of the Revolution and of the Left and in the formation of the rural vote for the Right. Subsequently, a segment of the traditional elites, particularly within the nobility, certainly attempted all through the nineteenth century to instrumentalize this peasant disappointment, using it to unreservedly stigmatize republican hypocrisies and to praise without qualification the merits of the Old Regime's ecclesiastical and civil institutions, all the better to preserve their own local power, sometimes

---

55. See P. Bois, *Paysans de l'Ouest. Des structures économiques et sociales aux options politiques depuis l'époque révolutionnaire dans la Sarthe* (Mouton, 1960); C. Tilly, *La Vendée. Revolution et contre-révolution* (Fayard, 1970).

56. See Bois, *Paysans de l'Ouest*, 89–135; Tilly, *La Vendée*, 307–320.

during elections by using their control over the peasants to get themselves elected or to favor other conservative and monarchist candidacies. The fact remains that the initial disappointment of the peasants with regard to the Revolution was profound and real, and it is from this recognition that we must begin.

After the Revolutionary Disappointment, the Peasant Disappointment with Working-Class Socialism

It is also logical that this disappointment with the first governments that came out of 1789 was extended to the Left in general, to the extent that the deputies who constituted the Left in the revolutionary assemblies were above all urban bourgeois (which is hardly surprising, given the semicensitary suffrage system in force at the time). Within the Left there was, of course, a group of Montagnard deputies in the 1790s, then Montagnard and Democratic Socialists in 1848–1852, — advocating in principle for an overall program of redistributing wealth and economic and political power—a program that could have benefited both the urban proletariat and poor peasants. But the fact is that this political tendency was never able to exercise power and set up a convincing program of land reform during either the First or the Second Republic. Obviously, it would not have been simple to implement and could also have met with countless obstacles when it was put into practice, but only such an experiment might have made it possible to reverse the negative impression left on rural people by the privatization of ecclesiastical property, which remained, until the nationalizations of 1945, the most radical (and to a certain extent, the most antiredistributive) attempt made in France to transform the property system. During the legislative elections of 1848 and 1849, the Democratic Socialist candidates tried to address in their speeches the questions of agrarian reform and access to land to the benefit of poor peasants, which allowed them to achieve certain successes in several rural territories, particularly in the Limoges area and in Périgord, not without frightening property owners. However, our results indicate that these successes obtained in a part of the rural world in 1848–1849 were very limited and localized, and that on average, the rural world voted heavily for the Right and not for the Left during these decisive elections (see figures 8.5–8.8). In chapter 9 we will return to these elections and see that these results can be explained in part by the fact that despite some people's efforts, in 1848–1849 the Democratic Socialist plan of action remained centered on the urban and workers' world, and in the end it proved to be very insufficiently receptive to the specific needs of the rural world of the time, especially considering the region's primordial demographic heft.

The fact is that as time went on, this urban and working-class bias only increased. Starting at the end of the nineteenth century and the beginning of the twentieth, the socialist and workers' movement emphasized more and more the importance of generalized state control over the means of production, in part under the influence of Marxism. This sometimes put it in conflict with the syndical movement, which dreamed of self-management, participation, and economic democracy, but it also and especially placed it in opposition to the peasant world, which increasingly saw the socialist movement (which was identified more and more with the Left) as the main obstacle to its primary objective in terms of emancipation and autonomy—namely, access to the ownership of land, which it saw as the central element that would allow it to live freely on its labor. We will return to these — questions, and in particular to the strengths and weaknesses of the Socialist and Communist programs of action in different periods, which were sometimes less narrowly statist than their adversaries claimed. It nonetheless remains that the peasant classes' profound disappointment with working-class socialism and its refusal to stress small private property and the redistribution of land undoubtedly constituted one of the principal factors (after the disappointment of the Revolutionary period) that helps to explain the rural world's historical distrust of the Left.

It is also worth noting that a structurally right-wing rural vote for the Right came at a very high political price for the Left, given that the rural world has always been characterized by rates of voter registration higher than those in the urban world and also by higher rates of turnout, with the sole exception of the period 1930–1960, when turnout was slightly higher in the urban world (see chapters 5 and 6). In that period, this corresponds to both a strong ability to mobilize the Left (in particular, the PCF), which then succeeded in better bringing together the urban working classes while at the same time reducing the electoral disparity with the rural world, as well as a powerful movement within the rural world tending toward salarization of the workforce, which made it possible to attenuate the conflict over access to the ownership of agricultural goods sought by the self-employed.

The Rural-Urban Cleavage: Socioeconomic and Not Religious Factors

We will return at length to these interpretations and their implications for the future when we study the different subperiods in greater detail. At this point, we will limit ourselves to making it clear that the general results that can be highlighted for the whole of the period 1848–2022 seem to be consistent with these hypotheses. Let us begin by examining the way the different political trends have distributed

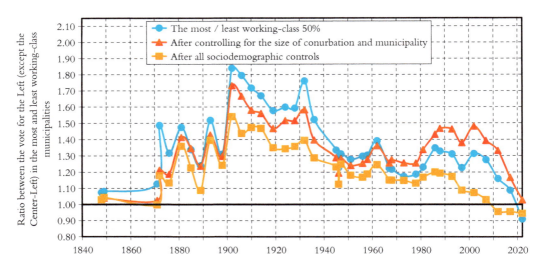

FIGURE 8.12. Vote for the Left (except the Center-Left) and working-class municipalities

From the legislative elections of 1848 to those of 2022, the vote for the Left (except for the Center-Left) has generally been much larger in municipalities with the largest proportions of blue-collar workers, with or without taking into account control variables. The effect is particularly great between 1900 and 1960, then clearly declines during recent decades, though less massively when the Center-Left is excluded.

Sources and series: unehistoireduconflitpolitique.fr

1.7 between 1900 and 1940 (see figure 8.12).[68] Quantitatively, the working-class vote for the Left is even greater than the rural vote for the Right. For more than a century, this was almost a definition of the vote for the Left. This conclusion applies to an even greater extent if we examine the ratio between the 20 percent of the most working-class municipalities and the 20 percent of the least working-class municipalities, and so on.[69]

We must also emphasize that this working-class vote for the Left is found in both the urban world and the rural world. The strongest working-class concentrations are, of course, situated historically in the urban world, but there have also always been large working-class populations within smaller conurbations. In both cases, a greater proportion of workers is associated with a larger vote for the Left,

---

68. Conversely, the effect is much smaller if we limit ourselves to the Center-Left, but with a large workers' vote for the SFIO during the interwar period and in the 1940s and 1950s (which is almost nonexistent in the 1970s). See unehistoireduconflitpolitique.fr, figures D1.8a–D1.8f.

69. See unehistoireduconflitpolitique.fr, figures D1.8a–D1.8f.

with a similar impact and magnitude in both worlds, as is shown by the fact that the electoral ratio is little affected by the inclusion of a control variable for the size of the conurbation and the municipality (see figures 8.11–8.12). Taking into account other factors (proportions of farmers and self-employed workers, income and real estate assets, education and diplomas, schools, and origins) also has only a limited effect on the overall profiles (except at the end of the period, which reflects the fact that it is the low level of the average income and not the share of industrial workers that becomes predictive of the vote for the Left in recent decades, as we will see later).[70]

During most of the period studied, municipalities with a larger proportion of industrial workers were not necessarily poorer than the rest of the country—quite the contrary. In the nineteenth century and most of the twentieth, the largest working-class populations corresponded to the sites of industrial development where the production of new sources of wealth was concentrated. In these municipalities and territories, it was not necessarily workers who benefited most from these sources of wealth—it was mostly engineers, managers, and especially stockholders (who may have lived not in the municipality but instead in a neighboring or even distant city), and that is precisely what fed the conflict. The data at our disposal at the municipal level does not enable us to settle this question, but everything suggests that within working-class municipalities, it was principally the workers and not the engineers or factory owners who voted most for the Left.

The situation changed radically during the last third of the twentieth century. Instead of being sites for the production of new kinds of wealth, the territories with large working-class populations became associated with deindustrialization, poverty, and unemployment. The production of wealth came to be concentrated in services and in new territories in the metropoles and wealthy suburbs, while industry saw its share in production and overall employment diminish after a historic peak reached in the 1950s and 1960s.[71] Starting in the 1970s and 1980s,

---

70. A frequent error of interpretation consists in identifying "the popular classes" with industrial workers (*ouvriers*), which amounts to forgetting the historical importance of poor peasants and also the fact that within the group of salaried workers it has been several decades since the average income of employees (*employés,* a category that includes particularly cashiers, waiters, cleaners, and so on) fell below that of industrial factory workers. It is by mobilizing criteria linked to wealth (income, property ownership) and correlating them with the socio-occupational category—a useful classification, to be sure, but one that suffers from being too inclusive—that we can give more precise substance to the term "popular classes," which is too often vague and poorly defined in public debate. See, for example, O. Schwartz, "Peut-on parler des classes populaires?," *La vie des idées,* 2011.

71. See chapter 2.

deindustrialization and the rise of unemployment led to relative and sometimes absolute losses of income in the former working-class municipalities. It is also at that time that the working-class electoral ratio began to decline in regard to the Left. It even became slightly negative in the 2000s, the 2010s, and at the beginning of the 2020s: the most working-class municipalities henceforth vote a little less for the Left than other municipalities do, even if the effect remains very weak compared with the earlier positive effects (see figures 8.11–8.12). The most obvious interpretation involves the immense disappointment of the working class with regard to a political group that had historically invested so much effort in the attempt to transform and emancipate the industrial world. Beyond the long-term factor, we can also consider that the policies pursued by the Left in power in the 1980s and 1990s considerably strengthened this feeling of abandonment. We will return to this when we study the legislative and presidential elections of this period, as well as the European referenda of 1992 and 2005, which certainly were major turning points.

The Concentration of Land Ownership and the Left: The Pursuit of Anti-aristocratic Mobilization

In addition to the proportion of workers, the second social characteristic that has been very strongly associated the vote for the Left over the long term and since the nineteenth century is the concentration of the ownership of agricultural land, measured here, as it was above, by the proportion of land held in the configuration of a farm of more than fifty hectares.[72] Concretely, in the nineteenth century and during most of the twentieth there was a larger vote for the Left in territories marked by a greater concentration of land ownership (see figure 8.13). By definition, the effect was visible especially in the rural world (and more generally, in territories where the agricultural sector played an important role) and it disappeared at the end of the twentieth century as the sector lost its influence. The most obvious interpretation of this result, which we have already encountered with electoral turnout during the referendum of 1793,[73] is that the presence of large landowners helped mobilize the vote of the poor rural classes, landless peasants, and agricultural workers to the benefit of the Left. As in 1793, the effect of

---

72. See chapter 7. As we did earlier, we use here the indicator observed at the municipal level and for the whole of the country during the census of 1962, but the results are similar to the partial cantonal data available for the distribution of agricultural lands in 1883.

73. See chapter 7, figure 7.18.

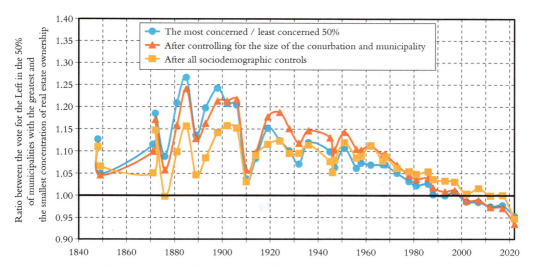

FIGURE 8.13. Vote for the Left and concentration of real estate ownership

In the nineteenth century and during most of the twentieth century, the vote for the Left was greater in the territories with the greatest concentrations of real estate ownership (in the sense of the proportion of agricultural land owned in the framework of properties of more than fifty hectares), with or without taking controls into account. The effect is disappearing as agriculture and the distribution of agricultural lands lose their importance.

Sources and series: unehistoireduconflitpolitique.fr

mobilization related to inequality thus seems to prevail over the impact of the landowners' grip on the rural population, contrary to what Siegfried had supposed.[74] On the other hand, our conclusion tends in the same direction as that obtained by Bois, who notes in his observational terrain of Sarthe that the cantons with large properties had a tendency to vote for the Left under the Third Republic (and particularly during the interwar period).[75]

To be sure, we must not exaggerate the magnitude of this effect of the concentration of property ownership, which is much less massive historically than the working-class vote for the Left, and especially less strong than the general propensity of the rural world to vote for the Left. The tendency to vote for the Left is on the order of 1.1 to 1.2 times stronger in territories with large properties than in other

74. Our result is an average result, which does not mean, of course, that the effect connected with the landowners' grip did not prevail in some territories. Here we reach the limits of the cartographic analysis developed by Siegfried, who did not have the technical means that could have enabled him to carry out a systematic statistical analysis.

75. See Bois, *Paysans de l'Ouest,* 9–30.

territories (see figure 8.13), but that usually it not enough to compensate for the fact that the rural world as a whole tends to vote between 1.2 and 1.3 times more for the Right, depending on the period (see figure 8.10). In other words, the dominant effect is that of a general distrust of the Left on the part of rural people, particularly in territories where rural people have already succeeded in gaining access to property. It is nonetheless interesting to note that in the territories with large properties, the propensity to vote for the Left is considerably stronger if the Center-Left is excluded and we concentrate on the Left of the Left (the Socialists up to 1919, the Communists starting with the elections of 1924).[76] That shows that the program of redistribution advocated by left-wing political trends has always been multiform (and not always perfectly coherent). Although this program has generally been centered on the working-class and industrial world (and on the objective of collectivizing the means of production), it has always also had a component dedicated to the rural world and access to land—which is insufficient, to be sure, to do away with the structural distrust of the Left, but nonetheless large enough to leave easily visible traces in the votes.[77]

The Left and Poor Municipalities: A Recent Evolution

We turn now to the question of the link between the vote for the Left and the level of wealth. As we have already seen, the existence of such a relation is in no way self-evident, insofar as the vote for the Left was defined historically as an industrial workers' vote above all, and for a long time territories with large concentrations of industrial workers were places where new forms of wealth were produced (even if the workers living there were not necessarily the main beneficiaries of this new wealth). The same goes, to a lesser degree, for territories that had large concentrations of property ownership; their average wealth can be greater than or equivalent to that in the zones with smaller properties, such that there is not necessarily a relation between the average wealth of a territory and the vote for the Left. On the national scale, if the country is divided into two equal halves according to the average municipal income per inhabitant, we find that in the nineteenth century and in the first half of the twentieth, the vote for

76. See unehistoireduconflitpolitique.fr, figures D1.8a–D1.8f.
77. In the same way as for the results of the referenda of 1793–1795 (see chapter 7), we must emphasize once again the limits of our sources. More detailed historical data concerning the transformations of real estate structures and the concentration of land ownership at the local level since 1789 might well make it possible to bring to light results that are more refined and differentiated than what is presented here.

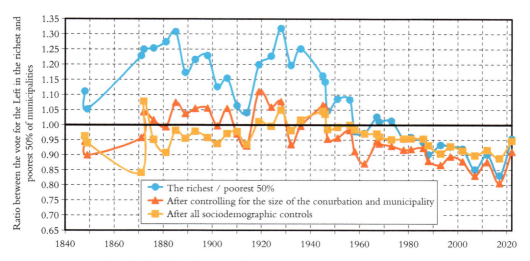

FIGURE 8.14. Vote for the Left and municipal income

In the nineteenth century and until the middle of the twentieth century, the vote for the Left was greater in rich municipalities than in poor ones, but this effect disappears as soon as we control for the size of the conurbation and municipality and for the other sociodemographic variables (particularly occupation). Since the 1980s, the poorest municipalities vote more for the Left than the rich municipalities do, in both the urban world and the rural world, before and after controls. Sources and series: unehistoireduconflitpolitique.fr

the Left was considerably greater on average in rich municipalities than in poor municipalities. But that is explained for the most part by the fact that the urban world votes more for the Left, and that it is also richer on average than the rural world. When we control for the size of the conurbation, then this effect disappears almost completely. In other words, for the same size of conurbation, the average municipal income had virtually no effect on the vote for the Left in the nineteenth century and in the first half of the twentieth (see figure 8.14).[78]

If we now add other sociodemographic characteristics, and specifically variables making it possible to control for occupation (in particular, the proportion of peasants and industrial workers), the effect even becomes slightly negative; in most of the elections conducted in the nineteenth century and the first half of the twentieth, the vote for the Left is a little greater in the poorest municipalities, all other things being equal. Then the gross effect of income on the vote for the

78. We obtain the same results by using the real estate capital per inhabitant rather than the income per inhabitant as a criterion of wealth. See unehistoireduconflitpolitique.fr, figures D1.3a–D1.3f.

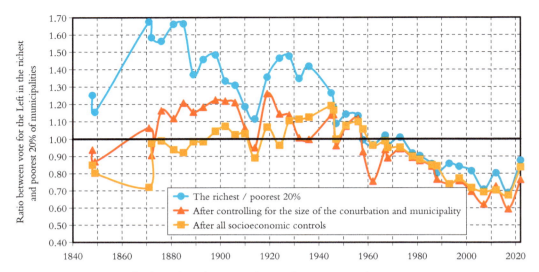

FIGURE 8.15. Vote for the Left: Rich municipalities and poor municipalities

Since the 1980s, the ratio between the vote for the Left in the richest and the poorest 20% of the municipalities has become more and more clearly inferior to 1, before and after controls.

Sources and series: unehistoireduconflitpolitique.fr

Left itself becomes negative starting in the 1960s and 1970s, and more markedly starting in the 1980s and 1990s. Ultimately, in the 2000s, 2010s, and 2020s, the vote for the Left is about 10–15 percent higher in the poorest 50 percent of the municipalities than in the richest 50 percent, both before and after taking control variables into account (see figure 8.14). The magnitude of the effect is, of course, smaller than it is on the rural vote for the Right or the workers' vote for the Left (at the time when this effect was at its apogee), but the contrast with the preceding periods is nonetheless striking. This effect is found again from the 1980s–1990s to the 2010s–2020s in all the categories of territories (villages, towns, suburbs, metropoles). In the rural world as in the urban world, poor municipalities now vote more for the Left than the rich municipalities do, and this holds true also for the poor suburbs in comparison with the rich suburbs, for the poor towns in comparison with the rich towns, and so on.[79] The effect is quantitatively even greater if we compare the poorest 20 percent of the municipalities with the richest 20 percent (see figure 8.15), rather than the poorest 50 percent and the richest 50 percent or the poorest and the richest 10 percent of the municipalities.[80]

---

79. See unehistoireduconflitpolitique.fr, figure D1.1h.

80. See unehistoireduconflitpolitique.fr, figures D1.2a–D1.2e.

Several factors can help explain this evolution, which runs counter to a certain number of received ideas. Generally speaking, it may be that we are witnessing a shift from a historical configuration based on the left-wing industrial worker vote (in territories that are sometimes richer than the national average) to a new configuration characterized by the impoverishment of the working class and a vote for the Left more connected with lower incomes and social transfers than it was in the past. This transformation can also be understood as the consequence of an increasingly complex social structure, with the growth of a patrimonial middle class and the formation of new cleavages within both the urban and the rural worlds. We will return in particular to the fact that the formation of the FN-RN vote in towns and villages continues to be closely related to access to suburban home ownership and the perception of a Left that is interested above all in the people considered less "meritorious," in groups in insecure situations, and in other "welfare recipients" (*cas sociaux,* beyond the question of origin).[81]

Let us review. We have drawn attention to two essential regularities in the structure of voting in the legislative elections held in 1848 and 2022. On the one hand, there is a vote for the Right that is structurally greater in the rural world than in the urban world, with a gap at the beginning of the twenty-first century that is equivalent to that observed in the nineteenth century, in connection with rural world's persistent (and largely understandable) distrust of the urban world, which was suspected of paying little attention to the rural world's aspirations and of caring mainly about itself. On the other hand, we see a vote for the Left in the rural world and the urban world determined historically by the proportion of industrial workers and the concentration of property ownership, and more recently by the level of income, in connection with the multiform and changing (and sometimes tentative and contradictory) program of redistribution advocated by the Left.

One of the questions that will now preoccupy us is how to better understand which of these two regularities is capable of prevailing over the other in the coming years, with considerable consequences for the political and electoral dynamics of the whole being at stake. When the cleavage related to wealth wins out over the

---

81. We have already briefly mentioned the importance of the role played by the rejection of "welfare" in the vote for the Right, which Luc Rouban characterizes as "considerations relating to the injustice of a system that fails to recognize its 'own' and their human and occupational investment, and wastes public funds on 'others.'" See Rouban, *La vraie victoire du RN.* See also the research of Louis Pinto, who refers to the support for a "nouvel ordre moral." L. Pinto, "La promotion d'un nouvel ordre moral," in *Les classes populaires et le vote FN,* ed. G. Mauger and W. Pelletier (Éditions du Croquant, 2017). We will return to these changes and interpretations in detail in the chapters devoted to the recent period.

rural-urban cleavage, the most working-class territories in the rural world and the urban world begin to merge politically and tend to vote together in favor of the Left bloc, so that the system is oriented toward the Left-Right bipartition, which we see during a large part of the twentieth century, probably in connection with the ambition of the redistributive program that was then advocated by the Left, but also linked with structural socioeconomic factors, such as the shift to the salarization of the workforce that is at work in the rural world. Conversely, when the rural-urban cleavage is the greatest—as it was in the nineteenth century and the beginning of the twenty-first—we observe a victory of tripartition. The two periods of tripartition compared here are, however, rather different from each other. The second is characterized particularly by the increasing complexity of social cleavages within both the urban and the rural worlds, especially concerning access to home ownership, public services, and social transfers, in terms that were obviously not the same in the nineteenth century, even if there are real analogies between the relationship to landed property in the past and suburbanization today. To go farther, we will have to study separately the three subperiods 1848–1910, 1910–1992, and 1992–2022, examining more precisely the elementary political families (moving beyond long-term reclassifications) that have competed for votes, the political battles, and the programs that might make it possible to explain the transformations of the electorates that the collected data reveal.

Social Determinants of the Increasing Vote over the Long Term

Before we do this, let us conclude this chapter by examining the evolution of the overall influence of the social determinants of the Left-Right vote in the legislative elections conducted from 1848 to 2022. In studying the structure of electoral turnout during that period, we have noted, over the long term and especially in recent decades, a large increase in the influence of social determinants, in connection with a very large cleavage in turnout associated with wealth, in proportions not seen for two centuries (see chapter 6). We obtain the same conclusion with the social determinants of the Left-Right vote (and its various subcomponents), with a particularly great influence exercised by the social determinants during the last elections, even if the increase is smaller than that for turnout.

Let us begin with the geosocial determinants by correlating the two dimensions of social class that are at the heart of our analysis: the rural-urban cleavage (the size of the conurbation and the municipality), and the cleavage related to wealth (average income, average real estate capital (total value of housing), proportion of property owners, and concentration of land ownership). If we include all these

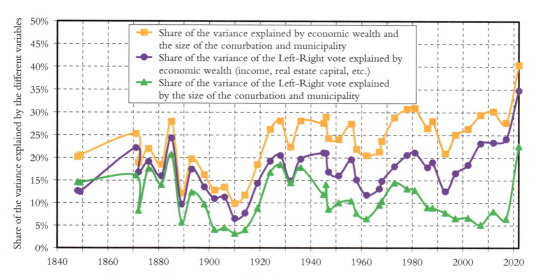

FIGURE 8.16. The geosocial determinants of the Left / Right vote

The explanatory power of the variables connected with economic wealth (income, real estate capital [the total value of housing], proportion of homeowners and real estate concentration) for explaining disparities in the municipal Left / Right vote in the legislative elections from 1848 to 2022 have generally been close to or superior to that of the size of the conurbation and municipality. In all, the geosocial class (wealth and territory) has never been as great as it is now.
Sources and series: unehistoireduconflitpolitique.fr

explanatory variables, we see that we can explain about 20 percent of the disparities in the Left-Right vote in 1848, and that the predictive power of these same factors reached 40 percent in the legislative elections of 2022, clearly surpassing the earlier high points reached during the elections of 1936, 1945, and 1981 (see figure 8.16).[82]

For electoral turnout, the explanatory power of these same variables barely exceeded 15 percent in 1848 and about 50 percent in 2022.[83] In other words, the geosocial determinants of turnout were less powerful than those for the Left-Right vote in the nineteenth century, and they have now become (somewhat) more powerful. In the past, geosocial class predicted the content of the vote more than turning out to vote did. Now, it is the fact of turning out to vote itself that is the most strongly predicted by geosocial determinants, and particularly by the level of wealth, which can hardly be considered an indication of the advance of democracy.

82. See unehistoireduconflitpolitique.fr, figure D1.2h.
83. See chapter 6, figures 6.15–6.16.

If we examine the predictive power of the Left-Right vote separately from the rural-urban cleavage and the cleavage related to wealth, we see that the latter has generally been more powerful than the former (particularly during recent elections). The explanatory power of the controls related to wealth (if they are used as the only explanatory variables) has thus risen from 13 percent of the variance in 1848 to 35 percent in 2022, whereas the explanatory power of the size of the conurbation and the municipality rose during the same period from 15 percent to 23 percent (see figure 8.16). It is particularly interesting to note that the explanatory power of the rural-urban cleavage was nearly the same as (and sometimes slightly greater than) that of the cleavage related to wealth in the nineteenth century and at the beginning of the twentieth century, before it clearly took the lead over the course of the twentieth century, as the Left-Right bipolarization gained the upper hand. From this point of view, the specificity of the current period is that in 2022 we see both a very strong rise in the predictive powers of both wealth and the size of the conurbation and municipality. Put another way, in recent elections it is the two components of geosocial class, the social component and the territorial component, that have acquired an unprecedented importance for predicting electoral behaviors.[84]

If we now include all the sociodemographic variables available to us (age and sex, occupations and sectors of activity, diplomas and education, proximity to Catholicism, origins, and so on), then the predictive power of the Left-Right vote increases considerably, rising from about 40 percent in 1848 to almost 55 percent in 2022. Once again, we note the preponderant weight of the socioeconomic factors, and particularly occupation (the proportions of peasants and factory workers in particular) in the nineteenth century and during the first half of the twentieth. In comparison, the weight of the variables measuring the proximity to Catholicism (refractory priests in 1791, children attending private schools in 1894 and 2021) clearly appears to be secondary. Of course, these variables gained importance in periods when the question of private schools was posed in a particularly pointed way, as it was in the 1880s–1890s, and even more in the 1950s and 1960s, when the Debré reform was being implemented and private schools were being put under contract, before it declined in recent decades. But the fact is that these characteristics never explained more than a clearly minor part of the total variance: always less than 10 percent, and generally less than 5 percent (see

84. It will be noted that the predictive power of the two dimensions considered together is inferior to the sum of the predictive powers of the two dimensions considered separately, which is explained by the fact that these dimensions are not totally independent of each other.

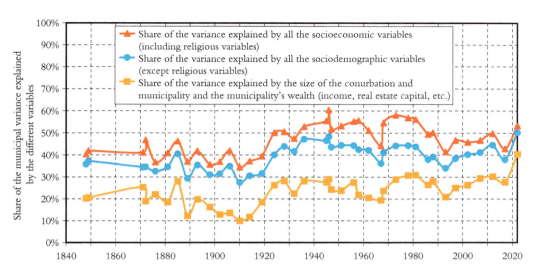

FIGURE 8.17. Social vs. religious determinants of the Left / Right vote

The inclusion among explanatory variables of controls connected with the Catholic religion (proportion of refractory priests, proportion of students in private schools, etc.) causes the explained share of the disparities in municipal votes for the Left in legislative elections to rise from 42% to 51% in 1962 and from 50% to 53% in 2022. In other words, the explanatory power of religious variables has diminished over time and has been gradually absorbed by other sociodemographic variables (particularly economic variables).

Sources and series: unehistoireduconflitpolitique.fr

figure 8.17). We arrive at the same conclusion, in an even more marked way, when we evaluate separately the predictive power of the variables related to origins (proportions of foreigners, immigrants, and naturalized citizens). It is always limited to a few percentage points of the total variance, even during the most recent period, when the conflict concerning the question of migrants and people of foreign origin present in the different territories seems so intense and so central (see figure 8.18). The same goes for the factors related to Catholicism—their limited predictive power is explained notably by the fact that in practice, the religious and identitarian variables are largely absorbed by the geosocial variables (the rural-urban cleavage, the cleavage associated with wealth). In other words, both sets of variables are certainly correlated, but their correlation remains very partial, and when they are not correlated, we realize that it is the geosocial variables that are dominant.[85] In the same way as for turnout, we also find a considerable long-term

85. All our regressions also include variables concerning family structures and in particular the proportion of complex households (that is, households that include several nuclear families,

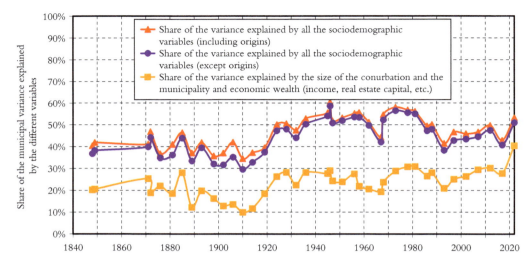

FIGURE 8.18. Social variables vs. origins as determinants of the Left / Right vote

The inclusion of variables connected with origins (proportion of people of foreign nationality, of immigrants, and of naturalized citizens) causes the explained share of disparities in the municipal vote for the Left to rise from 50% to 53% in 1936 and from 51% to 53% in 2022. In other words, the explanatory power of origins has changed little over a long period, and has always been relatively limited to other variables.

Sources and series: unehistoireduconflitpolitique.fr

decrease of the explanatory power of the department, which, if it is included in the list of controls, adds an explanatory capacity equivalent to approximately half the explanatory capacity of all the sociodemographic variables taken together in 1848, whereas in 2022 it increases explanatory capacity by only about a quarter (see figure 8.19).[86]

---

particularly in the context of multigenerational cohabitations) observed at the municipal level in the 1975 census. These variables sometimes play a significant role at the local level, in connection with the hypotheses developed in the works of Le Bras and Todd cited in the introduction, but their importance seems to be relatively limited (always less than 1 percent of the total variance).

86. Here we present the results obtained for the vote for the Left (Left and Center-Left), but the changes seen are very close to those seen in the vote for the Right and its different subcomponents. We also arrive at the same conclusion for the Center bloc, in which social determinants played a bigger role in 2017–2022 than during the period 1848–1910 (particularly because of the variables connected with wealth). See unehistoireduconflitpolitique.fr, figures D1.2f–D1.2j. The long-term decrease in the explanatory power of the department was already noted by Goguel on the basis of departmental maps for legislative elections ranging from 1849 to 1986. See F. Goguel, "Géographie électorale de la France (1849–1986)," *L'Histoire*, 1986.

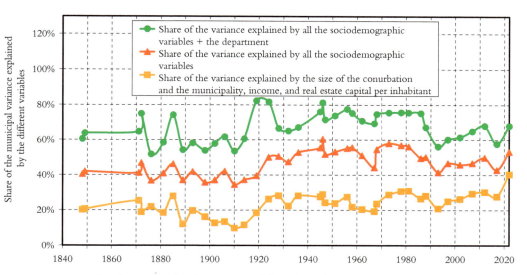

FIGURE 8.19. Social vs. geographic determinants of the Left / Right vote

From the legislative elections of 1848 to those of 2022, the share of the variance of the municipal vote for the Left explained by sociodemographic variables (in the sense of the R2 of the multifactorial regression) rose from about 40% to about 55%. The department has an additional explanatory power equivalent to about half the whole of the sociodemographic variables in 1848, but only a quarter in 2022.

Sources and series: unehistoireduconflitpolitique.fr

To sum up, these results confirm the structuring role of geosocial and socioeconomic determinants in long-term voting behavior (the rural-urban cleavage, the cleavage associated with wealth, the cleavage connected with occupation and sector of activity) and their primary importance in comparison to the geographical and identitarian factors. Let us be clear: the factors associated with religion and origins play a non-negligible role, but this role is quantitatively much less important than that of geosocial class, and it tends to be absorbed by the latter. These results contradict the notion of an "ethnicization" of French political conflict and an inexorable rise in the power of "communitarian" cleavages—a notion that is very widespread in public debate.[87] These results also contradict the idea of

---

87. See, in particular, J. Fourquet, *L'archipel français. Naissance d'une nation multiple et divisée* (Seuil, 2019). Many quantitative studies based on surveys have long since shown that instead, the weight of the social determinants had a tendency to grow over time, contrary to announcements regularly made in the different periods. See, for example, N. Mayer, "Pas de chrysanthèmes pour les variables sociologiques," in *Mars 1986: La drôle de défaite de la gauche,* ed. E. Dupoirier and G. Grunberg (Presses Universitaire de France, 1986); M. Franklin, "Vote sur

a decline in the role of social class and the idea of the growing importance of subjective variables such as "interpersonal trust."[88]

In this case, we note that the weight of the social determinants has risen rapidly over recent decades, for both voting and turnout, and particularly in the most recent elections. This may make a case for a future return toward a Left-Right bipartition centered on questions of the distribution of wealth and social inequalities, and not for a lasting continuation of tripartition. However, everything indicates that this question does not admit of a deterministic answer. In practice, the growing importance of class goes hand in hand with the increasing complexity of the class structure, and bipolarization is always the outcome of a complex and uncertain construction, depending in particular on the strategies of the actors (parties and voters, media and civil societies), their ability to mobilize, and the power relationships that flow from them. It is that question to which we will now devote our attention, first by summing up the discussion of the different subperiods, then by examining the subject in a more prospective manner.

clivage et vote sur enjeu," in *Sociologie plurielle des comportements politiques,* ed. O. Fillieule, F. Haegel, C. Hamidi, and V. Tiberj (Presses de Sciences Po, 2017). Our results confirm these general conclusions and enable us to clearly establish the growing weight of geosocial determinants of voting by situating our analysis in a historical period considerably longer than the data provided by surveys would allow.

88. See Y. Algan, E. Beasley, D. Cohen, and M. Foucault, *Les Origines du populisme. Enquête sur un schisme politique et social* (Seuil, 2020). It is not a question here of denying the potentially major role of "confidence" or other subjective variables. It is just that because these variables have been available only in very recent surveys, it is difficult to say whether their weight has increased, remained stable, or even decreased over the long term. On the other hand, the available data allow us to conclude that geosocial class and other social determinants of voting behavior make it possible to explain more than 50 percent of the variations in the municipal vote in the early twenty-first century, as opposed to 30–40 percent in the nineteenth century and at the beginning of the twentieth. See figures 8.16–8.18. Similarly, it is probable that psychological feelings about "the trials of life," analyzed by P. Rosanvallon in *Les épreuves de la vie. Comprendre autrement les Français* (Seuil, 2021), have always played a central role in shaping political attitudes. On this question, as on others, the central question is how to constitute an adequate empirical basis for making significant historical comparisons between periods.

CHAPTER 9

The First Tripartition, 1848–1910

We will now study more precisely the structure of the vote and electoral conflict during the period 1848–1910. Despite all that separates the two historical contexts, this period seems to us particularly rich in lessons for understanding the present world, especially with its socioeconomic inequalities that are increasing in both contexts and an electoral system marked by tripartition. From the legislative elections of 1848 to those of 1910, we can distinguish rather clearly three blocs: a bloc on the left bringing together the Socialists, the Democratic Socialists, and the Radical-Socialists, a bloc in the center consisting of Moderate Republicans, liberals, and Opportunists, and a bloc on the right consisting of conservatives, Catholics, and monarchists. For a time, the central bloc managed to keep its hold on power by playing on the divisions among its adversaries, particularly in the 1880s and 1890s, but it ended up losing its authority as the system was oriented to the Left-Right bipartition during the period 1910–1992, not without difficulties. Compared with the present period, an essential point in common is that between 1848 and 1910 the urban and rural working classes were deeply divided between the Left bloc and the Right bloc in proportions that were relatively close to what we see at the beginning of the 2020s, despite the profoundly different socioeconomic structures.

Among the many lessons that can be drawn from the study of the period 1848–1910, we will begin with the one that concerns the territorial cleavage. We will emphasize the objective difficulties of reconciling aspirations issuing from very different territories and geosocial classes, in particular those that came from the rural and urban worlds; these difficulties were expressed paradigmatically in the electoral and political struggles of the years between 1848 and 1852. We will also emphasize both the profound demand for equality and redistribution that was expressed by the electorate during this period of trying out universal suffrage, beyond the territories, and, at the same time, the powerful fear of risk and chaos, a fear that was certainly partly legitimate and comprehensible but which the property owners did not hesitate to instrumentalize to maintain their domination and ultimately to put an end to this democratic experiment in 1850–1852 (and to lock it up tight when the Third Republic was established in the 1870s). We will also see that powerful social and political forces were developed in the period 1848–1910 that paved the way for a rapprochement between the rural and urban working classes, and for moving beyond these antagonisms by rallying around a common program of redistribution. Everything indicates that these forces played an essential part in the exit from tripartition and the move to bipartition, and that the same could happen in the future.

The second key lesson of this period concerns the electoral and political strategies of the elites, as they can be understood on the basis of the vote of the richest municipalities. We will see that between 1848 and 1910 the elites' traditional support for the conservative bloc was transferred in part to the Moderate Republicans and Opportunists, who were perceived as more capable of safeguarding the social order. These vacillations and conflicts among elites also reflected different aspirations in connection with the productive specialties of the different dominant classes (agrarian, industrial, or military), as well as their attitudes regarding the religious and educational questions and their proximity to Catholicism. But finally, it is especially striking to note, during this period and over the long term, a certain plasticity of the elites, who were prepared to move rather rapidly from the Right bloc to the Center bloc if it corresponded to their fundamental socioeconomic interests, a phenomenon that is also found in 2017–2022 in still greater proportions than in 1848–1910. The complicated question is whether this plasticity and this pragmatism should be seen as an asset in political and electoral competition, or whether this "opportunism" and this supposed ability to aggregate all the elites (at the risk of being accused of social self-interest) is ultimately a weakness that contributed to the fall of the central bloc and the exit from the tripartition of the early twentieth century. We will defend the second hypothesis and the idea that such a phenomenon could be produced again in the future, but it goes without saying that the question is complex and deserves a differentiated analysis of the pros and cons.

The Elections of 1848–1849, the Rural-Urban Cleavage, and the Forty-Five-Centime Tax

Let us begin by putting ourselves back in the context of the elections of 1848–1849, which illustrate perfectly the difficulties connected with a possible alliance between the rural and urban working classes, taking into account the profoundly different aspirations separating territories and geosocial classes. Of course, the rural-urban cleavage had already been forcefully manifested in the 1790s. Whereas rural people had expressed in the *Cahiers de doléances* their hope to gain access to land ownership, rural people had been compelled to lower their sights when they saw that the new authorities had other priorities, starting with the auctioning off of ecclesiastical goods to the benefit of those who had the means to buy them, particularly rich city dwellers. The fiscal question, too, quickly led to intense territorial conflicts. The new government that issued from 1789 initially envisaged a fiscal system that was based primarily on the property tax created in 1790–1791 (the ancestor of the present-day property tax), which was levied proportionally on the value of land and all forms of buildings and real estate assets. It was soon recognized that such a property tax, if it alone was supposed to bring in all the required receipts, would have led in many departments to a considerable increase in the taxes paid by the rural world in comparison with the disparate system in force in the Old Regime, against all the hopes and all the promises of the Revolution. The new authorities very soon had to agree to resort to various indirect taxes and sales taxes (such as taxes on salt, beverages, and tobacco, and excise duties levied on entering a city), which weighed heavily on the poorest city dwellers, and which they had promised to abolish. All through the nineteenth century, the fiscal conflict turning on the respective burdens of the property tax and indirect taxes was to constitute one of the main points of tension that set the rural world against the urban world.

This question was central to the elections of 1848–1849. On the eve of the riots of February 1848, which were to hasten the flight of Louis-Philippe and the proclamation of the Second Republic, public finances were in a disastrous state and enormous tension reigned throughout the country. The agricultural crisis and the following industrial crisis of 1846–1847 caused tax receipts to plummet while at the same time leaving many poor peasants without resources to pay their rents and their bills and depriving hundreds of thousands of workers of their jobs. The situation was particularly explosive in the large cities, where high concentrations of factory workers had built up in the 1830s and 1840s, living in wretched conditions. This was notably the case in Paris, a veritable powder keg with more than a million inhabitants in 1848 (twice as many as in 1789), including more than 300,000 industrial factory workers, who rose up to demand better salaries and *ateliers nationaux* (production cooperatives) to provide jobs for unemployed workers. The dominant classes also had specific interests that were not necessarily totally aligned. The agrarian and industrial elites needed to get the level of economic activity increasing again, whereas the upper financial bourgeoisie (which held public debt securities in addition to industrial securities) had a primary interest in getting the state's credit and the interest payments reestablished as soon as possible and in dispelling the specter of bankruptcy. All these groups were naturally inclined to prevent the Revolution from going too far and to keep peasants' and workers' aspirations from ultimately posing a direct challenge to the private property system and the distribution of goods.

On the evening of 24 February 1848, when the insurrection announced that it had won and that the king had just abdicated, the editors in chief of the Republicans' two main daily newspapers (*Le National,* which was close to the Moderate Republicans and the liberals, and *La Réforme,* which was more receptive to the Democratic Socialists' theses) agreed on a list of eleven members to comprise the provisional government of the Second Republic, which was proclaimed at the Hôtel de Ville and published in one of the dailies on 25 February—"Au Peuple Français!" (see reproduction 9.1).[1] A Socialist and a factory worker—Louis Blanc and the worker "Albert"—were symbolic members, along with a Democratic Socialist, Ledru-Rollin, but essentially the list was composed of Moderate Republicans and liberals who were very hostile to socialism and who had taken part in the earlier censitary chambers, such as Arago, Lamartine, Marie, and Garnier-Pagès, who accepted the position of minister of finance. The Republic and universal suffrage were proclaimed, but on the economic and financial level, the main decision was the famous decree of 16 March issued by Garnier-Pagès, which included an increase of forty-five centimes in the property tax as its leading provision. Specifically, the decree raised the tax by 45 percent (each franc due as property tax was raised by forty-five centimes) and was applicable to all taxpayers. All peasants owning even the smallest parcels of land were affected, even if they were deeply indebted and already didn't know how they were going to pay their bills (including bills for seeds), all in the context of an acute agricultural crisis. The sharecroppers and landless peasants also had to bear the costs of this abrupt tax increase, insofar as their landlords frequently passed it on to them in rents, at least in part. The measure was supposed to bring in 160 million francs, a considerable sum for the period, and thus make it possible to reestablish public credit and ward off the danger of bankruptcy.[2]

---

1. On the development of these events, see, for example, M. Agulhon, *1848 ou l'apprentissage de la République* (Seuil, 1992); S. Hayat, *Quand la République était révolutionnaire. Citoyenneté et représentation en 1848* (Seuil, 2014). On the history of *Le National* and *La Réforme,* see C. Bellanger, J. Godechot, P. Guiral, and F. Terrou, eds., *Histoire générale de la presse française,* vol. 2, *De 1815 à 1871* (Presses Universitaire de France, 1969). *Le National,* "Journal officiel de la campagne réformiste" of 1840, which declared its opposition to any recourse to extralegal avenues, saw *La Réforme* rise up on its left in 1843, promoted by Ledru-Rollin, Arago, and also Louis Blanc (see in particular Bellanger et al., 129).

2. These 160 million francs represented about 1.5 percent of the national income in 1848 (around 10–12 billion francs), at a time when the totality of tax receipts barely reached 6–7 percent of the national income. See chapter 1, figure 1.7. For comparison, the receipts expected from the

Vendredi 25 Février 1848.

PRIX DE L'ABONNEMENT.

PRIX DES INSERTIONS :

LA RÉFORME

PROCLAMATION DU GOUVERNEMENT PROVISOIRE.
Au Peuple Français!

Reproduction 9.1: Proclamation of the provisional government, *La Réforme,* 25 February 1848

The figure reproduces the front page of the newspaper *La Réforme,* which proclaims the provisional government on the day after the victorious insurrection of 24 February 1848. On the evening of that eventful day, *La Réforme,* a republican daily, arrived at an agreement with *Le National* regarding the composition of this government.

Source: Gallica (digital library of the National Library of France).

Confirmed in May 1848 by a vote of the Constituent Assembly elected in April, the tax of forty-five centimes came to be seen by the rural world as the symbol of the new regime's deception. Cities were not asked to pay higher indirect taxes (even the salt tax was abolished on 15 April). All the sacrifices were made in the countryside, in the form of land taxes, in order to balance the budget and pay interest to the wealthiest bankers and urbanites, even though the country was in

---

carbon tax hikes planned for 2018–2019 (and later cancelled following the *gilets jaunes* movement) were about 10 billion euros initially (and were scheduled to reach 20 billion euros in the medium term), or between 0.5 percent and 1 percent of the national income, which is already very substantial, but has to be set against the fact that today, fiscal receipts represent around 50 percent of the national income. The 2023 pension reform also aims to achieve savings of the order of 10–15 billion euros per year by 2030 (or around 0.5 percent of the national income).

a severe economic and social crisis.[3] However, Garnier-Pagès did not give up: he saw raising direct taxes as the only way the government could cope with the collapse of bond prices and honor its debts, a sacred duty the country could not fail to respect.[4] The Moderate Republicans and liberals would pay a high price for this policy that they had devised and implemented on their own initiative. In practice, it was General Cavaignac—who had succeeded Arago as the head of the government in June 1848 while waiting for the presidential elections planned for December—who, in the name of the Republicans, attempted to tighten the fiscal screws by sending the army to collect taxes in the countryside during the summer of 1848. The tax collection was met with strong resistance throughout the country, especially in the West and in the South. In June a dozen people were killed in Creuse in a confrontation with the troops. These movements were sometimes locally instigated by Bonapartists and Legitimist landowners, who put up posters proclaiming that "landowners are not obliged to bear industry's losses."[5] The whole urban world, without any distinctions, was accused of selfishness: industrialists and workers, liberal Republicans and Democratic Socialists.

Observers at the time agreed that Louis-Napoléon Bonaparte's success in the presidential election of December 1848 could be explained in large measure by his resolute opposition to the forty-five-centime surcharge, which he promised to abolish, and which was in fact subsequently canceled (and replaced by gradual increases in indirect taxes, which were less visible and little debated during the electoral campaign). Thus Bonaparte won 75 percent of the votes in the first round, while Cavaignac (a Moderate Republican, a symbol of the established power) won 19 percent, Ledru-Rollin (Democratic Socialist) barely 5 percent, and Raspail (Socialist) only 0.5 percent. Many workers' fiefs voted massively for Bonaparte in order to ensure the elimination of Cavaignac, who, after closing the *ateliers nationaux* in June 1848, brutally put down the workers' revolt in Paris during the riots on 24–26 June (which resulted in 3,000–5,000 deaths, depending on the estimate). In many urban and rural territories, the cry "Down with Cavaignac,

3. Land tax (*taxe foncière*) were also levied on real estate (and therefore partly on the urban world), but at the time agricultural land represented 70 percent of the total tax base. Let us add that the forty-five centimes applied to the four direct taxes instituted in 1791 (the land tax, the personal tax (*contribution personnelle-mobilière*) , the business tax, and the tax on doors and windows), and not only the land tax, by far the most important and most visible parts of the total tax bill.

4. The Council of Ministers on 16 March thus reminded people of "the truth of this economic axiom: that land must be handled carefully in tranquil times in order to be able to deal with the necessities of great crises."

5. See R. Gossez, "La résistance à l'impôt: Les 45 centimes," *Revue d'histoire du 19e siècle*, 1953.

down with the rich!" exemplified the mood of the period.[6] We will return to the disparate structure of the vote for Bonaparte, which is explained above all by the rejection of Cavaignac and the liberal Republicans and the "Moderates" who had governed during the year 1848, and also by the fact that Louis-Napoléon made virtually no commitments (with the important exception of abolishing the forty-five centimes).[7]

The Central Difficulty: How to Unite the Working Classes in the Cities and the Countryside

The important point is that the democratic socialist and socialist trends, even though they achieved results in the legislative elections of April 1848 and May 1849 that were far superior to those they had achieved in the presidential election of December 1848, never succeeded in completely separating themselves from the opprobrium that weighed on the whole of the Republican camp in the rural world, and that was because of the forty-five centimes. Of course, the Democratic Socialist and Montagnard deputies denounced this unjust levy from the outset and defended the idea of a more ambitious tax reform based on the creation of a system of progressive taxes on income, inheritances, and wealth—that is, with zero or minimal taxes on persons in the lowest brackets and increasing rates as the level of wealth grew. Such an approach would have made it possible in principle to improve the lives of all the urban and rural working classes (industrial workers and peasants alike), and to shift the fiscal burden to the wealthy classes, whatever their territory. In that way, a territorial conflict would have become a class conflict, and it would have become possible to avoid the uniform increases in land taxes while at the same time releasing credit to lower indirect taxes, and thus to move beyond the binary conflict between the rural world and the urban world. How, then, can the failure of the Socialists and the Montagnards be explained? The proposals for a progressive tax system that they made were not always completely precise and well thought-out, which made criticizing them easier for the Moderate Republicans as well as the conservatives, monarchists, and Bonapartists of the Party of Order. They all decried the risk of chaos and a generalized challenge to the system of private property if the country were to engage in such an experiment. In fact, at that time, no progressive tax system had ever been tried out on such a large scale,

6. See A. J. Tudesq, *L'élection présidentielle de Louis-Napoléon Bonaparte (10 décembre 1848)* (A. Colin, 1965).
7. See chapter 12.

in France or elsewhere, so it was difficult to counter these fears and to leave behind the existing institutional framework. That framework was a fiscal system that in the nineteenth century was based on two principal tax instruments: the property tax (in practice, mostly a land tax) and the indirect taxes, both of which were proportional and regressive. It almost inevitably led to conflict between the rural world and the urban world and even exacerbations of this cleavage when new tax receipts were needed.

Beyond the fiscal question, which was difficult to deal with but crucial in order to escape the political dead end, some Democratic Socialists tried, despite everything, to emphasize specifically rural and agrarian problems, as did the novelist Eugène Sue, a "Red" candidate in Loiret in 1848 and the author of famous pamphlets on access to municipal lands, the development of rural credit, the creation of model farms, and the abolition of the system of "replacement" that allowed bourgeois youths to be replaced by rural men to meet their military obligations.[8] Generally, support for the demands of the poor peasants allowed Democratic Socialists to rack up some important successes in 1849 in several rural departments, notably in Limousin and Languedoc (in the Pyrénées-Orientales, the Democratic Socialists won more than 75 percent of the votes in many municipalities).[9] Further successes were registered in the partial elections of late 1849 and early 1850, as for example in December 1849 when a Red deputy was elected in Gard, replacing a Legitimist who had died, which spread panic in the Party of Order. Peasant petitions multiplied in 1848–1849 to demand that property owners "repay the

8. See E. Sue, *Le républicain des campagnes* (Librairie de la propagande démocratique et sociale, 1851). In 1850, Sue was elected as a representative for Seine in the legislative assembly. His life itself was worthy of one of his novels. Prince Eugène was his godfather, and his godmother was the Empress Joséphine. The son of a well-to-do family and a best-selling novelist in the 1830s–1840s, he retired to Sologne in 1840—following the ruin of his fortune and betrayal by a woman—where he became a Socialist. Back in Paris on the benches of the Assembly, he "protested against L. N. Bonaparte's *coup d'État*, went to give himself up as a prisoner at the fort of Vanves, even though L. Napoléon had struck his name from the list of representatives to be arrested, and went voluntarily into exile in Savoy," according to the entry on him in *Dictionnaire des parlementaires français*, ed. A. Robert, E. Bourlaton, and G. Cougny (Bourlaton, 1891).

9. It should be noted that in the presidential election of 1848, the two republican candidates—Cavaignac and Ledru-Rollin—together won more votes than Louis-Napoléon Bonaparte in Pyrénées-Orientales—a result just as exceptional as the votes won by the Montagnards during the legislative elections in 1849. On this detail of the Pyrénées-Orientales, see, in particular, P. McPhee, *Les semailles de la République dans les Pyrénées-Orientales, 1846–1952. Classes sociales, culture et politique* (Publications de l'Olivier, 1992).

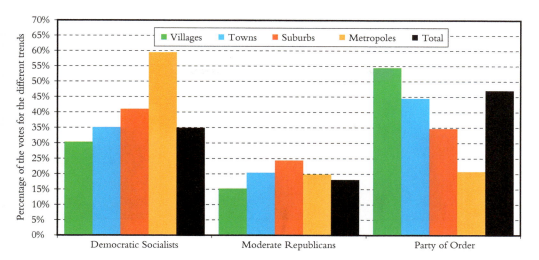

FIGURE 9.1. The legislative elections of 1849: Rural-urban conflict and tripartition

In the legislative elections of May 1849, the lists for the Democratic Socialists and their allies (Left bloc) came out on top in the metropoles and suburbs and were clearly behind those of the Party of Order and the conservatives (Right bloc) in the villages and towns (which rallied 48% and 40% the population, as against 7% and 5%, respectively, for the metropoles and suburbs). The lists for the Moderate Republicans and their allies lagged far behind almost everywhere.

Sources and series: unehistoireduconflitpolitique.fr

billion,"[10] which cannot fail to remind us of the watchword "return the ISF" during the *gilets jaunes* movement in 2018–2019.

Nonetheless, the successes of the Democratic Socialists in the rural world remained relatively limited. At the national level, the lists of the Democratic Socialists and similar groups rose from 31 percent in the legislative elections of April 1848 to 35 percent in May 1849, whereas the Moderate Republicans fell from 24 percent to 18 percent and the conservatives of the Party of Order consolidated their result of 45–47 percent. The latter nevertheless were seriously worried about what would follow, especially since they found themselves obliged to assume the burden of exercising power and implementing very unpopular direct tax increases, in particular the resurrected tax on salt. In the metropoles and suburbs, the Democratic Socialists clearly defeated the conservatives and often achieved by themselves an absolute majority (see figure 9.1). On the other hand, their result was two times lower in

10. In reference to the emigrants' billion voted in 1825 to compensate exiled nobles for rents lost during the Revolution, a payment that contributed to swelling the public debt and adding to the tax increases necessary to repay it, see R. Lévy, "Le milliard des émigrés et les 45 centimes," *Bulletin d'histoire de la Révolution de 1848,* 1912.

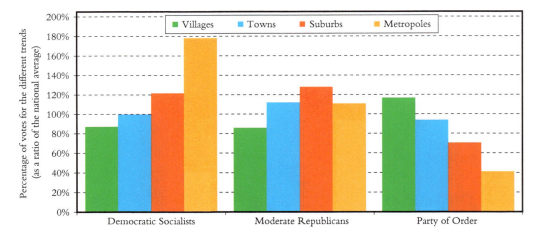

FIGURE 9.2. The legislative elections of 1848–1849 in the territories (as a ratio of the national average)

In the legislative elections in April 1848 and May 1849, the Democratic Socialists and their allies (Left bloc) achieved a store twice as high in the metropoles as in the villages, whereas the lists of the Party of Order (Right bloc) achieved a result almost three times higher in the villages than in the metropoles. The lists of the Moderate Republicans and their allies (Center bloc) achieved better results in the urban world and had a more balanced vote profile than the two other blocs.

Sources and series: unehistoireduconflitpolitique.fr

villages than it was in the metropoles, in 1848 and in 1849. Conversely, the conservatives of the Party of Order achieved a result that was almost three times higher in villages it was in metropoles. The Moderate Republicans, for their part, were in an intermediate situation. If their results in the different territories in the elections of 1848 and 1849 are expressed as percentages of their national average, which is the best way to make comparisons in time and between political trends, then we see that their vote profile is more urban than rural, but ultimately much better balanced than those of the other two blocs (see figure 9.2).[11]

The disappointing results achieved by the Democratic Socialists in the rural world can be explained by several factors. Of course, we must not neglect the organizational and financial superiority of the Party of Order and its electoral committee on the rue de Poitiers. Through the press they controlled and the pamphlets they distributed to condemn the Red Peril, the conservatives had an

---

11. The vote profiles for the territories are very similar for the elections of 1848 and 1849, and here we indicate the average profile. See unehistoireduconflitpolitique.fr, figures D3.1a–D3.1d. For the geographical distribution of the Democratic Socialist vote in 1849, see also map C9.1.

influence that far exceeded that of the Democratic Socialist bloc, not to mention the property owners' direct hold over voters. However, we should also emphasize the limitations of the discourses and programs of the Democratic Socialists and Montagnards in 1848–1849 with regard to the rural world. Despite all their efforts, these discourses and programs remained centered on the urban world and the problems encountered by the urban proletariat. The proposals bearing on fiscal justice and progressive taxes could definitely benefit the rural world as well, but the fact is that they were relatively abstract for many voters. The programs highlighted by the Democratic Socialists generally stressed workers' salaries and the workday and often failed to include any specific, concrete proposal to aid peasants and address the crisis that the agricultural world was going through at that time, such as a proposal concerning the construction of roads, irrigation problems, or access to land and credit. Research has also shown that the main republican daily newspapers in Paris, *Le National* and *La Réforme,* almost never took up issues that concerned the rural world; reading them, such issues hardly seem to exist. The question of the reform of the Code forestier of 1827, which considerably reduced the rights to make use of municipal goods and rights of access to private forests (in particular, the right to gather dead wood for heating, and leaves, berries, and roots for animals, food, and fertilizer), was thus almost never mentioned in these newspapers in 1848–1849, whereas in the countryside there was a demand for a complete reworking of this legislation.[12] This disregard of the

---

12. See G. Fasel, "The Wrong Revolution: French Republicanism in 1848," *French Historical Studies,* 1974. The subject of the Code forestier was discussed at length in provincial newspapers (unlike in the national press), starting with *La Gazette de Lyon, La Tribune de la Gironde,* and *Le Journal du Cher,* as shown by the archives of these newspapers available at Retronews. Thus, a newspaper like *L'Éclaireur des Pyrénées* (which leaned left in the Basses-Pyrénées) mentions on many occasions the proposals made to modify this Code forestier—for example, on 17 February 1849, 20 July 1849, 3 August 1849, 8 August 1849, 5 September 1849, and 7 October 1849. On 22 June 1849, it reports on a group of 200 or 300 individuals armed with rifles who gathered "on 31 May in the forest of Mixe to oppose a permit to cut timber to be sold by adjudication at the request of the syndical committee. The prefect has been asked to cancel this sale . . . because he has not acted with all the publicity required by the forest code." The article goes on to describe in great detail the (absurd) reasons for the cancellation of the sale, emphasizing above all the prefect's firm determination "to enforce the law and avoid any disorder." This firm determination is found again in the response of a woodcutter-voter published in *Le Spectateur de Dijon* (a Catholic-leaning newspaper) on 27 December 1849, which emphasizes "the obstacles to well-being that the government puts in the way of country people through humiliations by forest officials," stressing that decisions are always made "against the interests of country people" (and a priori without much interest from journalists in the capital).

rural world was all the more damaging because in the middle of the nineteenth century the villages and towns had far larger populations than the metropoles and suburbs, so in all logic, it was programs devoted to rural territories (and not to the urban proletariat) that should have made the headlines.[13]

It is interesting to note that a liberal-conservative as well informed as Tocqueville (who was an Orléanist deputy under the July Monarchy and was reelected deputy from Manche in 1848 after accompanying to the polling station the peasants of the village that bears his name)[14] explains candidly, in his *Souvenirs* published in 1850, that the peasants could have easily become revolutionaries in a few weeks if the Democratic Socialists had promised to immediately abolish mortgage debts— that is, by attacking creditors rather than property owners (which the peasants hoped to become). Tocqueville was still frightened by this, and he drew from it a harsh conclusion that has remained famous: "There were revolutionaries who were more wicked than those of 1848, but I don't think there have been any more foolish."[15] In fact, such a cancellation of the peasants' debts would probably have met with a certain success. We can also conclude that it would also have been necessary to propose a genuine agrarian reform that sought to redistribute to poor peasants the lands of domains exceeding a certain size.[16] However that may be, we are obliged to note that Eugène Sue's and Félix Pyat's proposals seeking to reform taxation or to develop rural credit were considerably less ambitious, and

13. Let us recall that in 1848, villages constituted 48 percent of France's population, towns 40 percent, and suburbs and metropoles 5 percent and 7 percent, respectively. See chapter 2, figure 2.6.

14. See chapter 1.

15. See A. de Tocqueville, *Souvenirs* (Henry, 1896),113–118. Reading this text, we understand especially the dread that seized property owners in 1848: "It was a great and terrible thing to see this whole immense city, full of so many riches, in the hands of those who owned nothing at all, or rather this great nation, for thanks to centralization, whoever reigns in Paris reigns in France. I do not believe that at any period of the Revolution the terror was as profound, and I think it can be compared only to the terror that the civilized cities of the Roman world must have felt when they saw themselves suddenly in the grip of the Vandals and the Goths. Since nothing comparable had been seen up to that point, many people expected acts of an unprecedented violence. A dark despair gripped the bourgeoisie thus oppressed and threatened." See also G. Lefebvre, "Le 24 février 1848," *1848 et les Révolutions du 19e siècle,* 1946.

16. We need only listen once again to the remarks of our "woodcutter-voter" published in late 1849 in *Le Spectateur de Dijon:* "Now be surprised that the people of the countryside allow themselves to be seduced by the candidates' promises at the time of the elections. They don't love the Republic for its beautiful eyes, but because of the good that it does them. Between two candidates, one who is as white as snow and the other red as scarlet, they will always choose the one who guarantees them the largest dose of freedom of movement."

in any case they were not in the first rank of the programs proposed by the Montagnards on the national scale.[17]

Proudhon, Thiers, Fiscal Reform, and the Party of Order

An episode that is particularly revealing of the difficulties the Democratic Socialists encountered in defining and promoting their program is the lively and illuminating exchange between Proudhon and Thiers at the rostrum of the Constitutive Assembly in July 1848. Proudhon was at the time one of the most prominent Socialist theorists and Montagnard deputies. In 1848–1850 Thiers was one of the main officials of the Party of Order and its electoral committee, and he repeatedly denounced "the vile multitude" during the debates that led to the adoption of the "Burgraves' law" in May 1850 to limit the right to vote and to exclude the poorest citizens (a law he had partly inspired).[18] Elected several times president of the Council, and a minister under the July Monarchy (he was minister of the interior when the Lyonnese silk workers' strike was put down in 1834), Thiers also would be the head of the executive during the crushing of the Paris Commune in the Bloody Week of May 1871. He incarnated the continuity of the conservative bloc in nineteenth-century France, beyond changes in regime. At this particular historical moment, when everyone was talking about socialism but its programmatic content remained largely to be defined, the exchange is all the more instructive because it left a trace in the pages of the *Moniteur universel,* where it was published despite the attempts to censor it made by the deputies of the Party of Order, who were stunned by the "immoralité" of the proposal made by Proudhon, who was accused of sapping the very foundations of society and making a frontal attack on the system of private property under the cover of a simple fiscal and financial measure.[19]

In fact, the originality of Proudhon's proposal for fiscal reform, which he had disseminated in a pamphlet published a few weeks earlier, was to make it possible to bring in substantial receipts for the public finances (and notably, to abolish the forty-five centimes) and deliver immediate, tangible benefits for the country's most

---

17. See F. Pyat, " Toast aux paysans," in Sue, *Le républicain des campagnes.* See also A. Bleton-Ruget, "Aux sources de l'agrarisme républicain: La propagande démocrate-socialiste et les campagnes (1848–1851)," *Cahiers d'histoire,* 1998.

18. See chapter 1.

19. See the complete text of the exchanges, collected in the *Rapport du citoyen Thiers précédé de la proposition du citoyen Proudhon relative à l'impôt sur le revenu, et suivi de son discours prononcé à l'Assemblée nationale le 31 juillet 1848 (conforme au Moniteur universel)* (Garnier, 1848).

disadvantaged social classes, and specifically for all the tenants in the rural and urban worlds. In concrete terms, Proudhon proposed to institute an income tax at the rate of one-third on all income from property, including rents, interest, dividends, and so on. The originality consists in the tax being deducted at the source, directly by farmers, tenants, and debtors, who were thus authorized to reduce immediately by one-third the rents, interest, and dividends that they owed their landlords and property owners. They were then expected to repay half this amount to the state (which thus collected a tax equal to one-sixth of the property's incomes), and they kept the other half for themselves, which procured for them, de facto, a decrease by one-sixth of the rent and interest they owed. Proudhon calculated that the measure would bring in 560 million francs for the state and 560 million francs for tenants, considerable sums for the period.[20] The proposal was completed by a progressive income tax on incomes issuing from public salaries and ministerial offices, with rates ranging from 5 to 50 percent, depending on the level of income. This supplementary levy was supposed to bring in 220 million francs, or 780 million francs in receipts for the state, almost five times as much as the forty-five centimes (160 million). This would have allowed Proudhon to immediately abolish the forty-five centimes, while massively reducing the taxes weighing on the world of work and production (the indirect taxes on consumption and trading licenses) and financing a vast network of public credit institutions, making it possible to restart economic activity. This last proposal played a central role in the decentralized, communalist, and federalist vision of socialism that the Montagnard deputy sought to promote (without giving more details concerning these credit institutions and their organization). For good measure, Proudhon also foresaw that farmers, tenants, and debtors would be able to delay by six months the payment of the rest of the rents and unilaterally prolong by three years the leases that bound them to the property owners.

For Thiers, this was too much. He deemed particularly "immoral" this license given to the poorest people to amend private deeds by themselves and to participate directly in the levying of taxes on property owners, by informing on them if necessary. Didn't Proudhon also suggest in the parliamentary debate that he would advise farmers, tenants, and debtors to apply his proposal themselves, should it not be adopted by the Assembly? That was proof that the Socialists would always go

---

20. Recall that national income was about 10–12 billion francs. Tax receipts going to the state were therefore on the order of 5 percent of national income, and similar for the transfer from property owners to tenants. The total amount paid by property owners was on the order of 10 percent of national income.

too far in their challenge to private property, and that they had to be stopped before it was too late. As was only proper, Thiers also denounced the economic incompetence of the Socialists in general and of Proudhon in particular, who was said to have grossly exaggerated the receipts his project would deliver. In this case, Thiers got tangled up in his figures and showed a degree of bad faith,[21] but he was right about one thing. If we examine today the various elements of the debate, we have to admit that Proudhon's calculations are plausible, but on the condition that the levy of one-third on the incomes from property would be applied not only to property owners who lent their land but also to property owners who cultivated it, no matter how modest they were, a condition that Thiers and the Party of Order did not fail to denounce. To exempt property owners who cultivated their land, or more generally all owners of small- and middle-sized properties up to a certain threshold, Proudhon would have had to apply a progressive scale with variable rates depending on the amount of the incomes issuing from the property (or on the size of the property itself), and not a proportional scale with a single, equal rate equal to one-third for everyone. Taking into consideration the extreme concentration of property ownership at the time, in reality, a progressive scale centered on the richest would have reduced only moderately the receipts envisaged (by a quarter or a third, depending on the option chosen), without calling the overall project into question.[22] The fact remains that Proudhon's project as it was formulated did threaten small property owners (in the same way that the forty-five-centime surcharge did, which is embarrassing for a proposal that meant to distance itself from the surcharge), and that weakened his position considerably. It is interesting to note that Proudhon declared that he preferred to stick to a proportional levy on property because he feared complicating his proposal and looking like a "sharer" if he opted for an explicitly progressive scale (a hidden and potentially limitless menace that the Party of Order sought to expose), to the point that the Socialist libertarian author preferred to keep his distance from it, unfortunately putting himself in a dilemma difficult to resolve.[23]

---

21. Proudhon had initially assessed his project as bringing in 1.5 billion, before correcting his evaluation to 1.340 billion (780 million for the state, 560 million for farmers, tenants, and debtors), or about 11–12 percent of the national income. Thiers pretended to believe that his adversary assessed his project at 3 billion (1.5 billion for the state, 1.5 billion for the farmers, tenants, and debtors), the better to discredit it, though this does not appear in any of the documents published by Proudhon.

22. In the nineteenth century, the least rich 90 percent held less than 20 percent of the total goods, as opposed to more than 80 percent held by the richest 10 percent. See chapter 1, figure 1.4.

23. Proudhon accepted the idea of a progressive tax on public salaries, but he was afraid of exposing himself to devastating criticism if he did the same for private property, whose exact distribution was, moreover, not well known at the time.

In addition to this discussion on tax progressivity, this debate also illustrates the violence of the power relationships that formed around these issues. For the great majority of the deputies in 1848—including, moreover, most of the Democratic Socialists—Proudhon had gone too far when he suggested that tenants could themselves decide to reduce their rents. The theorist of libertarian socialism and anarchist was reprimanded, and there was no vote on his proposal.[24] Clearly, it would have taken far more than a better technical formulation for his project to succeed, starting with significantly different power relationships, which only a very strong social and electoral mobilization could have provided, in the framework of a democratic socialist program that succeeded at better reconciling rural and urban aspirations. In this case, considering the very great advances registered by the Socialist and Montagnard candidates between 1848 and 1849 and the numerous successes seen during the partial elections of 1849 and 1850, as well as the increasingly evident disappointment generated by the Party of Order in power, it might have been possible that if the electoral process had followed its course in the 1850s and 1860s, then power relations could have continued to evolve in that direction. A successful trial of progressive taxation and the redistribution of wealth under the direction of the Democratic Socialists (no doubt in a form quite different from the one envisaged by Proudhon) could then have been established. History decided otherwise, with the very strong restriction of the right to vote adopted by the Party of Order in May 1850 and then the Bonapartist coup d'état in December 1851.

Marx, Class Struggles, and the Question of Democratic Socialism

Another illustration of the profound lack of understanding between the rural and urban worlds at that time—in addition to the fact that the notion of democratic and electoral experimentation was still far from being taken as self-evident—is provided by the valuable testimony that Karl Marx bequeathed to us with his work

---

24. Denouncing what it considered an unpardonable offense against the right of property, the Assembly interrupted the debate on Proudhon's proposals and adopted, almost unanimously, the following resolution: "The National Assembly, considering that Citizen Proudhon's proposal is an odious attack on the principles of public morality; that it violates property; that it encourages betraying others; that it appeals to the worst passions; considering, in addition, that the speaker has slandered the revolution of February 1848 by claiming to make it complicit in the theories that he has developed, moves on to the order of the day." Proudhon was subsequently dismissed from parliament and imprisoned for his involvement in the June 1848 uprising.

The Class Struggles in France. In this collection of articles published between March and October 1850 (before the coup d'état of December 1851), Marx analyzes in the heat of the moment events in France and Paris from 1848 and 1849. It is a genuine textbook case that allows the Socialist author to test and refine the theories he was forming regarding social classes and dialectical materialism applied to contemporary history.[25] The text is precious, because it includes subtle and convincing analyses of conflicts between dominating and dominated classes and also of conflicts within the dominant classes (in particular, regarding the driving role of the financial *haute bourgeoisie,* whose absolute priority was to reestablish the state mechanism for paying interest on the debt, itself inflated by the generous gifts that the state repeatedly gave property owners),[26] and because it is also full of negative, condescending prejudices regarding peasants, who are accused of having allowed the victory of reaction. This text [Marx] is precious because of its archaism and its jealous attachment to a small property. In pages that have remained famous, Marx stigmatizes the peasant voter, "oafish, burlesque, and pathetic, . . . who, by his backwardness and his petit-bourgeois aspirations, gave on 10 December 1848 the victory to Bonaparte and to the bloc of the conservatives and the property owners."[27] Generally, Marx's electoral analysis is not detailed. Cavaignac is naturally treated as the man who massacred protesting workers in June 1848, but the Democratic Socialist Ledru-Rollin is not treated much better: he is denounced for his feebleness, his naïve attachment to legality, and finally for his objective complicity with the Moderate Republicans and the Party of Order. Only the Socialist

---

25. See K. Marx, *The Class Struggles in France* (1850). See also *The Eighteenth Brumaire of Louis Bonaparte* (1852), in which Marx analyzes the coup d'état of 2 December 1851. *Capital* appeared in 1867.

26. Marx analyzes in particular the way the financial compensation accorded to slave owners that was adopted in 1848 at the same time as the abolition of slavery led to the growth of public debt, as did the billion francs given to the émigrés in 1825, and this increase in the debt was subsequently used by the government to justify tax increases on the mass of the population. The state certainly appears to have been in the service of the large property owners, or rather of various factions within that class, with variable power relationships, depending on the period.

27. "The tenth of December 1848 was the day of the peasants' insurrection. . . . The symbol that expressed their entry into the revolutionary movement, clumsy and cunning, rascally and naïve, oafish and sublime, a calculated superstition, a pathetic burlesque, a brilliant and insipid anachronism, a world-historic piece of buffoonery and an indecipherable hieroglyph for the understanding of civilized people—this symbol bore the unmistakable physiognomy of the class that represents barbarism amid civilization. . . . Napoleon was the only man who went all the way in representing the interests and imagination of the new peasant class that 1789 had created." See K. Marx, *The Class Struggles in France* (1850), part 2.

Raspail (0.5 percent of the vote) finds some grace in Marx's eyes, because he seemed not to be in the hands of the property owners.

To be sure, this dark and disabused analysis of the electoral process is understandable, at least in part, especially at a time when universal suffrage was very far from having proved itself as a force that could make possible social emancipation and the march toward equality. In addition, Marx had in front of him the law of 31 May 1850 eliminating the right to vote for the poorest people—the only defense that the Party of Order found to parry the rising power of its opponents—which shows rather clearly the hypocrisies of the elites in power when confronted on the question of the right to vote.[28] As early as 1848–1849, the Moderate Republican government relentlessly repressed the workers' movement and established a control over the press that was even more intrusive than it had been under the July Monarchy, particularly with the reintroduction of the "caution money" system, which was especially punishing for the popular press.[29] Facing these realities, it was not only justified but essential to avoid being naïve. The limits of electoral democracy deserve to be analyzed straightforwardly; above all, the social conditions for exercising the right to vote must be clarified and redefined. Specifically, without an egalitarian system for financing the press and electoral campaigns, and more generally, without a minimum of social and economic equality, the ideal of political equality in voting may prove illusory.

In the weeks that followed the insurrection of February 1848, many Socialists asked that the elections planned for April 1848 be postponed for a few months to implement fundamental structural reforms, such as cost-free education (without success) and laying the foundations for new rules concerning the system of labor and property (which was very partially realized with the *ateliers nationaux*). On 28 February, the Democratic Socialist fringe also achieved the creation of the Government Committee for Workers (also known as the Luxembourg Committee, because it was symbolically connected with the Luxembourg Palace, where the Chambre des Pairs met under the July Monarchy and where the Senate would later

---

28. In general, the Burgraves' laws had a very powerful effect on its contemporaries. For example, it is from this event that Victor Hugo's move to the left dates. In his youth, Hugo was a staunch monarchist, and in 1848 he had been elected a deputy on the basis of a confession of faith that was very clearly antisocialist: "I shall always be opposed to those who would like to substitute the red flag for the tricolor, ruin the rich without enriching the poor, abolish property and the family, and parade heads on pikes."

29. The caution system consisted of newspapers paying a large sum of money to obtain authorization to publish. This sum could be seized and thus lost in the event of the closure of the newspaper by the authorities. The system was canceled by the 1881 law on the freedom of the press.

meet), a committee led by Louis Blanc, composed of representatives of the various workers' occupations, and entrusted in principle with preparing proposals for new social legislation that was to be submitted to the future National Assembly.[30]

For all that, taking these essential and complex issues into account does not mean that we do not need to look into why Raspail and Ledru-Rollin convinced so few rural voters. To answer that question, it seems necessary to examine the limits of the Democratic Socialist discourses and programs and to understand in particular why they accorded too little place to the rural world, whose aspirations to property and autonomy cannot be simply dismissed as a sign of backwardness (unless we place ourselves outside any democratic logic). For Marx, the question of the Socialists' program and the future of the various social classes seemed to be already settled. He believed that the Revolution of 1848 failed because the process of industrial development and the concentration of capital had not yet reached its conclusion. When this process is sufficiently advanced, the workers' movement should be able to do without the peasant class and its archaism and would be able to take power all by itself and establish the dictatorship of the proletariat, at least for a time. The abolition of private property and the nationalization of the means of production would then open the way to a classless society. The problem with this strictly statist and hypercentralized view is that it does not correspond at all to the aspirations to participation, autonomy, and emancipation that were expressed in the nineteenth and twentieth centuries, in the urban world and in the rural world. After the failure of the attempt to take power during the Paris Commune in 1871, a failure attributed in part to the French Socialists' divisions and theoretical shortcomings, as well as to the weakness of the French industrial proletariat and the persistence of a numerous and backward peasantry, Marx and Engels shifted their expectations to Germany and its accelerated industrial development, the hope of the socialist movement in a German revolution that was still present after World War I and the Revolution of 1917.[31] Here again, the problem

---

30. In practice, the idea that such a committee might have real powers was fiercely opposed by most of the moderate and liberal Republicans, and this authority would be dissolved in June 1848 at the same time as the *ateliers nationaux*. See Hayat, *Quand la République était révolutionnaire*.

31. On these analyses, see, for example, the preface Engels wrote for the 1895 edition of *The Class Struggles in France*. For some authors, Marx's severe judgment of the agrarian world after 1848 helps explain his future obsession with industrial production and his lack of interest in questions concerning land and the environment, whereas in his early works he had taken more interest in the question of the common ownership of forests and the preservation of natural resources. See P. Charbonnier, *Abondance et liberté. Une histoire environnementale des idées politiques* (La Découverte, 2020), 241–267.

is that nothing guarantees that the hypercentralization of state power entailed by this strategy would be in alignment with the aspirations of the working classes, whether they resided in the cities or the countryside, in France, Germany, or the Soviet Union.

The Forces Working toward a Rapprochement between the Rural and Urban Working Classes

We now come to the evolution of the electoral cleavage between the rural world and the urban world during the first decades of the Third Republic.[32] Here, we must distinguish two subperiods. In the first, from the elections of 1871 to those of 1889, the differences in voting behavior between the countryside and the cities are extremely great. There were twice as many votes for Socialists, Radicals, and Radical-Socialists (the Left bloc) in the metropoles as there were in villages, whereas the conservatives, monarchists, Catholics, and Bonapartists (the Right bloc) won twice as many votes in the villages. The Moderate Republicans and Opportunists (the Center bloc) had a more balanced profile than the other two blocs, even as they gradually drew closer to the conservatives (see figure 9.3).

Then the distribution of votes began to evolve, starting with the elections of 1893 and 1898, as Socialist and Radical-Socialist candidates grew more numerous. Ultimately, if we examine the structure of the vote during the elections conducted between 1893 and 1910, we see that the electorates of the various blocs have become much closer. Specifically, the vote for the Left continues to be higher in the metropoles and suburbs than in the towns and villages, and inversely for the vote for the Right, but the gaps between them are now much more limited, on the order of 20 percent (see figure 9.4). The vote for the Center has lost its specificity as a balancing force between two votes that are very sharply divided on the territorial level, and its profile has become virtually identical with the vote for the Right.[33] We note here the advantage in having data at the level of the 36,000 municipalities, which alone allows us to realize the very great differences in electoral behavior that existed within the departments (see, for example, map 9.1 for an illustration in the case of the legislative elections of 1889) and to study in detail the transformations of the social and territorial structure of the vote.

32. We remind the reader astonished to see us pass over twenty years of legislative elections that the elections organized during the Second Empire left very little room for unofficial candidacies and so we have chosen not to study them. See chapter 5.
33. See unehistoireduconflitpolitique.fr, figures D3.1a–D3.1n, for the profiles vote by vote.

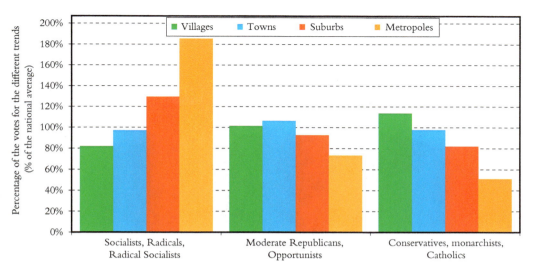

FIGURE 9.3. The legislative elections of 1871–1889 in the territories

In the legislative elections of 1871–1889, Socialist, Radical, and Radical-Socialist candidates (Left bloc) received twice as many votes in the metropoles as they did in villages, whereas the conservatives (Right bloc) received twice as many votes in villages. The Moderate and Opportunistic Republicans (Center bloc) had a more balanced profile than the other two blocs, even as they moved closer to the conservatives.

Sources and series: unehistoireduconflitpolitique.fr

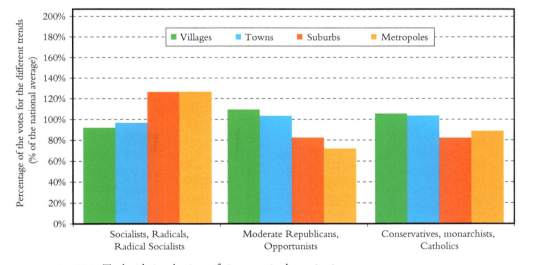

FIGURE 9.4. The legislative elections of 1893–1910 in the territories

In the legislative elections of 1893–1910, the Socialist, Radical, and Radical-Socialist candidates (Left bloc) achieved a result higher in the metropoles than in the villages, whereas the conservatives (Right bloc) had the inverse result. However, the disparities were for the most part more limited than in 1848–1849 and 1871–1899, and the Moderate and Opportunistic Republicans (Center bloc) moved much closer to the conservatives.

Sources and series: unehistoireduconflitpolitique.fr

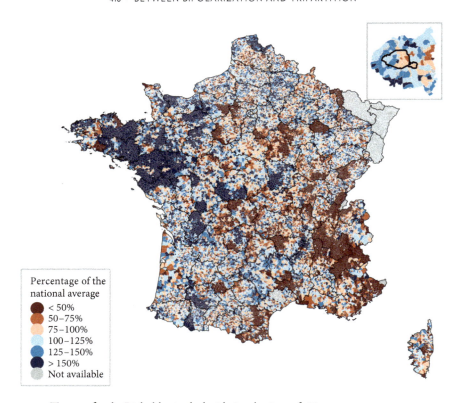

MAP 9.1. The vote for the Right bloc in the legislative elections of 1889
The map represents, for each municipality, the proportion of votes won by the Right bloc as ratio of the national average. Note the very large variations between departments and within departments.
Sources and series: unehistoireduconflitpolitique.fr

How should we account for this very clear process of rapprochement between the territorial structures of the different electorates? The question is important, because it involves the gradual passage from an electoral system based on a clear rural-urban cleavage to a system increasingly based on a social cleavage within both the rural world and the urban world, thus paving the way for a political conflict centered on the social question and the Left-Right bipartition that was to structure the political landscape more and more clearly over the course of the twentieth century. In practice, this rapprochement of the territorial structures of the electorates signifies in particular that the Left bloc was winning votes in villages and towns, especially in territories characterized by a greater proportion of workers and a great concentration of property ownership.[34] Conversely, the Right bloc gradually advanced in the metropoles and suburbs, in particular in the middle classes, in connection with its ideological repositioning on socioeconomic questions as well as on the problem of nationalism (to which we will return).

Generally, the most convincing explanation for the rapprochement of the territorial structures of the different electorates, and in particular between rural and urban working classes within the Left bloc, seems to us to reside in the transformations of the discourses and programs represented by the different political trends, precisely with a view to allowing convergences. At the beginning of the Third Republic, the rural-urban cleavage is extremely great; it is of the same order as it was in 1848–1849, and even greater in the case of certain elections.[35] The uprising and then the annihilation of the Paris Commune could only increase the mutual incomprehension between the metropoles and the villages, which had difficulty identifying with the demands made by the industrial workers in the capital, which were, in fact, not really intended for them. At the beginning of the 1870s, the advanced Republicans and the radical Republicans, as the most determined of the Republicans were called, also kept their distance from socialist ideas, and ultimately proposed a program that was not very ambitious on the socioeconomic level. This was notably the case with the "Belleville program" formulated in 1869 by the advanced Republican Gambetta, which is centered on the right to vote, public freedoms, and the separation of the church and state, and says nothing about the question of the property system, which was nonetheless central to the debates in 1848–1849 in both the rural world and the urban world.[36] To be sure, the program refers to the creation of a tax on income and the necessity of a major fiscal reform, like all the projects issuing from the Left bloc in the nineteenth century (and later on), but without making excessive commitments to a specific proposal, except concerning the suppression of excise duties, which was good news for urban taxpayers but could only arouse mistrust in the countryside.[37] In 1873–1875,

---

34. See chapter 8, figures 8.11–8.13.

35. See chapter 8, figures 8.4–8.10.

36. See A. Dontenwille-Gerbaud, "Le 'programme de Belleville,'" in *Les programmes politiques. Genèses et usages,* ed. K. Fertikh, M. Hauchecorne, and N. Bué (Presses Universitaires de Rennes, 2016).

37. The *octrois* were indirect taxes paid on goods and merchandise on entering certain large cities, such as Paris. Their suppression was supposed to be financed in a way that is not clarified by the program in question, whence the risk that the burden might be shifted to the land tax or the rural world in one way or another.

when Gambetta's Union républicaine approved the new compromise regarding the republican institutions that were emerging, the Socialist Louis Blanc bitterly accused it of having allowed a very small democratic chamber (the Senate) a veto right over all the legislation to come, with the risk that in many cases this would slow the adoption of essential social and fiscal reforms (which did in fact happen).[38]

Starting in the 1880s and 1890s, the programs of the Radicals (who presented themselves, with increasing frequency, as "Radical Socialists" even before the official creation of the Republican, Radical, and Radical-Socialist Party in 1901), became increasingly ambitious in their socioeconomic proposals, both to distinguish themselves from the moderates and Moderate Republicans on their right and to respond to the competition of the Socialists on their left. In comparison to mainstream Socialists (who focused their attention on industrial workers), the Radical-Socialists defined themselves as advocates of "social reform with respect to private property" and as the primary defenders of the small property owners in villages and towns, whether they were small farmers or small, self-employed, non-agricultural workers (merchants and artisans). The limitations of this program became clear during the interwar period, when the Radicals often served as a brake on the Socialists' and Communists' desire for reform, but for the time being, it showed that it was capable of drawing the rural world toward the Left.

Traumatized by the fiscal crisis of 1848 and the experience of the forty-five centimes, which had allowed the Right to appropriate the vote of the villages and towns, independent Radicals and other advanced Republicans in particular helped put in place major reductions in the land tax that benefited small rural property owners, first in 1881, then again in 1890 and 1897.[39] They were also and especially to join actively in the battle over the progressive tax. On this terrain, the progress had been nil in 1848–1849 and very limited in the 1870s. A timid "income tax on securities" was introduced in 1872 to tax interest, dividends, and other financial income that was taxed little or not at all under the system of direct taxation during the Revolution, which was based mainly on land and real estate wealth. But the principle of a general tax on income had once again been rejected by a coalition of moderate and conservative Republicans, for whom the question of progressivity

38. See chapter 1 and L. Blanc, *Histoire de la constitution du 25 février 1875* (Charpentier, 1882).

39. The land tax remained officially a proportional tax, but with reductions for the smallest tax liabilities that made it similar in certain respects to a progressive tax for the most modest property owners. On these reforms, see F. Goguel, *Le rôle financier du Sénat français. Essai d'histoire parlementaire* (Sirey, 1937), 12–30; B. Lignereux, *Les impôts sur le patrimoine de 1789 à nos jours* (LGDJ, 2022), 49–51.

and its possible excesses continued to be a bugaboo. The Radicals did not give up, and finally they succeeded in getting the principle of the progressivity of the inheritance tax adopted by the Chamber of Deputies in 1895, and then by the Senate in 1901, thanks to the patient work of electoral conquest in the countryside that allowed them to gradually attain a central place in the upper assembly. Specifically, in the framework of the law of 25 February 1901, the rate of taxation was limited to 1 percent for small legacies and gradually rose to 2.5 percent for the largest ones.

A breach had been opened that led to major increases in the following years and to rates of tens of percentage points on large inheritances during the interwar period, and to top it all off, a large deconcentration of patrimony and economic power over the long term.[40] This new philosophy of progressive taxation was inspired in particular by "solidarism," a Radical-Socialist doctrine par excellence advocated especially by Léon Bourgeois (the Radical president of the Council in 1895–1896) and Émile Durkheim (the founder of the French school of sociology, then in full development), according to which the creation of all wealth depends on the division of social labor and knowledge accumulated since the beginnings of humanity, for which no living person could claim to be responsible or to own.[41] For Jean Jaurès, one of the Socialist allies of the Radicals and the author of the contemporary *Histoire socialiste de la France contemporaine depuis 1789,* this was the beginning of a profound transformation of the property system that truly began with the law of 25 February 1901 that instituted the progressivity of the inheritance tax.[42]

The New Welfare State, the Exit from Tripartition, and the March toward Bipartition

More generally, it was during this period, in the years 1890–1910, that the first stages of what was to become the welfare state were gradually put in place in the

40. See T. Piketty, *Les hauts revenus en France au 20e siècle* (Grasset, 2001), 766–771.
41. On this "solidarist" conception of property considered as social property and the role played by these ideas in justifying progressive taxation of incomes and successions, see R. Castel, *Les métamorphoses de la question sociale. Une chronique du salariat* (Fayard, 1995), 444–449. We find the same emphasis on progressive taxation in the *Manuel républicain de l'homme et du citoyen* published in 1848 by Charles Renouvier, a philosopher who greatly influenced the Democratic Socialists of the time.
42. See chapter 1. In his "bilan social du 19e siècle" concluding the work published in 1908, Jaurès also stressed that Marx could not have anticipated the successes of electoral democracy, and that it was henceforth within that framework that the march toward socialist had to be envisaged.

twentieth century, with an eventual exponential growth of fiscal progressivity and public expenditures in matters of healthcare, education, and social transfers of a magnitude far greater than anything that could have been imagined in the time of the "immoral" proposals made by the Democratic Socialists and other Montagnards in 1848–1849. The adoption by the Radical-Socialists and the Socialists of the law of 6 April 1910 on "workers' and peasants' retirement pensions" thus marked the establishment of an initial general retirement system for the whole of the population. This was a major symbolic step, incarnating in its title the rapprochement of the urban and rural working classes. The rate of the inheritance tax applicable to the largest transmissions of wealth, which had already been raised from 2.5 percent to 5 percent in 1902, rose to 6.5 percent in 1910 to help finance the new retirement system. Thus it was the largest wealth holders (whether rural or urban) who contributed to the financing of welfare measures benefiting the workers of the rural and urban worlds. In conformity with the objectives of the Democratic Socialists of 1848, deputies symbolically left the territorial conflict to join in the class conflict (independent of the territory). The principle of the progressive income tax was also adopted by the deputies in 1895–1896, but the Senate did not lift its veto until 1914. In comparison with the debates of 1848–1849, an essential difference was that the parliamentary discussions now took place over time, which made it possible to pile up attempts, question opinions, win new seats, amend proposals, and finally, get them adopted.

In addition to measures of social and fiscal justice, the period 1890–1910 was also characterized by the development of public services and infrastructures that could certainly seem rudimentary from today's point of view—and that remained extremely inegalitarian in their territorial distribution, particularly in matters of roads, railroads, and educational and healthcare equipment—but which nonetheless represented a considerable transformation for the period. The establishment throughout the territory of free municipal public schools, financed in large measure by the state budget starting in the period 1880–1910, no doubt constituted the most powerful and most visible symbol of these new, universal public services benefiting villages and towns as much as the suburbs and metropoles. The Radicals also played a prominent role in the development of a more voluntarist approach to transportation infrastructure. Thus, between 1900 and 1910 they succeeded in approving the state's purchase of the Chemins de fer de l'Ouest, whose infamous malfunctioning was all the more scandalous because its private operator had received large guarantees from the state that increased his profits. The measure was less ambitious than the Socialists had hoped—they wanted nationalization over the whole territory, and less generous indemnities—but it paved the way for a public rail service.[43] With the development of public services, fiscal redistribution, and a new role for the state in the economy, the heart of political conflict shifted to these subjects and to the social welfare question, thus opening the way to moving beyond the rural-urban cleavage and to the rise of the Left-Right bipartition.

Although the Radical-Socialists were the most active political force in the Left bloc seeking to draw to the Left the working-class voters of the rural world,[44] we must not neglect the role played by the Socialists before 1914, and then by the Communists starting in the 1920s. Despite strong distrust of them, in some territories the Socialists and Communists succeeded in drawing support not only from the salaried classes of the rural world, but also from a fraction of the small farmers and other self-employed workers, whom they supported by developing local infrastructures and agricultural cooperatives adapted to their needs. Far from the official Marxist canons, which opposed individual property, starting in the late nineteenth century and the early twentieth, socialism and communism were often to develop at the municipal and departmental levels pragmatic and original forms of collective action.[45]

In chapter 10 we will come back to another factor capable of explaining the electoral rapprochement between the rural and the urban worlds at the end of the nineteenth century and the beginning of the twentieth—namely, the gradual decline in the proportion of farmers and self-employed workers in the rural world and the concomitant increase in the proportion of salaried workers (especially in industry and food processing). In fact, the increasing salarization of the rural world was able to facilitate the penetration of the discourses and programs of the socialistic trends, which were initially conceived for urban salaried workers and historically less attractive for small independent land owners.[46] To sum up, we will see that this structural evolution did in fact play a major role over a long period in reducing the cleavages between the rural and urban worlds and unifying the country around a single status of workers, but this alone was not great enough quantitatively to account for the changes in electoral structures observed over a

---

43. The measure was adopted by the deputies in 1900 and then blocked for several years by the Senate, which finally yielded in 1908. See Goguel, *Le rôle financier du Sénat français,* 104–126.

44. See chapter 8, figure 8.9 and unehistoireduconflitpolitique.fr, figures D1.1fa–D1.1fc.

45. See L. Boswell, *Le communisme rural en France. Le Limousin et la Dordogne de 1920 à 1939* (Pulim, 2006). These experiments at the beginning of the twentieth century often continued actions developed in 1848–1850 in the contexts of Democratic Socialist mobilizations. See A. Corbin, *Archaïsme et modernité en Limousin au 19e siècle. La naissance d'une tradition de gauche, 1845–1880* (Presses Universitaires de Limoges, 1975).

46. On the long-term evolution of the structure of employment and the active population by sector of activity, see chapter 2, figure 2.18.

few decades between 1880 and 1910, which seem to be connected more with inflections of the discourses and strategies of the various political trends. It was primarily by transforming their programs and political practices that the Radical-Socialists and the Socialists managed, at the end of the nineteenth century and the beginning of the twentieth, to bring together the rural and urban working classes and to start to leave tripartition behind, and not by relying on exogenous economic changes. Everything suggests that an identical conclusion could also be applied in this early twenty-first century: above all, it is by developing a program of redistribution as attractive to the working classes of the towns and villages as to those of the urban world that left-wing political trends could bring together the corresponding electorates and initiate an exit from tripartition and a return to the Left-Right bipolarization.

The Elites' Vote, from *Républicains opportunistes* to *La République en marche*

Let us now turn to the question of the elites for the different blocs. By construction, the numerical weight of the dominant classes is less than that of the average working classes, rural and urban, to which we have just referred. However, studying the elites' vote for the different blocs is very instructive, both because the influence of the dominant classes on political life can naturally go far beyond their strict demographic weight, particularly because of their role in the financing of medias, political parties, and electoral campaigns, and because the elites' vote provides us with valuable information on the way in which the different political blocs involved are perceived.

First, let us recall that the data at our disposal does not allow us to observe the vote directly, at the individual level. Over the long term, we observe the structure of votes only at the municipal level. Taking into account that France has 36,000 municipalities, that still enables us to analyze political behaviors in a very granular way in very specific territories.[47] To study the elites' vote, we will concentrate on the richest 1 percent of the country's municipalities, or more precisely, the 1 percent of the population living in the richest municipalities, in order to compare a con-

---

47. In addition, let us note that the data provided by surveys suffers from many limitations, particularly because of the small size of the sample, which is especially problematic for observing the political preferences of the richest 1 percent. To improve our understanding of their behaviors, municipal data are therefore extremely valuable. The other method, which is irreplaceable, consists in making use of field surveys and conducting interviews. See, for example, K. Geay, *Enquête sur les bourgeois. Aux marges des beaux quartiers* (Fayard, 2019).

stant fraction of the voters over time.[48] If the municipalities were all the same size, we would be dealing with the richest 360 municipalities. In practice, the wealthiest municipalities in the country also tend to be the largest (for example, since the middle of the nineteenth century we almost always find Paris's 7th, 8th, and 16th arrondissements in this group, along with well-known, very wealthy municipalities like Neuilly-sur-Seine), so the exact number of the municipalities is less than 360: it varies over time and is generally between 30 and 140 municipalities, usually about 100.[49] We have also reproduced all the results presented here, always focusing on the richest 100 or 200 or 300 municipalities (independent of their size), and the conclusions are identical. Moreover, we will focus on the presentation of the results obtained by classifying the municipalities in relation to their level of income per inhabitant, but we must add that the conclusions are similar if we choose to use other criteria, such as the real estate capital (total value of housing) per inhabitant (that is, the value of housing).[50] We will begin by presenting the estimates for the set of the richest 1 percent of the municipalities, and then we will examine in more detail the case of the capital's better-off neighborhoods, which are on the whole very representative of rich municipalities in general.

Let us also remember that the richest 1 percent of the municipalities are always much richer than the average. Thus, in 2002, the average income reached about 100,000 euros a year per inhabitant (including children) in the richest 1 percent of the municipalities, as opposed to scarcely 19,000 euros on average in the country as a whole and about 7,000 to 8,000 euros in the poorest 1 percent of the municipalities. Considering that there are disparities within municipalities (everyone is not rich in the former, and everyone is not poor in the latter), these are truly considerable gaps. As for the average value of housing, it comes close to 1 million euros in the richest 1 percent of municipalities, as opposed to 220,000 euros on average in the country, and barely 50,000 to 60,000 euros in the poorest 1 percent of the municipalities. In both cases, the gaps separating the richest 1 percent of the

48. As we did earlier, we will occasionally refer to the "the richest 1 percent of the municipalities" to simplify the exposition, but to avoid distorting temporal comparisons, the exact definition takes into account the sizes of the municipalities and designates in reality the 1 percent of the population living in the richest municipalities.

49. The exact number is on the order of 100–140 in the nineteenth century and at the beginning of the twenty-first, and it sinks to around 20–30 in the middle of the twentieth century, specifically because of the change in the capital's demographic weight.

50. For a detailed presentation of all the results obtained, see unehistoireduconflitpolitique.fr, figures D1.1ca–D1.1ci and appendix D1.

municipalities from the average and from the rest of the country were still greater in the nineteenth century and at the beginning of the twentieth century than they are at the beginning of the twenty-first.[51] Let us also add that the inequalities within rich municipalities (which have always had a tendency to be greater, as a rule, than in the rest of the country) were also even more marked at the time than they are today. This was especially the case in Paris, where in the nineteenth century and at the beginning of the twentieth an astronomical share of the country's wealth was concentrated, but which also included many very poor households living in lamentable conditions, sometimes in rich arrondissements.[52] Then the real estate operations (the destruction of working-class housing, the expulsion of poor families) and the rise in the price of housing led in the course of the twentieth century and until the beginning of the twenty-first to a relative social homogenization of the richest municipalities in comparison to earlier periods. To sum up, there were relatively few poor households in the richest municipalities at the beginning of the 2020s, whereas such a situation was more common in the nineteenth century and at the beginning of the twentieth.[53]

---

51. See chapter 2, figures 2.11–2.12 and maps 2.5–2.6.
52. See chapter 1 and T. Piketty, G. Postel-Vinay, and J. L. Rosenthal, "Wealth Concentration in a Developing Economy: Paris and France, 1807–1994," *American Economic Review,* 2006. In 1900–1910, Paris had 25 percent of the total patrimonies and inheritances of the country, and only 5 percent of its population, or an average wealth per inhabitant about five times higher than the national average. This ratio was approximately 3.0–3.5 at the beginning of the nineteenth century and 4.0–4.5 in the middle of the century. At the same time, in the nineteenth century and until the beginning of the twentieth, about 70 percent of the population of Paris died without having any patrimony to hand on (except for a few meager personal effects not registered in the successoral archives), as opposed to 40–50 percent in the rest of the country. In other words, Paris was both much richer and much more inegalitarian than the rest of the country.
53. The data available since 2000 on the redistributions of income within municipalities show that the average intramunicipal inequality increased only slightly with the level of average income (and with the size of the municipality). To put it another way, the municipalities whose average incomes were the highest are characterized, in a first approximation, by higher levels of income. These data regarding intramunicipal inequalities of income are unfortunately not available over the long term, but successoral sources indicate unambiguously a considerable decrease in intramunicipal inequalities over the long term. See unehistoireduconflitpolitique.fr, appendix B. On the worsening of the mutual spatial exclusion of the most socially segregated neighborhoods, see, for example, A. Fleury, T. Saint-Julien, J.-C. François, A. Ribardière, and H. Mathian, "Les inégalités socio-spatiales progressent-elles en Île-de-France?, *Métropolitiques.eu,* 2012. The question of residential segregation has been a central subject of urban sociology for several decades, and many quantitative studies have been conducted in France on spatial inequalities. See, for example, the research of Nicole Tabard, or that of Edmond Préteceille.

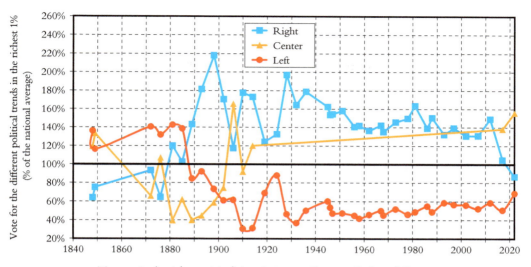

FIGURE 9.5. The vote in the rich municipalities, 1848–2022: Between Right and Center

Starting in the 1880s, the Right bloc almost always achieved better results than its national average in the richest 1% of the municipalities, except when the vote for the Center was dominant in these municipalities (as in 1906 and 2017–2022). Starting in the 1890s, the Left bloc systematically achieved a result lower than its national average in these municipalities. Note: The result obtained by the Center bloc was low and erratic during the period of bipartition and it has not been indicated for the 1919–2012 elections (for lack of representative candidates).

Sources and series: unehistoireduconflitpolitique.fr

Let us come to the results obtained. Two main conclusions emerge very clearly. First, the vote for the Left bloc (as it was defined above, thus including the Left and the Center-Left) within the richest 1 percent of the municipalities was, starting in the 1890s, systematically and massively weaker than the average result of the Left bloc at the national level. On the other hand, the Right bloc almost always achieved results far higher than its national average in the 1 percent of the richest municipalities, though with several exceptions in the period 1848–1910, and especially in 2017–2022, when the vote for the Center bloc established itself as the vote the most closely associated with the wealthiest municipalities (see figure 9.5). To sum up, the richest municipalities and the elites that reside in them rarely vote for the Left, but they may also choose to move rather rapidly from the Right to the Center if need be. From this point of view, the comparison between the situation seen during the first period of tripartition between 1848 and 1910 and the currently prevailing situation seems particularly pertinent. The central-liberal bloc appears to be an escape vote for elites in periods of tripartition, especially in the recent period, still more clearly than at the time of the first tripartition.

The Left and Redistribution: The Demonstration by the Elites

Before pursuing this comparison any further, several points are worth clarifying regarding these results. First, the fact that for more than a century, the vote for the Left bloc has been systematically and massively smaller in the richest 1 percent of the municipalities than in the rest of the country, and that this result is found in all the legislative elections from the 1890s to the 2020s, without exception, is an extremely striking result. In a certain way, it can be said that it is almost a definition of the Left, not as an abstract idea but as it has been incarnated historically and concretely in the electoral process. The Left has always been the bearer of a program for transforming the social order and for redistributing wealth and economic and political power, all topped off by a challenge to the position of the dominant classes, first the aristocratic and monarchical elites at the end of the eighteenth century and during the nineteenth, and then all the property-owning and capitalist elites, as socialist and communist trends took an increasingly prominent place in the Left bloc over the course of the nineteenth and twentieth centuries. Under these conditions it was logical that the richest municipalities, which thus collected the largest concentrations of the different dominant classes, would be less seduced by the Left than the rest of the country. All the interest of the data we have assembled is precisely that it allows us to test rigorously, for the first time, the extent to which this logic is found in the reality of electoral behaviors, and especially how this reality varies depending on the periods and the overall structure of political and electoral conflict.

In this case, it is interesting to note that the situation is different during the legislative elections held from 1848 to the 1880s, in the course of which the Left bloc achieved, on the contrary, a better result than its national average in the richest municipalities (see figure 9.5). Several factors may help explain this result. The most convincing and most plausible one is that this strong vote for the Left emanated mainly from the poorest populations (particularly worker-voters) living in the richest municipalities; these populations were in fact relatively larger in the rich municipalities of this period than during later periods (we have stressed above the decrease in intramunicipal inequalities over the long term). The second explanation is that during the period 1848–1890, the political trends that we have classified as Left (and particularly Center-Left) are sometimes characterized by programs that are centered on the question of the republican regime and relatively unambitious with regard to socioeconomic redistribution, which could allow them to attract votes in the richest municipalities (and not solely among the poorest voters there). Consider, for example, the "advanced Republicans" close to Léon Gambetta

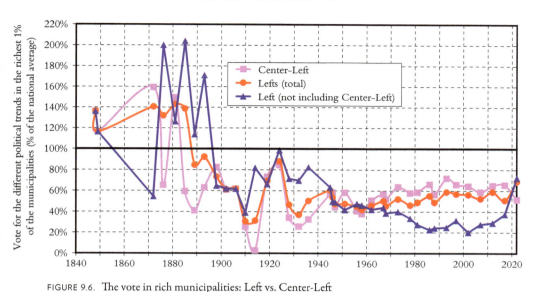

FIGURE 9.6. The vote in rich municipalities: Left vs. Center-Left

The Left bloc has systematically received a result lower than its national average in the richest 1% municipalities; up to the 1930s, the Left of the Left generally received a better result in these municipalities than the Center-Left, whereas the inverse has been true since 1945.

Sources and series: unehistoireduconflitpolitique.fr

and the Union républicaine at the end of the 1870s and in the early 1880s (which we have classified as Center-Left), as opposed to the Moderate and Opportunist Republicans close to Jules Ferry (classified as Center). The former were certainly further left than the latter regarding the socioeconomic stakes involved (particularly on the question of the income tax, which was supported by the former and rejected by the latter), but the difference was not always significant.

It is probable that these two complementary explanations were at work, with a relative importance that varied depending on the territories. The sources we have gathered together suggest, however, that the former played a more substantial role than the latter. We see, in fact, that it was the trends furthest to the left (in particular the Socialist candidates, workers, and Radicals), and not the Center-Left trends, who in the 1870s and 1880s obtained their best results in the richest 1 percent of the municipalities (see figure 9.6). If we examine the data in greater detail, we find in addition that the rich municipalities where the Left racked up its best results were also those that had the largest proportion of workers (relative to other rich municipalities), which also pleads for the first explanation.[54]

---

54. See unehistoireduconflitpolitique.fr, figures D1.1ca–D1.1ci and appendix D1.

Starting in the 1890s, the vote for the Left bloc became systematically and massively smaller in the richest 1 percent of the municipalities than it was on average
at the national level. This can be explained in part by the fact that the working
classes were gradually driven out of the wealthiest municipalities and arrondissements, as well as by the hardening of the social question and the programs for
redistributions borne by left-wing trends and parties, which helped to further distance the elites of the rich municipalities from this type of vote. In the 1870s or
1880s a bourgeois living in the 16th arrondissement might be tempted to vote for
an advanced Republican or a Radical, but it was much more rarely that he allowed
himself to be seduced by a Socialist or a Communist in the 1910s or 1920s. Thus
while the Radical Charles-Félix Frégault almost won an election in 1889 against
the monarchist Denys Cochin and the Boulangist Gabriel Terrail ("Mermeix") and
in 1893 was successfully elected in the 7th arrondissement of Paris over the reac-
tionary Paul Lerolle, it was conservative and nationalist candidates who won by a
landslide in the two districts of this same arrondissement in 1906—and moreover,
in the first round, Socialist candidates received at best a few hundred votes.

On average, from the 1890s to the 2020s, the Left vote in the richest 1 percent
of the municipalities was usually around 50–60 percent of the average result of
the Left on the national level (see figure 9.5). To sum up, the richest 1 percent
of the municipalities have been voting since the 1890s approximately twice less
often for the Left than the average of the country, and this gap has been relatively
stable, on first inspection, for more than a century. It will also be noted that in the
period 1890–1940, the vote for the Left of the Left was higher in rich municipalities (relative to its national average) than the vote for the Center-Left. The two
votes balanced each other from 1945 to 1960, and then the inverse configuration
was established. Since the 1960s and the 1970s, it has been the vote for the Left of
the Left (essentially, the Communist vote) that is particularly absent from the
richest municipalities (barely 20–30 percent of its national level from the 1980s
to the 2020s), whereas the vote for the Center-Left (mainly the Socialist vote) is
situated at levels that are clearly more significant, around 60–70 percent of its national level. All these cases involve results very inferior to their national results,
but the turnaround over the long term is particularly striking (see figure 9.6).[55]
The most convincing interpretation of this long-term transformation is here again

---

55. In 2022, the quasi-totality of the Left was brought together in NUPES (which we have classified as the Left of the Left rather than as Center-Left), such that the distinction between the
two components really no longer has any meaning.

the process of the social homogenization of the richest municipalities and the gradual exclusion of the working classes, from the nineteenth century to the beginning of the twenty-first.[56]

Is Property Better Protected by the Moderate Republicans or by the Right?

We come now to the choice between the Right and the Center in the rich municipalities between 1848 and 1910. During the elections of 1848–1849, the richest 1 percent of the municipalities voted more heavily for the Moderate Republicans than for the conservatives and monarchists, especially in Paris.[57] Considering the economic and financial policies conducted by the Moderate Republicans at that time under the direction of Garnier-Pagès, Arago, and Cavaignac, which were on the whole very favorable to the interests of property owners—and especially the wealthy financial bourgeoisie—this vote seems very logical. It must also be emphasized that that the borderline between the Center and the Right—that is, between the Moderate Republicans and the constitutional Republicans on the one hand, and the conservatives of the Party of Order on the other—was in practice rather porous, both on the electoral lists presented to the voters and in terms of the basic positions on economic and financial questions. When Thiers opposed Proudhon on the income tax in 1848, he did so as the head of the Party of Order, but he spoke at the same time in the name of all the Moderate Republicans who in any case wanted nothing to do with the socialist adventure and fiscal progressivity.

The same configuration is found in the 1870s, when the Moderate and Opportunistic Republicans once gain came in ahead of the conservative and monarchist Right in the richest municipalities (see figure 9.5), but with rather porous borderlines between the two groups. Moreover, it was precisely at this point that some

---

56. Note that the studies carried out on the basis of occupations also indicate a considerable increase in residential segregation from 1990 to 2015 (particularly in the Paris region). See H. Botton, P. Y. Cusset, C. Dherbécourt, and A. George, "Quelle évolution de la ségrégation résidentielle en France?," *France Stratégie*, 2020.

57. In Paris's 6th arrondissement (as it was in 1849), for example, during the legislative elections of May 1849 the Democratic Socialist Jean-Baptiste Boichot won with 12,246 votes, followed closely by Félix Pyat, Théodore Bac, and Victor Considérant (who were also Montagnards and each won more than 10,000 votes), ahead of Moderates such as Cavaignac and Jules Dufaure (about 9,000 votes), and especially far ahead of the representatives of the Party of Order (2,675 votes for General Piat, 3,186 for Louis-Lucien Bonaparte, and just barely 935 for General Adrien Aimé Fleury de Bar et al.).

of the former monarchists—especially within the Orléanists, who were traditionally closer to the urban and financial elites than the Legitimists, who were closer
to the landowners and rural elites—decided to go over to the Republican camp.
,One of them was Thiers, who had been a pillar among the Orléanist ministers in
the 1830s and 1840s, when he fiercely opposed the extension of the right to vote,
then was the head of the Party of Order in 1848–1849; in the 1870s he caused part
of the (Orléanist) Center-Right to move toward the (republican) Center-Left,
which was no doubt the most decisive stage in the constitution of a central bloc
relatively unified around the Moderates and Moderate and Opportunistic Republicans. The reasoning of the former Orléanists like Thiers and Broglie was perfectly
clear and explicit.[58] Considering the difficulties connected with a monarchical
restoration—because of the conflicts between rival dynasties and also because a
restoration would risk ultimately arousing new revolutions—it appeared more
promising and efficacious to combine the interests of social progressives with those
of property owners within a republican regime, but on the condition that the
latter include a structurally conservative chamber (the Senate) that had the right
to veto any legislation, which in fact slowed by several decades a number of crucial fiscal and social reforms. The discussions at the time were perfectly transparent on this point and on the role conferred on the upper assembly to restrain
as much as possible the movement in favor of redistribution. That is how the central bloc was constituted in the course of the first tripartition: as an alliance of the
different elites to preserve the social order in a republican framework, in a context
in which the prospect of a return to the monarchical order, whether censitary or
imperial, faded permanently into the distance and appeared less and less realistic.

However, all the old monarchists and conservatives of the Party of Order
did not show the same plasticity and pragmatism as Thiers did. Many of them accused the Moderate and Opportunistic Republicans of being hostile to Catholicism and religious schools. Some were also wary of the Republicans' excessive
tolerance of socialist or radical trends situated on their left, and they thought that
the conservative or moderate vote would provide better guarantees against any
excesses. Others, probably less and less numerous, continued to think that the
monarchical and dynastic principle was fundamentally superior to the elective
principle, in particular for preserving national unity and the social order, as well
as preventing the country from sinking into a hypertrophy of egos, an excessive

---

58. On this period, see, for example, O. Rudelle, *La République absolue. 1870–1889* (Publications
de la Sorbonne, 1982), 12–164.

quest for profit, and generalized competition.[59] *L'Union,* a conservative newspaper opposed to the republican regime, published in its issue of 10 February 1871—two days after the elections—an article by one of its most famous journalists, Jean-Joseph François Poujoulat (who was moreover twice elected deputy under the Second Republic), who wrote, "In France, the Republic is synonymous with revolution; that is what prevents it from being a government, why in our country it produces nothing but interregnums." Pierre-Sébastien Laurentie concurred with him on 14 February: "There can now be no possible doubt for any sensible man: France is monarchical, it wants to be monarchical; its nature, its thoughts, its instincts, its needs, everything incessantly leads it back to monarchy; experience has just testified once again that without monarchy, for France everything is fiction, violence, distress, impotence." If we believe the twenty-eighth edition of the *Annuaire de la Noblesse de France* published in 1872, there were no less than 225 noble deputies elected to the National Assembly (a third of the seats) in the legislative elections of 1871—elections that appear in retrospect to be the first of the Third Republic, though they were held at a time when it was not yet known whether the new regime, having issued from the military defeat by the Prussian armies, was going to go for a republican form or for another monarchical restoration. The *Annuaire*'s writer was enthusiastic in the face of what he saw as "the heartfelt cry of the nation, its spontaneous outburst: into whose arms could [the nation] throw itself with more confidence and sympathy than those of the nobility, whose offspring, the worthy heirs to the bravery and virtues of their ancestors, have so nobly shed their blood at Reichshoffen and Sedan? Also, although all the prominent figures who rallied to the Empire had retired from the battle, never, for more than forty years, has the elective Chamber been seen to offer such a brilliant collection of illustrious names of the aristocracy."[60] Yet, the proportion

---

59. The anthropologist Georges Dumézil, who was close to monarchist trends and Action française in the 1920s, summed up the argument this way in interviews conducted in 1986: "The principle not only monarchical, but dynastic, which shelters the state's highest position from caprices and ambitions seemed to me always preferable to generalized election in which we have been living since Danton and Bonaparte." See D. Eribon, *Faut-il brûler Dumézil? Mythologie, science et politique* (Flammarion, 1992), 67.

60. The *Annuaire* even goes so far as to count among the noble deputies no less than 9 princes or dukes, 31 marquis, 49 counts, 19 viscounts, 19 barons, and 80 elected members "provided only with *la particule,*" explaining that "we cannot completely guarantee the exactitude of this classification, even though it was drawn up, so far as possible, on the basis of authentic documents. A few deputies neglect or refuse to take up their titles, while on the contrary others take ones which are not even courtesy titles and to which they have no right." See *Annuaire de la noblesse de France,* 1872, 419–424.

of the noble deputies was to fall to less than 10 percent of the seats in 1914 and less than 5 percent during the interwar period.[61] The *Annuaire* itself was published for the last time in 1938.[62]

In practice, the most effective criticism of the Moderate Republicans, and the least commonly formulated on the right and on the left, no doubt concerns their wheeling and dealing and "opportunism." It is, moreover, to a conservative, the Marquis de Castellane, a deputy from Cantal and a member of the Union des droites (a parliamentary group that included, starting in 1876, the Legitimist and Orléanist monarchists, as well as some of the Bonapartists), to whom we owe one of the first uses of the term "opportunism," to describe the Moderate Republicans Jules Ferry and Jules Grévy, and in this case, it was a negative and pejorative use.[63] The Moderate Republicans sometimes tried to use the term positively, referring to a political strategy seeking to temporize and seize "opportunities" to move their program forward whenever they appeared (in particular, on educational and religious questions), in contrast to the Radicals, who adopted a maximalist posture that seemed to the Moderates excessively hasty. But the qualifier "Opportunist" remained a pejorative marker designating the central bloc's absence of principles— except that of remaining in power. Among the scandals that marred the Moderate and Opportunistic Republicans' image was, of course, the Panama affair, which bankrupted hundreds of millions of savers in the 1880s and 1890s and tarnished several of the Moderate Republicans' leaders (especially Charles de Freycinet and the family of the president of the Republic, Jules Grévy), and also of the scandal that exploded in 1887 with the revelations regarding the trafficking organized from the Elysée Palace by Daniel Wilson (Jules Grévy's son-in-law) in order to

---

61. See J. Bécarud, "Noblesse et représentation parlementaire: Les députés nobles de 1871 à 1968," *Revue française de science politique,* 1973.

62. An interesting indicator illustrating the long process of the rapprochement of the old and new elites is provided by the study of proper names with particules. Between 1890 and 1910, these names are twenty to thirty times more present among students at Sciences Po and the École polytechnique than their share of the general population (about 0.5 percent), whereas they are "only" twice as present among students at the École normale supérieure Ulm. Between 1980 and 2000, names with particules are about five times more present than their share in the population (still around 0.5 percent) in all these schools, a and still more than ten times more present in the most eminent business schools. See S. Benveniste, "Les grandes écoles au 20e siècle, le champ des élites françaises: Reproduction sociale, dynasties, réseaux" (PhD diss., Aix-Marseille Université, 2021), 69–71.

63. In a speech given in the Chamber, the Marquis of Castellane refers to "this politics that M. Jules Ferry has come to advocate at this rostrum, which he has described as a politics of results, and which I have heard called by another name that seems to me truer, the politics of opportunism." J. O. 13 July 1876, page 5090.

ensure businessmen's participation in his enterprises. The fall of Jules Ferry during the Tonkin scandal in 1885 is also emblematic of the accusations of wheeling and dealing formulated by both the Left and the Right (which voted together to cut off funds for the expeditionary force) with regard to the colonial projects of the Moderate Republicans. The latter were found guilty of having financed a distant and risky expedition in Indochina with the sole objective of providing new investment opportunities for French capital owners, thus responding to the pressures of business milieus and liberal economists who were enthusiastic supporters of colonialism, such as Leroy-Beaulieu.[64] Having just taken power, the new parliamentary elite was thus denounced as venal and corrupt, which between 1885 and 1889 fed the Boulangist movement, which defended a revision of the constitutional laws of 1875[65] in order to establish a strong executive power, a prospect that pleased some of the conservatives in the upper-crust quarters and former monarchists and Bonapartists,[66] without really leading to a concrete, mobilizing proposal for the Right.

From One Tripartition to the Next: The Question of the Durability of the Center

In the end, between 1880 and 1910, the richest municipalities voted chiefly for conservative, Catholic, and monarchist candidates, and secondarily for Moderate Republicans (see figure 9.5). But it must be emphasized that the Right and the Center were usually very close, particularly on economic and financial questions

---

64. See P. Leroy-Beaulieu, *De la colonisation chez les peuples modernes* (1874), a work in which the editor of the journal *L'Économiste français,* a professor at the École libre des sciences politiques and then at the Collège de France, and a leader of the liberal economists of the period, presented colonialization as an economic necessity to maintain the rate of profit. See also J. Ferry, *Le Tonkin et la mère patrie* (1890), a book in which the ex-president of the Council justified his policy and sought to present the Tonkin expedition that brought about his fall as having provided a major industrial outlet for French capital and the preservation of the profit margins of the French, continually repeating Leroy-Beaulieu's arguments.

65. The Third Republic was definitively adopted in 1875 with the votes on three constitutional laws organizing the republican regime (the Senate on 24 February, the public powers on 25 February, and finally the relations between the public powers on 16 July). See chapter 1.

66. Boulangism developed by drawing on anti-German nationalism and accusing parliamentary elites of preferring the policy of appeasement in order to protect their interests, which also allowed it to win support among workers and voters nostalgic about the Commune and continuing to fight the Prussians. To all this, General Boulanger added a display of a more humane treatment and better rations for the troops and a denunciation of the privileges of the princes and high-ranking military men, just as Louis-Napoléon Bonaparte had done before him.

lower than the national average in 2017. In the department Haute Savoie, we also see a sharp decrease in the vote for the Right of the Right over recent decades, particularly in the municipalities farthest east in the department—which are also the richest ones—like the valley of Chamonix-Mont-Blanc. However, there was a significant increase in the vote for the Right of the Right—around 50 percent of its national average—in 2022, which is explained entirely by the arrival of Reconquête (the party headed by Éric Zemmour), which we have classified as being in the Right of the Right, but which is developing a much more liberal program than that of the FN-RN on economic questions, and which is understandably realizing far better results in the upper-crust quarters.[72] In all, in 2022 the result obtained by the Right (excluding the Center-Right) in the richest 1 percent of the municipalities was twice as low as its average national result, which constitutes a considerable gap (see figure 9.7).

The contrast with earlier periods is spectacular. If we break down the Right into Center-Right and Right, in accord with the classifications introduced above, we see that the two components of the Right have always been favored by the richest municipalities, usually in comparable proportions, from the 1880s to the 1980s. At the beginning of the twentieth century and during the interwar period, it was the trends most on the Right (in particular the conservatives, monarchists, and Catholics) that came in above the Center-Right in the richest municipalities, with large variations. In the 1960s and 1970s and in the early 1980s, the Right (which at that time grouped together the Gaullist parties UDR, RPR, and so on) and the Center-Right (UDF, independents, and so on), achieved similar results (relative to their average national result). In the course of the recent period, the Center-Right (which since 1986 includes the Right except for FN-RN and closely related parties) continues to achieve excellent results in the richest municipalities relative to its average national result, even in 2017 and 2022, when the latter shifted toward the Center; nonetheless, given that the Center-Right's national result itself collapsed, this regularity no longer has much importance. The dominant phenomenon is that the Right as a whole received a (slightly) smaller result in the richest municipalities than it did in the rest of the country, a considerable transformation that allows us to take the measure of the regroupings that are taking place (see figures 9.6–9.7).

---

72. In his analysis of the presidential programs of the two candidates, Gilles Ivaldi shows that 43 percent of Éric Zemmour's measures are oriented toward the Right, including the IFI (impôt sur la fortune immobilière), taxes on inheritances, and retirement at the age of sixty-four—twice as many as Marine Le Pen's. See G. Ivaldi, "Marine Le Pen, Éric Zemmour: Social populisme contre capitalisme populaire" (working paper CEVIPOF, 2022).

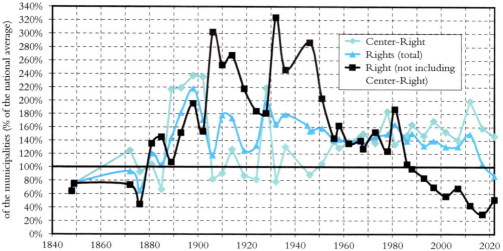

FIGURE 9.7. Vote for the various political trends in the richest 1 percent of the municipalities (percentage of national average)

Since the 1880s, the vote for the right bloc in the richest 1 percent of the municipalities has generally been greater than the national average. This applies at least as much to the Right of the Right as to the Center Right, with the exception of the period 1986–2022, when the Right of the Right (the FN and then the RN) received increasingly low scores in the richest municipalities by comparison with the national average.

Sources and series: see unehistoireduconflitpolitique.fr

The Upper-Crust Quarters in Paris, Emblems of the Right Sometimes Tempted by the Center

It is also interesting to examine more precisely the vote in the capital's richest arrondissements, and particularly the 7th, 8th, and 16th, which have always been among the richest 1 percent of France's municipalities since the nineteenth century, both in terms of average income and the average value of its housing. Generally speaking, we see very similar overall changes in the upper-crust neighborhoods of Paris and the richest 1 percent of the municipalities, which also include a great many well-off municipalities all over the territory,[73] particularly in the Paris region and in the largest agglomerations (notably around Lyon, Lille, and Bordeaux),

---

73. In chapter 2 we have already discussed the geography of the income per inhabitant (see, for example, map 2.6). For a visualization of the geography of the richest 1 percent of the municipalities at the beginning and end of this period, see unehistoireduconflitpolitique.fr, map C9.2.

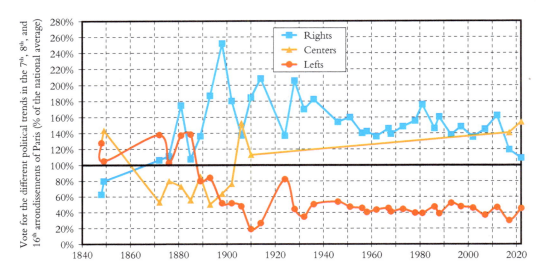

FIGURE 9.8. The vote in the upper-crust quarters, 1848–2022

Since 1890, the gap between the Right bloc and the Left bloc in the richest arrondissements of Paris (relative to their national average result) has remained even greater than in the richest 1% of the municipalities in general. The Center bloc (relative to its national average result) nonetheless came out ahead of the Right bloc on several occasions, notably in 1848–1849, 1906, and 2017–2022. Note: The result obtained by the Center bloc was low and erratic during the period of bipartition, and has not been indicated here for the 1919–2012 elections (for lack of representative candidates).

Sources and series: unehistoireduconflitpolitique.fr

but sometimes also in the rural world.[74] However, it will be noted that the gap between the votes for the Right bloc and the Left bloc was even greater in the upper-crust neighborhoods of Paris than in the richest 1 percent of the municipalities as a whole. From the 1890s to the 2010s, the Right bloc usually obtained about 150–170 percent of its national result in the 7th, 8th, and 16th arrondissements of the capital (sometimes as much as 180–200 percent or more), whereas the Left bloc usually obtained around 40–50 percent of its national result (see figure 9.8). That is, in a situation where the results of the Right and the Left were equal on the national level (which is approximately the case, on average), the Right

74. Generally, we observe no systematic, significant difference over the long term in the richest 1 percent of the municipalities in relation to the type of territory or the region considered. To sum up, the richest municipalities have always voted, in a first approximation, in the same way, whether they are part of the urban world or the rural world, the Paris region or the provinces. See unehistoireduconflitpolitique.fr, figures D1.1ca–D1.1ci and appendix D1.

would obtain a result on the order of three to four times higher than the Left in these arrondissements, which corresponds to crushing landslides such as 75 percent to 25 percent or 80 percent to 20 percent (in the absence of the Center).

The unqualified superiority of the Right in these arrondissements, particularly in the 16th, seen as a symbol of bourgeois Paris by the country, corresponds to a regularity so well established in the French political landscape that it has become almost a geographical definition of the Left and the Right. By definition, the Left has similar fiefs in the eastern part of Paris (especially the 19th and 20th arrondissements) as well as in the "Red" suburbs of the capital such as Aubervilliers and Saint-Denis, which are left-wing equivalents of Neuilly-sur-Seine on the Right.[75] Given the strength of this regularity, it is particularly striking to see that the Right bloc was clearly overtaken by the Center bloc in the 7th, 8th, and 16th arrondissements in the legislative elections of 2017 and 2022 (see figure 9.8). In the legislative election of 2022, Renaissance (the party formerly named LREM) won all the seats in these three emblematic arrondissements, which illustrates in a particularly extreme way the phenomenon of the plasticity of the elites already mentioned. This observation is so great that the interpretation is hardly in doubt: in 2017 and 2022, the voters in the upper-crust quarters thought that the Center bloc is now the best equipped to respond to their essential aspirations and to defend their fundamental economic interests.

If we go back in time and examine separately the different arrondissements, we can, of course, find other cases during the period 1848–1910 in which the upper-crust quarters placed Moderate and Opportunist Republicans ahead of conservative, monarchist, or Catholic candidates, but never so massively and systematically. Generally, although the 16th arrondissement is today the most emblematic and densely populated bourgeois arrondissement, it has not always been that way. The 8th arrondissement (around the Champs-Élysées) was long the historically richest, even if it has now been just barely overtaken by the 7th (near the National Assembly and Les Invalides) in terms of income per inhabitant and the value of the housing. Following these criteria, both are still situated quite clearly ahead of the 16th arrondissement, but with a much smaller population.[76] If we examine the votes, we also see that the 8th arrondissement was the first bourgeois arrondissement

---

75. We will return to this in the following chapters.

76. In 2022, the population of the 16th was about 165,000, with an average income of 75,000 euros per inhabitant and an average housing value of 1.1 million euros), whereas the 7th and the 8th had populations of 45,000 and 35,000 inhabitants, respectively, with average incomes of 108,000 and 107,000 euros and average housing values of 1.4 and 1.3 million euros, respectively. The complete historical series is available on unehistoireduconflitpolitique.fr.

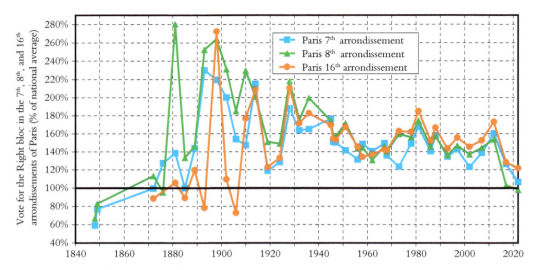

FIGURE 9.9. The vote for the Right in the upper-crust quarters

In the richest arrondissements of Paris (the 7th, 8th, and 16th) the vote for the Right bloc established itself as a massive and quasi-permanent reality, starting in the 1880s and 1890s (in the 7th and the 8th) and in 1910 (in the 16th). The vote for the Right bloc was nonetheless replaced by the vote for the Center in 2017–2022, as it had been on several occasions in during the period 1848–1910. Sources and series: unehistoireduconflitpolitique.fr

in which the Right won by a large margin while the Left disappeared almost completely, as early as the 1870s and 1880s. In the 7th and 16th arrondissements, it was not until 1890–1910 that this regularity was established (see figures 9.9–9.10).

In the case of the 16th arrondissement, during this period we continue to see for a long time alternations in power between Moderate and Opportunist Republicans deputies on the one hand, and conservative and monarchist deputies on the other. Thus in 1893 the Moderate Republican and administrator of mining companies Henri Marmottan won in the 16th arrondissement, defeating the former conservative deputy Louis Calla, the owner of manufacturing enterprises, a member of the royalist Central Committee, and president of the Association of Monarchist Conferences.[77] Subsequently, the fusion of the Right and Center

---

77. It is interesting to note that in 1881, Marmottan had already been elected as a deputy for the 16th arrondissement under a label close to Gambetta's Union républicaine (which we have classified as Center-Left in 1881), whereas in 1893 he appeared as a Moderate Republican (classified as Center).

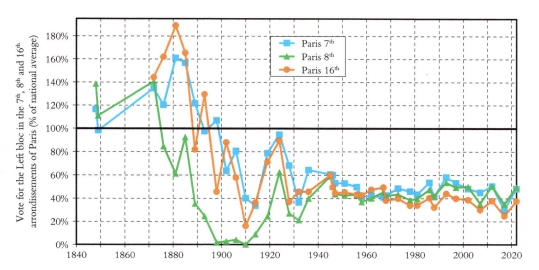

FIGURE 9.10. The vote for the Left in upper-crust quarters

In the richest arrondissements of Paris (7th, 8th, and 16th), the vote for the Left bloc collapsed in the 8th arrondissement starting in the 1870s and 1880s, then in the 7th and 16th arrondissements starting in 1890–1910. Since the 1950s, the vote for the Left bloc has been stabilized in the three arrondissements at around 40% of the Left's average result at the national level.

Sources and series: unehistoireduconflitpolitique.fr

trends simplified the situation and led to an undivided reign of the Right over the bourgeois arrondissements. In the case of the 16th arrondissement, which became part of the city of Paris only when new arrondissements were added in 1860, the real estate developments were still numerous at the end of the nineteenth century and the beginning of the twentieth. This explains a social homogenization that occurred somewhat later than that in the 7th and 8th arrondissements.[78] Despite these chronological differences, we note that the capital's three richest arrondissements converge politically during the interwar period and from then on are characterized by extremely close trajectories, from the point of view of both the very strong vote for the Right and the very weak vote for the Left, from 1910 to 2000–2010 (see figures 9.9–9.10). Of course, as we have said, this is not limited to the upper-crust quarters of Paris, which reflect more broadly the overall evolution of the richest 1 percent of the municipalities. Whether we examine Tourgéville in Cal-

78. The 7th and 8th arrondissements did not exist in their current forms before the redrawing of the map of Paris in 1860, and for the elections of 1848–1849 we have used the electoral results observed in the former 1st arrondissement (which corresponds, on the whole, to the current 8th and the former 10th arrondissements).

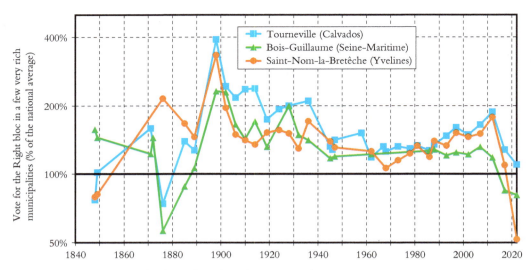

FIGURE 9.11. The vote for the Right in the richest municipalities

In the richest municipalities of the rural world and provincial conurbations, we find the same overall profile as we do in the upper-class quarters of Paris: the vote for the Right is systematically and massively higher than the national average from the 1890s to the early 2010s, before collapsing and being replaced by the vote for the Center in 2017–2022, as it had between 1848 and 1910. Sources and series: unehistoireduconflitpolitique.fr

vados, Bois-Guillaume in Seine-Maritime, or Saint-Nom-La-Bretèche in Yvelines, we find in a vote for the Right very clearly higher than the national average all through the twentieth century and as late as the middle of the 2010s—on average, between 120 and 160 percent of the national average, but sometimes over 200 percent—and then a recent turnaround (see figure 9.11).

When the Upper-Crust Quarters Fear the Right

The very sharp fall of the vote for the Right observed in 2017 and 2022 in these three municipalities, as well as in the 7th, 8th, and 16th arrondissements—a vote that is now only slightly greater in the upper-crust quarters of Paris than on average at the national level (but maintaining a significant advantage in the 16th in comparison with the 7th and 8th arrondissements)—is thereby all the more significant. If we examine in greater detail the changes seen for the different components of the Right, we find that in the same way as for the richest 1 percent of the municipalities as a whole, this fall of the Right is completely explained by the collapse of the Center-Right at the national level in 2017–2022, which certainly continues to rack up far better results in the upper-crust quarters (relative to its national average), but without having much effect on the overall results, taking into account the massive transfer of Center-Right voters to the Center.[79]

Over a longer period, the most important phenomenon is, here again, that the Right of the Right (excepting the Center-Right) has frightened the upper-crust quarters ever since it took on the colors of the FN-RN and closely related parties in 1986. This was a major historical change, insofar as the 7th, 8th, and 16th arrondissements had always voted massively for the Right of the Right (conservatives, monarchists, Catholics, liberals, Gaullists, and so on) from the 1890s to the beginning of the 1980s, a period during which the Right of the Right had also undergone a profound change on the ideological level (the Gaullists of the 1960s and 1970s had little in common with the monarchists of the 1880s and 1890s) but still continued to enjoy the confidence of the upper crust quarters. From this point of view, the reconfiguration that began in the 1980s with the appearance of the FN on the Right was an important rupture. To be sure, FN candidates won a respectable number of votes in the upper crust quarters in 1986, the first time they were on the ballot (and to a lesser degree, in 1988), a little higher than their average national result. But the decline began in 1988 and 1993, to the point that the FN's result in 2017 amounted to barely 20 percent of its national result in the 7th and 8th arrondissements and hardly more than 25 percent in the 16th arrondissement (see figure 9.12).[80]

A clear rise of the Right of the Right in the upper-crust quarters will be noted here, too, during the legislative elections of 2022, a phenomenon that is entirely due, as it was in the other rich municipalities, to the vote for the party Reconquête (Reconquest), but which here took on a still more significant magnitude, especially in the 16th arrondissement, where the Right of the Right rose to more than 60 percent of its national result. Here we see the (relative) importance of a wealthy electorate close to the identitarian theses of the Right of the Right and prepared to be oriented toward that trend if only it adopted an economic and financial program more in conformity with its aspirations and fundamental interests (for example, lowering the real estate tax and inheritance taxes). We will return to this question and to the possibility of such a trajectory

79. See unehistoireduconflitpolitique.fr, figures D1.1ca–D1.1ci and appendix D1.
80. For the geography of the change in the distribution of the FN / RN vote between 1986 and 2017, see unehistoireduconflitpolitique.fr, map C9.3. Map C9.4 puts in parallel the FN / RN vote in 2017 and the municipalities' incomes.

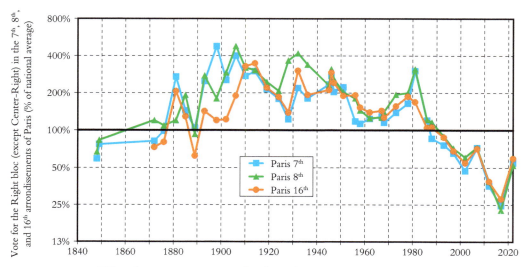

FIGURE 9.12. When the upper-crust quarters fear the Right

Historically, the vote for the Right of the Right (except the Center-Right) in the richest Paris arrondissements (7th, 8th, 16th) was very high from the 1890s to the early 1980s, before collapsing in the period 1986–2022, when the Right of the Right was constituted by the FN-RN and the parties close to it. However, we see a clear increase in 2022, entirely due to Reconquête.

Sources and series: unehistoireduconflitpolitique.fr

when we study the possible avenues for transforming the current tripartition and moving toward bipartition.

The Rise and Fall of the Catholic Right

Let us conclude this chapter by noting that the question of the proximity to Catholicism, which was one of the structural factors characterizing the vote for the Right during the 1848–1910 period, with regard to both the Center and other political trends, continued to play a significant role during a large part of the twentieth century before declining very steeply over recent decades. Again, we use several series of indicators that allow us to measure the proximity to Catholicism, and in particular, the proportion of refractory priests in 1791 and the proportions of students attending private schools in 1894 and 2021. Here, we present the results obtained with the proportion of girls attending religious primary schools in 1894, which are particularly convincing. Specifically, when we examine the ratio between the vote for the Right in the 50 percent of the municipalities with the largest and

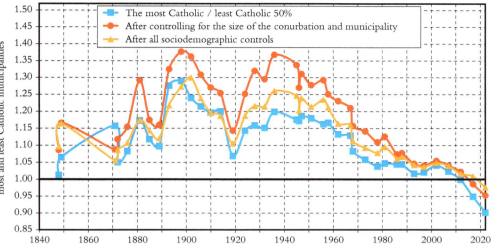

FIGURE 9.13. The vote for the Right and Catholicism, 1848–2022

From the legislative elections of 1848 to those of 2022, the vote for the Right has generally been larger in the municipalities characterized by the greatest proximity to Catholicism (measured here by the proportion of girls enrolled in private schools in 1894, before and after controls). The effect is particularly great from the 1880s to the 1960s, and disappears in the course of recent decades (or even becomes negative).

Sources and series: unehistoireduconflitpolitique.fr

smallest proportions of girls attending religious schools, we find that the vote for the Right has generally been significantly larger in the municipalities characterized by a greater proximity to Catholicism. The effect is particularly marked from the 1880s to the 1960s, then disappears in recent decades (see figure 9.13). In the legislative elections of 1881, for example, we see that the vote for the Right was far greater than the national average in the most Catholic of the departments in western France such as Vendée and Maine-et-Loire, but it was also particularly marked in the municipalities in Aveyron, where the proportion of girls attending private schools surpassed 60 or even 80 percent. It was more than 150 percent of the national average in the municipalities farthest east of Hautes Alpes, such as Monêtier-les-Bains, Briançon, and Aiguilles, where the proportion of girls attending private schools was far higher in 1894 than in the rest of the department—30 percent in Aiguilles as opposed to 18 percent in Embrun and 0 percent in Orcières, two municipalities where the vote for the Right was also zero in 1881 (see map 9.2).

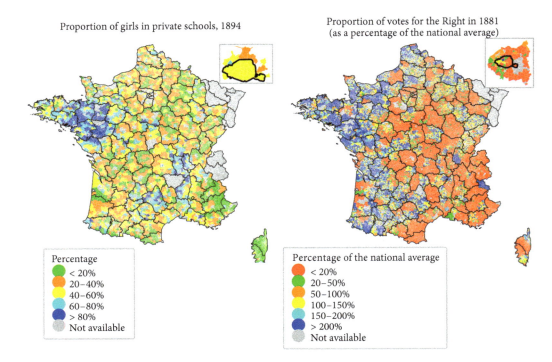

Proportion of girls in private schools, 1894

Proportion of votes for the Right in 1881
(as a percentage of the national average)

Percentage
- 🟢 < 20%
- 🟠 20–40%
- 🟡 40–60%
- 🔵 60–80%
- 🔵 > 80%
- ⚪ Not available

Percentage of the national average
- 🟠 < 20%
- 🟢 20–50%
- 🟠 50–100%
- 🟡 100–150%
- 🔵 150–200%
- 🔵 > 200%
- ⚪ Not available

MAP 9.2. The vote for the Right and Catholicism: Legislative elections of 1881
The map on the left represents the proportion of girls enrolled in private primary schools. The map on the right represents the proportion of votes won by the Right as a ratio of the national average.
Sources and series: unehistoireduconflitpolitique.fr

Several points regarding these results must be clarified. First of all, this very significant disparity is found both before and after taking into account control variables. That is, it is not explained by other sociodemographic variables that might be correlated with both Catholicism and the vote for the Right. Considering control variables would even tend to increase the magnitude of the effect, insofar as religious schools are on average less present in the rural world, which votes more for the Right. For a given size of agglomeration, the effect of private schools is thus larger than if we did not reason ceteris paribus.[81]

81. Whereas figure 9.12 compares the most Catholic 50 percent of the municipalities to the least Catholic 50 percent, we also see that the effect obtained is even more massive if we compare the 20 percent of the municipalities with the greatest and the least proximity to Catholicism, and so on. See unehistoireduconflitpolitique.fr, figures D1.14a–D1.17f and appendix D1 for the complete results.

It will also be noted that the effect achieves its maximal magnitude at the end of the 1870s and the beginning of the 1880s, at the time of the first laws concerning congregationalist schools and in favor of secular public schools, and especially between 1900 and 1910, at the time of the interdiction of congregational schools, the law on the separation of church and state, and the elimination of government financial support for religions.[82] However, the political context is quite different in the two cases, since the discontent of the Right bloc was expressed around 1880 with regard to the Moderate and Opportunist Republicans then in power, whereas in 1900–1910, it was the Radical-Socialists who were in control (with the support of the Socialists), at a time when the Central bloc was already considerably weakened and was getting ready to merge with other conservative and Catholic trends. In other words, the question of religious and educational policy was about to be permanently established as one of the elements of the Left-Right opposition within an electoral system on its way toward bipartition, rather than a structuring factor of tripartition. The 1900–1910 period was also the time when the secret files scandal (*l'affaire des fiches*) exploded and led to the fall of the government headed by the Radical-Socialist Émile Combes: in a context marked by the last epilogues of the Dreyfus affair (the innocence of the protagonist was to be officially established only by a judgment without appeal handed down by the Cour de cassation in 1906), the Radical government set up in 1900–1904 a system of information gathering within the army that allowed it to identify the conservative and Catholic officers in order to delay their promotions and to favor a new elite closer to the Radicals and the Left. The information-gathering system was developed with the active involvement of the Masonic lodges of the Grand Orient de France,[83] and this aroused the Right's fury and brought the religious conflict to the point of incandescence. In the end, though, the fall of the Combes ministry delayed for only a few months the vote on the law separating church and state in 1905.[84]

---

82. See chapter 3.
83. According to some estimates, 40 percent of the ministers of the period 1870–1914 were Freemasons. See J. Estèbe, *Les ministres de la République 1871–1914* (Presses de la FNSP, 1982), 201.
84. The information-gathering scandal returned again and again during the debates on separation. Thus, during the Senate's session on 13 November 1905, when Ernest Monis—who was minister of justice in the Waldeck-Rousseau government—said in his defense of separation that the Concordat of 1801 had instituted an oppressive regime, emphasizing that "the Concordat transformed the bishops into informers," Count Emmanuel de Las Cases retorted, "Daring to speak of denunciation in the aftermath of the *scandale des fiches!* Ah! If I were so inclined I could make some fine responses to that" (*La Croix,* 14 November 1905). The whole debate was rather salty, beginning with Las Cases's defense, in which he notes that "man cannot always

The magnitude of the religious cleavage remained important during the interwar period, when the controversies arose concerning educational questions (in particular secondary schools), and then again in the 1950s and 1960s, when the Debré law set up an unprecedented system of public funding for private schools (which retained, moreover, the right to choose their students and teachers). This law played an essential role in anchoring Gaullism in the Right.[85] Next, we note in the 1970s and 1980s a sharp decline of the religious cleavage, to the point that the effect is nearly zero in the 1990s and 2000s, or even slightly negative (but in a way that is not significant after taking control variables into account) in the 2010s (see figure 9.12).[86] A high rate of attendance in private schools has ceased to have a direct effect on the vote for the Right and the Left: other socioeconomic explanatory variables now play a dominant role and depending on the case, absorb the effect associated with attendance in private schools, which has become less and less connected with strictly religious reasons and more and more with socioeconomic factors.

To be sure, we must remember that the factors connected with geosocial class (the size of the agglomeration, the level of wealth, the proportions of workers and farmers, the concentration of land ownership, and so on) have always had an explanatory power regarding voting that is much greater than that of strictly religious factors, including during the period 1880–1960, when the latter did play an important role.[87] Political conflict has always been primarily a conflict opposing different geosocial classes, not a principally religious or identitarian conflict. The fact remains that proximity to Catholicism (for given social characteristics) has had a significant additional impact for structuring political conflict and making it more complex, and this factor has almost entirely disappeared over recent decades. Other parameters have provided new elements of complexity, beginning with the renewal of the territorial rural-urban cleavage and the emergence of new identitarian cleavages. From this point of view, it is interesting to note that the

---

walk hunched over the earth. . . . The Socialists have provided us with a solution that they want to implant by means of hatred. Catholicism is the religion of love."

85. See chapter 3. For interesting estimates of the connection between voting, social class, and religious practice, made on the basis of cantonal data issuing from the legislative elections of 1962 and 1968, see M. Dogan, "Le vote ouvrier en France: Analyse écologique des élections de 1962," *Revue française de sociologie*, 1965; D. Derivry and M. Dogan, "Religion, classe et politique en France," *Revue française de science politique*, 1986. See also G. Michelat and M. Simon, *Classe, religion et comportement politique* (Presses de la FNSP, 1977).

86. We get the same result if we use attendance in private schools in 2021 and not in 1894.

87. See chapter 8, figure 8.16.

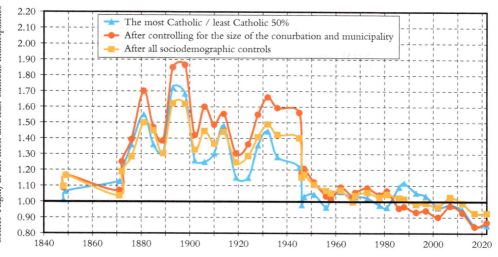

FIGURE 9.14. The vote for the Right (except the Center-Right) and Catholicism

From the 1880s to the 1930s, the relation between the vote for the Right and proximity to Catholicism (measured by the proportion of girls enrolled in private schools in 1894) is greater when the Center-Right is excluded. The inverse has been true since 1945, whether for the Gaullist Right (1946–1981) or the FN / RN Right (1986–2022), both of which have a weak or negative relation to Catholicism in comparison with the Center-Right.

Right of the Right was particularly associated with Catholicism at the end of the nineteenth century and in the first half of the twentieth century, more than the vote for the Center-Right, whereas the inverse equilibrium was established during the second half of the twentieth century and in the first decades of the twenty-first (see figures 9.13–9.14).

It will be noted that the shift took place as early as 1945; the vote for the Center-Right (in particular for the Christian Democrats of the MRP) became much more strongly connected with attendance in private schools than the vote for the Right of the Right (which included, in particular, the Gaullist parties). Then the relation became even slightly negative during the period between 1986 and 2022, when the Right of the Right included the FN-RN. After and before taking account of controls, we see above all that the effect is virtually nil (see figure 9.13). That is, it is no longer the relation to Catholicism that makes the structure of political conflict more complex, but rather new cleavages of a territorial and identitarian type. We will return at length to these questions, studying the difficult establishment of the Left-Right bipartition during the period 1910–1992, and then the rise to power of a new form of tripartition between 1992 and 2022.

CHAPTER 10

The Difficult Construction of Bipartition, 1910–1992

We will now study more precisely the structure of voting and of electoral conflict during the period 1910–1992. At first, this period seems to be characterized by a bipartition of the "classic" type, with a political confrontation centered on the social question and the redistribution of wealth. The Left bloc formed by the Socialists and Communists advocated greater equality among social classes, and to realize that objective, it proposed an overall transformation of the socio-economic system, whereas the Right bloc, including the conservative, liberal, and Gaullist trends, sought to contain these structural changes and to limit them to what it considered possible and desirable. It therefore instilled a dose of realism and a sense of measure that it claimed the Left lacked. It should not be idealized, but during the twentieth century this driving dialectic did make it possible to construct an unprecedented movement (albeit insufficient and incomplete) toward greater social equality and greater economic prosperity, all in the framework of a pluralist electoral democracy based on collective deliberation, political alternation, and respect for the diversity of points of view.[1]

For all that, the system of bipolarization that was established between 1910 and 1992 was always permeated by multiple weaknesses and contradictions that it is essential to analyze in order to better understand the system's collapse during the period 1992–2022, as well as the conditions of its possible resurgence. In practice, there are fundamental reasons explaining why bipartition is always incomplete and unstable; class conflict, like political conflict, is profoundly multidimensional and perpetually renewing, and such a reality cannot easily be organized on a single Left-Right axis, no matter what the merits of such a simplification might be for structuring coalitions and making social change possible. Only specific historical moments and programs for action that are particularly unifying can enable us to move temporarily beyond these contradictions in the framework of compromises that are always unstable and precarious.

Among the many factors of the weakening of bipolarization at work between 1910 and 1992, two deserve particular attention for what we can learn from them concerning the future. First of all, in practice, the Left-Right electoral cleavage

---

1. See chapter 1.

connected with wealth is always made more complex by a territorial rural-urban cleavage that partly contradicts it (the rural world being, on average, poorer and more likely to vote for the Right), in connection with different views of the productive structure and its long-term evolution. Now, although the rural-urban cleavage lost much its power between 1910 and 1992 in comparison to the periods 1848–1910 and 1992–2022—which to some extent allowed bipartition to emerge—it nonetheless continues to play a significant role and helps weaken the bipolar system. Besides, the Right bloc, like the Left bloc, is full of internal contradictions, which were especially deep during the interwar period and under the Fourth Republic, particularly in connection with the financial legacy of the wars, the inconsistencies of nationalism, the construction of the welfare state, and the question of democratic socialism. These difficulties of agreeing on a viable program often prevented clear alternations between the two blocs and regularly led to government by unstable coalitions. These two pitfalls associated with bipartition—the territorial pitfall and the programmatic pitfall—were closely related to each other and in the event of a return to bipartition, might be manifested in the future in similar forms in a context marked, of course, by new issues (like the climatic and environmental challenge or the questions of migration and identity), but one in which some of the fundamental contradictions seen in the twentieth century reappear.

We will begin by studying the social determinants of the Left-Right vote in the legislative elections of 1981, which constitute one of the emblematic moments in which the country's bipolarization was expressed. We will see that the cleavage associated with wealth is in fact obvious during these elections—the poor municipalities voted more for the Left—more so than in the election of 1936 or other elections of the period 1958–1992, for example. This social cleavage is nonetheless lessened by the persistence of a very clear territorial cleavage and a sectorial, occupational, and status-related (salaried or self-employed) cleavage. Then we will return to the way in which this multidimensionality of electoral conflict interacts with the programmatic question to explain the difficulties encountered by the coalitions in power during the interwar period and under the Fourth Republic, as well as during the period 1958–1992, which appeared to be more stable but nonetheless reflected the tensions connected with this structural complexity.

The "Classic" Left-Right Conflict: The Legislative Elections of 1981

Let us begin by examining the structure of voting in the legislative elections of 1981, which are among the historical elections in which bipolarization seems

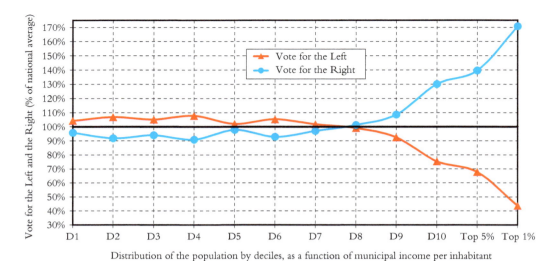

FIGURE 10.1. The classic Left-Right conflict and wealth: Legislative elections of 1981

In the legislative elections of 1981, the vote for the Left (relative to the national average) diminished with the municipality's average level of income, especially at the top of the distribution, whereas the inverse is true for the Right. Note: The results given here are after controls for the size of the conurbation and municipality.

Sources and series: unehistoireduconflitpolitique.fr

particularly pronounced in France, in the same way as the legislative elections of 1973 and 1978 and the presidential elections of 1974 and 1981, especially during Mitterand's and Giscard's closely fought duels, to which we will return.[2] For these elections as a whole, and more generally, for the quasi-totality of the elections of the period from 1910 to 1992, we see a relatively great electoral cleavage in function of wealth, in the sense that the vote for the Left diminished with the average income of the municipality, accompanied by a significant acceleration of the decrease at the peak of the distribution, whereas the inverse is true for the vote for the Right (see figure 10.1). The result is the same with other indicators of wealth, such as real estate capital (total value of housing) per inhabitant (that is, the average value of housing).[3]

2. These duels were characterized by a structure of the vote close to that seen in the legislative elections of 1973, 1978, and 1981. See chapters 12 and 13 on the analysis of the determinants of the vote in presidential elections.

3. See unehistoireduconflitpolitique.fr, maps C10.1 and C10.2.

Several points regarding this result must be clarified. First, we might be tempted to think that this electoral configuration is a little obvious and tautological: "Well, well, the poor municipalities vote more often for the Left than the rich ones do, who'd have thought it?" From the moment when the Left bloc relied primarily on a program of reducing social inequalities, and the Right bloc opposed it or tried to contain its magnitude, it isn't surprising that the poorest municipalities have voted more for the Left and the richest municipalities for the Right. However, it is crucial to be able to measure this reality precisely and rigorously, to study its exact magnitude and especially its variations over time, in order to better understand its wellsprings—something that the sources collected in this book enable us to do for the first time in a systematic way. We already know that the richest 1 percent of the municipalities vote very infrequently for the Left (relative to the national average) in the set of legislative elections conducted since the end of the nineteenth century.[4] The results presented here allow us to resituate this regularity in a broader perspective. We find, in fact, that the decline of the vote for the Left (relative to the national average) occurred gradually within the richest 30 percent of the municipalities, with a spectacular decrease among the richest 10 percent, until it reached a very low level within the richest 1 percent.[5] Inversely, within the poorest 70 percent of the municipalities, the vote for the Left is certainly higher than its average national result, but with a relatively small but constant divergence from the Right, at least in comparison to the chasm that developed within the richest 30 percent of the municipalities. We will see that this structural reality, which is found not only in 1981 but also over the whole period 1910–1992, provides us with valuable information regarding the nature of the electoral conflict that was formed in the framework of bipartition.

Before going further in the explanation of these regularities, it is useful to explain that presenting this electoral structure as the "classic" Left-Right conflict is in itself debatable and testifies to our situation in a specific sociohistorical context. In France—and more generally, in the European and Occidental world—it is often thought that the Left-Right bipartition that prevailed during a large part of the twentieth century constitutes the "normal" electoral structure, and that the irregularities observed in the course of recent decades are in some way unusual.[6]

---

4. See chapter 9, figure 9.5.
5. As before, we take into account here the sizes of the municipalities, so as not to bias the temporal comparisons. In other words, the richest 10 percent of the municipalities designate the 10 percent of the population living in the richest municipalities.
6. Let us add here that it is important not to confuse the bipolar structure of political conflict with the dualism of political parties. As has been stressed historically by Maurice Duverger, the

We do not disagree entirely with this point of view, since the bipolar Left-Right conflict centered on the social question seems to us particularly well adapted to structure collective deliberation and democratic transfers of power. However, we emphasize that this bipolar structure is not particularly normal or inevitable, and that it is in reality much more complex than it seems. It depends on socioeconomic and politico-ideological contexts, and especially on the strategies implemented by the different actors. Let us also recall how much the configuration seen in the United States during the twentieth century differs from European "normality," with, on the one hand, the Democrats—a party that issued in the nineteenth century from a slaveholding, segregationist, and social-differentialist (or social-nativist) trend that ended up occupying, beginning in the early twentieth century and especially from the New Deal of the 1930s, a place close to that of the European Social Democratic, Labor, and Socialist parties—and, on the other hand, the Republicans, who emerged from a pro-business tradition based on free (not servile) labor and moved closer to conservative parties before becoming, in recent decades, the party most hostile to minorities (after the Democrats supported the civil rights movement in the 1960s). In this work, our main objective is precisely to use the French case to highlight the multiplicity and complexity of the possible trajectories and configurations, emphasizing the similarities between the forms of tripartition seen in the early twenty-first century and the weaknesses of the bipolar schema dominant during the twentieth.

Between Bipartition and the Bipolar Quadrumvirate: The Cleavage Related to Wealth

We will now return to the electoral configuration described in figure 10.1 and try to understand the reasons for it. Let us recall that in 1981 the political landscape was structured around four main parties. The Left bloc consisted of the alliance of the Communists (PCF) and the Socialists (PS), whereas the Right bloc consisted of the Liberals and Christian Democrats of the UDF and the Gaullists of the

structure of electoral systems (for example, a uninominal election with one round versus a uninominal election with two rounds versus a proportional, plurinominal election) partly determines the form of partisan systems. But—beyond the limits of his approach—it is not because an electoral system is multipartite that its political confrontation cannot be bipolar. Thus, in the case of France that we are studying here, in each of the elections we have distinguished on average between ten and fifteen political nuances; nonetheless, during most of the twentieth century political conflict was characterized by bipolarity. In the context of this work, the terms "bipolarization" and "bipartition" (used as synonyms) refer to the division of political space into two main blocs, not to the formal dualism of party structures, which has never existed in France.

RPR.[7] What Jean-Marie Le Pen condemned at that time as "the gang of four," a bipolar quadrumvirate in which he was able, over the course of the 1980s and 1990s, to force the emergence of his own movement (the FN) as a fifth party and a third major pole. When the elections of 1981 approached, the Left bloc relied on a vast program of redistribution seeking to augment transfers of wealth for social welfare (such as family allocations and pensions, with a retirement age of sixty) and funding and personnel for public services (in particular, education and healthcare), all financed by greatly increasing the progressivity of the income tax (adding new brackets for the highest incomes) and creating a tax on large wealth holders (*impôt sur les grandes fortunes,* IGF). This program also included structural reforms, with nationalizations and a strengthening of the rights of salaried employees and syndical representatives in companies. The Right bloc denounced the risk of bankruptcy and the multiple dangers associated with these proposals. It also stigmatized the risks connected with the entry of Communist ministers into the government in the middle of the Cold War and reminded voters that it was possible to continue the march toward social progress begun decades earlier without, for all that, setting out on such an adventure. In the wake of the presidential election won by the Socialist candidate François Mitterand in May 1981, the Left bloc obtained a large majority of the seats in the legislative election held in June, thus leading to a particularly clear democratic transition from Right to Left.

Why were the disparities of the Left-Right vote during this election so large in the richest 20–30 percent of the municipalities, when they were more moderate in the rest of the distribution? The most obvious interpretation is that the very rich municipalities are considerably richer than the others, and that they are the only ones that felt directly and massively targeted by the program of the Union of the Left, and especially by the tax increases and the new rights given to salaried employees. That is particularly clear for the inhabitants of the upper-crust quarters and the richest 1 percent of the municipalities, where it is obviously very rare to find voters adhering to the PS-PCF program. Conversely, the disparities in wealth in the least rich 70 percent of the municipalities are smaller, so the variations in the average electoral behavior between municipalities are relatively limited.

It will also be noted that within the Left bloc, although the trends most markedly on the Left (essentially, the PCF in 1981) attracted the most votes in the poorest municipalities and the vote for the Center-Left (essentially, the PS) also diminished with the municipality's income, the decline was much less marked, particularly at the higher end of the distribution. Among the richest 1 percent of the

---

7. See chapter 8, table 8.1.

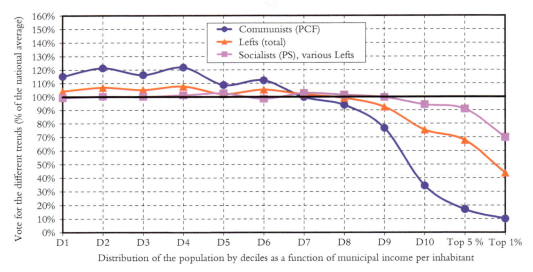

FIGURE 10.2. The vote and wealth in 1981: Left vs. Center-Left

In the legislative elections of 1981, the vote for the Left bloc diminished with the municipality's average income, especially at the top of the distribution. This is particularly true for the Left of the Left (PCF), and less marked for the Center-Left (PS, various Lefts)

Sources and series: unehistoireduconflitpolitique.fr

municipalities, the vote for the Left of the Left was thus equal to 10 percent of the national average, as against 70 percent for the Center-Left (see figure 10.2). On the contrary, within the Right bloc, the voting profiles for the Center-Right (UDF) and those more markedly on the Right (RPR) were almost identical (see figure 10.3). There again, the general result (a clear difference in profile in the Left, no clear divergence in the Right) is found not only for the elections of 1981 but also for the quasi-totality of the elections during the period 1910–1992 (with variations to which we will return). We find this conclusion again if we use other indicators of wealth, such as real estate capital per inhabitant.[8] Let us add that the spectacular fall of the vote for the Left (and particularly the vote for the PCF) within the richest 1 percent of the municipalities can also be reinforced by the knock-on effects and influence of the wealthier inhabitants on those who are less wealthy, even if the data available to us does not permit us to measure directly this type of factors internal to the municipalities.[9] Finally, we can note that support for the PCF in

8. See unehistoireduconflitpolitique.fr, figures D3.1a–D3.17i and appendix D3.

9. Continuing the work of Joseph Klatzmann ("Comportement électoral et classe sociale," *Les élections du 2 janvier 1956* [A. Colin, 1957]), Øystein Noreng remarks that "workers inhabiting

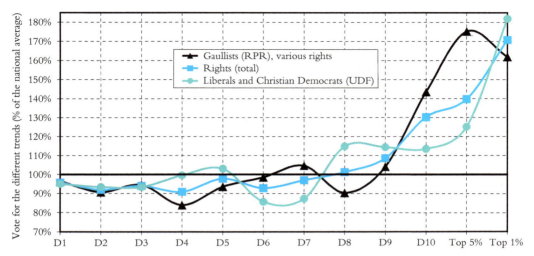

FIGURE 10.3. The vote and wealth in 1981: Right vs. Center-Right
In the legislative elections of 1981, the vote for the Right bloc increases with the municipality's average income, especially at the top of the distribution, in proportions comparable to the Right of the Right (RPR, various Rights) and to the Center-Right (UDF).
Sources and series: unehistoireduconflitpolitique.fr

the poorest 40 percent of the municipalities is relatively stable, which can again be explained by the fact that disparities in wealth are smaller at the bottom of the distribution than at its summit and thus generate political behaviors that are closer to one another.

A Left-Right Conflict That Is Situated in Specific Productive Structures

These interpretations centered on the position of municipalities in the distribution of wealth are nonetheless insufficient, because they shed no light on several essential factors. For the same average municipal income, numerous other dimensions

---

working-class neighborhoods vote Communist and Socialist by a much larger proportion than do workers living in mixed or bourgeois neighborhoods." Ø. Noreng, *Politisation et structure de classe. Essai d'analyse écologique comparée des élections sociales et des élections législatives en France de 1946 à 1962* (Presses de la FNSP, 1972). More generally, on the dynamics of electoral knock-on effects favoring the locally majoritarian social structure, see also J. Rivière, *L'illusion du vote bobo. Configurations électorales et structures sociales dans les grandes villes françaises* (Presses Universitaires de Rennes, 2022).

and social characteristics come into play to determine electoral behavior, in connection with the integration of municipalities into the territorial and productive structure of the country.[10] But these different factors often go in contradictory directions, and compensate one another, whence the misleading impression of a relative stability of the Left-Right cleavage in the poorest 70 percent of the municipalities. For a given income, rural municipalities and ones that include the largest proportions of self-employed workers (agricultural or nonagricultural) have a tendency to vote more heavily for the Right, whereas on the contrary, urban municipalities and those that have the highest proportions of salaried employees (and especially of blue-collar industrial workers) vote more for the Left. These general regularities are found in almost all the legislative elections held from 1848 to 2022, and particularly in 1981, but with temporal variations that, here again, must be analyzed in connection with the transformations of programs, discourses, and experiences of the various political forces.

Regarding the rural-urban cleavage, we have seen that it is the phenomenon that has most structured French political and electoral life since the Revolution. The fact that for two centuries the rural world has had an enduring tendency to vote more for the Right than the urban world is explained in large measure by deep differences in productive and socio-occupational structure and political positioning (blue-collar workers and the urban proletariat have been at the heart of left-wing programs since the nineteenth century, far more than peasants and other self-employed workers). This regularity can also be explained by the rural world's general feeling of being abandoned by the Left (a feeling that goes back to 1789 and continues to a certain extent, independent of the occupational structure). We have also noted that the rural world's tendency to vote more heavily for the Right was particularly marked in the period 1848–1910 and more limited between 1910 and 1992, and it has risen very sharply again since 1992.[11] Nonetheless, we must add that the rural-urban cleavage continued to play a significant role between 1910 and 1992; it has simply lessened in relation to the earlier and later periods. Thus, in the 1981 elections the vote for the Left (and especially for the PCF) was significantly smaller in the villages and towns than in the suburbs and metropoles, and vice versa for the vote for the Right (see figure 10.4).

---

10. Here it is a question of an important limit of the purely "visual" approach to the determinants of voting based on the construction of maps; on the contrary, statistical analysis allows us, thanks to the introduction of control variables, to study the effects of each of the determinants of voting, ceteris paribus.

11. See chapter 8, figures 8.5–8.10.

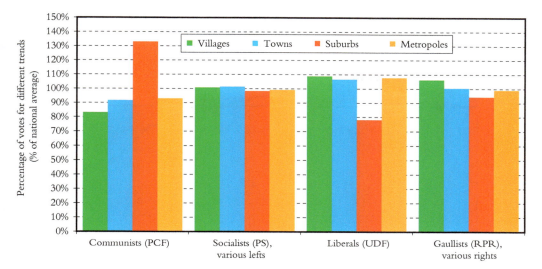

FIGURE 10.4. The elections of 1981 and the rural-urban cleavage

In the legislative elections of 1981, the result obtained by the PCF was considerably lower in villages and towns than it was in suburbs and metropoles, whereas the inverse is true for the UDF and the RPR. In comparison, the result obtained by the PS is about the same in the different territories.

Sources and series: unehistoireduconflitpolitique.fr

Because villages and towns are on average poorer than the suburbs and metropoles and vote more for the Right, this rural-urban cleavage runs opposite to the general relation between the level of income and voting for the Left, and thus tends to decrease it. For a given size of conurbation and municipality, the negative effect of income on the vote for the Left is thus greater than it is in the absence of any controls. In other words, within each type of territory, it is in fact the poorest municipalities that have a very strong tendency to vote more for the Left and the richest municipalities that tend to vote more for the Right. If we add the set of sociodemographic variables (in particular, those that bear on the socio-occupational composition), the negative effect of income becomes even clearer, and especially more regular. For example, in the absence of any controls, the poorest 10 percent of the municipalities actually voted slightly less for the Left than the national average in 1981, but that is entirely explained by the fact that these were in part rural municipalities that included a large number of agricultural workers. As soon as we control for the size of the conurbation and the socio-occupational structure, it appears that these municipalities voted for the Left much more than

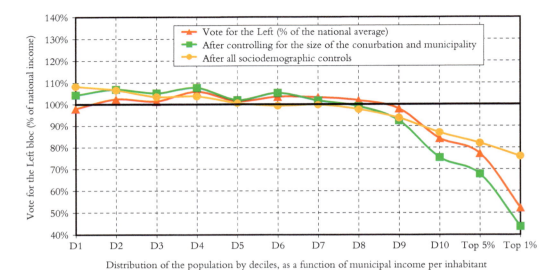

Distribution of the population by deciles, as a function of municipal income per inhabitant

FIGURE 10.5. The vote for the Right and level of income in 1981

In the legislative elections of 1981, the vote for the Left bloc diminishes with the municipality's average level of income, especially at the top of the distribution, before and after taking controls into account.

Sources and series: unehistoireduconflitpolitique.fr

the national average (see figure 10.5).[12] But we must add that apart from this, the general appearance of the curve remains largely unchanged.

Within the richest municipalities, we note as well that the negative effect of income on the vote for the Left is lessened by including control variables. In other words, if the richest municipalities vote so little for the Left, that is not only because they have a higher average income but also because they have a larger amount of real estate capital per inhabitant, a higher proportion of property owners, and a greater number of managers and people holding graduate degrees, and because all these characteristics are generally associated with a smaller vote for the Left. As a consequence, as soon as we reason ceteris paribus, the negative effect of income

12. As before, all the control variables were introduced in the form of categorial variables, taking twenty values corresponding to the ventiles of the distribution in question, in order to make it possible to take into account the most flexible and nonlinear effects involved. All the technical details regarding the regressions carried out, as well as all the codes making it possible to reproduce these results, are available online.

on the vote for the Left within these municipalities appears less massive, though it remains very substantial (see figure 10.5).[13]

To sum up, the relation between the level of wealth and voting for the Left remains largely the same when sociodemographic controls are introduced, but the negative effect of wealth becomes more regular from bottom to top. This reflects the fact that voting for the Left expresses both a position within the distribution of wealth (inhabitants of poor municipalities think they can expect more from the Left than do inhabitants of rich municipalities) and a position within the productive system and the territorial and socio-occupational structure (the inhabitants of urban municipalities, salaried employees, and blue-collar workers feel that the Left pays more attention to them than do those living in rural municipalities that are more agricultural and have more self-employed workers). The important point is that each of these variables plays an autonomous role—their effect remains significant even when we control for the other characteristics—which illustrates the multidimensionality of the political cleavages at work.

A Negative Effect of Wealth on the Vote for the Left, on the Whole Stable from 1910 to 1993

If we use the survey data at the individual level, this voting profile as a function of income or of real estate capital appears to be the same as it is at the municipal level. More precisely, in the totality of the postelectoral surveys conducted since 1958, the vote for the Left decreases with the individual level of income and wealth, with a relatively moderate dip among the 70–80 percent of the least rich voters and a much greater fall among the richest 20–30 percent and especially the richest 10 percent. Generally speaking, the individual voting profile as a function of wealth is even more marked than that as a function of income, which confirms the extent to which the question of the relation to property ownership is at the heart of political conflict. In all the surveys for which this information is available, we see that voters who have large property holdings very rarely vote for the Left, and conversely, that those who have no patrimony just as rarely recognize themselves in the Right, which confirms the centrality of the relation to property ownership in the construction of political affiliations.[14] In addition to the fact that they

---

13. Again, as before, the results are similar if we examine the effect of real estate capital per inhabitant (that is, the average value of housing). See unehistoireduconflitpolitique.fr, figures D3.1a–D3.17i and appendix D3.

14. A. Gethin, C. Martinez-Toledano, and T. Piketty, eds., *Clivages politiques et inégalités sociales. Une étude de 50 démocraties, 1948–2020* (EHESS / Gallimard / Seuil, 2021), 102–103, figures 2.6–2.7;

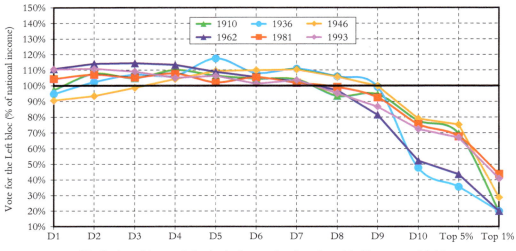

FIGURE 10.6. The vote for the Left by level of income, 1910–1993

From the legislative elections of 1910 to those of 1993, the vote for the Left (relative to the national average) generally diminishes with the level of the municipality's average income, especially at the top of the distribution. Note: The results given here are after controls for the size of the conurbation and municipality.

Sources and series: unehistoireduconflitpolitique.fr

are based on samples too small to satisfactorily combine all the available variables (in particular, to cross-reference income and wealth with the conurbation size and occupation), the great limitation of postelectoral surveys is that they first appeared only in the 1950s. In comparison, the sources we have collected at the municipal level allow us to adopt a long-term perspective, and in this case, to see that the voting profile for the Left as a function of the average municipal income was, in a first approximation, relatively stable all through the twentieth century (see figure 10.6).

More exactly, if we examine all the legislative elections conducted from 1910 to 1993, we see that the Left generally achieved a result superior to the national

T. Piketty, "Brahmin Left vs. Merchant Right. Rising Inequality and the Changing Structure of Political Conflict" (World Inequality Lab working paper 2018 / 07), figures 1.1a–1.1b. The comparative results presented in these works show that the Left's decreasing voting profile as a function of income is considerably more marked in other countries (in particular, in the United Kingdom and the United States) among the least rich voters, which can be explained by the particularly great weight of the rural and peasant factor in France.

average and relatively stable within the poorest 70 percent of the municipalities, and conversely, that its results systematically and massively fell in the richest 20–30 percent of the municipalities, and particularly in the richest 10 percent. This observation is valid from one end of the twentieth century to the other, whether or not control variables are taken into account. In other words, we find the negative effect of income on the vote for the Left in municipalities that have a certain size of conurbation (for example, in villages, towns, suburbs, or metropoles), as well as among municipalities with a certain occupational structure. In this case, we have indicated in figure 10.6 the average profiles obtained by controlling for the size of conurbation and municipality, but the overall picture is relatively close if we take no controls into account, or on the contrary, take all the controls into account, in the same way as for the elections of 1981 (see figure 10.5).[15]

However, we note a significant evolution: in the elections of the first half of the century, such as those of 1910, 1936, and 1946, the vote for the Left was slightly smaller among the poorest 20–30 percent than it was among the next-poorest 20–30 percent, even after controlling for the size of conurbation, a phenomenon that disappears in the elections of the second half of the century, such as those of 1962, 1981, and 1993. This is explained by the presence at the beginning of the century of a very large proportion of self-employed agricultural workers in the poorest municipalities, and a greater proportion of blue-collar industrial workers in the next-poorest municipalities (even with the same conurbation size). Thus we see the extent to which the transition from an electoral structure based on the territorial and sectorial cleavage to an electoral structure based on the cleavage connected with wealth (in a way that was increasingly independent of the territory and the sector of activity) is a gradual process that was far from complete in the first half of the twentieth century.[16] Let us add that for reasons of space, we have not shown here the detailed profiles observed for all the elections,

---

15. In order to allow a maximal comparability over time, we have also indicated in figures 10.1–10.3 the average profiles obtained by controlling for the size of the conurbation and the municipality. All the profiles obtained, election by election, before and after taking various controls into account, are available online. See unehistoireduconflitpolitique.fr, figures D3.1a–D3.17i and appendix D3.

16. In the elections of 1848–1849 and from the 1870s to the 1900s, a period in which the territorial cleavage won out over the cleavage connected with wealth, the vote for the Left was a growing function of the average municipal income in the absence of any control, but it takes on a form that increasingly resembled that of 1910 as soon as we control for the size of the conurbation. See unehistoireduconflitpolitique.fr, figures D3.1a–D3.17i and annex D3.

but they are available online and are very clearly part of this overall schema. In particular, the profiles for the elections of 1910, 1936, and 1946 are found again in 1914, 1919, 1924, 1928, and 1932, whereas those indicated for 1962, 1981, and 1993 are very close to those observed in 1958, 1967, 1973, 1978, 1986, and 1988.[17] If we examine synthetic indicators such as the ratio between the vote for the Left in the richest and the poorest 50 percent of the municipalities, we find relatively regular evolutions between the first half and the second half of the twentieth century.[18]

Let us also note that these overall regularities do not preclude interesting variations from election to election and from municipality to municipality, variations that deserve further analysis. For example, the decline of the vote for the Left among the richest 10 percent of the municipalities was much more marked (with a vote equal to only 50 percent of the national average) in 1936 and 1962 than in other elections (between 70 and 80 percent). In Bois-le-Roi in Seine-et-Marne, for instance, the vote for the Left was only 56 and 57 percent of the national average in 1936 and 1962, respectively, as opposed to 92 and 87 percent in 1910 and 1993. This can be connected to announcements made by Guy Mollet (then the SFIO's general secretary) on the eve of the first round in November 1962, which, paving the way for a new Popular Front, caused the anticommunist reflexes of the Right and Center-Right to flare up, as they had in 1936. In fact, the deputy mayor of Arras urged voters, in the event of a second round between a Communist candidate and a UNR candidate, to prefer the former to the latter, causing the editor in chief of *Le Figaro,* Louis-Gabriel Robinet, to write, "It is no longer a matter only of saying yes to de Gaulle, but also of saying no to the Popular Front."[19]

Beyond local particularities, the main lesson of the cartography of the municipal electoral data that we have collected no doubt concerns the very great variations of the structure of the vote within departments (see, for example, maps 10.1, 10.2, and 10.3 pertaining to the legislative elections of 1936, 1946, and 1981, respectively). But the fact is that these variations are far from random; to a large extent, they are connected with factors such as the size of conurbation and municipality, economic wealth, occupations and diplomas, and so on, which only municipal data allows us to reveal and measure in great detail.

---

17. See unehistoireduconflitpolitique.fr, figures D3.2a–D3.2r and appendix D3.
18. See chapter 8, figure 8.14.
19. See, for example, F. Goguel, *Le referendum d'octobre et les elections de novembre 1962* (Centre d'étude de la vie politique française, 1965).

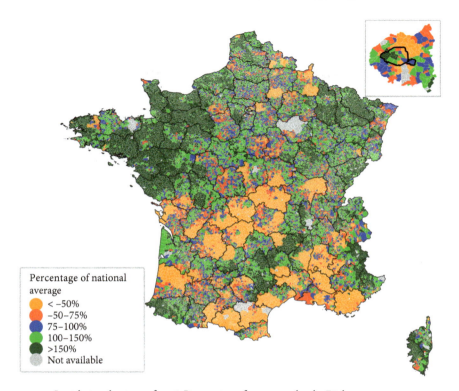

MAP 10.1. Legislative elections of 1936: Proportion of votes won by the Right

The map represents, for each municipality, the proportion of votes won by the rate as a ratio of the national average.

Sources and series: unehistoireduconflitpolitique.fr

The Left-Right Bipartition, Blue-Collar Workers, and Self-Employed Workers

To sum up, the Left-Right bipartition, as it is expressed in the elections of 1981 and in a more general way during the period 1910–1992, is characterized by three main regularities from the point of view of the social structure of the electorates. First, the poorest municipalities vote more for the Left than the richest municipalities, with an effect that is particularly marked at the peak of the distribution. Second, throughout the twentieth century we see a continuation of the rural vote for the Right and a significant rural-urban cleavage—less massive, to be sure, than it was during the earlier and later periods, but nonetheless important. Finally, in addition to the cleavages connected with wealth and the territory concerned, we see the persistence of a very pronounced socio-occupational cleavage: the municipalities

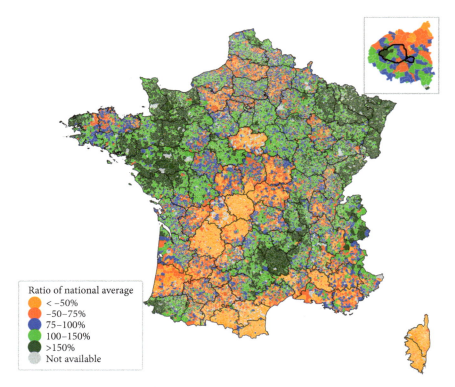

Ratio of national average
- < −50%
- −50−75%
- 75−100%
- 100−150%
- >150%
- Not available

MAP 10.2. Legislative elections of November 1946: Proportion of votes won by the Right

The map represents, for each municipality, the proportion of votes won by the Right as a ratio of the national average.

Sources and series: unehistoireduconflitpolitique.fr

with the largest proportions of salaried employees (and especially of blue-collar factory workers) vote more for the Left, whereas the municipalities with the most self-employed workers (agricultural and nonagricultural) vote more heavily for the Right.

Regarding the blue-collar vote, we have already noted that it has been constitutive of the vote for the Left since the nineteenth century. More generally, the ratio between the vote for the Left in the most blue-collar 50 percent of the municipalities and the least blue-collar 50 percent of the municipalities has almost always been more than 1 during the last two centuries, before and after taking the control variables into account. The effect is particularly great between 1900 and 1960, then begins to decline in the last decades of the twentieth century.[20] We

---

20. See chapter 8, figure 8.11.

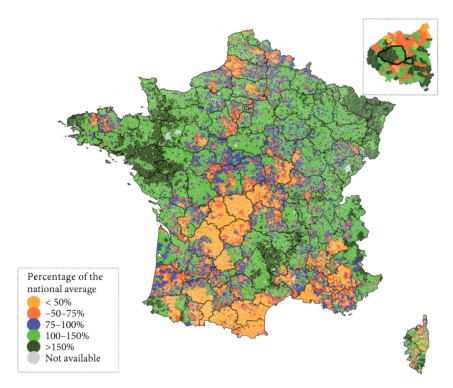

MAP 10.3. Legislative elections of 1981: Proportion of votes won by the Right

The map represents, for each municipality, the proportion of votes won by the Right as a ratio of its national average.

Sources and series: unehistoireduconflitpolitique.fr

can also analyze this singularity in a more refined way by classifying the municipalities by deciles, as functions of their proportions of blue-collar industrial workers. Then we note that the vote for the Left is a regularly growing function of the proportion of blue-collar workers throughout the distribution (and not only when comparing the most working-class 50 percent and the least working-class 50 percent of the municipalities). In the elections of 1936, for instance, the vote for the Left reached 130 percent of the national average in the 5 percent of the municipalities with the highest proportions of blue-collar workers. Among them, we find Hulluch, Haisnes, Wingles, and Liévin in Pas-de-Calais, where the vote for the Left surpassed, respectively, 137, 160, 175 and 196 percent of the national average; these are municipalities whose miners occupied the pits during the movements of May–June 1936. On the contrary, in Guinecourt, Sars-le-Bois, and

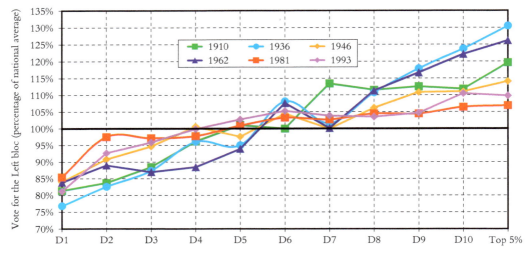

Distribution of the population by deciles, as a function of the proportion of workers in the municipality

FIGURE 10.7. The vote for the Left and working-class municipalities, 1910–1993

From the legislative elections of 1910 to those of 1993, the vote for the Left (relative to the national average) grows with the proportion of blue-collar workers in the municipality, but with a slope considerably less steep in 1981 and 1993 than in 1910, 1936, 1946, or 1962. Note: The results given here are after controls for the size of the conurbation and municipality.

Sources and series: unehistoireduconflitpolitique.fr

Wambercourt, municipalities in Pas-de-Calais that were among the least blue-collar in France, the vote for the Left did not exceed 50 percent of the national average. Between the two, in Cambrai in the department of Nord, a municipality that is median from the point of view of its proportion of workers, on average the citizens voted for the Left just as they did elsewhere in the country.

This regularity between voting for the Left and the proportion of blue-collar workers is found in all the legislative elections from 1910 to 1993 (see figure 10.7), whether or not the other explanatory variables are introduced.[21] This illustrates once again the extent to which electoral conflict goes beyond the territorial cleavage and the cleavage linked to wealth: for the same size of conurbation and municipality, and for a given average income, voting behavior also depends very much on occupational status and the sector of activity. It will also be noted

---

21. The results indicated in figures 10.7–10.8 are after controlling for the size of the conurbation and municipality. The profiles before any control and after the introduction of all the controls have a similar form and are available online. See unehistoireduconflitpolitique.fr, figures D3.1a–D3.17i and appendix D3.

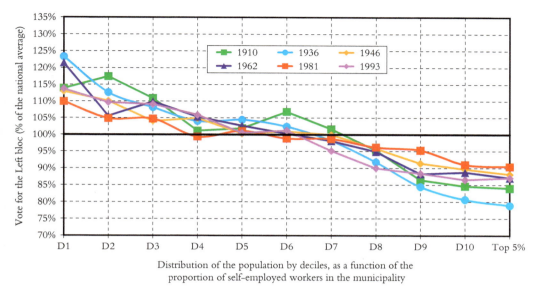

FIGURE 10.8. The vote for the Left and self-employed workers, 1910–1993

From the legislative elections of 1910 to those of 1993, the vote for the Left (relative to its national average) decreased with the proportion of self-employed workers in the municipality, with a slope hardly less steep in 1993 in comparison to 1946 or 1962. Note: The results given here are after controls for the size of the conurbation and municipality.

Sources and series: unehistoireduconflitpolitique.fr

that in working-class municipalities, voting for the Left is a phenomenon that is still very present in the elections of 1981 and 1993, but with a curve that nonetheless appears to be less steep than in 1910, 1936, or 1962. This gradual disaffection of blue-collar municipalities with regard to the Left has continued since the 1980s and 1990s; later on, we will return to the different factors capable of accounting for this fundamental transformation, whether it is a matter of the disappointment after the Union of the Left came to power or other, more long-term factors.

We come now to the question of self-employed workers. Again, we observe that all through the twentieth century, voting for the Left gradually declines with the proportion of self-employed workers in the municipality (see figure 10.8). If we examine the results in greater detail, we see that at the beginning of the twentieth century, agricultural workers play the leading role in generating this electoral profile, and then that self-employed, nonagricultural workers (artisans, merchants, businessmen, the liberal professions) take on an increasing importance starting in the interwar period and especially during the second half of the twentieth century.[22] The profile becomes slightly less steep over time, if we compare 1936 and 1981, for example, which can be interpreted as a consequence of the fact that the numerical and political weight of self-employed workers declined sharply between those two dates. However, unlike what we see for blue-collar workers, the evolution of the whole is much less clear. For example, the relation between voting for the Left and the proportion of self-employed workers observed in the legislative elections of 1993 is ultimately quite close to what it was in 1946 or 1962, despite the fact that the number and the composition of self-employed workers as a group underwent a profound change during this period.[23] We see also that although the vote for the Left diminishes with the proportion of self-employed workers, that implies symmetrically that it increases with the proportion of salaried workers in the active population (a proportion that is simply the inverse of the proportion of self-employed workers).

To sum up, although the working-class industrial vote ended up gradually moving away from the Left, there is a regularity that has remained practically unchanged over the long term—namely, that salaried employees (considered as a whole: blue-collar industrial workers, employees in the services, intermediary occupations and managers) still continue to vote more for the Left than for the Right, and that conversely, self-employed workers support the Right more than the Left, ceteris paribus. For example, if we examine the evolution of the ratio between the vote for the Left in the 50 percent of the municipalities with the most and the least self-employed workers in the legislative elections from 1848 to 2022, we see that this ratio has always been clearly less than 1 and shows no very clear tendency over the long term after the controls are taken into account (see figure 10.9). In the nineteenth century and the beginning of the twentieth, this ratio was particularly low, but that is explained mainly by rurality as such, and not by the proportion of self-employed workers. As soon as we control for the size of conurbation and a given municipality, the negative effect of the proportion of self-employed workers on the vote for the Right appears to be not very different at the end of the twentieth century and the beginning of the twenty-first than what it was in the nineteenth century and at the beginning of the twentieth.

This is a fundamental regularity that tells us about the deep structure of political and electoral conflict, and in this case, about self-employed workers' (and no longer just agricultural workers') persistent distrust of the Left, including self-employed workers who have low levels of income. This lack of understanding between the

---

22. See unehistoireduconflitpolitique.fr, appendix D3.
23. See chapter 2, figures 2.18–2.19.

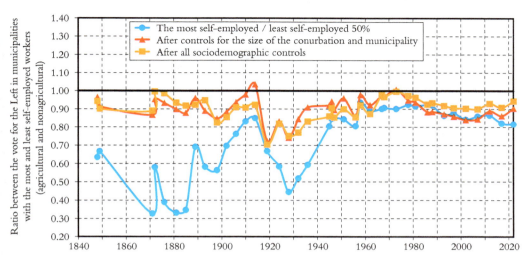

FIGURE 10.9. The vote for the Left and the self-employed, 1848–2022

From the legislative elections of 1848 to those of 2022, the vote for the Left has always been smaller in municipalities with the largest proportions of self-employed workers (agricultural and nonagricultural), particularly in the nineteenth century and the beginning of the twentieth. The control variables (especially the size of the conurbation) reduce the size of the effect without entirely erasing it. In the end, after the controls, the effect is relatively stable over a long period.

Sources and series: unehistoireduconflitpolitique.fr

Left and the self-employed suggests that bipartition has always been incomplete and fragile, insofar as the Left has always had difficulty bringing together people with the same levels of income but different statuses of employment and economic activity. Such divisions can prove to be particularly damaging to forming majority coalitions and government platforms, especially in periods when self-employed workers represent a considerable proportion of the active population (more than half at the beginning of the twentieth century and during the interwar period, and still more than a third under the Fourth Republic, as opposed to one-tenth at the beginning of the twenty-first century).[24]

The Difficult Establishment of Bipolarization: The Interwar Period

Let us go back and try to better understand the interaction between electoral cleavages, coalitions, and transfers of power in the course of the period 1910–1992,

---

24. See chapter 2, figures 2.18–2.19.

beginning with the prewar and interwar periods. In the preceding chapter, we emphasized that powerful forces driving toward bipartition were already in place around 1900–1910. On the right, the fusion of the former Moderate and Opportunist Republicans with the conservatives, monarchists, and Catholics was far advanced, particularly because the latter had rallied to the Republican regime, and also because both of them had always been relatively close on economic and financial questions and were increasingly wary of the Left's projects, and this incited them to unite. On the left, the Radical-Socialists and the Socialists constituted the two main poles. They voted together, not only for the laws concerning secularism and the separation of church and state (1905), but also for the draft of a program of redistribution and social security, with in particular the creation of a progressive inheritance tax (1901) and the law on retirement pensions for workers and peasants (1910), and then the income tax (1914) approved by the Senate on the eve of the war. This alliance of the Radical-Socialists and the Socialists also helped bring together the rural and urban working-class electorates, which were much less starkly divided in 1900–1910 than they were in the nineteenth century. The Radical-Socialists represented themselves as the best defenders of small property owners and self-employed workers of the rural and urban worlds, whereas the Socialists' base was the rapidly expanding urban and industrial proletariat. With these two components, which achieved excellent results in the legislative elections of 1910 and 1914, the Left bloc appeared to be capable of reconciling the rural and urban working classes and making a decisive contribution to the establishment of a political system centered on the social question and left-right bipolarization.

Nevertheless, the cleavage remained strong, and the Left's social and economic program was far from unified. The fact that the Left bloc was led by the Radicals, who (according to the syndical movement) did not always sufficiently emphasize working-class and industrial issues, was also a source of recurrent tensions with the Left between 1900 and 1910. Once again, this illustrates the difficulties connected with holding together a coalition that compounded such different statuses, territories, and productive structures.[25] The new challenges issuing from the

---

25. The explosion in the mine at Courrière, which occurred in March 1906 (1,009 dead, 696 injured) when the Left bloc was trying again to get the income tax adopted and to move toward solidarism, radicalized the syndical movement and led to the Charter of Amiens in October 1906 (syndical autonomy with regard to political parties, direct action to change the power relationships with the capitalists and to impose new rules on them through struggle). The additional fatalities in Villeneuve-Saint-Georges in 1908 during the strikes in the building trade and in the quarries in the Paris region definitively transformed Clemenceau (who subse-

military confrontation of 1914–1918 and from the Bolshevik Revolution of 1917 were to test this fragile unity and complicate a little more the establishment of the Left-Right bipartition. In practice, the interwar period was characterized not by serene transitions of power between two unified blocs, but rather by a series of unstable and precarious coalitions of the Right and Left, often with the participation of the Radicals, who, taking into account the electoral surge of the Socialists and Communists, once again found themselves de facto pushed to the center of the political chessboard. After the incontestable victory of the Right bloc gathered together in the "National Bloc" in the elections of 1919, conducted immediately after the military defeat of Germany, the Left bloc and the Center had two successes: the victories of the Cartel of the Left in 1924 and of the Popular Front in 1936. In each case, a majority was put in place (in 1924–1925 and 1936–1937) on the basis of parliamentary support from the Radicals, Socialists, and Communists, and then faded before passing the eighteen-month mark in government. In both cases, there was a second half of the legislative session, when the Radicals turned to the other side of the political chessboard and formed a new coalition with part of the right wing. Ultimately, it was the Right that governed most of the time during the interwar period, with or without the support of the Radicals. Considering the results of the different tendencies in the legislative elections, the interwar period might also be characterized as a period of weak tripartition (or an incomplete bipartition), with de facto a Center bloc consisting of Radicals, a Left bloc consisting of Communists and Socialists, and a Right bloc bringing together the different conservative, liberal, Catholic, and nationalist tendencies situated to the right of the Radicals. The crucial difference from the periods of real tripartition seen in the 1880s and 1890s and after the elections of 2017 and 2022 is that in the interwar period, the Radicals won barely 15–20 percent of the votes, such that the Center bloc was too weak to constitute a majority and at the same time too strong to allow the Left and Right blocs to govern on a long-term basis without it.[26]

To account for the chronic political instability seen in the interwar period as well as under the Fourth Republic (1946–1958)—during which the Center bloc was even weaker, with scarcely 10 percent of the votes for the Radicals and their allies—many observers have emphasized institutional factors and the inability of the actors of the time to agree on constitutional changes that would make it

---

quently moved toward the Right) and the Radicals (whence he came) into social traitors in the eyes of a large part of the syndical movement.

26. See chapter 8, figure 8.1.

possible to strengthen the executive and stabilize the parliamentary coalitions.[27] There is indeed little doubt that setting up the Fifth Republic in 1958 and electing the president by universal suffrage in 1962 greatly helped to stabilize parliamentary life around two large blocs, with a Center that continued to shrink for several decades.[28] Nonetheless, the elections of 2017 and 2022 show that the Fifth Republic did not necessarily entail bipartition, and the experience of 1848 reminds us that presidentialism does not guarantee political stability and social harmony—which explains to a large extent the hesitation during the interwar period to question the parliamentary system that had proved itself since the 1870s.

Public Debt, the Economic Crisis, and the Divisions of the Electorate

It seems to us essential to emphasize that the political instability of the interwar period is explained not just by institutional factors but also, and perhaps especially, by the fact that the different blocs were confronting immense difficulties in defining coherent responses to the challenges of the moment. The first challenge that was to dominate the political agenda of the 1920s was the financial legacy of the war. Emerging from four years of human and material destruction of an unprecedented magnitude, unrelated to any earlier war on French or European soil, the country found itself with a considerable public debt of a level not seen since the French Revolution.[29] The question of paying this debt constituted a redoubtable test for all the political camps, on the right and the left, and each one found itself making promises on this subject that it could not keep. And to top it all off, they were confronted with sharp conflicts over the distribution of the debt among the social classes—conflicts that are easy to analyze coolly with a century's distance, but which were extremely complex to resolve calmly in the heat of the moment. Then the 1930s were dominated by the consequences of the stock

---

27. See J. Garrigues, *Histoire du Parlement de 1789 à nos jours* (A. Colin, 2007).

28. Of course, here, too, history was not linear. Thus, during the presidential election of 1965, the centrists hesitated for a long time before presenting a candidate, unsure about the idea of "proving the existence or non-existence of this third political tendency between the Left and Extreme Left on the one hand, and Gaullism on the other." See R. Cayrol, *Les élections législatives de mars 1967* (Presses de la FNSP, 1970), 45. When de Gaulle was forced into a run-off election by Jean Lecanuet, the latter was convinced that a third way was possible (whence the constitution, in February 1966, of the Democratic Center, which in the legislative elections of 1967 won around 12–13 percent of the votes).

29. In the early 1920s, the public debt was between 1.5 and two years of the national revenue, as opposed to about one year of the national revenue in 1789. See T. Piketty, *Une brève histoire de l'égalité* (Seuil, 2021), figure 26.

market crash of 1929 and the worldwide economic and social crisis that resulted from it, once again with radically new challenges for all the political forces, in the context of an unprecedented rise in unemployment, a low level of industrial and agricultural activity, and the deflation of prices and salaries.[30]

To this we must add another radical novelty that may be even more important than the first two: the Bolshevik Revolution of 1917. In fact, the construction on the ruins of the czarist regime of the first "proletarian state" in history was to turn the political landscape upside down on the international scale, and especially in France. On the right, the Communist threat suddenly became real and no longer merely theoretical, and the new situation helped bind the ranks together and fed the arguments against the Left, even if other sources of division soon appeared. On the left, the first effect was the schism between the Communists (PCF) and the Socialists (SFIO-PS) at the Congress of Tours in 1920. The PCF embarked on a defense of the USSR and attracted an increasing share of a working class that was rapidly growing. For the first time, the PCF glimpsed the plausible prospect of a worldwide revolution and a regime under which proletarians would no longer be exploited. Following Jaurès and Blum, the SFIO set out to promote a more gradualist path toward socialism and rejected submission to the USSR. Nonetheless, during the interwar period, both the PCF and the SFIO were part of a Marxist perspective whose general objective was the collective ownership of the means of production, made inevitable by the growing concentration of capital in large production units, as predicted by Marx. Both of them sought to assure small-scale, independent producers that this socialization would not immediately concern them and would not necessarily take the form of a wholesale nationalization, but they did not completely calm their fears, insofar as the PCF's and the SFIO's conception of the place that small, private ownership of the means of production might have in a future society was never made truly explicit in the programs and discourses of the Communist and Socialist officials of the time.[31]

This ideological hardening brought on by the Revolution of 1917 may help explain why we see during the interwar period a growing distance between the

---

30. That is, a prolonged decline in prices and salaries, in contrast to the very high inflation seen during the war and in the early 1920s, a phenomenon that was in both cases traumatic and difficult for the general public to grasp, in view of the almost complete stability of prices between 1815 and 1914 under the gold standard.

31. See, for example, L. Blum, *Le congrès de Tours. Le socialisme à la croisée des chemins, 1919–1920* (Folio histoire, 2020). In these texts and speeches concerning the break with the Communists, Blum in no way challenged the prospect of a complete collectivization of the means of production.

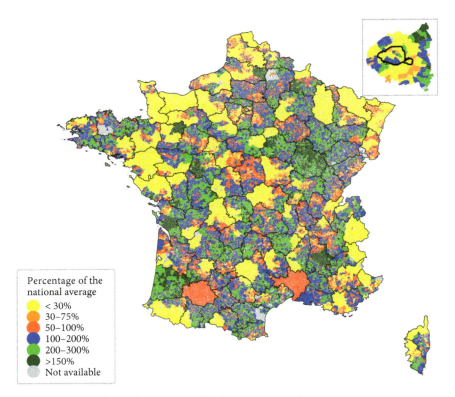

Percentage of the
national average
- < 30%
- 30–75%
- 50–100%
- 100–200%
- 200–300%
- >150%
- Not available

MAP 10.4. The Radical-Socialist vote in the legislative elections of 1928

The map represents, for each municipality, the proportion of votes won by the Radical-Socialist Party as a ratio of the national average. This vote is particularly concentrated in towns and villages.

Sources and series: unehistoireduconflitpolitique.fr

electorate of the Marxist parties (Socialists and Communists) and the Radical-Socialist electorate. What is particularly striking to note is the extent to which the Radical-Socialist vote was concentrated in towns and villages during the elections conducted from 1924 to 1936 (which the municipal electoral data allow us to measure precisely, taking into account the great variations within departments, illustrated by, for instance, map 10.4 in the case of the legislative elections of 1928) far more than before the war, and also far more than the vote for the conservative parties situated to the right of it, which is more surprising. The Radical-Socialist vote was in fact situated at the antipode of the vote for the Socialist and Communist Parties, which for their part were massively concentrated in the suburbs and metropoles (see figure 10.10).

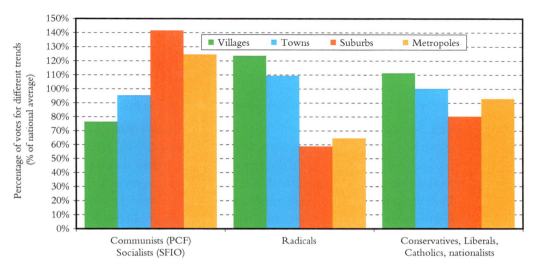

FIGURE 10.10. The elections of 1924–1936: Between bipartition and tripartition

In the legislative elections of 1924–1936, the Radicals constituted a bloc that was too weak to dominate the political system, but strong enough to participate in most of the coalitions. The structure of its electorate was massively oriented toward the villages and towns, even more than that of the Right bloc (conservatives, liberals, etc.), and it was situated at the antipodes of the Communist and Socialist electorate, which was based mainly in the suburbs and metropoles.

Sources and series: unehistoireduconflitpolitique.fr

Thus, we see a maximal sociological division of the electorates of the progressive parties, a great gap that could hardly help facilitate coherent coalitions. The Radical-Socialist party, which was an enthusiastic follower of prewar solidarist socialism,[32] claimed more than ever to be the defender of small-bore, independent producers, whereas the Socialist and Communist Parties opened up prospects for industrial workers and more generally for salaried workers in the urban world. Studies like those by Nonna Mayer have shown how the divorce between the Socialist and Communist Parties and the world of self-employed workers was aggravated and crystalized in an enduring way during the interwar period.[33] Our results confirm this conclusion in the sense that the negative effect that the

32. As we emphasized in chapter 9, under the Third Republic solidarism tried to propose a new path between liberalism and collectivization. See, for example, S. Audier, *La pensée solidariste. Aux sources du modèle social républicain* (Presses Universitaire de France, 2010).

33. See N. Mayer, *La boutique contre la gauche* (Presses de Sciences Po, 1986). See also N. Mayer and E. Schweisguth, "Classe, position sociale et vote," in *Explication du vote. Un bilan des études électorales en France,* ed. D. Gaxie (Presses de la FNSP, 1985).

proportion of self-employed workers had on the vote for the Left tended to peak before the war, and it also tended to grow again in the 1920s and 1930s (see figure 10.9).[34]

The Time of Blockages: Inconsistencies in Socialism and in Nationalism

To sum up, it was above all the contradictions within the alliance of the three progressive parties (Communists, Socialists, and Radical-Socialists) regarding the content of democratic socialism and the type of property regime they wanted to establish that limited the ability of this bloc to govern the country over the long term. These programmatic disagreements divided the electorate and considerably weakened the movement toward bipartition. However, we must add that the Right bloc was also shot through with multiple discords and inconsistencies that contributed at least as much to the blockages of the period as the Left's contradictions did. In fact, it was the three principal ideological systems that had structured public life since the nineteenth century that fell into crisis when confronted by the challenges of the interwar period: socialism, liberalism, and nationalism. In theory, the Right bloc remained united around the principles of economic liberalism and its opposition to the collectivists. In practice, the financial legacy of the war and the crisis of the 1930s fissured this consensus to a considerable degree. Confronted by a series of bankruptcies, widespread unemployment, and the obvious fragility of private capitalism when left to its own devices, new forms of state interventionism in economic life were required on all sides of political life. This took the form of the New Deal in the United States, nationalizations and state planning in France after 1945, and almost everywhere, economic and social policies that turned their backs on the unbridled liberalism of the pre-1914 era. However, during the interwar period, the various tendencies of the French Right balked at challenging liberal dogmas and long continued to believe in the return of the old world, and in particular in the reestablishment of the gold standard of 1914. This perspective, which was unrealistic and poorly adapted to the situation of the French economy, aggravated the crisis of the 1930s and was truly abandoned only with the devaluation of the franc imposed by the Popular Front in 1936—unfortunately, several years

---

34. This result is explained mainly by the fact that the Radical-Socialists are included in the Left bloc before the war, whereas they were pushed back toward the Center during the interwar period (in fact, we classify them as centrist starting in 1924) because of the growing space occupied by the Communists and Socialists.

after the United Kingdom and the United States devalued their currencies, in 1931 and 1933, respectively.[35]

The contradictions within nationalism were even more considerable. Since the war of 1870 and the first decades of the Third Republic, this theme had become increasingly structuring on the right. In the 1880s and 1890s, the monarchist and nationalist tendencies accused the Opportunist Republicans of privileging their business and financial interests, of neglecting the honor of the country and its army, and finally of writing off the major amputation of the national territory that occurred when Alsace and Moselle were reunited with the Reich.[36] As for the Socialists, they were stigmatized for their blind internationalism and the way in which they weakened the nation by aggravating the class struggle and internal divisions, whereas they should have united to confront the external enemy. In his *Enquête sur la monarchie* (the handbook of the militants of Action française, reprinted over and over between 1900 and 1924), Charles Maurras did not limit himself to stigmatizing the "four confederated states" (Jews, Protestants, Freemasons, and *métèques*) who were, according to him, responsible for undermining national unity. He intended to establish the superiority of the monarchical system on rational bases, proposing a historical analysis of the way in which the monarchy had made it possible to protect the nation's territory effectively and to avoid any invasion between 1650 and 1789 and from 1815 to 1848, whereas the republican regime had only weakened the country and permitted repeated incursions in 1792, 1814, and 1870, and then again from 1914 to 1918. This argument may surprise today's reader, but it shows the extent to which the question of protecting the national territory played a major role in the debates of the period.[37]

After the devastating conflict of 1914–1918, the question of nationalism and the astronomical reparations demanded of Germany were to play a structuring role.

---

35. On the narrative of the political-economic events of the period, see, for example, A. Sauvy, *Histoire économique de la France entre les deux guerres* (Fayard, 1965–1975). Although it is marred by multiple biases, this book nonetheless constitutes an interesting testimony given by the man who was the adviser of the minister of finance, Paul Reynaud, in 1938 (he was very opposed to the Popular Front and the forty-hour workweek), before becoming, after the war, the leader of French populationist demography.

36. This was particularly the case with Maurice Barrès, who had been elected as a Boulangist deputy from Nancy in 1889 and was the figurehead of French nationalism and anti-Germanism.

37. See, in particular, the "Discours préliminaire 1900–1924" that Maurras added to the final edition of his *Enquête sur la monarchie,* published in 1924 and supplemented with a statistical appendix with graphs and tables comparing the prewar French and German military budgets and predicted difficulties in the battles, which the Republican regime, which was not very respectful of the army and obsessed with internal struggles, was accused of having seriously neglected.

We know what happened next. The sums that the defeated country was required to pay by the Treaty of Versailles signed in 1919 reached truly incredible levels: the equivalent of about 300 percent of the German GDP in 1913—three years of national production—which with an interest rate of 5 percent would have meant that Germany had to pay France 15 percent of its annual production for an indefinite period of time, simply to repay the interest on the debt and without ever repaying the principal.[38] These reparations were never paid; they merely fueled German nationalism and the Nazis' rise to power in 1933. At the time, the most lucid observers (beginning with John Maynard Keynes) immediately predicted catastrophe. The French Right, and with it, the quasi-totality of the political class, did not give in; it was the only way to face up to France's immense debt and respect the "sacred word" given to all those who had lent their savings to finance the war and to support those who were shedding blood in the trenches. The sacred debt had to be paid back in 1914 gold francs—and to make that possible, Germany had to pay. Hadn't France paid in cash the equivalent of 30 percent of its national revenue to Prussia after the war of 1871? The devastation on French soil in 1914–1918 was far greater and justified the amounts demanded! When the Treaty of Versailles was ratified in the Chamber of Deputies on 2 October 1919, seventy right-wing deputies abstained in favor of larger reparations, an accelerated payment schedule, and more secure military and territorial guarantees (including various proposals for dismembering Germany). Louis Maurin, the head of the Republican Federation from 1925 to 1945 and a deputy from Meurthe-et-Moselle from 1905 to 1951—and whose lieutenant, Xavier Vallat, insulted Blum in 1936—went so far as to vote against the treaty, along with the Socialist deputies and a handful of radical pacifists, but for opposite reasons. The Socialists and pacifists were denounced for their duplicity and treachery in a climate where nationalism was white-hot and everyone was suspected of not doing enough to honor the dead and veterans.[39]

The alliance of nationalism and anticommunism allowed the Right to exercise power during most of the interwar period. But the nationalist program was based

---

38. See T. Piketty, *Capital et idéologie* (Seuil, 2019), 550–559. The amounts are all the more absurd because the 15 percent GDP trade surplus that Germany would have had to generate to cover this transfer would have severely hampered the recovery of French industry.

39. In 1918, the former Radical minister of finance, Joseph Caillaux (who was far from being a dangerous revolutionary internationalist), was stripped of his parliamentary immunity and imprisoned for "complicity with the enemy" simply because he had spoken in favor of making peace with Germany. The contradictions surrounding nationalism affected all the camps: before the 1914 elections, the left-wing parties (Socialists and Radicals) had promised to abrogate the law requiring three years of military service, and then a few months later they joined the Sacred Union's governments after Jaurès was assassinated and the war broke out.

on a fundamental contradiction that prevented it from succeeding, because ultimately, no one was ready to go back to war in order to seize further reparations when France had hardly begun to lick its wounds. An attempt to occupy the Ruhr was made between 1923 and 1925 in order to accelerate German payments, but without much success. No one dared go any further, because it was clear that extracting large amounts of Germany's wealth would require dispatching many more troops and a long-term occupation of the country that would ultimately risk triggering a new military conflict that French forces would have a hard time winning without support from other countries, considering the crushing demographic superiority of Germany (which was at that time over 50 percent more heavily populated than France). The fact is that the French nationalists lacked the human and military power that would permit them to carry out their projects.[40] That makes the French nationalism of the interwar period less offensive than Nazism or Fascism, but it nonetheless helped exacerbate the political blockages of the time, because neither the Left bloc nor the Right bloc had a coherent programmatic platform. There are, of course, other factors that might explain why French nationalism seems less offensive, starting with its stronger roots in the country's pluralist and parliamentary tradition.[41] However, even if it was less dangerous in the European context, that did not prevent multiple forms of violence and brutality in the colonies at the same time, which suggests that the country's demographic weakness played a certain role in moderating nationalist fervor in the European theater.

---

40. On this fundamental incoherence of French nationalism in the interwar period, see G. Richard's analyses in *Histoire des droites en France de 1815 à nos jours* (Perrin, 2017. See also J. L. Pinol, "1919–1958: *Le temps* des droites?," in *Histoire des droites en France,* vol.1, ed. J. F. Sirinelli (Gallimard, 1992).

41. We refer to the classic argument used by some French historians to counter the claim made by Zeev Sternhell and others that Fascism was French in origin. Z. Sternhell, *La Droite révolutionnaire, 1885–1914: Les origines françaises du fascisme* (Seuil, 1978). For a defense of the Parti social français (PSF) of Colonel de la Rocque, a party that emerged from veterans' movements and that might have been on the verge of winning the legislative elections of 1940 if they had taken place (the PSF is supposed to have had as many as 1.2 million members in 1938–1939, which would make it the largest party in the history of France, ahead of the PCF). see S. Bernstein and J. P. Thomas, *Le PSF: Un parti de masse à droite (1936–1940)* (CNRS Éditions, 2016). According to these historians, the PSF, a party that the Left of the period accused of being "fascist," can also be analyzed as an early form of Gaullism avant la lettre. On the idea that the nationalism inspired by Charles Maurras could not degenerate into expansionist Nazism because of its roots in an Old Regime tradition, an argument that is different from but related to the former, see M. Gauchet, *La droite et la gauche. Histoire et destin* (Le Débat / Gallimard, 2021), 99–101.

When the National Bloc Invented the 75 Percent Income Tax

Ironically, it was the parliamentary chamber furthest to the right in the history of the Republic—the famous *chambre bleu horizon* elected in 1919 as part of the National Bloc's majority—that set up the progressive tax on very large incomes with the highest rate the country had ever seen. It did this to cope with the difficult financial situation in which it found itself. That is all the more amazing because this majority was composed of parliamentary groups who before the war had rejected the very principle of progressive taxation and had long opposed the law of 15 July 1914 creating an income tax with a modest rate of 5 percent on the highest brackets. Since the nineteenth century, right-wing politicians had fiercely opposed progressive taxation, even at low rates, on the ground that once created, such a diabolical machine could never be stopped. But now it was the same parliamentary groups that had been opposed to any kind of progressivity who were pushing the machine further and faster than they could ever have imagined they would. After several rate hikes during the war years, the law of 25 June 1920 adopted by the majority of the National Bloc could truly be considered the second birth of the income tax. The rate applicable to the highest incomes was raised to 60 percent. If we include the supplemental tax of 25 percent applied to unmarried people (and 10 percent for married couples who were still without children after two years—proof of the governments' fiscal imagination if ever there was one!) also adopted by the National Bloc, in 1923 the top rate reached 75 percent for the highest incomes. In comparison, the "immoral" tax of one-third on incomes deriving from property, proposed by the Socialist Proudhon in 1848, looks very timorous. With the supplements, the National Bloc hit harder than even the Union of the Left and the Communist Left did after the elections of 1981 when they created 65 percent and 70 percent tax brackets.[42]

How can we explain why parliamentary groups that rejected a 5 percent income tax in 1914 ended up in 1920 adopting a tax of more than 60 percent, or even 75 percent with the supplements? Of course, the context had been completely transformed by the war, the destruction, and millions of dead. At a time when the budget deficit and the national debt had reached unprecedented proportions, when inflation was eroding purchasing power, when workers' salaries still had not regained their levels in 1914, and when several waves of strikes threatened to para-

---

42. For a detailed history of the legislation on income taxes and the political battles over them since the founding law of 1914, see T. Piketty, *Les hauts revenus en France au 20e siècle* (Grasset, 2001), 233–334.

lyze the country in May and June 1919, and then again in the spring of 1920, it almost seems that political nuances mattered very little. Beyond the slogans on the theme of "Germany will pay," which were facile and seldom had any effect, we had to come up with revenue, and no one imagined that the wealthiest would be spared. Here, the Socialist and Communist menace played an obvious role: it was better for the elites to accept a very progressive tax than to risk a general expropriation like the one that had just occurred with the Bolshevik Revolution.

However, it would be a mistake to see progressive taxation as simply the consequence of the war[43] and the Communist menace. The same evolution is found in all Western countries at that time, depending on diverse political modalities. In the United States, where the influence of the First World War and the Revolution of 1917 was much less crucial than it was in Europe, but where the demand for equality and justice was very strong starting in the 1890s and 1900s (a period when the feeling that a new industrial and financial oligarchy was on the verge of taking control of the country was spreading inexorably), and still more after the crisis of 1929, which left the impression that this elite had led the nation to disaster while enriching itself, fiscal progressivity also shot up, with a tax rate applicable to the highest incomes that reached 81 percent on average between 1932 and 1980. That in no way prevented the economic power of the United States from being deployed in an unparallelled way during this period; this essential historical episode demonstrates quite clearly that US prosperity was much more due to social and educational investment (the United States was at the time far ahead of the rest of the world in these areas) than to a stratospheric level of inequality. Everything also indicates that the establishment of this very strong fiscal progressivity made it possible to accelerate the development of the welfare state over the course of the twentieth century.[44] Finally, let us note that the proposals for progressive tax scales close to those that were to be adopted starting in the 1920s in Western countries, with rates ranging from less than 5 percent on the lowest brackets to 70–80 percent on the highest incomes and inheritances, had already been explic-

---

43. This is the thesis defended by Kenneth Scheve and David Stasavage in their works, in which they maintain that the establishment of higher tax rates for the rich can be seen as a form of "compensatory taxation," particularly following mass conscription during the two world wars. See K. Scheve and D. Stasavage, *Taxing the Rich: A History of Fiscal Fairness in the United States and Europe* (Princeton University Press, 2016). Their argument is interesting but insufficient: the examination of the different trajectories shows that it was above all the process of political mobilization seeking to reduce inequalities that had an essential impact, especially in countries like the United States and Sweden, where the 1914–1918 war played a far smaller role than it did in France and Germany, but where progressivity rose even more quickly and higher.

44. See Piketty, *Une brève histoire de l'égalité,* 185–200, figures 20–23.

itly formulated during the French Revolution.[45] But the power relationships at that time did not make it possible to adopt them. The experience of the 1920s shows that institutional upheaval can work very quickly and reminds us of the decisive importance of the historical context and social struggles, beyond the electoral results obtained by the various blocs.[46]

From the Cartel des Gauches to the Popular Front: The Assertion of the Left-Right Conflict

In addition to pursuing radical change in fiscal policy, the National Bloc also embarked on a race with the Left regarding social welfare questions, and in particular labor law, rent control, public housing, and pensions for veterans. On the eve of the elections in 1919, the Center-Right government had already secured the eight-hour workday, in a blatant exercise in triangulation with the Left. Here we see how a form of chaotic bipartition and a virtuous dynamic was set up. If we examine the maximalist version of its program, we see that each of the two blocs was marked by multiple contradictions and incoherencies, especially on the question of socialism and nationalism, which provoked numerous crises and changes in coalitions when the disagreements were expressed too overtly on the parliamentary scene, but in the end, the bipartisan electoral competition centered on the social welfare question made it possible to enter a dynamic dialectic and to advance a certain number of concrete policies.

The victories won by the Cartel of the Left in 1924 and the Popular Front in 1936 were also powerful symbolic stages in the assertion of the Left-Right bipartition. However, the two experiences were very different. In 1924, the Socialists were part of the parliamentary majority but they refused to join the government led by the Radical Édouard Herriot, in part because they did not want to be criticized by the Communists, who denounced any idea of direct participation in a bourgeois government. In 1936, the Socialists won the most votes and for the first time took over the direction of the government with Léon Blum, thanks to the sup-

---

45. See Piketty, *Une brève histoire de l'égalité,* 187, table`1.
46. The US economist Edwin Seligman, who played a major role in acclimatizing the idea of progressive taxation among reform-minded liberal elites on the global level before 1914, had in mind only a moderate progressivity (with maximal rates on the order of 10–20 percent) and would have stridently objected to the idea of marginal rates rising as high as 80–90 percent and an overall burden of the welfare state reaching 50 percent of the national revenue over the course of the twentieth century. See E. Seligman, *L'impôt progressif en théorie et en pratique* (Giard, 1909), a work that was translated into many languages and was very influential at the time.

port of the Radicals and the Communists. The riots provoked by the nationalist leagues on 6 February 1934 and the dangers posed by German rearmament had already taken their toll.[47] Above all, the Popular Front's record in the area of social welfare was far more substantial than that of the Cartel. This was due essentially to the unprecedented movement of strikes and occupations of factories that spontaneously arose after the elections. There is no doubt that the mobilization generated the greatest fear in property owners since the insurrections of 1848 and the Commune in 1871, but the effects were completely different. The great social welfare laws creating paid vacations and collective conventions were immediately approved by the parliament by a nearly unanimous vote of the deputies, including the Right, even though a few weeks earlier no one had had any idea of adopting such legislation. The experiment was historic, because it demonstrated to everyone the obvious complementarity of the labor movement and electoral democracy. Without the social struggles and occupations of factories, such a parliamentary consensus would never have occurred, and the Popular Front government probably would not have even tried to submit such laws for the approval of the Chamber and the Senate. Conversely, without an electoral victory by the Left and without Socialist leaders at the head of the state, it is difficult to see how a state power sure of its elective legitimacy would have reacted when faced by occupations and strikes (which in any case would no doubt not have happened in the same way).

The experience of the Cartel and the Popular Front also illustrates the importance of institutional factors in the establishment of the Left-Right bipartition and in the reduction of social inequalities. In 1924–1925, as in 1936–1937, the negative votes in the Senate (which then had a veto right extending to all legislation) blocked

---

47. The riots of 1934 followed the revelations, emerging in December 1933, of the twists and turns of "that nasty Stavisky affair" (to use the title of Paul Jankowsky's book), whose consequences were just as devastating in their own way as the great financial scandals of the 1880s and 1890s and the *affaire des fiches* in 1905, in a context in which the accusations of antipatriotism and treason made against the Radicals and the Left had taken on a new magnitude since the war. In a word, though it all began with the nth financial scandal—the affair of the Bayonne bonds, in which almost 500 million francs was stolen from the Caisses du Crédit Municipal—the campaign waged by the right-wing newspapers soon brought to light the role played by Alexandre Stavisky, a crook who presided over the destinies of the Crédit Municipal and had many protectors. After the press's revelations, Paris's general prosecutor, the brother-in-law of the Radical Party president of the Council of Ministers, Camille Chautemps, supposedly intervened seventeen times to prevent investigations of Stavisky—a Jewish financier and a Freemason to boot, which made him one of Maurras's favorite targets—as well as of the Radical deputy mayor of Bayonne, Joseph Garat. The Radicals in particular were weakened and criticized as a central group forever attached to power, like the Opportunist Republicans of the early Third Republic.

the establishment of multiple fiscal and social reforms supported by the majority of the Left deputies in the Chamber. In both cases, it was the Senate that provoked the fall of the Cartel's and the Popular Front's governments as well as the Radicals' swing toward the Right majorities. This was particularly the case in April 1925, when the Senate decided to bring down the Herriot government because of its fiscal and financial policy. When it took power in 1924, the Cartel had limited itself to pursuing the policy of raising the taxes on the highest incomes, which had been enacted by the National Bloc; in this case, it was difficult to go much further, since the top bracket had already been raised to 75 percent. But the Herriot government quickly realized that the receipts brought in by the income tax were insufficient to deal with the immense public debt resulting from the war, unless low and middle-range income levels were taxed very heavily. To significantly reduce the stock of public debt, the only way to proceed was to resort to an exceptional tax on the stock of private capital. The idea was natural for the Socialist and Communist deputies, who were already envisaging a general challenge to private ownership of capital; it was far less natural for the Radicals, who were afraid they would scare small, independent producers by putting in place a tool of this kind. In fact, the "diabolical machine" of the progressive tax on capital was potentially much more frightening than the progressive tax on the flow of income, since here it was a matter of redistributing property itself, potentially without limits.

When it took control in June 1924, it took months for the Herriot cabinet to make up its mind to resort to this extremity. After reaching the ceiling of the advances then authorized by the Banque de France, on 8 April 1925 Herriot finally decided to have the Chamber of Deputies adopt, with the help of the Socialists and Communists, the principle of an exceptional tax on private capital, with a rate rising as high as 10 percent for the largest patrimonies, a rate that might be raised in the future if it proved to be insufficient to reduce the public debt and honor the "sacred debt" owed savers. That was too much for the Senate, which decided to bring down Herriot and the Cartel des Gauches. François Goguel, a young administrator at the High Assembly in the 1930s who published in 1937 his first work on "the financial role of the French Senate," was aware of the democratic difficulty involved in challenging in this way a Chamber elected by universal suffrage. He was very afraid that the Senate might end up losing its right to veto if it abused this exorbitant power, as had the British House of Lords, which lost all its power in 1911 following the crisis of the "People's Budget."[48] Goguel nonetheless

---

48. This cocktail of progressive taxes on the privileged classes that made it possible to finance diverse social measures was imprudently censured by the House of Lords, which soon after-

attempted a justification: this fiscal measure, "Marxist" in inspiration, had not been explicitly proposed to voters before the election of 1924, and the Senate could thus legitimately be allowed to censure the Chamber and to make its own point of view prevail.[49] The argument is interesting but not entirely convincing; in the context of the economic and financial chaos peculiar to that period (and to many others), the parliament repeatedly adopted fiscal and financial measures that had not been explicitly debated and validated by the electors before the elections.[50]

With the historical distance that we now have, there can be little doubt that a progressive levy on private capital was the least bad way of solving the problem of public indebtedness, and above all, a fairer way of distributing the burden than the method consisting of relying implicitly on inflation and price rises, which is also a form of taxation on wealth, except that inflation relies more heavily on directly nibbling away at small and medium-sized savings than on taxing large portfolios invested in securities or real estate.[51] Several progressive taxes on private capital were applied with success in Europe (as well as in Japan) to reduce public debt after each of the two world wars. The example usually considered the most successful is the tax adopted in Germany in 1952, with a levy as high as 50 percent on the largest financial, business, and real estate wealth (in all its forms), which made it possible to pay off public debt without inflation (in a country where the trauma of hyperinflation in 1923 was still very much alive), and redistribute the contributions as justly as possible.[52] However, we must empha-

---

ward had to give up any right to veto future legislation following the dissolution of the House of Commons and the confirmation by universal suffrage of the popular support for this "people's budget."

49. See F. Goguel, *Le rôle financier du Sénat français. Essai d'histoire parlementaire* (Sirey, 1937), 182–249.

50. A certain irony can be discerned in the fact that Goguel—who was nonetheless not a revolutionary—thus defended an argument that one might be tempted to compare with the idea of an "imperative mandate" cherished by Jean-Jacques Rousseau and to the partisans of direct democracy, albeit in the context of a reflection on the necessary evolution of a bicameralism that emerged from the censitary tradition of the nineteenth century. It was also following a similar argument imprudently formulated by Lord Salisbury (the leader of the Tories) that the House of Lords lost its right to a veto during the British crisis of 1910–1911, which is very present in Goguel's analysis.

51. Thus, it is a question of taxation that is regressive, not progressive, with regard to the level of wealth. In practice, it was chiefly by inflation, the abandonment of the reference to the gold franc of 1914, and the increase of indirect taxes that the debt crisis was halted, particularly in the framework of the Poincaré stabilization (1926).

52. The mechanism of *Lastenausgleich* (sharing the burden) was adopted in the context of a compromise between Christian Democrats and Social Democrats, and it made it possible to finance compensations for small- and medium-sized patrimonies cut off by the destruction

size the great difficulties that this kind of situation always represents for democratic and parliamentary deliberation. It is never simple to agree on the social distribution of the burden when it reaches such an extent, and it is no doubt inevitable that the resolution of this kind of conflict involves moments of political and social tension of considerable magnitude. We can just hope that serene, peaceful examination of historical precedents might help guide the future conflicts that will not fail to occur in the twenty-first century.

1945: The PCF, Social Security, and the Question of Democratic Socialism

In 1945, the political and institutional context had changed substantially since 1924 and 1936. The Third Republic's parliamentary institutions had been scuttled by voting to give Marshal Pétain full powers in July 1940. The Constituent Assembly elected in October 1945 exercised all the legislative power of a regime that had suddenly become monocameral. This was the moment of "tripartism": the PCF, the SFIO, and the MRP (Christian Democrats) had three-quarters of the votes, and they undertook to govern together in order to rebuild the country. The Right was annihilated by the experience of Vichy and collaboration, and the Assembly leaned very far to the Left, with the Communists clearly dominating the Socialists. They were crowned with glory because of their unparalleled involvement in the Resistance and the Soviet Union's decisive contribution to the victory over Nazism. After the collapse of private capitalism during the depression of the 1930s, a crisis internal to capitalism that had led the world to the edge of the abyss, everyone felt that the future belonged to planning and a mixed economy, or even to socialism. In the three elections of October 1945, June 1946, and November 1946, the PCF won on average almost 28 percent of the votes (as opposed to 21 percent for the SFIO and 26 percent for the MRP).[53] The PCF was at the height of its influence. That was also the moment when structural reforms were adopted (1945–1946) that continue to play a central role in France today, beginning with the creation of a unified system of social security covering old age, illness, and accidents in the workplace, as well as family allocations, the status of public office, nation-

---

caused by war and monetary reform. In Japan, the exceptional levy applied in 1946–1947 affected 90 percent of the largest portfolios and made it possible to clear in an accelerated manner the debts resulting from the war. See Piketty, *Une brève histoire de l'égalité*, 212–216; and M. L. Hughes, *Shouldering the Burdens of Defeat: West Germany and the Reconstruction of Social Justice* (University of North Carolina Press, 1999).

53. The PCF won 27 percent of the votes in 1945, 26 percent in June 1946, and 29 percent in November 1946.

alizations, and the establishment of major public services such as EDF.[54] Without the PCF's 28 percent of the vote in 1945–1946—and without the 5 million members of the Confédération générale du travail (CGT, General Confederation of Labor) and the powerful social mobilization then present in the country, in a context in which most of the departmental liberation committees (CDL) were controlled by the Communists and demanded the immediate establishment of a true economic and social democracy in companies—it is difficult to say whether it would have been possible to adopt in this form social security and the other reforms. The Communist deputies were also in an ideal position to impose major fiscal reforms, particularly in order to increase the progressivity of the income tax in December 1945.[55] In addition, it was also in 1945 that the national solidarity tax was instituted, with rates as high as 20 percent for the largest patrimonies, as well as an exceptional levy on all the increases in wealth that occurred between 1940 and 1945, at rates reaching 100 percent for the largest ones.[56]

Following on from these wide-ranging social and fiscal reforms, the central question was obviously whether the country was going to undertake a wholesale transformation of its socioeconomic system. In the context of the period, the first thing to do was to decide whether the leader of the PCF, Maurice Thorez, was going to take over the direction of the government. As the head of the party that had come in first in the election of October 1945 and had the largest number of deputies, he could logically claim that role. This question was first raised at the end of 1945 and in early 1946, but the prospect of a Communist head of govern-

---

54. Électricité de France was created in 1946, whereas the SNCF (Société nationale des chemins de fer français, the national rail service) was created in 1937 by the Front populaire, the outcome of a long process that had begun in 1908 with the nationalization of the Chemins de fer de l'Ouest. See chapter 9.

55. With, in particular, the suppression of the deduction of the tax for the preceding year from the taxable income of the current year, a strange deduction that may seem technical but in reality drastically limited the application of fiscal progressivity in the interwar period. See Piketty, *Les hauts revenus en France*, 302–305.

56. Adjusting for inflation (prices had more than tripled between 1940 and 1945), this nominal levy amounted to taxing at a rate of 100 percent all those who had not been sufficiently impoverished. For André Philip, an SFIO member of the provisional government, it was in any case inevitable that this exceptional tax would weigh on "those who had not enriched themselves, and maybe even on those who, monetarily speaking, had become impoverished in the sense that their wealth had not increased in the same proportion as the general rise in prices, but who were able to preserve their overall wealth, whereas there were so many French people who had lost everything." See *L'Année Politique 1945*, 159. However, in practice, the national solidarity tax brought in less than the German *Lastenausgleich*, and it was especially the high inflation during the period between 1946 and 1949 that helped wipe out the enormous postwar debt.

ment and the warnings issued by French and US military men led the SFIO and the MRP to agree on the Socialist Félix Gouin. After the MRP came in first in June 1946, it took over the direction of the government with Georges Bidault and retained Thorez as deputy prime minister. Then the PCF won the election of November 1946, and this time succeeded in convincing the leaders of the SFIO to let Thorez be the head of government. But some of the SFIO deputies ultimately did not support him in the decisive vote in the Assembly on 5 December 1946 (where Thorez won 261 votes out of 579—thus he was short by 29 votes), so Léon Blum (who had recently returned from deportation, in a state of great exhaustion) had to agree to accept in extremis the position of president of the Council of Ministers, at a time when colonial war was flaring up in Indochina.[57]

Yet, Thorez had spared no pains to convince both sides. In a famous interview published in *Time* magazine on 18 November 1946, the leader of the PCF explained that the model of democratic, parliamentary socialism that he intended to construct in France had nothing to do with the Russian and Soviet path, and in particular that he would not touch peasants' small properties. However, the PCF and the SFIO did not undertake then—any more than at any other time— to describe precisely what their alternative model of socialism would be, and in particular, what place small private property and small independent producers would have in it.[58] According to Thorez, nationalizations should initially intend to concern only the largest enterprises, and different forms of self-management and decentralization would be retained for the smallest productive units, in particular in the agricultural sector in the form of cooperatives, for example. But the commitments lacked precision, which, considering the situation in the kolkhozes and sovkhozes in the Soviet Union, could legitimately arouse concerns among all those for whom ownership of land, a store, or a workshop remained the most common aspiration and the most convincing way to achieve emancipation and autonomy. The ambiguity also comes from the fact that whereas the SFIO had officially the same Marxist program based on the eventual collectivization of all the

---

57. See M. Winock, *La France libérée 1944–1947* (Perrin, 2021), 167–199.

58. Of course, we are not suggesting here that the PCF did not present a program for the legislative elections of 1946; on the contrary, in order to allay the fears of the masses, it worked out, "for the first time so realistically, a 'program of democratic action' including various precise measures (nationalization, price controls, fiscal reforms in order to achieve a balanced budget, industrial and agricultural investments, etc.)." J. Mischi, *Le parti des communistes. Histoire du Parti communiste de 1920 à nos jours* (Hors d'atteinte, 2020). But for all that, this program did not explain what socialism implies over the long term for small private property and the distribution of power in small- and medium-sized enterprises.

means of production—in the 1950s, Guy Mollet was known for his doctrinal inflexibility on this point—when it came time to form a government, the Socialists preferred to ally themselves with the MRP's Christian Democrats rather than with their Marxist coreligionists, which created a certain doubt regarding the desirability of this program. For a long time, these ambiguities concerning the nature of democratic socialism—and of the socioeconomic system that the Socialists and Communists really wanted to set up—helped postpone indefinitely the coming to power of the Union of the Left, and in that very way weakened the Left-Right bipartition.

When the Communists Were Not Left but East

In fact, during the whole period 1946–1958, when it had the opportunity to do so, the SFIO preferred to govern with the MRP and the Center-Right rather than with the PCF. This was notably the case between 1947 and 1951, with the SFIO-Radicals-MRP coalition called "the Third Force," whose objective was to outline a reasonable, intermediate path between the Communists to the left and the Gaullists to the right. As the Socialists saw it, the breakup in May 1947 and the expulsion of the Communists from the government were justified particularly by the support that the PCF and the CGT gave to increasingly serious strikes opposing the government's policies. Today, we know that neither the strikes at Renault in April 1947 (which turned mainly on a salary demand) nor the national strikes in November–December 1947 (which were violently suppressed by the government directed by the MRP member Maurice Schuman and his SFIO minister of the interior, Jules Moch)[59] had the revolutionary goals that the Socialist leaders attributed to them at the time.[60] In addition to the question of taking power and the model of socialism, another subject that especially fueled the conflict between the SFIO and the PCF was the extremely serious stakes involved in the maintenance of the colonial empire and the repression of national liberation movements. In May 1947 the head of government, Paul Ramadier (SFIO), sought the adoption of new military funds to put down the revolts in Madagascar and Indochina, which the PCF deputies refused to authorize, thereby contributing to the

---

59. See M. Zancarini-Fournel, *Les luttes et les rêves. Une histoire populaire de la France de 1685 à nos jours* (La Découverte, 2017), in which the historian refers in her introduction to the memories transmitted by her grandparents, who were anarcho-syndicalist workers during the interwar period, and by her parents, militant Communists who never forgave Moch and the Socialists for the violent repression of the strikes in 1947.

60. Winock, *La France libérée 1944–1947*, 311–337.

breakup in a way that was surely more decisive than the strikes in Metropolitan France. In fact, the Communists were then the only political force openly supporting the independence of the colonies and the end of the empire. The Socialists saw in this another proof of the PCF's duplicity and accused it of trying to push the colonies into the Soviet camp. The Cold War was raging and the two Marxist parties had chosen different camps.

We find the same configuration in October 1956, when the head of government, Guy Mollet (SFIO), allied himself with the British Conservative Anthony Eden to undertake a military expedition in Egypt in the hope of winning back the Suez Canal, which Nasser had just nationalized. The two colonial powers were ultimately abandoned by the United States, and under international pressure, they were forced to withdraw their expeditionary troops without having regained possession of the canal for its Franco-British stockholders. The PCF did not fail to criticize the pitiable action of the French Socialists and their leader, a fastidious Marxist playing the colonialist in chief in the service of capitalist interests. In a famous interview broadcast on television in November 1956, Guy Mollet defended his policy and accused the Communists of being " not Left but East."[61] Moreover, there was no lack of arguments against the PCF, which was at the same time supporting the Soviet repression of the Budapest insurrection. The increasingly hard-nosed war the French government was waging in Algeria under SFIO direction also helped exacerbate a violent antagonism with the Communists, who had long supported the demands of the Algerians fighting for independence.

We must stress that these tensions between the SFIO and the PCF, and this inability to govern together, were at that time explained far more by basic programmatic disagreements than by sociological divisions at the level of the electorates. From the point of view of the social structure of the latter, the two parties won more votes in the suburbs and metropoles than they did in the towns and villages, even if there were significant differences regarding the workers' vote (we will return to this). Generally speaking, the territorial divisions between the political trends on the left, center, and right were more moderate under the Fourth Republic (see figure 10.11) than they were during the interwar period (see figure 10.10). This is explained in part by the structural increase in the number of salaried workers and the decrease in the number of self-employed workers in the world of the villages and towns, which facilitated the improvement of the Social-

---

61. See "Guy Mollet à propos de la crise de Suez," interview of Mollet by Pierre Sabbagh, 12 November 1956, Institut nationale de l'audiovisuel, https://www.ina.fr/ina-eclaire-actu/video /i08164853/guy-mollet-a-propos-de-la-crise-de-suez.

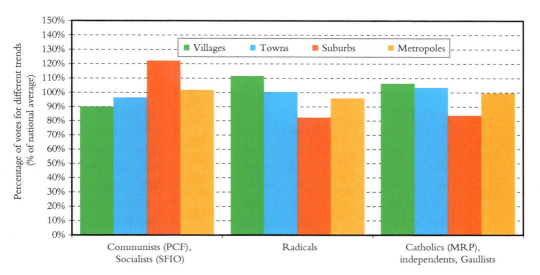

FIGURE 10.11. The territorial cleavage in the elections from 1946 to 1956

In the legislative elections of 1946–1956, the Radicals constituted a bloc that was even weaker than it was in the interwar period, and the territorial divisions from other electorates were attenuated. The Communist and Socialist vote nonetheless remained much smaller in the villages and towns than in the suburbs and metropoles, and the programmatic divisions within the left-wing parties remained considerable.

Sources and series: unehistoireduconflitpolitique.fr

ists' and Communists' results in the rural world and the convergence between the structures of the votes in the various territories.

The Fiscal Conflict between Salaried and Self-Employed Workers and the Poujadist Movement

We must point out that the conflicts between salaried and self-employed workers continued to play a significant role throughout this period, which was demonstrated in a perfectly clear way by the inroads the Poujadists made in the elections of 1956. In addition to the structural conflict pertaining to the question of the ownership of the means of production, numerous less existential but nonetheless significant conflicts were constantly arising, particularly concerning social and fiscal legislation that had been developing since the 1910s and 1920s in the context of a rapid increase in the power of the welfare state and the fiscal state, which accelerated again in 1945. But we have to note that in this process, the two Marxist parties (SFIO and PCF) often adopted positions that were excessively favorable to salaried workers and disadvantageous for self-employed workers (agricultural and nonagricultural), even when the self-employed lived in very modest conditions in comparison to certain salaried workers.

In general, the social welfare systems were conceived primarily for salaried employees, with contributions levied directly on payslips—requiring no additional effort on the part of salaried workers—whereas self-employed workers were required for the first time to keep complex accounts, without always knowing for sure that someday they would see again these contributions again. The result was often complex compromises in which the self-employed workers paid lower contributions than salaried workers (or at least lower than the sum of the so-called employees' and employers' contributions paid on behalf of wage earners, both of which were levied on payslips, with the employees' contributions being deducted from the gross salary and the employers' contributions being added to it), and on top of all that, an increase in the total cost of salaries for the employer, who was sometimes a small independent producer whose business was far from booming. In addition, the salaried workers had to be content with more limited social benefits for retirement and for healthcare and family allocations. It is sometimes difficult to say who gained from these arrangements, and self-employed workers often sensed that they were the fall guys. That is not always the case, but the simple fact that the social security system was conceived for salaried workers lends support to the notion that left-wing parties foresee a productive structure in which self-employed workers will have disappeared almost completely or will simply no longer count for much (which is not far from what the Socialists and Communists in fact envision, and it cannot be very pleasing for those most concerned).

Regarding fiscal questions, we must also remember that the income tax system that was debated at length between 1895 and 1914 included both a general tax on income (applicable to all forms of income) and so-called schedular taxes that separately applied to each category or "schedule" of income (salaries, self-employment income, profits, rents, dividends, interest, and so on). During the 1907–1908 debates in parliament this was already a subject of the recurrent conflicts between the Socialists and the Radicals, with the latter being traditionally more favorable to the self-employed and fearing that they would be treated worse than salaried workers. Caillaux long defended the idea of a neutral tax for the different kinds of incomes, such that the "salaried managers of big corporations" would not benefit from any privileged treatment compared to the "small industrialists" and "small merchants" whose income came from self-employment, and he went so far as to declare that "the schoolteacher, tax collector, and railway employee are often rich in comparison with the small farmer or self-employed trader."[62] But the system of schedular taxes, as it was adopted in 1917 and applied during the interwar period, was in fact much more favorable to salaried workers than to independents (that is, the self-employed). Whereas salaried workers benefited from major deductions (such that only the best remunerated 10–15 percent of them actually paid this tax), the self-employed were expected to pay the schedular tax starting with the first franc of income, which had to be carefully declared. Faced with such a flagrant injustice, small self-employed workers (peasants, craftsmen, shopkeepers) rallied energetically and managed to add a number of exceptional and compensatory measures during the 1920s and 1930s. But salaried workers, defended mainly by the Socialist and Communist Parties, which rejected the idea of a pure and simple alignment with the self-employed workers' system (because that would have implied tax hikes that were in their eyes unacceptable for small and medium-level salaried workers), continued to receive clearly privileged treatment.

This situation persisted after World War II. The fiscal reforms of 1948 and 1959 were supposed to unify the system with common rules for all incomes, but in reality, special deductions were instituted solely for salaried workers, who were also exempted from the "proportional tax." This issue was to a large extent the cause of the violent movement protesting taxes and defending the small independents who led the Poujadist inroads in the 1956 elections. It all began in July 1953, when Pierre Poujade, a stationer from Saint-Céré—a modest town in the department of Lot, which was then among the 5 percent of the municipalities with the highest proportions of the self-employed—mobilized for the first time the craftsmen and shopkeepers of his small town against the tax collectors, and a few months later founded the Union de défense des commerçants et artisans (UDCA). The apex of Poujadist agitation came in 1954–1955, with multiple "commando operations" intended to come to the aid of small shopkeepers or artisans driven into bankruptcy by the tax authorities' greediness. In January 1955, the UDCA announced the "taxpayers' strike," and in the elections held in January 1956 the movement achieved its greatest electoral penetration. The Poujadists denounced the adopted measures favoring salaried workers, and especially the "Parisian managers," who, in their view, were showing the extent to which the modernizing central government and its "heartless technicians"—no matter what their political labels—did not care

---

62. For a detailed analysis of these debates and the corresponding legislative developments, see Piketty, *Les hauts revenus en France*, 218–319.

what happened to small independent producers.[63] The Poujadist movement had few direct political descendants, but it illustrates once again the importance of the cleavage between salaried workers and the self-employed in the representation of the structure of production.[64]

From the point of view of the Socialists and the Communists, the advantages from which salaried workers benefited were officially justified by the fact that self-employed workers had an annoying tendency not to declare all their income, whereas salaried workers could not do the same. This argument is understandable, and at the same time, it has its limits. Instituting a special deduction to compensate salaried workers for alleged fraud by independents cannot end the fraud, and more generally, it will not make it possible to develop norms of fiscal justice acceptable to the different groups involved. These apparently technical debates played a central role in structuring electoral cleavages between salaried workers and the self-employed all through the twentieth century.[65] These conflicts show that the question of fiscal and social justice cannot be treated abstractly, independent of its institutional and administrative incarnations. The representations concerning a fair tax must be constructed historically and politically, in function of the mechanisms that can be used to compare the abilities of the various social groups to contribute to the common expenses, and in particular to measure and register the income and property of social categories that are in other respects very different (or, indeed, completely incomparable) on the level of their status and their economic activity. In the end, these conflicts explain to a large extent why the vote for the Left (and especially for the PCF) has always been a very clearly decreasing function of the proportion of independents in the municipality (see figures 10.12–10.13). Inversely, the

63. This takes nothing away from Poujade's very real anti-Semitism, lampooned particularly in the "Poujadolphe" cover of *L'Express,* the weekly news magazine favored by Parisian managers at the time.

64. Paradoxically, the Poujadist advance allowed Guy Mollet's SFIO to obtain slightly more deputies than Antoine Pinay's Independents (though both far were behind the PCF) and to take control of the government. Let us also recall that Jean-Marie Le Pen fought his first political battles as a Poujadist deputy in 1956, later returning to the National Assembly with the rise of the National Front in 1986.

65. The special 20 percent deduction in favor of salaried workers (on top of the 10 percent for "occupational costs") that emerged from the fiscal reforms of 1948 and 1959, which had been extended to the self-employed in the 1970s (on the condition that they agreed to have their accounts certified by an authorized business management center), was finally abolished and included in the tax scale in 2005.

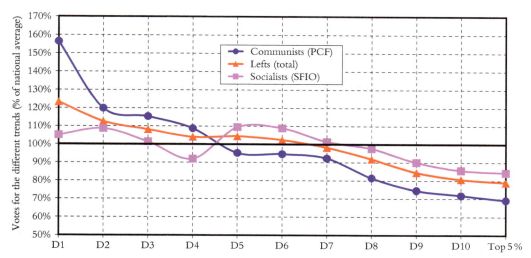

Distribution of the population by deciles, as a function of the proportion of independents in the municipality

FIGURE 10.12. The vote of the self-employed in 1936: PCF vs. SFIO

In the legislative elections of 1936, the vote for the Left diminished greatly with the proportion of independents (self-employed) in the municipality. This was particularly true for the vote for the Left of the Left (PCF), with a slope that was less steep but still significant.

Sources and series: unehistoireduconflitpolitique.fr

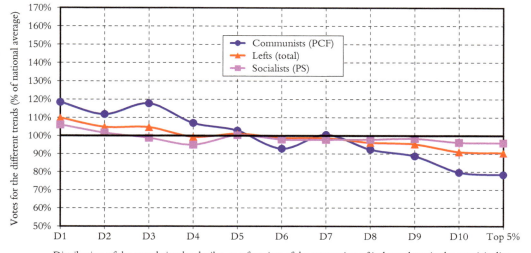

Distribution of the population by deciles, as a function of the proportion of independents in the municipality

FIGURE 10.13. The vote of the self-employed in 1981: PCF vs. PS

In the legislative elections of 1936, the vote for the Left diminished with the proportion of independents (self-employed) in the municipality, but that is explained mainly by the vote for the Left of the Left (PCF), and not much by the vote for the Center-Left (PS), which varied slightly with the proportion of independents.

Sources and series: unehistoireduconflitpolitique.fr

vote for the Right has always been a clearly increasing function of this same proportion, with an exceptionally steep curve for the Poujadist vote in 1956.[66]

The Period 1958–1995: Pure Bipartition and Its Limits

With the advent of the Fifth Republic, the French political system entered into its only period of pure, genuine bipartition. Between 1958 and 1995, each political tendency had to choose its camp within the bipolar Left-Right confrontation, particularly during the second round of the presidential elections, and the centrist parliamentary groups lost the pivotal role they had enjoyed under the Third and the Fourth Republics (although actually, their importance had already sharply declined since the period of real tripartition at the beginning of the Third Republic). There is something ironic in the fact that General de Gaulle, who sought to bring the French together beyond the Right and the Left, ended up contributing to the establishment of the purest bipolar system in the history of the country. He was probably aware of the driving role of bipartition for electoral democracy. In any case, the point is that in a few years, the Gaullist bloc succeeded in unifying all the Right, from the liberals to the Independents via the conservatives and the Christian Democrats. From this point of view, the most structuring and emblematic choice was to establish in 1959, with the Debré law, a major expansion of public financing to include private primary, middle, and high schools, thus fulfilling what had been the central demand of the Catholic tendencies since *La Croix* created the Justice-Equality Committee (JE) in 1896. The Right had never been able to satisfy it, because up to that point it had never been strong enough and unified enough to get such legislation adopted.[67] In a well-known interview in 1965, de Gaulle also explained that he expected to move beyond the old cleavages and reconcile the Right and Left, and in this case, the order and the movement dear to Goguel.[68] However, the language he used—recall the "housewife" who wanted to have a refrigerator and did not allow "girls to not come home at night"—betrays a old-fashioned outlook and a clear affiliation with the conservative bloc, and also a certain disconnect from the young people who would mobilize a few years later during the events of May 1968.[69]

---

66. See unehistoireduconflitpolitique.fr, appendix D3.
67. See chapter 3. The adoption of the Debré law also made impossible alliances between Socialists and Social Democrats of the Third Force type, and thus considerably strengthened bipartition.
68. See chapter 8.
69. "France is everything at once, it's all the French. France is not the Left! And it's not the Right!... As far as France is concerned, there's what happens in a household. The lady of the

Although Gaullism sought to embody a certain equilibrium as opposed to the excesses associated with the old Right (Vichyist and colonialist) and those associated with the Left (Socialist and Communist), the reality is that it very quickly brought together the quasi-totality of the Right. The bipolar dialectic and competition with the Left nevertheless made it possible to continue the construction of the welfare state, with the introduction of a new branch of the social security system in the form of unemployment insurance in late 1958, in the context of an agreement between labor unions and employers. This decision was made shortly after the creation of the basic old age pension in 1956, in a context in which the very high inflation of the postwar period had liquidated small savings and poverty was endemic among senior citizens, while the retirement system instituted in 1945 had not yet reached their full potential. The welfare state underwent another acceleration after the historic strikes and mobilizations of May 1968, which led to a major increase in the minimum wage and low salaries. These increases continued at a rapid pace during the 1970s and made possible a significant compression of salarial hierarchies. The period was also characterized by a continual increase in the resources allocated to the different systems of social security (particularly in the form of supplementary contributions), which made it possible to improve the level of social welfare coverage, especially in regard to access to healthcare, health insurance, and retirement pensions. In the electric social and political atmosphere of the late 1960s and the 1970s, the government, first under de Gaulle, then Pompidou, and then Giscard, felt obliged to give guarantees to salaried employees and labor unions, hoping to delay as long as possible the Left's electoral victory. This driving dialectic made a decisive contribution to the success of the Trente Glorieuses and, beyond that, to the movement toward greater social equality and greater economic prosperity that was established in the twentieth century.

We must also emphasize that this driving dialectic associated with the Left-Right polarization in no way implies a convergence toward the center. Each political bloc continued to have a distinct worldview and program of action. In this case, the Left set out to embody a project of transforming the economic system and reducing social inequalities that was much more ambitious than that of the Right, a project that the latter denounced as unrealistic and dangerous. To be sure,

---

house, the housewife, she wants to have a vacuum cleaner, she wants to have a fridge, she wants to have a washing machine, and even, if possible, a car. That's the movement. And at the same time, she doesn't want her husband to party all night, the boys to put their feet up on the table, and the girls not to come home at night. That's order. And the housewife wants progress, but she doesn't want chaos. And that's true for France. We need progress, not chaos." Interview with M. Droit, 1965, Institut nationale de l'audiovisuel. Available online at ina.fr.

the Right borrowed certain programmatic elements from the Left (particularly so-cial security and progressive taxation, as it already had done under the National Bloc in 1920), but it was careful to distinguish itself with respect to several essen-tial aspects (the tax on capital and labor union rights in 1924, the nationalizations and capital-labor power sharing in the 1960s and 1970s). Political conflict was fo-cused on the social question, but with two blocs proposing distinctly different projects to the country, which explains why the electorates remained extremely divided on the level of wealth and socioeconomic characteristics. It will also be noted that the end of the 1950s and most of the 1960s were marked by a broad-ening of the salarial hierarchy, with the salaries of managers and engineers regis-tering gains considerably greater than those of the worst-paid workers. It was not until 1968 that the Gaullist government, bowing to social and political pressure, agreed to invert the curve and undertake a vast revalorization of low salaries.[70]

On the other hand, the Left-Right polarization of the period 1958–1988 was characterized by a reduction of the territorial cleavage to an unprecedented level. During that period, the Left bloc continued to win more votes in the suburbs than in towns and villages, and vice versa for the Right bloc, but the disparities were relatively small (see figure 10.14) and in fact, they clearly diminished in relation to earlier periods (see figures 10.10–10.11). In other words, electoral behaviors were determined primarily by wealth and socio-occupational structure, and only very secondarily by the size of the conurbation and the municipality. It can also be seen that the metropoles voted more for the Right than for the Left during this period, which reflects a predominance of the effect of wealth.

Limits and Contingencies of the Union of the Left: The Decline of Communism

Yet, we must once again emphasize the limits and weaknesses of the system of bi-partition that was established during this period, and which owes a great deal to a particular strategic and programmatic configuration. Specifically, the Union of the Left that materialized in 1972 with the program of common government ap-proved by the PS and the PCF would probably not have been possible without

---

70. Conversely, the moment of "convergence toward the center" celebrated by certain authors at the end of the 1980s corresponds retrospectively to the beginning of the end of bipolarization: the disappointment of a large part of the working classes following what was perceived as a ral-lying of the Left to liberal economics helped weaken the Left-Right cleavage, and this drove the decrease in electoral turnout and the rise of tripartition. See F. Furet, J. Julliard, and P. Rosanvallon, *La République du centre. La fin de l'exception française* (Calmann-Lévy, 1988).

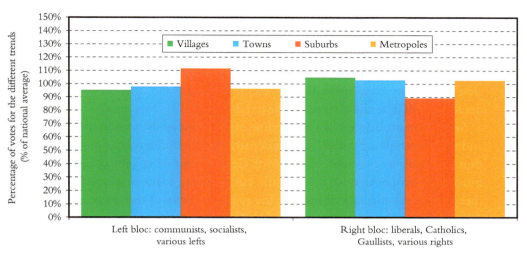

FIGURE 10.14. The elections of 1958–1988 in the territories: Toward pure bipartition and the end of the territorial cleavage?

In legislative elections from 1958 to 1988, the Center virtually disappeared, and almost all the political trends joined the Left or Right blocs. The Left bloc continued to achieve better results in the suburbs than in the villages and towns, and conversely for the Right bloc, but the territorial cleavages were much smaller than they were during the preceding and following periods.

Sources and series: unehistoireduconflitpolitique.fr

the already well-advanced decline of the Communist Party. In the late 1940s and in the 1950s, when the PCF was winning around 25–30 percent of the votes, compared with scarcely 15–20 percent of the votes for the SFIO, it was almost impossible for the Socialists to envision a union of the Left, which at that point could have been formed only under Communist leadership. The SFIO of Paul Ramadier and Guy Mollet preferred to govern with the Christian Democrats of the MRP, or with various partners in the Center or Center-Right. In the 1960s, the PCF had already begun to decline, but it still usually polled above 20 percent, at a time when the SFIO was hardly exceeding 15 percent. It was in the late 1960s that the prospect of the Socialists overtaking the Communists appeared to be within arm's reach. After taking leadership of the PS during the Epinay Congress in 1971, where he advocated a union of the Left, in 1972 François Mitterand negotiated a common program of government with the PCF. In the 1973 legislative elections, the PS trailed the PCF with 19 percent against 21 percent.[71] The historic victory

---

71. If we add the Mouvement des radicaux de gauche (MRG, Radical Left Movement) and the Parti socialiste unifié (PSU, Unified Socialist Party), which derived from several schisms

happened in 1978, with 25 percent of the vote for the PS against 21 percent for the PCF, which elicited very deep tensions within the Union of the Left.[72] Then the PS won 38 percent of the votes in the legislative elections of June 1981, a few weeks after the election of Mitterand as president of the Republic, while the PCF won only 16 percent. The two curves had just crossed, and over the following decades the PCF would not reverse the trend.[73]

Several factors help explain the decline of the Communist vote in the 1960s and 1970s, even though the PCF did not participate in the exercise of power and thus can hardly be criticized for its record. Generally speaking, in 1945 Communist and Soviet prestige was at its zenith, but it seemed to move inexorably further away as the memory of the war, the economic crisis of the 1930s, and the struggle against Fascism and Nazism faded. Above all, news coming from the East went from bad to worse. In the 1950s, Soviet Communism could continue to rely on impressive technological achievements (such as the first Sputnik in 1957) and a moral prestige that was still considerable, especially in the context of its support for independence movements and decolonization. But after the crushing of the uprising in Budapest in 1956, and then the new Russian intervention in Prague in 1968, it was perfectly clear that the Soviet regime had no intention of opening up to electoral pluralism. Naturally, the PCF continued to explain that the model of democratic socialism that it wanted to establish in France was very different from the Soviet model, but because its isolation on the French electoral scene prevented it from exercising power (missing out by only twenty-nine votes in 1946, as we have seen), it was never able to provide material proof of this. For the new generations,

---

within the SFIO (particularly after Guy Mollet's Algerian policy and then its support for the Fifth Republic in the late 1950s), the PS and its allies reached 23 percent.

72. In part because of these tensions, the common program of 1972 was officially denounced by Georges Marchais in late 1977. From that date, the PCF was no longer officially connected with the PS by a common program of government, even though the socialist project continued to be inspired by it and the PCF was represented in the Mauroy government responsible for implementing it from 1981 to 1983. When the breakup came in 1977, the PCF tried in vain to obtain an extension of the scope of nationalization (particularly to subsidiaries) and to increase union control over future managers of public enterprises, in order to demonstrate its difference from the PS and regain the upper hand politically and electorally. On these negotiations, see M. Fulla, "Le programme commun de gouvernement: Rupture économique ou artefact politique?," in *L'union sans l'unité. Le programme commun de la gauche, 1963–1978,* ed. D. Tartakowsky and A. Bergounioux (Presses Universitaire de Rennes, 2012). See also M. Fulla, *Les socialistes français et l'économie (1944–1981). Une histoire économique du politique* (Presses de Sciences Po, 2016).

73. At least not until the presidential election of 2022, when the PS candidate won only 1.7 percent of the vote, while the PCF candidate won 2.3 percent. We will return to this in part 4.

communism no longer inspired dreams. In view of young people's aspirations to autonomy, emancipation, and self-management, which were expressed so forcefully in the mobilizations of May 1968, the statist, hypercentralized model associated with the PCF seemed outdated.[74] In the eighth edition (1970) of his famous economics textbook used by generations of North American students, Paul Samuelson was still saying that it was possible that between 1990 and 2000, the GNP of the United States would be surpassed by the GNP of the Soviet Union, on the basis of trends observed from the 1920s to the 1960s.[75] But public opinion—which sometimes has more common sense than economists and is able to see beyond the GNP and more or less useless accumulations of concrete and steel—hadalready largely settled this issue: the Soviet model ceased to exist as a model of the future long before its final collapse and the dissolution of the USSR in 1991.[76]

To sum up, it was in large measure the decline of the Soviet model that made possible the establishment of the Union of the Left in the 1970s and the march toward a fully realized Left-Right bipartition. We must also underline the fragility of the bipartition that developed at that time, insofar as the program that the Socialists took over in 1981 was very classical and proved to be disappointing for the voters who had brought the Left to power. In addition to the continued construction of the welfare state with an increasing use of progressive taxation, the heart of the economic program rested primarily on nationalizations, with the state taking control of a large number of banks and major industrial enterprises that had not been nationalized after the Liberation.[77] That was no doubt the easiest way for

74. Especially since the PCF was attacked not only for its Stalinism during the events of 1968, but also for its moderation. In the eyes of many students and workers, it no longer appeared to be an avant-garde party that had a legitimate claim to be the bearer of a revolutionary radicalism. See Mischi, *Le parti des communistes.*

75. See P. Samuelson, *Economics,* 8th ed. (McGraw-Hill, 1970), 831.

76. In this case, the social and health indicators are probably more pertinent, and they reflect a worrisome stagnation of life expectancy in the Soviet Union from the 1950s on. We even see at the end of the 1960s and during the 1970s a slight tendency for men's life expectancy to decline, which is unprecedented for a country in peacetime, as well as an end to the decline in infant mortality. See E. Todd, *La chute finale. Essai sur la décomposition de la sphère soviétique* (R. Laffont, 1976). The whole picture testifies to a stagnation in living conditions and a healthcare system that is in great difficulty and seems to have reached its limits. In the 1980s, Gorbachev's attempts to tackle the overconsumption of alcohol played a central role in the last Soviet leader's loss of popularity and the final collapse of the regime. After presiding over the Russian people's emergence from czarism and poverty, Soviet Communism has become synonymous with a low level of well-being and shortened lives.

77. The great wave of nationalizations at the Liberation concerned in particular the banking sector, coal mines, and the automobile industry (especially with the nationalization / punishment of the Renault factories). The wave of nationalizations in 1981–1982 was intended to be a

the PS to construct the agreement to govern with the PCF and to establish its historical legitimacy to direct the Left, following the SFIO's blundering in the first decades after the war. However, this strategy posed several problems. First, the nationalizations produced few tangible social and economic results, whereas their cost weighed heavily on the public finances and made it difficult to conduct other social policies with more visible effects. When it returned to power in 1986, the Right was able to use this manna from heaven to privatize not only the enterprises nationalized in 1981 but also a large part of the 1945 public sector. In 1988, François Mitterand was reelected on a reassuring platform ("neither nationalizations nor privatizations"). Second, the emphasis on nationalizations was not in phase with the aspirations to self-management and decentralization that were expressed in 1968 and in the 1970s among a large segment of the youth and labor union activists. To be sure, the formulation of a viable program based on self-management produced many problems that could really be solved only by successful, large-scale experimentation—by starting with German and Swedish experiences with self-management and trying to carry them further, for example, which was certainly not easy, but had to be tried.[78] By clinging to a strategy centered on nationalizations alone, the Socialist government that emerged from the elections of 1981 no doubt weakened its own position and increased future disappointments.

The Great Arrival of the French Socialists in Power in the 1980s

In the following chapters we will return at length to the reasons for the erosion and then the collapse of bipartition over the course of the period 1992–2022. Among the most obvious explanations is, of course, the public's disappointment in the Left in power during the 1980s and 1990s, in connection with the inadequacies

---

continuation of the movement of 1945 and in particular to put almost the whole of the banking sector in the service of public planning and a strategy of industrial reconquest. See C. Andrieu, L. Le Van, and A. Prost, *Les nationalisations de la Libération: De l'utopie au compromis* (Presses de la FNSP, 1987).

78. In the 1970s (and beyond) there was an ambiguity—never truly resolved—between "self-management," which suggested that the employees would take control of the company, and the notion of "co-management," which denoted a simple sharing of votes between employees and stockholders that by construction turned to the advantage of the latter (as it had in West Germany since 1952) and which ultimately could be related to a not very revolutionary project of sharing capitalist profits and attitudes. On this point, see L. Bantigny, *1968. De grands soirs en petits matins* (Seuil, 2018), 330–341. To transcend these contradictions, we must consider going further than the German and Swedish models, by limiting the votes of the major individual stockholders and redistributing property itself, for example. We will return to this in chapter 13.

of its programmatic base and its performance in government. However, we will see that many other factors played a role, and that the question deserves to be considered in a broader historical framework. At this stage, it is important above all to stress that this disappointment was no doubt all the greater because French Socialists were in power for an unusually long time, and repeatedly, starting in the 1980s. Before this period, they had, of course, participated in several parliamentary coalitions since the beginning of the twentieth century and during the interwar period, particularly with the Radicals, but they had directed the government only intermittently, first in 1936–1937 and then on several occasions between 1946 and 1958, in the context of coalitions with the Center-Right. In comparison, the 1980s and 1990s represent this political movement's first real experience of the prolonged exercise of power. Between 1981 and 2002 the PS headed the government during fifteen full years: from 1981 to 1986 (the Mauroy and Fabius governments), from 1988 to 1993 (the Rocard, Cresson, and Bérégovoy governments), and from 1997 to 2002 (the Jospin government). It is very clear that when you are in power for fifteen years out of twenty, you can hardly exonerate yourself of responsibility for the evolution of the country's situation, both positive and less positive.

Power was next exercised by the Right from 2002 to 2012 (the Raffarin, Villepin, and Fillon governments under Chirac's and Sarkozy's presidencies), and then again by the Socialists, from 2012 to 2017 (the Ayrault and Valls governments, under Hollande's presidency). In all, the French Socialists held power for twenty years (four complete legislative five-year terms) during the period 1980–2020, which is considerable for a single political party. In the main neighboring countries, no Social Democratic or Labor party was in control for so long during the same period.[79] We will return to the way this particular longevity in government and the record of these experiences helped shape a specific evolution of the French political system in the recent period. If we seek to understand the general reasons for the French Left's rise to long-term power in the 1980s—which was simultaneously belated and prolonged—it can be tempting to refer to major socioeconomic and cultural factors, beginning with the long and powerful movement of the working population's salarization and de-Christianization. These two historic movements of primary importance have been ongoing since the nineteenth century, and both of them accelerated considerably beginning in the 1960s and

79. In comparison, the Social Democrats were in power for only seven years in Germany (1998–2005) and the Labour Party for thirteen years in the United Kingdom (1997–2010). It was only in Spain that the Socialists have governed longer, in the particular context of the post-Franco transition.

1970s.[80] Considering that the Independents, like the people closest to the Catholic Church, have always shown a greater propensity to vote for the Right,[81] this historical decline could only benefit the Left, and in particular the Socialists, who in fact operated during the period 1980–2020 in a political environment that was largely salaried and secularized—that is, radically different from the situation at the beginning or even the middle of the twentieth century. In particular, the very broad movement of the salarization of villages and towns, which at the end of the period had very large proportions of workers and employees, could only help reduce the historical electoral cleavage between the rural and urban worlds and facilitate the Left's electoral penetration into the rural world.[82]

As important as they may be, we must not overestimate the role played by these great structural changes. First, and generally, because we cannot reason ceteris paribus: all political tendencies constantly adapt their programs to the socioeconomic and cultural environments of which they are part, especially because they contribute to influencing the latter through their discourses and the policies and institutional systems that they set up.[83] In this case, it is properly political and programmatic factors, above all, that explain the French Socialists' coming to power between 1980 and 2020. It was the slow decline of the PCF, which had already begun in the 1960s and 1970s, that allowed the PS to gain hegemony over the Left and to unify it under its leadership, starting in the 1980s. In 1945–1946, the two big left-wing parties were extremely powerful on the electoral level, despite the fact that at that time, France had many self-employed workers and even more Catholics. If the Left bloc did not govern for long, that was primarily for political reasons—the SFIO refused to participate in a government under Communist direction. The second properly political factor explaining the grand arrival to power of the French Socialists during the period 1980–2020 is obviously the division of the Right bloc, which after the emergence of the FN in the 1980s and 1990s proved incapable of unifying around a common program (considering particularly the disagreements over migrants). That was what allowed the Left to

---

80. See chapter 2, figures 2.18–2.19, and chapter 4, figure 4.5.
81. See figure 10.9 and chapter 9, figure 9.13.
82. Compared to other European countries, in particular the United Kingdom and Germany, the agricultural and unsalaried sector remained important longer in France, such that this belated process of salarization might help explain why the French Socialists' rise to power came later than that of their Labour and Social Democratic counterparts.
83. For example, it's hard to imagine a right-wing official in 2023 giving the 1965 Gaullist speech about the housewife and the girls who don't come home at night.

win several legislative elections even though it had won only a minority of the votes.[84]

Basically, the situation was similar to the one the Left bloc had experienced in 1945–1970, except that whereas before the 1970s disunion was quasi-permanent on the Left, the Right had not experienced such an internal fracture since the conservatives and monarchists joined the Moderate Republicans and Opportunists around 1900–1910. To sum up, it was political and programmatic questions that played the primary role, not long-term determinist factors, even if there were, of course, major interactions between programmatic issues and transformations of socioeconomic and territorial cleavages, including, to be sure, those that occurred during recent decades.

When Did the Socialists Lose Industrial Workers?

Let us conclude this chapter by examining the extent to which the data we have collected enable us to determine when, and for what reasons, the Socialists lost the industrial workers' vote. The answer is more complex than it seems. One might be tempted to say that the Socialists lost the industrial workers in the 1980s and 1990s, following the disappointment caused by their inability to curb rising unemployment and the decline of industrial employment. In fact, after its historic result of 38 percent of the vote, reached in the first round of the legislative elections of 1981, the PS subsequently lost many votes, including, of course, among industrial workers. But the most interesting question concerns the industrial workers' vote relative to that in other categories. From that point of view, it is striking to see that the French Socialists had lost the industrial workers' vote long before they were in power in the 1980s. More precisely, if we study the evolution of the vote for the two main left-wing parties (PCF and SFIO-PS) in relation to the proportion of industrial workers in municipalities all through the twentieth century, we generally find that the Communist vote is always much stronger than the Socialist vote in working-class municipalities. During the interwar period, the SFIO nonetheless succeeded in preserving a significantly higher vote in the municipalities that had large proportions of industrial workers than it did in the others (see figure 10.15).

---

84. This was notably the case in 1988 and 1997, when the Left had only a (slight) minority of the votes, but thanks to numerous triangulations in the second round, it managed to put together a majority much larger than it would have been had the Right been unified.

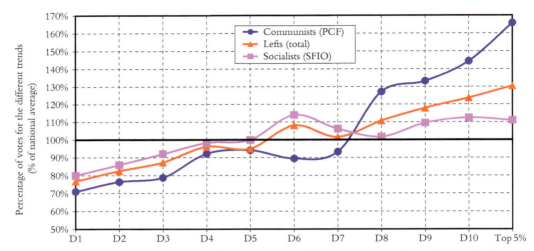

Distribution of the population by deciles, as a function of the proportion of workers in the municipality

FIGURE 10.15. The working-class vote in 1936: Communists vs. Socialists
In the legislative elections of 1936, the vote for the Left increased greatly with the proportion of blue-collar workers in the municipality. This was particularly true for the vote for the Left of the Left (PCF), but also for the vote for the Center-Left (PS), with a slope that was less steep but still significant.
Sources and series: unehistoireduconflitpolitique.fr

The fact is that the SFIO very quickly lost this working-class vote to the Communists. During the 1962 legislative elections, for example, we see that the PCF vote increased greatly with the proportion of workers in the municipality, whereas the curve became almost flat for the SFIO (see figure 10.16). If we examine in detail the results election by elections, we find that the SFIO's curve was already almost flat in the 1945–1946 elections.[85] In the legislative elections of 1981, the curves are nearly identical to what they were in 1962: the Socialist vote varies little with the proportion of industrial workers (or even seems to be slightly decreasing), whereas the Communist vote continues to be concentrated in the working-class municipalities (see figure 10.17). Things scarcely changed in the historic defeat suffered by the Left in the legislative elections of 1993. The PS fell to 18 percent of the votes, but the profile of its vote with regard to the proportion of industrial workers was still just as flat as it was in 1962 or 1981. As for the PCF, its result fell to 9 percent, three times lower than in 1945–1946, but the profile of its vote was still as concentrated in the working-class municipalities as it was before, with a

85. See unehistoireduconflitpolitique.fr, appendix D3, figures D3.14a–D3.14s.

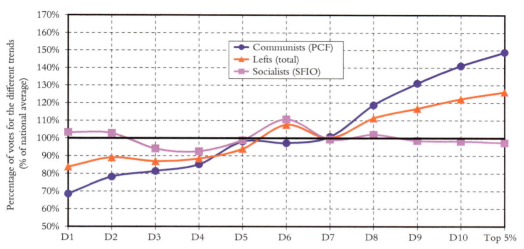

FIGURE 10.16. The working-class vote in 1962: Communists vs. Socialists

In the legislative elections of 1962, the vote for the Left increased greatly with the proportion of blue-collar workers in the municipality, but that is explained solely by the vote for the Left of the Left (PCF), and not at all by the vote for the Center-Left (SFIO), which varied little with the proportion of blue-collar workers.

Sources and series: unehistoireduconflitpolitique.fr

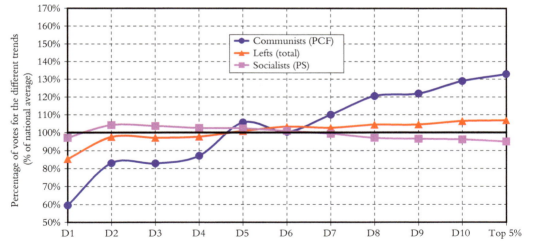

FIGURE 10.17. The working-class vote in 1981: Communists vs. Socialists

In the legislative elections of 1981, the vote for the Left increased with the proportion of blue-collar workers in the municipality, but that is explained solely by the vote for the Left of the Left (PCF), and not at all by the vote for the Center-Left (SFIO), which varied little with the proportion of blue-collar workers (or decreased slightly).

Sources and series: unehistoireduconflitpolitique.fr

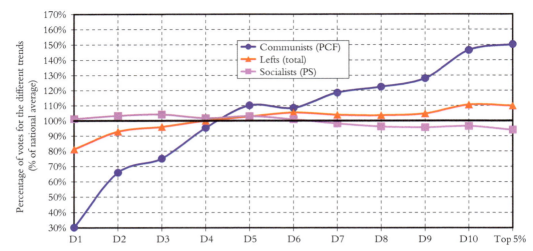

Distribution of the population by deciles, as a function of the proportion of workers in the municipality

FIGURE 10.18. The working-class vote in 1993: Communists vs. Socialists

In the legislative elections of 1993, the vote for the Left increased with the proportion of blue-collar workers in the municipality, but that is explained solely by the vote for the Left of the Left (PCF), and not at all by the vote for the Center-Left (SFIO), which varied little with the proportion of blue-collar workers (or decreased slightly).

Sources and series: unehistoireduconflitpolitique.fr

slope that had become even steeper than it was previously (see figure 10.18). That is, in 1993, the last Communist bastions appear to be even more working-class than the historic Communist vote, in a context in which the PCF vote as a whole was in free fall.

These results clearly indicate that the PCF powerfully preempted the industrial working-class vote, gradually, starting in the interwar period and quasi-hegemonically with regard to the SFIO between 1945 and 1960. Then the Communist vote began its historic decline starting in the 1960s, 1970s, and 1980s, as the old Communist voters gave way to new generations of voters who had not known the same historical moment in 1945, and who had never shared the same hope for a regime in which workers would no longer be exploited (in this case, in the form of the Soviet regime). This hope was disappointed, but the Communist vote remained surprisingly strong among workers and other voters, and even increasingly so. So far as the Socialists were concerned, they never really succeeded in taking working-class voters back from the Communists after 1945–1946—not in 1962, or in 1981, or in 1993, any more than they did later. Obviously, that does not imply that the policies conducted by the Socialist governments of the 1980s and 1990s bear no responsibility in this regard. In a context marked by the collapse of the Soviet model and the PCF vote, other policies more favorable to the working class might have allowed the PS to attract some of the blue-collar workers lost by the Communists and to finally be characterized by a voting profile increasing in function of the proportion of workers in the municipalities. The fact remains that this resituation in a historical perspective is essential for better understanding the immense hopes placed in Communism that were expressed within the French working class in the middle of the twentieth century, and also the immense disappointment that emerged at the end of the century. This historical perspective is also fundamental for analyzing the weakening of bipartition and the rise to power of a new tripartition in the period 1992–2022, a topic on which we will next concentrate our attention.

CHAPTER 11

Toward a New Tripartition, 1992–2022?

We will now analyze the bipartition's phase of weakening and the rise to power of a new form of tripartition that developed between 1992 and 2022, concentrating on the transformations of the social structure of the vote in the legislative elections during this period. We will start by continuing the study of the vote for the left-wing parties begun in the preceding chapter and assess the evolution of their electorates from the legislative elections of 1993 to those of 2022. Then we will examine the case of the vote for the Front national (FN), which became the Rassemblement national (RN) in 2018, and the transformations of its electorate from its entry into the legislative elections in 1986 to 2022. Next, we will examine the case of the rest of the Right (UDF and RPR, then UMP and LR), and finally, that of the new central liberal-progressive bloc that appeared during the elections of 2017 and 2022 (LREM-Modem-Ensemble). We will see that this vote is one of the most bourgeois in the whole of French electoral history, in the sense of both average income and real estate capital (total value of housing), which is its strength and perhaps also its principal weakness over the long term.

Finally, we will analyze the prospects of changes that might be reflected by either the long-term maintenance of tripartition (a scenario that does not seem to us the most probable, but which cannot, in all rigor, be excluded) or a return of bipartition, which might take one of two main forms: a social-ecological bloc against a liberal-nationalist bloc, or a social-nationalist bloc against a liberal-progressive bloc. The first configuration would be both closer to the earlier Left-Right bipartition and to a large extent more probable and desirable, but it would be a mistake to imagine that it is the only one possible.

When Did the Move from Bipartition to Tripartition Begin?

In the presidential and legislative elections of 1981, the Left-Right bipartition appeared to be so solidly established in France that it seemed almost eternal. Four decades later, similar elections organized in 2022 led to the emergence of a relatively clear tripartition of the country's political life, with a social-ecological bloc, a liberal-progressive bloc, and a nationalist-patriotic bloc, to use a terminology that of course can be debated and to which we will return, but which in any case makes the Left-Right bipolarization of 1981 look like a distant memory.

What happened, and when did the split begin? Let us explain at the outset that our approach to the history of political conflict is fundamentally interactionist and dynamic, and not deterministic. Several trajectories are always possible, particularly as a function of power relationships, the strategies of the actors (political parties, voters, activists, media, and so on), and the symbolic and material resources that the various groups are able to mobilize. These conflicts are not resolved in advance, and they always entail unstable, precarious compromises and incomplete and unforeseen bifurcations. To be convinced of this, it suffices to remember the results achieved in the last presidential elections: four candidates won between 20 and 24 percent of the vote in the first round of the presidential election of 2017, and three candidates won 22, 23, and 28 percent of the votes in 2022.[1] It is very clear that several second rounds could have taken place, in 2017 as in 2022, in function of more or less contingent and unpredictable campaign events, with a potentially significant impact on the structuration of public deliberation and following elections. We will return to the role of presidential elections and referenda in the overall electoral dynamics. In this chapter, we will concentrate on the legislative elections, which constitute our privileged long-term observation post.

When did the exit from bipartition begin? The first answer to this question, and the most precise, is that bipartition has always been fragile and incomplete. As we have already amply shown, class conflict and political conflict have always been profoundly multidimensional and can never be confined to a single axis for long. However, if one is interested in the emergence of an explicitly tripolar electoral structure, with three autonomous Left, Center, and Right blocs achieving approximately equal results, then one has to wait until the legislative elections of 2017 and 2022 to discern a balanced distribution approaching the three thirds observed in the 1880s and 1890s, with a Left bloc bringing together the Socialists and Radical-Socialists, a Center bloc consisting of Moderate Republicans and Opportunists, and a Right bloc consisting of conservatives, Catholics, and monarchists.[2]

---

1. To simplify, all the results are always rounded off to the nearest whole number. Generally speaking, in the context of this book we cite the results observed in the first round in continental France (in this case, however, the scores are identical in the overseas territories).

2. See chapter 8, figure 8.1. Note also a slight initial upturn of the Center starting in 2007, with the candidacy of François Bayrou in the presidential election (he won 19 percent of the votes in the first round, versus 26 percent for Ségolène Royale and 31 percent for Nicolas Sarkozy) and the development of Modem. See chapter 13.

However, it seems to us that this new episode of genuine tripartition became possible in 2017 and 2022 only because a deeper movement had begun much earlier. In this case, one might rather logically choose to place the beginning of the movement toward tripartition in the legislative elections of 1986, when the FN achieved its first electoral breakthrough with 10 percent of the votes.[3] We are still very far from a redistribution into three thirds, and it was not until the legislative elections of 1997 that the FN won 15 percent of the votes, and those of 2022 when its successor, the RN, won 19 percent of the votes (and more if we count the votes of the parties sympathetic to it).[4] Still, starting with the legislative elections of 1986, French political life has in fact been structured around three poles characterized by a certain hermetic closure and strategic autonomy: a Left bloc built around the PS and the PCF and other leftist and ecological parties that diversified over time and were generally prepared to govern together—under certain conditions—and to step aside for one another in the various elections; a right-wing liberal bloc consisting of the RPR and UDF, then the UMP and LR, movements that were also prepared to govern together, as they had always done; and finally, a right-wing nationalist bloc constituted essentially by the FN, which became the RN. The main characteristic of this third bloc is that, with a few rare exceptions, during this period no one in the liberal and conservative Right is openly planning to govern with it or promising to step aside for it (even if, for its part, the FN-RN has generally seemed more open on this question).[5] As long as this third bloc did not succeed in getting a significant number of deputies elected, which was the case until 2017, its impact on the parliamentary and political game would remain limited, were it not that its presence in numerous triangulations in the second

3. The very first breakthrough took place in the municipal elections of 1983 (with a result of 17 percent in Dreux, in the department of Eure-et-Loire), and especially in the European elections of 1984 (with a result of 11 percent at the national level). In the legislative elections of 1973, 1978, and 1981, there were in fact a few candidates to the Right of the Right (especially from the FN, a party founded by Jean-Marie Le Pen in 1972), but the national results were less than 1 percent of the votes. The breakthrough in 1986 was then confirmed by the presidential election of 1988, in which Jean-Marie Le Pen won 14 percent of the votes in the first round; we will return to this.

4. It was 26 percent of the votes if we include the votes for Reconquête (with whom the RN rejected any alliance), Debout la France, and the various right-wing candidates (not including LR), and 37 percent of the votes if votes for LR are counted. We will return later to the different groups and the flexible boundaries of the nationalist-patriotic bloc.

5. There are several exceptions (an RPR list allied with the FN won the second round in the municipal elections in Dreux in September 1983, and several UDF and RPR regional presidents were elected with FN votes in the regional parliaments in 1986, 1992, and 1998), but these occasional alliances became rare after 1998.

round raised the threshold of victory for the liberal and conservative Right (and slightly lowered it for the Left). As soon as it attained a substantial parliamentary group—which it has had since 2022—the political system entered a phase of active tripartition, after a long period of bipartition that could be called latent.[6]

Rather than arguing that the trajectory that led from bipartition to tripartition began in 1986, we will make a case for the pivotal date of 1992. This allows us to mark more clearly what we see as the decisive importance to the process of the 1992 European referendum on the Maastricht Treaty. This was in fact the first time that a large proportion of Center-Left and Center-Right voters (especially the voters best endowed with economic and financial capital and with diplomas) ended up so explicitly in the same political camp—in this case, to defend the Yes side and European integration in its liberal form. This bloc came together again in voting Yes in the European referendum of 2005, this time in a slimmed-down format. To a large extent, it prefigured the liberal-progressive LREM-Modem-Ensemble coalition that came to power in 2017 and 2022.[7] Conversely, the No bloc in the referenda of 1992 and 2005 comprised two groups that were irreconcilable and incapable of governing together, one from the Left and the other from the nationalist Right. In a certain way, the tripartition of 2017 and 2002 was already expressed relatively clearly in the European referenda of 1992 and 2005, with a central liberal-progressive bloc comprising socially privileged voters supporting liberal Europe and seeking to impose its views on the basis of the division of the lower and middle classes between the other two blocs. Given the centrality of the question of European and international economic integration in the movement toward tripartition, one might suppose that it will also play an essential role in a possible exit from tripartition.

We have already mentioned the main factors capable of explaining the weakening of the Left-Right bipartition and the rise of tripartition's power over the period 1992–2002. First, there are the disappointments connected with the exercise of power by the Left and Right blocs since the 1970s and 1980s, in the context of a steep increase in social and territorial inequalities; these disappointments favor

---

6. The FN had already obtained thirty-five deputies in 1986 in the context of the departmental election by party lists with proportional representation. From 1993 to 2012, the party oscillated between zero and three deputies, and then elected eight deputies in 2017 and eighty-nine in 2022. One of the structuring factors of this evolution was also the decline in turnout, which over time greatly reduced the number of triangulations (the threshold for qualifying for the second round is 12.5 percent of the registered voters, such that with declining turnout it becomes rarer that three candidates qualify for the second round).

7. Even if today some of the old Yes voters of 1992 and 2005 also ended up in the Left bloc. We will return in detail to these elections in chapter 14.

voting for new political trends that can present themselves as bearing no responsibility for the current situation. The dissatisfactions regarding the Left's record in power must also be resituated in a broader perspective emphasizing the strengths and weaknesses of the programmatic base conveyed by the Socialists and Communists since the beginning of the twentieth century. Among the structural factors contributing to the emergence of tripartition since the 1980s and 1990s is the rise to power of the issues of migration and cultural identity, and more generally the growing importance of the national question and questions connected with economic and commercial integration on the European and global scale.

By examining the evolution of the social structure of the vote for different political tendencies in recent decades, we will be able to refine and clarify some of these hypotheses. Our principal conclusion is this: even if new tensions related to migration and identity have played a significant role, the main factors allowing us to explain the passage to tripartition are above all socioeconomic in nature, connected with new territorial inequalities and uncertainty concerning the long-term evolution of the country's productive structure and its international integration. We emphasize in particular the growing complexity of the social structure and of class conflict, in relation with the redefinition of occupational and educational hierarchies, the distribution of property, and increased competition between territories for access to public services, infrastructures, and wealth. This new form of class conflict, which is characteristic of an advanced welfare state in the grip of unbridled international competition, has helped give the territorial cleavage and divisions among the rural and urban working classes a magnitude not seen since the nineteenth century. It is above all this social and territorial cleavage that has engendered a tripartition comparable to that observed then, and it seems that only platforms of redistribution and economic development that make it possible to bring these different geosocial classes together will allow us to escape it permanently. Thus, the central question is how these convergences will be situated with regard to the national question and the European question. Although there is every reason for redistribution, durable development, and European and international integration to move forward together, they will probably do so over the long term, and nothing guarantees that the same will be the case in the short and middle term.

A Negative Effect of Wealth on the Vote for the Left Increasing from 1993 to 2022

Let us begin by examining the evolution of the social structure of the vote for left-wing parties. These parties have undergone a significant renewal since the 1980s and 1990s: several movements have been added to the historical PS-PCF duopole, with the emergence of ecologist parties as well as new trends on the Left of the Left. On the ecologists' side, there is in particular the Greens party—which participated in the so-called plural Left government with the PS and the PCF from 1997 to 2002—and then Europe écologie–Les verts (EELV), which governed with the PS in the Left majority between 2012 and 2017. In the Left of the Left we find the Left Party (PG), founded in 2008 by Jean-Luc Mélenchon and other Socialist officials who left the PS following their commitment to vote No in the 2005 referendum. The PG allied itself with the PCF to form the Front de gauche (FG) in the legislative elections of 2012, then gave rise to La France insoumise (LFI) starting with the elections of 2017.[8] In the legislative election of 2022, the LFI and other left-wing parties (in particular, the PS, PCF, and EELV) joined together to present single candidates in most of the districts in the framework of NUPES (Nouvelle union populaire écologique et sociale).

If we examine first the total vote for the parties of the Left, whose combined result ran to about 40–45 percent of the vote from 1993 to 2012 and 30–35 percent from 2017 to 2022 (taking into account the departure of some of the PS voters who joined the Center bloc),[9] we see that throughout the period 1993–2022 the vote has been characterized by a very clearly decreasing profile in function of the average municipal income, especially at the height of redistribution (see figure 11.1).[10] That is, the poorest municipalities vote more for the Left than the national average, whereas the vote for the Left collapses in the richest municipalities, in particular in the richest 10 percent (and even more markedly in the richest 5 percent and the richest 1 percent) of the richest municipalities.

At first sight, it is striking to note that the voter profile on the Left as a function of the municipality's income is relatively stable over the period 1993–2022—just as much, moreover, as it was during the period 1910–1993.[11] If we examine

8. Let us also mention the small Trotskyist parties—particularly the LO's anti-Stalinist Communists and the LCR, which had become the NPA; they had been presenting candidates in the elections since the early 1970s and received as much as 3 percent of the votes in the legislative elections of the 1990s and 2000s.
9. See chapter 8, figures 8.1 and 8.3. The crumbling of the Left's overall result during the last decades is also explained by the escape into abstention and the rising power of the FN-RN vote, in addition to the question of the transfer of the PS vote toward the Center in 2017–2022.
10. As we did earlier, we arrive at the same conclusion if we use other indicators of wealth such as real estate capital per inhabitant (that is, the average value of housing). See unehistoireducon-flitpolitique.fr, appendix D, figures D3.3a–D3.3g and D3.6a–D3.6g for the whole set of profiles obtained, election by election, before and after the introduction of control variables.
11. See chapter 10, figure 10.6.

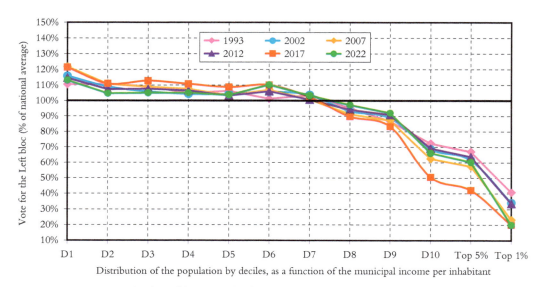

FIGURE 11.1. Vote for the Left by income level, 1993–2022

From the legislative elections of 1993 to those of 2022, the vote for the Left (relative to its national average) diminished sharply with the municipality's average income, especially at the top of the distribution and with a slope that increased slightly over time. Note: The results given here are after controls for the size of the conurbation and municipality.

Sources and series: unehistoireduconflitpolitique.fr

things more closely, we nonetheless see that the profile has become somewhat steeper over time. We have already mentioned this fact while examining the evolution of the curves over the course of the twentieth century: the poorest municipalities often included a large proportion of small, self-employed workers (agricultural or not) voting more for the Right in 1910, 1936, and 1946, an effect that largely disappears when we look at the legislative elections of 1962, 1981, and 1993. We find the same tendency in the course of the period 1993–2022; this phenomenon was conjuncturally strengthened during the most recent elections by the fact that the voters who abandoned the Left for the Center were not the poorest.[12] If we look at the evolution of the ratio between the vote for the Left and in the richest and poorest 50 percent (or among the richest and poorest 20 percent) of the municipalities over the last two centuries, from the legislative

12. It was particularly visible in 2017, when the Left's support fell to an unusually low level (28 percent of the votes, versus 39 percent in 1993, 47 percent in 1997, 41 percent in 2002, 40 percent in 2007, 49 percent in 2012, and 33 percent in 2022), and when the proportion of voters loyal to the Left appeared to be especially weak in the richest municipalities.

elections of 1848 to those of 2022, we see that it was at the end of the twentieth century and the beginning of the twenty-first that the negative effect of wealth on the vote for the Left tended to be the most marked, far more still than in the nineteenth century or at the beginning or the middle of the twentieth century.[13]

The fact that the negative effect of wealth on the vote for the Left tends to become more marked as time goes on, over the long term as well as in recent decades, is a result that may seem surprising or even paradoxical. When it has been in power, hasn't the Left driven the working class away with its betrayals and its support for the interests of the privileged classes? To really understand what is at stake here, we must remember three things. First, the least rich municipalities do indeed have a tendency to vote more heavily for the Left (and increasingly over time), but the gaps always remain relatively small in the least rich 70 percent of the municipalities—whose vote for the Left varies between 100 percent and 120 percent of the national average—and become greater only in the richest 30 percent and especially the richest 10 percent of the municipalities (where it may fall beneath half the national average). Second, the richest municipalities have never voted for the Left; they have systematically and massively voted for the Right since the end of the nineteenth century, except when they perceived that their interests and aspirations were better promoted by the Center, whether they are the Moderate Republicans and Opportunists of the early Third Republic or the LREM-Modem-Ensemble bloc in 2017–2022.[14] Finally, and above all, we must once again emphasize here that the Left was not constructed historically on the basis of the most economically disadvantaged territories. It was constituted on the basis of working-class municipalities in which the new productions of industrial wealth were developed starting in the nineteenth century and the beginning of the twentieth—that is, on the basis of municipalities that were, to be

---

13. See chapter 8, figures 8.14–8.15.
14. See chapter 9, figures 9.5–9.11. The idea that the modern Left now attracts the votes of the financially most favored voters is regularly brandished in conservative speeches. See, for instance, D. Brooks, *Bobos in Paradise: The New Upper Class and How They Got There* (Simon and Schuster, 2000), whose notion of the "bourgeois-bohemian" ("Bobo") has been widely adopted in France, for obvious reasons of political strategy. However, it has no serious factual basis, as the municipal data collected here show unambiguously, allowing us to confirm on a solid statistical basis the results emerging from our investigations. On this subject, see chapter 14, figures 14.24–14.25. For a critique of the use of the word "bobo," see also J.-Y. Authier, A. Collet, C. Giraud, J. Rivière, and S. Tissot, *Les bobos n'existent pas* (Presses Universitaires de Lyon, 2018), which underlines that from its origin, this word "has helped reorganize public debates around a certain vision of social spaces and groups . . . seeking to provide a basis for the legitimacy of a certain elite," and in this case, a conservative elite (88–89).

sure, less rich than the high-class quarters of the very well-off municipalities where the property owners lived, but which are often richer than the rural municipalities or which lack industrial activity. There is therefore nothing surprising about the fact that it was at precisely the time when industry was declining and when the industrial working class was moving away from the Left that the vote for the Left became a little more closely associated with poor municipalities than it was before; as the workers who continued to vote for the Left grew poorer, the Left henceforth brought together voters from occupations (particularly service employees) that are less well remunerated than workers were historically, in comparison with the rest of society.

A Vote for the Left by Employees, *Sociaux-Diplômés*, Women, and Young People

Generally, it is the whole socio-occupational structure associated with the vote for the Left that has been transformed over time. In the course of recent decades, voting for the Left has become less and less strongly associated with the vote of the industrial working class (*ouvriers* in the French sense) and more and more with the vote of employees working in the services (*employés* in the French sense), women, and young people. But the point is that the salaries of many employees like cashiers, waiters, cleaners, and paramedical employees are often lower than those of blue-collar industrial workers,[15] especially when they are women or young people, such that this discrepancy explains in part why the relation between the vote for the Left and municipal income has a tendency to grow larger over time.[16] In recent decades, the Left has also attracted a growing proportion of what we

---

15. According to INSEE's data, blue-collar industrial workers' average salary has been slightly higher than that of employees in the services since the early 2000s (the two having been close in the 1980s and 1990s), with especially large variations from one occupation to another within the general categories of industrial workers (*ouvriers*) and employees (*employés*). In 2020, the average net salary of employees was 1,785 euros, versus 1,855 euros for industrial workers. See "Les salaires dans le secteur privé en 2020" (*INSEE Première*, no. 1898, April 2022. Store cashiers—87 percent of whom were women—earned on average 1,600 euros per month net (when they worked full time, which was not often the case), and home help—96 percent women—1,400 euros per month net; by comparison, the monthly net income of a skilled electrical wiring specialist—85 percent men—amounted to 1,900 euros. See the data-visualization tool developed by INSEE at https://www.insee.fr/fr/outil-interactif/5369554/index.html.

16. The slope's tendency to grow steeper can also be seen after taking into account all the control variables (especially when these variables are socio-occupational). See unehistoireduconflitpolitique.fr, figures D3.3a–D3.3g.

propose to call *sociaux-diplômés* (that is, individuals who have the lowest incomes among those with higher education diplomas). This category includes in particular people holding diplomas who are employed in social work sectors (healthcare, education) and more generally in activities less well remunerated than the best paid jobs requiring diplomas in the commercial sector (finance, consulting, and the top management of large companies, for example).

Let us take things one at a time, beginning with the evolution of the vote of blue-collar industrial workers (*ouvriers*) and employees in service occupations (*employés*). Since the nineteenth century, the ratio between the vote for the Left in the 50 percent of the municipalities with the most and the fewest industrial workers has always been clearly higher than 1, with or without taking control variables into account, in both the urban world and the rural world. The effect was particularly important between 1900 and 1960 and then began to decline sharply in the 1980s–1990s.[17] Studying in greater detail the relation between the vote for the Left and the proportion of industrial workers, we have also noted that the curve was far steeper in 1936 and in 1962, for example, than in 1981 or 1993.[18] This development has continued in the meantime. Specifically, the vote for the Left (relative to its national average) has continued to increase slowly, in step with the proportion of industrial workers in the municipality during the period 1993–2022—an effect entirely due to the Left of the Left, as the Socialists have long since lost the workers' vote—but with an increasingly gradual slope over time, or even a slightly negative profile toward the end of the period in the municipalities with the most industrial workers (see figure 11.2).

Regarding the employees' vote, we see an evolution going in the opposite direction. The municipalities with a greater proportion of employees in the services already had a tendency to vote more heavily for the Left than those that had few employees at the beginning of the period, and the power of this relation has increased during the last three decades (see figure 11.3). Unfortunately, the available long-term data at the municipal level do not enable us to distinguish between different categories of employees—between secretaries, hospital assistants, and retail employees, for example—but considering the negative relation between the vote for the Left and the average municipal income, everything suggests that the increasing propensity to vote for the Left is due in particular to the employees who are paid the least. The more refined surveys conducted at the individual level, on the basis of representative samples or more detailed interviews, also confirm a large

17. See chapter 8, figure 8.11.
18. See chapter 10, figure 10.7.

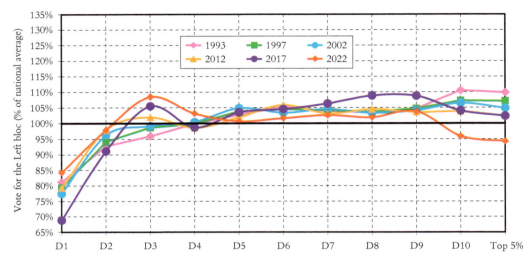

Distribution of the population by deciles, as a function of the proportion of workers in the municipality

FIGURE 11.2. Vote for the Left and working-class municipalities, 1993–2022

From the legislative elections of 1993 to those of 2022, the vote for the Left (relative to its national average) increased slightly with the proportion of blue-collar workers in the municipality, though with a slope less and less sharp over time, or even somewhat negative toward the end of the period in municipalities with more blue-collar workers. Note: The results given here are after controls for the size of the conurbation and municipality.

Sources and series: unehistoireduconflitpolitique.fr

proportion of the vote for the Left in the categories of employees whose situations are the most precarious, such as cashiers and cleaning and maintenance workers with irregular working hours and unstable incomes.[19]

We also note that the vote for the Left has always been a decreasing function of the proportion of managers (or more precisely, "managers and superior intellectual occupations") in the municipality.[20] This is particularly true at the peak of the distribution: in the 10 percent or 5 percent of the municipalities with the

19. See, for example, C. Braconnier and N. Mayer, *Les inaudibles. Sociologie politique des précaires* (Presses de Sciences Po, 2015). See also E. Agrikoliansky, P. Aldrin, and S. Lévêque, *Voter par temps de crise. Portraits d'électrices et d'électeurs ordinaires* (Presses Universitaires de France / Irisso, 2021); Collectif SPEL, *Le sens du vote. Une enquête sociologique (2011–2014)* (Presses Universitaires de Rennes, 2016).

20. Let us recall that the category "managers and superior intellectual occupations" includes both managers in the public and private sectors and the liberal professions. See chapter 2.

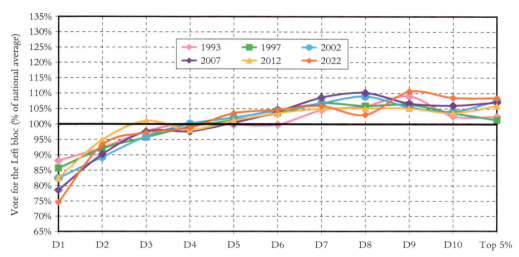

Distribution of the population by deciles, as a function of the proportion of service employees in the municipality

FIGURE 11.3. The vote for the Left and employees, 1993–2022

From the legislative elections of 1993 to those of 2022, the vote for the Left (relative to its national average) increased with the proportion of employees in the municipality, with a slightly increasing slope over time. Note: The results given here are after controls for the size of the conurbation and municipality.

Sources and series: unehistoireduconflitpolitique.fr

most managers, the vote for the Left collapses (see figure 11.4a),[21] a tendency that has grown over recent decades. This has been particularly the case between 2017 and 2022, because a large number of the managers who voted for the Left moved toward the LREM-Modem-Ensemble bloc. In the most high-class Paris arrondissements, as in many municipalities of Yvelines (Loges-en-Josas, Le Vésinet) and Hauts-de-Seine (Neuilly-sur-Seine, Vaucresson, Marne-la-Coquette), but also in Varois-et-Chaignot in Côte-d'Or, Lompret in Nord, Maumusson and Vritz in Loire-Atlantique, Saint-Ismier in Isère, and Roquefort-les-Pins in Alpes-Maritimes—all of which have some of the largest proportions of managers in the country—the vote for the Left did not surpass 50 percent of its national average in 2017. It was already below this average during the five preceding legislative elections, but less markedly (see figure 11.4b).

---

21. As we said earlier, all these results take into account the size of the municipalities in order to avoid biasing the developments. The 10 percent of the municipalities with the most managers designates the 10 percent of the population living in the municipalities with the greatest proportions of managers, and so on.

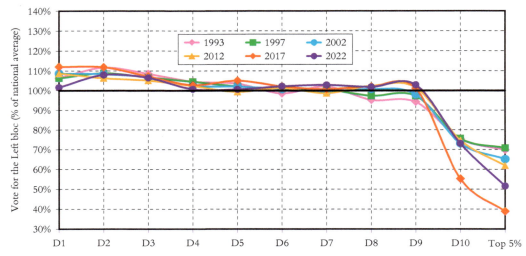

Distribution of the population by deciles, as a function of the proportion of managers in the municipality

FIGURE 11.4A. The vote for the Left and managers, 1993–2022

From the legislative elections of 1993 to those of 2022, the vote for the Left (relative to its national average) decreased with the proportion of managers in the municipality, with a slightly increasing slope over time. Note: The results given here are after controls for the size of the conurbation and municipality.

Sources and series: unehistoireduconflitpolitique.fr

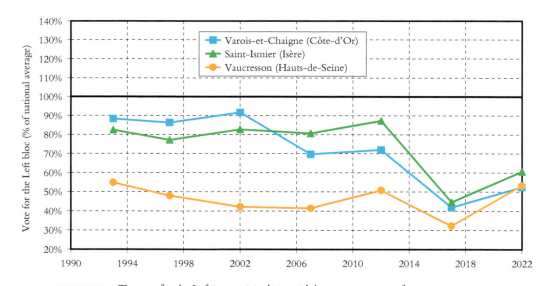

FIGURE 11.4B. The vote for the Left in municipalities with large proportions of managers

In municipalities with a very high proportion of managers—e.g., Varois-et-Chaigne (Côte-d'Or), Saint-Ismier (Isère), and Vaucresson (Hauts-de-Seine)—which are all among the 10% of municipalities with the highest proportions of managers, we see that the result obtained by the Left in the legislative elections from 1993 to 2022 is in general clearly lower than the national average.

Sources and series: unehistoireduconflitpolitique.fr

The negative correlation between the vote for the Left and the proportion of managers is similar to what we have seen in the case of income (see figure 11.1).[22] In general, the effects connected with wealth (income or real estate capital) and with the socio-occupational structure are partly correlated, but only partly; these two explanatory variables also play an autonomous role, in the sense that their effect persists at least in part after considering the other factors. Concerning managers, let us note, however, that their negative effect on the vote for the Left is greatly reduced when we control for the level of wealth (income or real estate capital), whereas the negative effect of wealth on the vote for the Left is not much affected by taking into account the proportion of managers.[23] In other words, whereas the vote for the Left is determined as much by socio-occupational identity (with, in this case, a gradual movement of blue-collar workers toward employees in the services) as by the low level of wealth, the vote against the Left—and thus for the Right or the Center, depending on the period—is determined mainly by the high level of wealth and only secondarily by the manager's identity, even if some elements that are not strictly speaking monetary (such as belonging to the private sector or having the status of an independent) also play an important role.[24] To put it still another way, while a retail sales employee with a high level of real estate capital—because of an inheritance, for example—will tend to vote for the Right, a freelance journalist who has trouble making ends meet, even though he is classified as a manager, will vote much more systematically for the Left.

In order to interpret these results correctly, it is important to put them back into the context of the transformations of the socio-occupational structure of recent decades. Between 1990 and 2022, blue-collar workers and the self-employed continued the decrease observed since the 1960s, and the decline in their share of

---

22. In both cases, the collapse is particularly pronounced in 2017, which reflects the fact that the voters who shifted from the PS to LREM were especially managers with high incomes.

23. See unehistoireduconflitpolitique.fr, appendix D3, figures D3.26a–D3.26h. From the point of view of the profile of the vote for the Left, the intermediate occupations move from a slightly decreasing relation in 1993 to a slightly increasing profile in 2022, and appear de facto in a median position between, on the one hand, blue-collar workers and employees (who have historically always had a clearly increasing profile that in recent decades is more and more distinct for employees and less and less distinct for blue-collar workers), and on the other hand, the managers and self-employed (who have always had a clearly decreasing profile of the vote on the Left).

24. Let us recall in particular the maintenance at an approximately constant level over recent decades of a negative association between the vote for the Left and the proportion of the self-employed, before and after taking into account all the controls (including income, real estate capital, and so on). See chapter 6, figure 10.9.

the population has been offset by the rise in the number of employees, people working in intermediary occupations, and managers.[25] In this context, blue-collar workers' move from their Left to the Left of employees must not be understood as just the negative consequence of industrial workers' disappointment with the Left and with Communism (even if that historical disillusionment naturally played a fundamental role), but also as a sign of support for the left-wing vote on the part of a large proportion of the employees in the various service sectors, and in particular in sectors connected with the development of the welfare state—for example, medical care and personal care. If we classify municipalities in accord with their proportions of people working in such intermediate occupations, we also note that the curve of the vote for the Left has grown much more clearly over time (although less steeply than for employees).[26] Moreover, the borderlines between categories are quite porous and can evolve within individual trajectories, with, for example, auxiliary nurses classified as employees and registered nurses as members of an intermediary occupation. In the educational sector, teaching assistants such as ATSEM (assistants in preschools and primary schools) are classified as employees, middle-school teachers are classified as members of the intermediate occupations, and teachers in high schools and higher education are classified as members of upper managerial and intellectual professions.

The data available at the municipal level over the long term do not allow us to make these fine distinctions, but surveys conducted at the individual level confirm the importance of the medical-social and educational sectors for the vote for the Left (carers, personnel serving the elderly, preschool aides, social workers, and so on), including in elections in which the vote for the Left falls to its lowest levels.[27]

The Swing to the Left of the Women's Vote

With the shift from the Left of blue-collar industrial workers to the Left of employees in the services, the other great transformation of recent decades is the swing to the left of the women's vote. Moreover, these two developments are closely linked from the point of view of the structure of economic activity, even if there is also a

---

25. See chapter 2, figure 2.19.
26. See unehistoireduconflitpolitique.fr, appendix D3, figures D3.3a–D3.3k and D4.20a–D4.20k, for the whole set of curves obtained before any control, after control for the size of the conurbation and municipality, and after the introduction of all the sociodemographic controls (including for the socio-occupational structure).
27. See Agrikoliansky, Aldrin, and Lévêque, *Voter par temps de crise.*

distinct factor connected with the women's vote as such. Let us also add that this is a structural development that is found in all Western electoral democracies. In all the countries for which we have exit polls at the individual level, we find that on average, in the 1950s and 1960s women had a tendency to vote more for the Right than men did, then this bias grew smaller in the 1970s and 1980s before finally being inverted in the 1990s, 2000s, and 2010s, with a women's vote for the Left more pronounced than men's.[28]

To account for this evolution, many researchers have emphasized the rise in the employment of women (especially in the service industries) as well as the increase in marital separations and precarious economic situations, particularly in the case of single mothers.[29] More generally, this development testifies to deep socio-economic and political-ideological transformations concerning family structures and the growing importance of gender equality. In particular, the objective of professional occupational equality has gradually replaced the patriarchal model and the ideology of the stay-at-home mother (which was largely dominant in the 1950s and 1960s, and strongly internalized by some women—aided by their husbands, who were quick to remind them of the economic and organizational benefits of retreating into the home), and feminist demands have been driven mainly by left-wing political trends since the 1970s and 1980s, which was not particularly the case in the nineteenth or early twentieth centuries.[30] Regarding France, taking into account socioeconomic control variables (diplomas, income, wealth, parents'

28. See A. Gethin, C. Martinez-Toledano, and T. Piketty, *Clivages politiques et inégalités sociales. Une étude de 50 démocraties, 1948–2020* (EHESS / Gallimard / Seuil, 2021), figure 1.25. The overall tendency is the same everywhere, but the levels differ. In the 1950s and 1960s, women voted on average much more rarely for the Right than men did in France, the United Kingdom, and Germany, and much more clearly in the United States.

29. See R. Inglehart and P. Norris, "The Developmental Theory of the Gender Gap: Women's and Men's Voting Behavior in Global Perspective," *International Political Science Review,* 2000. See also J. Mossu-Lavau, "Le vote des femmes en France (1945–1993)," *Revue française de science politique,* 1993; L. Edlund and R. Pande, "Why Have Women Become Left-Wing? The Political Gender Gap and the Decline in Marriage," *Quarterly Journal of Economics,* 2002.

30. At the beginning of the twentieth century, Radicals were particularly mistrustful of what they perceived as the Catholic grip on women, and Radical senators played an important role in delaying women's suffrage in the interwar period. In the nineteenth century, patriarchal and even masculinist discourses were very widespread on the political chessboard, in both the workers' movement and in bourgeois political trends. On the extreme violence of the misogynistic remarks made by Proudhon, for example, which were often hidden in the history of the labor movement, see B. Pavard, F. Rochefort and M. Zancarini-Fournel, *Ne nous libérez pas, on s'en charge! Une histoire des féminismes de 1789 à nos jours* (La Découverte, 2020), 101.

occupation, and so on) has little effect on the fact that the women's vote leaned toward the Right in the 1950s and 1960s, a regularity that we find at that time in almost all categories (among women who are well educated as well as among those who are not, for example). On the other hand, once we control for religion and the practice of religion, this effect disappears: among people who say they believe and practice their religion, women have never voted more for the Right than men. Nonetheless, we can conclude that the greater religiousness declared by some women in the surveys of the 1950s–1960s is itself connected with a system of beliefs concerning the role of mothers in families and the education of children, and with a process of internalizing these norms.[31]

From a methodological point of view, we note that it is very difficult to study this question of the women's and men's votes on the basis of the municipal data used here, and that it is highly preferable to turn to surveys conducted at the individual level. There are in fact relatively few variations among municipalities from the point of view of the male-female composition of the population, and the main variations are closely connected with the structure by age (municipalities with many elderly residents have more women) or the size of the conurbation (the rural world is a little more masculine), such that it is hard to isolate the effect of the women's vote on the basis of such data.[32] There are more variations between municipalities at the level of the age structure of the population (men and women taken together), which makes it possible to observe that the youngest municipalities generally vote more for the Left than older municipalities, and that this effect connected with age was particularly strong in the elections of 2017 and 2022 (see figure 11.5).[33] In France, exit polls conducted at the individual level confirm that since the 1950s, the youngest voters have voted on average more for the Left than older voters have, though there is a great degree of volatility over time concerning the magnitude of this effect. The gap in favor of the Left among young voters thus

---

31. See T. Piketty, "Brahmin Left vs. Merchant Right. Rising Inequality and the Changing Structure of Political Conflict" (World Inequality Lab working paper 2018/07), figures 2.2d–2.2g.

32. After taking into account all the control variables, the effect of the proportion of women in a municipality on the vote disappears entirely. See unehistoireduconflitpolitique.fr, appendix D3, figures D3.22p–D3.22r.

33. This effect is not much affected by taking into account the size of the conurbation and the municipality. On the other hand, it is largely absorbed when other sociodemographic variables are taken into account, especially income and occupational structure. See unehistoireduconflitpolitique.fr, appendix D3, figures D3.23p–D3.23r.

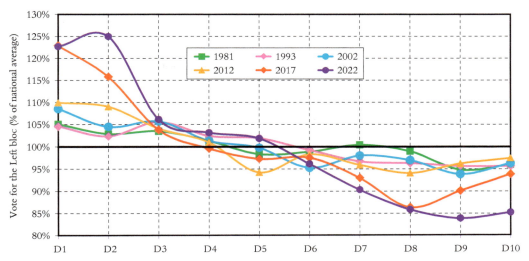

Distribution of the population by deciles, as a function of the average age in the municipality

FIGURE 11.5. The Left and young people, 1981–2022

From the legislative elections of 1981 to those of 2022, the vote for the Left (relative to its national average) is systematically higher in younger municipalities (in terms of the average age in the municipality) than in older municipalities, with a particularly strong relation at the end of the period of the elections of 2017 and 2022.

Sources and series: unehistoireduconflitpolitique.fr

seems to have been particularly great in the 1970s and early 1980s, and then again in the elections of 2002 and 2007, and especially in 2017 and 2022, whereas it is much more moderate in other periods.[34] This volatility is found in other countries, and it seems to be closely connected with political cycles and young people's waves of hope in view of possible changes in government.[35]

---

34. The effect is particularly clear if we compare voters younger than thirty-five years old to those over sixty-five. Its size diminishes after taking into account other variables (in particular, income and occupation), but it remains significant. On the other hand, since the 1980s it has been almost entirely absorbed when religion and religious practice are taken into account. See Piketty, "Brahmin Left vs. Merchant Right," figures 2.2a–2.2c.

35. Let us add that these variations reflect not only the effects of age but also, in certain cases, generational effects. In other words, the fact that one was born and socialized in a given period can have a significant and lasting impact on one's political position (an effect that is seen even when we control for occupation or education). See, for instance, V. Tiberj, *Les citoyens qui viennent. Comment le nouvellement générationnel transforme la politique en France* (Presses Universitaire de France, 2017).

Will the Left Become the Party of the *Sociaux-Diplômés?*

We come now to the question of the heavy vote for the Left among the *sociaux-diplômés*—that is, the people who have the least remunerative occupations among those with higher education diplomas. Generally speaking, having a smaller income increases the probability of voting for the Left, and that is true for diploma holders as well as for those who do not hold diplomas. It is thus perfectly logical that the worst paid of the diploma holders vote more for the Left than the best-paid diploma holders do. But the effect in question here is an additional effect that has appeared in the last decades: for a given level of income, holding a higher diploma increases the chances of voting for the Left, which was not the case previously. Let us begin by examining the situation that prevailed during the legislative elections of 1981. If we classify municipalities as functions of their proportion of higher education diploma holders, we see that the vote for the Left decreases greatly with the proportion of diploma holders, particularly at the peak of the distribution (see figure 11.6).

If we now control for a given size of conurbation, this negative effect of the proportion of diploma holders on the vote for the Left is even clearer, since small conurbations have on average fewer diploma holders and vote more heavily for the Right. An interesting point concerns the introduction of other sociodemographic variables, and in particular those connected with wealth (income and real estate capital) and with socio-occupational composition. We note that the effect connected with diploma holding disappears entirely when these control variables are taken into account (see figure 11.6). In other words, it is not because of their diplomas that the municipalities with the most diploma holders voted for the Right in 1981; it was solely because they had larger incomes or because they had more managers. For the same average income and the same proportion of managers, having more diploma holders had no effect on the vote, in one direction or the other. Let us add that this result observed in the legislative elections of 1981 is found in almost the same form for preceding elections (in 1910, 1936, 1962, and 1978, for example), and more generally in all elections until the 1970s, usually with a slight residual negative effect of the diploma on the vote for the Left, in historical contexts in which access to higher education concerned only a very small social elite and thus was associated with privileged backgrounds.[36]

---

36. For example, during the elections of 1936 and 1962, the municipalities with the most diploma holders voted a little more for the Right, even after taking into account all the other sociodemographic variables. However, the chief predictive factor for the vote for the Right was still

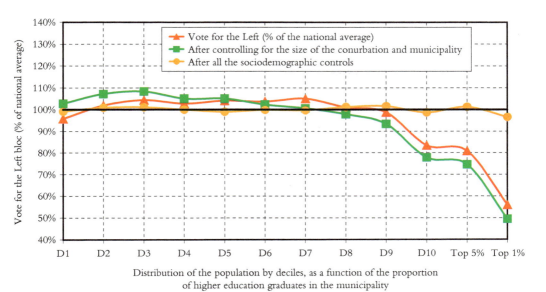

Distribution of the population by deciles, as a function of the proportion
of higher education graduates in the municipality

FIGURE 11.6. Vote for the Left and higher education graduates, 1981

In the legislative election of 1981, the proportion of higher education graduates in the municipality
has a negative effect on the vote for the Left before controls are taken into account, but this effect is
reduced to zero once all the controls are taken into account (in particular income and
occupation).

Sources and series: unehistoireduconflitpolitique.fr

If we reproduce the same operation for all the elections conducted since 1981,
we find a significant development going in the opposite direction. The swing gradually takes place in the 1980s and 1990s, at a time when the proportion of people
holding higher education diplomas was itself growing greatly. Thus, in the 1993
legislative election we see that the municipalities with the most diploma holders
continue to vote much less for the Left than the others (just as they did in all the
other elections up to 2022, moreover), but the effect changes its sign as soon as all
the control variables are introduced. The impact of the diploma is very significant:
before the controls, the vote for the Left in the 10 percent of the municipalities
with the most diploma holders was more than 10 percent smaller than the national
average; after taking the control variables into account, these same municipalities
voted 15 percent more for the Left than the rest of the country (see figure 11.7).
The fact is that we find the same result for all the legislative elections of the last

economic wealth (income and real estate capital) and the proportion of managers. For the
complete results, election by election, see unehistoireduconflitpolitique.fr, appendix D3.

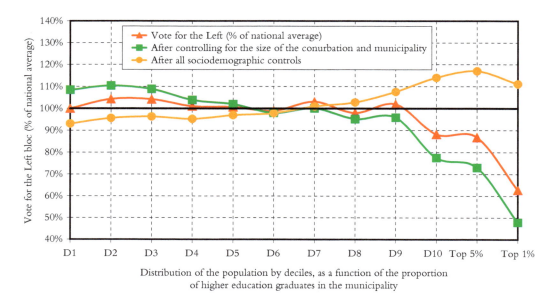

FIGURE 11.7. Vote for the Left and higher education graduates, 1993

In the legislative elections of 1993, the proportion of higher education graduates in the municipality has a negative effect on the vote for the Left, but the effect becomes positive once the all the explanatory variables are taken into account (particularly income and occupation).

Sources and series: unehistoireduconflitpolitique.fr

three decades: if we take the other explanatory factors into account, and in particular if we control for a given average income and a given proportion of managers, then the municipalities with the most diploma holders vote significantly and systematically more for the Left than the rest of the country (whereas the reverse is true in the absence of controls). The magnitude of the effect tends to grow until 2012 and diminishes a little in 2017 and 2022 when some left-wing voters moved toward the Center bloc, but it remains very significant (see figure 11.8).

It is particularly striking to note that we find similar transformations in exit polls conducted at the individual level. In all the surveys available since the 1950s, the probability of voting for the Left decreases greatly with income, especially at the peak of the distribution. The negative relation is still more marked if we consider the level of wealth. In comparison, the relation between the vote and the level of the diploma is more complex and has changed direction over time. In the 1950s and 1960s, the vote for the Left regularly diminished with the level of the diploma— less strongly, of course, than with the level of income or wealth, but nonetheless significantly (including for a given level of income and wealth). Then the relation

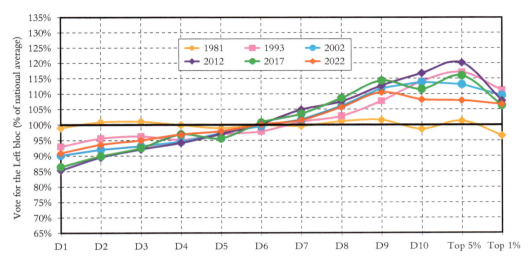

Distribution of the population by deciles, as a function of the proportion of higher education graduates in the municipality

FIGURE 11.8. Vote for the Left and higher education graduates, 1981–2022

From the legislative elections of 1993 to those of 2022, the proportion of higher education graduates had a residual positive effect on the vote for the Left (after taking into account all the sociodemographic controls, including income and occupation), whereas this residual effect was nil in the legislative elections of 1981 (and the preceding elections). Note: The results given here are after controls for the size of the conurbation and municipality after introducing all the sociodemographic controls.

Sources and series: unehistoireduconflitpolitique.fr

between the vote for the Left and diplomas gradually flattens out during the 1970s and 1980s, especially if we control for the level of income and wealth. This turnaround of the educational cleavage is also found in the United States, the United Kingdom, and in all the Western democracies. To sum up, we have moved from a situation in which all the dimensions of social stratification (income, wealth, diplomas) were pushing in the same direction to a new situation in which the groups richest in terms of income and wealth still continue to vote very heavily for the Right but those with the most diplomas (for a given income and wealth) tend on the contrary to vote more for the Left. This transformation is developing in a context of great educational expansion, in which higher education diploma holders now represent a very extensive group, have much more diverse backgrounds than they used to have, engage in very diverse activities, and receive extremely varied remunerations. It might be said that the electoral system that has been set up over the course of recent decades is based on the opposition between a "Merchant Right" (the richest voters) and a "Brahmin Left" (the voters with the most diplomas).[37] The expression is evocative, but on the condition that it is made clear that it is solely the "poor Brahmins"—or more precisely, the diploma holders engaging in the lowest-paid occupations—who vote more for the Left.[38] On reflection, and on the basis of the new sources we have collected here—which allow us in particular to show in a much more detailed way than the data provided by surveys that not only have the richest territories never voted for the Left but they even have had a tendency to move farther away from it over time—it seems to us more pertinent to speak of *sociaux-diplômés* to designate this group that has emerged in recent decades, the diploma holders who work in less remunerated activities (particularly in the health and education sectors) and who vote more for the Left.

The Vote of the *Sociaux-Diplômés:* A Specific Position in the Productive Structure

How do we interpret the fact that the richest voters in terms of income or real estate capital continue to vote for the Right (or the Center), whereas the *sociaux-diplômés* have drifted to the Left, and what can we conclude from this for the future? Generally, we must first insist on the complexity of the relation between diplomas, occupations, and economic wealth. To be sure, there is a positive correlation between these different dimensions of social stratification: the richest municipalities (in terms of average income or real estate capital per inhabitant) also tend to have a large proportion of inhabitants with higher education diplomas and a greater proportion of managers. However, in practice, this correlation is less important than one might imagine, for several reasons.[39] First, income depends

---

37. See Gethin, Martinez-Toledano, and Piketty, *Clivages politiques et inégalités sociales,* 42, figure 1.1; Piketty, "Brahmin Left vs. Merchant Right," figures 1.2a–1.2f. See also A. Gethin, C. Martinez-Toledano, and T. Piketty, "Brahmin Left vs. Merchant Right: Changing Political Cleavages in 21 Western Democracies 1948–2020," *Quarterly Journal of Economics,* 2022. Brahmins are the educated elites in the traditional Indian social system, as opposed to the warrior elites and commercial elites.

38. Here it is worthwhile to remember that the true Brahmins in India are both the most educated and the richest in wealth and income, and that they are by far the social group currently voting the most heavily for the Right, and in this case, for the probusiness Hindu nationalists of the Bharatiya Janata Party. See A. Banerjee, A. Gethin, and T. Piketty, "Caste, classe et représentation politique des inégalités sociales en Inde, 1962–2019," in Gethin, Martinez-Toledano, and Piketty, *Clivages politiques et inégalités sociales,* 306, figure 9.3.

39. In the municipal data that we have collected, the correlations between the ranks in the distribution of average income and average real estate capital and the proportion of managers or the proportion of higher education diplomas, is about 0.3 to 0.5, without a clear tendency over the

not only on income from work (salaries and nonsalaried activities) but also on wealth and receiving the flows of capital income that issue from it (dividends, interest, rents, profits, capital gains). Second, if we limit ourselves to income from work, the relation with diplomas is far from automatic. To be sure, on average, the absence of diplomas makes access to jobs more difficult, and the incomes of those with higher education diplomas are higher than those with general or technical secondary school degrees.[40] But for a given level of diploma, there are occupations and sectors of activity that are much less remunerative than others, in particular the social sectors (health, education), where salaries are clearly inferior to those in the commercial sector (including finance, consulting, and more generally, management positions in large private enterprises). But the fact is that this phenomenon has grown over time, taking into account the very great educational expansion ((with higher education diploma holders at 34 percent in the active population in 2022, compared with 2 percent in 1960 and 8 percent in 1980),[41] as well as the historical growth of the welfare state, which has, moreover, made educational democratization possible while at the same time leading to the development of new productive sectors organized, in large measure, outside the traditional lucrative and capitalist logic (particularly in the healthcare, social work, and educational domains). It seems relatively logical that the *sociaux-diplômés* see their aspirations and their worldview reflected more in the Left's political trends, insofar as the Left has historically supported the development of the welfare state, whereas the Right trends have tended to limit its growth and emphasize the necessity of a driving, dynamic commercial sector.

Several points regarding this interpretation must be clarified. First, most of the *sociaux-diplômés* concerned here work in the health and education sector,

---

long term, it being understood that a correlation equal to 0 corresponds to a complete absence of a statistical connection, and a correlation equal to 1.0 corresponds to a complete alignment of the two dimensions. Nevertheless, we see a decrease in the correlation between average income and the proportion of higher education diplomas during the period 1990–2020 (a correlation of almost 0.5 to barely 0.3), which seems to be consistent with the sharp increase in the proportion of diplomas and the interpretation proposed here. Note also that the correlations measured at the individual level in the exit polls are of the same order (0.3–0.5), with particularly weak connections between diplomas and patrimonies (0.1–0.2), which reflects quite clearly the fundamental multidimensionality of the inequalities between social classes.

40. On average, 30 percent higher for a *licence*, 60 percent higher for a master's degree, and 80 percent higher for graduates of the *grandes écoles*, according to G. Dabbaghian and M. Péron, "Tout diplôme mérite salaire? Une estimation des rendements privés de l'enseignement supérieur en France et de leur évolution" (Conseil d'analyse économique, Focus no. 075–2021).

41. See chapter 3, figure 3.6.

particularly in jobs at the middle or intermediate level, as nurses and as teachers in primary and elementary schools. Generally speaking, these occupations represent the largest groups in the sector of healthcare and teaching, a sector that comprised 25 percent of total employment in 2022, or more than industry, construction, and agriculture combined.[42] But the fact is that jobs in the healthcare, welfare, and teaching sector require multiple diplomas (bac+3 for nurses and bac+5 for primary school teachers), but their salaries are often smaller than the prevailing remunerations for jobs in the private sector based on the same levels of diplomas or sometimes even lower-level diplomas (jobs as salespeople or commercial managers, for example). We also find the same phenomenon at higher strata of diplomas and incomes. This is the case, for instance, for hospital physicians, who are generally paid less than independent physicians or managers in the private sector with equivalent or inferior training, or for secondary school teachers and teacher-researchers in higher education, who, although they have equivalent or superior diplomas (*agrégation, doctorat*), are usually paid less than people working in finance or consulting or as managers in the private sector after graduating from a school of business or engineering. The question here is not whether these differences in remuneration are justified; no doubt one could find reasons for the discrepancies, up to a point, in connection with the fact that the jobs of *sociaux-diplômés* could be considered more fulfilling, or that they provide more freedom or job security.[43] The essential point is that there are occupations that procure incomes lower than others for the same level of diploma. By construction, it is precisely these jobs that explain why and how municipalities with larger proportions of higher education diploma holders (controlling for average income and other socioeconomic characteristics) can end up voting more heavily for the Left, whereas in the absence of controls, the municipalities with the most diploma holders always vote more for the Right (see figure 11.7).

---

42. See chapter 2, figure 2.1

43. Let us note all the same that other countries have made different choices. In France, in 2021, the salaries of teachers with fifteen years of experience and the most extensive qualifications (CAPES) are 16 percent lower for the first cycle of secondary education (that is, middle school, or *collège*) than the average of the OCDE, and 19 percent for elementary school teachers. The gaps are greater than 50 percent if we compare France to Germany. See *Regards sur l'éducation 2022. Les indicateurs de l'OCDE* (OCDE, 2022). In the same way—even though in the second case the comparisons between countries are more difficult to interpret—France comes only twenty-third in the international ranking of nurses' salaries.

In addition to the healthcare, social work, and teaching sectors, which in the early 2020s comprised about half of all the jobs requiring diplomas in the country,[44] we must also take into account the existence of the *sociaux-diplômés* in multiple other sectors with workforces that are smaller but nonetheless significant, such as culture, media, and the nonprofit sector, as well as among the managers of local collectivities, the civil service, the public sector, and the semipublic sector (public transportation administrations, environmental agencies, and so on). What all these situations have in common is that the higher education diploma holders choose not to pursue the most remunerative jobs—apparently because they think that corresponds more to their aspirations—and that their inclinations themselves are positively correlated with voting for the Left (without that implying a systematic, deterministic connection). Alongside these "voluntary *sociaux-diplômés*" there are also people who, for a given diploma, do not succeed in securing a job as rewarding as they had hoped, whether it is because they suffer from discrimination, or because they do not have the required family networks and relational capital, or because of, we must add, of course, all the vicissitudes of life (separations, depression, health problems, and so on). These situations of "involuntary *sociaux-diplômés*" (or more simply, "poor diploma holders") may (or may not) be accompanied by a vote more to the Left (in addition to the usual effect of income). The data at our disposal are unfortunately not sufficient to study these different cases in a perfectly precise and satisfying manner. In particular, the available sources at the municipal level over the long term pertain to only the proportion of higher education diploma holders in general (without a supplementary breakdown of the diploma holders) and the socio-occupational composition by large categories (workers, employees, managers, and so on), without further clarification.

However, all the available data suggest that the interpretation in terms of "voluntary *sociaux-diplômés*" constitutes the most convincing and the most important explanation of the facts brought to light.[45] In particular, the surveys conducted at the individual level have long since proven that the salaried employees in

---

44. Healthcare, social work, and teaching constituted 25 percent of all employment in 2022. About two-thirds of these positions were occupied by people with higher education diplomas (bac + 2 or more), or about 17 percent of total employment, compared to 34 percent of diploma holders in the active population as a whole.

45. In passing, let us emphasize that access to higher education may give those who benefit from it many advantages that have to do with individual emancipation and not with a strictly monetary logic. Although access to the labor market—and the acquisition of specific qualifications—certainly constitutes one of the matrices of mass higher education, we might collectively wish that all those who want to are able to benefit from an increase in their knowledge, regardless of any "utilitarian" perception of the knowledge acquired.

institute selection and to increase registration fees at the universities—a project that young people interpreted as a desire to close society and to return to a form of elitism and Malthusianism—it led to large protests by high school and university students, and the plan was finally withdrawn in December 1986. It was especially on this issue that the Socialist president François Mitterand was reelected in 1988, despite his mixed record in coping with the economy and unemployment. That may also explain why many of the new diploma holders remained faithful to the Left, even when the diploma didn't lead to a job and a salary as lucrative as they expected. In any case, it will take decades for the proportion of higher education diploma holders to reach 70–80 percent in the whole of the active population (all ages included). Until then, and beyond—because the class of those who do not hold diplomas will no doubt increasingly be the class of the most precarious—the Left (like the Center and the Right) will have to find the means to address those without diplomas as much as those who have them, for reasons of justice and moral coherence as well as for reasons of political survival.

This question of the "class of the *sociaux-diplômés*" and the Left as the "party of the *sociaux-diplômés*" is closely connected with the reflections begun particularly by Bruno Latour on the notion of an "ecological class." In short, Latour proposes to move beyond the Marxist materialist analysis of social classes by placing at the heart of the analysis the conditions of the planet's livability (climate, biodiversity) rather than just the reproduction of human beings (food, clothing, shelter). The new ecological class that Latour wants has as its mission specifically to think about the livability of the planet and the new productive system, to win the battle of ideas, and to deny current extractivist classes any right to speak in the name of rationality. The ecological class is situated in the lineage of the working class and the movement to decommodify the economy and people's lives, which was launched with the welfare state in the twentieth century—but with the essential difference that now we have to restrain the relations of production in order to avoid environmental collapse. The ecological class includes in particular all the scientists who would like to be able to envision and invent without commercial and productivist constraints and to act in such a way that collective intelligence and rare resources are put in the service of the livability of the world (and not of advertising algorithms or high-frequency trading). Latour also emphasizes that the ecological class will have to bring together the working classes (the first victims of the environmental and energy crises), and to do that, it will have to fight on two fronts at the same time, against the globalizer-extractivists and against the reactionary-nationalists. The latter define the territory in relation to the dead and ancestors, not in relation to livability for all living creatures, such that their view of the planet seems to Latour even more sterile than that of the globalizer-extractivists.[48]

The perspective on the ecological class and its role in history that Latour describes is seductive, and to a certain extent it is already being realized, with the development of a class of *sociaux-diplômés* choosing to put their knowledge in the service of an alternative socioeconomic model, placing objectives of human development and sustainability before the lucrative logic, even if it means working in lower-paid jobs in the sectors of healthcare, education, culture, transportation, and the environment. Over the long term, in a world in which all voters hold higher education diplomas and have achieved better living conditions (in absolute terms), we can in fact imagine that the main political cleavage would be between the ecological *sociaux-diplômés* (adherents to the nonlucrative model) and the extractivist-productivists with business diplomas who are well versed in the commercial system. In such a political system, the social-ecologists and their families would possess, by construction, less wealth and financial and real estate capital than the extractivist-productivists, but they might have superior knowledge and diplomas (doctorates rather than MBAs), naturally with multiple class transitions in both directions.

We are, however, far from such a situation, for several reasons. Besides the fact that the great majority of the population in France and in the world does not hold higher education diplomas and will not before the end of the twenty-first century, we also have to take seriously the fact that the working and middle classes, more or less everywhere, are legitimately preoccupied with their living conditions, their income levels and purchasing power, access to housing and real estate property, transportation and public services, and so on. The productive system must certainly be radically transformed, especially in order to preserve the living conditions and livability on the planet for the poorest inhabitants, but that will be possible only if the most disadvantaged can be convinced that the distribution of efforts and benefits is as fair as possible, and not merely another pretext for putting pressure on the poorest and favoring even more the classes that are already privileged, whether they are social-ecological or globalist-extractivist. If so many voters vote for the reactionary-nationalists designated by Latour, particularly in rural territories, it is also and perhaps especially because they feel abandoned by the urban world, even in the context of well-intentioned social-ecological discourses that criticize living in a detached house and driving your own car, for example. Thus,

---

48. See, especially, B. Latour and N. Schultz, *Mémo sur la nouvelle classe écologique. Comment faire émerger une nouvelle classe écologique consciente et fière d'elle-même* (La Découverte, 2022).

of foreign origin—even in municipalities with the largest numbers of foreigners— it is probable that the effect of sociability plays an even more important role than does the direct effect.[51]

Generally speaking, the positive residual effect observed in the nineteenth century and during most of the twentieth must be related to the fact that left-wing political parties, along with the labor movement, played a major role in the integration and promotion of individuals from Italian and Spanish working-class immigrant backgrounds . Conversely, it is striking to note that the residual effect became virtually nil in the 1970s and early 1980s, and even slightly negative at the end of the 1980s and in the 1990s (see figure 11.9). In other words, the municipalities with a strong foreign presence then voted a little less for the Left than one might have expected on the basis of their occupational composition and their other characteristics. The natural interpretation is that the new waves of migrants from North and sub-Saharan Africa aroused a particular hostility in some of the inhabitants of the municipalities in question (we will return to this later, with our examination of the determinants of the FN vote), and all the more so in a context of economic crisis and increasing unemployment. Several researchers have also emphasized that in the 1970s, 1980s, and 1990s, the Left parties never really tried to help people from the Maghrebin immigration as much as they had the preceding waves, and thus they abandoned the field to negative prejudices and hostile discourses.[52] The weakening of the labor movement over several decades also helped diminish the social mechanisms that made it possible to create a link and solidarity between blue-collar workers or employees of different origins, which may have contributed to the development of new forms of prejudices and stigmatizations. The residual effect connected with foreign origins became nil again in the 2000s and then positive again in the 2010s and early 2020s, which can be interpreted as a defensive vote in the face of the rising power of anti-immigrant political trends, and perhaps especially as the slow advance of a positive effect—similar to

---

51. See the discussion in chapter 4. To go back to the principal orders of magnitude: on the eve of World War I, the 10 percent of municipalities with the largest proportions of foreigners consisted of, on average, around 16 percent foreigners, a figure that rose to 22 percent in 2022.

52. See, for example, F. Matonti, *Comment sommes-nous devenus réacs?* (Fayard, 2021), 31–55. On the minimal support (and indeed, sometimes outright hostility) shown by some of the Socialist leaders with regard to Maghrebin workers during several strikes in the late 1970s and the early 1980s, particularly in the automobile sector in Aulnay and Poissy, see also A. Hajjat and M. Mohammed, *Islamophobie. Comment les élites françaises fabriquent le problème musulman* (La Découverte, 2013), 133–139; R. Bertrand and P. Boucheron, *Faire musée d'une histoire commune* (Seuil, 2019), 396–397; S. Beaud and G. Noiriel, *Race et sciences sociales. Essai sur les usages publics d'une catégorie* (Agone, 2021), 157–161.

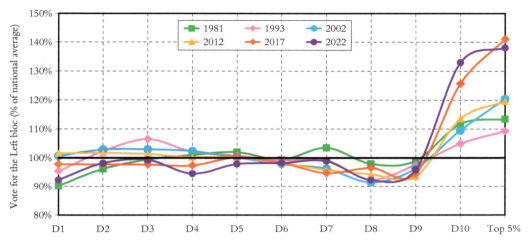

Distribution of the population by deciles, as a function of the proportion of foreigners in the municipality

FIGURE 11.10. Vote for the Left and foreign origins, 1981–2022 (before taking socioeconomic characteristics into account)

From the legislative elections of 1981 to those of 2022, the vote for the Left (relative to its national average) is higher in the 10% of municipalities with the largest proportions of persons of foreign nationality than in other municipalities. Note: The results given here are after controls for the size of the conurbation and municipality, but before introducing the other sociodemographic controls (income, occupation, etc.).

Sources and series: unehistoireduconflitpolitique.fr

the one observed in the first half of the twentieth century—connected with the sociability in municipalities with the greatest foreign presences. To put it another way, the sociability of the new migratory waves from North and sub-Saharan Africa required more time to take effect than it did for the preceding waves, but it now seems to be playing the dominant role again.

Finally, we must emphasize that these residual effects (generally positive from the nineteenth century to the 1960s, nil or slightly negative from the 1970s to the 2000s, then weakly positive again in the 2010s and 2020s) are still relatively moderate compared to the gross effects (see figure 11.9). In other words, it is above all the socioeconomic determinants (in particular, the average income and the socio-occupational composition) that explain the electoral behavior of the municipalities with the largest foreign presences (and in this case, their greater vote for the Left), and not foreign origins as such. This conclusion also emerges very clearly when we examine the detailed results, decile by decile, before and after taking controls into account (see figures 11.10–11.11). In particular, if the vote for the Left

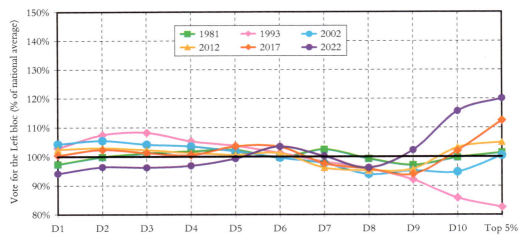

Distribution of the population by deciles, as a function of the proportion of foreigners in the municipality

FIGURE 11.11. Vote for the Left and foreign origins, 1981–2022 (after taking socioeconomic characteristics into account)

After taking into account all the socioeconomic variables (in particular income and occupation), the vote for the Left (relative to its national average) varies much less with the proportion of foreigners. The net effect is almost nil in 1981, 2002, and 2012, and negative in 1993 and positive in 2017 and 2022. Note: The results given here are after all the controls.
Sources and series: unehistoireduconflitpolitique.fr

grew substantially in 2017 and 2022 in the 10 percent of the municipalities with the largest foreign presences, compared to the elections of 1981 or 2022, that is explained above all by the sociodemographic variables (namely, an increasing concentration of the population of foreign extraction in the poor suburbs), and not by origins as such (the increase is much smaller after taking controls into account). This conclusion coincides with the results already obtained concerning the much greater predictive power of the socioeconomic variables compared to the variables connected with origin when we measure the role of the different determinants of the vote on the national scale.[53]

However, we must remember that although the residual effect of foreign origins on the vote for the Left (or more rarely, for the Right) still appears to be relatively moderate, the same cannot be said about the effects on electoral turnout. In fact, since the 1980s, we see a significant decline in voter turnout in the municipalities with the largest foreign presences. This phenomenon is explained in part by the

53. See chapter 8, figure 8.18.

more general decrease in the turnout in poor municipalities and working-class municipalities, but it also includes a significant autonomous component.[54] The most convincing explanation is a feeling of abandonment and discouragement in the working-class categories in general, with an additional effect in populations of foreign origin who confront discriminatory realities that have been recognized and demonstrated for decades without having led to any genuinely significant political and collective mobilization.

A Left on the Way to Unification?

We will conclude this examination of the Left vote by studying the evolution of the electoral cleavages between the different trends and parties of the Left. We have already noted that the structures of the votes for the Center-Left (PS) and the Left of the Left (PCF) were marked by significant differences all through the twentieth century. The decreasing relation between voting for the Left and level of income has always been clearly more pronounced for the Communist vote than for the Socialist vote. In addition, the Communist vote has always been much more closely linked to the industrial working-class municipalities (whereas since 1945 this has no longer been the case for the Socialist vote).[55] To a large extent, we find these divisions in the last decades, though they have a tendency to converge. In the legislative elections of 1993—which were particularly disastrous for the Left (see map 11.1)[56]—the divide between the Socialist / Green (PS-EELV) and the Communist electorates was even more marked than in 1981: the former was characterized by a profile that barely decreased with income, whereas the latter collapsed as soon as income increased. In 2012, the gap between the PS-EELV voters and those voting for the Front de gauche (PCF-PG) remained important, but it was less marked than it was in 1993 (see figures 11.12–11.13). In the 2017 election, the

---

54. See chapter 6, figures 6.11 and 6.13.
55. See chapter 10, figures 10.2 and 10.15–10.18.
56. The PS won only 18 percent of the votes in the first round—its worst result since the Epinay Congress—and only sixty-seven deputies' seats; in this election the Left as a whole fell to the lowest level in its history, with 9 percent of the votes for the PCF. In addition, the ecologists benefited only minimally from the Socialists' collapse, with barely 8 percent of the votes, far short of the hopes expressed a few months earlier. Several reasons may explain this defeat, beginning with the numerous internal divisions and the wear and tear of governing, but also the scandals that had multiplied over the preceding years. In the end, the RPR, the UDF, and the various Rights that were connected with them won 486 seats out of 577, or "the absolute record in French electoral history since 1876." See P. Habert, C. Ysmal, and P. Perrineau, *Le vote sanction: Les élections législatives des 21 et 28 mars 1993* (Presses de Sciences Po, 1993).

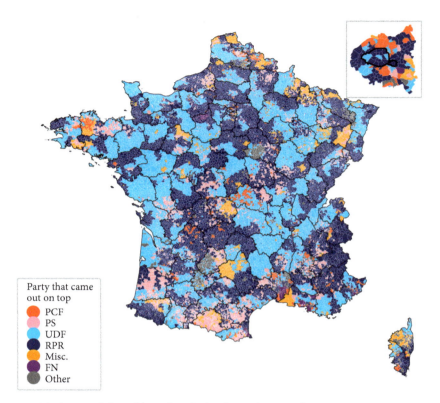

Party that came out on top
- ● PCF
- ● PS
- ● UDF
- ● RPR
- ● Misc.
- ● FN
- ● Other

MAP 11.1. The historic defeat of the Left in the legislative elections of 1993

The map represents the party that came out on top in each municipality, in the first round of the legislative elections of 1993.

Sources and series: unehistoireduconflitpolitique.fr

decreasing relation between the vote for the Left and municipal income was almost as strong as the vote for the Center-Left (PS-EELV) and the vote for the Left of the Left (PCF-LFI). In the 2022 elections, most of the Left was de facto unified in NUPES: four major parties (PS, EELV, PCF, LFI) joined the new alliance and a small number of diverse left-wing and ecologist candidates outside it won few votes.[57] It will be noted that the voter profiles in relation to income are once again very close (see figures 11.14–11.15).

57. In 2022, the NUPES candidates won 27 percent of the votes, as opposed to 6 percent for candidates outside of the alliance (see chapter 8, figure 8.3). Let us recall that the various left-wing and ecologist candidates were still classified as Center-Left (with the PS, the Greens, and EELV), with the exception of candidates of the NPA, LO, and LCR, who have been classified

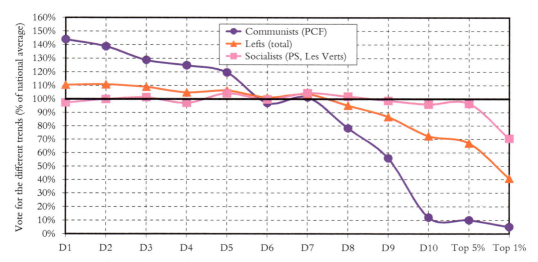

FIGURE 11.12. Vote and wealth in 1993: Left vs. Center-Left

In the legislative elections of 1993, the vote for the Left diminished with municipal income, especially at the top of the distribution. That is particularly true for the Left of the Left (PCF) and much less marked for the Center-Left (PS, Les yerts, various Lefts and ecological trends).

Sources and series: unehistoireduconflitpolitique.fr

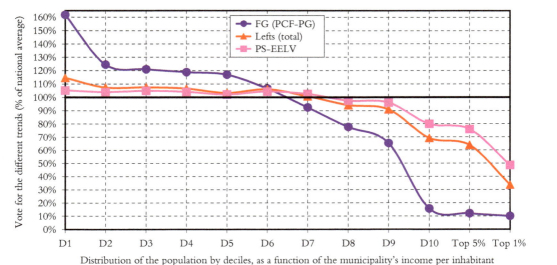

FIGURE 11.13. Vote and wealth in 2012: Left vs. Center-Left

In the legislative elections of 2012, the vote for the Left diminished with the municipal income, especially at the top of the distribution. That is particularly true for the Left of the Left (Front gauche, PCF-PG) and less marked for the Center-Left (PS-EELV, various Lefts, and ecological trends).

Sources and series: unehistoireduconflitpolitique.fr

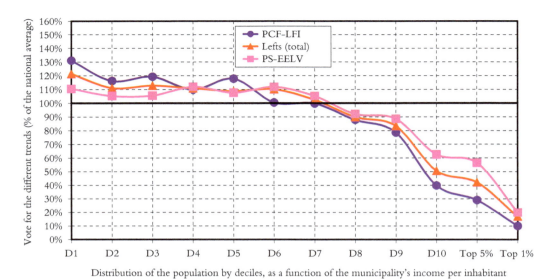

FIGURE 11.14. Vote and wealth in 2017: Left vs. Center-Left

In the legislative elections of 2017, the vote for the Left bloc diminished with the level of the municipality's average income, especially at the top of the distribution. That is particularly true for the Left of the Left (PCF-LFI), but it is also as marked for the Center-Left (PS-EELV).

Sources and series: unehistoireduconflitpolitique.fr

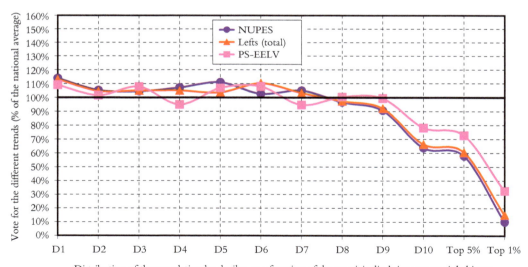

FIGURE 11.15. Vote and wealth in 2022: Left vs. Center-Left

In the legislative elections of 2022, the vote for the Left bloc diminished with the municipality's average income, especially at the top of the distribution. That is particularly true for the Left of the Left (NUPES), but it is also marked for the Center-Left (various Lefts and ecological trends).

Sources and series: unehistoireduconflitpolitique.fr

We observe similar convergences between the Left of the Left and the Center-Left during the period 1993–2022 if we examine the voter profiles in relation to the proportions of blue-collar workers, employees, or individuals of foreign nationality.[58] How can we explain this convergence, and can we see in it the sign of a Left on its way to unification, both sociological and programmatic, after the great break between Socialists and Communists that profoundly divided the Left during the whole existence of the Soviet Union (1917–1991)? The hypothesis is tempting and has its share of truth, even if we must not forget that the acceleration of the sociological convergence seen during the elections of 2017 and 2022 owes a great deal to the departure of the Center-Left toward the center of a large group of the wealthiest voters of the pre-2017 Center-Left. Were the Left as a whole to succeed in winning back these voters, a break similar to the one that prevailed in the past might reappear. That would depend, of course, on the durability of the NUPES electoral alliance and on the ability of the different left-wing trends to develop together a federative, democratic structure capable of deliberating collectively and making clear and convincing programmatic choices.

Regarding programs, one could think, in fact, that the breaks today are not as great as they could be in the past. Compared with the period 1945–1960, when Maurice Thorez's Communists and Guy Mollet's Socialists faced off over the Soviet model and the colonial empire, the disputes between Jean-Luc Mélenchon and Olivier Faure or François Hollande seem almost secondary.[59] In particular, neither of these two tendencies really presented options for transforming the socio-economic system and the property system. In addition, one could point out that neither of these tendencies proposed a clear perspective on this subject, either short-term or more long-term, which might be considered a problem in itself.

---

as Left of the Left (with the PCF, PG, and LFI). The results presented in figures 11.12–11.15 are after controlling for the size of the conurbation and the municipality. The gross profiles are a little different, and the profiles after the introduction of all the controls decrease more regularly with income. See, for example, chapter 10, figure 10.2. For all the results and the profiles by political tendency, see unehistoireduconflitpolitique.fr. We will return to the particular profile of the ecologist vote in chapter 12.

58. See unehistoireduconflitpolitique.fr., figures D3.15k–D3.15n, D3.19k–D3.19n, and D3.21k–D3.21n. At the beginning of the period, the vote for the Left of the Left was much more strongly linked to a major presence of blue-collar workers, employees, and individuals of foreign nationality than the vote for the Center-Left was. By the end of the period, the different profiles had moved much closer.

59. And moreover, even in 1962, these oppositions ultimately did not prevent Guy Mollet from calling for voting for a Communist candidate rather than his Gaullist adversary (see chapter 10).

However, it would be a mistake to underestimate the magnitude of the latent discords regarding the model of globalization and economic integration, as well as European and international policy. There again, the question is whether the currents of the Left will succeed in deliberating collectively and in making clear and ambitious choices concerning their socioeconomic and European program. We will return to this after studying the structure of the votes in the presidential elections (in particular, the persistent gaps between the votes for ecological candidates and other left-wing candidates) and the referenda of 1992 and 2005, which exemplify the magnitude of the conflicts within the Left regarding European questions.

The Return of the Territorial Cleavage and the Ruralization of the FN Vote

We come now to the structure of the vote for the FN-RN and its transformations from the legislative elections of 1986 to those of 2022. This issue is central for our investigation, because it is really the emergence of the FN during the legislative elections of 1986 that marked the first, decisive step toward the tripartition of French political life, with a Left bloc, a liberal Right bloc, and a nationalist Right bloc. But the fact is that the structure of the vote for the nationalist Right was completely transformed between 1986 and 2022, particularly at the territorial level. This was a spectacular revolution, rare in electoral history. In the legislative elections of 1986–1988, the FN vote was concentrated in the suburbs and the metropoles and was characterized by an electorate much more urban than the one observed for the Left bloc and the Right bloc, both of which were then relatively undivided at the territorial level (see figure 11.16). In the legislative elections of 2017–2022, the situation changed entirely: the social-ecological bloc that brought together the Left and ecological parties was now much more deeply implanted in the urban world than in the rural world, whereas conversely, the nationalist-patriotic bloc led by the FN-RN bloc achieved results almost twice as high in the villages and towns as in the suburbs and metropoles (see figure 11.17). In comparison with 1986–1988, the relation between the FN and the conurbation size was completely inverted.

This was a fundamental transformation, for several reasons. First, it was this ruralization by the FN-RN at top speed (and the concomitant, increasing urbanization of the Left vote) that explains why at the beginning of the twenty-first century the rural-urban cleavage between the Right and the Left as a whole regained a magnitude unseen since the end of the nineteenth century.[60] We have stressed at

---

60. See chapter 8, figures 8.5–8.10.

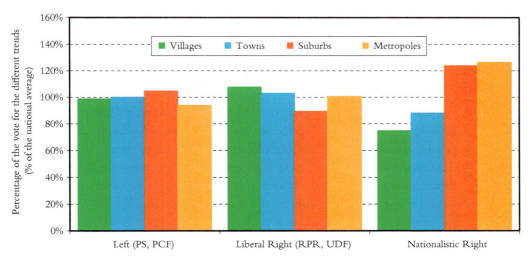

FIGURE 11.16. The legislative elections from 1986 to 1988: The emergence of the urban FN

In the legislative elections from 1986 to 1988, the result obtained by the FN (10% of the vote) was much greater in the metropoles and suburbs than in the towns and villages. In comparison, the result obtained by the Left (47% of the votes) varies little depending on the territories, and that of the liberal Right (43% of the votes) is a little higher in towns and villages than it is in suburbs and metropoles.

Sources and series: unehistoireduconflitpolitique.fr

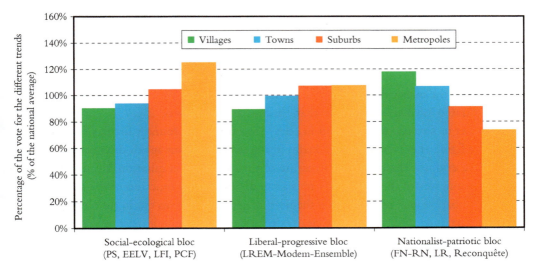

FIGURE 11.17. The legislative elections from 2017 to 2022: Territorial tripartition

In the legislative elections from 2017 to 2022, the result of the social-ecological bloc (32% of the votes) was much higher in the suburbs and metropoles than in the towns and villages. Conversely, the result of the nationalist-patriotic bloc (36% of the votes) was much higher in the towns and villages than in the suburbs and metropoles. The liberal-progressive bloc (32% of the votes) varied less depending on the territories but was more urban than rural.

Sources and series: unehistoireduconflitpolitique.fr

length that the very deep divide between the popular rural and urban classes seen in the nineteenth century was consubstantial with the system of electoral tripartition then in place. That was what allowed a central bloc constituted by Moderate and Opportunist Republicans to remain in power at the beginning of the Third Republic by relying on the divisions between the urban working classes voting for the Left bloc (Social Democrats, Socialists, Radical-Socialists) and the rural peasant classes voting for the Right bloc (conservatives, monarchists, Catholics). The similarities with the current situation are obvious, except that this new rural-urban division is taking place in a world whose productive structure has been totally transformed, with an agricultural and peasant universe that has almost completely disappeared, and this division is characterized by unprecedented forms of social, educational, occupational, and patrimonial stratification. It is therefore essential for our investigation to arrive at a better understanding of this new territorial division and its connection with the transformations of class structure.

Before going further, let us first make clear that in the early 2020s the nationalist-patriotic bloc is itself shot through with deep contradictions. Later, we will see that its three principal components (namely, LR, the RN, and Reconquête), as expressed in the legislative elections of 2022, are characterized by extremely different—or even wholly opposed—social, territorial, and programmatic bases. The reality is that LR is torn between the nationalist-patriotic bloc and the liberal-progressive bloc; it would like to be able to unite them in a liberal-nationalist bloc, as Right blocs have done in the past, but it is in danger of having to choose one or the other, or else disappear. Let us concentrate first on the component of the nationalist-patriotic bloc that is dominant today—namely, the FN-RN—and note at the outset that in 2017–2022, the FN-RN electorate was even more concentrated in villages and towns than the bloc as a whole was.

Let us also add that the shift in 2017–2022 from a profoundly urban FN vote (see figure 11.17) was made gradually, in stages, without any major discontinuity. If we examine the territorial structure of the electorate in question, election by election, we see that the FN vote is a rapidly increasing function of the size of conurbation in 1986–1988; then the relation gradually flattens out in the elections of 1993, 1997, and 2002 before clearly decreasing in the 2007 legislative elections, and then decreasing even more in 2012, 2017, and 2022.[61] We observe a certain acceleration of the tendency in 2012, coinciding with Marine Le Pen's arrival at the head of the FN in 2011. She emphasized the social turning point begun by her father Jean-Marie Le Pen (who founded the party in 1972) and sought to pre-

---

61. See unehistoireduconflitpolitique.fr, figures D2.3a–D2.3p.

sent herself as the best defender of the rural and peripheral territories abandoned by the globalized urban elites, in a context strongly marked by increased European and international competition and the awareness of the massive and partly irremediable nature of deindustrialization.[62] This evolution in the discourses expressed the party leaders' will to both broaden their electoral base and adapt to the country's electoral sociology and to the loss of votes recorded in the urban milieu. In the 1990s, 2000s, and 2010s, the growing emphasis on the denunciation of globalization and unrestrained liberalism, along with the defense of workers and the system of social protection (in particular, retirement pensions and family allocations) ultimately constituted a very significant change of direction in comparison with Jean-Marie Le Pen's discourse in the 1980s, which was centered on the denunciation of immigrants and an ultraliberal economic program.

The FN and Immigrants: From Conflict to Separation

It is interesting to note that at first, this strategic reorientation of the party did not lead to a noticeable improvement of its electoral result, which developed unevenly. The FN won 10 percent of the votes in the first round of the legislative elections in 1986 and 1988, then 13 percent in 1993, 15 percent in 1996, 11 percent in 2002, 4 percent in 2007, 14 percent in 2012 and 2017, and finally 19 percent in 2022. In 2007–2012, the result hardly budged from where it had been in 1986–1988, but the territorial profile was completely inverted. The social discourse centered on the abandonment of rural and peripheral territories was already well established in a political landscape marked by the European referenda of 1992 and 2005. In addition, the party consolidated its position in presidential elections by reaching the second round in the election of 2002, and then repeating the feat in 2017 and

---

62. Among the many studies devoted to the mutations of the Front's discourses and of its social and geographical structure, see, in particular, Crépon, Dézé, and Mayer, *Les faux-semblants du Front national;* and G. Mauger and W. Pelletier, *Les classes populaires et le FN. Explications de vote* (Croquant, 2016). In the 1980s, Jean-Marie Le Pen advocated reducing the state to its kingly functions and "de-stating" France by putting an end to the welfare state. See, for example, M. Charlot, "L'émergence du Front national," *Revue française de sciences politique,* 1986; N. Mayer, "De Passy à Barbes: Deux visages du vote Le Pen à Paris," *Revue française de sciences politique,* 1987. As Luc Rouban points out, its electorate was at that time very liberal on the level of economic liberalism—72 percent in 1974, or far more than either Giscard's electorate (58 percent) or that of Chaban-Delmas (61 percent). See L. Rouban, *La vraie victoire du RN* (Presses de Sciences Po, 2022). Marine Le Pen proved to be more aggressive in her discourse on the subject of purchasing power, defending a reevaluation of retirement pensions, increasing low salaries, and even providing free transportation for young workers.

2022, after winning 25 percent of the votes in the European elections of 2014 and almost 28 percent of the votes in the regional elections of 2015.[63]

The evolution of the voting profile as a function of the foreign presence in the municipality illustrates perfectly this repositioning of the FN. In the legislative elections of 1986–1988, the FN vote was not just urban, it was concentrated in urban municipalities with the greatest proportions of foreigners (see figure 11.8). This was the period when anti-immigrant rhetoric reached its maximal intensity, with the famous slogan that first appeared in a tract used during the legislative elections of 1978: "A million people out of work is a million immigrants too many! France and the French first! Vote National Front!" This simple, powerful message made it possible to capture the votes of the minority of voters who shared this view—and manifestly, this minority was the all the larger in municipalities with significant proportions of foreigners. Furthermore, on the level of economics, Jean-Marie Le Pen stood for an ultraliberal program centered on the denunciation of the size of the state and the labor unions, and the complete suppression of the income tax. The problem was that the liberal-national niche was already well filled by the right-wing RPR-UDF of the period; between 1986 and 1988, the prime minister, Jacques Chirac, privatized nonstop, abolished the tax on large fortunes, and proved that he was a serious competitor in the area of anti-immigrant diatribes.[64] Moreover, the reelection of François Mitterand in 1988 showed that the electorate had little appetite for an economic liberalism that was espoused too overtly. Starting in the 1990s and 2000s, the FN took a different position on the social terrain and centered its discourse on the denunciation of European and international

---

63. It is always easier for the FN to achieve high results in list-system elections at the regional or European level and the hyperpersonalized presidential election than in legislative elections that are ultimately based on 577 candidates and districts, with very few seats won by FN/RN before 2022. The social and territorial structure of the FN vote is roughly the same in the European and regional elections as it is in the legislative and presidential elections. Let us note that the relative similarity of the results obtained by the FN-RN in 1993 and 2022 (15 percent and 19 percent, respectively) does not accurately reflect the growing political influence of the movement, which had eighty-nine elected deputies in 2022and none at all twenty years earlier. This is due to the high rate of abstention in the last legislative elections, which, as we have already pointed out, increased the threshold of qualification for the second round and reduced de facto the number of triangulations; on the other hand, it led to the demise of the Republican Front—and this is essential in our investigation.

64. See chapter 4 on the famous speech he gave in Orléans in 1991. The FN's very low result in 2007 also illustrates the party's difficulty in competing with a muscular liberal-nationalist, anti-immigrant discourse like that of Nicolas Sarkozy taking power after his time at the Ministry of the Interior, his incendiary remarks about the suburbs that needed to be cleaned out "with a pressure washer," and the riots of 2005.

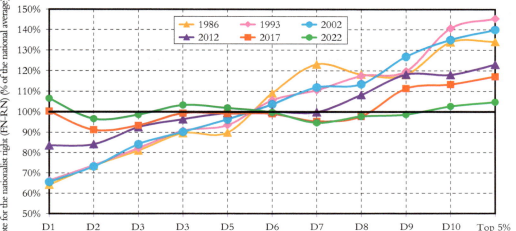

Distribution of the population by deciles as a function of the proportion of foreigners in the municipality

FIGURE 11.18. The nationalist Right and foreigners, 1986–2022 (before taking socioeconomic characteristics into account)

From the legislative elections of 1986 to those of 2022, the vote for the FN is all the higher as the proportion of foreigners in the municipality grows. This relation diminished in 2012 and 2017 and disappeared completely in 2022. Note: The results indicated here are after controls for the size of the conurbation and the municipality, but before controls for the other socioeconomic characteristics (income, occupation, etc.).

Sources and series: unehistoireduconflitpolitique.fr

economic integration and on the defense of peripheral territories. If we examine the voter profile, we see that starting in the 2000s and 2010s, the FN's result is less and less connected with the presence of foreigners, to the point that the relation disappears almost completely in 2017–2022 (see figure 11.18).

If we take into account the socioeconomic characteristics of municipalities (and in particular, the occupational composition and the proportion of industrial workers), we even see that the relation between the FN vote and the presence of foreigners in the municipality became clearly negative in 1986, 1988, and 1993. The inversion began in the 1990s and is already very visible in the voter profiles observed in the legislative elections of 2002 and 2012 (see figure 11.19).

To sum up, the FN vote shifted from being a vote about conflict with immigrants in one's community to being a vote that expressed the absence of any contact with immigrants, or a certain form of spatial segregation from immigrants.[65]

---

65. The available data do not allow us to make a direct connection between voting behaviors and moving from one municipality to another. However, considering that the general distribution

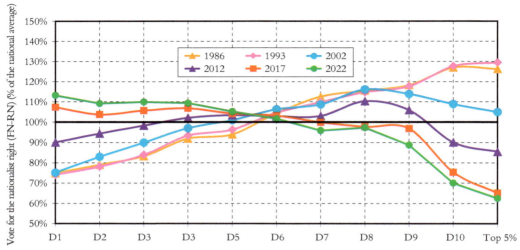

Distribution of the population by deciles as a function of the proportion of foreigners in the municipality

FIGURE 11.19. The nationalist Right and foreigners, 1986–2022 (after taking socioeconomic characteristics into account)

After taking into account all the socioeconomic variables (in particular income and occupation), we see that the FN-RN vote clearly diminishes with the foreign presence in the municipality in 2017–2022, whereas the relation was growing strongly in 1986–1988. Note: The results indicated here are after taking all the controls into account.

In the 1980s and at the beginning of the 1990s, the FN vote brought together an urban electorate that was living near populations of foreign origin and wanted to express their negative feelings about it. In the 2010s and at the beginning of the 2020s, on the contrary, the FN-RN vote united a rural electorate living in the towns and villages that had the fewest foreigners. For a given size of conurbation and municipality, a given proportion of industrial workers, and so on, the FN vote has become maximal in the municipalities with the smallest numbers of foreigners, inverting the situation at the beginning of the period.[66] This certainly does not

---

of the population among villages, towns, suburbs, and metropoles has been on the whole very stable over recent decades (see chapter 2, figure 2.6), it seems clear that these moves can explain at best only a limited part of the complete inversion of the rural-urban voter profile observed for the FN since the 1980s.

66. On the basis of his analysis of the results of the presidential election of 2017 at the level of the polling stations in thirty-five city centers, Jean Rivière shows that it is only in the cities of western France, such as Caen, Tours, and Rennes, where the proportion of immigrants is small, that the relation between the presence of workers and voting for the FN is strong; in contrast, this relation is small, even insignificant, in the cities of the Southeast, where the immigrant

imply that the subject of an excessive presence of immigrants in the country (in the absence of a presence in the municipality where they live) no longer plays any role in the FN vote. The subject remains very present in the party's discourses and in the perceptions of voters, and it may very well complement the general feeling that towns and villages have been abandoned to the supposed benefit of suburbs and metropoles with larger numbers of immigrants.[67] The fact remains that the subject is much less central than it was in the 1980s and the early 1990s, and that the FN-RN vote of the 2010s and early 2020s must first be analyzed in the specific social and territorial framework into which it has now been integrated.[68] We

presence is both strong and ancient. See J. Rivière, "L'espace électoral des grandes villes françaises," *Revue française de science politique*, 2017; J. Rivière, *L'illusion du vote bobo*. These results are consistent with those that we obtain at the level of the country, and particularly in the towns and villages.

67. As is emphasized by Emmanuel Pierru and Sébastien Vignon, who inquire into what they describe as an FN "over-vote" in the French countryside and examine in particular the case of the municipality of Saint-Vaast in the department of Somme, immigrants constitute a blank slate onto which what is experienced as a loss of status is projected: "The stigmatization of the populations of North African origin may then lead to the classical paradox of racism, in which the populations stigmatized are not present on the municipal territory." See E. Pierru and S. Vignon, "Comprendre les votes frontistes dans les mondes ruraux. Une approche ethnographique des préférences électorales," in Mauger and Pelletier, *Les classes populaires et le vote FN*. Thus, we encounter again a kind of tripartition of the political perceptions we have already mentioned, with an opposition not only between the most modest and the most favored, but also between the popular classes who perceive themselves as "deserving" and all those whom they think benefit from the system. Olivier Schwartz speaks in this regard of a "tripartition of the social consciousness in the modest categories." See O. Schwartz, "Vivons-nous encore dans une société de classes? Trois remarques sur la société française contemporaine," *La vie des idées*, 2009. In his novel on the decline of the working class, *Leurs enfants après eux* (*And Their Children after Them*), Nicolas Mathieu has Anthony, his hero from the lower middle class, tell jokes about the "*cassos*" (*cas sociaux*—that is, welfare recipients or other individuals in poverty), which he claims to do for fun as much as to "ward off evil, this insidious tide which seemed to gain little by little, from below." N. Mathieu, *Leurs enfants après eux* (Actes Sud, 2018).

68. An alternative interpretation might consist in saying that if the FN-RN vote no longer seems to be determined primarily by questions of identity and migration, that is not so much because the party has abandoned these questions as because the Left electorate's relation to immigration has changed. Thus, a recent report issued by the Jean Jaurès Foundation emphasizes the negative associations with immigration that many French people have, underlining, of course, the deep Left-Right cleavage over the question of how to receive migrants, but also noting an advance, even on the left, of the view that "there are too many immigrants in France today." A. Zulfikarpasic, "L'immigration, ce grand tabou (de la gauche)," Fondation Jean Jaurès, April 2023. Some conclude from this that a "good" model for the Left would be the Danish Social Democratic Party, which, over recent years, has implemented an extremely strict migration policy. R. Large, "Ambitieux sur les retraites, ferme sur l'immigration: Le modèle social-démocrate danois

will return to this question when we examine the structure of the votes in presidential elections, and we will stress that this transformation of the structure of the FN-RN electorate was initially more undergone than sought, in the sense that in 1986–1988 Chirac's Right, and then in 2007 Sarkozy's Right, largely absorbed the urban anti-immigrant vote most hostile to economic liberalism, leaving the FN-RN with a rural-social electorate that was not the one it had initially chosen, but which turned out to be very promising over the longer term.

Vote for the FN, Vote for the Left: Rural Popular Classes versus Urban Popular Classes

All the available data confirm the centrality of this social and territorial interpretation of the vote for the FN. If we examine the profile of the FN vote first as a function of the proportion of workers in the municipality, we find that the profile was already growing in the 1986 election, and it was to become larger and larger from 1986 to 2022 (see figure 11.20).

However, we must emphasize that the profile of the vote for the FN with regard to workers never reached the enormous magnitude observed in the vote for the PCF all through the twentieth century.[69] To be sure, the FN's electorate included a major working-class component, but it was more diversified in its sociooccupational structure and less centered on workers than the PCF vote was in its time. In addition, it was not the same working-class vote, in that the PCF vote was above all entirely urban and concentrated in the workers' suburbs of the great metropoles, whereas the FN vote was first of all a workers' vote that was primarily rural and peri-urban. It consisted particularly of blue-collar workers employed in industrial installations or logistics centers situated far from the metropoles and often near major highway crossroads. These new industrial territories developed starting in the 1960s and 1970s in the context of investment strategies betting on, depending on the case, less expensive real estate, the availability of adequate highway infrastructures, and a large labor supply issuing from the agricultural

---

(2016–2022)," Fondation Jean Jaurès, January 2023. Our analysis of the evolution of the structures of electorates over the long term—in particular, the fact that since 2000–2010, voting for the Left has once again become positively associated with foreign origins, as it had always been during the preceding waves (see figure 11.9)—leads us to think instead that it would be preferable that the Left bloc succeeded in enlarging its popular electorate by imposing a bipolar confrontation on a liberal-nationalist bloc and by centering its discourse on redistribution and the development of the welfare state. We will return to this in the next chapters.

69. See chapter 10, figures 10.15–10.18.

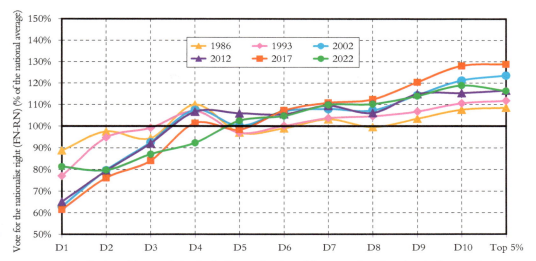

Distribution of the population by deciles as a function of the proportion of workers in the municipality

FIGURE 11.20. The nationalist Right and blue-collar workers, 1986–2022
From the legislative elections of 1986 to those of 2022, the FN vote has become ever more associated with the municipalities that have large proportions of blue-collar workers. The relation was stabilized later and turned slightly downward in 2022. Note: The results indicated here are after controls for the size of the conurbation and municipality.
Sources and series: unehistoireduconflitpolitique.fr

world, along with a desire on the part of CEOs, sometimes made explicit, to avoid the social and labor union protests associated with the suburbs and metropoles—all with the active support of the public authorities.[70] It was in this context that the proportion of workers in the villages and towns grew strongly between 1960 and 1990, reaching the levels observed in the suburbs and metropoles, which were themselves in steep decline during this period.[71] It was this new rural and peri-urban working class, which was less organized and less clearly on the Left than the working class of the suburbs and metropoles, and skeptical about the determination of the Socialist governments of the 1980s and 1990s to defend and promote it, that was to provide an increasing number of votes for the FN during the 1990s, 2000s, and 2010s.[72] Multiple ethnographic works and surveys on the basis of

---

70. See V. Girard, *Le vote FN au village. Trajectoires de ménages populaires du périurbain* (Éditions du Croquant, 2017), 24–56.

71. See chapter 2, figure 2.22, and unehistoireduconflitpolitique.fr, figures B1.6q–B1.6r.

72. See Girard, *Le vote FN au village.*

interviews have also shown the importance for the FN of the profile of rural workers who were not very organized and who thought they had scraped through on their own, in the framework of trajectories of promotion as supervisors or foremen, or as truck drivers who worked hard and harshly judged the actions of labor unions and left-wing parties that favored government officials and employees in the public sector or in other sectors benefiting from special status or protection in terms of job security.[73]

If we compare the FN's voter profile as a function of socio-occupational composition with the results obtained for the vote for the Left, another important difference is that the FN vote is an increasing function of the proportion of self-employed people in the municipality, whereas for the Left, the profile is decreasing. Inversely, the FN vote is a little less closely associated with the intermediary occupations than the vote for the Left. Even so, the FN vote and the Left vote also have points in common that are clearly discernable all through the 1986–2022 period: they are both clearly intersecting with the proportion of employees and steeply decreasing with the proportion of managers, especially at the peak of the distribution.[74]

Ultimately, in the recent period, the FN vote and the Left vote can be analyzed as two different forms of the popular vote within a social, occupational, and educational structure that is undergoing a profound renewal. In addition, aside from the fact that the Left attracts more employees' votes than blue-collar workers' votes while the FN does the opposite, the two main differences between the vote for the Left and the vote for the FN concern the relation to diplomas and the relation to property. For given sociodemographic characteristics, and in particular for a given size of conurbation and a given average income, we have seen that the Left vote became an increasing function of the proportion of people holding higher education diplomas in the municipality (see figure 11.8). This relation reflects the large vote for the Left among *sociaux-diplômés,* particularly in healthcare and education (nurses, schoolteachers, university professors, and others)—that is, among those holding higher education diplomas and having relatively low incomes compared with other diploma holders working in the private sector. As for the FN vote, the profile is completely inverted: for given characteristics, particularly in terms of the size of the conurbation and average income, the FN vote declines steeply

73. See, for example, the interviews collected by Agrikoliansky, Aldrin, and Lévêque, *Voter par temps de crise,* 281–305.

74. See unehistoireduconflitpolitique.fr, figures B1.6q–B1.6r.

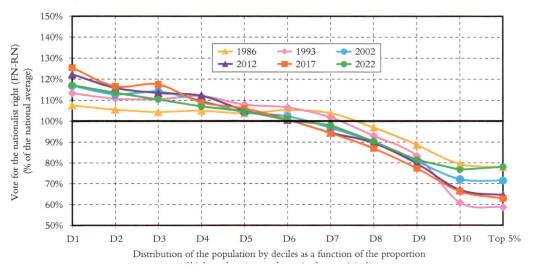

FIGURE 11.21. The nationalist Right and higher-education graduates, 1986–2022

From the legislative elections of 1993 to those of 2022, the proportion of graduates of higher education had a very clear residual effect on the vote for the FN-RN (after taking into account all the socioeconomic controls, including the size of the conurbation, income, and occupation). Note: The results indicated here are after taking all the controls into account.

Sources and series: unehistoireduconflitpolitique.fr

with the proportion of higher education diploma holders in the municipality (see figure 11.21).

This result reflects a specific integration into the productive structure: whereas the vote for the Left includes in particular voters who have advanced diplomas but receive small incomes, the FN vote brings together voters who have limited diplomas but receive incomes that are sometimes significant—for example, self-employed persons, truck drivers, and skilled workers who have been promoted to foremen, whose incomes may be higher than those received by nurses and school-teachers. These different trajectories may correspond in part to individual aspirations and distinct temperaments. Men and women who have grown up near great urban centers have thus been able to benefit from more opportunities to gain access to school and university infrastructures than rural populations have. This can lead people from the same working-class origins to follow different educational and occupational trajectories, and to end up engaging in processes of politicization and identification that are permanently separated and that help fuel territorial conflicts.

The FN: A Vote of People with Small Incomes Gaining Access to Property Ownership

With the differentiated relation to the educational system and diplomas, the second extremely clear distinction between the vote for the Left and the FN vote concerns the relation to property. Generally speaking, the proportion of households owning their homes rose from 37 percent to 58 percent between 1960 and 2022, with a particularly great increase in towns and villages. On average, the proportion of property owners is now nearly 70 percent in towns and villages, as opposed to barely 35 percent in metropoles.[75] Under these conditions, it is obvious that the question of access to property ownership, and particularly to the suburban habitat, is much more a concern for FN voters, who reside mainly in towns and villages, than it is for left-wing voters in the suburbs and metropoles, who are confronted by much higher real estate prices. The available data show that the positive relation between access to property ownership and the FN vote is also found for given social and geographic data. In other words, for the same sociodemographic characteristics, and in particular for a given size of conurbation and a given average income, we see that the FN vote increases regularly with the proportion of property owners in the municipality (see figure 11.22).[76] Inversely, the relation is negative in the vote for the Left.[77]

This is a particularly striking result—which we also find in the surveys conducted at the individual level[78]—and it can be explained by several factors.

---

75. See chapter 2, figure 2.17 and map 2.8.

76. As Marie Cartier and her coauthors document in their survey of the residential suburbs (on the basis of the example of the municipality of Gonesse, a poor suburb of 25,000 inhabitants northeast of Paris), some of the "pioneers" of the suburbs vote for the extreme Right now and then out of xenophobia, but especially because they see in foreigners the cause of the downgrading of their neighborhoods, whereas they had constructed their (small) social ascension around property ownership, and more precisely around the purchase of a single-family dwelling in this neighborhood that was then perceived as inhabited by "low-level managers." See M. Cartier, I. Coutant, O. Masclet, and Y. Siblot, *La France des "petits-moyens." Enquêtes sur la banlieue pavillonnaire* (La Découverte, 2008). We must also note the importance given the question of property in the FN's doctrine in its early years. In Pour la France (the FN's program, published in 1985), Jean-Marie Le Pen thus noted that he wanted to make citizens simultaneously free and responsible, and that responsibility can be developed only through property, which "secures, roots, stabilizes, and makes people responsible." See N. Mayer and P. Perrineau, *Le Front national à découvert* (Presses de Sciences Po, 1996), 207.

77. See unehistoireduconflitpolitique.fr, figures D3.34k–D3.34p.

78. Exit polls indicate that compared with left-wing voters, FN voters less often hold higher education diplomas and more often own their homes, both before and after controlling for other sociodemographic variables (and in particular for income, which in both cases is on average

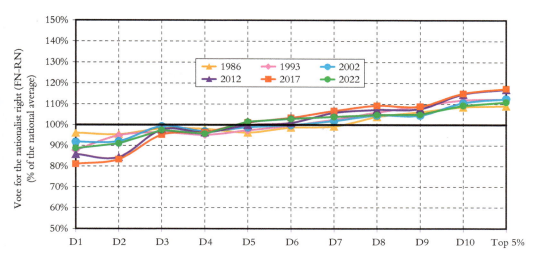

Distribution of the population by deciles as a function of the proportion of homeowners in the municipality

FIGURE 11.22. The nationalist Right and property, 1986–2022

From the legislative elections of 1993 to those of 2022, the proportion of homeowners had a very clear residual effect on the vote for the FN-RN (after taking into account all the socioeconomic controls, including the size of the conurbation, income, and occupation). Note: The results indicated here are after taking all the controls into account.

Sources and series: unehistoireduconflitpolitique.fr

Generally, access to property depends on a multitude of parameters, such as the availability of a small family patrimony (which can make a real difference, even if it does not involve a lot of money), more or less contingent factors like the existence of adequate real estate or projects to build suburban housing near the workplace (it being understood that a contingent choice to purchase property can subsequently help shape political preferences), and, of course, individual aspirations in connection with family and occupational life and how to use the available budget (lodging, vacations, leisure activities, culture, children, place of residence, and so on). Historically, individual property is particularly important to farmers—because of the complementarity between farm property, agricultural installations, and land—and they markedly tend to vote for the Right for reasons that have already been discussed at length (in connection with the perceived hostility of the Socialist and Communist Parties to individual property). The in-

considerably lower than that of Left and Center voters). See Gethin, Martinez-Toledano, and Piketty, *Clivages politiques et inégalités sociales,* 113, table 2.1.

teresting point here is that this connection between small property and voting for the Right has persisted despite the considerable transformation of the productive structure (as well as the transformation of the Left parties' programs, which essentially renounced any idea of collectivization long ago). This connection passes in part through the self-employed (who have a greater propensity to vote for the FN than for the Left), but it also involves blue-collar workers, employees, and people with intermediary occupations in the rural world who have gained access to suburban property and think it is obvious that their aspirations are better taken into account by the FN than by the Left, which is suspected of being interested only in rental property and large developments, and not in the world of the individual suburban dwelling.

From this point of view, the results that we obtain at the national level are perfectly consistent with the surveys conducted in several departments by researchers in political sociology such as Violaine Girard and Benoît Coquart. The interviews carried out show the existence of a large FN vote among the inhabitants of towns and villages who have succeeded in accessing property and who suspect that the Left does not support them in this ascension because it is concerned with more precarious populations above all.[79] These interviews also indicate that the movement toward the suburban habitat is experienced as a positive choice and a reason to be proud, a trajectory that compensates the efforts made in terms of occupational and familial stability, a choice that, moreover, has been strongly encouraged by the public authorities since 1977 with subsidies for access to property and since 1995 with the establishment of the no-interest loan (*prêt à taux zéro,* PTZ).[80] But the fact is that these mechanisms for supporting the suburban habitat, which were co-constructed by real estate developers and by the state starting in the 1970s, were generally created by right-wing governments, whereas when the Left was in power it devoted itself chiefly to the rental habitat.[81] How-

---

79. Or even that the Left denounces this choice of the peri-urban, which is often criticized as an act simultaneously "anti-aesthetic" and "anti-ecological." See, for example, F. Ripoll and J. Rivière, "La ville dense comme seul espace légitime? Analyse critique d'un discours dominant sur le vote et l'urbain," *Les annales de la recherche urbaine,* 2007.

80. See the interviews carried out in the Lyon region by Violaine Girard, in *Le vote FN au village,* 93–116. Girard emphasizes particularly that contrary to what is often claimed by certain authors (like Christophe Guilluy), the trajectories involving a departure from the suburbs to the residential peri-urban areas (trajectories that are, moreover, quite rare in the populations of towns and villages) are not experienced as flights forced on them but rather as positive and valorized choices.

81. On the political construction of the individual housing market, see the class studies by P. Bourdieu and R. Christin, "La construction du marché. Le champ administratif et la production de

ever, the people in question express great skepticism about the parties of the traditional liberal Right, which are perceived as addressing above all the high-ranking managers of the city centers and the well-off suburbs of large metropoles. In comparison, the people who purchased property in towns and villages perceive themselves as *petits-moyens,* people of slender means, intermediary between the working classes and the middle classes, with no connection to the genuine upper classes of the urban world, but who have nonetheless succeeded in rising above their initial condition, thanks to their efforts and their work.[82] Wary of both the traditional Right (too elitist) and of the Left (suspected of being interested only in people who are more precarious and less deserving, or indeed of *cas sociaux* of all kinds, whether they are of French or immigrant origin) these "people of slender means" often end up identifying with the FN, the only political party that supports their original trajectory of social ascent that does not involve either diplomas or labor unions, but which is nonetheless legitimate and worthy of public respect and support.[83]

We note also that in the elections of 2022, the RN proposed a major extension of the PTZ: each family could henceforth benefit from a state loan of 100,000 euros without interest, and most importantly, once the family's third child was born, this loan would no longer have to be repaid.[84] The measure mixes the key question of access to property with the party's traditional natalist themes, and

---

la 'politique du logement," and P. Bourdieu and M. de Saint-Martin, "Le sens de la propriété. La genèse sociale des systèmes de préférences," *Actes de la recherche en sciences sociales,* 1990. On the construction of the political conflicts surrounding property (and particularly real estate property), see also H. Michel, *La cause des propriétaires. État et propriété en France, fin 19e siècle–20e siècle* (Belin, 2006).

82. See Cartier et al., *La France des "petits-moyens."*

83. On the way in which FN voters who have succeeded through their own efforts in purchasing property negatively judge the Left for its inability to recognize their merit and for its naïveté (as FN voters see it) in dealing with those whose situations are precarious and other "welfare bums," see B. Coquard, *Ceux qui restent. Faire sa vie dans les campagnes en déclin* (La Découverte, 2019). The interviews carried out in Meuse and Haute-Marne show how a proclaimed "right-wing" (or even "100 percent Le Pen") identity becomes a legitimate way of displaying one's own efforts, of distinguishing oneself from all those who are "lost" in drugs or precarity (to a large extent, regardless of their French or immigrant origins), and of stigmatizing the "fantasy world" and the call to be lazy, which those who have "saved themselves" associate with the Left.

84. In the existing versions of the PTZ, the sums are usually smaller: they vary between 20 percent and 40 percent of the purchase price (with the maximum price of the property taken into account for the PTZ being, on average, around 200,000–300,000 euros, depending on the size of the family and the territories concerned) and are on average around 50,000 euros. Above all, the loans must still be fully repaid.

seems perfectly calibrated with the electoral realities that we have just examined. The RN also envisages reserving this loan for "young French families," defined as those "in which at least one of the two persons holds French nationality," which does not guarantee, of course, that people of immigrant origin will be excluded, but it nonetheless makes it possible to instill a kind of "national preference" (at least symbolic) at the heart of this policy.[85] Let us also remember that electoral turnout fell much less sharply over recent decades in the municipalities with the greatest proportions of property owners in comparison to others (even after controlling for all the other sociodemographic characteristics),[86] which makes this type of measure particularly strategic. Everything suggests that this question of the access to property will play an important role in coming electoral conflicts, and that it would be a great mistake for the Left to surrender this theme in advance to the RN.

The FN Vote, the Left Vote, and Wealth

On the whole, if we examine the relation between the FN vote and municipal income, we see that the curve was relatively uncertain in 1986 and 1993 but became clearly decreasing later on, particularly in 2017–2022 (see figure 11.23).

The profile found for the FN vote in the most recent elections is ultimately rather close to that observed for the Left vote (see figure 1.1). To sum up, the system of tripartition is characterized by the fact that the Left vote and the FN vote are both popular votes, in the sense that their voter profile diminishes with income, whereas the vote for the Center bloc (and also for the traditional Right) increases sharply with income, as we shall see later on. However, the popular votes for the Left and for the FN have very different characteristics: for a given income, Left voters are more often urban and have higher education degrees, and they are less often property owners, whereas the FN's voters have a tendency to be rural, not to have diplomas, and to own their own houses. In a certain way, these two popular voter profiles embody the fact that the two very powerful movements of expanding higher education and expanding property ownership that have taken place since the 1960s have not benefited the different territories and social classes in the same

---

85. Amendment no. 16719, filed 2 February 2023, to the proposed law to rectify the financing of Social Security, no. 760 for 2023. On the RN's willing politics of natality, see C. Alduy, "La natalité, une obsession lepéniste," AOC, 6 March 2023.
86. See chapter 6, figure 6.8.

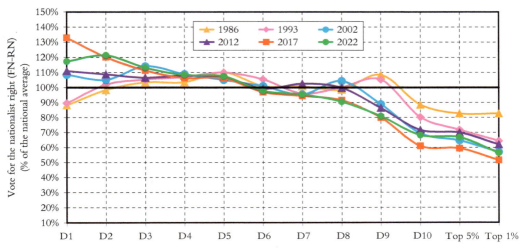

FIGURE 11.23 The nationalist Right and wealth, 1986–2022

In the legislative elections from 1986 to 2022, the vote profile for the FN becomes an increasingly declining function of the municipality's average income. However, in very rich municipalities the profile is nonetheless less sharply declining than the vote profile for the Left. Note: The results indicated here are after taking all the controls for the size of the conurbation and municipality into account.

Sources and series: unehistoireduconflitpolitique.fr

proportions. The expansion of education first concerned the urban popular classes, whereas the diffusion of property benefited primarily the rural popular classes. This is explained by a multiplicity of socioeconomic factors, beginning with the greater availability of university infrastructures in the urban world and the lower cost of real estate in the rural world. This diversity of trajectories has contributed to the deepening of the rural-urban electoral cleavage over recent decades, but it in no way reflects irremediable oppositions. We have already said what political conflict might look like in a world in which the expansion of education would continue all the way to the point that the quasi-totality of the population would hold higher education diplomas. The question of what a social and political universe in which the process of the diffusion of property had reached its endpoint might look like is just as decisive and complex, and it raises other issues that seem to us to have been insufficiently discussed.

In this case, contrary to the educational democratization that has involved almost the whole population, the patrimonial deconcentration has remained up to this point relatively limited: the proportion of households owning their own homes has certainly increased, but the amounts held remain extremely concentrated.[87] To sum up, the share held by the richest 10 percent fell from 80–90 percent of the total of patrimonies in 1910 to about 50–60 percent in the early 2020s, mainly to the benefit of the next-richest 40 percent, whose share has increased over the same period from scarcely more than 10 percent at the beginning of the twentieth century to about 40 percent currently. This is a significant increase, which corresponds in particular to the emergence of a "patrimonial middle class" composed of home-owning households. On the other hand, the poorest 50 percent still own almost nothing (hardly 5 percent of the total of patrimonies)—the same today as a century ago.[88] We will note in passing that this complexification of the social structure, with a large central group of property owners who are, to be sure, less rich than the upper classes situated above them, but at the same time much less poor than the popular classes below them, makes the political alliance of the popular and middle classes more complex today than it was a century ago. The new political division between the classes in the rural world that have few diplomas but generally own their homes and the classes in the urban world that hold diplomas but rent their homes is in a way the reflection of this new class structure. The FN's voters include in particular people who from the point of view of their wealth are capable of joining the world of the "patrimonial middle classes" (the 40 percent included between the richest 10 percent and the poorest 50 percent), but who from the point of view of diplomas held are instead part of the lowest 50 percent. We will return later to the uncertain and largely open question of the alliances and programmatic bases that make it possible to escape these contradictions.

If we compare the voter profiles for the Left and for the FN, we also see another significant difference—namely, a considerably greater decline in the vote for the Left than in the vote for the FN-RN in very rich municipalities (see figures 11.1 and 11.23). This difference can be explained by the fact that the left-wing parties propose much more explicitly than the FN-RN to raise taxes on the richest in order to finance their social programs, specifically by means of tax increases on the highest incomes and the largest fortunes. In the case of the FN-RN, the discourse is much

87. The concentration of spending on education has also decreased less than one might imagine—and the inequalities of access to higher education remain extremely great (in particular because of the French duality between universities and the elite institutions known as *grandes écoles*), but the level is incomparably lower than for patrimonial concentration. See chapter 3.

88. See chapter 1, figure 1.5.

more ambiguous and hesitant. To be sure, the party now defends the system of social protection (in particular, retirement pensions and family allocations) that it reviled in the 1980s, and it has long since abandoned Jean-Marie Le Pen's project of completely abolishing the income tax. Nevertheless, the FN-RN still has as many difficulties in formulating explicit propositions for raising taxes on the richest, because doing so would no doubt bring it too close to the Left and the class struggle, and also because the FN has another string to its bow: the denunciation of the undue largess from which immigrants supposedly benefit. By reserving social benefits for individuals of French nationality and putting an end to the "wave of migration," it should be possible, according to the FN-RN, to make considerable savings. Today as yesterday, nationalism is presented as a substantial attempt to valorize national and ethnoracial solidarities above all in order to avoid the class struggle.

As it was with the slogan "Germany will pay" during the interwar period, both voters and party leaders feel that a policy based on the slogan "the foreigner will pay" may not bring in resources as considerable as claimed. Under these conditions, it will be necessary to find other means of financing the party's social policy in the event that it takes power, whether it is a matter of retirement benefits, family allocations, or the PTZ—there are so many expensive measures that the FN-RN's adversaries on the Right and in the Center could not fail to attack them. It is in this context that we must see the party's recent evolution regarding the wealth tax (*impôt de solidarité sur la fortune,* ISF). The ISF was abolished in 2018 by the LREM government, or more exactly, it was replaced by a tax on real estate wealth (*impôt sur la fortune immobilière,* IFI) that entirely exempted financial portfolios, which constituted almost the totality of the largest fortunes.[89] This measure became emblematic of the "president of the rich," and it was difficult for the RN not to react without losing all credibility in broad segments of the popular electorate. Therefore, for the elections of 2022, the RN proposed replacing the IFI with a tax on financial wealth (*impôt sur la fortune financière,* IFF). As a sign of the party's rootedness in the territory, real estate wealth was henceforth to be entirely exempted, especially if it was in the form of the principal residence (whatever its value might be) or occupational or agricultural assets. Inversely, financial portfolios that fueled international speculation and were pampered by the current government would be taxed. Many observers noted that in practice, the IFI affects only those who own a principal residence valued at more than 1.9 million euros, so the reform proposed by the RN would result in a windfall for holders of very large real

89. See chapter 1, figure 1.5.

estate patrimonies, which are by definition above this threshold.[90] In the end, it is likely that such a reform—if it were applied—would cost the public finances more than it would bring in.[91] It is not certain that such largesse granted to the richest real estate owners would be appreciated by popular voters who have taken on heavy debts in order to purchase a house worth a few hundred thousand euros. Here we encounter the fundamental contradictions of the social turn of the FN-RN and the considerable limits of its programmatic platform.

The Contradictions of the Nationalist-Patriotic Bloc surrounding Economic Liberalism

This brings us to the more general question of the simultaneously sociological and programmatic contradictions within the nationalist-patriotic bloc. In the elections of 2022, the RN won 19 percent of the votes in the first round of the legislative elections, which was substantial but clearly insufficient to hope to someday win the majority of the seats. If the RN obtained a substantial number of deputies, it was in part because it was able to benefit from the transfer of votes from Reconquête (4 percent of the votes in the first round) and especially from LR (14 percent of the votes, if we count the 3 percent of the votes cast for various right-wing candidates), which allowed it to defeat a number of Left and Center candidates in the second round. But the fact is that this nationalist-patriotic bloc was riddled with such immense contradictions that one could ask whether LR should not be attached instead to the liberal-progressive bloc, as is suggested by the fact that a large number of its elected candidates had already joined the centrist bloc. However, what is true of the candidates elected is not necessarily true of voters, and that is why we have to begin by analyzing the structure of the electorates.

If we examine first the territorial structure, the most striking result is that in the legislative elections of 2022, the LR electorate became almost as rural as the RN electorate (see figure 11.24). This was a rather spectacular evolution in

---

90. The IFI concerns real estate patrimonies of more than 1.3 million euros, with a deduction of 30 percent on the principal residence, and thus it begins to apply only if the worth of the principal residence exceeds 1.9 million euros (assuming that it is the only property wealth).

91. Taking into account especially the RN's vagueness with respect to the financial assets affected by the IFF: the RN refers to a complete exemption of "occupational goods," which in practice might mean the quasi-totality of the largest financial patrimonies (which are by definition invested in enterprises), no matter what their amount, without any limit, just as for real estate assets held in the form of the principal residence, such that ultimately, the IFF could amount to very little.

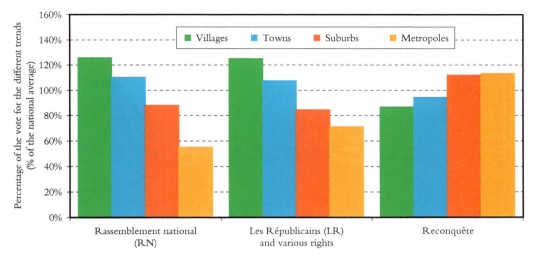

FIGURE 11.24. The components of the nationalist-patriotic bloc, 2022

In the legislative elections of 2022, the nationalist-patriotic bloc had three components that were very different from the point of view of their territorial and social composition. The RN won 19% of the vote, with a much higher result in the villages and towns than in the suburbs and metropoles. Les républicains won 14% of the vote (including 3% of various right-wing trends) with a similar territorial composition, whereas Reconquête had better results in the suburbs and metropoles than in the towns and villages.

Sources and series: unehistoireduconflitpolitique.fr

comparison to the preceding elections, insofar as the vote for the traditional liberal Right had certainly always been greater in the villages and towns than in the suburbs and metropoles, but with a distribution that was on the whole relatively balanced in recent decades (see, for example, figure 11.6). This evolution reflects the fact that in the legislative elections between 2017 and 2022 LR suffered a particularly massive hemorrhage of its urban electorate to the benefit of the LREM-Modem-Ensemble bloc, such that in 2022 it found itself with a much more rural vote than it had previously. On the contrary, we note that the Reconquête electorate gathered around Éric Zemmour is much more urban than rural; the results achieved are considerably higher in the metropoles and suburbs than in the towns and villages (see figure 11.24). This configuration resembles the FN vote united around Jean-Marie Le Pen in 1986–1988 (see figure 11.16).

Let us now examine the social profile of the different electorates, and in particular the relation with the municipality's level of economic wealth. We find that different electorates have radically opposed profiles. The Reconquête vote seems extremely bourgeois, with a particularly steep slope: the result achieved

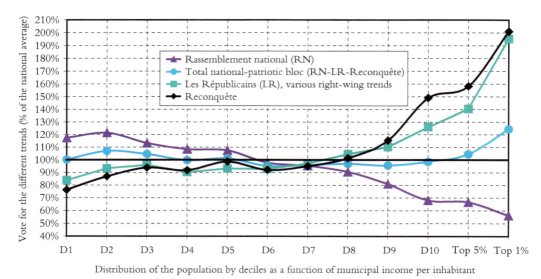

FIGURE 11.25. The nationalist bloc in 2022: Bourgeois or working class?
In the legislative elections of 2022, the vote for the RN was a decreasing function of the average municipal income, whereas the vote for LR and Reconquête was increasing with average income. Overall, the nationalist-patriotic bloc had a result that varied little with the municipal income (except for a slightly increasing part at the top of the distribution). Note: The results indicated here are after taking into account controls for the size of the conurbation and municipality.
Sources and series: unehistoireduconflitpolitique.fr

in the richest 1 percent of the municipalities is twice as high as the movement's average result at the national level, whereas it is almost 30 percent lower than the national average in the poorest municipalities (see figure 11.25). Reconquête's voter profile thus seems much more bourgeois than the FN's in 1986–1988, which was also urban but not especially bourgeois (see figure 11.23), and it achieved a considerably higher overall result. The Reconquête vote appears to be a niche vote (with only 4 percent of the votes in the legislative elections at the national level), but in this case, it is a golden niche concentrated in the upper-class quarters, the swanky city centers, and the richest suburbs, with (to take just a few examples from the richest 1 percent of the municipalities) 9 percent of the votes in the first round of the legislative elections of 2022 in the 8th arrondissement of Paris, 10 percent in the 16th, 12 percent in Neuilly-sur-Seine, Barbizon in Seine-et-Marne, and Saint-Jean-Cap-Ferrat in Alpes-Maritimes, 15 percent in Ferté-Saint-Cyr in Loir-et-Cher, and 26 percent in Ramatuelle in Var).

It is also very striking to see the quasi-similarity of the voter profile of LR and Reconquête as functions of the average income. The former is rural and the latter urban, but both of them achieve results that increase regularly and sharply with the municipalities' income, with extremely similar slopes (see figure 11.25).[92] The RN vote is just as rural as the LR vote, but the slope with regard to income is rigorously the inverse: the RN vote decreases regularly with the level of municipal income, in contrast to the LR vote. If we add up these three very heterogeneous components, we can see that the nationalist-patriotic bloc's overall profile with regard to income is relatively flat.[93] We obtain similar conclusions when we consider occupations. Both the Reconquête vote and the LR vote increase very sharply with the proportion of managers in the municipality, whereas the RN vote is clearly rising. The only notable point in common between the different votes of the nationalist-patriotic bloc is that all three of them rise with the proportion of self-employed independents in the municipality—in this case, with a steeper slope for the Reconquête vote than for the RN and LR votes.[94]

To sum up, the different components of the nationalist-patriotic bloc present radically opposed social characteristics. The RN vote is a popular vote, whereas the LR and Reconquête votes represent two different forms of the bourgeois vote. Moreover, it is interesting to note that the electorate of the traditional Right (RPR-UDF, then UMP, and finally LR) has become increasingly bourgeois since the 1980s and 1990s, as the right-wing popular vote was captured by the FN-RN. To be sure, the voter profile for the Right has always been a growing function of the level of the municipality's income—for example, in the paradigmatic illustration of the Left-Right bipartition represented by the legislative elections of 1981.[95] But if we look at the evolution of the profiles election by election, we see clearly that over time, the vote for the Right increases more and more steeply with income; for example, the relation is more marked in 2002 than in 1986 and 1993, and far more in 2012 than in 2002. The slope diminished a little in 2017 and 2022—a sign that a major portion of the wealthiest voters left for the LREM-Modem-Ensemble

92. Let us add that the profiles are almost identical after controlling for the size of the conurbation and the municipality. Before any controls, Reconquête's voter profile seems to be even more strongly increasing than LR's. See unehistoireduconflitpolitique.fr, appendix D3, figures D3.24a–D3.24r.

93. We find the same results when we use other criteria of wealth, like real estate capital per inhabitant instead of income.

94. See unehistoireduconflitpolitique.fr, appendix D3, figures D3.28a–D3.31r.

95. See chapter 10, figure 10.1.

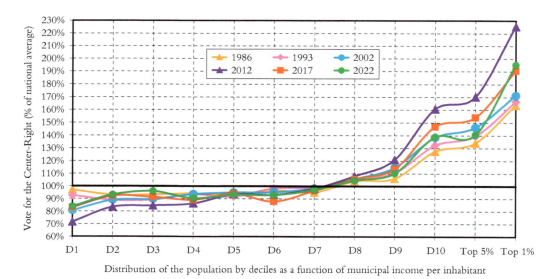

FIGURE 11.26. The liberal Right and wealth, 1986–2022

From the legislative elections of 1986 to those of 2022, the vote for the Center-Right (RPR, UDF, UMP, LR, various left-wing trends) has grown more and more with income, but with an inflection in 2017–2022 because of the richest municipalities' drift toward the liberal-progressive bloc. Note: The results indicated here are after taking into account controls for the size of the conurbation and municipality.

Sources and series: unehistoireduconflitpolitique.fr

bloc—while at the same time remaining larger than it was in 1986, 1993, and 2002 (see figure 11.26).

Let us return to the nationalist-patriotic bloc and its contradictions. The fact that the three components—RN, LR, and Reconquête—are characterized by electorates that are so radically different on the socioeconomic level must be related to deep programmatic discords. The three parties share, of course, a form of hostility toward Muslim and immigrant populations and are in principle in agreement about putting in place a policy of reducing migratory flows (although the modalities are not always set forth very clearly, and they vary depending on the candidates and the discourses). But apart from this subject, which in theory differentiates the nationalist-patriotic bloc from the liberal-progressive bloc, there are many disagreements. The programs of LR and Reconquête can be summed up as liberal, or even ultraliberal, economic policies centered on tax cuts and the reduction of public expenditures—which seems perfectly consistent with the profiles of their votes as a function of the wealth of the municipalities—while the RN defends a more social policy, with all the ambiguities that platform entails.

During the 2022 campaign, Éric Zemmour never stopped mocking the "leftism" he discerned in Marine Le Pen and the RN, particularly concerning the thoughtless promises made to workers on the subject of long careers and retirement at sixty or sixty-two for those who began working early in their lives. The current president of LR, Éric Ciotti, announced during the campaign that he would not hesitate to vote for Éric Zemmour if the second round of the presidential election turned out to be a contest between Zemmour and Emmanuel Macron. In the event of a second round between Le Pen and Macron, he confirmed that he would not in any case vote for the LREM candidate, but he did not encourage his supporters to vote for the president of the FN. Everything suggests that it would be difficult for LR and the RN to overcome their disagreements regarding the economic program to be adopted (but not the migratory program).[96]

To sum up, the so-called nationalist-patriotic bloc is not a truly political bloc, in the sense that its different components would find it very hard to govern together. If it functions de facto as an informal electoral bloc based on the transfer of support by voters seeking to defeat the candidates of the Left and Center, the proximities in the area of migration scarcely conceal completely opposite socio-economic priorities, which are, moreover, also found in extremely bourgeois electorates in the case of LR and Reconquête, and in much more popular electorates in the case of the RN. The central question for the future concerns the conditions under which these contradictions could be overcome, enabling this bloc (or a differently composed form of this group) to take power and exercise it over the long term. We will return to this subject after analyzing more precisely the role of presidential elections and referenda in the country's electoral and political dynamics.

The New Tripartition: Social and Territorial

We will now examine the overall structure of the electoral tripartition as it was expressed in the legislative elections of 2022. We have already referred to the territorial structure of the tripartition: the social-ecological bloc achieved by far its

---

96. Concerning the close proximity that developed between the UMP and the FN during the 2000s (and in particular during the election of 2007) regarding migration and identity, thus paving the way for a possible right-wing bloc of the "ethnocentric" type while at the same time freeing up a space for a central-liberal bloc (at that point, incarnated by François Bayrou), see the stimulating analysis by F. Gougou and P. Martin, "L'émergence d'un nouvel ordre électoral?," in *Des votes et des voix. De Mitterrand à Hollande*, ed. V. Tiberj (Champ social éditions, 2013). However, the results presented here emphasize the importance of economic disagreements within the "ethnocentric" bloc.

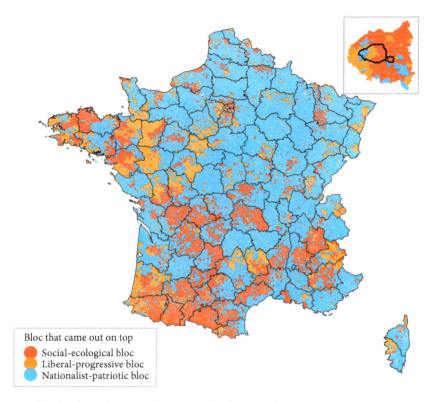

MAP 11.2. The legislative elections of 2022: Social and territorial tripartition

This map represents the bloc that came out on top in each of the municipalities in the first round of the legislative elections of 2022. The social-ecological bloc includes the PS, EELV, LFI, and the PCF. The liberal-progressive bloc includes Ensemble and UDI, and the nationalist-patriotic bloc includes the RN, LR, and Reconquête.

Sources and series: unehistoireduconflitpolitique.fr

best results in the suburbs and metropoles, the central liberal-progressive bloc had a more balanced distribution (albeit more urban than rural), and the nationalist-patriotic bloc obtained its best results in towns and villages (see figure 11.17). In addition to the regional variations in the structure of the vote (see map 11.2), this division between suburbs and metropoles on the one hand and villages and towns on the other is the central phenomenon on the territorial level, with very large differences in votes depending on the size of the conurbation and the municipality—differences that have returned to levels unknown since the nineteenth century.[97]

---

97. See chapter 8, figure 8.6.

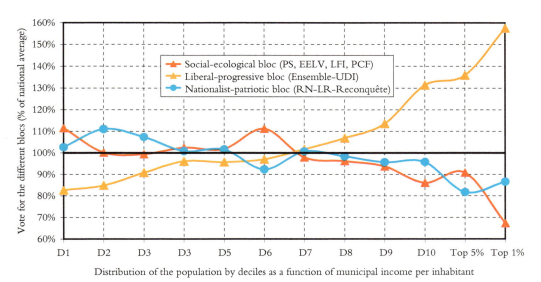

FIGURE 11.27. The legislative elections of 2022: Social tripartition

In the legislative elections of 2022, the liberal-progressive bloc (30% of the votes) was strongly increasing with the average municipal income, whereas the results of the social-ecological bloc (33% of the votes), and to a lesser extent, those of the nationalist-patriotic bloc (37%). diminished with income. Note: The results indicated here are before any controls.

Sources and series: unehistoireduconflitpolitique.fr

Let us now turn to the question of the social structure, and in particular to the voter profile as a function of wealth. If we classify municipalities by average income and examine the votes obtained by the different blocs, without any control for other characteristics, then we obtain a very sharp social tripartition (see figure 11.27).[98] The liberal-progressive bloc (Ensemble-UDI) recorded a result that crossed strongly with the municipality's average income, whereas the results of the social-ecological bloc (PS, EELV, LFI, PCF) and to a lesser degree, the nationalist-patriotic bloc (RN-LR-Reconquête), diminish with the wealth of the municipality. It should be noted that this observed diminution was smaller for the nationalist-patriotic bloc because of the increase in the LR-Reconquête vote with wealth; it is much clearer if we limit ourselves to the RN vote, but that narrows the overall electoral result of the group.

---

98. The results are similar if we use other indicators of wealth, such as real estate capital per inhabitant (that is, the average value of dwellings). See unehistoireduconflitpolitique.fr, appendix D3, figures D3.24a–D3.24t, for a detailed presentation of all the results obtained.

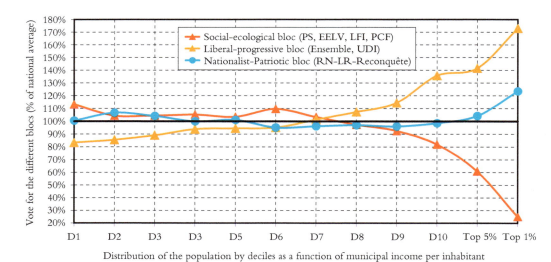

FIGURE 11.28. The legislative elections of 2022: Social tripartition (after controls for the size of the conurbation and municipality)

In the legislative elections of 2022, social tripartition between the three blocs appears even more clearly when we control for a given size of conurbation and municipality. Note: The results indicated here are after taking into account controls for the size of the conurbation and municipality. Sources and series: unehistoireduconflitpolitique.fr

If we compare this tripartition of 2022 with the classic form of Left-Right bipartition seen during the legislative elections of 1981,[99] the main difference is that the liberal-progressive bloc has taken the place of the Right (in the sense that this bloc henceforth brought together a vote that crossed strongly with income, and in particular with the vote of the richest municipalities and that of the upper-class quarters), whereas the popular vote is now divided between the social-ecological bloc and the nationalist-patriotic bloc. If we introduce controls for the size of the conurbation and the municipality, which amounts to neutralizing the effects of the territorial cleavage, then the vote for the social-ecological bloc seems to decrease even more clearly with the level of income, whereas inversely, the vote for the nationalist-patriotic bloc seems to be slightly increasing (see figure 11.28). If we control for all the sociodemographic variables—which amounts to focusing on the residual effect of income, after taking into account the effects of all the other variables (including the proportion of diploma holders, the proportion of managers,

99. See chapter 10, figure 10.1

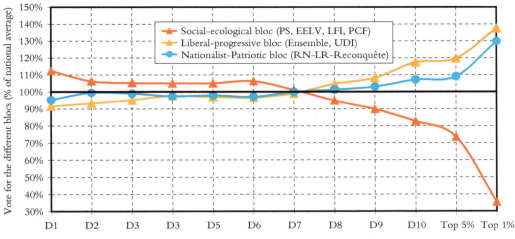

FIGURE 11.29. The legislative elections of 2022: Social tripartition (after all sociodemographic controls)

In the legislative elections of 2022, the social distribution between the three blocs appears even more clearly when we control for all the other sociodemographic characteristics (size of the conurbation, occupations higher education graduates, etc.). Note: The results indicated here are after all sociodemographic controls.

Sources and series: unehistoireduconflitpolitique.fr

the real estate capital per inhabitant, and so on)—then we see that the vote for the nationalist-patriotic bloc becomes almost as sharply increasing with income as the vote for the liberal-progressive bloc (see figure 11.29). Once again, this result is powered by the LR and Reconquête components of the nationalist-patriotic bloc, but we still have to note that the residual effect of income is virtually nil for the RN vote properly so called. This is a result that we find for all the legislative elections from 1986 to 2022: the residual effect of income on the FN-RN vote always appears to be virtually nil (indeed, sometimes slightly positive), which expresses that this vote is concentrated in the municipalities with few diploma holders and few managers, but once these factors are taken into account (reasoning for a given level of diploma holders, occupational composition, and so on), the FN-RN vote is not associated with smaller incomes, contrary to the Left vote. It is even sometimes associated with small financial successes achieved despite opposing winds—recall the "people of slender means" mentioned earlier.[100]

---

100. See unehistoireduconflitpolitique.fr, figure D3.24n.

Is the Ensemble Vote the Most Bourgeois in French History?

Let us now take up a question that is entirely central for our investigation. Is the vote brought together by the liberal-progressive bloc (LREM-Modem-Ensemble-UDI) during the legislative elections of 2017–2022 the most bourgeois in French electoral history, and more generally, how does it compare with other voter profiles observed in the past? Let us say at the outset that this question has a factual and historical dimension above all and does not necessarily lead to any moral and normative implications. Obviously, the fact that a project proposed to the country is based more on the richest classes than on others does not mean that it is not the most pertinent one, and inversely, the fact that a policy is based more on the middle or poor classes is certainly not a guarantee that that will be the right one. Economic and financial success can also be accompanied by solid personal experience that makes it possible to judge the reasonableness of different programs, and having succeeded in convincing a majority of voters who have been most successful from the point of view of wealth can be interpreted as a sign of credibility and seriousness. In the following chapters we will return to the strengths and the limits of the programmatic platform developed by the new liberal-progressive bloc. For the moment, we will simply point out that a voter profile too clearly and persistently bourgeois can pose serious problems from a democratic point of view, the main risk being getting used to the idea that the poorest people are structurally less capable than the richest when it comes to evaluating policies that concern them. In other terms, a voter profile that is growing sharply along with the level of wealth does not necessarily imply that a mistake has been made, but it does oblige the supporters of this vote to inquire seriously into the reasons for this situation and the ways of remedying it.

In this case, if we compare the Ensemble vote in the legislative elections of 2022 with the votes for the different right-wing blocs observed since the end of the nineteenth century, we see that if the Ensemble vote is in fact growing quickly along with the average municipal income, its slope is not always very different from that observed for the right wing in the past, especially at the peak of the distribution. On the other hand, we also see a relatively clear difference connected with the fact that in the past, these right-wing blocs generally achieved better results than the Ensemble bloc in the poorest municipalities (see figure 11.30). In other words, the most favored people did not vote more for Ensemble than they did for the different parts of the Right in the nineteenth and twentieth centuries, but the most modest are much less convinced that these groups represent their interests.

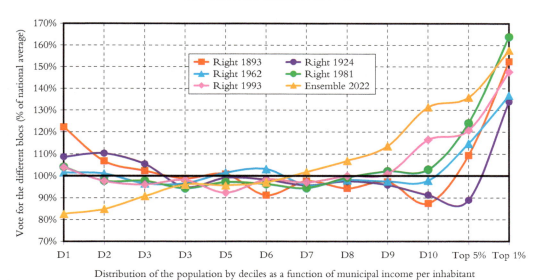

FIGURE 11.30. Is the vote for Ensemble the most bourgeois in French electoral history?

The vote for the liberal-progressive bloc Ensemble-UDI in 2022 is growing strongly with the average municipal income. The slope is on the whole comparable with the Right's vote profiles seen in the past, with the difference that it achieved better results in poor municipalities (and particularly in poor rural municipalities). Note: The results indicated here are without any control.

Sources and series: unehistoireduconflitpolitique.fr

This is explained particularly by the Right's historical ability to prove itself more convincing than the Left with regard to the peasant classes frightened by a left-wing party's attitude to individual property. Thus, the Right bloc brought together large numbers of votes in the poorest municipalities at the end of the nineteenth century and in the early twentieth, in the elections of 1893 and 1924, for example. The effect was not as strong in the second half of the twentieth century, especially in the legislative elections of 1962, 1981, and 1993, but it is nonetheless noteworthy that the results achieved by the Right in the poorest municipalities (relative to their national average result) during these elections was still considerably higher than the result obtained by the liberal-progressive bloc in 2022 (see figure 11.30). If we control for the size of the conurbation and municipality, which amounts to neutralizing the fact that the Ensemble vote is more urban than the Right votes in the past, we see that the difference is reduced while remaining significant (see figure 11.31).

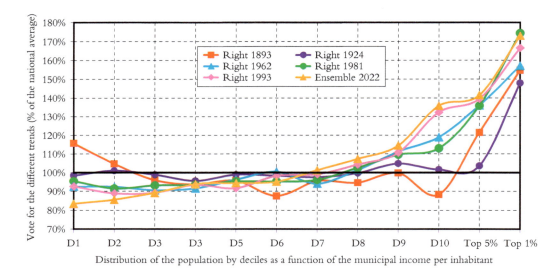

FIGURE 11.31. Is the vote for Ensemble the most bourgeois in French electoral history? (after controls for the size of the conurbation and municipality)

The vote for the Ensemble-UDI bloc is growing strongly with average municipal income. The slope is on the whole comparable with the Right's vote profiles seen in the past, with the difference that the latter achieved better results in the poorest municipalities, including for a given size of conurbation and municipality. Note: The results indicated here are after controls for a given size of the conurbation and municipality.

Sources and series: unehistoireduconflitpolitique.fr

To sum up, in comparison to the similar votes in the past, the Ensemble vote seems in fact more bourgeois, in the sense that it has approximately the same ability as the Right votes to attract the vote of the richest municipalities and the upper-class quarters (which were quickly transferred to the new liberal-progressive bloc in 2017–2022),[101] but it encountered greater difficulties in attracting a minimum of votes in the poorest municipalities (rural or urban). We find the same results when using other indicators of wealth such as real estate capital per inhabitant, and we will also obtain similar conclusions when we analyze the profile of presidential votes as a function of income or real estate capital.[102] This situation is explained in part by the fact that the vote for the liberal Right (RPR-UDF,

101. See chapter 9, figures 9.5 and 9.8.

102. See chapter 13. We obtain the same results using other criteria of wealth, such as the fraction of the population subject to the ISF (or the average amount of fortunes subject to the ISF). However, these data pertain to only a small fraction of the population and are not available before the 1990s, and that is why we privilege the results obtained with data pertaining to income and

then UMP and LR) has itself become more bourgeois since the 1980s and 1990s, as the vote of the poor municipalities became more and more drawn to the FN, especially in the rural world. The liberal-progressive has inherited this situation in part, even as it adds to it a political strategy of seeking to attract the most favored voters from the Center-Left, thus realizing a new form of the fusion of the elites. Let us note in passing that the correlation between the LREM-Modem vote and the level of income was already particularly strong in 2017, and that it became even stronger in 2022.[103] In 2017, one of the strengths of the LREM vote was that it presented itself as more "disruptive" than the traditional bourgeois vote, and in this way it sought to attract managers from the technological and financial sectors who wanted to distinguish themselves from the vote of the Catholic, conservative Right sometimes associated with their parents. In 2022, the upper-class quarters and the richest municipalities associated with the traditional Right continued to rally to the liberal-progressive bloc, such that this "disruptive" character largely disappeared.[104]

In comparison with the vote for the Moderate and Opportunistic Republicans of the 1880s and 1890s, who also presented themselves as attempting to achieve a rapprochement with the old and new elites, the vote for the liberal-progressive bloc of 2017–2022 also had a much more bourgeois profile and a much more marked slant with regard to economic wealth, because the Opportunistic Republicans had succeeded in winning over part of the upper-class quarters and the richest municipalities (although most of the latter continued to trust the traditional conservative and monarchist deputies), as well as a larger portion of their votes in modest and middle-level towns and villages.[105] In comparison with the tripartition that prevailed at the end of the nineteenth century, the tripartition at work at the beginning of the twenty-first century is based on divisions much more directly connected with the social question (whereas the question of the regime had a much more important role in the first tripartition), which gave it a specific character. Let us also note that the current tripartition is accompanied by an unprecedented collapse in electoral turnout in the most modest categories and in the poorest

---

real estate capital, which lend themselves better to overall historical comparisons regarding territorial inequalities.

103. See unehistoireduconflitpolitique.fr, figures D3.25m–D3.25n.

104. For interviews illustrating these generational cleavages within the bourgeoisie, particularly concerning the Macron-Fillon vote in 2017, as well as the convergences since 2017, see Agrikoliansky, Aldrin, and Lévêque, *Voter par temps de crise*, 49–69, 93–11.

105. See chapter 9, figures 9.5–9.8, and unehistoireduconflitpolitique.fr, figure D3.25r.

municipalities (particularly in the urban world).[106] At first, one might think this is an asset for the liberal-progressive bloc, in the sense that it allowed it to win elections with a limited number of registered voters.[107] In the longer term, however, it may contribute to weakening and challenging its social and democratic legitimacy.

An Unstable Tripartition versus Several Possible Bipartitions

Let us conclude this chapter by discussing the prospects of transforming the system of tripartition in the coming years and decades. The scenarios for an evolution are multiple and uncertain, and we can deal with this question only after examining the evolution of the social structure of the votes during presidential elections and referenda in recent decades. At this point, let us simply say that a long-term persistence of tripartition in its current form does not seem to us to be the most probable scenario. The tripartite system, with its division into three blocs of comparable size, is by nature extremely unstable, and the central liberal-progressive bloc appears to be particularly fragile, especially considering the plausible accusations of social self-interest. To be sure, it can try to keep itself in power for a time by playing on the divisions of its adversaries and the considerable contradictions and programmatic inconsistencies that exist in the nationalist-patriotic bloc as well as the social-ecological bloc. But over the more or less long term, it is hard to see how it can last if it does not accept some kind of a modulation of its policies and an alliance with one of the competing blocs. The privileged alliance in practice with LR since 2022 to compensate for the absence of an absolute majority in the National Assembly makes it impossible to respond fully to this contradiction, since it merely exacerbates the social bias and the narrowness of the electoral coalition in power. But it indicates that the most natural tendency is to come to an understanding with the Right, which is confirmed by the projects of hardening legislation on immigration, which may make it possible to bring together a majority with LR and the RN.

In the event of a return to bipartition, two principal scenarios are a priori conceivable: a social-ecological bloc versus a liberal-nationalist bloc, or a social-nationalist

---

106. See chapter 6, figures 6.1–6.3.
107. On the narrowness of the electoral base of the "bourgeois bloc," see also B. Amable and S. Palombarini, *L'illusion du bloc bourgeois. Alliances sociales et avenir du modèle français* (Raisons d'Agir, 2017). On the formation of the "bourgeois bloc," see also B. Amable, *La résistible ascension du néolibéralisme. Modernisation capitaliste et crise politique en France (1980–2020)* (La Découverte, 2021).

bloc versus a liberal-progressive bloc. In the first case, the current social-ecological bloc would succeed in broadening its popular electorate (in particular with regard to abstentionists in the urban world and the most social fraction of RN voters in rural territories) and in establishing a bipolar contest against a liberal-nationalist bloc issuing from the rapprochement between the liberal-progressive bloc and the LR and Reconquête segments from the nationalist-patriotic bloc (as well as RN voters who were less resistant to economic liberalism). In the second case, it is on the contrary the present nationalist-patriotic bloc led by the RN that would succeed in broadening its popular electorate (also with regard to abstentionists and the Left) and in imposing a bipolar confrontation between the new social-nationalist bloc thus constituted and the liberal-progressive bloc (reinforced by part of the former social-ecological bloc).

The first scenario is closer to the earlier Left-Right bipartition and seems to us by far the more desirable; it would make it possible to continue the virtuous dynamic toward social equality and prosperity begun in the twentieth century, and it seems more capable of developing the international cooperation indispensable for meeting the social and ecological challenges. Considering the convergences that we have brought to light between the electorates of the different components of the social-ecological bloc, and considering also the tendency of the present liberal-progressive bloc to broaden to the right, this prospect also seems the most probable one. However, this presupposes that Left parties and ecological parties succeed in developing a new, common organization capable of proposing an ambitious program (particularly concerning the European and international questions) and in attracting new voters, which is far from certain. The second scenario seems less likely than the first, considering particularly the profound divergences highlighted within the nationalist-patriotic bloc and the relative narrowness of its social component. However, this hypothesis cannot be excluded, especially if the Left and ecological parties are not able to unite and instead get lost in divisions that a majority of voters consider sterile—or else, if they succeed in uniting but once they are in power, they disappoint voters again. To move forward with the analysis of these different possibilities, we must first study the role of cleavages in presidential elections and referenda in the overall electoral and political dynamic.

PART IV

Between Representative Democracy and Direct Democracy

POLITICAL CLEAVAGES IN PRESIDENTIAL ELECTIONS AND REFERENDA

CHAPTER 12

The Twofold Invention of the Presidential Election, 1848 and 1965–1995

Up to this point, we have concentrated on the study of political cleavages and the social structure of electorates observed in the legislative elections that have taken place in France from 1848 to 2022. This is our preferred long-term vantage point because it allows us to study both the largest number of elections and the greatest diversity of political tendencies. However, presidential elections and referenda have also played a central role in the electoral and political dynamism of the country over the course of the last two centuries, and particularly in the recent period. In this fourth and last part of this work we will therefore focus on these elections and study the extent to which the results permit us to reorient and complete the interpretations and hypotheses developed earlier, as well as the prospects for future evolutions.

We will begin by analyzing in this chapter the formation of electoral cleavages during presidential elections, starting with the first introduction of the presidential election by direct universal male suffrage in 1848—which was a resounding failure and led to a coup d'état—and then during its second introduction in 1965, after which this much decried system succeeded in proving that it could structure bipolarization and repeated democratic transfers of power from 1965 to 1995. We will also see that the presidential election served to reveal the contradictions of the Right and the Left and, during the period 1965–1995, contributed to the emergence of a new form of nationalist Right and a multiform ecological tendency. Then in chapter 13 we will study the metamorphoses of the presidential elections from 2002 to 2022, the role they played in the establishment of tripartition, and the importance they might have in future evolutions (the continuation of tripartition or a return to bipartition). Finally, in chapter 14 we will examine the role of referenda and in particular the European referenda of 1992 and 2005, with European stakes whose importance for the weakening of bipartition and the transition to tripartition we have already noted, and which are very likely to have the same importance in future transformations.

The Election of 1848, the Rural-Urban Cleavage,
and the Harmful Nature of Presidentialism

We have already discussed at length the context of very high social and political tension in which the legislative elections of April 1848 and May 1849 took place; this was also true for the presidential election of December 1848. During the two legislative elections, three significant blocs divided up the votes: a Left bloc with the Democratic Socialists, a Center bloc with the Moderate and liberal Republicans, and a Right bloc with the conservatives, Catholics, and monarchists of the Party of Order. The Right bloc was dominant, but the Democratic Socialist bloc won a very substantial number of seats, particularly in May 1849, with about 35 percent of the vote (versus 47 percent for the Party of Order), and it was the Left's rapid advance in the partial elections of 1849–1850 that raised fears that the conservatives might be about to collapse, whence their decision to severely restrict the right to vote by excluding a third of the citizens from the electoral lists with the Burgraves' law of May 1850.[1] Compared with these hotly disputed legislative elections—so hotly disputed that the government saw no way of staying in power other than by calling into question the right to vote itself—the presidential election of December 1848 appears, on the contrary, to be an astonishing moment of national quasi-unanimity. In the first round, Louis-Napoléon Bonaparte won almost 75 percent of the votes cast, versus barely 20 percent for General Eugène Cavaignac (the candidate of the Moderate Republicans) and only 5 percent for the Democratic Socialist François-Vincent Raspail) (see figure 12.1 and map 12.1).

The concentration of votes in the first round is all the more surprising because the number of candidates participating in the election was relatively high; in addition to those already mentioned, we can add Alphonse de Lamartine, Louis Blanc, Armand Barbès, and General Nicolas Changarnier, who, despite his withdrawal, won a non-negligible number of votes. This was also the case for Marshal Bugeaud. An examination of the electoral records (all of which we have digitized) reveals a large number of surprises in this respect. With no lack of imagination, citizens sometimes voted not only for candidates who were no longer running (undeclared candidates like Adolphe Thiers and Napoléon Joseph Ney de la Moskowa), but also sometimes for dead men, such as Maximilien Robespierre, as is shown by the "record of the vote-count of sections of the cantonal assembly of Château-Thierry" in the department of Aisne (see reproduction 12.1a and 12.1b).

---

1. See chapter 9.

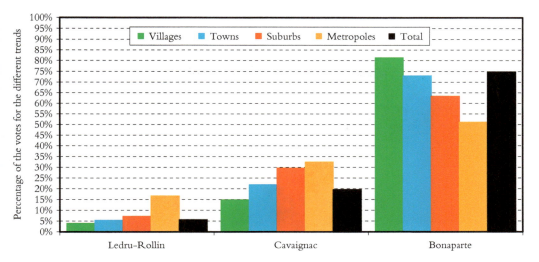

FIGURE 12.1. The presidential vote of 1848 in the territories

In the presidential election of 1848, Louis-Napoléon Bonaparte won 74.8% of the votes, followed by Cavaignac with 19.6% and Ledru-Rollin with 5.6% (including Raspail's 0.5% of the votes). Bonaparte achieved his best results in villages, followed by towns, suburbs, and metropoles, whereas the contrary is true for the other candidates. Note: The votes for Lamartine and Changarnier (0.1%) have been added to those for Cavaignac.

Sources and series: unehistoireduconflitpolitique.fr

Despite this great diversity of the political options and the voters' imaginations, the distribution of the votes proved to be extremely concentrated. There are some very good explanations for this indisputable result. The principal one is that the Moderate Republicans who held power from February to December 1848 made themselves immensely unpopular in only a few months. The most detested decision was the massive 45 percent increase in property taxes (the "forty-five centimes") weighing on the rural world. The objective was to reestablish the state's credit and pay the interest on the debt, but this choice was considered utterly iniquitous by the peasant classes who already faced a serious agricultural crisis. General Cavaignac, who led the government starting in June 1848, completely discredited himself by sending troops to levy the tax in the countryside during the summer of 1848. Like many conservatives and property owners in the rural world, Louis-Napoléon Bonaparte promised to do away with the "forty-five centimes," which had become the hated symbol of the selfishness of the urban world and the most important theme of the electoral

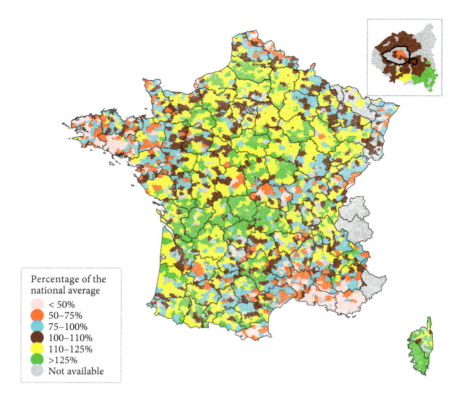

Percentage of the
national average

● < 50%
● 50–75%
● 75–100%
● 100–110%
● 110–125%
● >125%
● Not available

MAP 12.1. The invention of the presidential election in 1848
This map represents, for each municipality, the vote for Louis-Napoléon Bonaparte in proportion
to the national average in the presidential election of 1848.
Sources and series: unehistoireduconflitpolitique.fr

campaign.[2] In view of the fact that General Cavaignac had also won fame for violently putting down the workers' insurrection in June 1848, forcing the closure
of the *ateliers nationaux* and dispersing the workers, he was rejected by both the
peasant classes and the urban proletariat. But among the Social Democrats,
everyone was well aware that Ledru-Rollin and Raspail were little known outside
the world of the cities and had no chance of defeating Cavaignac or Bonaparte.
That is why, for tactical reasons, many urban workers voted for Bonaparte—to

2.   The forty-five-centime surtax was abolished after the election and replaced by higher indirect
     taxes. See chapter 9.

Reproduction 12.1: Original documents from the presidential election of 1848: Arrondissement of Château-Thierry (canton of Château-Thierry in the department of Aisne)

ensure the defeat of Cavaignac.[3] This tactical vote was all the greater because the constitution of 1848 did not provide for a second round, and because only a situation in which Bonaparte won more than 50 percent of the votes would guarantee the elimination of the "June Butcher," who might otherwise be elected

3. An observation made by, for example, the newspaper *La République* shortly after the election, on 13 December 1848—"A large number of workers who appeared, a few days ago, disposed to vote for M. Raspail voted for M. L.-N. Bonaparte"—as well as *Le Peuple* (edited by Pierre-Joseph Proudhon): "Most socialist workers, who were supposed to vote for Raspail or Ledru-Rollin, voted for Napoléon out of horror at the name of Cavaignac." The day before, *La République* expressed the Left's bewilderment: "What does it matter to us, the people, workers and proletarians? One will reduce the Republic and suffocate it, the other will kill it, and that won't take as long" (quoted in *Histoire générale de la presse française,* 2:225). *Le Peuple* ultimately supported Raspail's candidacy right down to the end, and in its issue for 10 December it advised its readers, "Voting for Bonaparte amounts to calling for civil war, because the People, which made the Republic, will not let it be taken away by a pretender. . . . We are voting for RASPAIL. By voting for a socialist martyr, we are protesting against the presidency, and demanding the right to work and the extinction of the capitalist privilege."

president by members of the parliament.[4] That explains why the candidacies of Ledru-Rollin and Raspail won little more than 5 percent of the votes in December 1848, even though the Democratic Socialists won 35 percent of the votes a few months later in May 1849 (and had won 26 percent in April 1848). Far from being a vote of support, this astonishing unanimity must be seen primarily as a consequence of a deliberate strategic vote.

If we compare the results in greater detail, we see that the tactical vote was equally great among the Social Democrats in rural zones. The small vote for Ledru-Rollin and Raspail in December 1848 was in fact heavily concentrated in urban centers (see figure 12.2), even more overwhelmingly than the Social Democrat vote during the legislative elections.[5] In the urban world, Ledru-Rollin's and Raspail's results grew in proportion to the number of blue-collar workers at the level of the municipalities, even if we also see very high numbers for Bonaparte in the most working-class municipalities.[6] Generally, in the context of the period, the rural-urban cleavage was so deep that it was extremely difficult for candidates from Social Democratic trends and from the industrial and workers' world to win, unless they completely redefined their programmatic base to reorient it toward the peasant classes and access to land and credit for rural workers. Some of the representatives of these trends tried to do this, but their attempts were insufficient.[7] In addition, Louis-Napoléon Bonaparte was clever enough to show that he was closer to the people than most of the conservative leaders, particularly by defending universal suffrage, which had been cut off by the Burgraves' law (this permitted him to condemn the hypocrisy and self-interest of the parliamentary elites), by promising to allow people to vote in their municipality rather than only in the canton's main town;[8] and by promising to end the practice of paying replacements

---

4. Article 47 of the Constitution provided that if no candidate obtained an absolute majority of the votes in the first and only round, the National Assembly would be called on to choose the president of the Republic from among the five candidates who received the most votes, which potentially opened the door to the election of Cavaignac, given the mistrust of Bonaparte among members of parliament.
5. See chapter 9, figures 9.1–9.2.
6. See unehistoireduconflitpolitique.fr, appendix E2, figures E2.1m–E2.1w, and E3.1a–E3.1i.
7. See chapter 9.
8. Holding the election at the level of the municipality rather than in the canton's main town was far from a purely technical issue: the choice of the main town in fact obliged the most isolated citizens to sacrifice several hours (and thus often a half- or even a full day of work) to go vote; otherwise, they were forced to renounce their electoral duty and, in this case, their right to vote. This problem is found again during the legislative elections of 1871, when the decision to return the election to the level of the canton's main town in February aroused anger and

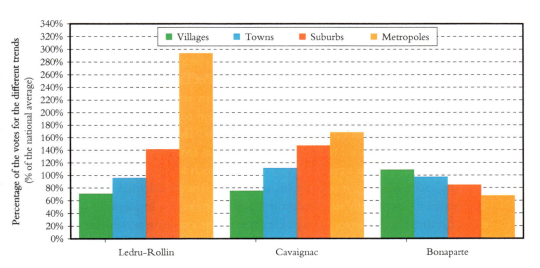

FIGURE 12.2. The presidential vote of 1848 and the territorial cleavage

In the presidential election of 1848, Ledru-Rollin obtained a result close to three times higher in the metropoles than his national average, Cavaignac a result more than 60% higher than his national average, and Bonaparte a result more than 30% lower than his national average. Note: The votes won by Raspail (0.5% of the votes) have been added to those of Ledru-Rollin, and those of Lamartine (0.2%) and Changarnier (0.1%) have been added to those of Cavaignac.

Sources and series: unehistoireduconflitpolitique.fr

for military service to allow the children of bourgeois families to avoid their obligations.[9] He missed no opportunity to criticize the "billion for émigrés" (without, however, proposing that it be repaid), and he reminded people of his absolute opposition to aristocratic and feudal privileges, as well as his faith in industrial development and an increase in workers' salaries—there again, without making any binding commitment of his own, but with an empathy more credible than Thiers's or Cavaignac's, especially since in 1848 he had not yet had to assume the burdens of power.[10]

incomprehension and was seen in the countryside as bullying against rural populations. See, for example, J. Gouault, *Comment la France est devenue républicaine.*

9. We find the same popular strand and the same sense of staging in 1886–1887 with General Boulanger, who knew how to skillfully evoke the necessary brotherhood between the troops and miners striking in Decazeville, and to denounce the military privileges of ecclesiastics— *curés sac à dos!* (Ecclesiastical students were permitted to continue their studies and to do only one year of military service.)

10. On the electoral campaign of 1848, see A. J. Tudesq, *L'élection présidentielle de Louis-Napoléon Bonaparte (10 décembre 1848)* (A. Colin, 1965). See also G. Renard, "La République de 1848," in *Histoire socialiste de la France contemporaine de 1789 à 1900,* ed. J. Jaurès (Rouff, 1908), 9:8–294.

We know what happened afterward. On the strength of having won 75 percent of the votes in 1848, and hurt by the Assembly's refusal to approve the constitutional amendment that would have allowed him to be a candidate for the presidency in 1852, Bonaparte organized the coup d'état of December 1851. He used a series of plebiscites to introduce an authoritarian regime and have himself proclaimed hereditary emperor, thus putting an end to electoral pluralism and to any genuine presidential or legislative elections. This disastrous experience convinced contemporaries that presidentialism was toxic, and it explains their reticence, for more than a century, to reintroduce such a system in France. Naturally, the sociopolitical context has since changed. The presidential election has shown that it can usefully supplement the legislative election by allowing citizens to choose directly the person who holds the supreme executive power. Today, no one really contemplates returning this right to the members of parliament. Nonetheless, this experience reminds us of the extent to which the twofold logic of the personalization of voting can sometimes lead to the illusion of individual omnipotence and to forgetting the necessarily collective, plural, and deliberative dimension of electoral democracy. In the last two presidential elections, Emmanuel Macron has defeated his opponent, Marine Le Pen, by large majorities (66 percent of the votes in 2017, 59 percent in 2022). But just as in 1848, this was a choice by default: the voters simply eliminated the candidate that worried them most.[11] This tactical vote does not entail any real support for the winning candidate's personal program, and obviously no particular illusion regarding a single individual's ability to make choices affecting the futures of tens of millions of people.

The Second Birth of the Presidential Election: The 1965 Election

The second introduction of the presidential election by universal suffrage was to prove much more conclusive. This time, the constitutional amendment of 1962 provided for a second round of the election between the two candidates with the most votes if neither of them had won an absolute majority of the votes in the first round. Above all, this new system was to take place in a completely transformed sociohistorical context in which no significant political force seriously considered putting an end to electoral pluralism and parliamentary sovereignty. In addition,

---

11. As the limited results obtained by Macron in the first round suggest (24 percent in 2017, 28 percent in 2022). These results were, moreover, partly the result not of support but of a strategic choice made by a certain number of voters to prevent a second round opposing Fillon and Le Pen in 2017, or Mélenchon and Le Pen in 2022.

since 1910, the party system had been increasingly oriented toward Left-Right bi-partition, with the development of the Socialist and Communist Parties and the rallying of the monarchists to the Republican regime. The election of the president by universal suffrage completed this evolution by obliging each camp to unite in the second round of the presidential election, thus contributing to an almost perfect bipolarity for several decades, and especially from 1965 to 1995.

Let us begin by examining the inaugural election of December 1965. The SFIO and the PCF were hostile to the election of the president by universal suffrage and were in no hurry to present a candidate. A centrist deputy who had served as a minister several times during the Fourth Republic, François Mitterrand, announced his candidacy and won the support of the Socialists and Communists. In the first round, he won 32 percent of the votes, compared with 44 percent for General de Gaulle (the candidate of the Gaullist party, UNR), while Jean Lecanuet, the candidate of the Christian Democrat party (MRP), won 16 percent and Tixier-Vignancour won 5 percent. Tixier-Vignancour was violently opposed to de Gaulle on the Algerian question (he had been the Vichy government's adjunct secretary-general for information, and had been sentenced after Liberation to ten years of *indignité nationale;* he also served as the lawyer of Louis-Ferdinand Céline and the putsch-minded generals of the OAS (Organisation de l'armée secrète). His campaign director was Jean-Marie Le Pen, who had been elected as a Poujadist deputy in 1956 before leaving to fight for French Algeria, and who was then waging his first presidential battle. Although Tixier-Vignancour's result was minimal, his case is still interesting, because he constitutes the link between the old, Vichyist and colonialist Right and the new, nationalist Right that was to develop significantly with the rise of the FN in the 1980s and 1990s. In addition, he made a decisive contribution to the emergence of a new form of tripartition in the recent period. We will return to the role played by the repatriates from Algeria in the development of this electoral trend in the election of 1965.

If we concentrate for the moment on the 1965 election, the very fact that there was a second round came as a great surprise to many contemporary observers who had bet on a broad victory by the General in the first round, to the point that for some of them, the question was whether de Gaulle would agree to participate in the second round (as it seems most people wanted, since what was at issue was the stability of institutions chosen by the General himself). It seems clear from the outset that the presidential election tended to simplify French political life, which was soon to be limited to two major trends. Commenting on the results of the first round in *Le Combat républicain,* François Mitterrand wrote in "L'enjeu du second tour" (What is at stake in the second round), "So the battle goes on, under very clear conditions: it is a battle between the Left and the Right." With support from the Socialists and Communists, in the first round of voting Mitterrand came out on top in the capital's Red belt and in territories traditionally favored by the Left (see map 12.2).

General de Gaulle won the second round, with 55 percent of the votes versus 45 percent for Mitterrand. Clearly, some of Lecanuet's and Tixier-Vignancour's supporters had chosen to oppose the General right to the end, even if it meant voting for a camp that was not theirs—Tixier-Vignancour himself urged his supporters to vote for the candidate of the Left "in order to ensure the defeat of General de Gaulle."[12] There is no doubt that the electorate that voted for Mitterrand was primarily that of the Communist and Socialist Left, whereas de Gaulle won the largest possible number of right-wing votes (except among those who still opposed his Algerian policy or did not forgive him for his authoritarianism). If we examine the social structure of the votes in the 1965 presidential election, we find two important facts that deserve our attention. First, as in the legislative elections conducted at that time, the territorial cleavage seems to be much attenuated compared to what it was in the nineteenth century and at the beginning of the twentieth. To be sure, the candidate supported by the SFIO and the PCF won more votes in the suburbs, whereas the Christian Democrat candidate and the Gaullist candidate obtained their best results in the villages and towns (see figure 12.3). But the differences are quite limited in comparison to the election of 1848 (see figure 12.2). This testifies to a world in which class conflict within each category of territory was greater than the territorial conflict itself. It will also be noted that the Tixier-Vignancour vote was mainly an urban vote driven by the new metropoles, which we have also seen in the case of the FN vote in the legislative elections of 1986 and 1988.[13]

The Election of 1965, the Left-Right Polarization, and Class Conflict

The second fact, which is even more important than the first, confirms the primacy of class conflict in the election of 1965, particularly in the second round. If we rank municipalities as a function of their average income, we see that the vote

12. Lecanuet's position during the period between the two rounds remained more moderate, but he did not declare himself in favor of François Mitterrand. The clear implication of his statements was that he wanted his supporters to avoid voting for General de Gaulle. See, for example, F. Goguel, "L'élection présidentielle de Décembre 1965," *Revue française de science politique,* 1966.

13. See chapter 11, figure 11.16.

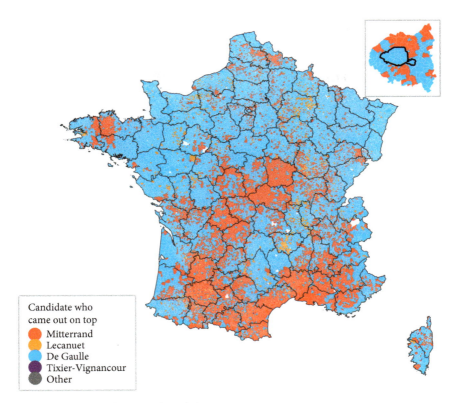

Candidate who
came out on top
- Mitterrand
- Lecanuet
- De Gaulle
- Tixier-Vignancour
- Other

MAP 12.2. The return of the presidential election in 1965

The map represents the candidate who came out on top in each municipality in the first round of the presidential election of 1965.

Sources and series: unehistoireduconflitpolitique.fr

for de Gaulle grew enormously in line with the wealth of the municipality, especially at the peak of the distribution, whereas inversely, the vote for Mitterrand declined consistently (see figure 12.4).

Several points regarding this result must be clarified. First, we have already observed similar conflicts in the votes for the Left and the Right in legislative elections such as the election of 1981, and more generally for all the legislative elections held during the twentieth century. The difference here is that in the second round of the presidential election, this Left-Right bipolar conflict appeared for the first time at the national level, with a highly symbolic choice between two major competitors who incarnated the two great trends that structured French political life. It was the first time in French electoral history that such a binary

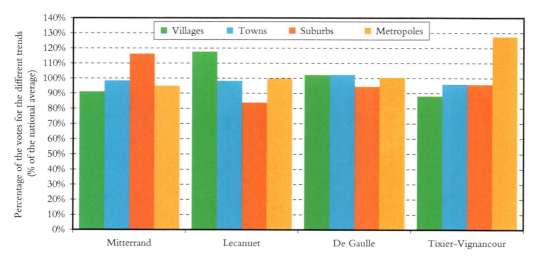

FIGURE 12.3. The presidential vote of 1965 and the territorial cleavage

In the presidential election of 1965, the left-wing candidate François Mitterrand (32% of the votes in the first round) achieved his best results in the suburbs, whereas the Christian Democratic candidate Jean Lecanuet (16%) and the UNR candidate Charles de Gaulle (44%) achieved their best results in the villages and the towns, and the Algérie française candidate Jean-Louis Tixier-Vignancour (5%) in the metropoles. In all, the territorial disparities were relatively limited.

Sources and series: unehistoireduconflitpolitique.fr

choice was set before the voters, and it constituted a major innovation in a country where a dozen significant parties or political tendencies were usually on the ballot.[14] We note also that the slope of the curve is greater and more regular for presidential elections (particularly for that of 1965) than for the legislative elections, especially at the low end of the distribution. The presidential election tends to eliminate the multiple local factors and to focus on the national dimension of the election, and thus class conflict over the redistribution of wealth. Let us add that the profiles indicated in figure 12.4 are found before taking into account any control variable, after taking into account the size of the conurbation and the municipality, and after the introduction of the whole set of sociodemographic variables. We also find the same results when we use other indicators of wealth, such as real estate capital (total value of housing) per inhabitant (the average value of housing).[15] It is also interesting to compare the vote profiles as a function of wealth for the various candidates during the first round of the elec-

---

14. Unlike countries with a two-party system, such as the United States and the United Kingdom.

15. See unehistoireduconflitpolitique.fr, appendix E3, figures E3.2a–E3.2k.

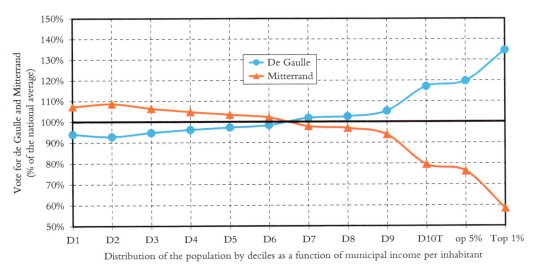

FIGURE 12.4. The presidential election of 1965 and wealth (second round)

In the second round of the 1965 presidential election, the vote for de Gaulle (relative to his national average) increased with the level of the municipality's average income, particularly at the top of the distribution, whereas the converse is true for the vote for Mitterrand. Note: The results indicated here are after controls for the size of the conurbation and municipality.

Sources and series: unehistoireduconflitpolitique.fr

tion. In particular, it is striking to see how much more rapidly the vote for the Christian Democrat Lecanuet grew in proportion to the municipal income than the vote for de Gaulle did, particularly in the country's richest municipalities (see figure 12.5).

Certainly, we must first take into account the fact that ultimately, de Gaulle won many more votes than Lecanuet—44 percent versus 16 percent, a considerable disparity that the difference in slope in relation to wealth does not suffice to bridge, even in the richest 1 percent of municipalities that in absolute terms placed the UNR candidate ahead of the Christian Democrat candidate.[16] The fact remains that the difference in slope is impressive: in the first round, the richest 1 percent of the municipalities voted little more than 1.1 times more often for de Gaulle than the country as a whole, whereas they voted almost twice as often for Lecanuet than the country as a whole did. This shows the extent to which a large

---

16. In all, in the first round Lecanuet came in on top with less than 4 percent of the municipalities (less than 1,400 municipalities out of 36,000), notably in Marne, Côte-d'Or, and Haute-Loire (see map 12.2).

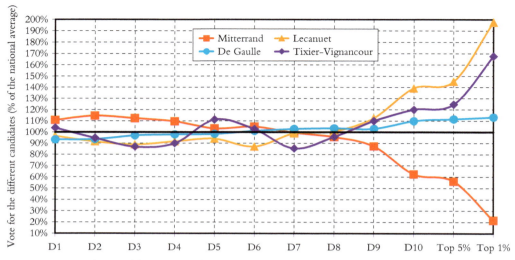

FIGURE 12.5. The presidential election of 1965 and wealth (first round)

In the first round of the 1965 presidential election, the vote for de Gaulle (relative to his national average) increased with the average income of the municipality, particularly at the top of the distribution, but less than the votes for Lecanuet and for Tixier-Vignancour. Note: The results indicated here are after controls for the size of the conurbation and municipality.

Sources and series: unehistoireduconflitpolitique.fr

part of the elites of the traditional Right still had reservations about de Gaulle and his tendencies to Caesarism at the time of the 1965 election. In the second round, we nonetheless see that in the richest 1 percent of the municipalities de Gaulle achieved a result that was 1.35 times higher than his national result, which shows that in the end, the transfers of votes to the Right made it possible to ensure a broad victory in municipalities like Bouc-Bel-Air in Bouches-du-Rhône, Villeneuve-Loubet in Alpes-Maritimes, and Drémil-Lafage in Haute-Garonne, whose inhabitants were among the richest 10 percent in terms of municipal income in the middle of the 1960s. In this sense, this was mainly a vote that was not only urban but also bourgeois, and not a working-class vote (see figure 12.5).[17] To be sure, the vote profile is a little less distinct than the one we have seen with the vote for the

17. For the distribution of the vote for Tixier-Vignancour, see unehistoireduconflitpolitique.fr, map C12.1. We will return to the other major determinant of the vote for Tixier-Vignancour—namely, a large number of Algerian repatriates. This was the case in the first two municipalities cited above.

Reconquête party led by Éric Zemmour in 2002, but in both cases it is nonetheless a vote that is very positively correlated with wealth.[18] We will return to the way the trends connected with the nationalist Right have oscillated between the bourgeois vote and the popular vote in French electoral history from the 1960s to the 2020s.

Absolute Bipolarity: Second Rounds in the Presidential Elections of 1965, 1974, 1981, 1988, and 1995

If the vote profile observed in the election of 1965 is so important, it is also and especially because this paradigmatic incarnation of the Left-Right bipolarization was to be reproduced in subsequent presidential elections. If we except the election of 1969, which was conducted immediately after General de Gaulle's resignation and in which the Left did not qualify for the second round,[19] the Fifth Republic's first five elections gave rise, in the second rounds, to extremely close Left-Right duels that soon became emblematic of French-style bipolarization. De Gaulle defeated Mitterrand in 1965 (55 percent to 45 percent), then Giscard d'Estaing defeated Mitterrand in 1974 (51 percent to 49 percent) and in 1981 (52 percent to 48 percent) before Mitterrand defeated Giscard d'Estaing in 1981 (52 percent to 48 percent) and Chirac in 1988 (54 percent to 46 percent). Lastly, Chirac defeated Jospin in 1995 (53 percent to 47 percent). It turns out that these five Left-Right presidential duels that took place between 1965 and 1995 were all characterized by vote profiles with regard to wealth that were extremely similar to those observed in 1965: the poor municipalities voted systematically more for the Left candidate than the national average, whereas the richest mu-

---

18. See chapter 11, figure 11.25.
19. Conducted one year after the historic defeat of the Left in the legislative elections of June 1968, in the context of a hardening of a large part of the country after the May movement, the presidential elections of June 1969 saw Georges Pompidou (UDR) come in first, with 44 percent of the vote, ahead of Democrat Alain Poher (23 percent), the Communist Jacques Duclos (21 percent), the SFIO candidate, Gaston Defferre (5 percent), and the PSU's Michel Rocard (4 percent). Pompidou won the second round, with 58 percent of the votes versus 42 percent for Poher and an unusually low turnout. See unehistoireduconflitpolitique.fr, figures E2.3a–E2.3j and E3.3a–E3.3l on the vote profiles, which have the usual characteristics. Note that both Pompidou and Poher have bourgeois vote profiles in the first round (increasing with wealth, particularly at the peak of the tripartition), but Pompidou's profile increases more than Poher's, and in the second round, the gap between the former and the latter is particularly great in the richest municipalities. After the events of May 1968, the Gaullist Pompidou seemed more reassuring to property owners than the Christian Democrat Poher, and again, this illustrates the repeated crossovers in the French Right.

nicipalities voted massively for the Right candidate, without exception. Although it ultimately lasted only three decades—a relatively short time on the scale of the country's electoral history since 1789—this period lasted long enough that those who experienced it considered it a new form of normality. During these years, French political life was explicitly bipolar and organized around the presidential duels, which were the key moments when each camp unified itself in an attempt to defeat the adverse camp in elections. Of the five duels of this golden age of bipolarity, the first two were won by the Right, the next two by the Left, and then the Right regained the upper hand in the fifth election. This is proof that the system allows repeated democratic transitions of power.

This fine edifice was blown up with the election of 2002. On the evening of 21 April, the FN candidate Jean-Marie Le Pen edged out the PS candidate, Lionel Jospin, such that in the second round the opponents were Le Pen and the candidate of the RPR, Jacques Chirac—that is, it was to be fought between the nationalist Right and the liberal Right, and no longer between the Left and the Right. This rupture was all the greater because this new situation became virtually the norm. Of the five elections held between 2002 and 2022, only two led to Left-Right duels (Royal versus Sarkozy in 2007 and Hollande versus Sarkozy in 2012) and three ended up in confrontations between candidates from the nationalist bloc and the liberal bloc (between Le Pen and Chirac in 2002, then between Le Pen and Macron in 2017 and 2022), such that no one was quite sure whether (or rather, when) the Left-Right duels would reappear. From every point of view, the shock of 21 April 2002 constitutes a major temporal landmark in the process leading from bipartition to tripartition, of the same order as the emergence of the FN in the legislative elections of 1986 and the European referendum of 1992. It was, in a way, the last line of defense for maintaining the fiction of an intangible Left-Right bipolarity that was shattered in the presidential election of 2002.

Before we take up this election and the following ones and study the extent to which the tripartition of 2017–2022 can be perpetuated or reconfigured in diverse new forms of bipartition in the future, we must still analyze in greater detail the electorates at the time of the presidential elections held from 1965 to 1995. This is because, in addition to the overall similarity of the whole set of the vote profiles in function of the wealth noted during the Left-Right duels, there were also several important changes that were manifested in this period.

Generally speaking, we must first remember that the Left-Right conflict can never be reduced to a conflict concerning the level of monetary wealth (income or real estate values). Just as in the legislative elections, in the presidential elections of this period there was always a residual territorial dimension (with a more urban and active Left vote, especially in the suburbs, and a larger Right vote in towns and villages, as well as in the centers of metropoles), even if it is greatly attenuated in the period from 1965 to 1995 in comparison with earlier and later periods. Above all, in both presidential and legislative elections we find that the Left and Right votes are always part of a specific productive and occupational structure. For example, given an average wealth and the same size of conurbation and municipality, we see that the right-wing presidential vote increases systematically with the proportion of self-employed workers in the municipality, and that inversely, the left-wing vote increases with the proportion of salaried workers, and especially with the proportion of blue-collar workers (and more and more over time, with the percentage of employees), whereas large numbers of managers are associated with large right-wing votes. Most of these effects of occupational composition persist after the impact of wealth is taken into account, and in the same way, the influence of wealth (income or real estate capital) on the Left-Right presidential vote is still found after the variables connected with occupational composition have been taken into account. We do not present all these results in detail here because they lead to essentially the same conclusions as those obtained for the legislative elections, but it is important to keep them in mind.

In addition to these overall regularities, several significant changes deserve closer inspection. First, if we study the presidential electorates for the period 1965–1995, we find multiple crossovers and inconsistencies within the French Right, especially concerning the relation to liberalism and nationalism, and also in connection with the emergence of the question of Europe, which also involved fractures within the Right and effects that were beginning to be felt during this period. These contradictions within the Right (and others within the Left) played an essential role in weakening bipartition and in future developments. Second, the presidential elections conducted from 1965 to 1995 enable us to note the development of two new political trends that were to play an increasingly important role over the course of the following decades: the construction of a new form of the nationalist Right that made a radical break with the traditional Right and with its evolving social and territorial profile, and the emergence of an ecological trend that took many forms and was imperfectly integrated into the Left.

The Presidential Elections of 1965–1995 and the Contradictions of the Right and of Liberalism

Let us first examine the case of the presidential election of 1974. François Mitterrand had been the leader of the PS since 1971 and in 1974 was the official candidate of the Union of the Left, PS-PCF, which had just completed its common program of government. In the first round, it received an impressive 44 percent of the votes, but for lack of votes transferred from other groups after the first round, it failed to win the second round. The Right was divided between Valéry Giscard d'Estaing, who came from the independent Republicans and gathered around him the liberal and Christian Democrat Right, and Jacques Chaban-Delmas, who was officially the candidate of the Gaullist party (UDR) until he was abandoned by several Gaullist officials, including Jacques Chirac, in favor of Giscard. After the election, Chirac became Giscard's prime minister, then resigned in 1976 to become the leader of the Gaullist party (renamed Rassemblement pour la République, RPR). During the first round in 1974, Giscard won 33 percent of the votes versus 15 percent for Chaban-Delmas, who withdrew in his favor. In total, the three main candidates won 92 percent of the votes. The territorial distribution followed the regularities that our investigation has already set forth: Mitterrand achieved his highest results in the suburbs, whereas Giscard and Chaban-Delmas were particularly strong in the villages and towns (see figure 12.6), although the urban orientation was less obvious than in the Tixier-Vignancour vote in 1965 (see figure 12.3). But the differences between territories were not very great among the main candidates; this was the heart of the period of a very strong Left-Right bipolarization, where the class cleavage was clearly more important than the territorial cleavage.

The presidential election of 1974 also witnessed the arrival of several "little candidates" who were to play an important role later on. Jean-Marie Le Pen, who had just founded the FN in 1974, was a candidate for the first time, and he won scarcely 1 percent of the votes, with higher results in the metropoles than in the villages and towns (see figure 12.6), although the urban orientation is less pronounced than in the case of the Tixier-Vignancour vote in 1965 (see figure 12.3). The election of 1974 also corresponds to the first candidacy of Arlette Laguiller, in the name of the Trotskyist (anti-Stalin Communist) party Lutte ouvrière (LO). She won more than 2 percent of the votes, four times as many as Alain Krivine (0.5 percent), another Trotskyist who belonged to the Revolutionary Communist League (Ligue communiste révolutionnaire, LCR). We note that whereas the LCR had a rather urban vote profile (relatively close to that of the PS-PCF), the LO candidate achieved better results in the villages, followed by the towns, and then the suburbs and metropoles.[20] Interestingly, this very clearly rural vote is found in almost all the LO candidacies, from the 1974 election to that of 2022. The data at

---

20. See unehistoireduconflitpolitique.fr, map C12.2.

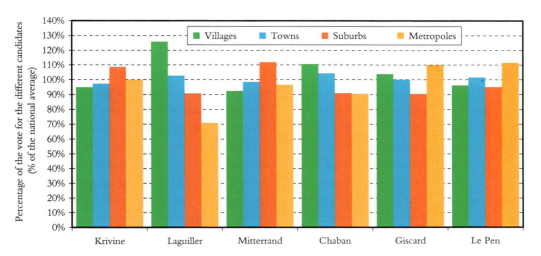

FIGURE 12.6. The presidential vote of 1974 and the territorial cleavage

In the 1974 presidential election, the left-wing candidate François Mitterrand (44% of the votes in the first round) achieved his best results in the suburbs, whereas the right-wing candidates Chaban-Delmas (15%) and Valéry Giscard d'Estaing (33%) got their best results in the village and towns, and Jean-Marie Le Pen (1%) did best in the metropoles. However, we note that the Trotskyist LO candidate, Arlette Laguiller (2%), got her best result in the villages and towns, whereas the Trotskyist LCR candidate Alain Krivine (0.5%) had a territorial profile closer to that of Mitterrand.

Sources and series: unehistoireduconflitpolitique.fr

our disposal do not allow us to break down the part of this vote corresponding to the neoruralists and the old ruralists.[21] In the second round, which was very close, Mitterrand's and Giscard's vote profiles were particularly distinct in terms of wealth, especially in the richest municipalities (see figure 12.7), even more strongly than in 1965 (see figure 12.4). Clearly, the prospect of seeing the Socialists-Communists take power and implement their common program of government—and only a few years after the events of May 1968—was in no way reassuring to the upper-class neighborhoods and very wealthy municipalities. We also note that during the first round of the election, the result obtained by the candidate of the Union of the Left, like those realized by the LO and LCR candidates, declined

---

21. If we divide up the municipalities (and particularly the villages) by centiles in function of the evolution of their population during the five or ten years preceding the election, there seems to be no significant effect on the LO vote. See unehistoireduconflitpolitique.fr, appendix E2. We will return to the territorial vote profile of the Trotskyist vote from 1974 to 2022 (see figure 12.24 below).

steeply with municipal income, again in all the categories of the territory. Thus, in the richest 1 percent of the municipalities the vote for Mitterrand barely reached a third of his national average, with 14 percent and 20 percent of the votes cast in the first round in the villages of Gambaiseuil in Yvelines and Humbauville in Marne, respectively, and 20 percent, 26 percent, and 27 percent in the much more heavily populated and just as wealthy municipalities of Neuilly-sur-Seine in Hauts-de-Seine, Bondues in Nord, and Saint-Cloud, respectively. Among the right-wing candidates, Giscard is the one for whom we find the clearest relation between the votes won and the wealth of the municipality. In particular, the future president won the maximum number of votes possible in the richest municipalities (see figure 12.8). Conversely, Chaban-Delmas's vote profile was virtually flat. His way of talking about the "new society" (an attempt to be open-minded regarding the Left and the labor unions that made him a dangerous centrist in the eyes of the most right-wing Gaullists and led to his being replaced by Pompidou as prime minister in 1972) did not reassure the well-off municipalities, which instead bet on Giscard to protect them against the Socialists and Communists.[22] Finally, it should be noted that in 1974, Le Pen achieved higher results in the richest municipalities than in the poorest municipalities (see figure 12.8). The first Le Pen vote in a presidential election was a primarily bourgeois vote, even if it was less bourgeois than the vote for Tixier-Vignancour in 1965 (see figure 12.5).

In the presidential election of 1981, the PCF nominated its own candidate, Georges Marchais,[23] who won 16 percent of the votes, with an overrepresentation in the suburbs, versus 26 percent for the PS candidate, François Mitterrand, whose votes were distributed very evenly in the different categories of territories (see figure 12.9 and map 12.3). The Right was divided between the outgoing president, Valéry Giscard d'Estaing (UDF), who won 28 percent of the votes versus 18 percent for his former prime minister, Jacques Chirac (RPR). In contrast to the UDF candidate, the representative of the RPR achieved his best results in both the villages and the metropoles. Because he was unable to gather the necessary number of sponsors, Le Pen could not be a candidate, and he denounced "the gang

---

22. In his famous speech delivered in 1969, which the new prime minister had not thought it necessary to ask the president of the Republic to review, Chaban-Delmas had mentioned a reform of the ORTF (the French national broadcaster) intended to give it more independence and open the airwaves to opposition political parties and the labor unions. He also supported emblematic social demands such as the monthly payment of salaries.

23. This followed the breakdown of the Union of the Left in 1977, after the PCF's relative failure, with the PS hot on its heels in the legislative elections of 1973 and then overtaking it for the first time in 1978 (see chapter 10).

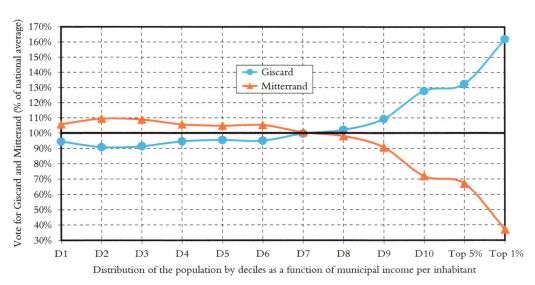

FIGURE 12.7. The presidential election of 1974 and wealth (second round)

In the second round of the 1974 presidential election, the vote for Valéry Giscard d'Estaing (relative to his national average) increased with the municipality's average income, particularly at the top of the distribution, while the reverse is true for the vote for François Mitterrand. Note: The results indicated here are after controls for the size of the conurbation and municipality.

Sources and series: unehistoireduconflitpolitique.fr

of four."[24] In the second round, the vote profiles for Giscard and Mitterrand are very clear with respect to wealth (see figure 12.10), almost as stark as in 1974 (see figure 12.7). In the first round, as in the legislative elections, we see that the vote for the PCF candidate decreases greatly with the municipality's average income, much more so than the vote for the PS candidate, which seems in comparison almost flat, except in the richest municipalities: it varies from 90 percent of

24. The law of 18 June 1976 raised from 100 to 500 the number of sponsors required in order to become a candidate, following the gradual increase in the number of candidates during the preceding presidential elections (six in 1965, seven in 1969, twelve in 1974). The law of 6 November 1962 concerning the election of the president of the Republic by universal suffrage provides that the state will subsidize the costs of the campaign materials for candidates who have won at least 5 percent of the votes cast—and also will subsidize "the same facilities for the campaign" for all candidates; the organic law of 18 June 1976 can be read as an effort to limit these expenses for the state—or more simply, to avoid the multiplication of frivolous candidacies. However, let us note that despite Le Pen's accusations, this new law did not prevent ten candidates from running in 1981.

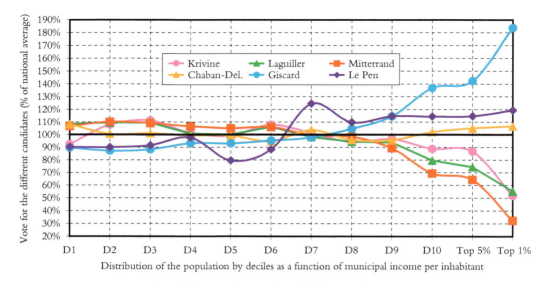

FIGURE 12.8. The presidential election of 1974 and wealth (first round)

In the first round of the 1974 election, the vote for Valéry Giscard d'Estaing (relative to his national average) increased with the municipality's average income, particularly at the top of the distribution, and more strongly than the votes for Jacques Chaban-Delmas or Jean-Marie Le Pen). Note: The results indicated here are after controls for the size of the conurbation and municipality.

Sources and series: unehistoireduconflitpolitique.fr

its national average in the wealthiest 10 percent and even 5 percent of the municipalities before collapsing to only 60 percent in the richest 1 percent (see figure 12.11). Concerning the Right, we see a complete inversion in relation to the preceding elections. It is the candidate of the Gaullist Right (Jacques Chirac) who has the clearer vote profile with respect to wealth compared to the candidate of the non-Gaullist Right (Valéry Giscard d'Estaing), whereas in 1965, Jean Lecanuet had a vote profile more bourgeois than de Gaulle's, and in 1974, Giscard's vote profile was more bourgeois than that of Jacques Chaban-Delmas. This new situation must be seen in relation to the fact that the Gaullists, under the guidance of Chirac, never stopped criticizing the weakness and compromises of the Giscard government and presenting themselves as the best rampart against the Left. It will also be noted that it was the dissident RPR candidate, Marie-France Garaud, Georges Pompidou's éminence grise, who opposed Chaban-Delmas's "new society" and attacked Chirac himself for his weakness and compromises with Giscardism, who

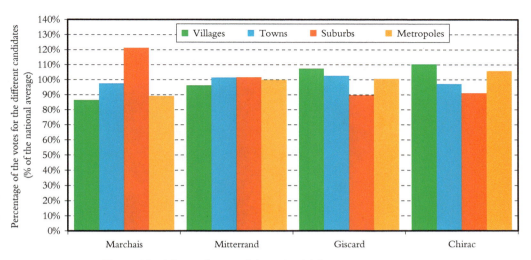

FIGURE 12.9. The presidential vote of 1981 and the territorial cleavage

In the presidential election of 1981, the PCF candidate Georges Marchais (16% of the votes in the first round) achieved his best results in the suburbs, whereas the PS candidate François Mitterrand (26% of the votes) had a relatively balanced territorial profile. The UDF candidate Valéry Giscard d'Estaing (28% of the vote) and the RPR candidate Jacques Chirac (18%) achieved their best results in the villages and town (but also, to a lesser degree, in the metropoles).

Sources and series: unehistoireduconflitpolitique.fr

obtained the most urban and most bourgeois vote profile, particularly in the richest municipalities (see figure 12.11).[25]

From the Gaullist "Participation" to the "Social Fracture," by Way of Reaganism

Generally, the evolution of the structure of electorates illustrates the contradictions of the French Right during the period 1965–1995, and in particular its difficulties

---

25. Garaud's vote profile is also more bourgeois than the vote for Michel Debré, another dissident Gaullist candidate in the election of 1981. Emblematic of her line, which claimed to be "hard," in an open letter to the head of state, Marie-France Garaud attacked the unraveling of "our will" and "our means" (for example, the judicial system and the police), whom she accused of being "so hung up that they often can't make up their minds whether to crack down or look the other way, so that getting beaten up on a street corner one evening or being the victim of a burglary no longer arouses an emotion and that only the victim's death—or worse, that of the aggressor—still excites compassion." Between the two of them, Garaud and Debré won less than 3 percent of the votes, but they weakened Chirac against Giscard.

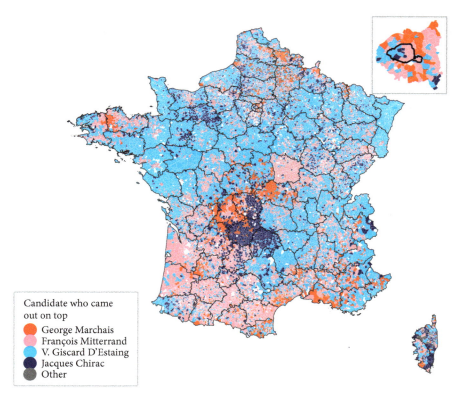

Candidate who came
out on top
🔴 George Marchais
🔴 François Mitterrand
🔵 V. Giscard D'Estaing
⚫ Jacques Chirac
⚫ Other

MAP 12.3. The victory of the Left in the presidential election of 1981

This map represents the candidate who came out on top in each municipality in the first round of
the 1981 presidential election.

Sources and series: unehistoireduconflitpolitique.fr

positioning itself with regard to the question of liberalism and nationalism. In
theory, the issues had become considerably clearer since the interwar period. The
question of nationalism with regard to Germany had been completely redefined,
and in 1963 the leaders of the two countries, Charles de Gaulle and Konrad Ade-
nauer, met to sign with great pomp the Élysée Treaty, thereby putting their seal
on Franco-German reconciliation and friendship. In France as in Germany, the
Right had changed its relation to economic liberalism since the trauma of the
crisis in the 1930s. Both the Gaullists and the Christian Democrats played active
roles in the development of the welfare state, albeit in the framework of an intense
electoral competition with the left-wing parties and under very strong pressure
from the labor movement. In France, General de Gaulle did not want to leave the
social initiative to the Left, and he tried to propose his own middle way between

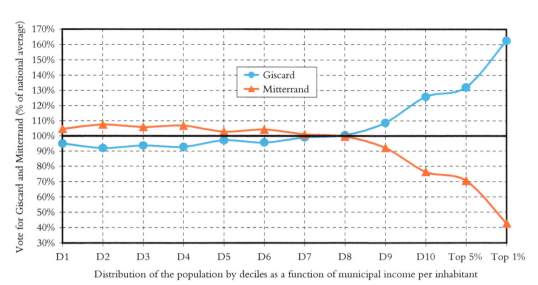

FIGURE 12.10. The presidential election of 1981 and wealth (second round)

In the second round of the 1981 presidential election, the vote for Valéry Giscard d'Estaing (relative to his national average) increased with the municipality's average income, particularly at the top of the distribution, whereas the converse is true for the vote for François Mitterrand. Note: Distribution of the population as a function of the municipal income per inhabitant.

Sources and series: unehistoireduconflitpolitique.fr

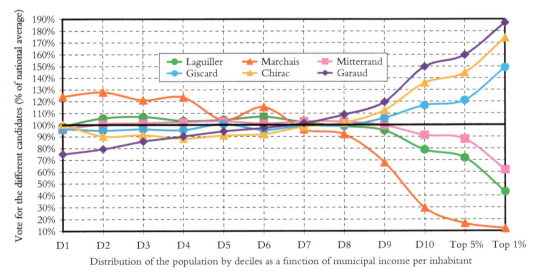

FIGURE 12.11. The presidential election of 1981 and wealth (first round)

In the first round of the 1981 presidential election, the vote for Valéry Giscard d'Estaing increased with the level of the municipality's average income, particularly at the top of the distribution, but less strongly than the vote for Jacques Chirac or Marie-France Garaud. The vote for Georges Marchais (PCF) fell far more steeply with income than the vote for François Mitterrand (PS).

Sources and series: unehistoireduconflitpolitique.fr

liberal capitalism and Soviet-style Communism, emphasizing the idea of profit sharing.

In practice, however, the 1977 ordinance concerning "the participation of salaried workers in the fruits of the expansion of enterprises" was limited to urging companies to transfer part of their profits to their salaried workers in the form of bonuses and profit sharing. No actual power sharing was envisaged, contrary to the law on co-management (or "co-determination") that the German Christian Democrats had agreed to support in 1952 under intense pressure from labor unions and the Social Democrats. In addition, up to half the seats on the governing bodies of large companies (boards of directors or supervisory boards) were reserved for representatives of salaried workers, and therefore there was a risk that the stockholders might lose the majority if the employees succeeded in forming alliances with some of the stockholders (or even if the employees themselves or a local collectivity became a minority stockholder).[26] French stockholders did not want to hear any talk about this kind of challenge to their power, or to grant even one seat in their governing bodies to employees, and the Gaullists had no intention of imposing on them anything at all regarding this matter, which quite clearly indicated the limits of the concept of power sharing then being promoted by this political trend. The fact remains that the Gaullist discourse on this question demonstrates that at that time, the French Right needed to distinguish itself from liberalism pure and simple, and to try to formulate an alternative doctrine—or at least give the impression that it was trying to do so.

The crisis of the 1970s and the end of the Trente Glorieuses would help put the cards on the table. In the 1960s and 1970s, the liberals, independents, and Christian Democrats brought together in the non-Gaullist Right appeared to be more liberal and less social than the Gaullists, as is shown by Lecanuet's more bourgeois vote profile versus de Gaulle's in 1965, and by Giscard's versus Chaban-Delmas's in 1974. But in the 1980s, the Gaullists following Chirac chose on the contrary to stake everything on ultraliberalism. In this we can see the importation to the French political scene of the movement that followed the election of Margaret Thatcher in the United Kingdom and the election of Ronald Reagan in the United States in 1980, but we must also take into account the peculiarly French context. The Gaullists of the RPR sought to regain the upper hand versus the Giscardians and to show that they were the most resolute adversaries of the Union of the Left. The

---

26. The first measures of this kind had been imposed on German stockholders in 1919, again in a context of very strong social and political pressure and a considerable weakening of the stockholders' camp.

program based on across-the-board privatization (even if it meant questioning nationalizations) that was set up under de Gaulle's provisional government and the suppression of the wealth tax that was proposed by Jacques Chirac as the elections of 1986 approached allowed the RPR to capture the public's attention and to move past both the Socialist-Communist episode and the Giscardian parenthesis. Like its Anglo-Saxon counterparts, the French Right was also seeking new ideas to cope with the stagflation of the 1970s and the apparent exhaustion of countercyclical policies associated with Keynesianism. The return of a revised version of economic liberalism postponed after the crisis of the 1930s and the invention of unprecedented forms of "neoliberalism" were naturally part of the repertory of solutions on which officials would draw.[27]

It was in this context that in the presidential election of 1981 Jacques Chirac put together a vote profile that was appreciably more bourgeois than Giscard d'Estaing's (see figure 12.11). A similar scenario was repeated in the presidential election of 1988. At that time, the Right was divided between another Chirac candidacy supported by the RPR and a Raymond Barre candidacy supported by the UDF, with territorial divisions close to those related to wealth (see figure 12.12) and a second-round vote deeply split in relation to wealth (see figure 12.13). In the first round, we see that the Chirac vote increases much more with the wealth of the municipality than the Barre vote does (see figure 12.14). The steepness of the slope for income even seems to have become greater over time: whereas the vote in 1974 for Valéry Giscard d'Estaing reached 140 percent of the national average in the richest 5 percent of the municipalities and 180 percent in the richest 1 percent, for Jacques Chirac in 1988 it was 160 percent and 220 percent, respectively. We also note that the vote for the PCF candidate, André Lajoinie, still decreased massively with the municipal income (although the Communist result collapsed at the national level, Lajoinie's social profile is still just as clear as it was in the legislative elections) and that Le Pen's breakthrough—with 14 percent of the votes at the national level—was a little more limited in the richest municipalities than it was in the rest of the country.

The crushing defeat in 1988 led the Gaullist party and its leader to make further U-turns. Convinced, not without reason, that the excesses of economic liberalism had not persuaded voters and had allowed he Left to return to power after only two years of RPR-UDF government, Chirac did not hesitate in undertaking a new social about-face. After the Right's victory in the legislative elections of 1993,

---

27. In 1984 Jacques Chirac received Friedrich von Hayek (a neoliberal thinker and Pinochet's supporter in the 1970s and 1980s) at the Paris Hôtel de Ville to award him the Médaille de la Ville.

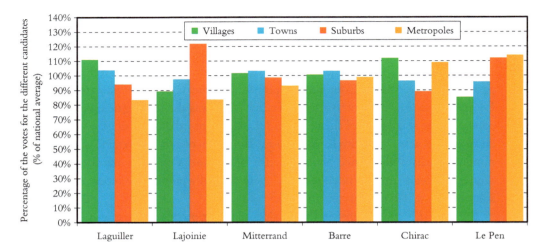

FIGURE 12.12. The presidential election of 1988 and the territorial cleavage

In the 1988 presidential election, the PCF candidate André Lajoinie (7% of the votes in the first round) achieved his best results in the suburbs, whereas the PS candidate François Mitterrand (34% of the votes) had a relatively balanced territorial profile, while the RPR candidate Jacques Chirac (20%) got his best results in the villages and metropoles. The UDF candidate Raymond Barre (18%) had a balanced profile and the LO candidate Arlette Laguiller (2%) was centered on the villages and towns, while the FN candidate Jean-Marie Le Pen (1%) was, on the contrary, centered on the suburbs and metropoles.

Sources and series: unehistoireduconflitpolitique.fr

he appointed his former minister of finance (who had also been in charge of the privatizations of 1986–1988), Edouard Balladur, as prime minister, in preparation for the presidential elections of 1995. But Balladur decided he would run for president as well, with the support of the UDF. At the risk of losing everything, Chirac developed an offensive discourse based on denouncing the "social fracture" and the damage done by the elitist liberalism incarnated, according to him, by Balladur. This allowed him to defeat Balladur by a nose on the evening of the first round of the presidential election in 1995. The territorial structure of the vote was close to the one observed in the preceding elections (see figure 12.15), and the vote in the second round, which pitted Chirac against Jospin, was still deeply divided in accordance with wealth (see figure 12.16). It is striking to note that in the first round, the *frères ennemis* Chirac and Balladur had almost exactly the same vote profile—right-wing voters who were completely disoriented by these repeated changes of position and who divided their vote almost equally between the two former allies (see figure 12.17), even if the geography of their vote differs (thus Chirac won in almost all the municipalities of the departments of Haute-Vienne,

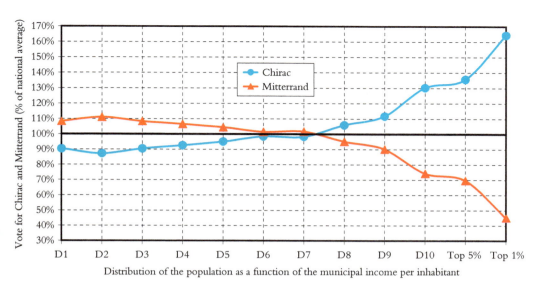

FIGURE 12.13 The presidential election of 1988 and wealth (second round)

In the second round of the 1988 presidential election, the vote for Jacques Chirac (relative to his national average) increased with the average level of the municipality's income (particularly at the top of the distribution), whereas the converse was true for the vote for François Mitterrand. Note: The results indicated here are after controls for the size of the conurbation and municipality.

Sources and series: unehistoireduconflitpolitique.fr

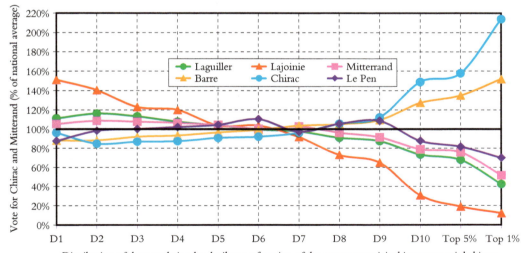

FIGURE 12.14. The presidential election of 1988 and wealth (first round)

In the second round of the 1988 presidential election, the vote for Jacques Chirac (relative to his national average) increased with the municipality's average income, particularly at the top of the distribution, more steeply than the vote for Raymond Barre or Jean-Marie Le Pen (which even diminished at the top). The vote for André Lajoinie (PCF) declined with income even more sharply than the vote for François Mitterrand (PS). Note: The results indicated here are after controls for the size of the conurbation and municipality.

Sources and series: unehistoireduconflitpolitique.fr

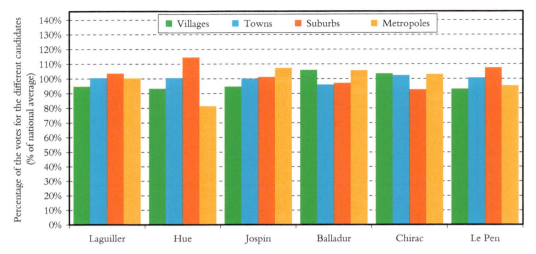

FIGURE 12.15. The presidential election of 1995 and the territorial cleavage

In the 1995 presidential election, the PCF candidate Robert Hue (9% of the votes in the first round) achieved his best results in the suburbs, whereas the PS candidate Lionel Jospin (23% of the votes) had a relatively balanced territorial profile, as did the right-wing candidates Édouard Balladur (19%) and Jacques Chirac (20%) (both of whom came from the RPR) as well as the FN candidate Jean-Marie Le Pen (15%) and the LO candidate, Arlette Laguiller (5%).

Sources and series: unehistoireduconflitpolitique.fr

Creuse, Cantal, and, of course, Corrèze, whereas Balladur's strongholds were more in Maine-et-Loire and Haute-Saône; see map 12.4). We also see that Jean-Marie Le Pen slightly improved his result, with 15 percent of the votes (once again, with a weaker outcome in the richest municipalities than in the rest of the country), while the PS candidate, Lionel Jospin, fell to 23 percent of the votes in the first round (versus 34 percent for Mitterrand in 1988), a decrease partly compensated by a slight recovery of the PCF vote (with 9 percent of the votes for Robert Hue in 1995 versus 7 percent for André Lajoinie in 1988), and by a very high result for the LO candidate Arlette Laguiller (more than 5 percent of the votes in 1995, versus about 2 percent in 1974, 1981, and 1998).[28]

There is scarcely any doubt that these repeated U-turns made by the Right and its leaders contributed to the impression of a camp that cared more about

28. Note that the multiplication by 2.5 of the LO result was accompanied by a relatively balanced territorial profile, contrary to the earlier elections in which the LO vote—as we have seen—was much higher in the villages and towns than in the suburbs and metropoles. The LO vote subsequently resumed its rural profile starting in 2002. We will return to this point later on (see figure 12.24 below).

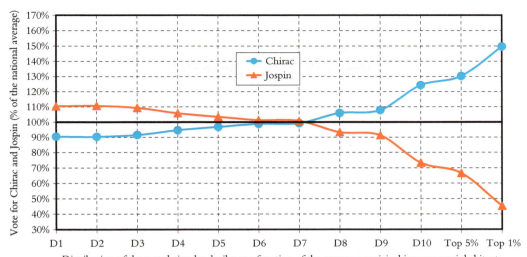

FIGURE 12.16. The presidential election of 1995 and wealth (second round)

In the second round of the 1995 presidential election, the vote for Jacques Chirac (relative to his national average) increased with the municipality's average income, particularly at the top of the distribution, whereas the converse was true for the vote for Lionel Jospin. Note: The results indicated here are after controls for the size of the conurbation and municipality.

Sources and series: unehistoireduconflitpolitique.fr

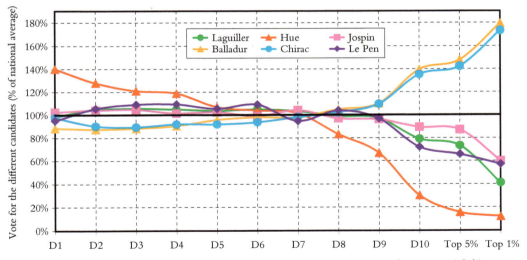

FIGURE 12.17. The presidential election of 1995 and wealth (first round)

In the first round of the 1995 presidential election, the vote for Jacques Chirac increased with the municipality's average income, particularly at the top of the distribution, as did the vote for Édouard Balladur. The vote for Robert Hue (PCF) declined much more steeply with income than did the vote for Lionel Jospin (PS). Note: The results indicated here are after controls for the size of the conurbation and municipality.

Sources and series: unehistoireduconflitpolitique.fr

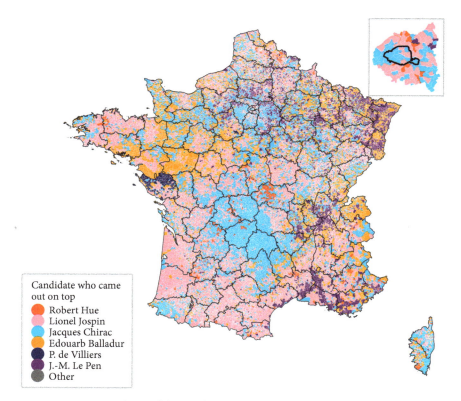

Candidate who came
out on top
● Robert Hue
● Lionel Jospin
● Jacques Chirac
● Edouarb Balladur
● P. de Villiers
● J.-M. Le Pen
● Other

MAP 12.4. The metamorphoses of the presidential cleavages in 1995

The map represents the candidate who came out on top in each municipality in the first round of the presidential election.

Sources and series: unehistoireduconflitpolitique.fr

winning power than about the reality of the policies to be managed for the good of the country. From this point of view, the presidential election of 1995 is emblematic. Elected on the basis of denouncing the policy of austerity associated with the Balladur government and promising to reduce the "social fracture," President Chirac and his first minister, Alain Juppé, made another U-turn immediately after the election, decreeing that starting in July, the VAT (value-added tax) would be increased by two points, an increase that would weigh heavily on the lower and middle classes and handicap the hesitant recovery from the historic recession of 1993. The announcement of a new austerity plan for social security was to lead to a historic strike and the government's retreat in December 1995. The Juppé government never recovered from this catastrophic beginning. Jacques Chirac tried to take matters in hand with a surprise dissolution of the National

Assembly in 1997, but confronted by the electoral victory of the Gauche plurielle (Plural Left) coalition (PS, PCF, the Greens), he found himself forced yield to the reality of his new prime minister, Lionel Jospin. Whereas the Right never stopped stigmatizing the Left for its economic incompetence and budget negligence, the irony of history is that it was the government of the Plural Left— which, it is true, benefited from a buoyant international situation from1998)— that was to succeed in reducing the budget deficit to 3 percent of the GDP (a necessary condition for France to qualify for the single European currency, which was to come into force on 1 January 1999 for businesses and 1 January 2002 for households), while at the same time conducting social policies such as Emploi des jeunes (Youth employment) and reducing the VAT by one point in 2000. The other side of the coin was that the Left positioned itself as the best pupil in the European class with its policies of liberalization and privatization, which contributed to its scattering and ultimately to the elimination of Jospin from the first round of the 2002 presidential election (and to Chirac's easy election over Le Pen, though he had no clear programmatic agenda for governing). The flagship policy of the Jospin government, the "thirty-five-hour workweek," was criticized for sometimes benefiting managers (who were to be paid on the basis of the total number of working days, and secured several additional weeks of paid vacation time) more than employees and blue-collar workers, who also were confronted with forced flexibility and may have preferred more purchasing power in a context of stagnation and industrial job losses in the face of new European and international competition.

The Emergence of the European Question and the Rapprochement of the Center-Right and Center-Left

Generally, it was during the period 1965–1995 that the European question gradually assumed the centrality it still has today for defining the memberships and divisions between political blocs. In the 1960s the Gaullist government had already sought to distinguish itself from the pro-Europe liberals and Christian Democrats by imperiously insisting on the necessity of preserving national independence and France's status as a great autonomous power in opposition to supranational logics. In the 1970s the conflict was aggravated when the Gaullists accused the Giscardians of seeking to sacrifice national sovereignty on the altar of a new European commercial order that cared nothing for the identity of the country and its strategic independence. This was the moment when the liberal Valéry Giscard d'Estaing was negotiating with his German Social Democratic counterpart, Helmut Schmidt, to set up the European Monetary System (Système monétaire européen, SME), a system of quasi-fixed exchange rates among European currencies established in 1979 that was to pave the way for the single currency instituted by the Maastricht Treaty (ratified by referendum in 1992) and the entry into effect of the euro in 1999–2002. It was in December 1978, while the debates about the SME were raging between the different components of the right-wing majority, that Jacques Chirac made his famous "Call from Cochin," in which he denounced in exceptionally virulent terms "the foreigner's party" incarnated, according to him, by the Giscardians prepared to sell off the country's monetary and economic sovereignty.[29]

Inspired in part by the advice of Marie-France Garaud, who was very angry at the Giscardians, the position adopted by Chirac and the Gaullists regarding Europe was not always limpid and easy for the public to understand—like the whole series of European debates agitating both the Left and the Right during this period and in the following decades. Although the abuse of monetary creation certainly may have fueled inflation (and the major rise in prices in the 1970s was not unrelated to the new reflections on the single currency and the independence of the central banks), the need to keep one's own national currency can be justified in various ways, including particularly to cope with unforeseen crises without having to depend on the goodwill of one's partners. In the late 1980s and at the beginning of the 1990s, French Socialists bet that having a common monetary policy, with a European Central Bank making its decisions by majority vote, would in the long run make it possible to provide new areas of shared sovereignty, thanks to a public monetary authority operating at the same transnational level as the financial markets themselves. In the absence of an adequate social, fiscal, and democratic anchorage, it can be legitimately claimed that this bet was in part turned against its authors and only exacerbated liberal excesses. We will return to this when we examine the cleavages resulting from the European referenda of 1995 and 2005. At this point, let us simply note that the position taken by the RPR in the 1970s

---

29. "As always when the goal is to debase France, the foreigner's party is at work with its peaceful and reassuring voice. I ask the French people not to listen to it. It is the numbing that precedes the peace of death." Chirac issued this call on 6 December from the Cochin hospital, where he was recuperating from injuries suffered in a traffic accident, the day after the European Council of Brussels adopted a resolution regarding the SME's installment and operating rules. The reference to de Gaulle's "Call of 18 June 1940" is obvious; the goal was to condemn the traditional liberal Right to the status of inveterate "collaborators" prepared to make all kinds of compromises in order to preserve their little businesses and debase the country, in contrast to the Gaullists, who incarnated the surge of nationalist energy.

and 1980s was far from limpid, insofar as opposition to Europe was accompanied in this case by an ultraliberal discourse on economic questions. But if the objective is to disconnect the state from economic life, then the Giscardian strategy of seeking to accelerate the free circulation of goods and capital seems relatively suitable. However, the Gaullists emphasized the need to preserve room for maneuver to support national champions in world competitions or to avoid sacrificing farmers on the altar of liberalism. In a way, the point of view of Chirac's "Call from Cochin" in 1978 would be more understandable had he made it in connection with his 1995 remarks on the "social fracture."[30] But on European issues, Jacques Chirac had already moved on in the 1990s: he called for a Yes vote in the referendum on the euro in 1992—while at the same time saying that his "heart" was pushing him to vote No—and left it to Philippe Séguin to conduct the No campaign in the name of "social Gaullism."

It must be stressed that these contradictions, which began to agitate the Right on the subject of European questions in the late 1970s, also did not spare the Left. A seminal moment occurred during the electoral campaign for the first elections to the European Parliament by universal suffrage in 1979. While the debate over the proposed SME and the deepening of European integration was raging, Antenne 2 organized a major televised debate on 4 May 1979 among the heads of the four main lists: Georges Marchais for the PCF, François Mitterrand for the PS, Simone Veil for the UDF, and Jacques Chirac for the RPR. During this debate it became clear that the PS and the UDF were the two political forces most favorable to European integration. The UDF candidate defended, of course, the European record of the president in office, while the RPR candidate—following the line of the *appel de Cochin*—deplored the relinquishment of sovereignty that the Giscard government had accepted and the dangers of a supranational power that General de Gaulle never would have accepted and that sincere Gaullists were bound to oppose. The secretary-general of the PCF denounced the excesses of liberal Europe and the European Commission's total absence of political will to conduct a social policy, and especially to oppose the plans to eliminate jobs that were then threatening the European steel industry. The PS candidate also deplored the absence of a social policy, even as he refused to make Europe a "scapegoat" for the economic crisis and defended a constructive approach to European issues as ma-

---

30. The RPR's discourse in the late 1970s and 1980s can be interpreted as an exacerbated version of the liberal nationalist discourse: it assumes the priority of the market but also unstinting support for the national champions and a stubborn rejection of supranational authorities, like Reagan and Trump in the United States; in both France and the United States, this discourse was met with mitigated results and inegalitarian liberal policies.

jorities gradually succeeded in being constituted to reorient the construction currently going on. He called on the RPR and PCF candidates to say whether they wanted to leave a Europe that they considered harmful to French interests, and he insisted that all the members of his list supported the Treaty of Rome.

Thus, during these debates about the SME in 1979 we see the basis of a European bloc bringing together large segments of the Center-Left and the Center-Right that were in favor of a Yes vote in the European referenda of 1992 and 2005, as well as an outline of the liberal-progressive bloc that was to be constituted in 2017–2022. Of course, there was something artificial about the notion of a "European" bloc, insofar as everything depended on the specific content of the European policies about which decisions had to be made and for which the strategies for doing so had to be created. On this subject, more than all others, the question of what was possible and alternative programs that might lead to plausible political outcomes played a central role in structuring political conflict. We will return to this in the next chapters.

The Construction of the Nationalist Right, from Tixier-Vignancour to the Rassemblement National

We come now to the two principal innovations of the period 1965–1995 in terms of political trends: the development of a new form of the nationalist Right and the emergence of a multiform ecological trend. In both cases we see multiple programmatic contradictions and sociological transformations in the structure of the electorates concerned, with major consequences for the structuring of electoral and political policy in the first decades of the twenty-first century. Let us begin with the case of the nationalist Right. Examining the votes for the FN and then the RN during the legislative elections from 1986 to 2022, we have already noted in chapter 11 that the nature of this political trend had completely changed since the 1980s. Its profile gradually shifted from being an urban vote to being a massively rural vote, and from a vote in reaction to a perceived excessive presence of immigrants at the local level to a vote manifested chiefly in the towns and villages without an immigrant presence, but marked by a strong feeling of socioeconomic abandonment and a desire for a different way of gaining social standing, especially through access to property.[31] The study of presidential elections allows us to confirm these results while refining the analysis, considering in particular that the account of the emergence of the contemporary nationalist Right may be sup-

---

31. See chapter 11, figures 11.16–11.25.

planted in a longer perspective, starting with the vote for Tixier-Vignancour in 1965 and Le Pen in 1974.

With regard to the territorial distribution of the vote, the most striking result is the complete inversion of the structure of the vote for the nationalist Right over the past half century. The contemporary nationalist Right clearly has urban origins: the vote for Tixier-Vignancour in 1965 was much greater in the metropoles than in the towns and villages, and so was the vote for Le Pen in 1974 and 1988.[32] The tipping point occurred during the presidential elections of 1995, 2002, and 2007. The result in the metropoles was close to that in the villages and towns in 1995, then it decreased in 2002, and then in 2007 Jean-Marie Le Pen's result declined regularly as we move from the villages to the towns, suburbs, and metropoles. Although the slope became steeper and the FN-RN vote more rural with the Marine Le Pen's candidacies in 2012, 2017, and 2022, the fact is that the shift had already taken place with Jean-Marie Le Pen, before the handover to his daughter (see figure 12.18).

As we have already noted when we were analyzing the results in the legislative elections, this shift in the structure of the FN vote beginning in the 1980s–1990s must be connected to the party's social turn, with its discourse increasingly centered on abandoned territories and the loss of industrial jobs arising from globalization and European and international competition. On the evening of 21 April 2002, when the stunned country had just learned that he had qualified for the second round of the presidential election, Jean-Marie Le Pen launched a call to "the humble," "the small fry," "the excluded," and "the workers in all these industries ruined by Maastricht euro-globalism."[33] Nonetheless, we must emphasize the extent to which this strategic turning point was determined by the circum-

---

32. The nationalist Right has a long history that began long before 1965, of course, specifically with Action française (which defended "complete nationalism" but seldom took part in elections), and more generally with the various conservative, monarchist, Boulangist, Catholic, anti-Dreyfusard, and other trends that existed in the nineteenth century, at the beginning of the twentieth, and during the interwar period. These trends enjoyed diverse and changing relationships with nationalism and were usually characterized by vote profiles that were much more rural than the urban votes for Tixier-Vignancour. However, in both cases we find very good results in the richest municipalities and the upper-class neighborhoods. See chapters 8 and 9.

33. "Vous, les petits, les sans grade, les exclus, ne vous laissez pas enfermer dans les vieilles divisions de la gauche et de la droite. Vous qui avez supporté depuis vingt ans toutes les erreurs et les malversations des politiciens, vous, les mineurs, les métallos, les ouvrières et les ouvriers de toutes ces industries ruinées par l'euro-mondialisme de Maastricht, vous, les agriculteurs aux retraites de misère et acculés à la ruine et à la disparition, vous aussi, qui êtes les premières victimes de l'insécurité dans les banlieues, les villes et les villages."

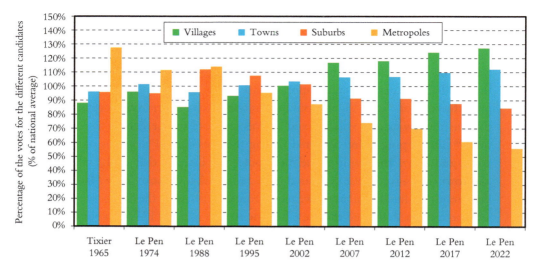

FIGURE 12.18. The nationalist Right and the territorial cleavage, 1965–2022

The representatives of the nationalist Right in the presidential election had a principally urban profile with Tixier-Vignancour in 1965 (5% of votes) and Jean-Marie Le Pen in 1974 (1%) and 1988 (14%), then the profile was inverted and ruralized with Jean-Marie Le Pen in 1995 (15%), 2002 (18%), and 2007 (11%), before becoming increasingly rural with Marine Le Pen in 2012 (18%), 2017 (22%), and 2022 (23%).

Sources and series: unehistoireduconflitpolitique.fr

stances. In the late 1980s, the political niche combining economic ultraliberalism and strong anti-immigrant rhetoric was already occupied by the RPR, leading Jean-Marie Le Pen to step up his criticism of globalization, the common market, and European integration. The same phenomenon is found in 2007. By combining a liberal discourse on the economy and violent diatribes against the "rabble," references to the need for a "pressure washer," and the defense of national identity, Nicolas Sarkozy was elected hands down and succeeded in siphoning off a large part of Jean-Marie Le Pen's electorate, which fell from 17 percent of the vote in 2002 to less than 11 percent in 2007. It is interesting to note that it was precisely at this low point in 2007 that there appeared for the first time a vote profile characterized by a maximal result in the villages, followed by the towns and then the suburbs and metropoles (see figure 12.18).

In other words, it was the voters who chose this vote profile, not the party itself. Actually, Sarkozy managed to attract the most urban segments of Le Pen's electorate in 2002, which were composed of the lower classes and blue-collar workers in the towns and villages, who hardly identified with the UMP candidate's uninhibited liberal discourse. Although Marine Le Pen was able to build on this legacy by emphasizing the social discourse, it is important to note that the party inherited from this configuration more than it wanted. To sum up, the FN was originally a party of the liberal-nationalist type, but the stiff competition maintained by the RPR and then the UMP from the 1980s to the 2000s helped transform it into a social-nationalist, or even social-rural vote. More than the party's leaders, it was the voters in the peripheral territories who decided on this configuration (for lack of another option that would make it possible, in their view, to express more effectively their feeling of having been abandoned by the urban world), and this helps us understand the difficulties the FN-RN encountered in trying to construct a programmatic platform consistent with this sociological reality.

If we now examine the vote profile for the nationalist Right in relation to wealth, we see once again a considerable long-term decline. The vote for Tixier-Vignancour in 1965 was a bourgeois vote, in the sense that it grew rapidly with the average wealth of the municipality, especially at the peak of the distribution. This was again the case—though to lesser extent—for the Le Pen vote in 1974; after that, the curve is inverted at the peak of the distribution, starting in 1988 and continuing in the elections of 1995 and 2002. From 2007 on, the curve declines throughout the distribution, from bottom to top, and not only at the peak (see figure 12.19). In other words, the Le Pen vote diminishes systematically as the municipality's wealth increases. For the presidential as for the legislative elections, this vote profile decreasing with respect to wealth (or increasing with regard to the proportion of industrial blue-collar workers) is less steep, to be sure, than the equivalent profiles historically seen for the Left (and in particular for Communist candidates), but we nonetheless find a spectacular evolution from the starting point of the bourgeois nationalist Right in the 1960s and 1970s.[34] Note also that the profiles indicated in figure 12.19, like the earlier ones, have been generated after taking into account the effects of the size of the conurbation and the municipality. Considering that rural municipalities are on average poorer than urban municipalities, the decreasing profiles seen since 2007 would be even more steeply decreasing in the absence of any controls.[35]

---

34. The profiles are on the whole very close to those for the legislative elections (see chapter 11, figure 11.23). However, we note that the decreasing profile of the FN vote with respect to wealth is slightly greater for legislative elections than it is for presidential elections, which is explained mainly by differentials in turnout, which falls particularly steeply in the legislative elections in the poor suburbs, and more generally, more steeply in poor municipalities voting for the Left and less steeply in those voting for the FN.

35. See unehistoireduconflitpolitique.fr, appendix D3, for all the profiles obtained in this way.

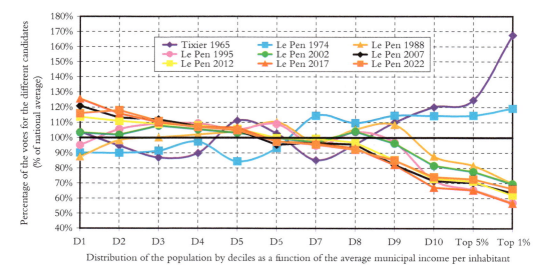

FIGURE 12.19. The nationalist Right and wealth, 1965–2022

In the presidential election of 1965, the vote for Tixier-Vignancour was higher in the richest munici-palities than in the rest of the country. That was the case again with the Le Pen vote in 1974, but starting in 1988, the curve was inverted at the top of the distribution, and then starting in 2007, it be-came decreasing over the whole of the distribution, from bottom to top. Note: The results indicated here are after controls for the size of the conurbation and municipality.

Sources and series: unehistoireduconflitpolitique.fr

From the Postcolonial Right to the Social-Nationalist Bloc: The Case of People Repatriated from Algeria

We must also stress the way in which the postcolonial and identitarian question, which played a central role in the initial development of the nationalist Right (with Tixier-Vignancour in 1965 and the first candidacies of Jean-Marie Le Pen in 1974, 1988, and 1995), has in the interim lost much of its importance. In the 1965 elec-tion, Tixier-Vignancour's candidacy expressed in particular the very strong animus felt by the supporters of French Algeria against General de Gaulle, who had just accepted Algerian independence by signing the Évian Accords of 1962. This was particularly the case for people repatriated from Algeria—that is, the population of French colonists (*pieds-noirs*) who arrived in Metropolitan France in 1962 under conditions that were frequently catastrophic. These repatriates were audited sep-arately at the level of the 36,000 municipalities during the census of 1968, when they represented about 1.5 percent of the total population (or about 800,000 individuals).[36] If we classify the municipalities in accord with their proportions of repatriates (as measured in 1968), we see that the vote for Tixier-Vignancour in 1965 increased very strongly with these proportions (see figure 12.20). It was 2.2 times larger than his national average in the 10 percent of the municipalities with the largest proportions of repatriates from Algeria, and 2.6 times greater in the 5 percent of the municipalities with the most repatriates. Thus it exceeded 20 percent in Roque d'Anthéron and Marignan in Bouches-du-Rhône, in Castelnau-le-Lez in Hérault, and in Six-Fours les Plages in Var.

We note as well that the profile grows massively in all the categories of territories; adding controls for the size of the conurbation and the municipality hardly affects the curve at all. Taking into account the set of other sociodemographic controls attenuates the slope very slightly (which is due essentially to the fact that the repatriates are represented a little more in the municipalities with larger proportions of the self-employed, and that a greater proportion of self-employed persons is generally associated with a higher vote for Tixier-Vignancour), but it does not make much difference. In any case, the presence of repatriates had a huge effect: Tixier-Vignancour's result in the 10 percent of the municipalities with the most repatriates was about twice as high as his average result at the national level, even after taking into account all the control variables (see figure 12.20).[37] We also see that the proportion of repatriates at the municipal level continued to have a significant impact on the vote for Le Pen in 1974, and to a lesser degree in 1988 and in all the elections until 2022 (see figure 12.21). In the presidential elections of 2022, the vote for Marine Le Pen was thus about 15–20 percent higher in the 10 percent of the municipalities where a greater number of repatriates had historically settled than it was in the rest of the country (after taking into account the size of the conurbation and the municipality), and about 10 percent higher after taking into account the whole set of sociodemographic characteristics.[38]

---

36. See chapter 4, map 4.2.

37. As above, the size of the municipalities is taken into account here: the 10 percent of the municipalities with the most repatriates designate the 10 percent of the population living in municipalities with the largest proportions of repatriates. The average proportion of repatriates reaches 7.3 percent in these municipalities, almost five times the national average (1.5 percent). In other words, these municipalities taken together constitute almost 50 percent of the repatriates as a whole.

38. See unehistoireduconflitpolitique.fr, figures E3.2m–E3.2u, for all the results, before and after taking into account various controls.

15–20 percent of the Tixier-Vignancour vote, which was very substantial but nonetheless in the minority. It is also possible that the repatriates helped raise awareness of their cause among some inhabitants of the municipalities where they resided, which could have led to a strong Tixier-Vignancour vote in the municipalities in question.[41] In any case, the majority of the Tixier-Vignancour vote responds to other motivations. This is particularly the case in the upper-class quarters and the richest municipalities, where the repatriates were few,[42] but where Tixier-Vignancour realized his best results. For example, the proportion of repatriates is almost two times lower than the national average in the 7th, 8th, and 16th arrondissements of Paris, but Tixier-Vignancour's result there is nearly twice as high as it is in the rest of the country. The motivation for this vote may be connected with nostalgia for the erstwhile colonial empire or the Vichy regime, or with other themes of the anti-Gaullist Right represented by Tixier-Vignancour, but it is clearly not a *pied-noir* vote.

Even if the *pied-noir* vote is a minority within the Tixier-Vignancour vote—and even more in the FN-RN electorates of recent decades—the fact remains that this very distinct vote with regard to particular origins illustrates the magnitude of the traumas associated with decolonization, and more generally, the importance of the colonial heritage. Most of the *pieds-noirs* were not very rich, and in theory, one could certainly imagine that certain kinds of compensation might be paid to them for the goods they left behind in Algeria (housing, businesses, small farms, and so on). These compensations could have been financed by raising taxes on the minority of *grands colons,* and more generally on the financial assets, real estate, and occupational goods held by the largest metropolitan property owners (all of whom, in one way or another, profited from their international and colonial integration,

---

41. We see a disparity on the order of five percentage points between the Tixier-Vignancour vote in the 90 percent of the municipalities with the smallest number of repatriates (about 4.5 percent of the Tixier-Vignancour vote) and the 10 percent of the municipalities with the most repatriates (about 9.5 percent of the Tixier-Vignancour vote). Considering that the former had on average 0.9 percent repatriates and the latter about 7.3 percent, this difference in the vote can be explained by the fact that almost all the repatriates voted for Tixier-Vignancour, or else that about half of them voted for Tixier-Vignancour and convinced individually one other voter (or lived near an additional Tixier-Vignancour voter in relation to other locations), or any other combination. The data at our disposal do not allow us to go further in the analysis of the vote.

42. Generally, the proportion of repatriates is relatively large in both poor towns and rich ones, as well as in poor suburbs and rich ones, but small in villages and much higher in rich metropoles and poor ones. See unehistoireduconflitpolitique.fr, annex B5, figure B5.3n.

without which neither France nor the West could have gotten so rich). We see how difficult it would have been to determine by democratic deliberation the amount and structure of fair compensation—all the more so because such a deliberation on compensation would scarcely have been able to ignore the far more considerable injustices suffered by the colonized Algerian populations that had paid the price, during almost a century and a half, for a structurally discriminatory and segrega- tionist system, especially in regard to the educational system, access to land, and political and electoral rights. It would also have been necessary to take into account the existence of profound patrimonial inequalities in Metropolitan France, where a young person without inherited wealth would no doubt not have understood why the children of *pieds-noirs,* and no one else, should be compensated. It's clear that gradually, the whole question of the distribution of wealth and property would have to be debated, with the objective of finding reasonable compromises accept- able to most people. But the magnitude of the task must not lead us to abandon any democratic and deliberative perspective of this kind, especially since there are sociohistorical contexts in which compromises have been found to compensate populations that have been ill treated by history.[43] In the absence of such compro- mises, the risk is, of course, that the initiative regarding these questions would be left to national law—which in this case would mean acting without any universalist perspective and focusing on the repatriates alone. In 1962, in Nice, at the invitation of the committee to aid repatriates that had been put under the moral sponsorship of Antoine Pinay, it was Jean-Marie Le Pen, then a deputy representing Seine, who demanded "full compensation by the state for the material losses suffered by the repatriates."[44] This is a position that we find again in Tixier-Vignancour and that explains in large measure his electoral success among the *pieds-noirs.*[45]

43. See chapter 10 and M. L. Hughes, *Shouldering the Burdens of Defeat: West Germany and the Reconstruction of Social Justice* (University of North Carolina Press, 1999), on the German system of *Lastenausgleich,* which sought to finance compensations in connection not only with monetary reform and the elimination of public debt, but also with war damage and losses suffered by German populations repatriated into the Federal Republic of Germany, with in all cases a progressive scale depending on the level of wealth.

44. D. Olivesi, "L'utilisation des rapatriés dans les Alpes-Maritimes (1958–1965)," *Bulletin de l'Institut d'Histoire du Temps Présent,* no. 79, 2002.

45. However, we must note that that both Lecanuet and Mitterrand, though they emphasize the "Algerian betrayal" less than Tixier-Vignancour does, also promise to indemnify the repatri- ates. See, for example, *L'élection présidentielle de décembre 1965* (Cahiers de la FNSP, 1970). A 1962 law indemnifying the repatriates was finally adopted in France in 1970 and amended repeatedly, in particular in the framework of the 2005 law (see chapter 13). On these laws, see,

It is interesting to note that the first postelectoral surveys conducted in France in the 1950s and 1960s included questions addressed to the voters of Metropolitan France on the subject of the continuation of French colonial domination in Algeria and West Africa. In the framework of the 1958 survey, we see that it was blue-collar workers who most favored immediate independence—in that respect, following the position defended at the time by the PCF. Inversely, self-employed workers were more for the continuation of French Algeria and colonial trusteeship in Africa (perhaps because they identified more with the fate of the repatriated colonists and their property).[46] We should also note that cohabitation in the metropolitan territory (in particular, in the southern part of the country) of the repatriates from Algeria and immigrant North African workers (particularly Algerians), who were themselves rapidly increasing in numbers in the 1960s and 1970s, in some cases contributed to the rising tensions that also fueled the advance of the FN vote in the 1980s and 1990s. The difference in the terminology used ("repatriates" versus "immigrants") is in itself symptomatic—it says a lot about the fact that the two groups were not perceived as having the same legitimate right to inhabit the territory, even if in practice the *pieds-noirs* also had to cope with discrimination and were not always welcome (far from it!).

Here again, we must emphasize that the identitarian and anti-immigrant dimension of the FN vote must not be exaggerated, To be sure, in the presidential elections of 1988 and 1995, as in the legislative elections of 1986, 1988, and 1993, we see that the FN vote is considerably higher in municipalities with the largest numbers of foreign inhabitants (in particular, of North African origin), but this positive effect of the proportion of foreigners on the FN-RN vote for the nationalist Right was very weak in the case of the Tixier-Vignancour vote in 1965, and almost nil in the Le Pen vote in 1974; in both cases, the proportion of repatriates was far more important. Above all, it would disappear, and then become negative in the presidential elections conducted from 2002 to 2022, while the FN-RN vote

---

for example, Y. Scioldo-Zürcher, "L'indemnisation des biens perdus des rapatriés d'Algérie," *Revue européenne des migrations internationales,* 2013.

46. Nevertheless, let us emphasize that aside from this opposition between blue-collar workers and the self-employed, their answers to these questions concerning independence are on the whole not very divergent from a socioeconomic point of view. In particular, the salaried employees with the most diplomas and the highest incomes are in an intermediate situation between these two groups. See T. Piketty, "Brahmin Left vs. Merchant Right. Rising Inequality and the Changing Structure of Political Conflict" (World Inequality Lab working paper 2018 / 07), technical appendix.

became more rural and was associated with the absence of immigrants, and no longer with their presence.[47]

Can Political Ecology Be Working Class?

The study of presidential elections since 1965 also allows us to shed new light on the vote for political ecology. In the same way as for the nationalist Right, political ecology historically lacks strong roots at the local level and candidates to embody it in the electoral districts, such that the analysis of the results achieved in legislative elections is not always sufficient to evaluate the response to this political trend. The advantage of presidential elections (along with the drawbacks that it includes in terms of personalization and the illusion of individual omnipotence) is that all the country's voters make judgments regarding the same candidates (by definition, present in all the districts), and this is particularly valuable for studying political trends that are underrepresented or absent in the legislative elections. It also sometimes makes it possible to go further back in time—in this case, to 1965 for the emergence of the nationalist Right with Tixier-Vignancour, or to 1974 for the advent of political ecology with the candidacy of the agronomist René Dumont. Dumont's candidacy was truly historic and a major political innovation, insofar as it was the very first time in France (and to a certain extent, in the world) that such a trend was proposed to voters on the national scale.[48]

René Dumont's result was, of course, limited (1.3 percent of the votes), but the electoral campaign of 1974 allowed him to set forth his ideas on the unsustainable nature of industrial growth and the unrestrained speed with which natural resources were being consumed. From then on, political ecology candidates participated in almost every presidential election, with Brice Lalonde in the name of the Mouvement d'écologie politique (MEP, Political Ecology Movement) in 1981 (4 percent of the vote), Antoine Waechter for the Greens (Les verts, LV) in 1988 (4 percent), Dominique Voynet (LV) in 2007 (2 percent), Eva Joly (Europe écologie–Les verts, EELV) in 2012 (2 percent), and Yannick Jadot (EELV) in 2022 (5 percent). In 2002, ecology even had two candidates, with—in addition to Noël

---

47. See unehistoireduconflitpolitique.fr, figures E3.2w–E3.2z. The results were similar to those already presented for the legislative elections. See chapter 11, figures 11.18–11.19.

48. It is generally thought that the first "green" party on the regional scale was created in 1971 in Neuchâtel, Switzerland, with the Mouvement populaire pour l'environnement (Popular Movement for the Environment), and the first national party in 1972, in New Zealand, with the Values Party. The German Greens participated for the first time in national elections in 1980 and entered the Bundestag in 1983.

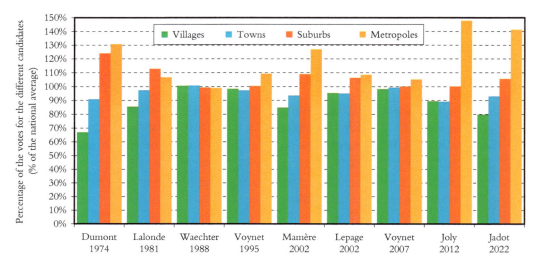

FIGURE 12.22. Political ecology and the territorial cleavage, 1974–2022

The representatives of political ecology in the presidential elections conducted from 1974 to 2022, whether it was Dumont (1% of the vote), Lalonde (4%), Waechter (4%), Voynet (3%), Mamère (5%), Lepage (2%), Voynet (2%), Joly (2%), or Jadot (5%), have almost always achieved higher results in the metropoles and suburbs than in the towns and villages, with even an acceleration of this tendency toward the end of the period.

Sources and series: unehistoireduconflitpolitique.fr

Mamère (a member of the Gauche plurielle majority that governed from 1997 to 2002) for the Greens—the candidacy of Corine Lepage, Alain Juppé's former minister of the environment, representing an ecology closer to the Center-Right. In 2017, the EELV candidate, Jadot, withdrew in favor of Benoît Hamon (PS).

If we examine the structure of the votes for the various representatives of political ecology from 1974 to 2022, we find two major regularities. First, ecologist candidates have almost always achieved much higher results in metropoles and suburbs than in towns and villages. That is particularly true of Dumont, and we find the same regularity in almost all the candidacies, with the exception of Waechter in 1988 and, to a lesser degree, Voynet in 2007, both of whom obtained relatively balanced results in the different territories. The urban profile of the ecologist vote had the same tendency to increase in 2012 and 2022, with a concentration of the vote in the metropoles even clearer than Dumont's in 1974 (see figure 12.22).

The second regularity concerns the relation between political ecology and wealth. In the founding vote for Dumont in 1974, it is striking to note the extent to which the support accorded political ecology grew in an extremely pronounced way with the municipality's average income. This was particularly the case in very rich municipalities: in the richest 1 percent of the municipalities, Dumont achieved a result twice as high as in the rest of the country, and inversely, his result was almost 40 percent lower than his national average among inhabitants of the poorest 10 percent of the municipalities (see figure 12.23 and map 12.5). To be sure, we have to take into account the very low level of the Dumont vote at the national level (1.3 percent, so a vote twice as high is still less than 3 percent of the votes cast) and also remember that with the sources at our disposal, we are not able to say who the Dumont voters were in the richest municipalities.[49] For example, we cannot exclude the possibility that this is partly a matter of the least rich voters in these municipalities being convinced by their everyday contacts that a break with productivism and consumerism was necessary.[50] Nonetheless, the fact remains that the curve of the Dumont vote in function of municipal wealth is exceptionally strong. If we examine later ecologist candidacies, we find none that have such a distinct profile. The situation that comes closest to it is the vote for Lepage in 2002—but as we have noted, this candidate was associated with the Center-Right and presented herself as having broken with the left-wing ecologist Mamère—and to a lesser degree, the vote in 2022 for Jadot, a candidate often described as relatively accommodating in regard to the logics of the market and liberalism; he obtained a vote 1.4 times higher than his national average in the richest 5 percent of the municipalities. Generally speaking, it is striking to note that on the whole, the vote for the ecologist candidates declines in the richest 10 percent of the municipalities or, at a minimum, in the richest 1 percent (except in the cases of Dumont and Lepage), but increases systematically in the least rich 90 percent of the municipalities, including for candidacies coming from the Left (see figure 12.23).[51] In other words, the richer the municipality, the more it votes for political ecology, except at the peak of the distribution of income.

---

49. Unfortunately, the survey data cannot help us much here, since the low level of the Dumont vote as a function of wealth makes it impossible, because of the small number of voters queried, to carry out a significant study of the characteristics of his electorate.

50. Hence, we will not agree with Jacques Ozouf's ironic remark, made after the elections in his analysis of the geography of the Dumont vote, that it seems that "to defend the quality of life, one first had to taste it." See J. Ozouf, "L'élection présidentielle de mai 1974," *Esprit,* 1974.

51. Let us explain that the vote profiles indicated in figure 12.23 correspond to the curves obtained after taking into account the size of the conurbation and the municipality, and that they would be even more clearly increasing before the introduction of controls. See unehistoireduconflit-politique.fr, appendix E2, for all the profiles obtained.

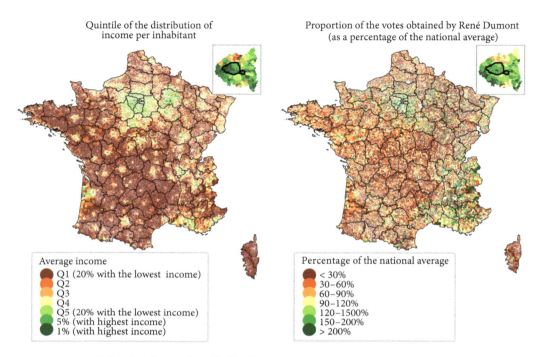

Average income
- Q1 (20% with the lowest income)
- Q2
- Q3
- Q4
- Q5 (20% with the lowest income)
- 5% (with highest income)
- 1% (with highest income)

Percentage of the national average
- < 30%
- 30–60%
- 60–90%
- 90–120%
- 120–1500%
- 150–200%
- > 200%

MAP 12.5. Political ecology and wealth: The Dumont vote, 1974

The map on the left represents the municipalities as a function of their quintile of the income per inhabitant. Q1 corresponds to the poorest 20%, Q2 to the next-poorest 20%, etc., and Q5 to the richest 20% of the municipalities. The map on the right shows the proportion of the votes won by René Dumont as a ratio of the national average.

Sources and series: unehistoireduconflitpolitique.fr

Before trying to explain these results, we must emphasize that the vote profile found for the ecologist candidates is considerably different from that observed for the other components of the Left. We have already examined at length the characteristics of the electorates of the traditional parties of the Left in the presidential elections conducted during the period 1965–1995, in particular for the candidates from the Socialist and Communist Parties (see figures 12.5, 12.8, 12.11, 12.14, and 12.17). In the preceding chapters,[52] we have done the same for the structure of the votes in the legislative elections. In every case, the results are the same. The Communist and the Left of the Left vote always declines very sharply with wealth, from the poorest municipalities to the most well-off municipalities;

---

52. See chapter 10, figures 10.2, 10.6, and 10.12–10.14, and chapter 11, figures 11.1 and 11.12–11.15.

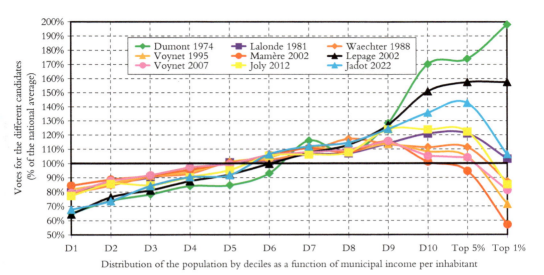

FIGURE 12.23. Political ecology and wealth, 1974–2022

In the 1974 presidential election, the vote for Dumont was a sharply increasing function of the municipality's income, all through the distribution. Subsequently, the vote for the ecological candidates was generally an increasing function of municipal income, except for the richest municipalities. Note: The results indicated here are after controls for the size of the conurbation and municipality.

Sources and series: unehistoireduconflitpolitique.fr

and the vote for the Socialists and Center-Left less clearly decreases with wealth than the Communist vote, particularly in the least rich 90 percent of the municipalities, but it is still decreasing, at least a little. In other words, it is never characterized by the very clearly increasing profile systematically found in the vote for the ecologists in the least rich 90 percent of the municipalities (see figure 12.23). The ecologists' vote profile certainly does not increase with wealth as much as the right-wing vote can, and its decrease at the level of the municipalities (except in the votes for Dumont and Lepage) reflects its attachment to the Left coalitions that apparently did not inspire confidence in upper-class milieus. The profile of the ecologist vote is an unusual one that does not completely resemble either the Right or the Left, and that expresses the fact that the ecologists are located on the borders of the Left—and in general, far from the popular classes.

How should these results be interpreted? A pessimistic explanation might consist in saying that it is inevitable that only the wealthy can afford to worry about the environment and ecology, bringing to mind the famous dichotomy between those who fret about the "end of the world" and those who are primarily anxious about "making ends meet." However, the regularity brought out here extends over half a century, and nothing seems to portend a turnaround any time soon. Above all, such an explanation seems a little elitist and cynical, and out of phase with the democratic and popular ambitions of political ecology from the outset. A more convincing explanation is that despite their initial ambition, ecological trends have not succeeded in convincing working-class voters and the most disadvantaged territories of their desire and ability to improve workers' lot (perhaps because of an excessive determination to distinguish themselves from the earlier socialist and communist traditions and rhetorics centered on social classes). At a minimum, these results lead us to question the strategies used up to now by ecologists of various tendencies. In theory, nothing prevents us from pursuing both an ambitious ecological policy and an equally ambitious policy seeking to redistribute wealth and reduce inequalities between social classes and territories. We might even say that the former cannot really accomplish its objectives without the latter, and vice versa. These results suggest that the ecologist trends have not gone far enough in that direction, and that only fundamental changes in their socioeconomic program could reverse this state of affairs. Generally speaking, it is striking to note to what extent measures intended to expand the welfare state and radically reduce inequalities—including, if necessary, by taxing the highest incomes and patrimonies at a rate of 80–90 percent, as was done in the twentieth century—are not really part of the policies usually associated with this political family. For many voters coming from popular categories or disadvantaged territories, the ecologist vote is often associated with a discourse that is, to be sure, respectable and even indispensable on the level of objectives, but that in practice tends to neglect the question of social inequalities and is in danger of turning against the humblest people, who seem not always to be among this political trend's priorities, and who are generally considered to be closer to the relatively favored urban classes.

In view of these results, we might add that the very fact of speaking about a "social-ecological bloc" to characterize the Union of the Left and ecological parties in force since the 1990s, from the Gauche plurielle of 1997 to the NUPES (Nouvelle union populaire écologique et sociale) instituted in 2022, can constitute an obstacle to uniting voters from the popular categories (especially in rural territories, but not only there). In comparison, the notion of a "Socialist-Communist bloc" or a "Left bloc" makes it possible to express more clearly the centrality of the social message and the objective of reducing inequalities. Even so, the notion of a "social-ecological bloc" is indispensable, insofar as the objective of preserving the habitability of the planet appears as a central component of any effort to develop an alternative, just, and emancipatory socioeconomic system in the twenty-first century. The fact remains that it is clearly not obvious to voters how these social and environmental objectives are to be realized. The results presented here suggest that the increased power of the ecological issue is one of the factors that have contributed to the weakening of Left-Right polarization over recent decades, and that only the establishment of programmatic platforms that are far more ambitious and convincing regarding the redistribution of wealth might enable us to overcome these contradictions. To sum up, in the 1980s and 1990s the Left has had a tendency to scale back its redistributive ambitions, even though the ecological challenge would, on the contrary, have demanded a deepening of the redistributive agenda in order to reassure working-class voters that environmental ambitions would not get in the way of the social objectives.

Wealthy Urban Ecologists, Rural and Disadvantaged Trotskyists

To continue this analysis, we will now compare the structure of the ecologist Trotskyist electorates that have been formed in presidential elections since the 1970s. Two main Trotskyist parties competed in these elections. One was Lutte ouvrière (LO), which systematically nominated a candidate (always a woman) in all the presidential elections held from 1974 to 2022, first Arlette Laguiller from 1974 to 2007, and then Nathalie Arthaud from 2012 to 2022. The other was the Ligue communiste révolutionnaire (LCR), which nominated a candidate in 1969 and 1974 (Alain Krivine), in 2002 and 2007 (Olivier Besancenot), and from 2012 to 2022 (Philippe Poutou), after which the party changed its name to become the NPA (Nouveau parti anticapitaliste) in 2009.[53] To be sure, the results obtained by these candidates were relatively modest (each generally winning around 1–2 percent of the votes), but in the end their cumulative result was not very different from that of the ecologists, which justifies the comparison. Let us also add that Laguiller attained results of 5–6 percent in 1995 and 2002, and that the vote for Besancenot exceeded 4 percent in 2002—that is, a total of more than 10 percent for the two Trotskyist candidates in 2002—which is explained by both the disappointments caused by the Left when it was in power and the decline of the PCF's result since 1981. This Trotskyist peak in 1995–2002 did not last long: the two

---

53. The LCR did not nominate a candidate in 1981, 1988, and 1995, and it called on its supporters to vote for the LO or the PCF in these elections.

candidates fell back to results of barely 1–2 percent each in 2007 and 2012.[54] To say that these Trotskyist parties qualified is somewhat reductive. Although they were attached to an anti-Stalinist communist tradition historically associated with Trotskyism, the reality is that these movements represented chiefly an inventive attempt to incarnate the communist, international idea, in connection with the specificities of the French social and political context.

In terms of the structure of the Trotskyist electorate, two principal characteristics appear very clearly. First, it is a vote that is characterized by a very distinct rural profile. In particular, in virtually all the presidential elections from 1974 to 2002, the LO vote for Laguiller and then for Arthaud is clearly higher in the villages and towns than in the suburbs and metropoles (see figure 12.14). The only exception concerns the election of 1995, in which Laguiller achieved more than 2.5 times her result from 1988 and brought together a new, very balanced electorate in the various territories. The LO electorate returned to its rural profile in 2002, and that tendency was subsequently amplified. In 2002, the LO vote was 1.2 times higher in villages than its national average, whereas it barely reached 70 percent of this average in the metropoles. This same profile is found for the LCR vote, and then for the NPA's, from 2002 to 2022: Besancenot and Poutou got their best results in villages and towns, followed by suburbs and metropoles.[55]

This particular territorial profile of the Trotskyist vote, which reached is high point in the villages, followed by towns, suburbs, and metropoles, was situated at the exact opposite of the ecologist vote, which was on contrary maximal in the metropoles, followed by the suburbs, towns, and villages (see figure 12.22). The Trotskyist vote is also differentiated from the classic vote profile of the Left, and particularly from the PCF vote, which is always maximal in the suburbs, followed by the metropoles and then by the towns and villages.

In addition to this unusual territorial profile, the second characteristic of the LO, LCR, and NPA vote is that in all the presidential elections held between 1974 and 2002 it decreases systematically and regularly in accord with the municipality's wealth (see figure 12.22). The contrast with the ecologists' profile, which

---

54. This rapid decline may be related to the growth of the FG-PG vote, and then the LFI vote from 2012 to 2017, even if the territorial distributions of the different votes are not the same, and these effects of inclination must not be exaggerated.

55. This was not the case with the LCR vote for Krivine in 1974, which at that time had a more classical urban profile (see figure 12.6), as did the votes for the LCR (Krivine) and the PSU (Rocard) in 1969 (see unehistoireduconflitpolitique.fr, appendix E2, figure E2.3g). Moreover, everything indicates that the return to a rural LO vote in 2002 is explained in part by a transfer of LO's urban vote to Besancenot's LCR in 2002.

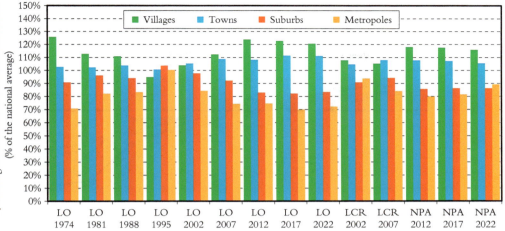

FIGURE 12.24. Trotskyism and the territorial cleavage, 1974–2022

In 1974, the Trotskyist party LO was represented in the presidential elections by Arlette Laguiller (2% of the votes), and again 1981 (2%), 1988 (2%), 1995 (5%), 2002 (96%), and 2007 (1%), and by Nathalie Artaud in 2012 (1%), 2017 (1%), and 2022 (1%). The LCR was represented by Olivier Besancenot in 2002 (5%) and 2007 (4%), and the NPA by Philippe Poutou in 2012 (1%), 2017 (1%), and 2022 (1%). The votes for LO, LCR, and NPA were systematically higher in the villages and towns than in the suburbs and metropoles for all these elections, except for the LO's initial breakthrough in 1995.

Sources and series: unehistoireduconflitpolitique.fr

systematically and regularly increases in accord with wealth (except in the richest 10 percent of the municipalities), is particularly striking (see figure 12.23).[56] On the other hand, the profile of the Trotskyist vote with regard to wealth is quite close to the decreasing profile traditionally associated with the vote for the Left parties. In this case, the Trotskyist profile is slightly less decreasing than the PCF's vote profile, but distinctly more than the PS profile.[57]

The comparison with the ecologist vote is all the more interesting because the LO, LCR, and NPA parties have long denounced the capitalist system's extractivism

---

56. Let us explain that we indicate here the profiles after taking into account the size of the conurbation and the municipality. In the absence of any control, the profile of the Trotskyist vote with regard to wealth is even more steeply decreasing, and inversely, the profile of the ecologist vote is even more strongly increasing. For all the profiles obtained, see unehistoireduconflitpolitique.fr, appendix E3.

57. Note the weight of the Communist electorate in the Mitterrand vote in the first round in 1974, which appears to decrease even more sharply with wealth than the Trotskyist vote does. See figure 12.8.

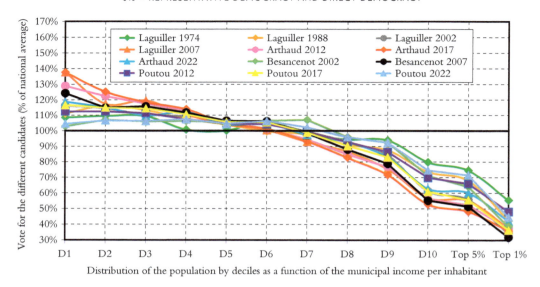

FIGURE 12.25. Trotskyism and wealth, 1974–2022

From the presidential election of 1974 to that of 2022, the Trotskyist candidates have systematically had a vote profile that sharply decreases as a function of municipal wealth, whether it is a question of the LO candidates (Arlette Laguiller or Nathalie Arthaud), the LCR candidate (Olivier Besancenot), or the NPA candidate (Philippe Poutou). Note: The results indicated here are after controls for the size of the conurbation and municipality.

Sources and series: unehistoireduconflitpolitique.fr

and seizure of natural sources, such that at first, one could imagine a rather considerable closeness between their electorates and the ecologist vote. But the Trotskyist and ecologist electorates have almost entirely opposed profiles: the former is composed above all by rural people from relatively poor municipalities, whereas the latter relies chiefly on urban people from well-off municipalities. The explanation for this no doubt resides both in the parties' programmatic discourses and in the strategies of voters seeking to convey this or that message, or to associate themselves with different groups. In this instance, the Trotskyist parties have a discourse centered around challenging capitalism, redistributing wealth, and taxing bosses to the benefit of workers, which can, of course, help explain the greater success they enjoy in poor municipalities and peripheral territories. Conversely, the ecologists' parties' discourses are much less focused on the social question. Let us immediately add that our aim is not in any way to idealize the Trotskyist program of moving beyond capitalism and setting up an alternative socioeconomic and political system (a program that is in many respects extremely vague and brings together only a very small proportion of the voters), but simply to point out that different discourses are associated with different electorates. In theory, we can certainly imagine that other proposals that succeed in combining the strengths of the different programs and worldviews in a better way might be able to rally these various electorates (and others), even if the task is obviously anything but easy. The results presented here illustrate the complexity and diversity of the programmatic and sociological recompositions that characterize the multiple political trends and heritages that make up the social-ecological bloc at the beginning of the twenty-first century.

How 21 April Came About: The Left's Divisions and Contradictions

To sum up, the reintroduction in 1965 of the presidential election by direct universal suffrage was far more conclusive than the disastrous experience of 1848. The presidential elections conducted from 1965 to 1995 helped strengthen the logic of the Left-Right polarization that had already been at work since the beginning of the twentieth century. They also helped structure a driving political dialectic and multiple democratic alternations in power, and they also favored the emergence on the national level of new trends like the nationalist Right and political ecology. These new trends can be seen as signs of democratic vitality, but they can also be seen as factors weakening the Left-Right cleavage. Ultimately, the logic of personalization and the balkanization of the first round implies that the presidential election can help fuel extremely diverse political identities and recompositions, far beyond the tendency to strengthen bipolarization that is generally stressed.

The 1965–1995 phase, marked by Left-Right second rounds emblematic of bipolarization, came to an end on 21 April, with the nationalist Right candidate qualifying for the second round against the liberal Left candidate. In 2002–2022, the presidential election played a major role in structuring the transition from bipartition to tripartition, with second rounds between the candidates of the liberal-progressive bloc and the nationalist-patriotic bloc; we will return to this topic in chapter 13. At this point, let us simply say that 21 April 2002 was above all the outcome of the Left's divisions and contradictions. We have already noted the disappointments with the Gauche plurielle, which did succeed in winning at the ballot box after the failed dissolution in 1997 and in qualifying France for the euro, but they also helped deepen commercial liberalization and privatization.

In a context marked by the closures of industrial sites such as the one at Vilvoorde in Belgium and job losses at Michelin, Lionel Jospin's statements to the effect that "the state cannot do everything" sounded like a coldhearted surrender to liberalism and a renunciation of all political will. In many sectors, the "thirty-five-hour workweek" gave managers more vacation days but obliged low-paid workers and employees to accept additional "flexibility." The negative effects of the lack of sufficient recruitment in the public sector, and particularly in hospitals, were also being felt. The most disconcerting turning point undoubtably came in 2000, when Laurent Fabius, the president of the National Assembly, was made minister of finance. As election day 2002 approached, Fabius explained that "the Left is not in much danger of being beaten by the Right, but it might be beaten by taxes." For the first time in French history, a left-wing government had decided in 2000–2002 that its new political priority consisted in reducing income taxes, including the rates applicable to the highest incomes, at the very time when there were immense unsatisfied needs in the areas of healthcare and education.[58]

As soon as it came to power, the Left was beaten—not by taxes, but by the feeling of abandonment experienced by its traditional supporters, a large majority of whom now turned in the second round to candidates other than Lionel Jospin. Indeed, the candidates' logic of balkanization and especially the division of the Left reached its extreme in the presidential election of 2002. On 21 April, voters had to choose between sixteen candidates—a record number the likes of which had not been seen since 1965 and which has remained unmatched. On the left, in addition to the outgoing prime minister, Lionel Jospin (PS), who obtained 16 percent of the votes, six candidates had significant results: the two Trotskyists Arlette Laguiller (LO, 6 percent) and Olivier Besancenot (LCR, 4 percent), the PCF candidate, Robert Hue (3 percent), the Greens' candidate, Noël Mamère (5 percent), the candidate of the Mouvement des citoyens (MDC), Jean-Pierre Chevènement (5 percent), and the candidate of the Parti radical de gauche (PRG), Christiane Taubira (2 percent). In all, these alternative candidates of the Left won 26 percent of the votes,[59] or 42 percent of the votes if we add

---

58. The top rate of the income tax was reduced from 54 to 52 percent (that is, to a level considerably lower than the one set by the nationalist bloc in 1920, for example). This measure is all the more surprising because the two-point increase in the VAT decided on in 1995 by the Chirac-Juppé government—an increase that weighed very heavily on the most modest taxpayers—has still not been canceled, contrary to the promises to do so (only a one-point decrease took place in 2000). This episode reminds us of the increase in the VAT François Hollande instituted in 2014—after having canceled in 2012 the increase foreseen by Nicolas Sarkozy—particularly in order to finance the competitiveness and employment tax credit (CICE) for business enterprises.

59. We even approach 27 percent if we include the 0.5 percent of the votes for Daniel Gluckstein (another Trotskyist candidate, coming from the Workers' Party). Gluckstein had the same vote profile as the other Trotskyist candidates, with higher results in villages and towns than in the